NML/HPP
70·00

THE VICTORIA HISTORY
OF THE
COUNTIES OF ENGLAND

A HISTORY OF
WILTSHIRE

VOLUME XVI

OXFORD
UNIVERSITY PRESS

Great Clarendon Street, Oxford OX2 6DP

*Oxford University Press is a department of the University of Oxford. It furthers the University's
objective of excellence in research, scholarship, and education by publishing worldwide in
Oxford New York
Athens Auckland Bangkok Bogotá
Buenos Aires Calcutta Cape Town Chennai
Dar es Salaam Delhi Florence Hong Kong
Istanbul Karachi Kuala Lumpur
Madrid Melbourne Mexico City Mumbai
Nairobi Paris São Paulo Singapore
Taipei Tokyo Toronto Warsaw*

*with associated companies in
Berlin Ibadan*

Oxford is a registered trade mark of Oxford University Press in the UK and certain other countries

*Published in the United States
by Oxford University Press Inc., New York*

British Library Cataloguing in Publication Data
Data available

Library of Congress Cataloging in Publication Data
ISBN 0 19 722793 7

*Printed by H Charlesworth & Co Ltd
Huddersfield, England*

THE VICTORIA HISTORY
OF THE
COUNTIES OF ENGLAND

EDITED BY C. R. J. CURRIE

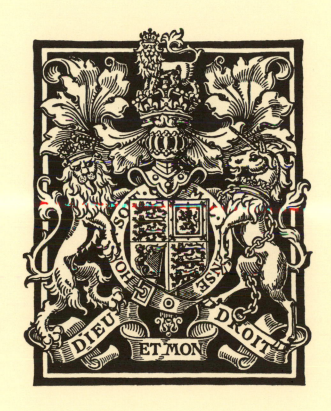

THE UNIVERSITY OF LONDON
INSTITUTE OF
HISTORICAL RESEARCH

INSCRIBED TO THE

MEMORY OF HER LATE MAJESTY

QUEEN VICTORIA

WHO GRACIOUSLY GAVE THE TITLE TO

AND ACCEPTED THE DEDICATION

OF THIS HISTORY

LITTLE BEDWYN
St. Martin's church, Chisbury, looking east

A HISTORY OF

WILTSHIRE

EDITED BY D. A. CROWLEY

VOLUME XVI

KINWARDSTONE HUNDRED

PUBLISHED FOR

THE INSTITUTE OF HISTORICAL RESEARCH

BY

OXFORD UNIVERSITY PRESS

1999

CONTENTS OF VOLUME SIXTEEN

LIST OF ILLUSTRATIONS

Thanks are rendered to the following for permission to reproduce material: Aerofilms Ltd.; the earl of Cardigan; the Conway Library, Courtauld Institute of Art, for photographs of paintings by John Buckler in Devizes Museum; Country Life (©Country Life Picture Library); A. F. Kersting; Roger Pope, for the photograph of North Street, Pewsey; the Royal Commission on the Historical Monuments of England (©Crown Copyright. RCHME); the bishop of Salisbury; Wiltshire County Council. Material in Devizes Museum is reproduced by permission of Devizes Museum (the Wiltshire Archaeological and Natural History Society).

LIST OF ILLUSTRATIONS

LIST OF MAPS

The maps listed below were drafted by D. A. Crowley, Jane Freeman, and Janet H. Stevenson, and were digitized by R. A. Canham, County Archaeologist for Wiltshire, and his colleagues in the Archaeology service of the Libraries and Heritage branch of Wiltshire County Council's Education department. The parish and other boundaries are taken from inclosure award and tithe award maps and from Ordnance Survey maps of the later 19th century.

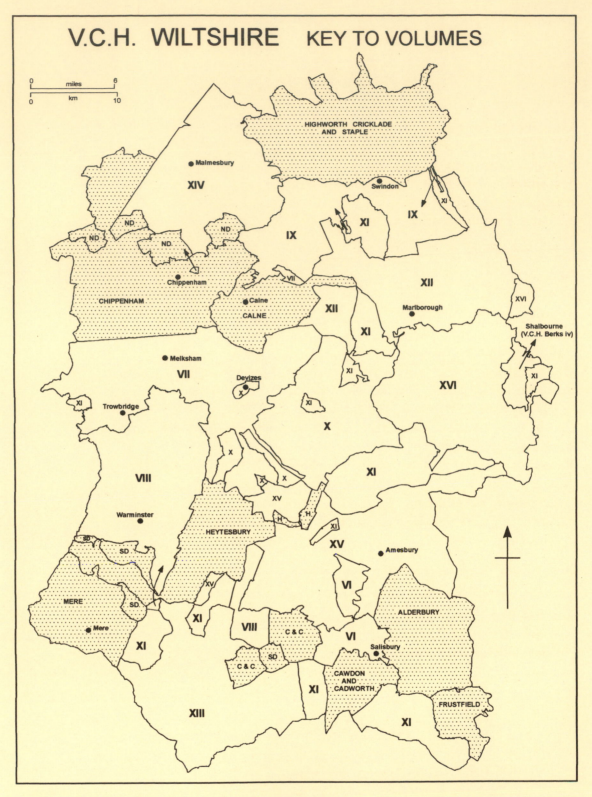

V.C.H. WILTSHIRE KEY TO VOLUMES

Detached parts of hundreds:

C & C Cawdon and Cadworth   **ND** North Damerham   **SD** South Damerham   **H** Heytesbury

EDITORIAL NOTE

Like the sixteen earlier volumes of the *Victoria History of Wiltshire*, this volume has been prepared under the supervision of the Wiltshire Victoria County History Committee. The origin and early constitution of that Committee are described in the Editorial Note to Volume VII, the first to be published. New arrangements introduced in 1975 are outlined in the Editorial Note to Volume XI, and further modifications in 1990 and 1993 are described in the Editorial Notes to Volumes XIV and XV respectively. The Local Authorities retaining representation on the Committee in 1998 were Wiltshire County Council and the District Councils of Kennet, Salisbury, North Wiltshire, and West Wiltshire. To them the University of London again offers its profound thanks for their continued support of the Wiltshire V.C.H. Committee, whose collaboration in the enterprise is once more warmly acknowledged. In 1998 the Wiltshire Victoria County History Appeal, under the patronage of the Lord Lieutenant, Sir Maurice Johnston, was launched to seek supplementary funding for the Committee's work.

In 1997 Mr. M. O. Holder resigned as Honorary Secretary of the Wiltshire V.C.H. Committee, and Mr. S. P. Milton succeeded him in 1998. Grateful thanks are owed to Mr. Holder for his five years' service to the Committee. Also in 1997 Miss Janet Stevenson retired, and in 1998 Dr. Jane Freeman resigned, as assistant editors after 32 and 20 years' service respectively. The extent of their contribution is reflected in the table of contents of this, as of earlier, volumes. In January 1999 Dr. Carrie Smith took up the post of Assistant Editor.

Thanks are also offered to the many people who have helped in the compilation of this volume by granting access to documents and buildings in their ownership or care, by providing information, or by giving advice. Most of them are named in the footnotes to the articles with which they helped. Special mention must be made of the assistance given by the staff of the Wiltshire and Swindon Record Office and by the Trowbridge Reference and County Local Studies Librarian of Wiltshire County Council (Mr. M. J. Marshman) and his assistants. Special thanks are also due to Mr. R. A. Canham, County Archaeologist for Wiltshire, for his help in preparing maps, and to Mr. P. Williams, Mr. M. Hesketh-Roberts, and Mr. J. O. Davies, all of the Royal Commission on the Historical Monuments of England, for their work as photographers.

The *General Introduction* to the *Victoria County History*, published in 1970, and its *Supplement* published in 1990 give an outline of the structure and aims of the series as a whole, with an account of its progress.

WILTSHIRE
VICTORIA COUNTY HISTORY COMMITTEE

As at 16 September 1998

COUNCILLOR MRS. V. C. S. LANDELL MILLS, *Chairman* *Representing the Wiltshire County Council*

COUNCILLOR C. NEWBURY
COUNCILLOR MRS. P. RUGG
COUNCILLOR MRS. M. E. SALISBURY

COUNCILLOR MRS. P. E. G. COURTMAN   *Representing the Kennet District Council*

COUNCILLOR T. F. COUPER   *Representing the Salisbury District Council*
COUNCILLOR MRS. J. GREVILLE

COUNCILLOR MRS. M. F. LLOYD   *Representing the North Wiltshire District Council*
COUNCILLOR MISS D. J. MATTHEWS

COUNCILLOR MRS. J. REPTON   *Representing the West Wiltshire District Council*

DR. C. R. J. CURRIE   *Representing the Central Committee of the Victoria County History*

MRS. P. COLEMAN   *Representing the Wiltshire Archaeological and Natural History Society*

MR. I. M. SLOCOMBE   *Representing the Wiltshire Local History Forum*

Co-opted Members

DR. J. H. BETTEY   MISS S. REYNOLDS
DR. J. H. CHANDLER   MR. K. H. ROGERS
MR. D. F. HODSON   MR. M. SCOTT
MR. M. J. LANSDOWN

MR. S. P. MILTON, *Hon. Secretary*
MR. F. R. MARSHALL, *Hon. Treasurer*

xiv

LIST OF CLASSES OF DOCUMENTS
IN THE PUBLIC RECORD OFFICE

USED IN THIS VOLUME
WITH THEIR CLASS NUMBERS

LIST OF CLASSES OF DOCUMENTS

NOTE ON ABBREVIATIONS

Among the abbreviations and short titles used are the following:

Abbrev. Rot. Orig.	*Rotulorum Originalium in Curia Scaccarii Abbreviatio* (Record Commission, 1805)
Acct. of Wilts. Schs.	*An Account of Schools for the Children of the Labouring Classes in the County of Wiltshire*, H.C. 27 (1859 Sess. 1), xxi (2)
Acts & Ords. of Interr. ed. Firth & Rait	*Acts and Ordinances of the Interregnum*, ed. C. H. Firth and R. S. Rait
Alnwick Castle Mun.	Muniments at Alnwick Castle, Northumberland
Alum. Cantab.	*Alumni Cantabrigienses*, ed. J. and J. A. Venn
Alum. Oxon.	*Alumni Oxonienses*, ed. J. Foster
Arch. Jnl.	*Archaeological Journal*
archd. Wilts.	archidiaconal court of Wiltshire
Aubrey, *Topog. Colln.* ed. Jackson	*The Topographical Collections of John Aubrey*, ed. J. E. Jackson (Devizes, 1862)
B.L.	British Library
Add. Ch.	Additional Charter
Add. MS.	Additional Manuscript
Add. Roll	Additional Roll
Harl. Ch.	Harleian Charter
Harl. MS.	Harleian Manuscript
Harl. Roll	Harleian Roll
Maps	Map Library
Stowe MS.	Stowe Manuscript
Bk. of Fees	*The Book of Fees* (H.M.S.O. 1920–31)
Burke, *Commoners*	J. Burke and others, *A History of the Commoners* (London, 1833–8)
Burke, *Ext. & Dorm. Baronetcies*	J. Burke and others, *Extinct and Dormant Baronetcies*
Burke, *Land. Gent.*	J. Burke and others, *Landed Gentry*
Burke, *Peerage*	J. Burke and others, *A Dictionary of the Peerage*
Cal. Chart. R.	*Calendar of the Charter Rolls preserved in the Public Record Office* (H.M.S.O. 1903–27)
Cal. Close	*Calendar of the Close Rolls preserved in the Public Record Office* (H.M.S.O. 1892–1963)
Cal. Cttee. for Compounding	*Calendar of the Proceedings of the Committee for Compounding, etc. 1643–1660* (H.M.S.O. 1889–92)
Cal. Cttee. for Money	*Calendar of the Proceedings of the Committee for the Advance of Money, 1642–1646* (H.M.S.O. 1888)
Cal. Doc. France, ed. Round	*Calendar of Documents preserved in France, illustrative of the History of Great Britain*, ed. J. H. Round (H.M.S.O. 1899)
Cal. Fine R.	*Calendar of the Fine Rolls preserved in the Public Record Office* (H.M.S.O. 1911–62)
Cal. Inq. Misc.	*Calendar of Inquisitions Miscellaneous (Chancery) preserved in the Public Record Office* (H.M.S.O. 1916–68)
Cal. Inq. p.m.	*Calendar of Inquisitions post mortem preserved in the Public Record Office* (H.M.S.O. 1904–95)
Cal. Inq. p.m. Hen. VII	*Calendar of Inquisitions post mortem, Henry VII* (H.M.S.O. 1898–1955)

Cal. Lib.	*Calendar of the Liberate Rolls preserved in the Public Record Office* (H.M.S.O. 1916–64)
Cal. Papal Pets.	*Calendar of Papal Registers: Petitions to the Pope* (H.M.S.O. 1896)
Cal. Papal Reg.	*Calendar of Papal Registers: Papal Letters* (H.M.S.O. and Irish Manuscripts Commission, 1893–1994)
Cal. Pat.	*Calendar of the Patent Rolls preserved in the Public Record Office* (H.M.S.O. 1891–1986)
Cal. S.P. Dom.	*Calendar of State Papers, Domestic Series* (H.M.S.O. 1856–1972)
Calamy Revised, ed. Matthews	*Calamy Revised: being a Revision of Edmund Calamy's Account of the Ministers and others Ejected and Silenced, 1660–2*, by A. G. Matthews (1934)
Camd., Camd. Soc.	Camden Series, Camden Society
Cat. Anct. D.	*Descriptive Catalogue of Ancient Deeds in the Public Record Office* (H.M.S.O. 1890–1915)
Cat. of Drawings Colln. of R.I.B.A.	*Catalogue of the Drawings Collection of the Royal Institute of British Architects: a Cumulative Index*, ed. J. Bettley
Cath. Rec. Soc.	Catholic Record Society
Ch. Com.	Church Commissioners
Char. Com.	Charity Commission
Chron. Mon. Abingdon	*Chronicon Monasterii de Abingdon*, ed. J. Stevenson (Rolls Series, 1858)
Close R.	*Close Rolls of the Reign of Henry III preserved in the Public Record Office* (H.M.S.O. 1902–75)
Colln. Topog. et Geneal.	*Collectanea Topographica et Genealogica* (London, 1834–43)
Complete Peerage	G. E. C[ockayne] and others, *The Complete Peerage* (2nd edn. 1910–59)
Compton Census	*The Compton Census of 1676: a critical edition*, ed. A. Whiteman (British Academy Records of Social and Economic History, N.S. x)
cons. Sar.	consistory court of Salisbury
Crockford	*Crockford's Clerical Directory*
Cur. Reg. R.	*Curia Regis Rolls preserved in the Public Record Office* (H.M.S.O. 1922–91)
D. & C. Windsor Mun.	Muniments of the dean and canons of St. George's chapel, Windsor
D. & C. Winton. Mun.	Muniments of the dean and chapter of Winchester
D.N.B.	*Dictionary of National Biography*
Dugdale, *Mon.*	W. Dugdale, *Monasticon Anglicanum*, ed. J. Caley and others (1817–30)
Educ. Enq. Abstract	*Abstract of Returns relative to the State of Education in England*, H.C. 62 (1835), xliii
Educ. of Poor Digest	*Digest of Returns to the Select Committee on the Education of the Poor*, H.C. 224 (1819), ix (2)
Endowed Char. Wilts.	*Endowed Charities of Wiltshire*, H.C. 273 (1908), lxxx (northern division); H.C. 273–i (1908), lxxxi (southern division)
Ex. e Rot. Fin.	*Excerpta e Rotulis Finium in Turri Londinensi asservatis*, ed. C. Roberts (Record Commission, 1835–6)
Feud. Aids	*Inquisitions and Assessments relating to Feudal Aids preserved in the Public Record Office* (H.M.S.O. 1899–1920)
Finberg, *Early Wessex Chart.*	H. P. R. Finberg, *Early Charters of Wessex* (Leicester, 1964)
First Pembroke Survey, ed. Straton	*Survey of the Lands of William, First Earl of Pembroke*, ed. C. R. Straton (Roxburghe Club, 1909)
G.E.C. *Baronetage*	G. E. C[ockayne], *Complete Baronetage* (1900–9)
Gent. Mag.	*Gentleman's Magazine* (1731–1867)
Geol. Surv.	Geological Survey
H.C.	House of Commons

NOTE ON ABBREVIATIONS

H.M.S.O.	Her (His) Majesty's Stationery Office
Harl. Soc.	Harleian Society
Hist. MSS. Com.	Royal Commission on Historical Manuscripts
Hist. Parl.	*The History of Parliament*
Hoare, *Mod. Wilts.*	Sir Richard Colt Hoare and others, *The History of Modern Wiltshire* (London, 1822–44)
Inq. Non.	*Nonarum Inquisitiones in Curia Scaccarii*, ed. G. Vandersee (Record Commission, 1807)
L.J.	*Journals of the House of Lords*
L. & P. Hen. VIII	*Letters and Papers, Foreign and Domestic, of the Reign of Henry VIII* (H.M.S.O. 1864–1932)
Land Util. Surv.	Land Utilisation Survey
Le Neve, *Fasti*	J. Le Neve, *Fasti Ecclesiae Anglicanae* (revised edition issued by the Institute of Historical Research)
Leland, *Itin.* ed. Toulmin Smith	*Itinerary of John Leland*, ed. L. Toulmin Smith (1907–10)
Lewis, *Topog. Dict. Eng.*	S. Lewis, *Topographical Dictionary of England*
Lond. Gaz.	*London Gazette*
Lond. Metro. Archives	Corporation of London, London Metropolitan Archives
Longleat Mun.	Longleat House Muniments
Misc. Geneal. et Her.	*Miscellanea Genealogica et Heraldica* (London, 1866–1938)
N.S.	New Series
Nat. Soc. *Inquiry, 1846–7*	*Result of the Returns made to the General Inquiry made by the National Society, 1846–7* (1849)
Nightingale, *Wilts. Plate*	J. E. Nightingale, *The Church Plate of Wiltshire* (Salisbury, 1891)
O.S.	Ordnance Survey
Orig. Rec. ed. G. L. Turner	*Original Records of Early Nonconformity under Persecution and Indulgence*, ed. G. L. Turner (1911–14)
P.N. Berks. (E.P.N.S.)	M. Gelling, *Place-Names of Berkshire* (English Place-Name Society, xlix–li)
P.N. Wilts. (E.P.N.S.)	J. E. B. Gover, A. Mawer, and F. M. Stenton, *Place-Names of Wiltshire* (English Place-Name Society, xvi)
P.R.O.	Public Record Office (see above, pp. xv–xvi)
P.R.S.	Pipe Roll Society
Pat. R.	*Patent Rolls of the Reign of Henry III preserved in the Public Record Office* (H.M.S.O. 1901–3)
Pevsner, *Lond. NW.*	B. Cherry and N. Pevsner, *Buildings of England: London 3, North West*
Pevsner, *Wilts.* (2nd edn.)	N. Pevsner, *Buildings of England: Wiltshire*, revised by B. Cherry (1975)
Phillipps, *Wilts. Inst.*	*Institutiones Clericorum in Comitatu Wiltoniae*, ed. Sir Thomas Phillipps (priv. print. 1825)
Plac. de Quo Warr.	*Placita de Quo Warranto*, ed. W. Illingworth (Record Commission, 1818)
Poor Law Abstract, 1804; 1818	*Abstract of Answers and Returns relative to the Expense and Maintenance of the Poor*, H.C. 175 (1804), i; H.C. 82 (1818), xix
Poor Law Com. 1st Rep.	*First Annual Report of the Poor Law Commissioners for England and Wales*, H.C. 500 (1835), xxxv
Poor Law Com. 2nd Rep.	*Second Annual Report of the Poor Law Commissioners for England and Wales*, H.C. 595 (1836), xxix (1)
Poor Rate Returns, 1816–21	*Poor Rate Returns, 1816–21*, H.C. 556, Supplementary Appendix (1822), v
Poor Rate Returns, 1822–4	*Poor Rate Returns, 1822–4*, H.C. 334, Supplementary Appendix (1825), iv
Poor Rate Returns, 1825–9	*Poor Rate Returns, 1825–9*, H.C. 83 (1830–1), xi

Poor Rate Returns, 1830–4	*Poor Rate Returns, 1830–4*, H.C. 444 (1835), xlvii
Princ. Regy. Fam. Div.	Principal Registry of the Family Division of the High Court of Justice
R.O.	Record Office
Rec. Com.	Record Commission
Red Bk. Exch.	*The Red Book of the Exchequer*, ed. H. Hall (Rolls Series, 1896)
Reg. Ghent	*Registrum Simonis de Gandavo, Diocesis Saresbiriensis*, ed. C. T. Flower and M. C. B. Dawes (Canterbury and York Society, 1934)
Reg. Hallum	*The Register of Robert Hallum, Bishop of Salisbury*, ed. J. Horn (Canterbury and York Society, 1982)
Reg. Langham	*Registrum Simonis Langham, Cantuariensis Archiepiscopi*, ed. A. C. Wood (Canterbury and York Society, 1952–6)
Reg. Langton	*The Register of Thomas Langton, Bishop of Salisbury*, ed. D. P. Wright (Canterbury and York Society, 1985)
Reg. Martival	*The Registers of Roger Martival, Bishop of Salisbury*, ed. K. Edwards and others (Canterbury and York Society, 1959–75)
Reg. Pontoise	*Registrum Johannis de Pontissara, Diocesis Wyntoniensis*, ed. C. Deedes (Canterbury and York Society, 1913–24)
Reg. Regum Anglo-Norm.	*Regesta Regum Anglo-Normannorum, 1066–1154*, ed. H. W. C. Davis and others (1913–69)
Reg. St. Osmund	*Vetus Registrum Sarisberiense alias Dictum Registrum Sancti Osmund Episcopi*, ed. W. H. R. Jones (Rolls Series, 1883–4)
Reg. Waltham	*The Register of John Waltham, Bishop of Salisbury*, ed. T. C. B. Timmins (Canterbury and York Society, 1994)
Rep. Com. Eccl. Revenues	*Report of the Commissioners appointed to Inquire into the Ecclesiastical Revenues of England and Wales* [67], H.C. (1835), xxii
Return of Non-Provided Schs.	*Return of Schools Recognised as Voluntary Public Elementary Schools*, H.C. 178-xxxi (1906), lxxxviii
Returns relating to Elem. Educ.	*Returns relating to Elementary Education*, H.C. 201 (1871), lv
Rot. Chart.	*Rotuli Chartarum in Turri Londinensi asservati*, ed T. D. Hardy (Record Commission, 1837)
Rot. Cur. Reg.	*Rotuli Curiae Regis, 6 Richard I to 1 John*, ed. F. Palgrave (Record Commission, 1835)
Rot. Hund.	*Rotuli Hundredorum temp. Hen. III & Edw. I*, ed. W. Illingworth (Record Commission, 1812–18)
Rot. Litt. Claus.	*Rotuli Litterarum Clausarum in Turri Londinensi asservati*, ed. T. D. Hardy (Record Commission, 1833–44)
Rot. Litt. Pat.	*Rotuli Litterarum Patentium in Turri Londinensi asservati*, ed. T. D. Hardy (Record Commission, 1835)
Rot. Parl.	*Rotuli Parliamentorum* [1783]
Sar. Almanack	*The Sarum Almanack and Diocesan Kalendar*
Sar. Chart. and Doc.	*Charters and Documents illustrating the History of the Cathedral, City, and Diocese of Salisbury, in the Twelfth and Thirteenth Centuries, etc.* ed. W. Dunn Macray (Rolls Series, 1891)
Sar. Dioc. Dir.	*The Sarum Diocesan Directory*
Sar. Jnl.	*Salisbury Journal*
Soane Mus.	Sir John Soane's Museum, Lincoln's Inn Fields, London
Tax. Eccl.	*Taxatio Ecclesiastica Angliae et Walliae auctoritate P. Nicholai IV circa A.D. 1291*, ed. T. Astle, S. Ayscough, and J. Caley (Record Commission, 1802)
Topog. and Geneal.	*The Topographer and Genealogist* (London, 1846–58)
V.C.H.	*Victoria County History*
val.	valuation

NOTE ON ABBREVIATIONS

Valor Eccl.	*Valor Ecclesiasticus temp. Hen. VIII*, ed. J. Caley and J. Hunter (Record Commission, 1810–34)
W.A.M.	*Wiltshire Archaeological and Natural History Magazine*
W.A.S. (Libr.)	Wiltshire Archaeological and Natural History Society (Library in the Museum, Long Street, Devizes)
W.N. & Q.	*Wiltshire Notes and Queries* (Devizes, 1896–1917)
W.R.O.	Wiltshire and Swindon Record Office

Principal classes used:

A	Quarter Sessions records
D	Salisbury Diocesan records
EA	Enclosure Awards
F	County Council records
G	Records of Rural District, Borough, and other councils
J	Hospital records
L	Delegated and presented public records

W.R.S.	Wiltshire Record Society (*formerly* Records Branch of W.A.S.)
Walker Revised, ed. Matthews	*Walker Revised: being a Revision of John Walker's Sufferings of the Clergy during the Grand Rebellion, 1642–60*, ed. A. G. Matthews
Walters, *Wilts. Bells*	H. B. Walters, *The Church Bells of Wiltshire* (Devizes, 1927–9)
Williams, *Cath. Recusancy*	J. A. Williams, *Catholic Recusancy in Wiltshire, 1660–1791* (Catholic Record Society, 1968)
Wilts. Cuttings	Volumes of newspaper and other cuttings in W.A.S. Libr.
Wilts. Gaz.	*Wiltshire Gazette*
Wilts. Inq. p.m. 1242–1326	*Abstracts of Wiltshire Inquisitiones post mortem in the reigns of Henry III, Edward I, and Edward II, 1242–1326*, ed. E. A. Fry (Index Library, xxxvii)
Wilts. Inq. p.m. 1327–77	*Abstracts of Wiltshire Inquisitiones post mortem in the reign of Edward III, 1327–77*, ed. Ethel Stokes (Index Library, xlviii)
Wilts. Inq. p.m. 1625–49	*Abstracts of Wiltshire Inquisitiones post mortem in the reign of Charles I, 1625–49*, ed. G. S. and E. A. Fry (Index Library, xxiii)
Wilts. Q. Sess. Rec. ed. Cunnington	*Records of the County of Wiltshire from the Quarter Sessions Rolls of the 17th Century*, ed. B. H. Cunnington (Devizes, 1932)
Winch. Coll. Mun.	Muniments of Winchester College, Hampshire

INTRODUCTION

ALL the parishes in Kinwardstone hundred in east Wiltshire contain chalk downland. In the west part of the hundred six parishes lie in the east part of the Vale of Pewsey; other parishes lie in the valleys of the rivers Bourne, Dun, and Kennet. There are hill forts at Chisbury in Little Bedwyn parish and at Fosbury in Tidcombe parish, and the sites of several Roman villas have been found, but, compared with the downland of south Wiltshire, the hundred is not rich in prehistoric remains. Before the Conquest much of the land lay in four large royal estates, Bedwyn, Collingbourne, Pewsey, and Wootton, which were granted away, wholly or in portions, mainly between the 10th century and the 12th. Settlement was mostly in small villages beside streams. In the west part of the hundred, between East Sharcott in Pewsey parish and West Grafton in Great Bedwyn parish, c. 10 villages stand, as north–south streets, in the form characteristic of the Vale of Pewsey. There is evidence of colonization from Burbage, Chilton Foliat, and Pewsey, and there was probably colonization from Great Bedwyn and Collingbourne Kingston. On the north-west the woodland of Savernake forest, and on the south-east that of Chute forest (until 1544 including Hippenscombe), belonged to the Crown until the 16th century and the 17th respectively.

The land of the hundred is generally fertile. Each of about 45 villages and hamlets on it had its own set of open fields and its own common pasture. Several sets of open fields were apparently of less than 200 a., some were of over 500 a., and Burbage's was over 1,000 a. Most of the lowland common pasture was inclosed in the 17th century, most of the open fields and of the downland pasture in the 18th. Sheep-and-corn husbandry predominated in the hundred until the 19th century, when, after a railway was built through the Dun valley and the Vale of Pewsey, dairy farming for the London market became important. In the late 20th century most farming was arable, in some places combined with beef, dairy, or sheep farming, and much of the land lay in farms of over 1,000 a.; by then large farmsteads had been built outside the villages, and the sites of smaller ones within the villages had been used for housing. No industry has developed in the hundred and no town stands in it. Great Bedwyn was an early borough and retains a small market square, and Pewsey had a market from the 19th century and became a local shopping centre in the 20th, but the principal market towns for parishes in the hundred were Marlborough, Hungerford (Berks.), and Andover (Hants).

Between the Conquest and the Dissolution the owner with the most land in the hundred was Hyde abbey, Winchester, which held Collingbourne Kingston and Pewsey manors. Members of the Sturmy family held land in the hundred from 1086 or earlier and became hereditary wardens of Savernake forest. Their estate passed by marriage to the Seymour family, and later likewise to the Bruce and Brudenell-Bruce families. Edward Seymour, duke of Somerset (d. 1552), greatly increased it by purchase and, especially, by the acquisition of the estates of Hyde abbey and Easton priory and the addition of Savernake forest, Hippenscombe, and other Crown land. The estate was diminished by alienations in the later 17th century, and increased by purchases in the later 18th century and earlier 19th. Tottenham House was built on it in the 1720s and the park around the house was redesigned by 'Capability' Brown from the 1760s. About 1840 Charles Brudenell-Bruce, marquess of Ailesbury, owned, besides land outside the hundred, most of Great Bedwyn, Little Bedwyn, Burbage, Collingbourne Kingston, Easton, and Savernake parishes, and land in several other parishes. The estate was greatly reduced by sale in 1929, by a 999-year lease of woodland to the Forestry Commission in 1939, and by a sale to the Crown in 1950.

In the Middle Ages only 12 parish churches stood in the hundred, and most of their revenues were taken by religious houses and prebendaries of Salisbury cathedral. The benefices of only Buttermere, Chilton Foliat, and Pewsey remained rectories. Great Bedwyn church had six dependent chapels, but most villages and hamlets lacked a church. In the 19th century five new churches, Chute Forest, Fosbury, East Grafton, Savernake (Christchurch), and Savernake Forest (St. Katharine's), were built and an ecclesiastical district was assigned to each. Many villages had one or more nonconformist chapel, but no centre of religious dissent grew in the hundred. An almshouse for 50 widows stands in Froxfield: it was built in the 1690s and endowed by Sarah, duchess of Somerset (d. 1692).

KINWARDSTONE HUNDRED

Kinwardstone hundred was a large and compact hundred in east Wiltshire which possibly took its name from a stone that marked its meeting place.[1] At 196¼ hides it was the second most highly assessed hundred in Wiltshire in 1084,[2] and it was later among Wiltshire's largest hundreds.[3] Estates known to have been part of the assessment in 1084 lay at East Grafton, West Grafton, or both, Marten, Wolfhall (all four later in Great Bedwyn parish), Burbage, Collingbourne Kingston, Ham, Pewsey, Stitchcombe (later in Mildenhall parish), Shalbourne, South Standen (Standen Hussey later in Hungerford parish), and Wootton Rivers.[4]

In 1332 the hundred apparently included the whole of some parishes, most of some others, and a smaller proportion of others. Ham and Stitchcombe, parts of the hundred in 1084, had been transferred respectively to Elstub hundred by 1332 and Selkley hundred by 1243;[5] Everleigh and Collingbourne Ducis, both in Kinwardstone hundred in 1249 and 1275,[6] were withdrawn by an earl of Lancaster and in 1332 were part of Everleigh liberty.[7] The parishes apparently wholly in Kinwardstone hundred in 1332 were Little Bedwyn, Burbage, Buttermere, Chute, Collingbourne Kingston, Easton, Froxfield, Pewsey, and Wootton Rivers. The lands of all the villages and hamlets of Great Bedwyn parish as it was from the 16th century, except Great Bedwyn village, were part of the hundred in 1332; Great Bedwyn village had borough status and was not part of a hundred in the Middle Ages.[8] From c. 1130 to 1522, from 1547 to 1552, and from 1783 the lord of the hundred was also lord of the borough,[9] and in the 18th and 19th centuries the village, although not represented at the hundred court, was an accepted part of the hundred.[10] The whole of Milton Lilbourne parish except Clench apparently lay in the hundred in 1332:[11] Clench had been withdrawn in the mid 13th century by Battle abbey (Suss.), which held the land, was added to the abbey's liberty of Bromham, which survived the Reformation,[12] but was apparently part of Kinwardstone hundred from the late 18th century[13] or earlier. The whole of what was Tidcombe parish from 1894 lay in Kinwardstone hundred in 1332 with the probable exception of Hippenscombe, which was part of Chute forest;[14] Hippenscombe was part of the hundred in the 17th century and later.[15] Three fifths of Chilton Foliat parish lay in Wiltshire, the rest in Berkshire: the Wiltshire part lay in Kinwardstone hundred from 1332 or earlier; the Berkshire part lay in Kintbury (later Kintbury Eagle) hundred in 1086 and remained part of it.[16] Of six estates at Shalbourne in 1086 the two largest lay in Kintbury hundred and in Berkshire, the

---

[1] *P.N. Wilts.* (E.P.N.S.), 331.

[2] *V.C.H. Wilts.* ii, pp. 178–216.

[3] e.g. ibid. iv. 326–30; *Tax List, 1332* (W.R.S. xlv), *passim.*

[4] *V.C.H. Wilts.* ii, pp. 213–14; for Great Bedwyn, below, Great Bedwyn, intro.; for Stitchcombe, *V.C.H. Wilts.* xii. 125; for S. Standen, *V.C.H. Berks.* iv. 195.

[5] *Tax List, 1332* (W.R.S. xlv), 62; *V.C.H. Wilts.* xii. 62.

[6] *Crown Pleas, 1249* (W.R.S. xvi), p. 218; *Rot. Hund.* (Rec. Com.), ii (1), 259.

[7] *Tax List, 1332* (W.R.S. xlv), 115–16; *V.C.H. Wilts.* xi. 106, 137.

[8] *Tax List, 1332* (W.R.S. xlv), 8–9, 123–8; cf. below, Great Bedwyn, intro.

[9] Below, this section; Great Bedwyn, manors (preamble; Borough; Wexcombe).

[10] *Q. Sess. 1736* (W.R.S. xi), p. 142; *Poor Law Abstract, 1804*, 564; *V.C.H. Wilts.* iv. 329; W.R.O. 9/18/8–12.

[11] *Tax List, 1332* (W.R.S. xlv), 123–4.

[12] *Rot. Hund.* (Rec. Com.), ii (1), 260; *V.C.H. Wilts.* vii. 177; below, Milton Lilbourne, local govt.

[13] W.R.O., A 1/345/299.

[14] *Tax List, 1332* (W.R.S. xlv), 126; below, Tidcombe, intro.; Hippenscombe, intro.

[15] W.R.O. 9/18/8–12.

[16] *V.C.H. Berks.* i. 340, 345; iv. 157; *Tax List, 1332* (W.R.S. xlv), 126–7; below, Chilton Foliat, intro.

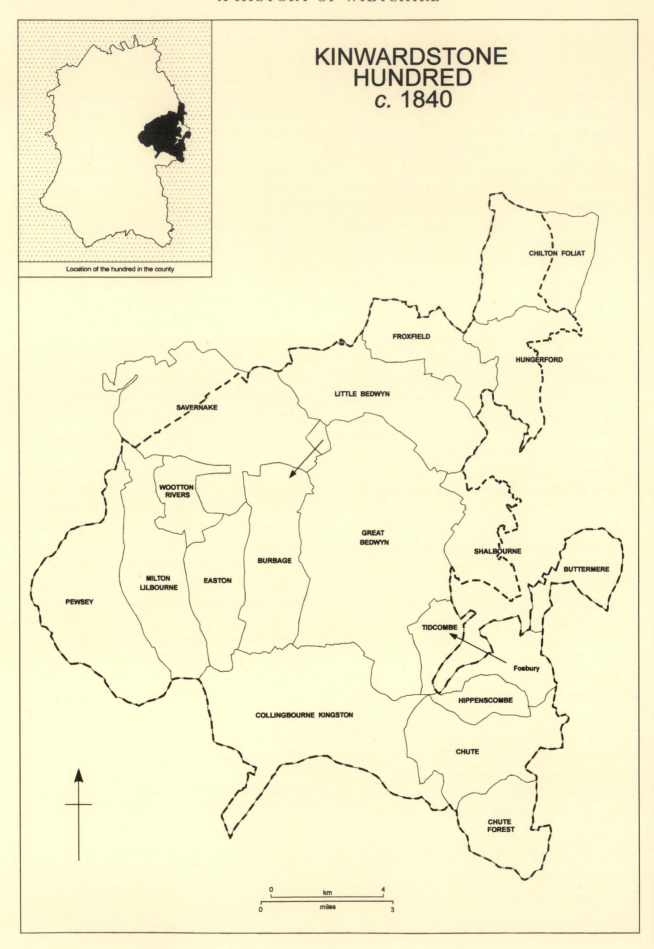

KINWARDSTONE HUNDRED
c. 1840

Location of the hundred in the county

CHILTON FOLIAT

FROXFIELD

HUNGERFORD

LITTLE BEDWYN

SAVERNAKE

WOOTTON RIVERS

GREAT BEDWYN

SHALBOURNE

BUTTERMERE

BURBAGE

MILTON LILBOURNE

EASTON

PEWSEY

TIDCOMBE

Fosbury

HIPPENSCOMBE

COLLINGBOURNE KINGSTON

CHUTE

CHUTE FOREST

four smallest in Kinwardstone hundred:[17] about a third of Shalbourne parish, including most of Shalbourne village, remained part of Kinwardstone hundred.[18] South Standen, Charlton (later Charnham Street), which was in the hundred in 1249, and North Standen, which was in it in 1268, remained parts of the hundred although most of Hungerford parish, in which they lay, was in Berkshire.[19] In 1255 Savernake forest was expressly said to lie in Kinwardstone hundred:[20] much land was excluded from the forest in the early 14th century, from 1330 the forest consisted only of the king's woods,[21] and for long after 1330 no part of the forest seems to have lain in the hundred; the west part of the forest was converted to agriculture in the 17th century,[22] and by the 19th century the southern part of that land had been assigned to Kinwardstone hundred.[23] Other parts of Savernake forest were added to Great Bedwyn, Little Bedwyn, and Burbage parishes and thus to the hundred.[24] Chute forest, which was a royal forest until the 17th century,[25] never seems to have been part of Kinwardstone hundred. Although in 1784 the owner of the land of the forest may have succeeded in a disputed claim that his land there was exempt from obligations imposed by the hundred court,[26] as an extra-parochial place and civil parish called Chute Forest it was accepted as part of the hundred for purposes of county government in the 19th century.[27] This volume deals with the whole of Kinwardstone hundred except the part which lay in Hungerford and Shalbourne parishes; it includes the whole of Chilton Foliat parish, Chute Forest parish, and the whole of Savernake parish, only part of which became part of the hundred. The history of the whole of Hungerford and Shalbourne parishes has been written elsewhere.[28]

Jurisdiction over Kinwardstone hundred was granted by Henry I with his estate called Bedwyn, which included the lordship of Great Bedwyn borough and the lordship in demesne of Wexcombe manor in Great Bedwyn parish, to John FitzGilbert, his marshal, probably c. 1130.[29] It descended with Wexcombe manor until 1522: it was then held by the Crown after the execution of Edward Stafford, duke of Buckingham, for high treason and was retained when Wexcombe manor was granted.[30] In 1523 the Crown granted the hundred to William Cary (d. 1528) in tail male,[31] and in 1544 granted the reversion to Edward Seymour, earl of Hertford.[32] Cary's heir was his son Henry, who in 1547, when he came of age, sold his interest in the hundred to Seymour, then duke of Somerset.[33] The hundred passed back to the Crown on Somerset's execution and attainder in 1552, and in that year the Crown granted it to William Herbert, earl of Pembroke.[34] It descended with the Pembroke title to 1783, when Henry Herbert, earl of Pembroke and of Montgomery, sold it to Thomas Bruce, earl of Ailesbury.[35] It thereafter descended

[17] *V.C.H. Berks.* i. 331, 348; *V.C.H. Wilts.* ii, pp. 156, 163–4, 166.
[18] e.g. *Tax List, 1332* (W.R.S. xlv), 126; O.S. Maps 6", Wilts. XXXVII, XLIII (1882–7 edns.).
[19] *Crown Pleas, 1249* (W.R.S. xvi), p. 218; *V.C.H. Berks.* iv. 183; *P.N. Berks.* (E.P.N.S.), ii. 302; *Tax List, 1332* (W.R.S. xlv), 126–7; O.S. Maps 6", Wilts. XXX, XXXVII (1887 edns.); P.R.O., HO 107/1180; ibid. JUST 1/998, rot. 34d. [20] *Rot. Hund.* (Rec. Com.), ii (1), 231.
[21] *V.C.H. Wilts.* iv. 399–400, 419, 450–1.
[22] Below, Savernake, econ. hist.
[23] *Poor Law Abstract, 1804*, 566; W.R.O., A 1/345/354.
[24] Below, Great Bedwyn, intro.; Little Bedwyn, intro.; Burbage, intro.
[25] Ibid. Chute Forest, estates.
[26] W.R.O. 9/18/14.
[27] *Poor Law Abstract, 1804*, 564; *V.C.H. Wilts.* iv. 329.
[28] *V.C.H. Berks.* iv. 183–200, 228–34.
[29] H. M. Cam, *Liberties and Communities in Medieval Eng.* 68–9; below, Great Bedwyn, manors [preamble].
[30] Below, Great Bedwyn, manors (Wexcombe); *Rot. Hund.* (Rec. Com.), ii (1), 231, 260; *Cal. Pat.* 1281–92, 351; *Cal. Inq. p.m.* iii, p. 234; v, p. 328; ix, p. 55; xiii, p. 181; xvii, p. 93; xviii, p. 269; P.R.O., E 36/150, rot. 2.
[31] P.R.O., C 142/48, no. 107.
[32] W.R.O. 1300/172B.
[33] P.R.O., C 142/48, no. 107; ibid. E 326/7567.
[34] *Cal. Pat.* 1550–3, 357–8; *Complete Peerage*, xii (1), 63–4.
[35] W.R.O. 9/18/6–7.

in the Bruce and Brudenell-Bruce families with Tottenham House in Great Bedwyn.[36]

Of the places in Kinwardstone hundred in the later Middle Ages some were exempt from the jurisdiction of the hundred courts. Besides the exemption of Great Bedwyn borough, from 1340 or earlier a manor held by the prebendary of Bedwyn and based in Great Bedwyn village was also exempt, and the lord of the hundred, and later other owners of Wexcombe manor, held a separate view of frankpledge for Wexcombe and, also in Great Bedwyn parish, Stock, Ford, Wilton, and West Bedwyn manor.[37] The overlord of Chilton Foliat manor, which was the Wiltshire part of Chilton Foliat parish, held the honor of Wallingford (Berks., later Oxon.) and until *c.* 1520 his men of Chilton Foliat attended a view held for part of the honor; after *c.* 1520 a separate view was held for Chilton Foliat.[38] While Conholt manor was held by Battle abbey in the 13th and 14th centuries the men of Conholt attended views held by the abbey;[39] in the 16th century and later the tithingman of Conholt attended Kinwardstone hundred courts.[40] The men of a manor in Easton parish held by Bradenstoke priory were also exempt from the jurisdiction of the hundred courts, and from the mid 16th century leet jurisdiction over the whole parish was exercised at a view held privately; a tithingman of Easton nevertheless attended the hundred courts.[41] Oakhill, in Froxfield parish, and North Standen were parts of one manor and of the duchy of Lancaster and had been withdrawn from the jurisdiction of Kinwardstone hundred courts by the 15th century.[42] No tithingman expressly said to be of South Standen attended the hundred courts;[43] South Standen may have been exempt or part of Charnham Street tithing.

Despite those exemptions the courts of Kinwardstone hundred were attended in the 16th century by 31 tithingmen, in the 17th by 32, and in the 19th by 33; only three tithings, Buttermere, Easton, and Wootton Rivers, were apparently conterminous with parishes. In the part of Great Bedwyn parish not exempt there were four tithings, Crofton, East Grafton, West Grafton, and Wolfhall, and the tithingman of Wilton also attended the courts; Marten in Great Bedwyn was part of a composite tithing with Tidcombe. In Little Bedwyn there were four tithings, Little Bedwyn, Chisbury, Henset, and Puthall; either Henset or Puthall included Rudge in Froxfield. There were four tithings in Pewsey parish (Down Pewsey, Kepnal, Sharcott, and Southcott), three in Collingbourne Kingston parish (Collingbourne Kingston, Collingbourne Valence, and Collingbourne Sunton) and Milton Lilbourne parish (Milton Lilbourne, Milton Abbot's, and Fyfield), and two in Burbage parish (Burbage Savage and Burbage Sturmy) and Chute parish (Chute and Conholt). Tidcombe was part of Tidcombe and Marten tithing, and Fosbury in Tidcombe parish was a separate tithing. Froxfield (excluding Oakhill and Rudge), Charnham Street, and the Wiltshire part of Shalbourne parish were also tithings. Between 1567 and 1696 a tithingman of Hippenscombe began to attend the courts, and in the 19th century a tithingman of Brimslade and South Savernake attended.[44]

[36] W.R.O. 9/18/12; below, Great Bedwyn, manors (Tottenham).

[37] Above, this section; below, Great Bedwyn, manors (Prebendal); local govt.

[38] Below, Chilton Foliat, manors (Chilton Foliat); local govt.   [39] Ibid. Chute, manors (Conholt); local govt.

[40] *First Pembroke Survey*, ed. Straton, i. 191; W.R.O.

9/18/8–12.

[41] Below, Easton, manors (Easton Bradenstoke); local govt.; W.R.O. 9/18/8–12.

[42] Below, Froxfield, manors (Oakhill); local govt.

[43] Cf. W.R.O. 9/18/8–12.

[44] *First Pembroke Survey*, i. 190–1; W.R.O. 9/18/8–12; for Rudge, below, Little Bedwyn, local govt.

Two hundred courts were held, one, at which leet jurisdiction was exercised and the tithingmen paid cert rent, twice a year, and one every three weeks.[45] The early meeting place of the hundred may have been in or near Burbage village, which lies near the centre of the hundred, and in the late 17th century Kinwardstone gate led to the part of Burbage parish where Kinwardstone Farm was built in the earlier 19th century;[46] in the mid 19th century the biannual court met at the White Hart, Burbage. One tithingman for each tithing was required to attend when each court was held. Records of the biannual court survive for 1696–1719, when it was called the court of view of frankpledge, and 1842–71, when it was called the court leet and view of frankpledge. In the earlier period the court met each spring and autumn. It was attended by the tithingmen and some of the free suitors, and new tithingmen were appointed at the autumn meeting. The tithingman of Wolfhall and the tithingman of Puthall were required to keep, respectively, a bloodhound and a mastiff for the use of the men of the hundred, and by custom each showed his dog at the view of frankpledge: presumably for meeting the requirement each was excused attendance at the court held every three weeks. At each meeting of the view of frankpledge a jury was empanelled and it presented under leet jurisdiction. Most presentments concerned the poor condition of boundaries, highways, watercourses, hedges, pounds, and stocks; in 1716 the dangerous condition of chimneys in Charnham Street was presented. The number of presentments declined through the period. In the later period the court leet met alternately in spring and autumn, but only 15 times. Besides amercing those who failed to attend, its only business was to nominate officers and tithingmen. Records of the court held every three weeks survive for 1706–20 and 1737–63. The court was held by the lord's steward, met before two free suitors of the hundred, and was usually attended by several tithingmen. Apparently the court's only business was to hear pleas and to amerce the tithingmen who failed to attend, and until the 1750s the progress of several pleas was recorded at most meetings. From 1760 no tithingman attended and the court's only business was to amerce each one.[47]

In 1275 the hundred was valued at £20: £2 4s. was received by the lord of the hundred as tithing penny, £3 14s. as sheriff's aid, and the rest as perquisites of the courts.[48] In the 1390s it was valued at £17: £9 10s. was received as tithing rent, £3 as sheriff's aid, and the rest from the perquisites.[49] In 1567 the tithingmen attending the courts paid £9 1s. 4d. as cert rent and £4 10s. 10½d. as sheriff's aid.[50] In 1783 the combined payments, then called law silver, amounted to £13 13s. 10d.[51]

The bailiwick of Kinwardstone hundred descended in the Homedieu family in the 13th and 14th centuries.[52] Constables were being appointed in the mid 14th century.[53] From the later 16th century or earlier two were appointed each year,[54] and from the later 17th century or earlier they were chosen by the steward at the autumn meeting of the view of frankpledge and one served for the east part of the hundred and one for the west.[55]

---

[45] P.R.O., SC 6/1117/8; W.R.O. 9/18/8–12.
[46] W.R.O. 9/18/8, ct. 20 Apr. 1697; ibid. EA/68; below, Burbage, intro. (other settlement).
[47] W.R.O. 9/18/8–12.
[48] Rot. Hund. (Rec. Com.), ii (1), 260.
[49] Cal. Inq. Misc. vi, p. 145.
[50] First Pembroke Survey, i. 190–2.
[51] W.R.O. 9/18/6–7.
[52] Cal. Pat. 1354–8, 438; Extents for Debts (W.R.S. xxviii), pp. 20–1, 23; P.R.O., JUST 1/1001, rot. 11; JUST 1/1006, rot. 38.
[53] V.C.H. Wilts. v. 24.
[54] Sess. Mins. (W.R.S. iv), 81, 89, 113.
[55] W.R.O. 9/18/8; 9/18/12.

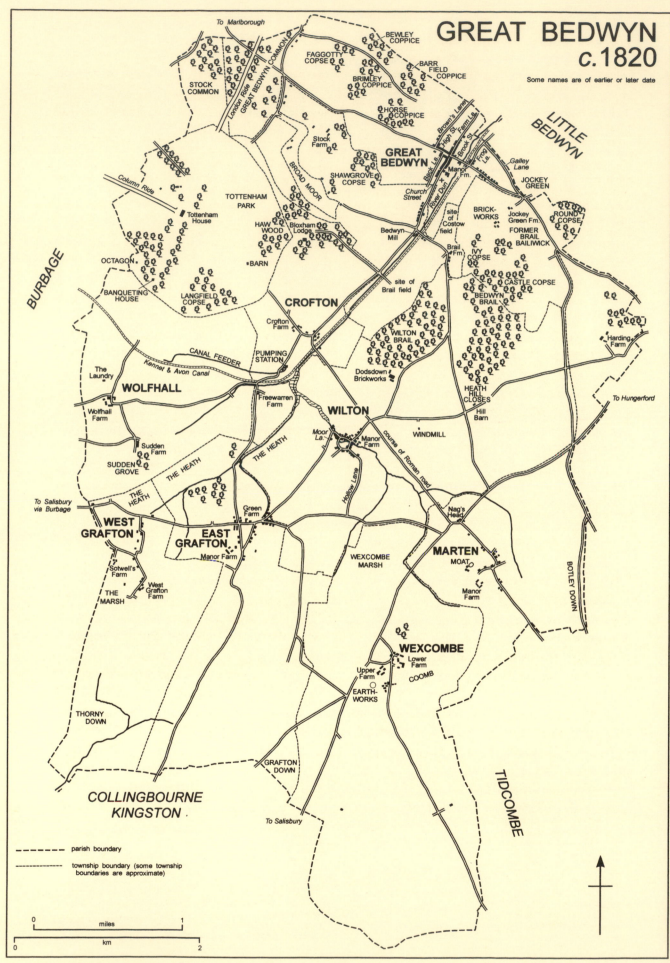

GREAT BEDWYN
c.1820

Some names are of earlier or later date

To Marlborough

BEWLEY COPPICE

FAGGOTTY COPSE

BARR FIELD COPPICE

BRIMLEY COPPICE

STOCK COMMON

HORSE COPPICE

Brown's Level

LITTLE BEDWYN

Farm La

High St.

Stock Farm

GREAT BEDWYN

Galley Lane

JOCKEY GREEN

Column Ride

TOTTENHAM PARK

SHAWGROVE COPSE

Manor Fm.

Brook St.

Frog La.

BROAD MOOR

Church Street

BRICK-WORKS

Jockey Green Fm.

ROUND COPSE

Tottenham House

HAW WOOD

Bloxham Lodge

Bedwyn Mill

site of Costow field

FORMER BRAIL BAILIWICK

River Dun

Brail Fm.

IVY COPSE

OCTAGON

BARN

Brail field

CASTLE COPSE

BURBAGE

BANQUETING HOUSE

LANGFIELD COPSE

CROFTON

BEDWYN BRAIL

Crofton Farm

WILTON BRAIL

Harding Farm

CANAL FEEDER

PUMPING STATION

Dodsdown Brickworks

Kennet & Avon Canal

The Laundry

WOLFHALL

HEATH HILL CLOSES

To Hungerford

Freewarren Farm

WILTON

Hill Barn

Wolfhall Farm

Moor La.

Manor Farm

WINDMILL

Sudden Farm

THE HEATH

SUDDEN GROVE

THE HEATH

course of Roman road

Hollow Lane

Nag's Head

THE HEATH

Green Farm

To Salisbury via Burbage

WEST GRAFTON

EAST GRAFTON

WEXCOMBE MARSH

MARTEN

MOAT

BOTLEY DOWN

Sotwell's Farm

Manor Farm

Manor Farm

THE MARSH

West Grafton Farm

Manor Farm

WEXCOMBE

Lower Farm

Upper Farm

COOMB

EARTH-WORKS

THORNY DOWN

GRAFTON DOWN

TIDCOMBE

COLLINGBOURNE KINGSTON

To Salisbury

- - - - parish boundary

- - - - township boundary (some township boundaries are approximate)

0   miles   1

0   km   2

8

GREAT BEDWYN

GREAT BEDWYN village stands 10 km. south-east of Marlborough and 7 km. south-west of Hungerford (Berks.).[1] In the Middle Ages Great Bedwyn parish apparently consisted of most of what became Great Bedwyn, Little Bedwyn, and Grafton parishes.[2] As Little Bedwyn the northern third of it had become a separate parish by the 16th century.[3] Great Bedwyn parish adjoined Savernake forest, which was extra-parochial,[4] and a part of the forest, and two areas which were almost certainly parts of the forest, were added to it: Bedwyn Brails bailiwick was a detached part of the forest embraced by the parish, Tottenham park was presumably part of the forest in the 16th century,[5] and north of the park Bedwyn common and Stock common were apparently part of the forest in the 18th century although a dubious claim was then made that they were not.[6] All those lands had been absorbed by the parish by the 19th century.[7] Including them Great Bedwyn was then a parish of 9,933 a. (4,020 ha.). As East Grafton the southern half of that parish became a separate ecclesiastical district in 1844 and as Grafton a civil parish in 1895.[8] From 1895 Great Bedwyn parish measured 4,007 a. (1,622 ha.) and Grafton 5,927 a. (2,399 ha.). In 1987 Great Bedwyn parish was increased to 1,679 ha. by transfers from it to Burbage and to it from Little Bedwyn, Burbage, and Grafton, and Grafton parish was decreased to 2,263 ha. by transfers from it to Great Bedwyn and Burbage.[9] This article deals with Great Bedwyn parish as it was from the 16th century to 1895 when, besides Great Bedwyn village, it contained villages and hamlets called Crofton, Ford, East Grafton, West Grafton, Harding, Marten, Stock, Wexcombe, Wilton, and Wolfhall. Burgage tenure in it gave Great Bedwyn borough status.[10]

The boundary of a large estate called Bedwyn was recited in 968. Attempts to relate much of it to modern parish boundaries are unconvincing, but it had some points in common with the boundary of Great Bedwyn parish as it was from the 16th century.[11] On the east the parish boundary follows a prehistoric ditch for c. 1 km., was drawn very near to two barrows, follows a Roman road for c. 60 m., and is marked by other roads for c. 1.25 km., on the south it runs along the bottom of two deep dry valleys, and on the

west at the south end it is marked by a track which is possibly ancient, but for most of its length, c. 35 km., it ignores both relief and major features.[12] The boundary drawn between Great Bedwyn and Grafton parishes in 1895 followed a railway line, the Roman road, and other roads.[13]

Chalk outcrops at the south end of the parish, Upper Greensand in much of the centre. In the north part of the parish chalk outcrops as the lower land, the sands and clay of the Reading Beds, London Clay, and Bagshot Beds as the higher. There are deposits of clay-with-flints in the north-west and south-east parts of the parish, of gravel in dry valleys north-west and south-east of Great Bedwyn village, and of a small amount of alluvium immediately south-east of the village.[14] The relief is broken and most of the valleys are dry. Most of the parish drains north-eastwards towards the river Kennet. Several streams rising in the centre of the parish come together as a river known locally in the 18th century as the Bedwyn river or the Bedwyn brook,[15] downstream called the Dun in the 19th century;[16] in the later 20th century the name Dun was applied to the whole river.[17] In the north part of the parish the highest land is at 197 m. on the western boundary, several ridges reach c. 160 m., and the lowest point is at c. 120 m. where the Dun leaves the parish. The chalk downland in the south part of the parish includes some escarpments and deep dry valleys; the highest point is at 267 m. near the eastern boundary. South of the scarps the land drains southwards, and a feeder of the river Bourne rises in the south-west corner of the parish; the lowest land is at c. 140 m. where the feeder leaves the parish. Most, if not all, of the villages and hamlets in the parish had open fields and common pasture, most of the land is suitable for arable or pasture,[18] and in much of the parish, especially in the south part, there were few areas of dense woodland until the late 18th century.[19] There have been several parks in the parish, mainly in the north-west part.[20]

In 1377 the parish had 398 poll-tax payers.[21] The population was 1,632 in 1801. It had risen to 2,191 by 1831, it remained roughly constant from 1831 to 1871, when it was 2,068, and it had fallen to 1,627 by 1891. In 1901 Great Bedwyn

[1] This article was written in 1996. Maps used include O.S. Maps 1", sheet 14 (1817 edn.); 1/50,000, sheet 174 (1993 edn.); 6", Wilts. XXXVI–XXXVII, XLII–XLIII (1882–8 and later edns.).
[2] *Chandler's Reg.* (W.R.S. xxxix), pp. 31–3; cf. below, manors (Prebendal).
[3] Below, Little Bedwyn.
[4] Ibid. Savernake, intro.
[5] Ibid. this section [Savernake forest]; manors (Brail; Tottenham); econ. hist. (Brail; Tottenham park).
[6] W.R.O. 9/3/388; 9/3/393H.
[7] O.S. Maps 6", Wilts. XXXVI–XXXVII (1887–8 edns.).
[8] *Lond. Gaz.* 20 Aug. 1844, pp. 2904–6; *V.C.H. Wilts.* iv. 349.
[9] *Census,* 1991; Statutory Instruments, 1987, no. 619, Kennet (Parishes) Order.
[10] Below, this section (Great Bedwyn); local govt.; parl. rep.

[11] *W.A.M.* xli. 281–300; *Arch. Jnl.* lxxvii. 75–80; cf. below, manors [preamble], where, in n. 28, there is comment on the chart. of 968.
[12] For the track, *Arch. Jnl.* lxxvii. 62; for the ditch, inf. from Arch. section, Co. Hall, Trowbridge.
[13] For roads, railways, and prehist. remains, below, this section.
[14] Geol. Surv. Maps 1", drift, sheet 267 (1971 edn.); 1/50,000, drift, sheet 283 (1975 edn.).
[15] W.R.O. 9/3/386–7.
[16] *P.N. Berks.* (E.P.N.S.), ii. 302–3.
[17] Cf. O.S. Maps 6", Wilts. SU 26 SE. (1961 edn.); 1/10,000, SU 26 SE. (1982 edn.).
[18] Below, econ. hist.
[19] *Andrews and Dury, Map* (W.R.S. viii), pl. 12; below, econ. hist.
[20] Below, econ. hist. (E. Grafton; Marten; Wolfhall; Tottenham park).
[21] *V.C.H. Wilts.* iv. 309.

parish had 877 inhabitants, Grafton parish 663. Great Bedwyn's population fell from 880 in 1911 to 789 in 1931, but thereafter the building of new houses in Great Bedwyn village caused it to rise: from 847 in 1951 it had increased to 974 by 1981 and, after the boundary changes of 1987, it stood at 1,093 in 1991. Grafton's population fell steadily from 1911, when it was 684, to 1971, when it was 547; it was 583 in 1981 and, after the boundary changes of 1987, 603 in 1991.[22]

The course of the Roman road between Cirencester and Winchester via Mildenhall runs north-west and south-east across the parish.[23] In 1996 it was used by roads south-east of Wilton and of Marten and by a track north-west and south-east of Crofton; in the north-west part of the parish it was imparked, probably before the mid 16th century,[24] and went out of use. The road between Oxford and Salisbury via Hungerford, important in the 17th century, crosses the south-east part of the parish;[25] it was turnpiked in 1772 and disturnpiked in 1866.[26] As a continuation eastwards of a road from Pewsey and Burbage a new road was made between 1773 and 1817, partly or wholly c. 1792, to link East Grafton village to the Hungerford road west of Marten.[27] In 1886 the section of it east of its junction with the Marlborough–Salisbury road at Burbage was declared a main road,[28] and, avoiding a steep gradient on the old turnpike road west of Wexcombe, it became the main Hungerford–Salisbury road. In the 20th century, especially after the London and south Wales motorway was opened in 1972,[29] the road took much traffic between London and the centre part of Wiltshire.

The Kennet & Avon canal was opened from Hungerford to Great Bedwyn in 1799, from Great Bedwyn to Devizes in 1809, and completely in 1810.[30] A wharf was built in Great Bedwyn village,[31] and four locks were built south-west of it in the parish. The reach west of Crofton is the highest part of the canal, and a pumping station was built south-west of Crofton to supply water to it from the Dun. The pumping station, of three storeys and red brick, housed a steam-powered beam engine which began pumping in 1809; a second engine began pumping in 1812. From 1836–7 the canal was fed from Wilton Water, an 8-a. reservoir made south of the canal by damming head streams of the Dun. A new red-brick chimney was built in 1856. In 1968 the Kennet & Avon Canal trust bought the pumping station, which by 1971 had been restored by the Crofton Society. The canal was reopened across the parish in 1988.[32]

The Berks. & Hants Extension Railway, operated by the G.W.R., was opened across the parish in 1862; it was built along the north side of the canal, and Bedwyn station was built in Great Bedwyn village near the wharf. The line led from Reading to Devizes and from 1900 to Westbury; from 1906 it has been part of a main line between London and Exeter.[33] In 1882–3 the Swindon, Marlborough & Andover Railway, in 1884 vested in the Midland & South Western Junction Railway, was opened as a single-track line across the west part of the parish; it ran north–south, at West Grafton had a station called Grafton and Burbage, and used the G.W.R. line from a junction north-east of Wolfhall to Savernake station in Burbage. In 1898 a new double-track line, bridging the G.W.R. line and converging on the single-track line at a point a little north of Grafton and Burbage station, was opened for Swindon–Andover trains. To improve services to new army camps on Salisbury Plain the track south of that point was doubled in 1902 and the Grafton curve, a new section of line bridging the canal south-west of Crofton, was built in 1905 to enable trains to run directly between Bedwyn station and Grafton and Burbage station. A tramway between Grafton and Burbage station and Dodsdown brickworks north-east of Wilton village was opened in 1902 and closed in 1910. In 1933 the line built in 1898 was singled, and in 1961 the whole north–south line across the parish was closed.[34] In the late 20th century Paddington–Exeter trains did not stop at Bedwyn station, which was then the terminus for trains from Reading.

Many prehistoric remains, including artefacts of the Neolithic period and the Bronze Age, have been found in the parish.[35] The many barrows on the downland in the south-east include a long barrow 1 km. south of Wexcombe village.[36] An Iron-Age field system also south of Wexcombe village covers 100 a., and another on downland east of Wilton village covers c. 150 a.[37] A Neolithic enclosure has been found south-west of Crofton village,[38] and there are other prehistoric enclosures west of Great Bedwyn village and between West Grafton and Wolfhall.[39] The prehistoric ditch on the parish boundary at the south-east end of the parish may be one of a group mainly in Tidcombe and Fosbury parish.[40] In the north part of Great Bedwyn parish two Roman villas have been discovered, neither far from the Cirencester–Winchester road.[41] That SSE. of Great Bedwyn village was excavated 1983–6: it was built in the 1st century A.D., was enlarged to incorporate a courtyard, and was given luxury fittings in the 4th century.[42] There

[22] V.C.H. Wilts. iv. 340, 349; Census, 1961; 1971; 1981; 1991; for the new hos., below, this section (Great Bedwyn).
[23] I. D. Margary, Rom. Roads in Brit. (1973), pp. 98–9.
[24] W.R.O. 1300/372, ff. 38–9; below, econ. hist. (Tottenham park).   [25] J. Ogilby, Brit. (1675), pl. 83.
[26] V.C.H. Wilts. iv. 257, 262, 270.
[27] Andrews and Dury, Map (W.R.S. viii), pl. 12; O.S. Map 1", sheet 14 (1817 edn.); W.R.O., EA/68.
[28] W.R.O., A 1/110/1886/E.
[29] Rep. Co. Surveyor, 1971–2 (Wilts. co. council), 3.
[30] K. R. Clew, Kennet & Avon Canal (1985), 60, 71, 73.
[31] O.S. Map 1/2,500, Wilts. XXXVII. 5 (1880 edn.).
[32] Clew, op. cit. 69–71, 173; Kennet & Avon Canal Trust (Crofton Branch), Crofton Beam Engines (1993), 9, 21.

[33] V.C.H. Wilts. iv. 286–7, 289.
[34] Ibid. 289–90; D. Bartholomew, Midland & SW. Junction Rly. i. 162–3, 165; C. G. Maggs, Midland & SW. Junction Rly. 55, 74–6, 89–90; for the brickworks, below, econ. hist. (Wilton).   [35] V.C.H. Wilts. i (1), 72–3.
[36] Ibid. 140, 176–7, 209, 218.
[37] Ibid. 276.
[38] W.A.M. lxx/lxxi. 124–5; lxxxviii. 18, 23–4.
[39] V.C.H. Wilts. i (1), 266.
[40] Inf. from Arch. section, Co. Hall, Trowbridge.
[41] V.C.H. Wilts. i (1), 73.
[42] W.A.M. lxxix. 233–5; lxxx. 97–102; lxxxi. 52–6; E. Hostetter and T. N. Howe, Romano-Brit. Villa at Castle Copse.

is a 6th- or 7th-century cemetery near Crofton village.[43]

The whole parish lay within Savernake forest; Great Bedwyn borough, although within the bounds, was exempt from the forest law. When the boundary of the forest was redefined in 1300 all but Bedwyn Brails bailiwick, an area south-east of Great Bedwyn village, was excluded, and, with that exception, the parish was finally disafforested in 1330. Land at the north-west end of the parish, as Tottenham park, Bedwyn common, and Stock common later part of it, almost certainly remained part of the forest in 1330.[44]

A gibbet was standing north-east of Wilton village in 1773.[45]

GREAT BEDWYN. In the early 12th century there was a tradition at the abbey of Abingdon (Berks., later Oxon.) that a grant of land probably near Abingdon by King Cissa between 674 and 685 was a prelude to the founding of the abbey. The tradition was possibly based on fact,[46] but the statement that Cissa ruled from Bedwyn and gave his name to Chisbury, where he built a castle, was apparently first made in the 13th century,[47] was presumably made in the knowledge that Bedwyn belonged to the abbey in the 10th century[48] and that a hill fort had been made at Chisbury,[49] and was almost certainly fantasy. In the late 10th century there may have been a guild at Great Bedwyn: a document of that date in which ordinances of a guild were listed does not name Great Bedwyn but probably relates to it.[50] In the mid 11th century Great Bedwyn was a borough comprising 25 burgages and containing a mint.[51] The borough stood on the north-west bank of the Dun.[52] In the mid 18th century Great Bedwyn village consisted of a rectangular market place and of five streets leading from it. The market house stood at the south-east end of the market place, most of the streets was built up, and there seem to have been only one or two farmsteads in the village.[53] Those urban characteristics may have survived from the 11th-century borough; some of them were retained in the late 20th century, but no evidence of long and narrow burgage plots survived then.[54]

A church may have been standing in the late 10th century. The site of one which was standing in 1066[55] is not known. In the 12th century the church stood 250 m. south-west of the market place[56] at what may then have been, and was from the 18th century to the 20th, the south-west edge of the built-up area.[57] A manor house for the prebendary of Bedwyn, and Manor Farm, a farmstead which was part of the Prebendal estate, were built beside the 12th-century church,[58] and a vicarage house was built nearby. Of Manor Farm, the farmhouse standing in 1996 was a square red-brick house of the mid 19th century; the farm buildings were demolished in the late 20th century.[59]

In the late 11th century Great Bedwyn's mint was apparently transferred to Marlborough,[60] and thereafter Great Bedwyn seems to have been stunted by its proximity to Hungerford and Marlborough. It was damaged by fire in 1201,[61] had only 87 poll-tax payers in 1377,[62] and c. 1545 was called by Leland 'a poor thing to sight'.[63] A fire destroyed 28 houses in 1716,[64] and in 1754 Great Bedwyn was 'a poor town of farmers, maltsters, and publicans'.[65] The market house was rebuilt, or built anew, probably in the early 17th century.[66] It was open on the ground floor and had a first-floor timber-framed room supported on turned columns; its roof was hipped and surmounted by an open cupola in which a bell hung. A large brick chimney stack had been built against the north-west end by 1770, when the building was repaired and a new bell was hung. The building was demolished in 1870.[67] A hospital in which St. John the Baptist was invoked from the 13th century to the 15th was said to stand in Bedwyn; the most likely site for it is one in Great Bedwyn village. It seems that the hospital, which in the 13th century was given a small estate in Crofton, was poorly endowed, and it may have been dissolved before the Reformation.[68]

Great Bedwyn's wide market place[69] and the street leading north-west from it were called Chipping Street or Cheap Street,[70] from 1841 or earlier High Street.[71] One house or more stood in the middle of High Street in the earlier 18th century,[72] two in 1751,[73] apparently none in 1773[74] or later. Church Street leads south-westwards from the market place's south corner, Brook Street south-eastwards, and Farm Lane north-eastwards, from its east corner, and Back Lane south-westwards from its west corner: those streets were first so called in 1759, 1552, 1730, and 1675 respectively.[75] Farm Lane was

43 V.C.H. Wilts. i (1), 73.
44 Ibid. iv. 399–400, 418, 448, 450–1.
45 Andrews and Dury, Map (W.R.S. viii), pl. 12.
46 F. M. Stenton, Early Hist. Abbey of Abingdon, 9–18.
47 Chron. Mon. Abingdon (Rolls Ser.), ii. 268.
48 Below, manors [preamble].
49 Ibid. Little Bedwyn, intro. [prehist. remains].
50 W.A.M. lii. 360, 363–4; Eng. Hist. Doc. i, ed. D. Whitelock (1979), pp. 605–6.
51 V.C.H. Wilts. ii, pp. 16, 115–16.
52 Cf. W.A.M. xlix. 394.
53 W.R.O. 9/3/393H; cf. below, econ. hist. (Great Bedwyn).
54 Below, plate 45.
55 Ibid. churches.
56 Ibid. [archit.].
57 Cf. W.R.O. 9/3/393H; below, plate 45.
58 Ibid.; for the manor ho., below, manors (Prebendal); for the prebendary, below, church.
59 Cf. O.S. Map 1/25,000, SU 26/36 (1983 edn.).

60 V.C.H. Wilts. ii, pp. 16–17.
61 Pipe R. 1201 (P.R.S. n.s. xiv), 295.
62 V.C.H. Wilts. iv. 309.
63 Leland, Itin. ed. Toulmin Smith, v. 79.
64 E. L. Jones, Gaz. Eng. Urban Fire Disasters, 1500–1900, p. 20.
65 Travels through Eng. of Dr. Ric. Pococke, ii (Camd. Soc. [2nd ser.], xliv), 157.
66 Below, plate 44.
67 W.R.O. 9/3/394; 2320/6.
68 V.C.H. Wilts. iii. 334; W.A.M. xxxix. 380–1; Chandler's Reg. (W.R.S. xxxix), p. 102.
69 For the mkt. place and the streets leading from it, below, plate 45.
70 Cat. Anct. D. ii, C 2891; W.R.O. 9/3/53; 1308/5.
71 P.R.O., HO 107/1180/1, f. 6.
72 W.R.O. 79B/8, deed, Streat to Streat, 1722.
73 Ibid. 9/3/393H.
74 Andrews and Dury, Map (W.R.S. viii), pl. 12.
75 W.R.O. 9/1/95, p. 58; 9/1/158; 9/3/215; 9/3/282.

renamed Jubilee Street, presumably in 1887, and reverted to Farm Lane in the later 20th century.[76] Brown's Lane, in which stand three buildings possibly of 17th-century origin, was made before 1751,[77] possibly as an alternative to Farm Lane, which was narrow and on lower ground south-east of it. In the 18th century the right to vote at parliamentary elections in Great Bedwyn was attached to tenements which stood in each part of the village.[78]

In 1648 the alehouses in Great Bedwyn, presumably the village, were regarded as a nuisance and too numerous by the inhabitants of neighbouring parishes.[79] In the 18th century c. 14 inns or alehouses were open at various times, including six in Church Street. In 1763 the Cross Keys in Brook Street was replaced by an inn of that name on the corner of High Street and Farm Lane, and in 1784 the Three Tuns was open on the corner of High Street and Brown's Lane.[80] In the 1790s the White Hart, on the north-west side of Church Street, the Cross Keys, and the Three Tuns were apparently the only inns open in the village;[81] the White Hart was closed in 1867,[82] and the other two remained open in 1996.

The houses in High Street and Church Street in 1996 were characteristically small, of red brick, and with tiled roofs. A few may have been 17th-century, many were ostensibly 18th-century, and a few had been enlarged in the 20th century. In the 19th century 14 estate cottages replaced buildings which were standing in 1751.[83] The houses stood close together, there were several terraces, and on the south-east side of Church Street there was an unbroken row of what in the later 19th century was c. 15 houses.[84] The largest house to be built in the two streets is apparently that on the corner of High Street and Church Street which was built in the later 18th century with a main north-east front of seven bays. On the north-east side of High Street, part of a large house which has a main south-east front of six bays seems to consist of altered 18th-century cottages. Two terraces of four estate cottages, one terrace being dated 1871, stand on the north-east side of High Street, and three pairs stand in Church Street near the church. A school built in Church Street in the earlier 19th century[85] is one of the few stone buildings in the village.

In Farm Lane c. 16 houses and cottages built between the 17th century and the 19th were standing in 1996. Two of the cottages, timber-framed and thatched, are apparently 17th-century; two houses of red brick and thatch, in one of which timber framing is visible, and two rows of cottages, each of a single storey and attics and of red brick and tiles, may be 18th-century. On the south-east side of the street a large red-brick malting, diapered with blue brick, was built in 1868 and converted to several

No. 12 FARM LANE

dwellings c. 1975.[86] Immediately south-west of it what was probably the maltster's house is apparently contemporary with it and was built in similar style; it has its back to the street, and to the front has heavily carved bargeboards and a deep central recess. Nearby on the north-west side of the street there is a pair of red-brick mid 19th-century cottages with decorations of buff brick. Also on the south-east side of the street a small house, no. 12 Farm Lane, has at its west corner a tall early 17th-century chimney stack of stone and flint. The house of which the stack was part was replaced, probably in the later 17th century, by a smaller and lower house, largely timber-framed, in which the two fireplaces served by the stack were incorporated. The house standing in the earlier 17th century is reputed to have been the birthplace of Thomas Willis (1621–75), who discovered diabetes mellitus and was a founder of the Royal Society.[87]

Between the market place and the Dun two small 17th-century houses, each of one storey and attics, survived on the north-east side of Brook Street in 1996. Off the south-west side c. 26 houses were built in the late 20th century. Off that part of Brook Street to the north-east four pairs of red- and blue-brick estate cottages were built in 1870.[88] They are arranged in a symmetrical composition of two smaller and two larger pairs, face the railway line, were known as Railway Terrace in 1891,[89] and in 1996 remained conspicuous on the approach to the village from the south-east.[90]

At the north-east end of Back Lane a row of about six cottages had been built by 1751. One of the cottages was rebuilt in the 19th century; the others are of the earlier 18th century. Of the possibly 17th-century buildings in Brown's Lane two cottages, each of a single storey and attics, stand at the south-west end, a house at

76 O.S. Maps 6", Wilts. XXXVII. NW. (1900 and later edns.).   77 W.R.O. 9/3/393H.
78 Cf. ibid.; for elections, below, parl. rep.
79 Wilts. Q. Sess. Rec. ed. Cunnington, 194.
80 P.R.O., E 134/3 Anne Trin./20; W.R.O. 9/3/99; 9/3/298; 9/3/347; 9/3/354; 9/3/367; 9/3/393H; 9/3/397, p. 38; 9/4/86; 9/26/520A, pp. 27, 29, 31; 1300/372, ff. 3–4; ibid. A 1/326/3; ibid. D 21/2/3/125.
81 Early Trade Dir. (W.R.S. xlvii), 11.

82 W.R.O. 1308/5, p. 22.
83 Cf. ibid. 9/3/393H.
84 O.S. Map 1/2,500, Wilts. XXXVII. 5 (1880 edn.).
85 Below, educ.
86 Dates on bldg.
87 D.N.B.; Gent. Mag. lxviii (2), 1013.
88 Date on bldgs.
89 P.R.O., RG 12/972, f. 15.
90 Below, plate 35.

the north-east end; two other thatched houses stand on sites occupied by buildings in 1751.[91] A nonconformist chapel was built at the south-west end of the lane in the 19th century.[92]

In the 17th century Great Bedwyn village extended itself south-east of the Dun. Galley Lane, running north-west and south-east along the parish boundary and presumably fording the Dun and taking Marlborough traffic away from the village, was joined to the village by a south-east extension of Brook Street;[93] the junction, at which the Horse and Jockey inn stood in Little Bedwyn parish, took the name Jockey Green. By 1773 the two ends of Brook Street had been linked by a bridge over the Dun c. 50 m. north-east of the present bridge;[94] the site at which the Dun was bridged was apparently changed when the Kennet & Avon canal was built c. 1800. South-east of the river Frog Lane, so called in 1742, links Brook Street and Galley Lane. By 1751 a row of five cottages had been built on the waste at the south-west end of Frog Lane and 21 small houses on the verge beside the extension of Brook Street.[95] Most of the buildings survived in 1996. Of those which did all were thatched; a few were apparently 17th-century, most early 18th-century; most walling was of red brick, and several houses incorporated timber-framed attics. In the 19th century a pair of estate cottages was built at Jockey Green, and in the 20th nine houses and bungalows were built beside Brook Street.

In the 20th century Great Bedwyn village grew much more than in the 19th. North-west-wards from the junction of High Street and Brown's Lane, where the road was given the name Forest Hill, settlement was extended c. 100 m. to where a block of six estate cottages was built in 1845;[96] a large brick house was built c. 1920, and 10 other houses, some of them large, were built in the mid and later 20th century. Also c. 1920 eight pairs of council houses were built on the north-west side of Church Street and linked the village to the buildings which stood on or near what was probably the site of Ford hamlet.[97] At Jockey Green two pairs of council houses were built in 1926,[98] in Farm Lane two pairs in 1936.[99] Between 1948 and 1996 nearly all the land between Brown's Lane and the railway line was used for housing. North-west of Farm Lane 36 houses and 7 bungalows were built in Castle Road by the rural district council between 1948 and 1954;[1] south-east of Farm Lane 45 private houses and bungalows were built in the later 1960s;[2] near the railway 26 council bungalows for old people were built

in the Knapp, 12 in 1969, 14 in 1971;[3] north-east of Castle Road 37 private houses and bungalows were built in the 1970s and 1980s,[4] a school and other houses in the 1990s. Small estates of private houses and bungalows were built off High Street and Church Street in the 1980s and 1990s.[5]

A friendly society which had been started by 1821 met until c. 1906 or later.[6] A Comrades hall had been built in High Street by 1922;[7] a British Legion club stood on the site in 1996. On a 3-a. field off Frog Lane which belonged to Cox's charity until 1923 a hall was built c. 1926 and used mainly as the headquarters of a summer camp for children from London. It was used partly as a village hall until 1949, solely as one thereafter. It was replaced by a new village hall built in 1982. The land was a cricket field from 1962 and in 1996. Land off Castle Road has been used as a public recreation ground from 1946 or earlier.[8]

A conservation area designated in 1975 and amended in 1996 included the whole village except the north-east end.[9]

CROFTON. Standing beside the Dun, in the Middle Ages Crofton was apparently a small village comprising several small farmsteads.[10] It had a chapel in the 14th and 15th centuries[11] and 25 poll-tax payers in 1377.[12] In the 19th and 20th centuries it was no more than a hamlet.

In 1773 Crofton's buildings stood in an arc formed by the road from Great Bedwyn and the Roman road, and there were two mills on the Dun, which was bridged between them.[13] Three cottages standing in 1773 survived in 1996. Two on the north-west side of the Great Bedwyn road were thatched, timber-framed, probably 17th-century, and extended in brick; one on the south-east side of the road was of red brick and probably 18th-century. The only farmstead in the hamlet in the later 19th century and 1996 was Crofton Farm, which stood beside the Roman road. The surviving farmhouse was built in the later 19th century. Two pairs of 19th-century estate cottages had been built beside the Great Bedwyn road by 1879.[14]

One of the mills at Crofton was demolished c. 1773, the other probably c. 1800.[15] The Kennet & Avon canal was bridged c. 100 m. south-west of the site of the bridge over the Dun.[16] From c. 1862, when the railway was built beside the canal,[17] the new bridge was approached from Crofton village over a level crossing; a crossing keeper's cottage was built.

[91] W.R.O. 9/3/393H.
[92] Below, nonconf.
[93] Cf. W.R.O. 9/3/386; 9/3/393H; 1300/372, f. 3.
[94] Andrews and Dury, Map (W.R.S. viii), pl. 12.
[95] W.R.O. 9/1/204, p. 525; 9/3/393H; for the canal, above, this section.
[96] Date on bldg.
[97] O.S. Map 1/2,500, Wilts. XXXVII. 5 (1924 edn.); cf. below, this section (Stock and Ford).
[98] W.R.O., G 8/600/1.
[99] Ibid. G 8/505/1.   [1] Ibid. G 8/602/1.
[2] Ibid. A 1/355/420; A 1/355/440.
[3] Ibid. G 8/602/1.
[4] Ibid. A 1/355/470/1; A 1/355/545/2.
[5] Ibid. A 1/355/520/3; A 1/355/570/3; below, educ.
[6] W.A.M. xlviii. 507; B. Sheldrake, 'Hist. Great Bed-

wyn' (copy in Wilts. local studies libr., Trowbridge), 297–8.
[7] O.S. Map 1/2,500, Wilts. XXXVII. 5 (1924 edn.).
[8] H. E. Bracey, Social Provision in Rural Wilts. 175–6; Sheldrake, 'Great Bedwyn', 314; inf. from Mr. M. Scott, Wessex Ho., 7 Church Street; for the char., below, educ.
[9] Inf. from Dept. of Planning and Highways, Co. Hall, Trowbridge.
[10] Cf. below, econ. hist. (Crofton).
[11] Ibid. churches.
[12] V.C.H. Wilts. iv. 309.
[13] Andrews and Dury, Map (W.R.S. viii), pl. 12.
[14] O.S. Map 1/2,500, Wilts. XXXVI. 12 (1880 edn.).
[15] Below, econ. hist. (Crofton).
[16] Cf. Andrews and Dury, Map (W.R.S. viii), pl. 12.
[17] Above, this section [railways].

EAST GRAFTON. In the Middle Ages a chapel and probably a manor house stood at East Grafton, the chapel on land called Chapel mead in 1792.[18] A large demesne farmstead, adjoined by gardens, extensive inclosed lands, and a park, stood near Chapel mead in the 17th century;[19] in the mid 19th century the farmhouse was replaced by that called Manor Farm. Until the 19th century nearly all the other buildings of East Grafton village stood north-east of Manor Farm along the sides of a large triangular green formed by the junction of roads from Burbage, Collingbourne Kingston, Crofton, and Wilton.[20] The village may have shrunk between 1377, when it had 45 poll-tax payers,[21] and 1792, when only c. 20 houses and cottages stood around the green.[22] A pond on the east side of the green was drained in the earlier 20th century.[23]

In 1792 there were, in addition to Manor Farm, large farmsteads on the north side of the green and at the east corner. The farmhouse of that on the north side was rebuilt in the earlier 19th century; there remains part of a timber-framed barn converted for residence. Of the other houses and cottages around the green in 1792 it seems that c. 14 survived in 1996. All are thatched. A timber-framed house at the south end is of c. 1600 and may be the oldest. On the east side two other timber-framed houses may be 17th-century; most of a third was replaced by a red-brick range bearing the date 1723. On the west side of the green a timber-framed and possibly 17th-century cottage stands in a row of three cottages. A short distance along the Crofton road a row of about four cottages, of brick and thatch, was standing in 1792.[24]

A church and a school in the 1840s, and between 1847 and 1860 a house for the incumbent, were built on the east side of the green.[25] By 1886 new farm buildings and a terrace of four cottages had been erected beside the Hungerford road east of the green, and a pair of cottages had been built beside the Burbage road west of the green.[26] The village expanded further in the 20th century. Beside the Wilton road 16 council houses called the Severals were built in four lots between 1936 and 1948, and 2 council bungalows were built in 1965; off the Hungerford road 6 houses in 1948, 9 houses in 1967, and 6 bungalows in 1973 were also built by the rural district council.[27] A private estate of 7 bungalows was built off the west side of the green c. 1970,[28] and in the late 20th century other small private estates were built off the Burbage road, to replace farm buildings on the north side of the green, and between the council houses in the Wilton and Hungerford roads. Other buildings erected in the mid and later 20th century include several thatched houses, of which one stands at the south end of the green and one beside the Burbage road, a few other houses and bungalows beside the Burbage, Hungerford, and Wilton roads, a village hall beside the green, and large farm buildings, disused in 1996, beside the Crofton road.[29] In 1996 the only farmsteads in East Grafton village were Manor Farm and that beside the Hungerford road. A conservation area designated in 1974 includes nearly all the village.[30]

WEST GRAFTON. Like many villages west of it in the Pewsey Vale,[31] but like no other settlement in Great Bedwyn parish, West Grafton village stood beside a north–south lane. Its lands were not extensive[32] and the village, which had 19 poll-tax payers in 1377,[33] was never large.

Near its north end the lane had been diverted eastwards by 1792. Apparently only two or three farmsteads then stood beside the lane; four cottages had apparently been built on its verge, and two houses stood on what was probably its old straight course. The age of the two houses, which survive, suggests that the diversion was made in the 18th century. By 1864 a nonconformist chapel had been built on the site of one of the cottages, and between 1792 and the mid 20th century no new site beside the lane was used for building.[34] In the later 20th century on new sites a pair of houses and a bungalow were built near the north end of the lane and large farm buildings at the south end.

Of the buildings standing in 1792 four houses and cottages survived in 1996. One at the south end of the lane was then the only farmstead. The farmhouse is timber-framed and 17th-century; in the mid or later 18th century it was refronted in brick and altered inside. The houses beside the old course of the lane are each 17th-century, timber-framed, thatched, and of a single storey and attics. One of the cottages standing on the verge in 1792 survives at the north end of the lane.[35]

Three sites west of West Grafton village had buildings on them in 1792. A farmstead stood beside the parish boundary in the later 17th century and a large farmstead stood there in 1792; nearly all its buildings were removed, mainly in the late 19th century and early 20th. Between it and the south end of the lane a cottage stood in 1996 on the site of a building standing in 1792, and beside the Burbage road at the parish boundary a building was replaced by a pair of cottages probably in the 19th century. Also beside the Burbage road a small cottage was built in the 18th century and other buildings, near Grafton and Burbage station, were erected

18 W.A.M. vi. 270–1; O.S. Map 6", Wilts. XLII (1888 edn.); W.R.O., EA/68; below, churches.
19 W.R.O. 2203/13; ibid. EA/68; below, econ. hist. (E. Grafton).
20 W.R.O., EA/68.
21 V.C.H. Wilts. iv. 309.   22 W.R.O., EA/68.
23 O.S. Maps 6", Wilts. XLII. NE. (1926 edn.); 1/25,000, 41/26 (1949 edn.).
24 W.R.O., EA/68.
25 Below, churches; educ.
26 O.S. Map 6", Wilts. XLII (1888 edn.).
27 W.R.O., G 8/600/1; G 8/602/1.

28 Ibid. A 1/355/445/2; A 1/355/450/2.
29 Cf. O.S. Map 6", Wilts. XLII. NE. (1926 edn.).
30 Inf. from Dept. of Planning and Highways, Co. Hall, Trowbridge.
31 e.g. below, Burbage; Easton; Milton Lilbourne; Pewsey.
32 Below, econ. hist. (W. Grafton).
33 V.C.H. Wilts. iv. 309.
34 O.S. Map 1/25,000, SU 26 (1961 edn.); W.R.O., EA/68; below, prot. nonconf.
35 Dept. of Environment, list of bldgs. of hist. interest (1986); W.R.O., EA/68.

in the late 19th century and early 20th.[36] In 1996 the main building at the station was a private house.

HARDING. It seems that Harding Farm was built on the downland of a village which stood on a site now in Shalbourne parish. A farmstead stood on the downs in the 16th century.[37] The present farmhouse incorporates an early 17th-century house which was almost certainly timber-framed, had a main east–west range on a three-roomed plan, and had a large chimney stack, which survives. The outer walls were encased in brick, some of the brickwork being of the late 17th century. In the later 18th century a west wing was built and extended northwards to provide a three-bayed west entrance front, with a central door, and a rear kitchen wing. Minor additions were made to the house in the earlier 19th century. Near the house in 1996 stood a large, 18th-century, and timber-framed barn, and a group of brick farm buildings erected in the mid 19th century. North-west of the farmstead a pair of cottages was built in the mid 19th century.[38]

MARTEN was probably the site of the battle of Meratun fought between the Saxons and the Danes in 871.[39] The village stands between two head streams flowing north-westwards to the Dun. On the ridge between the streams a platform c. 50 ft. square had a steep-sided moat, c. 15 ft. deep, with a returned entrance causeway and ditch against the north-east side. The platform may be the site of a manor house standing in the Middle Ages. North-east of it a grid of low banks was bounded by a ditched bank, and south-west of it there is an isolated mound and traces of ditches or hollow ways: those features may survive from those of the garden of such a house.[40] A short distance south-east of the platform a chapel stood in the Middle Ages.[41] A farmstead standing immediately south-west of the platform c. 1815[42] had been partly demolished by 1879, wholly by the mid 20th century.[43] Also on high ground another farmstead, in 1996 called Manor Farm, was built c. 200 m. south-east of the platform. A farmhouse built there in the 17th century was timber-framed and survived in 1996 as an east–west range incorporated in the house called the Manor. The inside of the farmhouse was refitted in the earlier 18th century, the date of doors and a staircase which remain in it. In the earlier 19th century a south service range was built; it extended further east than the earlier range, which was encased in brick in the mid 19th century. In the late 20th

century the old range was extended eastwards to the length of the new range, extensive alterations were made to the inside of the house and to a walled kitchen garden south of the house, and a timber-framed barn north-west of the house was dismantled.[44]

On lower ground beside the north-eastern head stream farmsteads, cottages, and houses stood along a lane, and by 1773 the Roman road between the lane and the farmsteads on the ridge south-west of it had gone out of use.[45] About 1815 two farmsteads and nine houses and cottages were standing beside the lane and beside the Roman road south-east of the lane's junction with it.[46] In 1996 a farmstead and 11 houses and cottages occupied the same sites as, or sites near to, those of the earlier buildings. A thatched house of 18th-century origin stood on the south-west side of the lane, and an 18th-century, timber-framed, and thatched cottage stood on the north-east side of the Roman road, but otherwise none of the buildings of c. 1815 survived. Four council houses were built on the north-east side of the Roman road in 1955.[47] On the south-west side of the lane one of the buildings standing c. 1815, or its site, was used for a school in the later 19th century.[48]

West of the junction of the lane and the Roman road a few buildings were standing in a short lane in 1773 and c. 1815.[49] Only one, an 18th-century cottage of brick and thatch, stood there in 1996. At the north-west end of the village, where the lane rejoins the Roman road at an elongated crossing of the Hungerford–Salisbury road, the Nag's Head inn was open in 1724;[50] it was rebuilt in 1902[51] and was called the Tipsy Miller in 1996.

STOCK AND FORD. A village called Stock, the site of which is uncertain, apparently had a strip of land running north-west and south-east. Open fields lay on either side of the Dun south-west of Great Bedwyn's, and common pasture probably lay on the high ground towards the north-west end of the parish.[52] By analogy with the many Wiltshire villages which had open fields and common pasture in a strip of land stretching from a river to downland it is possible that Stock village stood beside the Dun, and possible that its site there was deserted in the late Middle Ages. By analogy with Chisbury in Little Bedwyn, and Rudge in Froxfield, settlements nearby,[53] it is more likely that in the Middle Ages and later Stock's open fields were worked from farmsteads on the high ground north-west of them. A manor house stood on the high ground in the 17th century and probably earlier.[54]

36 O.S. Maps 6", Wilts. XXXVI, XLII (1888 and later edns.); W.R.O., EA/68; ibid. 9/16/73.
37 Below, manors (Harding); econ. hist. (Harding).
38 Cf. O.S. Map 6", Wilts. XXXVII (1887 edn.).
39 Arch. Jnl. lxxv. 191–2.
40 O.S. Map 1/10,000, SU 26 SE. (1982 edn.); Camb. Univ. Libr., air photo., print no. ANB 29; cf. below, manors (Marten).
41 W.A.M. vi. 273–4; O.S. Map 1/2,500, Wilts. XLIII. 1 (1880 edn.); below, churches.
42 W.R.O., EA/99.
43 O.S. Maps 1/2,500, Wilts. XLIII. 1 (1880 edn.); 1/25,000, SU 26 (1961 edn.).
44 Inf. from Mr. B. R. Taylor, the Manor, Marten.

45 Andrews and Dury, Map (W.R.S. viii), pl. 12.
46 W.R.O., EA/99.   47 Ibid. G 8/602/1.
48 Ibid. EA/99; O.S. Map 1/2,500, Wilts. XLIII. 1 (1880 edn.); below, educ.
49 Andrews and Dury, Map (W.R.S. viii), pl. 12; W.R.O., EA/99.
50 W.R.O. 9/3/397, p. 38.
51 Date on bldg.
52 Sar. Chart. and Doc. (Rolls Ser.), p. 216; W.R.O. 9/3/393H; below, econ. hist. (Stock).
53 Below, Little Bedwyn, intro. (Chisbury); Froxfield, intro. (Rudge).
54 Aubrey, Topog. Colln. ed. Jackson, 374; cf. below, manors (Stock).

Its site was probably that of Stock Farm, from which much of Stock's land was later worked, and in the Middle Ages other farmsteads probably stood nearby. In 1751 there were several groups of buildings on the high land mostly south and south-west of Stock Farm. The farmhouse at Stock Farm was apparently built in the 17th century and altered and enlarged in the 18th and 19th centuries.[55] It was called Stokke Manor in 1996, when a few houses of the 19th or 20th century, large farm buildings, and what was apparently a service building converted for residence stood near it. Among the other buildings on the high land in 1996 were a timber-framed and thatched cottage of the 17th century and three thatched cottages, mostly of brick and partly timber-framed, probably of the 18th. Pairs of estate cottages built in the 19th century, some on the site of buildings standing in 1751,[56] include one west and five in various styles north-west of Stokke Manor.

A hamlet called Ford probably stood on Stock's land. In the Middle Ages Stock was linked in assessments for taxation with a settlement called Ford,[57] a manor was later called Stock and Ford,[58] and the 32 poll-tax payers ascribed to Ford in 1377[59] presumably included inhabitants of both places. A mill standing at Ford in the 1230s[60] probably stood where, between Great Bedwyn village and Crofton, the Great Bedwyn to Wilton road forded the Dun immediately below a mill in 1751, and the hamlet standing near the mill and on the north-west bank of the Dun in 1751 was probably on or near the site of Ford. In 1751 the mill and c. 20 cottages and houses stood beside the Great Bedwyn road.[61] By 1773 the Dun had been bridged on the site of the ford.[62] At the northeast end of the hamlet nine cottages standing in 1751 had apparently been built on the waste at the junction of Back Lane and Church Street;[63] they were replaced c. 1870 by three pairs of small red-brick villas. The mill was demolished between 1879 and 1899,[64] and on each side of the road other cottages were replaced in the 19th century. On the north-west side of the road a timber-framed cottage and a red-brick cottage, both thatched and apparently 18th-century, were standing in 1751 and 1996.[65] In the 20th century the council houses built in Church Street linked Great Bedwyn village to the hamlet,[66] in which 13 new houses and bungalows had been built by 1996.

WEXCOMBE. Its name suggests that the village originated in a coomb, and earthworks at the head of an east–west coomb[67] presumably mark where most of its buildings stood in the Middle Ages. In the 13th and 14th centuries it may have been larger and more populous than at any time later. A timber-framed hall, possibly part of a manor house or demesne farmstead, was built there c. 1235,[68] there was a prison there in 1277,[69] and in the early 14th century the court of an honor may have been held there by the lord of Wexcombe manor.[70] It seems that a large demesne farm was worked from the village and that tenants of the manor held small farmsteads there.[71] In 1377 there were 68 poll-tax payers.[72] The village grew between 1773 and the 1840s, when it consisted of c. 22 houses and had c. 140 inhabitants.[73]

On the ridge north of the coomb a new farmstead, later called Lower Farm, was built in the 17th century, and another, Upper Farm, was built in the early 19th. The farmhouse of Lower Farm was timber-framed and consisted of a main east–west range. In the early 19th century the house was encased in brick and extended northwards; in 1911 a new wing was built on the west,[74] the 19th-century extension was extended eastwards, and a new south gable was built at the east end of the house. In 1996 most of the farm buildings were 20th-century. A small redbrick farmhouse was built as part of Upper Farm; it was extended in the late 19th century and much altered in the early 1970s.[75] Large farm buildings stood around the house in 1996. On the high ground near Lower Farm two 18th-century cottages and an early 19th-century house, each of red brick and thatch, were standing in 1996. A chapel of ease at Upper Farm was served in the late 19th century and early 20th.[76]

On the floor of the coomb few buildings were standing in the later 18th century or early 19th.[77] In 1847 eight buildings, a total of 16 cottages, stood there.[78] Apparently the only one to survive in 1996 was a pair of cottages possibly of the early 19th century. A nonconformist chapel was built in the late 19th century; two pairs of houses were built in the mid 20th. Between Lower Farm and the floor of the coomb two pairs of estate cottages were built in the mid 19th century; one pair was rebuilt in the early 20th.[79]

In 1899 W. C. Finch, the lord of Wexcombe manor, provided waterworks for the village. A circular pump house was built.[80]

55 Dept. of Environment, list of bldgs. of hist. interest (1986); W.R.O. 9/3/393H.
56 W.R.O. 9/3/393H.
57 V.C.H. Wilts. iv. 300; Tax List, 1332 (W.R.S. xlv), 125.
58 e.g. W.R.O. 9/3/393H.
59 V.C.H. Wilts. iv. 309.
60 Sar. Chart. and Doc. (Rolls Ser.), p. 216.
61 W.R.O. 9/3/393H.
62 Andrews and Dury, Map (W.R.S. viii), pl. 12.
63 W.R.O. 9/3/393H.
64 O.S. Maps 1/2,500, Wilts. XXXVII. 9 (1880 edn.); 6", Wilts. XXXVII. SW. (1901 edn.).
65 W.R.O. 9/3/393H.
66 Above, this section (Great Bedwyn).
67 Air photo. in possession of Arch. section, Co. Hall, Trowbridge.
68 Close R. 1234–7, 131.
69 Gaol Delivery, 1275–1306 (W.R.S. xxxiii), p. 49.

70 Cal. Close, 1323–7, 389–90; Wilts. Inq. p.m. 1327–77 (Index Libr.), 112–13.
71 Wilts. Inq. p.m. 1242–1326 (Index Libr.), 339–41, 403–6; Tax List, 1332 (W.R.S. xlv), 125; below, econ. hist. (Wexcombe).
72 V.C.H. Wilts. iv. 309.
73 Ibid. 340; Andrews and Dury, Map (W.R.S. viii), pl. 12; W.R.O., tithe award.
74 Date on bldg.
75 Inf. from the occupier.
76 O.S. Map 1/2,500, Wilts. XLIII. 5 (1880 edn.); below, churches.
77 Andrews and Dury, Map (W.R.S. viii), pl. 12; O.S. Map 1", sheet 14 (1817 edn.).
78 W.R.O., tithe award.
79 Ibid.; O.S. Maps 1/2,500, Wilts. XLIII. 5 (1880, 1924 edns.); below, nonconf.
80 Dept. of Environment, list of bldgs. of hist. interest (1986); below, manors (Wexcombe).

WILTON. The village stands in the valley of a head stream of the Dun, on the course of which a pond served it from the 18th century or earlier and remained a feature of it in 1996. South-east of the pond a rectangle of *c.* 3 a. bordered by a lane and with five roads joining it at the corners may have been a village green; it had been inclosed and partly built on by the late 18th century[81] and was further built on later. In the Middle Ages the village apparently comprised many small farmsteads,[82] and it had 71 poll-tax payers in 1377.[83] In the late 20th century it was notable for its pond and the survival of *c.* 20 cottages and small houses of the 18th century and earlier. It was designated a conservation area in 1985.[84]

In 1792 buildings stood beside the lane bordering what may have been the green and beside the roads leading north-east to Great Bedwyn, south towards Wexcombe, and north-west towards Crofton. The road leading southwards was later called Hollow Lane. Before 1792 a new section of road called Moor Lane was built from north-west of the pond to link the Crofton road to a road leading south-west to East Grafton,[85] and in the later 20th century most traffic through the village used the Great Bedwyn road, the north side of the rectangle, the Crofton road, Moor Lane, and the East Grafton road. Between 1792 and *c.* 1820 a new farmstead was built at the south-west corner of the rectangle,[86] and in the earlier 19th century a nonconformist chapel and a schoolroom were built on the east side of Moor Lane.[87] In the mid 19th century a large red-brick house was built south-west of the pond, and in 1849 a terrace of four estate cottages was built *c.* 200 m. along the Great Bedwyn road.[88] In 1955 the rural district council built four bungalows and two houses at Upper Brooklands on the west side of Moor Lane.[89] A few other houses were built in most parts of the village in the 20th century.

The only farmstead in the village in 1996 was Manor Farm, standing in the angle of the Great Bedwyn road and what in the 18th century was a road leading towards Marten.[90] The farmhouse, of red brick and thatch, was built in the earlier 18th century, incorporates an older house, and was extended in the 19th century. South of the house a large barn, aisled, timber-framed, and thatched, is of the early 18th century; other large farm buildings are 20th-century. On the north side of the rectangle Batts Farm is a former farmhouse,[91] timber-framed, of the 17th or 18th century, and now with a principal south front of red brick and a tiled roof. Of the older cottages and small houses to survive most are thatched and apparently 17th-century. In some, timber framing with brick nogging is visible; from the 18th century or the 19th the brick walls of some others may have encased or replaced timber framing.

The Swan inn was open in 1724,[92] in the late 19th century and early 20th occupied a house on the north side of the rectangle,[93] and in 1996 occupied a mid 20th-century house at the north-east corner of the rectangle. In the late 18th century and earlier 19th cottages in the village were used as a parish workhouse.[94]

WOLFHALL. In the earlier Middle Ages Wolfhall, which possibly had open fields and common pasture, was probably a small village consisting of several farmsteads. Its lands amounted to *c.* 750 a.[95] Their boundary on the south, with East Grafton and West Grafton, followed a ridge.[96] On the north, by analogy with Wolfhall's western neighbours Burbage and Durley, they may have included, north of a line which was probably that of an upper reach of the Dun and was later followed by the Kennet & Avon canal, the steep north side of the valley of the Dun but not, north of that, the high flat land which was almost certainly part of Savernake forest and became Tottenham park.[97] Wolfhall had 14 poll-tax payers in 1377.[98]

In the late Middle Ages the Seymour family lived in a manor house at Wolfhall,[99] and by the 16th century much of Wolfhall's land had been imparked and the village apparently deserted.[1] The manor house was visited by Henry VIII in 1535, 1539, and 1543.[2] John Aubrey, writing in 1672, related that the king's wedding to Jane Seymour in 1536 was observed in a long barn at Wolfhall. The manor house was partly demolished in the 1660s,[3] wholly probably by 1723.[4]

Where Wolfhall village stood is uncertain. The most likely site is one in an east–west valley, in which a head stream of the Dun may have flowed in the Middle Ages, about where a house called Wolfhall Farm stood in 1996. The house was built in the early 17th century: it was called the Laundry in 1633[5] and may have been built on the site of an earlier laundry, but its architecture suggests that it was built solely as a dwelling house. It was built of brick with stone dressings, with two storeys and attics, and on an L-shaped plan with a short north–south range from which a short east range projected at the north end. The principal rooms on all floors were at the north end of the north–south range, and their fireplaces were served by a large stack in the north wall. Alterations of the 19th and 20th centuries included the blocking of a doorway in the west wall and the building of a porch in the angle between the ranges and of a new staircase.

81   W.R.O., EA/68.
82   Below, econ. hist. (Wilton).
83   *V.C.H. Wilts.* iv. 309.
84   Inf. from Dept. of Planning and Highways, Co. Hall, Trowbridge.
85   W.R.O., EA/68.
86   Ibid.; Savernake estate map, *c.* 1820 (copy in W.R.O.).
87   Below, nonconf.   88   Date on bldg.
89   W.R.O., G 8/602/1.
90   Ibid. EA/68.
91   Cf. O.S. Map 6", Wilts. XXXVI (1888 edn.).
92   W.R.O. 9/3/397, p. 38.
93   O.S. Maps 1/2,500, Wilts. XXXVI. 16 (1900, 1924

edns.).
94   *Endowed Char. Wilts.* (N. Div.), 37.
95   Below, econ. hist. (Wolfhall).
96   W.R.O., EA/68.
97   Below, econ. hist. (Wolfhall; Tottenham park); Burbage, intro.
98   *V.C.H. Wilts.* iv. 309.
99   *W.A.M.* li. 503.
1   Below, econ. hist. (Wolfhall).
2   *W.A.M.* xv. 164; li. 517.
3   Aubrey, *Topog. Colln.* ed. Jackson, 379.
4   W.R.O. 9/22/109.
5   Ibid. 9/22/21.

THE OLD BARN AT WOLFHALL

Where the Seymours' manor house stood is also uncertain. The most likely site of that is one on the ridge south of Wolfhall Farm about where Wolfhall Manor stood in 1996. A long thatched barn which stood on the site was dilapidated in the 1870s and had largely collapsed by the 1920s;[6] there is no direct evidence that it was standing in 1536, but it was almost certainly the barn referred to by Aubrey. Wolfhall Manor, consisting of a timber-framed north–south range, was built as a farmhouse in the early 17th century. Much of the outer walling of the house was rebuilt in brick, possibly in the early 18th century, when additions were made to the east side. A new north front was built of brick in the early 19th century, and minor additions were made to the north part of the east side c. 1900. There were extensive farm buildings around the house in the 19th and 20th centuries.[7]

Between Wolfhall Farm and Wolfhall Manor a pair of 19th-century estate cottages[8] was replaced by a house built in 1984.[9]

OTHER SETTLEMENT. On the common pastures of Wilton on high ground north-east of the village a new house was begun in 1548 for Edward Seymour, duke of Somerset, who owned most of the land in the parish. Bricks were made nearby at Dodsdown, quarries were opened, foundations were laid, a conduit c. 500 m. long was dug to supply water, and plans to impark land with a circumference of c. 3 miles around the house were drawn up. Apparently work on the house ceased on or before Somerset's death in 1552 and was not resumed.[10]

In the north-west part of the parish Totten-ham House was built in the early 18th century on the site of a lodge which was standing in the 16th century and until then. It was enlarged in the 18th and 19th centuries and, standing in a large park which extended into Burbage parish, was the mansion of the earls and marquesses of Ailesbury.[11] North of the mansion, on the edge of the park, and on the boundary with Burbage parish a church, a vicarage house, a school, and two other houses were built in the later 19th century;[12] the vicarage house stands in Burbage, the rest in Great Bedwyn.

Bloxham Lodge was built in the mid 18th century on high ground east of Tottenham House. In 1773 it was described as newly built, bore its present name, and belonged to John Bloxham.[13] It is a brick house with a centre block of three bays and two storeys; it has single-storeyed wings in line which are possibly additions. In 1773 formal gardens lay south-west of it.[14]

A farmstead and seven houses and cottages stood as a group south of Great Bedwyn village in 1751.[15] The group was called Brail in 1773.[16] The farmstead, at the north end of the group, was called Brail Farm in 1879, when it included large farm buildings.[17] The farmhouse, of the early 18th century, survived in 1996; most of the farm buildings had been demolished by 1899.[18] New farm buildings were erected in the 20th century, and, apart from the farmhouse, none of the buildings standing in 1751 survived in 1996.

Several farmsteads were built outside the villages and hamlets of the parish. South of Wolfhall a lodge standing in Sudden park in the 17th century[19] was probably on or near the site of Sudden Farm, which was a farmstead c. 1718.[20]

6 W.A.M. xv. 144; xlii. 352–3.
7 O.S. Maps 6", Wilts. XXXVI (1888 and later edns.).
8 Ibid. 6", Wilts. XXXVI (1888 edn.); cf. Savernake estate map, c. 1820 (copy in W.R.O.).
9 Date on bldg.
10 W.A.M. xv. 178–86; Cal. Pat. 1550–3, 358; for land ownership, below, manors; for Wilton's pastures, below, econ. hist. (Wilton); for the duke, Complete Peerage, xii (1), 59–64.
11 Below, manors (Tottenham).

12 Ibid. churches (St. Katharine's); educ.
13 W.R.O. 9/14/58.
14 Andrews and Dury, Map (W.R.S. viii), pl. 12.
15 W.R.O. 9/3/393H.
16 Andrews and Dury, Map (W.R.S. viii), pl. 12.
17 O.S. Map 1/2,500, Wilts. XXXVII. 9 (1880 edn.).
18 Ibid. 6", Wilts. XXXVII. SW. (1901 edn.).
19 W.A.M. xv. 158 n.
20 W.R.O. 1300/372, ff. 1–2.

The farmhouse, called Suddene Park Farm in 1996, was rebuilt in the mid 19th century. South-west of Jockey Green a farmstead was called Brail Farm in 1773, later Jockey Green Farm. In 1996 a pair of 19th-century cottages stood on its site, and a few farm buildings stood nearby. Freewarren Farm had been built south-west of Crofton village by 1773;[21] its farmhouse was replaced in the early 19th century by a house of brick and thatch which was extended east-wards in 1996. Hillbarn Farm in the east part of the parish originated between 1773 and 1817,[22] Bewley Farm in the north part between 1820 and 1879.[23]

At Dodsdown, north-east of Wilton village, a pair of cottages was built in the mid 19th century on each side of the Great Bedwyn to Wilton road near a brickworks.[24] Other isolated houses in the parish include several 19th-century houses and estate cottages and several 20th-century houses. Fairway, built beside the Marlborough to Great Bedwyn road in the early 20th century,[25] is a large buff-brick house in vernacular style.

MANORS AND OTHER ESTATES.

In the 8th century lands called Bedwyn were almost certainly in the hands of the king of Wessex. In 778 King Cynewulf granted away 13 *manentes* of them, apparently the land of Chisbury.[26] Other land at Bedwyn was given by Byrhtelm to Ealhmund, bishop of Winchester, and his see in an exchange between 801 and 805: it was possibly the estate said to lie at Stock by Shalbourne which Denewulf, bishop of Winchester, gave to King Edward in an exchange in 904.[27] A large estate called Bedwyn was, by his will made 879 × 888, given by King Alfred (d. 899) to his son Edward (d. 924), who succeeded him as king. It apparently passed with the crown, and in 968 King Edgar (d. 975) gave 72 *cassati* at Bedwyn to Abingdon abbey. In 968 the estate included the land of apparently all the villages which lay in Great Bedwyn parish in the 16th century, that of Burbage, probably that of Tidcombe, and, apparently lying almost detached after Chisbury was alienated in 778, probably that of Little Bedwyn. On Edgar's death the estate was taken from the abbey by force and assigned to his younger son Ethelred, king from 978.[28] Apparently it again passed with the crown and in 1086 it was held by William I.[29] By 1086 the land of

Crofton, East Grafton, West Grafton, Harding, Marten, Wolfhall, Burbage, and Tidcombe had been granted in fee, almost certainly separately as individual estates,[30] and the king's estate called Bedwyn seems to have comprised then the lordship of the borough of Great Bedwyn, which consisted of the tenements of 25 burgesses,[31] and the lordship in demesne of Stock, Wexcombe, and Wilton and of what became West Bedwyn and Little Bedwyn manors.[32] The estate was held by the Crown until, probably c. 1130, Henry I granted it to John FitzGilbert, his marshal.[33] Little Bedwyn manor may have been excluded from that grant; West Bedwyn manor, Stock manor, and some of Wilton's land were probably subinfeudated after c. 1130.[34]

The lordship of the *BOROUGH* descended with Wexcombe manor until 1403, except that the Crown held it between 1314 and 1317 and Margaret de Audley probably held it from 1317; it apparently descended with Wexcombe manor from 1403 to 1553,[35] and from 1553 to the 19th century descended with Tottenham Lodge and Tottenham House.[36]

The tenements in Great Bedwyn village to which the right to vote as a burgess in parliamentary elections was attached became attractive to those wishing to influence elections. The lord of West Bedwyn manor and of Stock manor owned many from the 17th century or earlier until 1766, when he sold them to Thomas Brudenell, Lord Bruce, the lord of the borough.[37] Those tenements, others already owned by Lord Bruce, and others later bought by Lord Bruce and his successors in title, descended with Tottenham House and the lordship of the borough, and in the early 20th century Henry Brudenell-Bruce, marquess of Ailesbury (d. 1911), owned nearly all the houses and cottages in the village.[38]

The land of Great Bedwyn village lay mainly in two manors, West Bedwyn and one which was part of the Prebendal estate.[39] *WEST BED-WYN* manor was probably subinfeudated after c. 1130.[40] It was held by Richard Collingbourne (d. 1418), probably from 1408 or earlier, and passed to his son Robert (d. 1459).[41] It was held by William Collingbourne, who was executed and attainted in 1484. In 1485 Richard III granted it to Edmund Chadderton (d. 1499) for William's heirs, his daughters Margaret, wife of George Chadderton, and Jane, wife of James

21   *Andrews and Dury, Map* (W.R.S. viii), pl. 12.
22   Cf. ibid.; O.S. Map 1", sheet 14 (1817 edn.).
23   C. Greenwood, *Map of Wilts.* (1820); O.S. Map 1/2,500, Wilts. XXXVI. 8 (1880 edn.).
24   O.S. Map 1/2,500, Wilts. XXXVII. 13 (1880 edn.); for the brickworks, below, econ. hist. (Wilton).
25   Cf. O.S. Maps 6", Wilts. XXXVII. NW. (1900, 1926 edns.).
26   Finberg, *Early Wessex Chart.* p. 71; *Arch. Jnl.* lxxvi. 151–5; below, Little Bedwyn, intro. [boundary]; Little Bedwyn, manors (Chisbury).
27   Finberg, *Early Wessex Chart.* pp. 72, 80; *V.C.H. Wilts.* ii, pp. 86–7.
28   *Eng. Hist. Doc.* i, ed. D. Whitelock (1979), pp. 534–7, 582–4; Finberg, *Early Wessex Chart.* p. 96; *Arch. Jnl.* lxxvii. 75–80. The first two sources give reasons to believe that the chart. of 968 is authentic; the authenticity is denied in P. H. Sawyer, *Anglo-Saxon Chart.* (revised S. E. Kelly; priv. circulated 1996), no. 756.
29   *V.C.H. Wilts.* ii, pp. 115–16.

30   Ibid. pp. 141, 143, 149, 164–6.
31   Ibid. p. 116.
32   Cf. below, this section; local govt. [Wexcombe]; Little Bedwyn, manors.
33   *Rot. Hund.* (Rec. Com.), ii (1), 259; *Complete Peerage*, x. 358–67; x, App. G, 93–7.
34   Below, Little Bedwyn, manors; for Wexcombe manor, below, this section.
35   *Cal. Inq. p.m.* xviii, p. 269; *Feud. Aids*, v. 203; *Cal. Close*, 1313–18, 415; below, this section (Wexcombe).
36   *Wilts. Inq. p.m.* 1625–49 (Index Libr.), 344–5; W.R.O. 9/3/367; below, this section (Tottenham).
37   Below, parl. rep.
38   Ibid.; W.R.O. 9/3, *passim*; ibid. Inland Revenue, val. reg. 56; for the descent, below, this section (Tottenham).
39   For the Prebendal estate, below, this section.
40   Above, this section [preamble]; below, local govt. [Wexcombe].
41   *Cal. Close*, 1441–7, 43; *Hist. Parl., Commons* 1386–1421, ii. 631–2.

Lowther, and the Chaddertons and Lowthers held it in 1502–3.[42] The manor passed to Margaret's son Edmund Chadderton (d. 1545), whose son William sold it in 1568 to Anthony Hungerford[43] (d. 1589). From 1582 it descended with Stock manor and from 1766 to 1950 with Tottenham House; in 1996 its farmland belonged to the Crown.[44] The manor house, near which there was a pasture called Spain's, may have stood in the north-east part of Farm Lane, possibly on the site of no. 12 Farm Lane which in 1996 incorporated a tall early 17th-century chimney stack.[45] In 1408 the oratory in it was licensed for divine service.[46]

In 1086 Crofton was held by Alfred of Marlborough and of him by Hugh.[47] The estate may have been acquired soon after 1086 by Edward of Salisbury. It may have passed to Edward's daughter Maud, wife of Humphrey de Bohun, to Maud's son Humphrey de Bohun, and in the direct line to Humphrey, Henry (cr. earl of Hereford 1200, d. 1220), and Humphrey, earl of Hereford and of Essex (d. 1275). In 1229 Humphrey's right to Crofton was confirmed following a dispute with Ela Longespée, countess of Salisbury, Edward of Salisbury's great-great-granddaughter.[48] By 1300 Crofton's land had been divided between two manors, each of which had been subinfeudated.[49] The overlordship may have descended with the Hereford and Essex titles and the overlordship of Newton Tony to Humphrey de Bohun, earl of Hereford, of Essex, and of Northampton (d. 1373).[50] If so, it was presumably allotted to his daughter Eleanor (d. 1399), the wife of Thomas of Woodstock (cr. earl of Buckingham 1377, duke of Gloucester 1385, d. 1397); in 1479 Anne (d. 1480), the relict of Eleanor's grandson Humphrey Stafford, duke of Buckingham (d. 1460), was overlord.[51]

In 1300 *CROFTON FITZWARREN* manor was held of a mesne lord, William Keynell, by William FitzWarin; no other mesne lord of the manor is known. FitzWarin (d. 1300) was succeeded by his son Alan,[52] who granted the manor to Richard of Polhampton (d. 1317) and his wife Margaret (d. 1331) for life.[53] The manor passed to Sir Fulk FitzWarin (d. 1349), who granted it for life to Robert Hungerford (d. 1352). It

presumably reverted to Fulk's son Sir Fulk (d. 1374),[54] and it descended in the direct line to Sir Fulk (d. 1391), Fulk (d. 1407),[55] and Fulk (d. 1420):[56] each of the last four Fulks was a minor at his father's death. The last Fulk's heir was his sister Elizabeth (d. 1426 × 1428), the wife of Sir Richard Hankford (d. 1431),[57] and hers were her daughters Thomasine and Elizabeth (d. unmarried 1433). The manor passed to Thomasine (d. 1453), the wife of William Bourghchier (from 1449 Lord FitzWarin, d. 1469),[58] to her son Fulk Bourghchier, Lord FitzWarin (d. 1479), and to Fulk's son John, Lord FitzWarin (cr. earl of Bath 1536, d. 1539).[59] John's relict Elizabeth (fl. 1542) held the manor for life.[60] In 1540 his son and heir John, earl of Bath, sold the reversion to Edward Seymour, earl of Hertford (cr. duke of Somerset 1547),[61] who already owned Crofton Braboef manor.

In 1275 *CROFTON BRABOEF* manor was held by William Braboef (d. 1284), a prominent justice,[62] after whose death his relict Joan de St. Martin (fl. 1289) held it for life.[63] In 1332 it was probably held by William Braboef.[64] Hugh Camoys and his wife Joan conveyed it to Thomas Warrener in 1365.[65] It was afterwards acquired by Easton priory, which in an exchange licensed in 1390 gave it to Sir William Sturmy (d. 1427).[66] From Sir William's death the manor descended in the Seymour family like Burbage Sturmy manor.[67]

On Somerset's attainder and execution in 1552 Crofton Fitzwarren and Crofton Braboef manors passed by Act to his son Sir Edward Seymour (cr. earl of Hertford 1559, d. 1621);[68] thereafter they descended with Tottenham Lodge and Tottenham House.[69] Crofton's lands lie north-west and south-east.[70] About 1929 George Brudenell-Bruce, marquess of Ailesbury, sold 60 a. at the south-east end as part of Freewarren farm;[71] in 1996 Freewarren Farm and that land belonged to Mr. A. J. Mills.[72] In 1950 land at the north-west end and *c*. 300 a. in the centre were sold, respectively as parts of Warren farm, based in Burbage parish, and Crofton farm, by Lord Ailesbury to the Crown, the owner in 1996.[73] Other land in the north-west continued to descend in the Brudenell-Bruce family with Tottenham House, of which it was part of the park, and in 1996

42 *Cal. Pat.* 1476–85, 542; *V.C.H. Wilts.* xiv. 110–11; A. B. Emden, *Biog. Reg. Univ. Oxf. to 1500*, i. 382–3; P.R.O., C 1/259, no. 10.
43 W.R.O. 9/26/2; below, Collingbourne Kingston, manors (Chaddertons).
44 Below, this section (Stock; Tottenham); for the woodland, ibid. (Bedwyn common).
45 W.R.O. 9/1/95, p. 59; 9/3/393H; above, intro. (Great Bedwyn).
46 *Reg. Hallum* (Cant. & York Soc.), p. 96.
47 *V.C.H. Wilts.* ii, p. 141.
48 Ibid. xv. 146; *Complete Peerage*, v. 135; P.R.O., CP 25/1/250/8, no. 11.   49 Below, this section.
50 *V.C.H. Wilts.* xv. 146.
51 *Complete Peerage*, ii. 388–9; v. 136; vi. 473–6; xii (1), 179–81; P.R.O., C 140/73, no. 76, rot. 2.
52 *Cal. Inq. p.m.* iii, p. 438.
53 *Wilts. Inq. p.m.* 1242–1326 (Index Libr.), 416–17; *V.C.H. Wilts.* xi. 153.
54 *Wilts. Inq. p.m.* 1327–77 (Index Libr.), 231; for the FitzWarins, Hankfords, and Bourghchiers, *Complete Peerage*, v. 499–511.
55 *Cal. Inq. p.m.* xvii, pp. 23–4.

56 Ibid. xix, pp. 153–4.
57 P.R.O., C 138/52, no. 106, rot. 20.
58 Ibid. C 139/51, no. 54, rot. 9; C 139/65, no. 40, rot. 10.
59 Ibid. C 140/73, no. 76, rot. 2.
60 Ibid. C 54/392, no. 10; *Complete Peerage*, ii. 16.
61 W.R.O. 9/14/43–4.
62 *Rot. Hund.* (Rec. Com.), ii (1), 259; *Cal. Inq. p.m.* iii, p. 310; E. Foss, *Judges of Eng.* iii. 60–1.
63 *Cal. Close*, 1279–88, 277–8; P.R.O., JUST 1/1006, rot. 27d.
64 *Tax List, 1332* (W.R.S. xlv), 125.
65 *Feet of F.* 1327–77 (W.R.S. xxix), p. 129.
66 *V.C.H. Wilts.* iii. 326; P.R.O., C 139/28, no. 22.
67 Below, Burbage, manors (Burbage Sturmy).
68 *Complete Peerage*, vi. 505–7; P.R.O., E 328/117.
69 Below, this section (Tottenham).
70 Ibid. econ. hist. (Crofton).
71 W.R.O. 9/1/521.
72 Local inf.
73 Inf. from the agent for the Crown Estate Com., 42 High Street, Marlborough; for the woodland, below, this section (Bedwyn common).

belonged to David Brudenell-Bruce, earl of Cardigan.[74]

In 1086 the lands of East Grafton and West Grafton lay in four or more estates. William of Eu (d. c. 1095) held one, in 1066 assessed at 1 hide, which Hugh held of him.[75] Three were held by serjeants of the king: Ralph de Halvile held 3 hides and 1½ yardland, Robert son of Ralph held 1 hide and 2½ yardlands, and Richard Sturmy held 1 hide. In 1066 Ralph de Halvile's undertenants were Alwin, Alwold, Lewin, and Celestan; Robert's land was then held by Ulmar.[76] Of those estates only Richard's can be identified with a later one.[77]

In 1167 *EAST GRAFTON* manor was held by Alan de Neville (d. c. 1178).[78] It descended to his son Alan (d. c. 1190), who added to it land formerly held by Thomas Martigny.[79] The manor was held by the younger Alan's relict Gillian,[80] passed to his heir, his brother Geoffrey (d. c. 1225),[81] and descended to Geoffrey's son John (d. c. 1253)[82] and presumably to John's son Geoffrey de Neville (d. 1267). The younger Geoffrey's heir was his cousin Sir Hugh de Neville, who subinfeudated the manor in 1271.[83] The overlordship apparently descended to Sir Hugh's son Geoffrey (d. 1316), to that Geoffrey's son Philip (d. 1345), and to Philip's heir John de Neville, Lord Neville, who was overlord in 1359.[84] It has not been traced further.

From 1271 the lordship in fee of East Grafton manor belonged to John Havering (d. apparently between 1302 and 1316) and his wife Joan (fl. 1316).[85] By 1324 it had passed to Sir Richard Havering[86] (fl. 1349),[87] who in 1347 was granted free warren in his demesne at East Grafton.[88] The manor descended in the Havering family until 1405 or later.[89] In 1428 a moiety was held in fee by Sir Thomas Barnardiston (d. c. 1461), who was succeeded in turn by his son Thomas and grandson Sir Thomas Barnardiston (d. 1503).[90] In 1530 the moiety was held by Sir Thomas's relict Elizabeth Barnardiston.[91] It reverted to his son Sir Thomas[92] (d. 1542), whose son Thomas[93] sold it in 1543 to Edward, earl of Hertford (cr. duke of Somerset 1547).[94] The second moiety was held in 1411 by Sir William Butler (d. 1415), passed to his son Sir John (d.

1430), and was held for life by Sir John's relict Isabel (d. 1441). It descended in turn to Sir John's son Sir John Butler[95] (d. 1463) and to that Sir John's sons William (d. 1471) and Sir Thomas (d. 1522).[96] Later it was held with the first moiety by Edward, duke of Somerset. On Somerset's execution and attainder in 1552 the whole manor was classified as an estate which he had acquired by 1540 and as such passed by Act to his son Sir Edward Seymour (cr. earl of Hertford 1559, d. 1621).[97] The classification was wrong for the first moiety and possibly for the second, it was apparently reversed, and the manor belonged to the Crown until 1611, when it was sold through agents to Gilbert Prynne.[98] Prynne was apparently a trustee of Lord Hertford, who held East Grafton manor in 1613. The manor passed in 1621 to Lord Hertford's grandson Sir Francis Seymour[99] (cr. Baron Seymour 1641, d. 1664) and descended in turn to Sir Francis's son Charles, Lord Seymour (d. 1665), Charles's sons Francis, Lord Seymour (duke of Somerset from 1675, d. 1678), and Charles, duke of Somerset (d. 1748), and that Charles's son Algernon, duke of Somerset (cr. earl of Northumberland and of Egremont 1749, d. 1750).[1] In 1750 it passed to Algernon's half-sister Frances, from 1750 wife of John Manners, marquess of Granby, his half-sister Charlotte, from 1750 wife of Heneage Finch (from 1757 earl of Aylesford), and his nephew Sir Charles Wyndham, Bt., who succeeded him as earl of Egremont, as tenants in common. In 1779 it was allotted to Charlotte,[2] who in 1787 sold it to Thomas Bruce, earl of Ailesbury.[3] From 1787 the manor, to which other estates in East Grafton were added,[4] descended with Tottenham House.[5] About 1929 George Brudenell-Bruce, marquess of Ailesbury, sold his land at East Grafton as the main parts of Manor farm, 518 a. apparently including c. 180 a. of West Grafton's land, Green farm, 390 a. including c. 35 a. of Wilton's land, and East Grafton farm, 439 a. including c. 140 a. of Wilton's land.[6] Mr. R. Browning bought Manor farm in 1965 and Green farm in 1970; in 1996 the combined holding, c. 800 a., belonged to Mr. Browning and members of his family.[7] In 1996 East Grafton farm belonged to Mr. B. R. Taylor, the owner of Manor farm, Marten.[8]

74   Inf. from the earl of Cardigan, Savernake Lodge, Savernake; below, econ. hist. (Crofton).
75   *V.C.H. Wilts.* ii, p. 149; I. J. Sanders, *Eng. Baronies,* 119.   76   *V.C.H. Wilts.* ii, p. 166.
77   Below, this section.
78   *Pipe R.* 1168 (P.R.S. xii), 159; for the Nevilles, *Complete Peerage,* ix, at pp. 502–3.
79   *Red Bk. Exch.* (Rolls Ser.), ii. 483–4.
80   *Pipe R.* 1190 (P.R.S. N.S. i), 121.
81   *Red Bk. Exch.* (Rolls Ser.), ii. 483–4; *Rot. Litt. Pat.* (Rec. Com.), 65.
82   *Sar. Chart. and Doc.* (Rolls Ser.), pp. 307–8.
83   *Cal. Chart. R.* 1257–1300, 178; *Rot. Hund.* (Rec. Com.), ii (1), 259.
84   *Feet of F.* 1327–77 (W.R.S. xxix), pp. 114–15.
85   *Cal. Chart. R.* 1257–1300, 178; *Rot. Hund.* (Rec. Com.), ii (1), 259; *Wilts. Inq. p.m.* 1242–1326 (Index Libr.), 286–7; *Feud. Aids,* v. 203.
86   *Feud. Aids,* v. 218.
87   *Wilts. Inq. p.m.* 1327–77 (Index Libr.), 217–18.
88   *Cal. Chart. R.* 1341–1417, 69–70.
89   *Chandler's Reg.* (W.R.S. xxxix), p. 33.
90   W. A. Copinger, *Suff. Man.* v. 258; *Feud. Aids,* v. 262;

Cal. Inq. p.m. Hen. VII, ii, p. 492.
91   P.R.O., STAC 2/17/331.
92   *Cal. Inq. p.m. Hen. VII,* ii, p. 492.
93   P.R.O., C 142/69, no. 198.
94   Ibid. C 54/434, no. 20; *Complete Peerage,* xii (1), 59–64.
95   *Feud. Aids,* v. 262; P.R.O., C 139/47, no. 11, rot. 2; for the Butlers, *V.C.H. Lancs.* i. 346–9.
96   *Cal. Close,* 1485–1500, p. 296.
97   *Complete Peerage,* vi. 505–6; P.R.O., E 328/117.
98   *Cal. Pat.* 1566–9, pp. 156, 385–6; 1569–72, pp. 388–9; P.R.O., C 66/1845, no. 2; Alnwick Castle Mun. X.II.11, box 2, deed, Whitmore to Prynne, 1611; cf. above, this section.
99   Alnwick Castle Mun. X.II.11, box 2, deed, Prynne to Hertford, 1613.
1   *Complete Peerage,* xi. 640–2; xii (1), 76–81.
2   Ibid. i. 365; v. 36; xi. 268; *V.C.H. Wilts.* xii. 169; Som. Estate Act, 19 Geo. III, c. 46 (Priv. Act).
3   W.R.O. 9/16/28.   4   Below, this section.
5   Ibid. (Tottenham).   6   W.R.O. 9/1/521.
7   Inf. from Mr. R. Browning, Old Coach Ho., E. Grafton.
8   Inf. from Mr. B. R. Taylor, the Manor, Marten.

The estate held by Richard Sturmy in 1086[9] was probably that at East Grafton which Robert Doygnel held by serjeanty in 1198.[10] Warin Doygnel (d. by 1235) held 4 hides there c. 1210. His heirs were his daughters Alice (d. by 1243) and Joan, wife of Richard Baxman (fl. 1243).[11] The estate was probably that held by Stephen Baxman in 1275 and 1289,[12] by William Baxman in 1303, and by another William Baxman[13] (d. c. 1312). The second William was succeeded by his grandson John Holt.[14] In 1350 John granted his estate in East Grafton to St. Margaret's priory, Marlborough,[15] which held it until it passed to the Crown at the Dissolution.[16] In 1539 the estate was granted to Anne of Cleves and in 1541 to Edward, earl of Hertford (cr. duke of Somerset 1547).[17] On Somerset's execution and attainder in 1552 it passed to the Crown, and in 1553 it was assigned to his son Sir Edward Seymour.[18] It thereafter descended with Tottenham Lodge and Tottenham House, from 1787 also with East Grafton manor.[19]

In 1336 Robert Hungerford gave 1 carucate probably in East Grafton to Easton priory,[20] and land in East Grafton was given to, or bought by, the priory c. 1349.[21] The priory was dissolved in 1536, when, with Easton Druce manor in Easton, its estate in East Grafton was granted to Edward Seymour, Viscount Beauchamp (cr. earl of Hertford 1537, duke of Somerset 1547). On Somerset's execution and attainder in 1552 the estate passed by Act to his son Sir Edward.[22] From 1553 the estate, which in 1634 consisted of a farm accounted 112 a. with feeding rights,[23] descended with Tottenham Lodge and Tottenham House, and from 1787 also descended with East Grafton manor.[24]

In 1245 St. Margaret's priory was taking two thirds of the great tithes of East Grafton manor and giving 2 a. of wheat to the prebendary of Bedwyn. In exchange for 2s. a year to be paid by the priory to the prebendary, presumably in addition to the 2 a. of wheat, those tithes were confirmed to the priory in 1246.[25] Between 1412 and the earlier 16th century the priory also became entitled to the estate, consisting of ½ yardland, the remaining tithes from East

Grafton manor, and other tithes, held in 1405 by the chaplain serving East Grafton chapel. The priory's estate passed to the Crown at the Dissolution. In 1541 it was granted to Edward, earl of Hertford,[26] on whose execution and attainder in 1552 it again passed to the Crown.[27] In 1591 the Crown sold it through agents to John Blagrave,[28] who in 1594 sold it to Edward, earl of Hertford.[29] From 1613 the estate descended with East Grafton manor,[30] and the tithes were merged with the land from which they arose.[31]

In 1198 Nicholas Monk held 1 carucate in West Grafton by serjeanty.[32] That was possibly the estate which Alan FitzWarin and his wife Margery conveyed to St. Margaret's priory, Marlborough, in 1260.[33] The priory acquired other land in West Grafton,[34] and in the 16th century its estate there was called *WEST GRAFTON* manor.[35] The manor passed to the Crown at the Dissolution, was granted in 1541 to Edward, earl of Hertford (cr. duke of Somerset 1547),[36] and was forfeited on Somerset's execution and attainder in 1552. In 1553 it was assigned to Somerset's son Sir Edward Seymour[37] (cr. earl of Hertford 1559, d. 1621). It thereafter descended with Tottenham Lodge and Tottenham House,[38] and other land was added to it.[39] In 1929 George Brudenell-Bruce, marquess of Ailesbury, sold his land at West Grafton mostly as West Grafton farm, 428 a., and Kingston farm, 73 a.; c. 180 a. was part of Manor farm, East Grafton.[40] In 1963 West Grafton farm was bought by members of the Curnick family, and in 1996 it belonged to Mr. T. W. Curnick, the owner of Southgrove farm, Burbage, which adjoined it.[41]

Before 1275 Robert Fosbury held 1 carucate at West Grafton by serjeanty.[42] It passed to John Fosbury (d. c. 1294) and to John's son Peter[43] (d. 1352), whose coheirs conveyed it c. 1352 to John Malwain (d. 1361) and his wife Margery. John Malwain also held land at Marten, with which the estate at West Grafton descended to his son John (d. by 1378).[44] The estate at West Grafton had passed by 1380 to that John's sister Margery and her husband Helming Leget,[45] and

9 Above, this section.
10 *Bk. of Fees*, i. 13; *W.A.M.* xxxix. 60.
11 *Red Bk. Exch.* (Rolls Ser.), ii. 487; *Bk. of Fees*, i. 586; *Close R. 1234–7*, 145; *W.A.M.* xxxix. 64; *Ex. e Rot. Fin.* (Rec. Com.), i. 408.
12 *Rot. Hund.* (Rec. Com.), ii (1), 260; P.R.O., JUST 1/1006, rot. 51.
13 *Cal. Pat. 1301–7*, 104.
14 *Wilts. Inq. p.m. 1242–1326* (Index Libr.), 392.
15 *Cal. Pat. 1348–50*, 444.
16 P.R.O., SC 6/Hen. VIII/3985, rot. 66.
17 *L. & P. Hen. VIII*, xiv, p. 154; xvi, pp. 380–1.
18 P.R.O., E 328/117.
19 Above, this section (E. Grafton); below, this section (Tottenham).
20 *Cal. Pat. 1334–8*, 225.
21 Ibid. *1348–50*, 303; P.R.O., C 143/293, no. 13.
22 *V.C.H. Wilts.* iii. 326; Longleat Mun., Seymour papers, xii, f. 323 and v.; below, Easton, manors (Easton Druce).
23 Alnwick Castle Mun. X.II.11, box 6, survey, 1634, pp. 6–7.
24 Above, this section (E. Grafton); below, this section (Tottenham).
25 *Sar. Chart. and Doc.* (Rolls Ser.), pp. 307–8; for the prebend, below, this section (Prebendal); ibid. churches.

26 *Chandler's Reg.* (W.R.S. xxxix), pp. 33, 120; P.R.O., E 305/15/C 18.
27 P.R.O., E 309/1/5 Eliz. I/27, no. 2.
28 Ibid. C 66/1374, mm. 2–4, 8; Alnwick Castle Mun. X.II.11, box 2, deed, Downing to Blagrave, 1591.
29 Alnwick Castle Mun. X.II.11, box 2, deed, Blagrave to Hertford, 1594.
30 Ibid. X.II.11, box 2, deed, Hertford to Seymour, 1617; above, this section.
31 Cf. W.R.O., tithe award.   32 *Bk. of Fees*, i. 13.
33 P.R.O., CP 25/1/251/20, no. 7.
34 Below, this section.
35 P.R.O., SC 6/Hen. VIII/3985, rot. 66.
36 *L. & P. Hen. VIII*, xvi, pp. 380–1.
37 P.R.O., E 328/117.
38 Below, this section (Tottenham).
39 Ibid. this section (Sotwell's).
40 W.R.O. 9/1/521.
41 Inf. from Mrs. I. S. Curnick, Southgrove Farm, Burbage.
42 *Rot. Hund.* (Rec. Com.), ii (1), 259.
43 *Cal. Inq. p.m.* iii, pp. 142–3.
44 Ibid. xi, pp. 129–30; *Cal. Pat. 1350–4*, 271; *Wilts. Inq. p.m. 1327–77* (Index Libr.), 227; below, this section (Marten).
45 *Cal. Pat. 1377–81*, 546.

with land at Marten it had been conveyed by 1399 by John Lovel, Lord Lovel and Holand, to St. Margaret's priory.[46] It was apparently merged with the priory's other estate in West Grafton.[47]

A farm in West Grafton later called *SOT-WELL'S* belonged to Thomas Sotwell in 1543.[48] It may have passed to Thomas's son William (d. 1589–90), passed to John Sotwell (d. 1598), the younger of two sons of William so called, and was held for life by John's relict Anne. The farm passed in turn to John's sons Richard (d. 1628) and Robert (d. 1630) and to Robert's son Robert,[49] who in 1648 sold it to John Durnford.[50] John held the farm in 1679, when it was accounted 185 a. including 15 a. in Burbage.[51] In 1719 John's son John sold it to Francis Hawes, a director of the South Sea Company.[52] After the collapse of the company in 1720 Hawes's estates were confiscated by parliamentary trustees, who sold the farm in 1729 to John Hopkins.[53] From 1729 to 1788 the farm passed with Wexcombe manor.[54] In 1788 Benjamin Bond Hopkins sold it to Thomas Bruce, earl of Ailesbury,[55] who added it to West Grafton manor.

Alvric the huntsman held Harding in 1066. Richard Sturmy held it in 1086, when Robert held it of him.[56] It apparently descended in the Sturmy family, was held by Walter Sturmy (d. 1243), and was divided between Walter's sisters Alice, wife of Robert Kernet, and Letewarie.[57] Alice's moiety descended with, and apparently became part of, Westcourt manor in Shalbourne, and apparently lay mainly in Shalbourne parish.[58] Letewarie subinfeudated her moiety, the later *HARDING* farm, which lay mainly in Great Bedwyn parish, to Richard of Harding (d. c. 1250), whose heir was his son Richard.[59] It passed to another Richard Harding (d. c. 1294), whose heir was his uncle Roger Harding[60] (d. c. 1331). The estate passed to Roger's niece Maud, wife of Thomas Alresford[61] (d. 1361),[62] and in 1336 was settled on Thomas and Maud for life and on Thomas's son Roger and other members of his family in tail.[63] The descent of the estate from 1361 to the mid 15th century is obscure. Sir John Seymour (d. 1464) settled it on Roger Seymour in tail male, and on the death of Roger's son John in 1509 it reverted to Sir John's

great-grandson Sir John Seymour[64] (d. 1536). Harding farm thereafter descended with Burbage Sturmy manor,[65] and from 1553 with Tottenham Lodge,[66] until the death of John Seymour, duke of Somerset, in 1675. Under a settlement of 1672 the farm passed in 1675 to Somerset's relict Sarah (d. 1692), and from 1692 to c. 1767 descended in the Seymour family with Pewsey manor.[67] In 1767 Hugh Percy, duke of Northumberland, and his wife Elizabeth, by direction of Joseph Champion, sold it to John White.[68] It descended in the direct line to John (d. 1797) and Thomas White, who in 1801 sold it to Thomas Bruce, earl of Ailesbury.[69] It thereafter descended with Tottenham House to George Brudenell-Bruce, marquess of Ailesbury, who sold it c. 1929. It then measured 396 a. and included c. 70 a. of Wilton's land and c. 65 a. of the former Bedwyn Brails bailiwick.[70] In 1996 the land was part of a large estate based at Stype Grange in Shalbourne and belonged to Mrs. V. L. Duffield.[71]

At Marten in 1086 there were three estates, held by Odolina, Ralph de Halvile, and Turbert. Lewin held Turbert's estate in 1066. Ralph and Turbert held by serjeanty. Odolina may have given her land to Westminster abbey in the late 11th century,[72] but there is no evidence that the abbey later held land at Marten. Before 1187 one of the estates seems to have been held by Philip de Chartrai.[73]

An estate later called *MARTEN* manor was held by John de Palerne, whose son Henry conveyed it to William Brewer (d. 1226) c. 1200.[74] In 1227 Brewer's son William gave it to Mottisfont priory (Hants),[75] and the priory held the manor, with land at Wilton, until the Dissolution. In 1536 the Crown granted it to William Sandys, Lord Sandys (d. 1540), and his wife Margery (d. 1539).[76] It passed to the Sandyses' son Thomas, Lord Sandys (d. 1560),[77] on whose daughter-in-law Elizabeth (fl. 1598), wife of Ralph Scrope, it was settled for life in 1572,[78] and to Thomas's grandson William Sandys, Lord Sandys (d. 1623). In 1602 Lord Sandys sold the manor to Sir Edward Hungerford[79] (d. 1607). It passed to Sir Edward's grandnephew Sir Edward Hungerford (d. 1648), to that Sir Edward's half-brother Anthony Hungerford (d. 1657), and to Anthony's son Sir Edward,[80] who

46 Ibid. 1396–9, 560; below, this section (Marten).
47 Above, this section.
48 P.R.O., E 318/13/574, rot. 11; for the Sotwells, *Wilts. Pedigrees* (Harl. Soc. cv/cvi), 185–6.
49 *Wilts. Inq. p.m.* 1625–49 (Index Libr.), 141–2; P.R.O., PROB 11/91, ff. 367–8.
50 W.R.O. 9/16/72. 51 Ibid. 9/16/73.
52 Ibid. 9/16/99. 53 Ibid. 9/16/101.
54 Below, this section (Wexcombe).
55 W.R.O. 9/16/136.
56 *V.C.H. Wilts.* ii, p. 166; iv. 392.
57 *Ex. e Rot. Fin.* (Rec. Com.), i. 393, 400.
58 For the descent, *V.C.H. Berks.* iv. 231; cf. *Wilts. Inq. p.m.* 1327–77 (Index Libr.), 275; W.R.O. 9/1/95; 9/1/509.
59 *Cal. Inq. p.m.* i, p. 45; *V.C.H. Berks.* iv. 231.
60 *Cal. Inq. p.m.* iii, p. 100.
61 Ibid. vii, pp. 254–5.
62 Ibid. xi, pp. 2–3.
63 *Feet of F.* 1327–77 (W.R.S. xxix), pp. 46–7.
64 P.R.O., C 142/24, no. 38; below, Burbage, manors (Burbage Sturmy).

65 Below, Burbage, manors (Burbage Sturmy); cf. Longleat Mun., Seymour papers, xii, f. 301 and v.; P.R.O., E 328/117.
66 Below, this section (Tottenham).
67 W.R.O. 1300/290; 1300/299; below, Pewsey, manor (Pewsey). 68 W.R.O. 9/3/170–1.
69 Ibid. 9/3/173; 9/3/175; 9/3/179–81.
70 Ibid. 9/1/521; below, this section (Tottenham); for Wilton and Bedwyn Brail bailiwick, ibid. this section.
71 Local inf.
72 *V.C.H. Wilts.* ii, pp. 164, 166.
73 *Pipe R.* 1187 (P.R.S. xxxvii), 180.
74 Ibid. 1200 (P.R.S. N.S. xii), 161; *D.N.B.* (s.v. Brewer).
75 *Cal. Chart. R.* 1226–57, 40; *Cur. Reg. R.* xiv, p. 261.
76 *L. & P. Hen. VIII*, xi, p. 87; below, this section (Wilton); for the Sandyses, *Complete Peerage*, xi. 441–6.
77 P.R.O., CP 25/2/66/547, no. 33.
78 Ibid. C 66/1281, m. 23.
79 Ibid. CP 25/2/262/44 Eliz. I Trin.
80 *V.C.H. Wilts.* xv. 205; W.R.O. 415/163; 490/1540, ff. 65v.–66.

sold it in 1674 to Edmund Pyke. In 1690 Edmund's son and heir Henry Pyke sold part of the manor in portions, and in 1692 sold the rest to the executors of Evelyn Fanshawe, Viscount Fanshawe (d. 1687). Lord Fanshawe's heir was his uncle Charles Fanshawe, Viscount Fanshawe (d. 1710), who in 1693 bought one of the portions sold in 1690. Charles's heir was his brother Simon, Viscount Fanshawe[81] (d. 1716), who devised Marten manor to Thomas Fanshawe (d. 1726). From Thomas the manor descended in the direct line to Simon (d. 1777), whose relict Althea held it until her death in 1805,[82] Henry (d. 1828), and Henry (d. 1857). From 1815, when additional land at Marten was received in exchange for tithes and for land at Wilton, the manor measured c. 545 a.[83] The younger Henry Fanshawe was succeeded in turn by his brother the Revd. Charles Fanshawe (d. 1859) and Charles's sons the Revd. Charles Fanshawe (d. 1873) and the Revd. John Fanshawe (d. 1892). From John the manor descended in the direct line to Henry (d. 1913) and Charles Fanshawe, who in 1920 sold it to Gordon Crees (d. 1961). In 1980 Crees's executors sold Manor farm, c. 360 a., to Faccombe Estates, a company from which Mr. B. R. Taylor, the owner in 1996, bought it in 1985. North-east of the village c. 150 a., formerly part of Manor farm, belonged to Mr. J. R. Crook in 1996.[84]

In 1242–3 William Longespée (d. 1250), styled earl of Salisbury, was overlord of ⅕ knight's fee at Marten. William was succeeded by his son Sir William Longespée (d. 1257) and he by his daughter Margaret, from 1261 countess of Salisbury (d. by 1310), wife of Henry de Lacy, earl of Lincoln (d. 1311).[85] The overlordship descended to Margaret's daughter Alice de Lacy, countess of Lincoln and of Salisbury. In 1325 Alice and her husband Sir Ebles Lestrange granted it to the younger Hugh le Despenser, Lord le Despenser,[86] who forfeited it in 1326.[87] It was presumably granted in 1337 with the earldom of Salisbury to William de Montagu (d. 1344). William's great-grandson Thomas de Montagu, earl of Salisbury, was overlord in 1428.[88] The lordship in fee of the estate was held by John Malwain in 1242–3[89] and by William Malwain in 1275.[90] In 1313 it was held by Ralph Malwain and his wife Maud,[91] and it passed to their son John[92] (d. 1361), who also held land at West Grafton. That John was succeeded by his

son John[93] (d. by 1378),[94] whose heirs were his sisters Joan, wife of Peter Tebaud, and Margery, wife of Helming Leget. In 1385 the Legets conveyed their part of the estate to John Lovel, Lord Lovel and Holand,[95] who by 1399 had conveyed it to St. Margaret's priory, Marlborough.[96] There is no evidence that the priory later held land at Marten. In 1397 Peter Tebaud conveyed Joan's part of the estate to John Malwain[97] (d. by 1426), and thereafter it descended in the Malwain and Ernle families with Etchilhampton manor to Michael Ernle[98] (d. 1594). In 1610 Michael's son Sir John Ernle[99] sold his estate at Marten, then described as a third part of Marten manor, to Sir Anthony Hungerford.[1] Either at Sir Anthony's death in 1627 or by conveyance in 1620–1 it passed to his son Sir Edward Hungerford[2] (d. 1648), who added it to Marten manor.[3]

In 1246 Mottisfont priory was taking all the tithes arising from its estate at Marten and giving 2 a. of wheat to the prebendary of Bedwyn. The tithes were confirmed to the priory in 1246, from when additionally it was to give 1 a. of barley and 1 a. of oats to the prebendary.[4] The tithes apparently descended with Marten manor, and at inclosure in 1815 Henry Fanshawe was allotted 90 a. to replace them.[5]

Land at Bedwyn given by Byrhtelm to the bishop of Winchester and his see by exchange in the early 9th century was possibly the 20 *manentes*, then said to lie at Stock by Shalbourne, given by the bishop to the king in 904: if so, it was presumably added or restored to the king's estate called Bedwyn.[6]

STOCK manor was probably subinfeudated after c. 1130.[7] In the early 14th century Thomas de St. Vigeur held it, and in 1335 his relict Maud held a third of it in dower. Thomas conveyed the manor to Adam of Stock (d. c. 1313) and Adam's wife Gena (d. c. 1335) and son Patrick. About 1313 it passed to Gena, who married Robert Hungerford, and c. 1335 to Adam's grandson Edward Stock[8] (d. 1361). Edward's heir was his son John, at whose death in 1376 his lands were divided between his aunt Margaret Stock, wife of John Weston, and his cousin Nicholas Danvers (d. by 1387), a chaplain. Nicholas's moiety reverted to Margaret, who by 1387 had settled the manor on herself for life with remainder to John Comberwell in tail.[9] The

81 *Complete Peerage*, v. 255–6; W.R.O. 212A/27/20/3, Fanshawe's abstr. of title.
82 W.R.O. 212A/27/20/3, Fanshawe's abstr. of title; P.R.O., PROB 11/1027, f. 131 and v.; for the Fanshawes, Burke, *Land. Gent.* (1965), i. 253–4.
83 W.R.O., EA/99.
84 Inf. from Miss S. D. Crees, Coppers, Marten; Mr. B. R. Taylor, the Manor, Marten.
85 *Bk. of Fees*, ii. 709; *V.C.H. Wilts.* xv. 246; *Complete Peerage*, xi. 382–4.
86 *Feet of F.* 1272–1327 (W.R.S. i), pp. 132–3; *Complete Peerage*, xi. 385.
87 *Complete Peerage*, iv. 267–70.
88 Ibid. xi. 385–95; *Feud. Aids*, v. 263.
89 *Bk. of Fees*, ii. 709, 719.
90 *Rot. Hund.* (Rec. Com.), ii (1), 260.
91 *Feet of F.* 1272–1327 (W.R.S. i), p. 83.
92 *Cal. Close*, 1349–54, 523.
93 *Cal. Inq. p.m.* xi, pp. 129–30; above, this section.

94 Hist. MSS. Com. 55, *Var. Colln.* iv, p. 114.
95 Ibid. pp. 116–17; *Cal. Close*, 1402–5, 6–7.
96 *Cal. Pat.* 1396–9, 560.
97 Hist. MSS. Com. 55, *Var. Colln.* iv, p. 119.
98 *V.C.H. Wilts.* x. 72–3.
99 P.R.O., C 142/240, no. 77.
1 Ibid. CP 25/2/369/8 Jas. I Trin.
2 *Wilts. Inq. p.m.* 1625–49 (Index Libr.), 57–9; W.R.O. 490/1540, ff. 64–8.
3 Above, this section.
4 *Sar. Chart. and Doc.* (Rolls Ser.), pp. 309–10; for the prebend, below, this section (Prebendal); ibid. churches.
5 W.R.O., EA/99; above, this section.
6 Finberg, *Early Wessex Chart.* pp. 72, 80; *V.C.H. Wilts.* ii, pp. 86–7; above, this section [preamble].
7 Above, this section [preamble]; below, local govt. [Wexcombe].
8 *Cal. Inq. p.m.* v, p. 211; vii, p. 457.
9 Ibid. xi, pp. 167–8; xiv, p. 279; *Cal. Fine R.* 1368–77, 371; *Cal. Pat.* 1385–9, 295–6.

manor was held by Thomas Stock in 1428 and formerly by William Stock.[10] In the period 1429–31 Thomas conveyed it to Walter Hunger-ford, Lord Hungerford (d. 1449).[11] From Walter it descended in the direct line to Sir Edmund (d. 1484),[12] Sir Thomas (d. 1494), Sir John (d. 1524), Sir Anthony (d. 1558), Sir John (d. 1582), Anthony (d. 1589), and Sir John Hungerford (d. 1635).[13] Anthony's relict Bridget (d. 1621) held it for life.[14] In 1630 Sir John sold it to Sir John Danvers[15] (d. 1655), a regicide. Danvers's estates were confiscated at the Restoration, and in 1661 the Crown conveyed Stock manor to trustees, who in 1664 sold it to William Byrd[16] (d. 1692).[17] After c. 1716 Byrd's son William sold the manor to Francis Stonehouse[18] (d. 1738),[19] in 1741 Stonehouse's son Francis sold it to Lascelles Metcalfe,[20] in 1753 Metcalfe sold it to Ralph Verney, Earl Verney,[21] and in 1766 Lord Verney sold it to Thomas Brudenell, Lord Bruce.[22] The manor thereafter descended with Tottenham House.[23] About 1929 George Brudenell-Bruce, marquess of Ailesbury, sold Stock's land south-east of the Dun as Brail farm, 120 a.[24] In 1996 the farm, then c. 200 a., belonged to Mr. J. J. Hosier.[25] In 1950 the rest of Stock manor, except the woodland, was sold by Lord Ailesbury to the Crown, the owner in 1996.[26]

A manor house stood on the high ground west of Great Bedwyn village. In the mid 17th century it was said that it had earlier been moated[27] and, if so, it was presumably lived in by the Stock family in the 14th and 15th centuries; it was apparently lived in by Sir John Hungerford (d. 1582).[28] Stokke Manor probably occupies its site and nothing of it is known to survive.[29]

In the 1230s the executors of Sir John Dacy gave an estate including Ford mill and a nominal 33 a. in the open fields of Stock to Salisbury cathedral.[30] The cathedral owned the mill and 21 a. in the open fields in 1751.[31] By an exchange of 1800 it gave its estate at Stock to Thomas Bruce, earl of Ailesbury, who added it to Stock manor.[32]

WEXCOMBE manor, which, probably *c.*

1130, Henry I granted to John FitzGilbert (d. 1165), his marshal, probably passed in turn to John's sons Gilbert FitzJohn (d. 1165–6) and John (d. 1194).[33] In 1189 Richard I confirmed it to John the marshal,[34] at whose death it passed to his brother William Marshal, earl of Pem-broke (d. 1219). It descended to William's son William, earl of Pembroke (d. 1231), whose relict Eleanor (d. 1275), the wife of Simon de Mont-fort, earl of Leicester (d. 1265), held it for life.[35] On Eleanor's death the manor passed to Gilbert de Clare, earl of Gloucester and of Hertford (d. 1295), the grandnephew of William, earl of Pembroke (d. 1231).[36] It was held for life by Gilbert's relict Joan (d. 1307) and passed to his son Gilbert, earl of Gloucester and of Hertford (d. 1314),[37] whose relict Maud held it until her death in 1320.[38] The manor passed to the younger Gilbert's sister Margaret (d. 1342), one of his heirs and the wife of Hugh de Audley (cr. earl of Gloucester 1337, d. 1347), whose estates were held between 1321 and 1326 by the king because of Hugh's contrariance. In 1347 the manor passed to Margaret's daughter Margaret de Audley (d. 1348), the wife of Ralph de Stafford (cr. earl of Stafford 1351, d. 1372), and in 1372 to that Margaret's son Hugh de Stafford, earl of Stafford (d. 1386).[39] It descended with the Stafford title to Hugh's sons Thomas (d. 1392), William (d. 1395), and Edmund (d. 1403). Edmund's heir was his son Humphrey, earl of Stafford[40] (cr. duke of Buckingham 1444, d. 1460), a minor until 1423. Humphrey was suc-ceeded by his grandson Henry Stafford, duke of Buckingham, whose estates passed to the Crown in 1483 when he was executed and attainted.[41] Wexcombe manor was probably held by the Crown until 1485 and was probably among the lands restored then by Act to Henry's son Edward, duke of Buckingham. It passed to the Crown again in 1521 when Edward was executed for high treason.[42] In 1522 it was granted in tail male to Sir Edward Darell (d. 1530),[43] in 1544 the reversion was granted to Edward Seymour, earl of Hertford (cr. duke of Somerset 1547),[44] and in 1545 Sir Edward's grandson and heir Sir

10 *Feud. Aids*, v. 264.
11 *Cal. Close*, 1429–35, 163; *Complete Peerage*, vi. 616; W.R.O. 9/26/2.
12 P.R.O., C 141/6, no. 25, rot. 2.
13 *Wilts. Pedigrees* (Harl. Soc. cv/cvi), 90–3: corrected by *Hist. Parl.*, *Commons*, 1509–58, ii. 411.
14 *Colln. Topog. et Geneal.* v. 28, 30; P.R.O., C 2/Jas. I/L 15/48.
15 S. R. Ranson, *Verney Papers* (cat. for Claydon Ho. trust), p. 423.
16 *D.N.B.*; W.R.O. 9/26/3–6.
17 P.R.O., C 5/113/14.
18 W.R.O. 9/26/15–23; 9/27/54.
19 *Colln. Topog. et Geneal.* v. 361.
20 W.R.O. 9/26/29–30.
21 Ibid. 9/26/32. 22 Ibid. 9/26/34.
23 Below, this section (Tottenham).
24 W.R.O. 9/1/521.
25 Inf. from Mrs. A. J. H. Smith, Brail Farm.
26 Inf. from the agent for the Crown Estate Com., 42 High Street, Marlborough; for the woodland, below, this section (Bedwyn common).
27 Aubrey, *Topog. Colln.* ed. Jackson, 374.
28 W.R.O. 9/26/511.
29 Above, intro. (Stock and Ford).
30 *Sar. Chart. and Doc.* (Rolls Ser.), pp. 215–17; for the mill, above, intro. (Stock and Ford); below, econ. hist.

(Stock); for the rest of the estate, below, this section (Wilton).
31 W.R.O. 9/3/393H.
32 Ibid. 9/3/165.
33 *Complete Peerage*, x, App. G, 93–7; above, this section [preamble].
34 P.R.O., C 52/21, no. 10.
35 *Complete Peerage*, vii. 546–7; x. 360, 363, 365, 367–8; *Pipe R.* 1195 (P.R.S. N.S. vi), 136; 1220 (P.R.S. N.S. xlvii), 178; *Close R.* 1227–31, 498; *Rot. Hund.* (Rec. Com.), ii (1), 259.
36 *Rot. Parl.* i. 8; *Wilts. Inq. p.m.* 1242–1326 (Index Libr.), 210–11; P.R.O., E 159/50, rot. 5; for the earls of Glouc. and of Hert., *Complete Peerage*, v. 694–719.
37 *Wilts. Inq. p.m.* 1242–1326 (Index Libr.), 339–41, 403–6.
38 *Cal. Close*, 1313–18, 131; *Feud. Aids*, v. 203; *Complete Peerage*, v. 714–15.
39 *Cal. Inq. p.m.* ix, p. 55; xiii, pp. 181–2; *Complete Peerage*, v. 715–17; xii (1), 174–9.
40 *Cal. Inq. p.m.* xvi, pp. 159, 161; xvii, pp. 88, 93, 478, 485; xviii, p. 269; for the earls of Staff., *Complete Peerage*, xii (1), 179–81.
41 *Complete Peerage*, ii. 388–90.
42 Ibid. 390–1; P.R.O., C 142/80, no. 4.
43 P.R.O., C 142/51, no. 2; W.R.O. 1300/172.
44 *L. & P. Hen. VIII*, xix (2), pp. 313–14; *Complete Peerage*, xii (1), 59–62.

Edward Darell conveyed the manor to Seymour in an exchange.[45] In 1552 the manor passed to the Crown on Seymour's execution and attainder. In 1553 it was assigned to his son Sir Edward[46] (cr. earl of Hertford 1559, d. 1621), and it descended to that Edward's grandson and heir William Seymour, earl of Hertford (cr. marquess of Hertford 1641, restored as duke of Somerset 1660, d. 1660),[47] who devised it to trustees to pay debts and legacies. The duke's trustees held the manor until 1719 when, by order of Chancery, it was sold to John Hopkins (d. 1732). Hopkins devised it in trust for the children of his cousin John Hopkins. The trustees held it until 1772; they then conveyed it to that John's grandson Benjamin Bond, who took the additional surname Hopkins.[48]

In 1788 Benjamin Bond Hopkins sold Upper farm and Lower farm, which together included nearly all the land of Wexcombe, to Ralph Tanner and Daniel Tanner respectively.[49] On Ralph's death in 1800[50] Upper farm passed to Edward Tanner; c. 1808 Lower farm passed from Daniel to Thomas Tanner[51] (d. 1822), who devised it to William Tanner, and c. 1829 passed from William to Edward Tanner[52] (d. 1843), the owner of Upper farm. Both farms were devised by Edward Tanner to J. B. H. Tanner (will proved 1846),[53] and remained in the Tanner family until the 1880s.[54] They were owned in 1889 by W. C. Finch, who conveyed them in 1904 to Florence Parker, later wife of J. L. Baskin, and Florence owned them in 1907.[55] K. A. MacAndrew owned them from 1908 or earlier to c. 1920.[56] In 1920 they were bought by the brothers A. J. Hosier (d. 1963) and Joshua Hosier.[57] Both farms descended in the Hosier family, and in 1996 belonged to Mr. P. Hosier, A. J. Hosier's grandson.[58]

The land of *WILTON* was probably granted c. 1130 as part of the king's estate called Bedwyn. As tenant in chief of the estate granted c. 1130 the lord of Wexcombe manor retained the lordship in demesne of some of Wilton's land and apparently subinfeudated the rest.[59] In the 13th century Wilton's land lay in three estates, and for long periods one belonged to the lord of East Grafton manor, one to the lord of Marten manor, and one to the lord of Wexcombe manor.

William de Ros (d. by 1229) held an estate at Wilton of which part descended to his son Hugh, whose heirs held ½ knight's fee of Pain de

Chaworth in 1275.[60] Hugh's was probably the estate at Wilton which John Havering held in 1302.[61] Havering's estate thereafter descended with East Grafton manor.[62] When it was sold by Charlotte, countess of Aylesford, to Thomas, earl of Ailesbury, in 1787 it was accounted c. 9 yardlands.[63]

By 1225 William de Ros had given land at Wilton to Mottisfont priory,[64] and from 1227 the land descended with Marten manor.[65] After inclosure in 1792 Althea Fanshawe held c. 200 a. at Wilton.[66] In 1815 Henry Fanshawe gave 148 a. of it by exchange to Charles Brudenell-Bruce, earl of Ailesbury,[67] who, as heir to his father Thomas, earl of Ailesbury, already owned nearly all the other land of Wilton.[68]

In 1275 Gilbert de Clare, earl of Gloucester and of Hertford, the lord of Wexcombe manor, held 1 knight's fee in Wilton which William Rivers held of him.[69] There is no later evidence of an undertenant, and the lordship in demesne of the estate descended with Wexcombe manor.[70] In 1778 Benjamin Bond Hopkins sold the estate, then accounted c. 412 a., to Thomas, earl of Ailesbury.[71]

From 1815 nearly all Wilton's land descended with Tottenham House.[72] About 1929 George, marquess of Ailesbury, sold it mainly as three farms, Manor, 408 a., Wilton Bank, 268 a., and Batt's, 224 a., and as c. 250 a. of woodland consisting of Wilton Brail, 107 a., and about two thirds of Bedwyn Brail. In addition c. 175 a. was sold as part of East Grafton farm and of Green farm, East Grafton, and c. 70 a. as part of Harding farm.[73] In the 1950s half of Manor farm, most of Wilton Bank farm, Wilton Brail, and the whole of Bedwyn Brail belonged to Sir William Rootes (cr. Baron Rootes 1959, d. 1964), who in 1958 sold that estate to Seymour Egerton, earl of Wilton. In 1962 Lord Wilton sold it to Victor Warrender, Lord Bruntisfield, in 1971 Lord Bruntisfield sold it to Mr. A. J. Buchanan, and in 1984 Mr. Buchanan sold it to Mr. R. M. Charles, who in 1996 owned the agricultural land as Hillbarn farm, 360 a., and the woodland, 361 a.[74] In 1948 the other half of Manor farm, and c. 1962 the rest of Wilton Bank farm, were bought by D. L. Lemon. As Manor farm they passed to his son Mr. P. D. L. Lemon, who added most of Batt's farm to them by purchase c. 1993 and owned Manor farm, c. 500 a., in 1996.[75]

A fourth estate at Wilton, consisting of 1

45 P.R.O., C 142/51, no. 2; ibid. E 211/9.
46 Ibid. E 328/117.
47 *Complete Peerage*, vi. 505–7.
48 W.R.O. 9/16/114; 9/16/135.
49 Ibid. A 1/345/24; cf. ibid. 9/16/136.
50 Ibid. 1836/6. 51 Ibid. A 1/345/24.
52 Ibid.; P.R.O., PROB 11/1661, ff. 66v.–70.
53 P.R.O., PROB 11/1981, ff. 340–5; PROB 11/2036, ff. 303–5; W.R.O. 1836/6.
54 W.R.O., A 1/345/24.
55 *Kelly's Dir. Wilts.* (1889, 1907); deeds in possession of Knowle hosp., Fareham, Hants, in 1957.
56 *Kelly's Dir. Wilts.* (1915); W.R.O., G 8/760/5; ibid. Inland Revenue, val. reg. 56.
57 A. J. and F. H. Hosier, *Hosier's Farming System*, 7.
58 Inf. from Mr. P. Hosier, Wexcombe Manor.
59 Above, this section [preamble]; ibid. (Wexcombe); cf. below, local govt. [Wexcombe].
60 *Cur. Reg. R.* xii, p. 190; xiii, p. 528; *Rot. Hund.* (Rec.

Com.), ii (1), 260; below, Little Bedwyn, manors (Puthall).
61 *Wilts. Inq. p.m. 1242–1326* (Index Libr.), 286–7.
62 Above, this section (E. Grafton).
63 W.R.O. 9/16/28; 9/16/238.
64 *Cur. Reg. R.* xii, p. 190; xiii, p. 528.
65 Above, this section (Marten).
66 W.R.O., EA/68.
67 Ibid. EA/99.
68 *Complete Peerage*, i. 63–4; above and below, this section.
69 *Rot. Hund.* (Rec. Com.), ii (1), 259.
70 Above, this section (Wexcombe).
71 W.R.O. 9/16/136.
72 Below, this section (Tottenham).
73 W.R.O. 9/1/521; cf. ibid. EA/68; for the farms of E. Grafton and for Harding farm, above, this section.
74 Inf. from Mr. A. J. Buchanan, Hillbarn Ho., Great Bedwyn; Mr. R. M. Charles, Hillbarn Farm, Wilton.
75 Inf. from Mr. P. D. L. Lemon, Manor Farm, Wilton.

yardland and a meadow, was part of an estate given in the 1230s by the executors of Sir John Dacy to Salisbury cathedral.[76] In 1800 Thomas, earl of Ailesbury, gave an additional 34 a. at Wilton to the cathedral by exchange.[77] The estate passed to the Ecclesiastical Commissioners, who in 1911 sold their land at Wilton as a 64-a. farm.[78] In 1996 that land belonged to Mr. P. D. L. Lemon as part of Manor farm.[79]

Turold and Alwin held 4 hides at *WOLF-HALL* in 1066, Turold held all or part of the estate in 1084, and the whole estate was probably held by Ralph de Halvile in 1086.[80] In the 1180s land at Wolfhall was claimed from William de Coleville by William Dauntsey, who in 1189–90 apparently succeeded in his claim.[81]

In 1242–3 Robert de Beauchamp, Hugh le Poer, and Richard Benger held 1 knight's fee at Wolfhall.[82] Benger's title has not been traced further. Beauchamp (d. 1264) was succeeded by his son John, of whom Henry Sturmy held ½ knight's fee at Wolfhall in 1275; the lordship in demesne of that estate apparently passed from Henry (d. *c.* 1296) in the direct line to Henry (d. *c.* 1305), Henry (d. *c.* 1338), and Henry Sturmy (d. 1381),[83] who was granted free warren in his demesne at Wolfhall in 1359.[84] Hugh le Poer's estate may have been the land in Wolfhall held by Sir Philip Basset (d. 1271); in 1294 Ela Longespée, Sir Philip's relict, who held it for life, and his grandson Sir Hugh le Despenser (cr. earl of Winchester 1322), who held the reversion, conveyed Sir Philip's land there to Adam of Stock (d. *c.* 1313) and his brother Roger.[85] In 1316 the estate, assessed at ½ knight's fee in 1313, was conveyed by Adam's relict Gena and her husband Robert Hungerford to Roger Stock[86] (d. *c.* 1333), probably Adam's son. In 1360 Roger's son Edward conveyed it to Henry Sturmy (d. 1381).[87]

Wolfhall manor presumably passed from Henry Sturmy to his nephew Sir William Sturmy,[88] on whose death in 1427 a moiety passed to his grandson Sir John Seymour (d. 1464) and a moiety to his daughter Agnes, wife of John Holcombe (d. 1455). Agnes, her son William Ringbourne, or William's son Robert

apparently exchanged her moiety for a rent charge of 13 marks from the whole manor. About 1485 the rent charge passed at Robert Ringbourne's death to his brother William (fl. 1491); it has not been traced further. Sir John Seymour's heir was his grandson John Seymour, who held the whole manor at his death in 1491.[89] From then the manor descended with Burbage Sturmy manor, from 1553 also with Tottenham Lodge, until 1675.[90] John Seymour, duke of Somerset (d. 1675), devised Wolfhall manor to his second cousin Francis Seymour, duke of Somerset, on whose death without issue in 1678 it reverted to John's niece Elizabeth Bruce. From 1678 it descended with Tottenham Lodge and Tottenham House.[91] About 1929 George, marquess of Ailesbury, sold 235 a. as Sudden farm, and 88 a. probably part of the manor as part of Freewarren farm; as most of Suddene Park farm all that land belonged to Mr. P. J. Devenish in 1996.[92] In 1950 Lord Ailesbury sold *c.* 230 a. as part of Wolfhall farm to the Crown, the owner in 1996.[93] The rest of Wolfhall manor, *c.* 200 a. between the Kennet & Avon canal and the park of Tottenham House, descended with Tottenham House, was sold in the early 1970s[94] to Mr. D. C. F. Gent, and in 1996 belonged to Mr. A. Day.[95]

The manor house which stood at Wolfhall in the late Middle Ages[96] may have been timber-framed and built around a great court and a little court. It incorporated a chapel, a long gallery, and a tower. The tower was demolished in 1569. The gallery and an evidence room survived the partial demolition of the house in the 1660s;[97] the whole house had probably been demolished by 1723.[98]

Woodland called the *BRAIL*, assessed at 212 a. in 1568,[99] stood south-east of Great Bedwyn village.[1] When the bounds of Savernake forest were revised in 1300 it was defined as a detached part of the forest,[2] and as Bedwyn Brails bailiwick it belonged to the Crown.[3] In 1544 it was granted to Edward Seymour, earl of Hertford[4] (cr. duke of Somerset 1547), on whose execution and attainder in 1552 it passed back to the Crown.[5] In 1552 it was granted to William Herbert, earl of Pembroke,[6] and it descended

[76] *Sar. Chart. and Doc.* (Rolls Ser.), pp. 215–17; for the rest of the estate, above, this section (Stock).

[77] W.R.O. 9/3/165.

[78] Ch. Com. file 35914.   [79] Inf. from Mr. Lemon.

[80] *V.C.H. Wilts.* ii, pp. 166, 213–14.

[81] *Pipe R.* 1180–1 (P.R.S. xxx), 95; 1190 (P.R.S. N.S. i), 118, 121.

[82] *Bk. of Fees*, ii. 711, 745.

[83] I. J. Sanders, *Eng. Baronies*, 51; *Rot. Hund.* (Rec. Com.), ii (1), 260; below, Burbage, manors (Burbage Sturmy).

[84] *Cal. Chart. R.* 1341–1417, 164.

[85] *Cat. Anct. D.* iii, A 4605; *Cal. Inq. p.m.* v, p. 211; *Complete Peerage*, iv. 261–6.

[86] *Cal. Inq. p.m.* v, p. 211; *Cal. Close*, 1313–18, 131, 135; *Feet of F.* 1272–1327 (W.R.S. i), p. 95; above, this section (Stock).

[87] *Feet of F.* 1327–77 (W.R.S. xxix), p. 117; *Cal. Inq. p.m.* vii, p. 312; cf. ibid. v, p. 211.

[88] Cf. *Cal. Inq. p.m.* xv, p. 202.

[89] *Cal. Inq. p.m. Hen. VII*, i, pp. 35–6, 327–9; *V.C.H. Hants*, iv. 84, 419; P.R.O., C 139/28, no. 22, rot. 6; C 140/14, no. 32; below, Burbage, manors (Burbage Sturmy).

[90] Below, this section (Tottenham); Burbage, manors

(Burbage Sturmy).

[91] *Complete Peerage*, xi. 642; xii (1), 76–7; W.R.O. 1300/295; below, this section (Tottenham).

[92] W.R.O. 9/1/521; inf. from Mr. P. J. Devenish, Suddene Park Farm.

[93] Inf. from the agent for the Crown Estate Com., 42 High Street, Marlborough.

[94] Inf. from the earl of Cardigan, Savernake Lodge, Savernake.

[95] Local inf.

[96] Above, intro. (Wolfhall).

[97] Aubrey, *Topog. Colln.* ed. Jackson, 379; *W.A.M.* xv. 194–5; li. 518; W.R.O. 9/22/21; 9/22/40.

[98] Cf. W.R.O. 9/22/109.

[99] *First Pembroke Survey*, ed. Straton, i. 186.

[1] Cf. *Andrews and Dury, Map* (W.R.S. viii), pl. 12; W.R.O. 9/3/393H.

[2] *V.C.H. Wilts.* iv. 422, 451, where the interpretation of the boundaries of Bedwyn Brails bailiwick needs revision.

[3] For the ownership of Savernake forest, below, Savernake (estates).

[4] *L. & P. Hen. VIII*, xix (2), pp. 313–14.

[5] *Complete Peerage*, xii (1), 59–64.

[6] *Cal. Pat.* 1550–3, 358.

with the Pembroke title.[7] By *c.* 1625 most of the land had been converted to agriculture and was worked as Brail farm.[8] The farm was sold in 1783 by Henry Herbert, earl of Pembroke and of Montgomery, to Thomas, earl of Ailesbury.[9] It thereafter descended with Tottenham House.[10] About 1929 George, marquess of Ailesbury, sold *c.* 75 a. as part of Bedwyn Brail and *c.* 65 a. as part of Harding farm, and in 1930 he sold 101 a. as part of Jockey Green farm.[11] Jockey Green farm was bought by E. B. Gauntlett and added to Little Bedwyn manor, of which it remained part in 1996.[12]

West of Great Bedwyn village land which was almost certainly part of Savernake forest in the Middle Ages had been inclosed as *TOTTEN-HAM* park by the earlier 16th century.[13] All or most of it was later part of Great Bedwyn parish, and Tottenham Lodge and Tottenham House, which replaced Tottenham Lodge in the 1720s, were built on it.

Tottenham park was presumably included in Savernake forest when the reversion of the forest was granted to Edward Seymour, earl of Hertford, in 1547[14] and when the forest was assigned in 1553 to his son Sir Edward Seymour[15] (cr. earl of Hertford 1559, d. 1621), a minor until 1558. The park descended with the earldom to the younger Edward's grandson William Seymour (cr. marquess of Hertford 1641, restored as duke of Somerset 1660, d. 1660),[16] and with the dukedom to William's grandson William Seymour (d. 1671), a minor, and the younger William's uncle John Seymour (d. 1675).[17] On John's death Tottenham Lodge and the park passed to the younger William's sister Elizabeth (d. 1697), from 1676 the wife of Thomas Bruce (earl of Ailesbury from 1685, d. 1741). Elizabeth's heir was her son Charles Bruce, Lord Bruce (a minor until 1703, earl of Ailesbury from 1741, d. 1747), from whom Tottenham House and the park passed to his nephew Thomas Brudenell (later Bruce), Lord Bruce (cr. earl of Ailesbury 1776, d. 1814). Thomas was succeeded by his son Charles Brudenell-Bruce (cr. marquess of Ailesbury 1821, d. 1856), and thereafter the house and park descended with the marquessate to Charles's sons George (d. 1878) and Ernest (d. 1886), to Ernest's grandson George Brudenell-Bruce (d. 1894),[18] and to George's uncle Henry Brudenell-Bruce (d. 1911). They descended in the direct line to George (d. 1961), Chandos (d. 1974), and Michael Brudenell-Bruce, marquess of Ailesbury, who in 1987 transferred them to his son David, earl of Cardigan, the owner in 1996.[19]

In Tottenham park stood a lodge which was large enough to accommodate the mother and children of Edward, earl of Hertford, when Henry VIII visited Wolfhall in 1539.[20] About 1580 Tottenham Lodge superseded the manor house at Wolfhall as one of the principal houses of Edward's son Edward, earl of Hertford,[21] and in the 1660s materials of the manor house, part of which was then demolished, were used to alter, enlarge, or rebuild Tottenham Lodge. The work on Tottenham Lodge was apparently in progress in 1672, when the house was expected to become 'a complete new pile of good architecture'.[22] The expectation may not have been fulfilled: soon after 1676 Elizabeth Seymour, who on the death of John, duke of Somerset, in 1675 inherited Tottenham park and other lands of his, and her husband Thomas Bruce were said by Elizabeth's mother Mary Somerset, duchess of Beaufort, to lack a house in Wiltshire in which they could live.[23] In the early 18th century Tottenham Lodge was apparently in poor repair and in 1712 part of it was damaged by fire.[24] In 1716 it was rectangular, incorporated an inner courtyard, and had two short wings, one at each end of its south-east front; in plan it was smaller than its stable block, which stood north-east of it.[25]

About 1720 Charles Bruce, from 1741 earl of Ailesbury, invited his brother-in-law Richard Boyle, earl of Burlington, to design a new house, and in the 1720s Tottenham Lodge was demolished and Tottenham House was built on its site to designs by Lord Burlington. Previously Lord Burlington had designed features only at his own houses, Chiswick House (Mdx.) and Burlington House (Piccadilly). Tottenham House was built of brick with stone dressings and was square in plan and of moderate size. It was of one tall storey between attic and basement, except at the angles where each wide outer bay rose an additional storey to form a tower with a pyramidal roof. On the north-west a cramped three-bayed entrance front was slightly recessed from the outer bays; on the garden front to the south-east the five centre bays were pedimented, projected slightly, and had an attached hexastyle Ionic portico to attic level. The entrance front was set within a walled forecourt flanked by service pavilions, one on the north-east side and one on the south-west, each of one tall storey. In the 1730s the house was enlarged to new designs by Lord Burlington. Four narrow wings, each of one tall storey over a basement, were built to extend both the north-west and south-east fronts north-eastwards and south-westwards, thus making deep open-ended north-east and south-

7 For the earls of Pembroke, *Complete Peerage*, x. 405–26.
8 W.R.O. 2057/S41, p. 19.
9 Ibid. 9/18/6–7.
10 Below, this section (Tottenham).
11 W.R.O. 9/1/521; cf. 9/3/393H; ibid. EA/68; for Harding farm, above, this section (Harding); for Bedwyn Brail, above, this section (Wilton).
12 W.R.O. 1010/22; inf. from Mr. R. H. Tucker, Manor Ho., Little Bedwyn; for Little Bedwyn manor, below, Little Bedwyn.
13 *V.C.H. Wilts.* iv. 419; Hist. MSS. Com. 58, *Bath*, iv, p. 328.
14 *Cal. Pat.* 1547–8, 124–33.

15 P.R.O., E 328/117.
16 *Complete Peerage*, vi. 505–7; *Wilts. Inq. p.m. 1625–49* (Index Libr.), 20–31.
17 *Complete Peerage*, xii (1), 74–5.
18 Ibid. i. 59–66; W.R.O. 1300/372, ff. 38–9.
19 *Debrett's Peerage and Baronetage* (1995), 14–16; inf. from the earl of Cardigan, Savernake Lodge, Savernake.
20 *W.A.M.* xv. 145–6.
21 Ibid. 156–7.
22 Aubrey, *Topog. Colln.* ed. Jackson, 379.
23 *W.A.M.* lii. 149; *Complete Peerage*, i. 59–60; ii. 52.
24 Earl of Cardigan, *Wardens of Savernake Forest*, 230.
25 W.R.O. 1300/372, ff. 38–9.

west courts; the two wings extending the north-west front were linked to the existing pavilions to become **L**-shaped.[26] Between *c.* 1740 and the early 19th century the house was little altered.[27] Alterations and rebuilding begun in the 1820s[28] almost entirely destroyed its external features and its plan, and in 1996 all that could be seen of it were a length of rusticated walling in the cellars and panelling in a room south-west of what was then the entrance hall.[29]

Between *c.* 1823 and 1870 Tottenham House was converted to a stone-clad mansion, and enlarged, to designs by Thomas Cundy (d. 1867), whose father designed new stables in 1816, and probably by Thomas Cundy (d. 1895).[30] On each main front the bays between the towers were raised to the height of the towers, the wings built in the 1730s were raised to two storeys, the two courts were built on to produce continuous north-east and south-west elevations, and the pavilions built in the 1720s were altered. A giant tetrastyle Ionic portico was added to the entrance front, and a single-storeyed one of paired columns replaced that on the south-east front. The fenestration was altered, new Venetian windows in the outer bays of the main fronts recalling the original design. Dates on rainwater hoppers suggest that the exterior work on the centre and south-west parts of the house was completed in 1825, that on the north-east in 1860. Two convex single-storeyed quadrant wings, one extending west from the south-western of the pavilions built in the 1720s, the other extending north from the north-eastern, were completed *c.* 1870.[31] Each wing has a large pavilion at its far end: that on the west is an orangery connected to the main part of the house by a lean-to conservatory along the back wall of the wing, and that on the north forms one side of an enclosed garden. Inside the house rooms lead off a central hall in which there is a flying stair. The interior decoration in 1996 was nearly all of the later 19th century. In the principal rooms it was very rich and showed French and Russian influences.

In 1716 Tottenham Lodge stood in the north-west part of a roughly circular park of 600 a., most of which was used for agriculture and in which a farmstead stood *c.* 300 m. north of the house. The only features of the park to survive in 1996 were, south-west of the house, woodland with a north-east and south-west walk through it and, respectively south and east of the house, Langfield copse and Haw wood.[32]

The park was redesigned between the 1720s, when Tottenham House was built, and the 1740s. A banqueting house, which was built near the far end of the walk through the woodland south-west of the house, an octagonal temple, which was built on a circular lawn north-west of the banqueting house, and possibly other features were designed by Lord Burlington. The other new features included an exedra-ended lawn on axis with the south-east front of the house, a curved forecourt to the north-west front, a broad walk on axis with the north-east side of the house to match the walk on the south-west side, north-east of the house a plantation of trees arranged geometrically and a short canal, and south-west of the house two canals and parterres. Three straight rides were made, each leading from the house across and beyond the park. North-east of the house the broad walk was extended *c.* 1730 as an avenue called London ride to join the road to London from Bath and Bristol in Little Bedwyn parish; two rides led to Marlborough, one, later called Column ride, on axis with the entrance front and one, later called the Grand Avenue, roughly on the course of the Roman road. New stables, *c.* 1740 depicted as in Palladian style, were built between the house and the farmstead north of it.[33] They were demolished *c.* 1816,[34] and the banqueting house was demolished in 1824;[35] the octagonal temple, which was used as a summer house,[36] was standing in 1996.

From 1764 the park was altered and enlarged to designs by Lancelot Brown.[37] It was extended north-westwards and *c.* 1768 part of Durley heath was impaled as the New (later Durley) park; further north-west the rest of Durley heath and the woodland of Savernake forest were brought into the overall design of the landscape. The park was brought up to the two main fronts of the house, trees were planted informally around the house, and the principal drive, the ride leading to Marlborough from the north-west front of the house, was developed as a vista of which the main feature was a column erected in 1781 at the highest point of the ride. Straight drives, meandering paths, and consciously irregular clearings, Ludens Lye, Ashlade, Woolslade, and Bagdens Lawn, were made in the woodland; four drives, including the Grand Avenue, met in Ludens Lye; Woolslade and Bagdens Lawn were later called Savernake Lawn. To abut the farmstead and stables north of Tottenham House a walled kitchen garden was made, and a neoclassical greenhouse was built between the stables and the house. Between 1786 and *c.* 1818 new buildings were erected in the kitchen garden, and a menagerie was built between the garden and the Grand Avenue.[38]

Between 1816 and 1818 the stables were re-

26   *Arch. Jnl.* cii. 154; H. Colvin, *Dict. Brit. Architects* (1995), 147–50; J. Bold, *Wilton Ho. and Eng. Palladianism* (Royal Com. Hist. Mon. Eng.), pp. 140–3; J. Harris, *Artist and Country Ho.* pp. 63–4; *Country Life*, 28 May 1987; for the site, cf. W.R.O. 1300/372, ff. 38–9.
27   J. Harris, 'Bldg. Works of Lord Bruce', *Lord Burlington and his Circle* (Georgian Group symposium, 1982), p. 43; J. Buckler, watercolour in W.A.S. Libr., vol. x. 17; W.R.O. 1300/359; below, plate 17.
28   Below, this section.
29   Cf. Harris, 'Bldg. Works of Lord Bruce', p. 29.
30   Below, plates 16, 18; *Cat. of Drawings Colln. of R.I.B.A., C–F,* 56–7; Colvin, *Brit. Architects,* 286; for the stables, below, this section.

31   Date on bldg.
32   W.R.O. 1300/372, ff. 38–9.
33   Ibid. 9/3/388; 1300/358; Harris, *Artist and Country Ho.* p. 63; Harris, 'Bldg. Works of Lord Bruce', pp. 29, 46–7; cf. Pevsner, *Lond. NW.* 400.
34   Below, this section.   35   W.R.O. 1300/361.
36   O.S. Map 1/2,500, Wilts. XXXVI. 11 (1900 edn.).
37   D. Stroud, *Capability Brown,* 100–2; papers giving details of proposals by Brown are in W.R.O. 1300/1910–51; 1300/1961–2005; cf. below, plate 16.
38   W.R.O. 1300/359–60; Savernake estate map, *c.* 1820 (copy in W.R.O.); for Durley heath, below, Burbage, econ. hist. (Durley); for Savernake Lodge, built in Savernake Lawn, below, Savernake, intro.

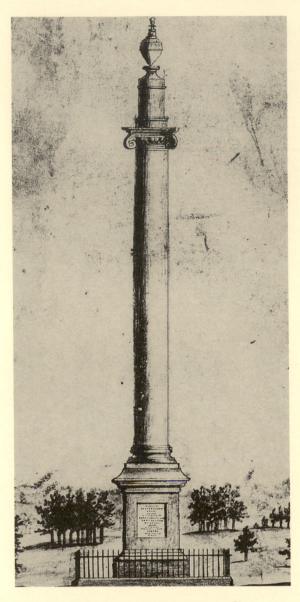

THE COLUMN ERECTED IN 1781

around private gardens on three sides of the house, and the north-east walk and part of the south-west walk were obliterated. Between *c.* 1820 and 1886 a circular plantation was made around the rond-point, called Eight Walks, where the drives met in Ludens Lye.[40] No lodge was ever built on the perimeter of Tottenham park.

In the late 19th century the park seems to have been informally extended north-westwards over the rest of Durley heath, on the north-west part of which woodland increased. In the 20th century nearly all the park was used for farming and from 1939 most of the woodland of Savernake forest north-west of it was used for commercial forestry.[41] In 1996 the enclosed gardens still lay on three sides of the house, north-west of the house *c.* 300 a. of grassland grazed on by sheep lay as a park crossed by the road from Durley to Warren Farm, and deer were kept in the woodland south-west of the house;[42] the column still stood in Column ride and the gates in the Grand Avenue, and near the house the stables quadrangle and the walls of the kitchen garden survived.

At the north-west end of the parish *BED-WYN COMMON* and *STOCK COMMON*, so called in the 18th century,[43] almost certainly belonged to the Crown as part of Savernake forest in the Middle Ages and from the 16th century to the owner of Tottenham Lodge and Tottenham House.[44] About 1760 Ralph, Earl Verney, the lord of West Bedwyn and Stock manors, tenants of whom had the right to feed animals on the commons, claimed the freehold against Thomas Brudenell, Lord Bruce, the owner of the forest and of Tottenham House.[45] The claim had presumably lapsed by 1766, when Lord Bruce bought the two manors from Lord Verney, and the commons thereafter descended with Tottenham House.[46] In 1939 George Brudenell-Bruce, marquess of Ailesbury, leased the woodland on the commons, *c.* 265 a., with *c.* 200 a. of woodland of West Bedwyn, Crofton, and Stock manors and of the Prebendal estate, to the Forestry Commission for 999 years.[47] In 1950 Lord Ailesbury sold the farmland on the commons, *c.* 60 a., to the Crown, which in 1996 owned it as part of Warren farm based in Burbage parish.[48] The reversion of the woodland descended with Tottenham House and in 1996 was held by David, earl of Cardigan.[49]

In 1086 Great Bedwyn church belonged to Bristoard the priest, whose father had held it in 1066. It was acquired by Osmund, bishop of Salisbury, who gave it to the cathedral in 1091. By 1179 the church's estate had been used to endow a prebend in the cathedral, and it was

placed on the same site by a new stables quadrangle designed by Thomas Cundy (d. 1825).[39] Shortly before 1820 Warren Farm was built 1.5 km. north of Tottenham House, and probably *c.* 1820 a new road was made across the New park between Durley village and Warren Farm; where the road crossed it the Grand Avenue was gated. The farmstead north of the house was demolished before *c.* 1820, presumably when Warren Farm was built. Between *c.* 1820 and 1879 the greenhouse was demolished and new buildings, probably glasshouses, were erected on the site of the farmstead; a boundary was made

39 *Cat. of Drawings Colln. of R.I.B.A., C–F*, 56–7; Colvin, *Brit. Architects*, 286; W.R.O. 1300/359.
40 O.S. Maps 1/2,500, Wilts. XXXVI. 8 (1880 edn.); 6", Wilts. XXXVI (1888 edn.); Savernake estate map, *c.* 1820 (copy in W.R.O.); for the road and Warren Farm, below, Burbage, intro. (roads; other settlement).
41 Below, econ. hist. (Tottenham park); Savernake, econ. hist.; cf. O.S. Map 6", Wilts. XXXVI (1888 and later edns.).
42 Inf. from the earl of Cardigan.
43 W.R.O. 9/3/393H.

44 Cf. above, this section (Tottenham); below, Savernake, estates.
45 W.R.O. 9/3/388.
46 Above, this section (W. Bedwyn; Stock; Tottenham).
47 W.R.O. 9/33/5; for W. Bedwyn, Crofton, and Stock manors, above, this section; for the Prebendal estate, below, this section.
48 Inf. from the agent for the Crown Estate Com., 42 High Street, Marlborough.
49 Inf. from the earl of Cardigan.

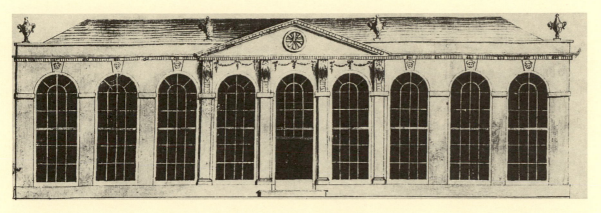

THE NEOCLASSICAL GREENHOUSE

later called the *PREBENDAL* estate. It consisted of all or nearly all the tithes from the whole of what was Great Bedwyn parish from the 16th century, of tithes from what became Little Bedwyn parish, and of a manor assessed at 1½ hide in 1086 and comprising mainly land of Great Bedwyn village.[50] By 1246 great tithes arising from lands of East Grafton and Marten had been alienated,[51] and small tithes were assigned to the vicar. The tithes from the demesne of Crofton Braboef manor, to which the chaplain serving the chapel at Crofton was entitled in 1405, apparently reverted to the prebendary when the chapel went out of use.[52] The prebend was dissolved in 1543,[53] and in 1544 the Prebendal estate was granted to Edward, earl of Hertford (cr. duke of Somerset 1547).[54]

In 1547 Somerset gave the great tithes which were part of the estate, except those from Crofton and Wolfhall, to the king in an exchange,[55] and in the same year the king gave them to St. George's chapel, Windsor.[56] Under an Act to resolve disputes between them, the chapel leased those tithes to Edward, earl of Hertford (d. 1621), for 99 years from 1603 at a rent of £77,[57] and it made successive leases at the same rent to Lord Hertford's successors as owner of Tottenham Lodge and Tottenham House.[58] In 1790, when there was said to be doubt about which tithes were held by the lease, the freehold of the chapel's tithes was transferred by Act to Thomas, earl of Ailesbury, subject to a rent charge of £77 and a corn rent of 5 loads 1 qr. 1 bu. of wheat.[59] The tithes descended with Tottenham House.[60] Under an inclosure award of 1815 those arising from Marten were exchanged for 148 a. in Wilton,[61] and by 1847 most of the other tithes had been merged with the land

from which they arose. In 1847 the tithes which had not been exchanged or merged, arising mainly from Wexcombe, were valued at £394 and commuted.[62] The 148 a. in Wilton was sold *c.* 1929 by George Brudenell-Bruce, marquess of Ailesbury, as part of Wilton Manor farm and of Wilton Bank farm.[63]

About 1550 Somerset gave away *c.* 88 a. of the manor which formed part of the Prebendal estate in exchanges at an inclosure.[64] In 1552 the manor and the tithes from Crofton and Wolfhall should have reverted to the Crown on his execution and attainder[65] but were concealed from it. From 1552 to 1565 they were held by Somerset's son Sir Edward Seymour (cr. earl of Hertford 1559), a minor and a ward of the Crown until 1558;[66] in 1565 they were sold by the Crown to Thomas Blagrave,[67] and in 1567 Blagrave sold them to Lord Hertford.[68] They thereafter descended with Tottenham Lodge and Tottenham House.[69] By 1847 the tithes had been merged with the land from which they arose.[70] In 1718 the land of the manor was accounted 419 a., of which 355 a. was Great Bedwyn's land, 5 a. Crofton's, and 24 a. Wilton's; 35 a. lay in Little Bedwyn parish. Of the 355 a., 337 a. lay in Manor farm.[71] In 1950 George, marquess of Ailesbury, sold Manor farm, then *c.* 320 a., to the Crown, the owner of that land in 1996.[72]

From 1547 the manor house of the Prebendal estate passed with the land. In 1552, when it was becoming dilapidated, it was of stone and was said to be large.[73] Its hall was reroofed with stone slates in 1502–3.[74] In the later 17th century that house or a replacement was standing immediately north-east of the church on the site occupied later by Manor Farm. It was burned

50   *V.C.H. Wilts.* ii, p. 119; *Reg. St. Osmund* (Rolls Ser.), i. 199, 252; for the content of the estate, below, this section; Little Bedwyn, manors [tithes].
51   *Sar. Chart. and Doc.* (Rolls Ser.), pp. 307–10.
52   *Chandler's Reg.* (W.R.S. xxxix), p. 32; below, churches.
53   Le Neve, *Fasti, 1300–1541, Salisbury,* 30.
54   *L. & P. Hen. VIII,* xix (1), p. 14; *L.J.* i. 265; *Complete Peerage,* xii (1), 59–62.
55   P.R.O., E 305/15/F 42–3.
56   *Cal. Pat.* 1547–8, 148–50.
57   W.R.O. 9/4/17; 9/4/39.
58   e.g. ibid. 9/4/39; 9/4/50; 9/4/94–5.
59   Great Bedwyn Incl. Act, 30 Geo. III c. 45 (Priv. Act).
60   Above, this section (Tottenham).

61   W.R.O., EA/99.
62   Ibid. tithe award.
63   Ibid. 9/1/521; for the farms, above, this section (Wilton).   64   W.R.O. 9/1/95, p. 60.
65   *Complete Peerage,* xii (1), 62–4; P.R.O., E 328/117.
66   *Complete Peerage,* vi. 505; W.R.O. 9/4/18.
67   W.R.O. 9/4/19–20.
68   Ibid. 9/4/24.
69   Above, this section (Tottenham).
70   W.R.O., tithe award.
71   Ibid. 1300/372, pp. 3–6.
72   Inf. from the agent for the Crown Estate Com.; for the woodland, above, this section (Bedwyn common).
73   W.R.O. 9/1/95, p. 61.
74   P.R.O., SC 6/Hen. VII/974.

down between 1674 and 1695 and was replaced *c.* 1695. The new house was enlarged *c.* 1705[75] and was presumably demolished in the mid 19th century when Manor Farm was built.[76]

ECONOMIC HISTORY. In 1086 the king's estate called Bedwyn, which apparently included several parts of what became Great Bedwyn and Little Bedwyn parishes, had land for 79 ploughteams. In demesne there were 12 teams and 18 *servi*; 80 *villani*, 60 coscets, and 14 coliberts had 67 teams. There were 8 mills, 2 woods assessed at 2 square leagues, 200 a. of meadow, and 72 square furlongs of pasture.[77]

GREAT BEDWYN. The land of Great Bedwyn village, probably *c.* 600 a., apparently lay as a north-west and south-east strip, crossed near its south-east end by the Dun.[78]

Agriculture. In the Middle Ages Great Bedwyn apparently had four open fields, all near the village. Tile field, 37 a., and Barr field, 30 a., lay north-west of Brown's Lane; Harding field, 19 a., and Conyger field, 8 a., lay south-east of the Dun. Land south-west of the road leading from the village towards Marlborough was also arable. Meadows lay beside the Dun, and Spain's, a pasture probably of *c.* 20 a., lay north-east of the village. The land north-west of Tile field and of Barr field, and some land south-west of the Marlborough road, was probably pasture. By *c.* 1550 the arable south-west of the Marlborough road, and some of the pasture, had been inclosed; Spain's had been inclosed and divided. The open fields and additional pasture were inclosed, and previously inclosed lands were exchanged, *c.* 1550.[79]

Great Bedwyn and Stock were among the villages on the periphery of Savernake forest for each of which a particular part of the forest was designated for their sheep to feed on in common. The commons lay open to the forest and the deer in it. The part assigned for the men of Great Bedwyn and Stock, *c.* 325 a., lay immediately north-west and west of the lands of those villages; in 1703 it was cut off from the unfenced parts of the forest by the inclosure of a rabbit warren north-east of Durley in Burbage parish, and by 1751 it had been divided between Great Bedwyn and Stock. Great Bedwyn's part, Bedwyn common, *c.* 200 a., included Broad moor, *c.* 65 a., south-west of Stock Farm. The men of Great Bedwyn also had the right to feed cattle at large in the forest.[80]

Most of Great Bedwyn's land was part of the Prebendal manor or of West Bedwyn manor.[81]

Great Bedwyn church had land for 1 ploughteam in 1086.[82] In the earlier 16th century the demesne of the Prebendal manor, later called Manor farm, was probably of *c.* 100 a., and customary tenants held *c.* 50 a. About 1550 the demesne farm was reduced to *c.* 55 a.[83] From 1582 West Bedwyn manor belonged to the lord of Stock manor,[84] and its land in Great Bedwyn was apparently added to holdings worked from Stock or elsewhere. In 1718 Manor farm included 20 a. of watered meadow, 202 a. of arable, 3 a. of pasture, and, presumably, feeding rights on the common pasture. Its farmstead, later called Manor Farm, stood in Church Street,[85] and in 1751 was almost certainly the largest on Great Bedwyn's land.[86] About 1770 Manor farm had 206 a., of which 49 a. was part of Stock's land, and included 19 a. of meadows and all Great Bedwyn's former open fields; 67 a. in four closes, three of which were called Bewley, were not then part of the farm as they had been.[87]

Feeding rights over Bedwyn common were presumably extinguished in the late 18th century or early 19th, after the lord of the Prebendal manor had bought Stock manor and West Bedwyn manor,[88] and most of the land was afforested in the 19th century.[89] By the early 19th century Great Bedwyn's agricultural land north-west of its former open fields had been added to Stock farm, and Stock's former open-field land north-west of the Dun had been added to farms based in Great Bedwyn village. In 1847 two farms had farmsteads in the village and all their land nearby. Manor farm had 271 a., and a farm with buildings on the north-west side of Church Street and on the south-west side of High Street had 264 a. The tenant of Manor farm also held Jockey Green farm, 132 a.[90] In the early 20th century Manor farm was held with Harding farm.[91] Bewley Farm was built on Great Bedwyn's north-western land in the mid 19th century,[92] and in the 20th century nearly all Great Bedwyn's remaining agricultural land, and most of Stock's north-west of the Dun, was worked from it. In 1996 Bewley farm was an arable and beef farm of 587 a.; from that year it was worked in conjunction with Manor farm, Chisbury, 446 a. The part of Bedwyn common which was not afforested, *c.* 35 a. of Broad moor, was then used from Burbage as part of Warren farm.[93]

Woodland. Between the open fields in the south-east and the common pasture at the north-west end the Prebendal manor included 36 a. of woodland in five coppices in 1552.[94] In 1718 the manor had 101 a. of woodland in six coppices, including Barr Field coppice adjoining Barr

75 W.R.O. 9/4/55; 9/4/57; 1300/372, p. 3.
76 Above, intro. (Great Bedwyn).
77 *V.C.H. Wilts.* ii, pp. 115–16; for the estate, above, manors [preamble].
78 Cf. W.R.O. 9/3/393H.
79 Ibid.; ibid. 9/1/95, pp. 57–60; 1300/372, ff. 3–4.
80 Ibid. 9/3/388; 9/3/393H; for the econ. hist. of Stock, below, this section (Stock); for the warren, below, Burbage, econ. hist. (Durley).
81 Cf. W.R.O. 9/3/393H; above, manors.
82 *V.C.H. Wilts.* ii, p. 119.
83 W.R.O. 9/1/95, pp. 58–60.
84 Above, manors. 85 W.R.O. 1300/372, ff. 3–4.
86 Ibid. 9/3/393H.

87 Ibid. 9/4/88, pp. 26, 29. 88 Above, manors.
89 C. Greenwood, *Map of Wilts.* (1820); O.S. Maps 1", sheet 14 (1817 edn.); 6", Wilts. XXXVI (1888 edn.); Savernake estate map, *c.* 1820 (copy in W.R.O.).
90 W.R.O., tithe award; ibid. 9/1/107, ff. 31–2; cf. 9/3/393H; for Stock and Stock farm, below, this section (Stock); for Jockey Green farm, below, this section (Brail).
91 W.R.O., Inland Revenue, val. reg. 56; for Harding farm, below, this section (Harding).
92 O.S. Map 1/2,500, Wilts. XXXVI. 8 (1880 edn.); Savernake estate map, *c.* 1820 (copy in W.R.O.).
93 Inf. from the agent for the Crown Estate Com., 42 High Street, Marlborough; cf. W.R.O. 9/3/393H.
94 W.R.O. 9/1/95, p. 60.

field, Horse coppice adjoining Tile field, Bewley coppice north-west of Barr Field coppice, and Brimley coppice and Faggotty coppice north-west of Horse coppice.[95] All that woodland was standing in 1996. Between *c.* 1880 and 1899 trees were also planted between Barr Field coppice and Horse coppice, and between those three coppices and Brimley coppice, a total of *c.* 19 a., all of which was also standing in 1996.[96] Of Bedwyn common *c.* 165 a. had been afforested by 1886,[97] and it remained woodland in 1996.

Markets. A market was held at Great Bedwyn in the later 13th century, when the village was sometimes called Chipping Bedwyn. The lord of the borough was entitled to the tolls.[98] In 1468 a Monday market was granted to the burgesses;[99] in 1641 a Tuesday market was granted to the lord of the borough and apparently supplanted it.[1] A market house stood in the market place from the 17th century or earlier;[2] butchers' shambles were mentioned in the mid 15th century and in 1740.[3] The market was held on Tuesdays in the late 18th century and early 19th.[4] In the 1840s and 1850s the market house was disused and there was no more than a corn market for samples held at the Three Tuns. That had apparently been discontinued by 1859.[5]

Fairs. In 1468 a four-day fair beginning on the first Monday after 25 March, and a six-day fair at Michaelmas, were granted to the burgesses of Great Bedwyn,[6] and in 1641 annual fairs, one on 24 April and one on 28 October, were granted to the lord of the borough.[7] In 1792 the fairs were held on 23 April and 15 July, each apparently for only one day;[8] in the 1830s and 1840s they were held on 23 April and 26 July.[9] The spring fair had lapsed by the 1880s.[10] That held on 26 July was then a pleasure fair; it lapsed in the earlier 20th century.[11]

Trade and industry. Burel, a coarse woollen cloth, was made at Great Bedwyn in the early 13th century.[12] There is no later evidence that more than the usual rural trades flourished there. John Bushel, a mercer of Great Bedwyn, issued a trade token in 1669, and in 1670 was indicted at quarter sessions for making and uttering brass and copper farthings of very low value.[13] There were two clothmakers in the village in the later 17th century[14] and a weaver in 1711,[15] and

members of the Newman family were tailors in the mid 18th century.[16] There were six hopyards in the village in 1675,[17] in the 18th century each of several inns incorporated a malthouse,[18] and there were several maltsters in the village in the earlier and mid 19th century.[19] A new malting was built in Farm Lane in 1868.[20] From 1851 or earlier and in 1996 members of the Lloyd family were in business in Church Street as stonemasons.[21] Other trades in Great Bedwyn included wig makers in the mid and later 18th century and a clock and watch maker in 1842.[22]

CROFTON. In 1086 Crofton had land for 5 ploughteams. There were 3 teams and 3 *servi* on the demesne; 2 *villani* and 5 coscets had 2 teams. There was 10 a. of meadow, and there was pasture which was said to lie 6 a. long and 6 a. broad.[23]

The land of Crofton village, which stands beside the Dun, was disposed like Great Bedwyn's and Stock's which lay north-east.[24] It consisted of a small common meadow beside the river, in the earlier 16th century probably *c.* 50 a. which lay in closes near the village, and, also near the village, two open fields north-west of the Dun and two south-east. About 1536 the fields north-west were North, which was probably bounded to the north-west by Haw wood, and Hatchet; those south-east were Sands, which probably lay on the greensand south-west of the village, and the field beyond the water, which was later called Mill field and probably lay south-east of the village. Crofton also had an extensive common pasture which presumably lay north-west of its open fields.[25]

In the Middle Ages Crofton FitzWarren manor and Crofton Braboef manor each included demesne and customary land.[26] About 1536 Crofton Braboef manor consisted of seven holdings, of which the largest was nominally of 47 a., the smallest nominally of 13 a.; the tenants had the right to feed 415 sheep on the open fields and the common pasture.[27] By the early 16th century demesne land of Crofton FitzWarren manor had apparently been inclosed;[28] it was possibly the land south of the Dun on which Freewarren Farm had been built by 1773.[29]

Nearly all the land north-west of the open

95 Ibid. 1300/372, ff. 3–4.
96 O.S. Maps 6", Wilts. XXXVII (1887 edn.); XXXVII. NW. (1900 edn.).
97 Ibid. 6", Wilts. XXXVI (1888 edn.).
98 *Wilts. Inq. p.m.* 1242–1326 (Index Libr.), 210–11; *P.N. Wilts.* (E.P.N.S.), 332.
99 P.R.O., C 66/3140, no. 15.
1 Ibid. C 66/2895, no. 8.
2 Above, intro. (Great Bedwyn).
3 B.L. Add. Ch. 27679; 28005; W.R.O. 9/3/366.
4 *Rep. Com. Mkt. Rights and Tolls* [C. 5550], p. 214, H.C. (1888), liii; Lewis, *Topog. Dict. Eng.* (1831), i. 133.
5 *Kelly's Dir. Wilts.* (1848 and later edns.).
6 P.R.O., C 66/3140, no. 15.
7 Ibid. C 66/2895, no. 8.
8 *Rep. Com. Mkt. Rights and Tolls,* p. 214.
9 Lewis, *Topog. Dict. Eng.* (1831), i. 133; (1848), i. 196.
10 *Rep. Com. Mkt. Rights and Tolls,* p. 214.
11 *Kelly's Dir. Wilts.* (1889 and later edns.).
12 *V.C.H. Wilts.* iv. 117–19; *Pipe R.* 1218 (P.R.S. N.S. xxxix), 10; 1219 (P.R.S. N.S. xlii), 17; 1220 (P.R.S. N.S. xlvii), 180; 1221 (P.R.S. N.S. xlviii), 165.
13 G. C. Williamson, *Trade Tokens,* ii. 1237; Hist. MSS. Com. 55, *Var. Colln.* i, p. 150.

14 W.R.O. 9/3/18.
15 Ibid. 9/26/261.
16 Ibid. 9/26/364; 9/26/380; 9/26/411; 9/26/415–16; 9/26/418–19.
17 Ibid. 9/26/85.
18 Ibid. 9/3/295; 9/4/88, p. 2; 9/26/164; 1300/372, ff. 3–4.
19 *Early Trade Dir.* (W.R.S. xlvii), 63–4, 102–3; P.R.O., HO 107/1686, ff. 181–2, 196.
20 Date on bldg.
21 *Kelly's Dir. Wilts.* (1855 and later edns.); P.R.O., HO 107/1686, f. 202.
22 *Early Trade Dir.* (W.R.S. xlvii), 11, 103; W.R.O. 9/3/108; 9/26/137; 9/26/141.
23 *V.C.H. Wilts.* ii, p. 141.
24 Cf. above, this section (Great Bedwyn: agric.); below, this section (Stock).
25 Longleat Mun., Seymour papers, xii, ff. 298–300v.; W.R.O. 9/14/223–4; for Haw wood, below, this section.
26 *Wilts. Inq. p.m.* 1242–1326 (Index Libr.), 156, 243–4, 416–17.
27 Longleat Mun., Seymour papers, xii, ff. 298–300v.
28 Hist. MSS. Com. 58, *Bath,* iv, p. 326; W.R.O. 9/14/223.
29 *Andrews and Dury, Map* (W.R.S. viii), pl. 12.

fields, presumably Crofton's common pasture, and part of Hatchet field south-west of Haw wood were inclosed in Tottenham park, possibly in the mid 16th century. The inclosure had certainly taken place by the earlier 17th century, and in the early 18th those lands lay within the park, the boundary of which came to within *c.* 650 m. of Crofton village.[30]

In the 17th century and the earlier and mid 18th Crofton's land still seems to have been worked as farms of less than 100 a. In 1764 Crofton farm, probably the largest, was of *c.* 95 a.[31] In the 18th century the open fields measured 174 a.: Upper (formerly North) measured 60 a., Middle (formerly Hatchet) 63 a., Mill 31 a., and Sands 19 a. They were inclosed by private agreement in 1764.[32] In the mid 18th century Bloxham Lodge was built on land formerly in or adjoining Upper field,[33] and land around it was later planted with trees.[34]

In the early 19th century Crofton farm, 172 a., was almost entirely arable. Other land in Crofton lay in holdings of 67 a., 57 a., 30 a., and 19 a.; only one included a farmstead and it is likely that the others were worked as parts of farms based elsewhere. The land around Free-warren Farm was then apparently part of Wolfhall farm.[35] In 1910 a farm of 168 a. and one of 153 a. were worked from Crofton village, and Freewarren was then a separate farm of 97 a. Most of Crofton's other land was part of Wolfhall farm, and some was worked from Wilton.[36] In 1929 Freewarren was a dairy farm of 148 a. including 88 a. of what was probably Wolfhall's land.[37] It remained a dairy farm until *c.* 1990. In 1996 Freewarren Farm and the 60 a. of Crofton's land were used for keeping horses,[38] and Crofton farm, *c.* 150 a. of which was Stock's land, was an arable and dairy farm of 463 a. Much of Crofton's land inclosed in Tottenham park was then farmland, some of which was worked from Burbage parish as part of Warren farm.[39]

In 1086 there was woodland 3 furlongs by 1 furlong at Crofton.[40] Haw wood, 19 a. in 1716, was standing in the earlier 17th century and stood in Tottenham park in the earlier 18th.[41] Immediately north-east, east, and south-east of Haw wood additional woodland was planted around Bloxham Lodge. Most of it had been planted by *c.* 1820;[42] *c.* 55 a. of woodland stood in several copses there in 1886, and another 4 a. was planted in the early 20th century.[43] Haw wood and all that other woodland was standing in 1996.

A mill stood at Crofton in 1086.[44] In the 13th century a mill there was part of Crofton Braboef manor,[45] in the late 15th century the lord of the manor offered to share with the tenant the cost of adding a malt mill to it,[46] and in the earlier 16th century the manor included two mills probably under one roof.[47] A new mill at Crofton was built *c.* 1598,[48] and in 1773 Upper mill and Lower mill stood on the Dun *c.* 400 m. apart.[49] Upper mill was possibly the mill said in 1773 to have been recently demolished.[50] The source of the water used to drive both was used to feed the Kennet & Avon canal, one of the mills was bought *c.* 1800 by the owner of the canal,[51] and neither mill is known to have worked in the 19th century.

EAST GRAFTON. In 1086 the four estates in which East Grafton's and West Grafton's land lay had land for 8 or more ploughteams; there were 5 or more teams on demesne land. There were 4 *servi*, 9 coscets, and 3 bordars on the estates, but no *villanus*. Pasture was assessed at 3 square furlongs, woodland at 2 arpens.[52]

East Grafton's lands, *c.* 1,000 a., lay as a north–south strip bounded on the north by a ridge between two head streams of the Dun and on the south by the parish boundary. In the Middle Ages extensive open fields lay south of the village; east and west of the village land called the Sands was probably common pasture; north of the village there was a common pasture called the Heath, probably the land, *c.* 100 a., north-west of one of the streams; Grafton down, which rises in the south-east corner of East Grafton's land, was a common pasture for sheep. There were home closes in the village, the green was apparently used as a common pasture on which sheep fed in winter, and there was meadow land used in common probably beside a head stream which flowed northwards from the east end of the village.[53]

In 1347 the lord of the manor was licensed to impark a wood at East Grafton.[54] A park of *c.* 70 a. was made north-west of the village and in the mid 16th century contained woodland and was stocked with deer.[55]

In the 16th century the Heath may have been used as pasture for sheep and cattle. It was inclosed, divided, and allotted between 1571 and 1623, and the Sands had also been inclosed by the earlier 17th century. Sheep continued to be fed in common on the open fields and the downland, but allotments of the Heath, and

30 W.R.O. 9/14/224; 1300/372, ff. 38–9; below, this section (Tottenham park).
31 W.R.O. 9/14/223–4; 9/14/228.
32 Ibid. 9/14/47–8.
33 Above, intro. (other settlement).
34 Below, this section. 35 W.R.O. 9/1/107.
36 Ibid. Inland Revenue, val. reg. 56; *Kelly's Dir. Wilts.* (1911). 37 W.R.O. 9/1/521; cf. 1300/372, f. 1.
38 Local inf.
39 Inf. from the agent for the Crown Estate Com., 42 High Street, Marlborough; the earl of Cardigan, Savernake Lodge, Savernake; for Warren farm, below, Burbage, econ. hist. (Durley).
40 *V.C.H. Wilts.* ii, p. 141.
41 W.R.O. 9/14/224; 1300/372, ff. 38–9.
42 Savernake estate map, *c.* 1820 (copy in W.R.O.).
43 O.S. Maps 6", Wilts. XXXVI (1888 and later edns.).

44 *V.C.H. Wilts.* ii, p. 141.
45 *Wilts. Inq. p.m.* 1242–1326 (Index Libr.), 156.
46 W.R.O. 1300/151.
47 Longleat Mun., Seymour papers, xii, f. 299v.
48 W.R.O. 9/14/72.
49 *Andrews and Dury, Map* (W.R.S. viii), pl. 12.
50 W.R.O. 9/14/146; cf. ibid. 1644/27H.
51 Ibid. 9/14/68; above, intro. [canal].
52 *V.C.H. Wilts.* ii, pp. 149, 166.
53 Alnwick Castle Mun. X.II.11, box 6, survey, 1634, p. 7; Longleat Mun., Seymour papers, xii, f. 301; P.R.O., SC 2/208/28, f. 33v.; W.R.O. 2203/13; ibid. EA/68; for the Sands, cf. below, this section (W. Grafton).
54 *Cal. Chart. R.* 1341–1417, 69–70.
55 Alnwick Castle Mun. X.II.11, box 1, E. Grafton ct. bk. 1552–65; P.R.O., STAC 2/17/331; W.R.O. 2203/13; ibid. EA/68.

probably of the Sands, replaced all rights to feed cattle in common: one holding was allotted 5 a. of the Heath to replace feeding for 8 cattle.[56] From the earlier 17th century to the later 18th there remained *c.* 700 a. of open fields and common downland south of the village. The open fields were Home, which extended north almost to the south corner of the green, and Further, which extended south to the parish boundary. Grafton down was probably of *c.* 100 a.[57]

From the 16th century several of the farms based in East Grafton seem to have been moderately large. In 1611 a farm of 299 a. was apparently the demesne of East Grafton manor.[58] In 1657 the demesne of the manor was accounted 446 a., of which *c.* 175 a. lay in closes west and north-west of the village. To the north-west 37 a. of the Heath had apparently been allotted as demesne and added to the park, then accounted 106 a., of which 27 a. was coppices and woody ground, 59 a. meadow and pasture, and 20 a. arable; the closes to the west were apparently allotted as demesne when the Sands was inclosed. The 446 a. also included a nominal 140 a. in East Grafton's open fields, and it included land in West Grafton of which a nominal 88 a. lay in open fields.[59] In 1631 a copyhold of 3 yardlands was said to include 80 a., one of 2 yardlands 56 a., and another of 2 yardlands 51 a.[60] In 1634 a farm was assessed at 112 a. with feeding for 160 sheep.[61] In 1786 East Grafton manor included Grafton farm, 503 a. including the park, and farms of 121 a. and 105 a.;[62] the farm of *c.* 112 a. in 1634 may have remained over 100 a.

In 1792 the open fields, Grafton down, and 7 a. of common meadow were inclosed by Act,[63] and in the early 19th century most of East Grafton's lands lay in Grafton (later Manor) farm, 507 a. worked from the buildings later called Manor Farm, and a composite farm of 456 a. probably worked mainly from the buildings, later called Green Farm, on the north side of the green. Grafton farm apparently included *c.* 180 a. of the former open fields of West Grafton. Together the farms had 725 a. of arable.[64] By 1886 a new farmstead had been built beside the Hungerford road.[65] In the early 20th century Manor farm, 503 a. in 1910, and Green farm, 381 a. in 1910, were worked together, and the farmstead beside the Hungerford road was that of East Grafton farm, 439 a. including *c.* 140 a. of Wilton's land.[66] In 1996 Manor farm, *c.* 800 a. including most of Green farm and *c.* 180 a. of West Grafton's land, was devoted to arable farming and the production of organic beef.[67] The land of East Grafton farm was then worked in conjunction with Manor farm, Marten, as a holding of *c.* 775 a. devoted to arable farming.[68]

Little of East Grafton's land was wooded. Two copses standing north-west of the village in the late 18th century, Round, 4 a., and Culversleaze, 7 a., may have survived from the medieval park.[69] Round copse was grubbed up in the mid 20th century;[70] Culversleaze copse was standing in 1996. Grafton clump, 12 a. of which half was East Grafton's land, was planted on the border with Collingbourne Kingston apparently between 1820 and 1843[71] and was standing in 1996.

A water mill called Big mill stood at East Grafton in the early 16th century,[72] a windmill *c.* 1593.[73] There is no later evidence of either mill.

In 1347 a Thursday market at East Grafton was granted to the lord of the manor.[74] There is no evidence that a market was held.

WEST GRAFTON. The lands of West Grafton, *c.* 700 a., lay, like those of East Grafton, as a north–south strip from the ridge between two head streams of the Dun to the parish boundary. Like East Grafton, West Grafton had a common pasture called the Heath north of the village. It had a common pasture called the Sands probably east of the village, south of the village it had a lowland pasture called the Marsh adjoining the west boundary of the parish, and further south, adjoining the same boundary, Thorny down was a common pasture which, despite its name, lay on low and flat land. In 1638 the Heath was estimated at 30 a. or 80 a., the Sands at 34 a. or 50 a., the Marsh at 18 a. or 40 a., and Thorny down at 40 a. or 50 a.; Thorny down is known to have been 43 a. The Marsh was for sheep the whole year; the other three pastures were for cattle in summer and sheep in winter.[75] South of the village and mainly east of the common pasture West Grafton had *c.* 400 a. of arable in open fields. In the 16th century there were fields called Home, which stretched north nearly to the village, and Further, which lay south of Home; respectively those fields adjoined the Home field and Further field of East Grafton.[76] Later there was a third field, Hazelditch, 22 a., south of Thorny down and adjoining the parish

[56] Alnwick Castle Mun. X.II.11, box 1, survey of E. Grafton, 1611; X.II.11, box 6, survey, 1634, p. 7; Longleat Mun., Seymour papers, xii, f. 301; W.R.O. 9/15/326.
[57] W.R.O., EA/68; ibid. 9/1/107. The boundary between the open fields of E. Grafton and of W. Grafton is obscure.
[58] Alnwick Castle Mun. X.II.11, box 1, survey of E. Grafton, 1611.
[59] W.R.O. 2203/13; ibid. EA/68.
[60] Alnwick Castle Mun. X.II.11, box 7, survey of E. Grafton, 1631.
[61] Ibid. X.II.11, box 6, survey, 1634, pp. 6–7.
[62] W.R.O. 9/16/32.
[63] Ibid.; ibid. EA/68.
[64] Ibid. 9/1/107, ff. 5–7; 9/1/109, ff. 1–2; ibid. EA/68.
[65] O.S. Map 6", Wilts. XLII (1888 edn.).
[66] W.R.O., Inland Revenue, val. reg. 56; ibid. 9/1/521; cf. ibid. EA/68.

[67] Inf. from Mr. R. Browning, Old Coach Ho., E. Grafton.
[68] Inf. from Mr. B. R. Taylor, the Manor, Marten.
[69] W.R.O., EA/68; above, this section.
[70] O.S. Maps 6", Wilts. XXXVI. SE. (1926 edn.); 1/25,000, SU 26 (1961 edn.).
[71] Greenwood, *Map of Wilts.*; W.R.O., Collingbourne Kingston tithe award.
[72] P.R.O., SC 2/208/28, f. 33v.
[73] Alnwick Castle Mun. X.II.11, box 17, memo. bk. *c.* 1593.
[74] *Cal. Chart. R. 1341–1417*, 69–70.
[75] W.R.O. 9/1/104, ff. 3, 5; 9/14/224; ibid. EA/68; above, this section (E. Grafton).
[76] Alnwick Castle Mun. X.II.11, box 17, memo. bk. *c.* 1593; W.R.O., EA/68. The boundary between the open fields of E. Grafton and of W. Grafton is obscure.

boundary west and south.[77] In the 17th century there were closes of meadow near the village, and there was a small amount of common meadow land.[78]

In 1361 the demesne of an estate at West Grafton consisted of 63 a. of arable, $3\frac{1}{2}$ a. of meadow, and feeding for 12 cattle and 200 sheep.[79] In 1611 there was a holding, later called West Grafton farm, of 102 a. including 22 a. in closes and 79 a. in the open fields.[80] In 1638 the farm included a nominal 124 a. in the open fields, 31 a. of meadow of which 2 a. was in Broad mead, and the right to feed 300 sheep and 36 beasts in common, and Robert Sotwell's farm was assessed at 200 a. with feeding for 230 sheep and 28 cattle.[81] There were probably a few smaller farms with land in West Grafton.[82]

Between 1638 and 1657 the common pastures of West Grafton were inclosed. In 1679 Sotwell's farm included 58 a. in closes and nominally 115 a. in the open fields; it also had 15 a. in Burbage, and its farmstead stood near the parish boundary west of West Grafton village.[83] The open fields were inclosed by Act in 1792, and about then the principal farms were rearranged. Sotwell's became a long and narrow farm of 202 a. lying along the Burbage boundary and consisting mostly of old inclosures. West Grafton farm, 306 a., lay east of it, was worked from the farmstead at the south end of the village, and included 163 a. of the former open fields. The east part of the open fields was apparently added to, and remained part of, Manor farm, East Grafton.[84]

In 1867 the management of West Grafton farm, then 299 a. including 258 a. of arable, was said to be rather slovenly. Sotwell's farm had 282 a., including 98 a. in Burbage, of which c. 214 a. was arable.[85] Most of Sotwell's farm was added to West Grafton farm, probably in the late 19th century.[86] In 1910 West Grafton farm had 434 a., and Kingston farm, worked from buildings at the north end of West Grafton village, had 47 a. in West Grafton. In 1929 West Grafton farm was a mixed farm of 428 a., Kingston a pasture farm of 73 a. including 23 a. in Burbage.[87] In 1996 West Grafton farm, the buildings of which were then called Manor Farm, was part of a large arable and poultry farm based at Southgrove Farm, Burbage.[88]

HARDING. In 1086 Harding had land for 1 ploughteam. All its land was demesne and 1 team was on it.[89] The village probably had open fields, a common pasture for cattle, and a common down for sheep,[90] and it seems that when the lordship of Harding was partitioned c. 1243 most of the north-east part of the village's land, including the open fields, was allotted to one lord, and most of the south-west part, consisting mainly of the downland, to the other. The north-east part was later in Shalbourne parish, the south-west in Great Bedwyn.[91]

In 1331 the demesne of the estate on which Harding Farm was built included 150 a. in the open fields, 6 a. of meadow, and a pasture worth 3s. 4d.[92] By the 16th century the downland had been inclosed and Harding Farm built on it. About 1536 Harding farm consisted of the farmstead, 46 a. of arable, 5 a. of meadow, 109 a. of pasture in eight closes, feeding for cattle in a common pasture, and feeding for 300 sheep in the open fields. It is almost certain that the arable lay in open fields in Shalbourne, that the sheep could be fed on the same fields, and that the pasture lay in Great Bedwyn parish.[93] It is not clear how much of Harding's land in Great Bedwyn parish lay in farms worked from Shalbourne. A new farmhouse was built on the downland in the early 17th century,[94] probably on or near the site of that standing c. 1536. In the mid 18th century Harding farm had c. 257 a., including 44 a. in open fields in Shalbourne: by an agreement which remained voidable at pleasure the 44 a. had been inclosed and the farm's feeding for 200 sheep on the rest of the fields had been given up. The farm included 18 a. of meadow and 217 a. of arable, much of the downland around the farmstead having apparently been ploughed up.[95]

Harding farm was estimated at 287 a. in 1825.[96] In 1910 it measured 351 a., including 12 a. in Shalbourne, and was held by the tenant of Manor farm, Great Bedwyn.[97] In 1929 it measured 396 a., of which c. 70 a. was Wilton's land and c. 65 a. was part of what was formerly Bedwyn Brails bailiwick: the farm included 203 a. of arable and 165 a. of pasture.[98] In 1996 the land which was Harding farm's in 1929 was worked from Shalbourne parish[99] and was arable.

Harding copse, 10 a. north-east of Harding Farm, was standing in 1820[1] and 1996.

MARTEN. In 1086 Marten had land for $3\frac{1}{2}$ ploughteams. Most of the land seems to have been demesne, and there were 2 *servi*, 4 coscets, and no *villanus*. There were 6 a. and 2 arpens of meadow, 30 a. 'between meadow and pasture', and 12 a. of pasture. The land lay in three estates.[2]

77 W.R.O. 9/16/73; ibid. EA/68.
78 Ibid. 9/14/224.
79 *Wilts. Inq. p.m.* 1327–77 (Index Libr.), 290.
80 Alnwick Castle Mun. X.II.11, box 1, survey of E. Grafton, 1611.
81 W.R.O. 9/14/224.
82 e.g. ibid. 9/1/107, f. 8; ibid. EA/68.
83 Ibid. 9/14/224; 9/16/73; 2203/13.
84 Ibid. 9/1/104, ff. 1–9; ibid. EA/68.
85 Ibid. 9/1/110, ff. 46, 55.
86 Cf. above, intro. (W. Grafton).
87 W.R.O. 9/1/521; ibid. Inland Revenue, val. reg. 56.
88 Inf. from Mrs. I. S. Curnick, Southgrove Farm, Burbage.
89 *V.C.H. Wilts.* ii, p. 166.

90 *Wilts. Inq. p.m.* 1327–77 (Index Libr.), 67–8; Longleat Mun., Seymour papers, xii, f. 301 and v.; W.R.O. 9/24/32.
91 Above, manors (Harding).
92 *Wilts. Inq. p.m.* 1327–77 (Index Libr.), 67–8.
93 Longleat Mun., Seymour papers, xii, f. 301 and v.
94 Above, intro. (Harding).
95 Alnwick Castle Mun. X.II.11, box 22, survey of Harding farm.
96 W.R.O. 9/3/184.
97 Ibid. Inland Revenue, val. regs. 2, 56.
98 Ibid. 9/1/521; for the bailiwick, below, this section (Brail).
99 Local inf.
1 Greenwood, *Map of Wilts.*
2 *V.C.H. Wilts.* ii, pp. 56, 164, 166.

Marten village stood roughly in the centre of its lands, *c*. 725 a. Open fields lay south and east of the village, meadow and pasture lay around the village and west and north-west of it, and the easternmost part of the lands was a north–south scarp face, Botley down, *c*. 100 a., which was rough pasture for sheep. In the Middle Ages the meadow presumably lay beside the head stream of the Dun north-east of the village.[3] A park, which in the earlier 13th century was said to lie between Wilton and Marten, was presumably north-west of, and possibly not far from, Marten village.[4] Both Marten manor and the Malwains' estate included a demesne farm, the buildings of each of which stood on high ground immediately south-west of the rest of the village;[5] *c*. 140 a. south, west, and north-west of the farmsteads was probably demesne pasture lying in closes, and possibly the 13th-century parkland.[6] The Weares, a common pasture probably of 25–40 a. and apparently for the cattle of customary tenants, lay north-west of the village and apparently mostly north-west of the Salisbury road. It had been inclosed, divided, and allotted by 1601.[7]

In 1410 the demesne of Marten manor included 118 a. of sown arable and had on it 7 cows and calves and 318 sheep and lambs.[8] In 1621, in addition to the two demesne farms, there were eight holdings with a nominal 162 a. in the open fields, 18 a. of meadows, 40 a. of inclosed pasture, and feeding for 360 sheep on Botley down. The largest holding was of *c*. 38 a., the smallest of *c*. 14 a.;[9] each presumably had a farmstead in the lane between the course of the Roman road and the head stream. In the mid 18th century, when they were called Great farm and Little farm, the two demesne farms were held by one tenant, and there seem to have remained a few small farms.[10]

In 1765 the lord of the manor unsuccessfully sought an agreement to inclose Botley down and the open fields. The fields were then Hill, Middle, and South,[11] later North, *c*. 100 a., Little, *c*. 65 a., and South, *c*. 125 a. In 1815 they and the down were inclosed by Act and many exchanges of old inclosures were made. Then and later most of Marten's land seems to have lain in Manor farm, which was worked from a farmstead on the high ground south-west of the Roman road and incorporated the two demesne farms and probably some former customary land.[12] In the 19th century two smaller farms seem to have been worked from buildings on the north-east side of the lane through the village.[13] Manor farm had *c*. 600 a. in 1861,[14] 630 a. in

1910,[15] and *c*. 500 a. in 1920, when it was a mainly arable and beef farm.[16] In 1910 there was also a farm of 63 a.[17] Manor farm was reduced to *c*. 360 a. in 1980; in 1996 it was worked in conjunction with the land of East Grafton farm as an arable holding of *c*. 775 a.[18] In 1996 *c*. 150 a. north-east of Marten village was arable worked from outside the parish, and there was a cattle farm of *c*. 60 a. with new buildings on the north-east side of the lane through the village.[19]

Marten had no woodland in the early 19th century.[20] By 1899 *c*. 14 a. had been planted with trees in several small copses,[21] all of which survived in 1996.

STOCK. Stock's land, *c*. 500 a. in 1751, lay as a north-west and south-east strip south-west of Great Bedwyn's and, like Great Bedwyn's, was crossed by the Dun near the south-east end. There were four open fields, Town, 34 a., and Coward, 39 a., north-west of the river, and Costow, 18 a., and Brail, 54 a., south-east. Beside the river and between the open fields lay *c*. 35 a. in closes and a few acres of meadow. North-west of the open fields the land was probably pasture in the Middle Ages. The men of Stock, along with the men of Great Bedwyn, had the right to feed sheep on *c*. 325 a. of Savernake forest immediately north-west and west of the land of those villages. By 1751 that part of the forest had been cut off from the unfenced parts and, as Stock common, 125 a. of it had been assigned to Stock. The 125 a., north-west of, and detached from, Stock's other land, could be fed on by 300 sheep.[22]

In the Middle Ages Stock's open fields were probably worked from farmsteads standing on the high ground north-west of them.[23] The pasture on the high ground was possibly inclosed in the 16th century, as was some similar pasture of Great Bedwyn.[24] On one of the upland closes Stock Farm probably replaced a manor house and had apparently been built by the 17th century;[25] the demesne farm of Stock manor was worked from it in the 18th century.[26] In 1751 there were apparently two or three other farmsteads among the upland inclosures.[27] In the 17th century or earlier 18th Stock Farm was held with *c*. 85 a. in closes around it; most of the land in the open fields was part of copyholds.[28]

Stock's open fields were inclosed by private agreement in 1769.[29] By the earlier 19th century most of their land north-west of the Dun had been added to Manor farm and the other farm based in Great Bedwyn village; in the later 20th

3   W.R.O., EA/99.
4   *Cal. Chart. R.* 1226–57, 40.
5   W.R.O. 490/1540, ff. 65v.–67; above, intro. (Marten).
6   W.R.O., EA/99.
7   Ibid.; ibid. 490/1540, ff. 64–65v., 67v.–68.
8   *Edington Cart.* (W.R.S. xlii), p. 31.
9   W.R.O. 490/1540, ff. 64–8.
10   Ibid. 212A/27/20/3, art. of agreement, 1765.
11   Ibid.
12   Ibid. EA/99.
13   Ibid.; O.S. Map 1/2,500, Wilts. XLIII. 1 (1880 edn.).
14   P.R.O., RG 9/724, f. 49.
15   W.R.O., Inland Revenue, val. reg. 56.
16   Sale cat., 1920, in possession of Miss W. S. D. Crees, Coppers, Marten.

17   W.R.O., Inland Revenue, val. reg. 56.
18   Inf. from Mr. B. R. Taylor, the Manor, Marten.
19   Local inf.
20   Greenwood, *Map of Wilts.*; O.S. Map 1", sheet 14 (1817 edn.); W.R.O., EA/99.
21   O.S. Map 6", Wilts. XLII. NW. (1901 edn.).
22   W.R.O. 9/3/388; 9/3/393H; for Great Bedwyn, above, this section (Great Bedwyn).
23   Cf. above, intro. (Stock and Ford).
24   Cf. W.R.O. 9/1/95, pp. 57–60.
25   Above, intro. (Stock and Ford).
26   W.R.O. 9/26/516.
27   Ibid. 9/3/393H.
28   Ibid. 9/26/516.
29   Ibid. 9/26/203.

century it was shared between Bewley farm and Crofton farm.[30] Of the land south-east of the Dun, Brail field became part of Brail farm, for which buildings had been erected on Stock's land by 1751. In 1929 Brail farm was a dairy farm of 120 a., and it remained a dairy farm until the 1980s; in 1996 it had *c.* 200 a., was mainly arable, and was worked from outside the parish.[31] In 1996 Costow field was part of Crofton farm.[32]

By 1769 Stock farm had been increased by the addition of other inclosures north-west of the open fields to those around the farmstead. In 1769 the farm, 320 a., included the feeding rights on Stock common and almost certainly some of Great Bedwyn's land.[33] There were 390 sheep on the farm in 1787.[34] In 1807–8 it had 390 a., of which *c.* 300 a. was arable, and included the closes called Bewley, other land in Great Bedwyn, and feeding for 200 sheep on Stock common.[35] By 1879 most of Stock common had been afforested.[36] In the 20th century most of Stock farm became part of Bewley farm and some, including that part of Stock common not afforested, part of Warren farm based in Burbage parish.[37]

In 1575 the lord of Stock manor sold 430 oak trees growing near his manor house. Most of them may have stood in Shawgrove copse, which in 1751 and 1996 was a wood of 19 a. south-east of Stokke Manor. Several other small copses stood on Stock's land in 1751[38] and 1996. Of Stock common *c.* 75 a. was afforested before 1879, *c.* 25 a. later;[39] both areas remained woodland in 1996.

Ford mill, which was standing in the 1230s, belonged to Salisbury cathedral from then until 1800, when it was given to Thomas Bruce, earl of Ailesbury, in an exchange.[40] In the 18th century the mill, then called Bedwyn mill, stood on the Dun near the probable site of Ford hamlet.[41] There is no evidence that it worked in the 19th century[42] and it was demolished between 1879 and 1899.[43]

WEXCOMBE. Of Wexcombe's 1,700 a. *c.* 1,150 a. is chalk downland.[44] There were open fields, probably lying east of the village in the coomb and north of it on the lower slopes of the chalk, and downland presumably south of the village was used to feed cattle and sheep in common.

Further north Wexcombe marsh, low land on the greensand, was a common pasture which in the late 16th century was used for sheep in winter and for horses and cattle at other times.[45]

In the Middle Ages large flocks of sheep were kept on the demesne of Wexcombe manor: in 1165–6 it was stocked with 458 sheep and 30 oxen,[46] and *c.* 1322 it had on it a flock probably of *c.* 700 or more sheep.[47] In 1296 the demesne arable was estimated at 164 a., in 1307 at 300 a., and in 1314 at 478 a.: if those figures are accurate the increase was probably caused by the ploughing of downland. In 1296 the demesne also included 15½ a. of meadow, and pasture worth 60s. and presumably extensive. The customary tenants then either paid rents totalling £5 4s. 2d. or worked on the demesne.[48] In the late 13th century the men of Wexcombe's claim to have pasture for cattle free of charge in the king's forest at Hippenscombe was disputed.[49] In the earlier 15th century there was said to be, or to have been, 11 yardlands in Wexcombe held customarily. The demesne was then held on lease, in portions or collectively, by four men.[50] In the later 15th century it was apparently a single farm.[51] A hare warren was made, probably in the early 16th century and almost certainly on the downland immediately south-west of the village where four fields totalling 145 a. bore the name Hare warren *c.* 1847.[52]

In 1682 there were at Wexcombe the demesne farm, accounted 479 a., and 18 copyholds and 2 leaseholds assessed at between 10 a. and 48 a.[53] About 1716 the copyholds and leaseholds included feeding rights for 120 cattle and horses and *c.* 1,125 sheep, and by then some had been merged to form two or more farms of over 100 a.[54]

By 1780 all Wexcombe's land had been shared between Lower and Upper farms[55] and common husbandry presumably eliminated. A new farmstead was built for Upper farm in the early 19th century.[56] The farms lay several *c.* 1847, when Lower farm had 775 a., Upper farm 885 a. Each lay as a north–south strip, Lower farm to the east. Lower farm included 533 a. of arable, 56 a. of meadow and pasture, and 168 a. of downland pasture; Upper farm included 537 a. of arable, 63 a. of meadow and pasture, and 275 a. of downland pasture.[57]

From 1920 Lower and Upper farms were

30 W.R.O., tithe award; inf. from the agent for the Crown Estate Com., 42 High Street, Marlborough; for Bewley farm and farms based in Great Bedwyn, above, this section (Great Bedwyn: agric.); for Crofton farm, above, this section (Crofton).
31 W.R.O. 9/1/521; 9/3/393H; inf. from Mr. R. M. Charles, Hillbarn Farm, Wilton.
32 Inf. from the agent for the Crown Estate Com.
33 W.R.O. 9/26/202, *Sar. Jnl.* 30 Jan. 1769.
34 Ibid. 212A/11.
35 Ibid. 9/1/107, ff. 31–2; cf. above, this section (Great Bedwyn: agric.).
36 O.S. Map 1/2,500, Wilts. XXXVI. 8 (1880 edn.).
37 Inf. from the agent for the Crown Estate Com.; for Warren farm, below, Burbage, econ. hist. (Durley).
38 W.R.O. 9/3/393H; 9/26/511.
39 O.S. Map 1/2,500, Wilts. XXXVI. 8 (1880 and later edns.).
40 *Sar. Chart. and Doc.* (Rolls Ser.), pp. 215–17; W.R.O. 9/3/165.
41 *Andrews and Dury, Map* (W.R.S. viii), pl. 12; W.R.O.

9/3/393H; above, intro. (Stock and Ford).
42 e.g. *Kelly's Dir. Wilts.* (1848 and later edns.).
43 O.S. Maps 1/2,500, Wilts. XXXVII. 9 (1880 edn.); 6", Wilts. XXXVII. SW. (1901 edn.).
44 Cf. W.R.O., tithe award.
45 Ibid. 9/3/356; 9/27/52–4.
46 *Pipe R.* 1165–6 (P.R.S. ix), 71.
47 P.R.O., SC 6/1145/12.
48 *Wilts. Inq. p.m.* 1242–1326 (Index Libr.), 211, 339, 403.
49 *V.C.H. Wilts.* iv. 426; *Rot. Hund.* (Rec. Com.), ii (1), 260.
50 B.L. Add. Ch. 28005.
51 Ibid. Add. Ch. 28007–8.
52 Hist. MSS. Com. 58, *Bath*, iv, p. 335; W.R.O., tithe award.
53 W.R.O. 9/27/52–3.
54 Ibid. 9/27/54.
55 Ibid. A 1/345/24.
56 Above, intro. (Wexcombe).
57 W.R.O., tithe award.

worked together by A. J. Hosier and Joshua Hosier, brothers who at Wexcombe developed a method of dairy farming which, compared to the existing method, required fewer buildings and less labour. Most of the arable and downland was converted to fenced pastures, a water supply to the downland was installed, and cows were kept on the pastures the whole year and milked in mobile sheds which were taken to the pastures. Each shed contained bails and a milking machine, from which milk was pumped into churns for immediate transport to London by road. The dairy herd at Wexcombe was increased from 80 c. 1923 to 320 in 1927 and, in the same period, the average yearly yield of each cow rose from 633 to 725 gallons. The Hosiers set up a company to make milking sheds and to sell them to other farmers. About 1930 they also introduced a folding system for poultry; in 1933 there were 160 mobile pens and c. 4,000 laying hens at Wexcombe.[58] In 1996 Wexcombe farm, c. 1,550 a., was an arable and beef farm.[59]

In 1521–2 there was 12 a. or more of woodland at Wexcombe.[60] About 1847 there was c. 45 a. including Picked plantation, 7 a., and Scotspoor wood, 23 a., in the extreme south-east. Those two woods were apparently planted after 1820[61] and were standing in 1996.

WILTON had c. 1,650 a., by far the greater part of which was used for sheep-and-corn husbandry in common until the late 18th century. The village stood roughly in the centre of its open-field land, c. 800–950 a. North-east of the fields lay an arc of common pasture, c. 535 a., and along the boundary with Crofton's land west of the village the Heath was a common pasture of c. 25 a. The head stream of the Dun crossing the land from south-east to north-west provided meadow land.[62]

Most of Wilton's land belonged to the lords of manors with demesne farms based elsewhere,[63] and it was shared mainly by customary tenants with farmsteads in the village and with holdings which were not extensive. There were apparently many such holdings. In the later Middle Ages the lord of Wexcombe manor had 16 or more customary tenants holding 15 yardlands or more at Wilton;[64] in the late 17th century he had 12 holding c. 18 yardlands.[65] In 1621 the lord of Marten manor had copyholds of 2 yardlands, 1 yardland, and 20 a. at Wilton,[66] and in 1631 the lord of East Grafton manor had eight copyholders with 10 yardlands.[67] In the earlier 16th century there was also a holding of

12½ a., assessed at ½ yardland, which was part of Crofton Braboef manor.[68] By the 18th century holdings had been agglomerated, and in 1765 all Wilton's land lay in 10 farms.[69] Farms of 218 a. and 195 a., each with pasture rights, were held together in 1773;[70] they had been merged by 1787, when the land included 45 a. of meadow and 367 a. of arable.[71]

In Wilton village 45 a. lay in the home closes of the farmsteads,[72] and by the earlier 17th century the Heath and some meadow land had also been inclosed.[73] The Heath was divided into c. 20 closes, each of c. 1 a.[74] In 1765 the occupiers of the land made new regulations governing the use of the open fields and common pastures,[75] and in the 1770s 131 a. of arable and 60 a. of meadow lay inclosed and there were 815 a. of open-field arable and 41 a. of common meadows. There were then c. 11 open fields, including south-west of the village, on the greensand, Upper Sandy and Lower Sandy, south-east of the village Overland, Little Prior Croft, and Great Prior Croft, north of it Dodsdown and Underdown, and east of it Stony Way, Forehill, Underhill, and Yonderhill. The north part of the arc of common pasture was the cow common, c. 300 a., the east part the sheep common, c. 200 a. Where the two commons and Stony Way field and Yonderhill field met c. 10 a. had been inclosed as seven closes called Heath Hill closes.[76]

The open fields, common meadows, and common pasture were inclosed in 1792 by Act. About 200 a. of the cow common and c. 50 a. of the sheep common was immediately planted with trees. Immediately after inclosure Manor farm had 555 a., including c. 44 a. of meadows, 347 a. of arable, and 158 a. of the two commons. There were holdings of 63 a., 42 a., 35 a., and 32 a. worked from buildings in the village, and 175 a. adjoining Marten's land south-east of Wilton village may also have been worked from there; 52 a. was worked from Crofton.[77]

In 1828 there were seven farms in Wilton; the largest had 304 a., the smallest 50 a.[78] In 1867 there were five, all mainly arable. Manor, 388 a., was poorly farmed; Wilton Bank, 241 a., and Batt's, 143 a., were well farmed. The other farms had 100 a. and 96 a., and it was thought desirable to add their lands to larger farms.[79] In 1929 Manor farm, 408 a., lay east of the village, Wilton Bank, 268 a., mainly north-east and south of the village, and Batt's, 224 a., north and west of the village. All were worked from farmsteads in the village and were mixed farms.

[58] A. J. and F. H. Hosier, *Hosier's Farming System*, 8, 10–29, 35–6; *W.A.M.* xlv. 387–8; *Country Life*, 24 Oct. 1925, pp. 617–19; 31 Oct. 1925, pp. 658–60; 14 Aug. 1926, pp. 261–2; 10 Dec. 1932, pp. 655–6; 18 Mar. 1933, p. 285; *The Times*, 26 July 1926; 1 Nov. 1927.
[59] Inf. from Mr. P. Hosier, Wexcombe Manor.
[60] P.R.O., E 36/150, f. 2.
[61] Greenwood, *Map of Wilts.*; W.R.O., tithe award.
[62] W.R.O. 9/27/56; ibid. EA/68; for the Heath, Longleat Mun., Seymour papers, xii, f. 298v.
[63] Above, manors (Wilton); this section (E. Grafton; Marten; Wexcombe).
[64] B.L. Add. Ch. 26873; 28005; P.R.O., SC 6/1145/12.
[65] W.R.O. 9/27/52–3.
[66] Ibid. 490/1540, f. 64 and v.
[67] Alnwick Castle Mun. X.II.11, box 7, survey of E.

Grafton, 1631.
[68] Longleat Mun., Seymour papers, xii, f. 298v.
[69] W.R.O. 9/27/33.
[70] Ibid. 9/14/228, p. 39.
[71] Ibid. 9/16/241.
[72] Ibid. 9/27/56.
[73] Ibid. 490/1540, f. 64 and v.; Alnwick Castle Mun. X.II.11, box 7, survey of E. Grafton, 1631.
[74] Cf. W.R.O., EA/68.
[75] Ibid. 9/27/33.
[76] Ibid. 9/27/56; 9/27/59; ibid. EA/68.
[77] Ibid. 9/1/104, pp. 16–25; 9/27/59; 1355/17; ibid. EA/68.
[78] Ibid. 9/27/57.
[79] Ibid. 9/1/110, pp. 43–4, 47, 54; *Kelly's Dir. Wilts.* (1867); cf. P.R.O., RG 9/724, ff. 55–6, 70.

Manor farm included Hill Barn.[80] Later the east part of Manor farm and the part of Wilton Bank farm north-east of the village were worked as Hillbarn farm, which in 1996 was an entirely arable farm of 360 a.[81] In 1996 the rest of Manor farm, the part of Wilton Bank farm south of the village, most of Batt's farm, and other land, an entirely arable holding of *c.* 500 a., were worked as Manor farm, the principal buildings of which remained in the village. In partnership or under contract the farmer also worked other arable holdings; machinery was housed at Manor Farm, and a large building to house equipment to dry grain stood south of the village.[82] In 1929 *c.* 140 a. of Wilton's land south and south-west of the village and *c.* 70 a. north-east was part of East Grafton farm and Harding farm respectively,[83] and in 1996 was worked with the land of those farms.[84]

Wilton had very little woodland[85] until *c.* 1792, when *c.* 200 a. of the cow common and *c.* 50 a. of the sheep common were afforested. Of the new woodland 107 a. stood as Wilton Brail.[86] The rest of the woodland adjoined woodland in the former Bedwyn Brails bailiwick[87] and, with that, a total of 212 a., later bore the name Bedwyn Brail.[88] Wilton Brail and Bedwyn Brail comprised *c.* 361 a. of woodland in 1996.[89]

A windmill,[90] a tower mill of red brick, was built *c.* 750 m. east of Wilton village in 1821. In 1828 it contained three pairs of stones, a flour machine, and a dressing mill. It ceased to work *c.* 1908 and became dilapidated. Between 1971 and 1976 it was restored to working order by the Wiltshire Historic Buildings Trust.[91]

At Dodsdown, where in 1548 bricks were made for the house begun for Edward, duke of Somerset, a new brickworks *c.* 750 m. north-east of Wilton village had been opened by *c.* 1820.[92] A tramway linking it to the railway at West Grafton was constructed in 1902 to enable bricks to be taken to North Tidworth for use in the army barracks being built there. The tramway was closed in 1910,[93] the brickworks *c.* 1930.[94]

WOLFHALL. In 1086 Wolfhall had land for 3 ploughteams. The demesne of the estate there had no stock; there were 4 *villani* and 4 coscets.[95]

Wolfhall had *c.* 750 a.[96] On chalk north of the line followed by the Kennet & Avon canal it may have had steep land used as pasture for sheep; that was possibly the land called Tottenham Hill, 40 a. of which was sheep pasture *c.* 1550.[97]

On greensand south of that line, which was probably that of an upper reach of the Dun, the land is undulating and may have been the site of open fields; Wolfhall field was mentioned in 1289.[98] The upper reach of the Dun and a tributary flowing north-eastwards to it may have provided meadow land.

In 1333 a moiety of Wolfhall manor was said to include 800 a. of demesne arable, 30 a. of demesne meadow, and no land held customarily.[99] In 1341 formerly cultivated land assessed at 4 carucates lay fallow,[1] and by the mid 16th century much land had been imparked. The Home park was mentioned in 1536[2] and was possibly the park called the Horse park *c.* 1550. The Horse park, 20 a., may have embraced the site of Wolfhall village, and in the early 17th century a house called the Laundry (in 1996 Wolfhall Farm) was built on it. The south-western part of Wolfhall's land was inclosed in Sudden park, accounted 240 a. *c.* 1550; Red Deer park, 40 a. *c.* 1550, may have lain at Wolfhall or in Savernake forest. In the mid 16th century, when the manor house was used as a residence by Edward Seymour, duke of Somerset (d. 1552),[3] all Wolfhall's land lay in demesne.[4] There were 126 a. of arable and 14 a. of meadows; the rest of the land, including that in the parks, was pasture.[5] In the earlier 17th century red and fallow deer were kept in Sudden park.[6]

In 1633 demesne land north and probably north-east of Sudden park was leased as a farm. The lease included the site of the manor house, and the farm was probably worked from Wolfhall Manor, which was built as a farmhouse in the early 17th century, and buildings near it.[7] The farm was later called Wolfhall farm. Sudden park was leased as a farm in 1654; a farmstead, probably incorporating the lodge, stood in the middle of the park.[8] The Laundry was leased with meadow land in 1675.[9] In 1673 Wolfhall farm had *c.* 645 a. including land probably in Crofton and Burbage: all its land, including 483 a. of arable and 158 a. of meadow and pasture, lay in severalty.[10] In 1718 Sudden farm, 243 a., included *c.* 173 a. of arable and *c.* 57 a. of meadow and pasture, and Laundry farm consisted of the farmstead and 41 a. of meadows.[11]

In 1807–8 Wolfhall farm had 678 a., of which 52 a. lay in Burbage, and included 528 a. of arable, 122 a. of meadow, and 13 a. of pasture.[12] In 1867 it had 692 a. including 97 a. in Burbage.[13] In 1910 Wolfhall farm had 549 a.,

80 W.R.O. 9/1/521.
81 Inf. from Mr. R. M. Charles, Hillbarn Farm, Wilton.
82 Inf. from Mr. P. D. L. Lemon, Manor Farm, Wilton.
83 W.R.O. 9/1/521.
84 Inf. from Mr. B. R. Taylor, the Manor, Marten; local inf.; for E. Grafton farm and Harding farm, above, this section.
85 W.R.O. 9/27/56; ibid. EA/68.
86 Ibid. 9/27/59; 1355/17; ibid. EA/68.
87 Below, this section (Brail).
88 W.R.O. 9/1/521.
89 Inf. from Mr. Charles.   90 Below, plate 36.
91 M. Watts, *Wilts. Windmills*, 34–42; *Wilton Windmill* (copy in Wilts. local studies libr., Trowbridge), 3–4, 21.
92 Savernake estate map, *c.* 1820 (copy in W.R.O.); above, intro. (other settlement).
93 C. G. Maggs, *Midland & SW. Junction Rly.* 74–6.
94 *Kelly's Dir. Wilts.* (1927, 1931).
95 *V.C.H. Wilts.* ii, p. 166.

96 Cf. W.R.O. 1300/372, ff. 1–2, 38–9; the boundary with Crofton is obscure.
97 *W.A.M.* xv. 166.
98 P.R.O., JUST 1/1006, rot. 51.
99 *Wilts. Inq. p.m. 1327–77* (Index Libr.), 81–2.
1 *Inq. Non.* (Rec. Com.), 173.
2 Hist. MSS. Com. 58, *Bath*, iv, p. 326.
3 *W.A.M.* xv. 140–51, 166; above, intro. (Wolfhall).
4 W.R.O. 192/53, f. 1.
5 *W.A.M.* xv. 166.
6 P.R.O., STAC 8/255/2; STAC 8/271/6.
7 W.R.O. 9/22/21; above, intro. (Wolfhall).
8 *W.A.M.* xv. 158 n.; P.R.O., E 134/30 Chas. II East./7; cf. W.R.O. 1300/372, ff. 1–2.
9 W.R.O. 9/22/46.
10 Ibid. 9/22/40.
11 Ibid. 1300/372, ff. 1–2.
12 Ibid. 9/1/107, ff. 21–3.
13 Ibid. 9/1/110, ff. 57–8.

Sudden farm still 243 a.[14] In 1929 Sudden was a mixed farm of 235 a., and 88 a. of what was probably Wolfhall's land was part of Freewarren farm, the buildings of which stood on Crofton's land.[15] About 1990 the 88 a. was added to Sudden farm, which in 1996 was called Suddene Park farm, measured 390 a., and was entirely arable.[16] In 1996 Wolfhall farm was an arable and dairy farm of 333 a. including c. 100 a. in Burbage.[17] Wolfhall's land north of the Kennet & Avon canal, c. 200 a. which was worked with Wolfhall farm until c. 1990, was arable in 1996.[18]

Woodland at Wolfhall was accounted 4 square furlongs in 1086.[19] In 1333 one of the moieties of Wolfhall manor included 100 a. of woodland.[20] The only woodland later known to have stood on Wolfhall's land is Sudden grove, a circular plantation of 10 a. standing near Sudden Farm in 1718.[21] It was grubbed up between c. 1820 and 1886,[22] and no woodland has since been planted.

There was a mill at Wolfhall in 1086,[23] and a miller amerced at a court of Wolfhall manor in 1264 may have had a mill there.[24] No later mill is known.

BRAIL. Woodland south-east of Great Bedwyn village in which there were deer in the earlier 13th century was part of Savernake forest and, after the boundaries of the forest were redefined in 1300, stood as a detached part. As Bedwyn Brails it became a separate bailiwick of the forest.[25] In 1568 the woodland, 212 a., stood in four coppices which contained many oaks and were planted with hazel, ash, and willow. Another coppice, 3 a., had been cut to provide timber for a new house built at Ramsbury by William Herbert, earl of Pembroke.[26]

By c. 1625 most of the woodland had been cleared, a farmstead had been built, and the land had become Brail farm. In 1645 the farm had 145 a. of arable, 7 a. of pasture, and 6 a. of meadow.[27] It was later called Jockey Green farm.[28] In 1929 it was a mixed farm of 157 a., of which 101 a. lay in Great Bedwyn parish and the rest in Little Bedwyn; in 1996 the 101 a. was used for arable and dairy farming as part of Manor farm, Little Bedwyn. In 1929 c. 65 a. of what was formerly Brail farm was part of Harding farm, and in 1996 it was worked with the land of that farm.[29]

In 1645 there remained five copses, then assessed at 33 a. and including Castle copse and Ivy's copse south of the farmstead.[30] In 1773 the woodland stood in two areas, that south of the farmstead and as Round copse east of it.[31] Castle copse and Ivy's copse adjoined woodland planted on Wilton's land c. 1792 and were part of the woodland later called Bedwyn Brail. In 1879 Castle copse measured 33 a., Ivy's copse 7 a., and there was a circular copse of 7 a. near them. In 1929 and 1996 c. 75 a. of Bedwyn Brail stood on what was formerly Bedwyn Brails bailiwick. Round copse measured 20 a. in 1879.[32] It adjoined woodland in Little Bedwyn and was standing in 1996.

In the early 19th century there was a brickworks west of Jockey Green Farm.[33] It had been closed by 1879.[34]

TOTTENHAM PARK. Land almost certainly part of Savernake forest in the Middle Ages had been imparked as Tottenham park by the earlier 16th century.[35] A lodge stood in the park in 1539 and Tottenham House was built in it later.[36] The park was estimated at 300 a. c. 1550.[37] Possibly about then a small part of Crofton's open fields, and much land north-west of them, presumably common pasture, were added to it,[38] and c. 1560 c. 260 a. of woodland was said to stand on it.[39] In 1716 the park had in it 600 a., all but c. 30 a. of which lay in Great Bedwyn parish. There were 386 a. of arable, 60 a. of pasture, 28 a. of meadow, and 116 a. of woodland, including Haw wood. A farmstead stood c. 300 m. north of Tottenham Lodge.[40] From the 1720s, when Tottenham House was built, there was apparently less agriculture in the park, which was enlarged north-westwards to take in part of Burbage parish.[41] In 1786 a farmstead stood on or near the site of that standing in 1716. It was demolished before c. 1820, presumably shortly before when Warren Farm was built 1 km. north of it.[42] Of the park as it was in 1716 the only farmland in the 19th century was apparently c. 70 a. in the south part near Crofton, and possibly land north of the house and in Warren farm.[43] Other parts of that park were converted to farmland in the 20th century: in 1996 c. 150 a. in the north-east part was part of Warren farm,[44] there was c. 230 a. of farmland south and

14   Ibid. Inland Revenue, val. regs. 56, 59.
15   Ibid. 9/1/521; for Freewarren farm, above, this section (Crofton).
16   Inf. from Mr. P. J. Devenish, Suddene Park Farm.
17   Inf. from the agent for the Crown Estate Com., 42 High Street, Marlborough.
18   Local inf.
19   *V.C.H. Wilts.* ii, p. 166.
20   *Wilts. Inq. p.m.* 1327–77 (Index Libr.), 81–2.
21   W.R.O. 1300/372, ff. 1–2.
22   O.S. Map 6", Wilts. XXXVI (1888 edn.); Savernake estate map, c. 1820 (copy in W.R.O.).
23   *V.C.H. Wilts.* ii, p. 166.
24   P.R.O., SC 2/183/56, rot. 1.
25   *V.C.H. Wilts.* iv. 450–1; *Close R.* 1231–4, 1.
26   *First Pembroke Survey*, ed. Straton, i. 186; *V.C.H. Wilts.* xii. 20.
27   W.R.O. 2057/S41, pp. 19–20.
28   Cf. *Andrews and Dury, Map* (W.R.S. viii), pl. 12; W.R.O. 9/1/521.
29   W.R.O. 9/1/521; inf. from Mr. R. H. Tucker, Manor Ho., Little Bedwyn; local inf.

30   W.R.O. 2057/S41, pp. 19–20.
31   *Andrews and Dury, Map* (W.R.S. viii), pl. 12.
32   O.S. Maps 1/2,500, Wilts. XXXVII. 5, 16 (1880 edns.); W.R.O. 9/1/521; above, this section (Wilton).
33   Savernake estate map, c. 1820 (copy in W.R.O.).
34   O.S. Map 1/2500, Wilts. XXXVII. 9 (1880 edn.).
35   Hist. MSS. Com. 58, *Bath*, iv, p. 328; *V.C.H. Wilts.* iv. 419.
36   Above, manors (Tottenham).
37   *W.A.M.* xv. 166.
38   Above, this section (Crofton).
39   W.R.O. 192/53, f. 2.
40   Ibid. 1300/372, ff. 38–9.
41   J. Harris, *Artist and Country Ho.* p. 63; above, manors (Tottenham).
42   W.R.O. 1300/360; 1300/372, ff. 38–9; Savernake estate map, c. 1820 (copy in W.R.O.); below, Burbage, intro. (other settlement).
43   O.S. Map 6", Wilts. XXXVI (1888 edn.); Savernake estate map, c. 1820 (copy in W.R.O.).
44   Inf. from the agent for the Crown Estate Com.; for Warren farm, below, Burbage, econ. hist. (Durley).

south-east of Tottenham House, sheep grazed on *c*. 50 a. of grass north-west of the house, and red and fallow deer were kept in a park of *c*. 75 a. SSW. of the house; *c*. 100 a., including Haw wood, was woodland.[45]

LOCAL GOVERNMENT. Great Bedwyn borough was incorporated by charter in 1468; the charter was confirmed in 1673. The borough developed no institution for self government although its bailiff was given the powers of a justice of the peace.[46] A new matrix for the borough seal was given by Daniel Finch, M.P. for the borough, probably in 1673. It is 9.5 cm. in diameter and depicts a castle, domed, embattled, and with a round-headed doorway, surmounted by a griffin on a mantled helm and surrounded by the legend THE COMMON SEALE OF THE CORPORATION OF GREAT BEDWIN.[47]

The lord of the borough apparently held a court for it in the late 12th century[48] and was granted regalian rights over it in 1200.[49] He presumably exercised leet jurisdiction over it, in the 12th and 13th centuries the borough was sometimes called a hundred,[50] and in 1275 the lord claimed the assize of bread and of ale in respect of it.[51] Records of the view of frankpledge or court leet held for the borough by the lord exist for the 16th century to 1837. From the mid 18th century the court was held yearly in autumn in the market house. It enforced the assize of bread and of ale and heard pleas of debt and of trespass, but was concerned mainly with good order and safety in the village. Nuisances brought to its attention included thoroughfares fouled with dung, blocked watercourses, unsafe chimneys and wells, dilapidated buildings, roads and bridges in need of repair, unlawful under-tenants, unlawful grazing in the streets, and wandering animals. The limits of the borough were described in 1748, and in 1758 some waste grounds were defined and protected from encroachment. The court also ordered that the instruments of punishment and restraint should be maintained: there was a blindhouse, a cage, and a cuckingstool in the 17th century, stocks in the 18th and 19th centuries, and a pillory in 1740. The principal officers of the court were the portreeve and the bailiff. In the early 17th century the court also appointed an aletaster, from *c*. 1675 two aletasters; in the 18th century those minor officers were called aletasters, bread weighers, and keepers of weights and measures.[52]

In 1281 and 1289 the prebendary of Bedwyn claimed view of frankpledge, the assize of bread and of ale, and pleas of vee de naam in respect of his manor in Great Bedwyn. The Crown denied his right to the pleas.[53] The prebendary's right to hear pleas in the court of his manor and to punish offences under leet jurisdiction was confirmed in 1340.[54] Records of the court of the Prebendal manor survive for the 1570s, when view of frankpledge was also held, and for the 18th century and early 19th, when it was called a court baron. In the 1570s the court transacted the normal business of a manor, and in 1575 heard a plea of debt; in 1576 the view punished an assault and a theft and elected a tithingman. The court was usually held yearly 1738–70. It met mainly to hear presentments that tenants had died, to order repair of buildings and amendment of minor nuisances affecting holdings of the manor, and for conveyancing; occasionally a tithingman was elected and the lord required to repair the pound. From 1770 to 1814 the court did no more than witness four admittances and surrenders, the last in 1800.[55]

Records of the court of either Crofton FitzWarren manor or Crofton Braboef manor survive for 1354, 1455–6, and 1459–62. The court regulated the use of common pasture and transacted the normal business of a manor; in 1456 the homage agreed that no trout under a foot long should be taken from the water of the manor. In the mid 16th century the courts of the two manors were merged. As part of its normal business the composite court regulated common husbandry and concerned itself with boundaries and hedges. In the mid 18th century the condition of gates was of particular concern. Apart from occasionally witnessing an admittance the court did very little business in the late 18th century and early 19th. It apparently ceased in 1818.[56]

The court of East Grafton manor, of which records exist for the later 16th century to the earlier 18th, dealt mainly with transfers of copyholds, including those in Wilton held of the lord. In the 16th and 17th centuries other business included the occasional presentment of minor nuisances and of breaches of manorial custom. In the 18th century the unsatisfactory condition of hedges and gates was also presented.[57]

The records of the court held for Marten manor survive for 1628–40. The court was held twice a year. Its jurisdiction extended over the lord's land at Wilton, and its main business was to deal with minor breaches of agrarian custom and minor nuisances; it heard presentments that buildings were dilapidated and that holdings had been sublet without licence.[58]

Of the estate called Bedwyn held by the king in 1086 the lands of Wexcombe, Stock (includ-

45 Inf. from the earl of Cardigan, Savernake Lodge, Savernake.

46 P.R.O., C 66/3140, no. 15; cf. *Wilts. Q. Sess. Rec.* ed. Cunnington, 13.

47 The matrix is in mus. of W.A.S., Devizes; for Finch, *Hist. Parl., Commons, 1660–90*, ii. 312–15.

48 *Cur. Reg. R.* 1194–5 (Pipe R. Soc. xiv), 66.

49 *Rot. Chart.* (Rec. Com.), 47.

50 *Cur. Reg. R.* 1194–5 (Pipe R. Soc. xiv), 66; *Plac. de Quo Warr.* (Rec. Com.), 809; cf. *Crown Pleas, 1249* (W.R.S. xvi), p. 221.

51 *Rot. Hund.* (Rec. Com.), ii (1), 260.

52 W.R.O. 9/1/135; 9/1/140; 9/1/144; 9/1/146; 9/1/148–56; 9/1/158; 9/1/162; 9/1/165; 9/1/169; 9/1/173–4; 9/1/187;

9/1/197–202; 9/1/204; 9/3/364–7; 192/24A.

53 *Plac. de Quo Warr.* (Rec. Com.), 809; P.R.O., JUST 1/1006, rot. 51d.

54 *Cal. Pat.* 1338–40, 555.

55 W.R.O. 9/1/204, pp. 55–63; 9/4/84–6; for other jurisdiction over Great Bedwyn, below, this section [Wexcombe].

56 W.R.O. 9/1/134; 9/1/140; 9/1/144; 9/1/146; 9/1/153; 9/1/156; 9/1/161–3; 9/1/170–1; 9/1/174; 9/1/189; 9/1/200; 9/1/202; 9/1/204; 9/14/215–17; 9/14/219–20; 192/24B.

57 Ibid. 9/1/135–6; 9/1/139; 9/16/235; 2203/13–14; Alnwick Castle Mun. X.II.11, box 1, E. Grafton ct. bks. 1552–65; 1621–6; X.II.11, box 7, E. Grafton ct. bks. 1582–1611; 1621–3; 1631–5.

58 W.R.O. 490/1541.

ing Ford), Wilton, and what became West Bed-wyn manor had apparently not been infeudated by 1086 and were probably included in the grant to John FitzGilbert *c.* 1130. Stock, some of Wilton's land, and West Bedwyn manor were probably subinfeudated after *c.* 1130;[59] the lord of Wexcombe manor retained leet jurisdiction over them and exercised it with that over Wex-combe at a view of frankpledge. That part of Wilton which belonged to him was also within the lord's jurisdiction.[60] In the 15th century two views were held each year.[61] In the later 16th century and earlier 17th separate presentments were made by the tithingman of Wexcombe and Wilton and by the tithingman of Stock and Ford, whose presentments included matters relating to West Bedwyn manor and thus Great Bedwyn village. The view dealt with breaches of the assize of bread and of ale, assault, and stray animals, and orders were made to remove unli-censed undertenants, to repair buildings and the highway, to make hedges, and to ring pigs. The only direct record of the view after 1619 is for 1673, when little leet business was done at it. The view was held with the court of Wexcombe manor, in which matters relating to the lord's holdings in Wilton were also dealt with. In addition to recording the death of tenants and witnessing transfers of copyholds, in respect of Wexcombe the court made regulations for com-mon husbandry, ordered the repair of the pound and a gate, and appointed tellers of sheep and overseers of common pastures; Wilton matters included misuse of the common pasture and orders to make a pound and to identify what lands there belonged to the lord of Wexcombe manor and what to the lord of Marten manor.[62] In 1766 Thomas Brudenell, Lord Bruce, whose predecessors as owners of Tottenham park were lords of Wexcombe manor until 1660, bought Stock and West Bedwyn manors[63] and in respect of them began to hold what was called a court leet and view of frankpledge. A jury made a few presentments in 1766 but no other business was done at the court, which was last convened in 1808.[64]

Records of the court of a manor of Wolfhall survive for 1263–5. The court dealt with the normal business of a manor and particularly with the use of pastures.[65]

There was a workhouse in Great Bedwyn village in the mid 18th century,[66] and from 1786 or earlier cottages at Wilton were used as a parish workhouse. A master of the workhouse was appointed and the services of a surgeon were provided for the inmates. The workhouse con-tained 11 beds and 8 spinning wheels in 1795,

housed 19 paupers in 1802–3 and 12 in 1812–13, and remained open until 1835. In 1797 inmates were forbidden to leave it without permission, to receive visitors, or to collect wood for fuel.[67]

In 1775–6 the parish spent £799 on relief of the poor, in the three years to Easter 1785 an average of £697 a year. In 1802–3 it spent £987 on outdoor relief and £80 on indoor relief. Out of the workhouse 88 adults and 144 children were relieved regularly, 21 occasionally.[68] In the late 18th century and early 19th monthly doles cost more than extraordinary expenses.[69] In 1812–13 the parish spent £3,076 on outdoor relief for nearly half the population: 150 were relieved regularly, 760 occasionally. Thereafter total expenditure and the number of paupers fell. Expenditure was £1,988 in 1813–14 and £1,116 in 1814–15.[70] Between 1815 and 1834 it was between £1,000 and £2,000 in all but three years, in each of which it was higher.[71] In 1835 Great Bedwyn parish joined Hungerford poor-law union.[72] In 1974 Great Bedwyn parish and Grafton parish became part of Kennet district.[73]

PARLIAMENTARY REPRESENTATION. Great Bedwyn returned two burgesses to parlia-ment in 1295 and was represented at six of the 17 parliaments summoned between then and 1315. The borough returned two members in 1362 but, having failed to answer a summons in 1378, was otherwise unrepresented in parlia-ments summoned between 1315 and 1379. It returned two members in 1379 and, although it again failed to answer summonses in 1381 and 1388, was represented at most parliaments which met between 1379 and 1390. Between 1390 and 1419 it is known to have returned members to only one of 25 parliaments. From 1420 it seems to have been represented at all parliaments, except one of 1421, one of 1425, and those of 1653–6, until it was disfranchised in 1832.[74]

In 1295 and the 14th century elections are likely to have been initiated by a precept sent by the sheriff of Wiltshire to the bailiff of the lord of the borough, and most of those elected were probably burgesses of Great Bedwyn. In the 15th century members included men who, al-though they may have owned burgage tenements in Great Bedwyn, bore the surnames of local landowners. Other members, whose local con-nexion is less obvious, may have been elected through the patronage of the lord of the borough or his lessee.[75]

The right to vote for candidates at parliamen-tary elections at Great Bedwyn was attached to tenements in the village. In the 18th century, when the right could not be extended to any

59 Above, manors (preamble; W. Bedwyn; Stock; Wil-ton); for Ford, above, intro. (Stock and Ford).
60 W.R.O. 9/1/134, ff. 42–3, 143–5; 9/1/137; 9/1/139–41; 9/3/365.
61 B.L. Add. Ch. 27679; 28005; 28008.
62 W.R.O. 9/1/134, ff. 42–3, 143–5; 9/1/137; 9/1/139–41; 9/1/157; 9/3/365; 9/27/51.
63 Above, manors (W. Bedwyn; Stock; Wexcombe; Tot-tenham).   64 W.R.O. 9/26/514.
65 P.R.O., SC 2/183/56.
66 W.R.O. 9/3/21–2; 9/3/262.
67 Ibid. 1355/17–18; *Endowed Char. Wilts.* (N. Div.), 37; *Poor Law Abstract, 1804,* 564–5; *1818,* 498–9.

68 *Poor Law Abstract, 1804,* 564–5.
69 W.R.O. 1355/17–20.
70 *Poor Law Abstract, 1818,* 498–9; *V.C.H. Wilts.* iv. 340.
71 *Poor Rate Returns, 1816–21,* 188; *1822–4,* 228; *1825–9,* 218; *1830–4,* 212.
72 *Poor Law Com. 1st Rep.* App. D, 242.
73 O.S. Map 1/100,000, admin. areas, Wilts. (1974 edn.).
74 *W.A.M.* xlvii. 177–258; *Hist. Parl., Commons,* 1386–1421, i. 698–700; *V.C.H. Wilts.* v. 299, 301.
75 *Hist. Parl., Commons,* 1386–1421, i. 700–1; for M.P.s called Collingbourne, Stock, Sturmy, cf. above, manors (W. Bedwyn; Stock; Wolfhall).

building erected on a new foundation, there were *c.* 120 voters.[76] Elections were conducted by the portreeve, a principal officer of the borough court,[77] and in the 18th century were held at the market house.[78]

In the 16th century the lord of West Bedwyn manor may have owned many of the tenements in the village, as he did in the 18th.[79] Anthony Hungerford, from 1582 lord of Stock manor, bought West Bedwyn manor in 1568:[80] Hungerfords were M.P.s for Great Bedwyn at several parliaments in the later 16th century and earlier 17th,[81] and in 1660 representatives of the lord of West Bedwyn manor thought mistakenly that they had enough tenants in the village to win both seats.[82] The lordship of the borough, and possibly some tenements in the village, descended in the Seymour family from 1545,[83] and some M.P.s in the 16th and 17th centuries were apparently nominees of successive Seymours.[84] Elections were contested in 1640, 1660, and 1661.[85] From 1676, when it was acquired by Thomas Bruce, from 1685 earl of Ailesbury, successive lords of the borough were Tory.[86] Some non-Tory members were returned, including the republican John Wildman in 1681 and in 1689,[87] when the borough was described as open;[88] in 1705 clothiers of Newbury (Berks.) successfully bribed electors to return candidates opposed by Lord Ailesbury.[89]

In the earlier and mid 18th century successive lords of West Bedwyn manor and Thomas Bruce, earl of Ailesbury, and his successors as lord of the borough and owner or lessee of an increasing number of tenements in the village shared or disputed influence at elections. Francis Stonehouse, who may have had an interest in West Bedwyn manor from 1699, was elected several times 1679–1702 and Lascelles Metcalfe, lord of the manor 1741–53, was elected in 1741 and, after a contest, in 1747.[90] Of 155 properties in the village listed in 1751 Metcalfe owned 52, Thomas Brudenell, Lord Bruce, 32.[91] In 1754 Ralph Verney, Earl Verney, owner of West Bedwyn manor 1753–66, and Lord Bruce promoted a candidate each by agreement. Lord Bruce bought other tenements after 1751, and in 1761 candidates promoted by him won both seats at a contested election. In 1766 Lord Verney sold West Bedwyn manor, including his tenements in Great Bedwyn village, to Lord Bruce subject to an agreement by which a nominee of Lord Verney was returned at a by-election in that year and at the following general election. Thereafter Lord Bruce (cr. earl of Ailesbury 1776, d. 1814) and his son Charles Brudenell-Bruce, earl of Ailesbury (cr. marquess of Ailesbury 1821), controlled elections held in the borough. No election was contested after 1761 and members acceptable to the government were usually returned.[92]

CHURCHES. A minster church may have stood at Great Bedwyn in the late 10th century, when God's servants at Bedwyn were referred to.[93] A church stood there in 1066.[94] Its revenues were given to Salisbury cathedral in 1091 and became an endowment of Bedwyn prebend.[95] The prebendary was rector of the church,[96] in which a vicarage had been ordained by 1316.[97]

The prebendary of Bedwyn exercised archidiaconal jurisdiction, triennially inhibited by the dean of the cathedral, over Great Bedwyn parish, including what became Little Bedwyn parish. From 1543, when the prebend was dissolved, the jurisdiction descended with the Prebendal manor and, from 1567, with Tottenham Lodge and Tottenham House. The area over which it was exercised, Great Bedwyn, Little Bedwyn, and Collingbourne Ducis parishes, was called the peculiar of the Lord Warden of Savernake Forest: the name echoes the hereditary title of the owners and their forbears. The visitation court was competent in testamentary matters, was often held by the vicar of Great Bedwyn, and was usually held in Great Bedwyn church or Collingbourne Ducis church. In 1675 it was held at the King's Head, probably in Great Bedwyn village. The jurisdiction ceased in 1847.[98]

Little Bedwyn had become a separate parish by the 16th century,[99] in 1844 a church was built at East Grafton and the south part of Great Bedwyn parish was assigned to it as a district,[1] and in 1861 the church of St. Katharine, Savernake Forest, was built and in 1864 the northernmost part of Great Bedwyn parish and parts of other parishes were assigned to it as a district.[2] In 1982 the vicarages of Great Bedwyn, Little Bedwyn, and Savernake Forest were united.[3]

[76] *Hist. Parl., Commons,* 1754–90, i. 413; *W.A.M.* vi. 305.
[77] *Hist. Parl., Commons,* 1660–90, i. 446; above, local govt.
[78] W. Cobbett, *Rural Rides,* ed. G. D. H. and Margaret Cole, i. 13; W.R.O. 9/26/329.
[79] Below, this section.
[80] Above, manors (W. Bedwyn; Stock). From 1582 W. Bedwyn manor descended with Stock manor.
[81] *W.A.M.* xlvii. 209–10, 214–15.
[82] *Hist. Parl., Commons,* 1660–90, i. 446.
[83] Above, manors (Borough).
[84] *V.C.H. Wilts.* v. 115, 129, 135.
[85] *Hist. Parl., Commons,* 1660–90, i. 446; M. F. Keeler, *Long Parl.* 202; T. Carew, *Rights of Elections* (1754), 41.
[86] *Complete Peerage,* i. 59–63; *V.C.H. Wilts.* v. 159.
[87] *Hist. Parl., Commons,* 1660–90, i. 447.
[88] *V.C.H. Wilts.* v. 209.
[89] Ibid. 213.
[90] *W.A.M.* xlvii. 223–4, 226–9; *Hist. Parl., Commons,* 1715–54, i. 346; W.R.O. 9/26/15–23; above, manors (Bor-

ough; Stock); for the purchase of tenements, W.R.O. 9/3, *passim.*
[91] W.R.O. 9/3/393H.
[92] *Hist. Parl., Commons,* 1754–90, i. 413–14; 1790–1820, ii. 419–20; above, manors (Stock).
[93] *W.A.M.* lii. 362–4.
[94] *V.C.H. Wilts.* ii, p. 119.
[95] *Reg. St. Osmund* (Rolls Ser.), i. 199, 252.
[96] *Plac. de Quo Warr.* (Rec. Com.), 809; *Valor Eccl.* (Rec. Com.), ii. 150; Le Neve, *Fasti, 1066–1300, Salisbury,* 47; *1300–1541, Salisbury,* 30.
[97] *Reg. Martival* (Cant. & York Soc.), iv, p. 2.
[98] *W.A.M.* vi. 261; W.R.O., D 21/1–4; above, manors (Tottenham; Prebendal); for the title, *V.C.H. Wilts.* iv. 421.
[99] Above, intro.; below, Little Bedwyn, intro.; church.
[1] *Lond. Gaz.* 20 Aug. 1844, pp. 2904–6; W.R.O., D 1/2/33, ff. 121v.–128.
[2] *Lond. Gaz.* 12 Apr. 1864, pp. 2018–21; W.R.O., D 1/60/7/25.
[3] Ch. Com. file, NB 34/156B/2.

Vicars of Great Bedwyn were presented to the dean, until 1543 presumably by the prebendary. From 1544 the advowson of the vicarage descended with the Prebendal manor. The Crown presented in 1574, for a reason which is obscure, and in 1595 and 1611 by lapse. The dean collated by lapse in 1784 and 1796.[4] George Brudenell-Bruce, marquess of Ailesbury, who sold the land of the Prebendal manor to the Crown in 1950, transferred the advowson of the vicarage to the bishop of Salisbury in 1953. The bishop was appointed patron of the united benefice formed in 1982.[5]

The vicarage, valued at £9 in 1535,[6] c. £20 in 1678,[7] and £212 c. 1830,[8] was poor. It was augmented in 1823 by £600 given by parliament and £400 given by the patron; Queen Anne's Bounty and the patron each gave a further £400 in 1828.[9] The vicar was entitled to small tithes, probably from the whole parish. In 1792 those arising from Wilton were valued at £13 and commuted to a rent charge. In 1847 the rent charge and the rest of the tithes were valued at £212; in 1849 they were commuted to a rent charge on c. 900 a. lying mainly around Great Bedwyn village and at Wilton.[10] The vicar had no glebe.[11] A vicarage house, designed by G. G. Scott (d. 1897), was built in 1878–9[12] and sold in 1968. A new house was built in the garden of the old c. 1966.[13]

In the Middle Ages several churches, in addition to that of Little Bedwyn, were dependent on Great Bedwyn church as chapels.[14] Presumably because they received great tithes the chaplains of Crofton, East Grafton, and Marten were each called a rector.[15]

The chapel at Crofton was mentioned first in 1317.[16] St. Catherine was invoked in it and it stood on Crofton Braboef manor, the lord of which was the patron. The chaplain was prohibited from administering any sacrament, and mass might only be said when the lord of the manor was present. The chaplain was entitled to all tithes from the demesne of Crofton Braboef manor and had a barn, 1 a., and a croft: in return he paid 13s. 4d. a year to the prebendary and 7d. to the lord of the manor. The chapel was dilapidated in 1405[17] and last mentioned in 1414.[18]

At East Grafton a chapel was standing in 1302, when St. Mary was invoked in it and the lord of East Grafton manor was licensed to give 1 yardland and 4 marks rent to it.[19] Later the chaplain was entitled to the small tithes, the hay tithes, and a third of the great tithes from East Grafton manor and from 64½ a.; he held ½

yardland and paid 2s. a year to the prior of St. Margaret's, Marlborough. He was instituted and inducted by the prebendary of Bedwyn, to whom he was presented by the lord of East Grafton manor, and was entitled to administer the sacraments to members of the lord's household at East Grafton and officiate at their burial at St. Margaret's priory. The chapel, in which St. Nicholas was invoked in 1405, was not served in 1468 or 1486. It was in use in 1480 but apparently not thereafter.[20]

At Marten a chapel was standing in 1313 on the estate which was held then by Ralph Malwain and was later conveyed by Peter Tebaud to John Malwain.[21] By 1405 the altar had been dedicated to the Assumption. The owner of the estate, his household, and his tenants had all rights in the chapel except burial; the chaplain had 8 a. and was given 1 a., a croft, and 1 load of corn yearly by the prebendary. The chapel was not served in 1486 and is not known to have been served thereafter.[22]

At Wilton in 1405 a chapel in honour of the Assumption stood on the land which belonged to the lord of East Grafton manor. As in the case of the chapel at East Grafton, the lord of the manor presented the chaplain to the prebendary for institution and induction. The chaplain had 1 yardland and was entitled to all tithes from Port mill, presumably the mill of that name in Marlborough. The chapel was vacant 1403–5, was not served in 1412, and had ceased to exist by c. 1440.[23]

In the Middle Ages Ralph Randall gave land to Great Bedwyn church for prayers, and another donor gave 3 a. and a rent of 2s. for a light.[24] In the early 15th century the church was rich in plate, books, and vestments, and had a box covered in silk and containing relics of saints. In 1409 the vicar was accused of frequenting taverns, an accusation which he denied, and in 1412 he was failing to appoint a chaplain because of the poverty of the vicarage.[25] The vicar was not resident in 1758, when the curate read prayers and preached every Sunday and held a communion service eight times,[26] or in 1812, when a single service was held each Sunday, a communion service was held four times a year, and there were 100 communicants.[27] In 1832, when the vicar was required to officiate at a chapel in Tottenham House, two services were held each Sunday in Great Bedwyn church.[28] In 1851 on Census Sunday 324 attended morning service, 374 afternoon service.[29] In 1864 the vicar and his assistant curate served Great Bedwyn

4 W.R.O., D 5/1/2.
5 Ch. Com. files, NB 34/156B/1–2; above, manors (Prebendal).   6 Valor Eccl. (Rec. Com.), ii. 150.
7 P.R.O., E 134/30 Chas. II East./7.
8 Rep. Com. Eccl. Revenues, 824–5.
9 C. Hodgson, Queen Anne's Bounty (1845), pp. cc, ccix, cccxxxv.
10 W.R.O., EA/68; ibid. tithe award.
11 Ibid. D 5/10/1/6.
12 Ibid. D 1/11/255; G. Stamp and A. Goulancourt, Eng. Ho., 1860–1914 (1986), 80–1; below, plate 27.
13 Inf. from Ch. Com.; inf. from the vicar.
14 For Little Bedwyn, below, Little Bedwyn, church.
15 Chandler's Reg. (W.R.S. xxxix), pp. 32–3, 120.
16 W.R.O. 9/14/40.
17 Feet of F. 1327–77 (W.R.S. xxix), p. 129; Chandler's

Reg. (W.R.S. xxxix), p. 32; cf. above, manors (Crofton Braboef).
18 Reg. Hallum (Cant. & York Soc.), pp. 61–2.
19 Wilts. Inq. p.m. 1242–1326 (Index Libr.), 286.
20 Chandler's Reg. (W.R.S. xxxix), p. 33; cf. above, manors (E. Grafton).
21 Feet of F. 1272–1327 (W.R.S. i), p. 83; above, manors (Marten).
22 Chandler's Reg. (W.R.S. xxxix), p. 32.
23 Ibid. pp. 33, 120; cf. above, manors (E. Grafton; Wilton); for Port mill, V.C.H. Wilts. xii. 177.
24 P.R.O., E 310/26/156, f. 49.
25 Chandler's Reg. (W.R.S. xxxix), pp. 63–4, 102, 120.
26 W.R.O., D 5/28/125/2.   27 W.A.M. xli. 129.
28 Ch. Com. file, NB 34/156B/1.
29 P.R.O., HO 129/121/2/3/2.

church and St. Katharine's, but not East Grafton church. At Great Bedwyn the average congregation at the two services each Sunday was 250; services were also held on Wednesdays and Fridays, on holy days, and in Lent and Holy Week. A communion service was held twice a month, when the average attendance was 24, and at five principal festivals, when it was 31.[30]

A chapel of ease at Wexcombe had been built by 1879.[31] Services in it were held by the vicar of Tidcombe in 1899 and later. Its closure took place apparently between 1920 and 1923.[32] The vicarage of Great Bedwyn was held in plurality with that of Little Bedwyn from 1953 to 1958, with that of Savernake Forest from 1958, and with both from 1965.[33]

A tenement or more in Great Bedwyn village belonged to the church in 1564,[34] and in the 18th century the incumbent and churchwardens held an estate in trust for repairs to the church. It consisted of a parcel of land called St. John's at Crofton which was possibly part of the estate given to St. John's hospital in the 13th century, several tenements on the north-west side of Church Street in Great Bedwyn village, 4 a. at Great Bedwyn, some of which was allotted to replace open-field arable in Stock, and a nominal 9 a. in open fields in Shalbourne parish. In 1792 that estate was exchanged for 14 a. in Little Bedwyn,[35] of which 4 a. was sold in 1893–4.[36] From 1835 income from the cottages at Wilton owned by the parish, and until then a workhouse, was also used for repairs to the church.[37] The cottages were sold in 1923.[38] In the 18th century the church received c. £20 a year for repairs from its estate, in the earlier 20th c. £39.[39] In 1996 the income from its land and from the capital accruing from the two sales yielded c. £300 for repairs.[40]

The church of *ST. MARY*, so called in 1405,[41] is built of ashlar and flint with ashlar dressings and consists of a chancel with south vestry, a central tower with transepts, and an aisled and clerestoried nave.[42] The church standing in the 12th century, when the aisles were built, was already large. The chancel was rebuilt in Chilmark stone in the mid or later 13th century. The crossing was built in the mid 14th century, presumably to replace a tower, and the transepts are contemporary with it. In the 15th century the clerestory was built, the aisles were altered, and all the roofs, until then steep, were reconstructed with a lower pitch and covered with lead. The stair turret at the north-east corner of the tower

was built in 1840, and the west front of the church was rebuilt in 1843. The church was restored between 1853 and 1855 to designs by T. H. Wyatt.[43] A new east window in 14th-century style was inserted, the vestry was built, and the stair turret was rebuilt; a north porch and a south porch were removed from the respective aisles, the walls of the aisles were apparently rebuilt, and a doorway in the south aisle and one at the west end of the north aisle were blocked; all the roofs abutting the tower were restored to their earlier pitch. The church was refitted, and galleries, for which timber was given in 1702,[44] were removed. By 1894 the chancel screen, which was made in the 14th century, had been moved to the south aisle;[45] it was removed from the church c. 1905,[46] and in 1975 was placed across the north aisle.[47] A pair of tomb recesses in the south wall of the south transept are apparently for members of the Stock family and coeval with the transept; memorials of the Seymour family include a tomb chest of c. 1590 on which lies an effigy of Sir John Seymour (d. 1536).[48]

In the early 15th century the church had three chalices each with a paten,[49] and Peter de Testa (d. 1467), the prebendary, by his will directed that a gilt cup should be bought.[50] In 1553 the king took 42 oz. of plate, and 14 oz. was retained for the parish. By c. 1890 that plate had been replaced by two chalices hallmarked for 1785, a plate hallmarked for 1712 and given in 1831, a flagon hallmarked for 1805 and given in 1840, and an almsdish hallmarked for 1846.[51] All that plate was held for Great Bedwyn parish in 1996.[52]

Money for bells for the church was being collected in 1405.[53] There were five bells in 1553. Possibly in 1623, when the present tenor was cast by John Wallis, the ring was increased to six. Of the other five bells in the ring one was cast by William Purdue and Nathaniel Boulter in 1656, the others by Henry Knight of Reading in 1671. A sanctus bell was cast by John Cor in 1741.[54] Those seven bells hung in the church in 1996.[55]

There are registrations of burials from 1538, of marriages from 1540, and of baptisms from 1554. Apart from burials and baptisms of 1635–6 and burials of 1769–79 the registers are complete.[56]

The church of *ST. NICHOLAS* was built at East Grafton, and a district was assigned to it, in 1844. It was served by a perpetual curate,

30 W.R.O., D 1/56/7.
31 O.S. Map 1/2,500, Wilts. XLIII. 5 (1880 edn.).
32 *Kelly's Dir. Wilts.* (1899 and later edns.).
33 Ch. Com. files, NB 34/156B/1–2.
34 W.R.O. 9/3/364.
35 Ibid. EA/68; for the land in Stock, ibid. 9/3/393H; 9/26/203; for St. John's hosp., above, intro. (Great Bedwyn).
36 *Endowed Char. Wilts.* (N. Div.), 36.
37 Ibid. 37–8; above, local govt. [poor relief].
38 W.R.O., L 2, Great Bedwyn.
39 *Endowed Char. Wilts.* (N. Div.), 33, 36, 38.
40 Inf. from the vicar.
41 *Chandler's Reg.* (W.R.S. xxxix), p. 32.
42 Below, plates 1–2; description based partly on J. Buckler, watercolours in W.A.S. Libr., vol. iv. 15; viii. 35, 49.

43 *W.A.M.* xli. 130–1.
44 Notebook of J. Ward, vicar 1826–50, in church.
45 *W.A.M.* xxviii. 144.
46 Ibid. xxxiv. 146, 348.
47 *Church Guide* (1985).
48 *W.A.M.* xxviii. 142, 144; above, manors (Stock).
49 *Chandler's Reg.* (W.R.S. xxxix), p. 63.
50 *N. Country Wills* (Surtees Soc. cxvi), 47; Le Neve, *Fasti, 1300–1541, Salisbury,* 29.
51 Nightingale, *Wilts. Plate,* 164.
52 Inf. from the vicar.
53 *Chandler's Reg.* (W.R.S. xxxix), p. 33.
54 Walters, *Wilts. Bells,* 20.
55 Inf. from the vicar.
56 W.R.O. 1836/1–6; 1836/9–12; dean's transcripts for some of the years 1769–79 are in W.R.O.

ST. NICHOLAS'S CHURCH, BUILT IN 1844

from 1868 called a vicar, presented by the vicar of Great Bedwyn.[57] In 1962 the vicarage was united with the vicarage of Tidcombe with Fosbury, and in 1979 the united benefice became part of Wexcombe benefice. Between 1962 and 1979 the vicar of Great Bedwyn shared the patronage of the united benefice, and from 1979 was a member of the board of patronage for Wexcombe benefice.[58] The vicarage house, built between 1847 and 1860 on a site assigned for it in 1844,[59] was sold in 1978.[60]

On Census Sunday in 1851 morning service was attended by 480, afternoon service by 300.[61] In 1864 the perpetual curate held a service twice on each Sunday and held additional services in Holy Week and on each Wednesday and Friday in Advent and Lent. He held a communion service c. 20 times with a congregation averaging 44 at great festivals, 34 at other times.[62] From 1955 the vicarage was held in plurality with that of Tidcombe with Fosbury.[63]

The church, of Bath stone, was built in Romanesque style to designs by Benjamin Ferrey.[64] It has an apsidal chancel, an aisled and clerestoried nave, and a north-west tower with a pyramidal roof.

By will proved 1894 Elizabeth Carter gave the income from £100 for repairs to the church.[65]

Two chalices, a paten, a flagon, and an almsdish, all hallmarked for 1843, were given by the vicar of Great Bedwyn in 1844 and remained for the use of East Grafton parish in 1996.[66] A ring of tubular bells was hung in the tower in 1902 and remained there in 1996.[67]

57 Ibid. D 1/2/33, ff. 121v.–128; D 1/2/34, ff. 209v.–210; *Lond. Gaz.* 20 Aug. 1844, pp. 2904–6; *W.A.M.* vi. 270; Incumbents Act, 31 & 32 Vic. c. 117.
58 Ch. Com. file, NB 34/371B/2; inf. from Ch. Com.
59 *W.A.M.* vi. 270; W.R.O., D 1/2/33, f. 125; ibid. tithe award.
60 Inf. from Ch. Com.
61 P.R.O., HO 129/121/2/3/3.

62 W.R.O., D 1/56/7.
63 *Crockford* (1961–2); Ch. Com. file, NB 34/371B/2.
64 W.R.O., D 1/2/33, f. 128.
65 *Endowed Char. Wilts.* (N. Div.), 39–40; W.R.O., L 2, Great Bedwyn.
66 Nightingale, *Wilts. Plate*, 168; W.R.O., D 1/2/33, f. 125v.; inf. from Mrs. A. Beese, Church Ho., E. Grafton.
67 *Kelly's Dir. Wilts.* (1903); inf. from Mrs. Beese.

The church of *ST. KATHARINE* was built at the north end of Great Bedwyn parish in 1861. It was served by the vicar of Great Bedwyn until 1864, when a district called Savernake Forest and consisting of parts of Great Bedwyn, Little Bedwyn, and Burbage parishes was assigned to it, the patronage was vested in George Brudenell-Bruce, marquess of Ailesbury, and a perpetual curate, from 1868 called a vicar, was presented.[68] In 1953 George, marquess of Ailesbury, transferred the advowson to the bishop of Salisbury. The vicarage was united with the vicarages of Great Bedwyn and Little Bedwyn in 1982. A vicarage house built in 1879–80 was sold in 1950.[69]

In earlier 1864 most services were probably held by the assistant curate of Great Bedwyn. Two services were held each Sunday with a congregation which averaged *c.* 160; additional services were held at festivals and on saints' days, those held in the morning being attended by a congregation of 12–20, those in the evening by one of 40–80. About 1864 communion was celebrated *c.* 20 times a year; of *c.* 90 communicants 66 received the sacrament at Easter 1864.[70] The vicarage was held in plurality with the vicarage of Savernake (Christchurch) from 1947 to 1949,[71] with Great Bedwyn from 1958, and additionally with Little Bedwyn from 1965.[72]

The church, of flint with ashlar dressings, was built in early 14th-century style to designs by T. H. Wyatt. It has an apsidal chancel with north vestry, a nave with north and south transepts and north aisle, and a south tower with spire. The interior is richly provided with coloured floor tiles, stone screens with marble shafts and foliage capitals, and varnished pine benches with decorated ends. The north aisle has been walled off and is used as a vestry and a meeting room. Mary, marchioness of Ailesbury (d. 1892), is commemorated by a monument designed by Alfred Gilbert.[73]

The church was given two chalices, each with a paten, and a flagon and an almsdish, all hallmarked for 1861 and retained in 1996,[74] and it has a peal of five bells cast by G. Mears & Co. in 1862.[75]

NONCONFORMITY. Recusants living in Great Bedwyn parish included one at Marten in the 1590s,[76] one at Wexcombe in 1639,[77] and one at Wolfhall in the 1660s.[78] Two who were papists in the 1670s may also have lived in the parish.[79]

In Great Bedwyn village a Methodist chapel was opened *c.* 1810. It stood on the north-west side of Church Street near the church, and on Census Sunday in 1851 it was attended by 150 in the morning and 140 in the evening.[80] It was presumably replaced by the Methodist chapel, small and of red brick with stone dressings, built in Brown's Lane *c.* 1874.[81] A schoolroom was built beside that chapel between 1899 and 1922.[82] The chapel was closed in 1967.[83] West of the village a house on Bedwyn common was certified in 1825 for worship by Methodists.[84] A single service, attended by 56, was held in it on Census Sunday in 1851[85] and it had apparently been closed by 1864.[86]

At West Grafton a chapel for Primitive Methodists had been opened by 1864.[87] It was open in 1939 and had been closed by 1964.[88] At Wexcombe a building was certified in 1844 for worship by Primitive Methodists.[89] A small chapel was built apparently between 1880 and 1885.[90] It was open in 1939 and had been closed by 1966.[91] At Wilton the Bethel chapel, small and of red brick, was built in 1811 and was used by Wesleyan Methodists. A school was built in 1843.[92] Two services were held in the chapel on Census Sunday in 1851; 179 attended in the afternoon, 180 in the evening.[93] The chapel was closed *c.* 1994.[94]

EDUCATION. There was a schoolmaster at Great Bedwyn *c.* 1580,[95] in 1758 there were said to be many schools in the parish,[96] and for many years until 1791 a Swiss held a school there.[97]

By a deed of 1799 William Cox (d. 1812) gave 3 a. off Frog Lane to provide money after his death for 10 children aged between 5 and 10 to be taught to read. The income from the land was allowed to accumulate until 1824, when a schoolmaster was appointed; because the teaching of girls was provided for well enough at other schools only boys were taught. In 1834 the charity's income was £7, and 10 boys were taught. From 1847 the rent from the land was divided equally between the master and the mistress of the National school. In 1904 the income was still *c.* £7.[98] By a Scheme of 1913 £3 a year was given to the Sunday school and the rest of the income spent on travelling expenses and maintenance allowances for pupils

68 *Lond. Gaz.* 12 Apr. 1864, pp. 2018–21; *Clergy List* (1870); Incumbents Act, 31 & 32 Vic. c. 117; W.R.O., D 1/56/7; D 1/60/7/25.
69 Ch. Com. files, NB 34/156B/1–2; inf. from Ch. Com.
70 W.R.O., D 1/56/7.
71 *Sar. Dioc. Dir.* (1949, 1950).
72 Ch. Com. file, NB 34/156B/1.
73 Pevsner, *Wilts.* (2nd edn.), 462–3; *Complete Peerage*, i. 65; *St. Katharines, Savernake* (church guide: copy in Wilts. local studies libr., Trowbridge); below, plate 11.
74 Nightingale, *Wilts. Plate*, 163; inf. from the vicar.
75 Walters, *Wilts. Bells*, 194; inf. from the vicar.
76 *Recusant R.* ii (Cath. Rec. Soc. lvii), p. xcii.
77 W.R.O., D 21/2/2.
78 Williams, *Cath. Recusancy* (Cath. Rec. Soc.), p. 307.
79 W.R.O., D 21/2/3/125.
80 Ibid. tithe award; P.R.O., HO 129/121/2/3/6.
81 W.R.O. 1464/25.
82 O.S. Maps 6", Wilts. XXXVII. NW. (1900, 1926 edns.).
83 W.R.O. 2193/12.
84 *Meeting Ho. Certs.* (W.R.S. xl), p. 109.
85 P.R.O., HO 129/121/2/3/4.
86 W.R.O., D 1/56/7.   87 Ibid.
88 *Kelly's Dir. Wilts.* (1939); inf. from Meth. Church Property Div., Central Bldgs., Oldham Street, Manchester.
89 *Meeting Ho. Certs.* (W.R.S. xl), p. 159.
90 *Kelly's Dir. Wilts.* (1880, 1885); O.S. Maps 1/2,500, Wilts. XLIII. 5 (1880, 1900 edns.).
91 *Kelly's Dir. Wilts.* (1939); inf. from Meth. Church Property Div.
92 Dates on bldgs.
93 P.R.O., HO 129/121/2/3/7.
94 W.R.O. 2928/23.
95 Ibid. D 1/43/5, f. 18.
96 Ibid. D 5/28/125/2.
97 *Coroners' Bills, 1752–96* (W.R.S. xxxvi), p. 112.
98 *Endowed Char. Wilts.* (N. Div.), 33–4, 37; *W.A.M.* vi. 290; notebook of J. Ward, vicar 1826–50, in church; for the Nat. sch., below, this section.

and on school equipment.[99] The charity sold its land in 1923. It continued to receive a small income, and in 1991 £70 was given away, mostly to the schools at Great Bedwyn and East Grafton.[1] It was wound up in 1993–4.[2]

W. G. Pike (d. 1839) gave by will the income from £50 to the National school.[3] The income, £1 10s., was still being paid to Great Bedwyn school in 1984. The charity's assetts were probably transferred to a day centre for old people with those of Pike's eleemosynary charity in 1987.[4]

In the parish in 1818 there were three or four day schools attended by a total of c. 70 children; clothes were given at a school for c. 20 girls.[5] In 1833 there were 13 day schools attended by 145 children.[6] The number of schools declined after National schools were opened in the 1830s and 1840s.[7]

In Great Bedwyn village a National school in Church Street was built in 1835.[8] It had c. 30 pupils in 1846–7.[9] A room for infants was added in 1856,[10] and in 1858 the school had c. 130 pupils.[11] Between 1906–7 and 1926–7 average attendance fell from 139 to 104. In the 1930s it was c. 150.[12] The school was closed in 1993 when a new one in Farm Lane was opened. The new school had 108 pupils on the roll in 1996.[13]

At East Grafton a National school was opened in 1846.[14] It was attended by children living in the district served by East Grafton church, and in 1858 its 70–80 pupils came from Crofton, East Grafton, West Grafton, and Wexcombe.[15] In the period 1898–1901 the schoolmaster taught commercial arithmetic, elementary science, and horticulture at a night school.[16] Average attendance at the day school was highest at 101 and lowest at 77 between 1906–7 and 1926–7, and was c. 125 in the 1930s.[17] There were 24 children on the roll in 1996.[18]

At Marten a school was attended by 25–30 young children in 1858.[19] The school probably remained open in 1879 but not in 1899.[20]

At Wilton the upper room of the Methodist school built in 1843 was used for a day school in 1858, when there were c. 30 pupils and an untrained teacher.[21] The day school apparently ceased between 1880 and 1885.[22]

In the park of Tottenham House a wooden building used as a school had been converted to a summer house by 1858.[23] A new school was built near St. Katharine's church between 1861 and 1864.[24] In the late 19th century it was for girls.[25] In the 20th it was mixed. Between 1906–7 and 1926–7 average attendance was highest at 78 and lowest at 41; in the 1930s it was c. 106.[26] In 1996 there were 53 children on the roll.[27] From 1946 to 1994 Tottenham House was used as Hawtreys preparatory school for boys.[28]

CHARITIES FOR THE POOR. By deed of 1604 Sir Anthony Hungerford (d. 1627) gave £10 a year to apprentice two children born in Great Bedwyn village. In the earlier 19th century an average of one boy a year was apprenticed, and one boy was apprenticed in each of the years 1899–1902.[29] By a Scheme of 1914 the income was used to equip young people for a trade or to prepare them for a career. In the late 20th century occasional gifts of money were made; three beneficiaries shared £142 in 1986 and one received £30 in 1989.[30]

By the early 19th century John Bushell had given a rent charge of 10s. to provide 6d. a year for poor widows of Great Bedwyn village at Christmas; each year in the earlier 19th century fewer than 20 received money.[31] W. G. Pike (d. 1839), Georgina Pike (will proved 1871), and John Sawyer (will proved 1880) each gave by will £100 for the poor of Great Bedwyn parish. In 1903 the income from those three charities and from Bushell's was c. £9, of which the share of Grafton parish was £1 10s. In Great Bedwyn parish £3 was given to a clothing club and the rest of the income was given away in sums of 5s. or less.[32] Income and the pattern of expenditure had changed little by 1928.[33] In the 1970s sums of 50p were given.[34] Under a Scheme of 1987 the income and assetts of all four charities were given to a day centre for old people in 1987–8.[35]

By will proved 1877 John Miles gave £200 to provide gifts of 1s. to 20 widows or widowers of East Grafton, West Grafton, Wexcombe, and Wilton and gifts of money or coal to labourers working on Upper farm, Wexcombe. In 1904 £6 was distributed among 17 widows, 14 widowers, and 16 labourers;[36] 20 widows and widowers each received 1s., and 17 labourers each 5s. 4½d., in 1923.[37] The charity had been wound up by 1993.[38]

99 Char. Com. file.
1 Sale cat. and acct. bk. in church; inf. from Mr. M. Scott, Wessex Ho., 7 Church Street; for the schs., below, this section.　　　　　　　　　2 Char. Com. file.
3 *Endowed Char. Wilts.* (N. Div.), 38; *W.A.M.* vi. 290.
4 W.R.O. 2649/1; Char. Com. file; below, charities.
5 *Educ. of Poor Digest*, 1018.
6 *Educ. Enq. Abstract*, 1028.
7 e.g. Nat. Soc. *Inquiry, 1846–7*, Wilts. 2–3; below, this section.　　　　　　8 Date on bldg.
9 Nat. Soc. *Inquiry, 1846–7*, Wilts. 2–3.
10 P.R.O., ED 7/130, no. 133.
11 *Acct. of Wilts. Schs.* 5.
12 *Bd. of Educ., List 21, 1908–38* (H.M.S.O.).
13 Inf. from Director of Educ., Co. Hall, Trowbridge.
14 P.R.O., ED 7/130, no. 132.
15 *Acct. of Wilts. Schs.* 5.
16 W.R.O., F 8/500/130/2/1.
17 *Bd. of Educ., List 21, 1908–38* (H.M.S.O.).
18 Wilts. co. council, *Sched. of Educ. Establishments* (1996), p. 4.　　　　19 *Acct. of Wilts. Schs.* 5.
20 O.S. Maps 1/2,500, Wilts. XLIII. 1 (1880, 1900 edns.).

21 *Acct. of Wilts. Schs.* 5; above, nonconf.
22 *Kelly's Dir. Wilts.* (1880, 1885).
23 *Acct. of Wilts. Schs.* 41.
24 W.R.O., D 1/56/7; the date of the opening of the sch. is given as 1865 in *St. Katharines, Savernake* (church guide); as 1867 in P.R.O., ED 7/130, no. 134.
25 O.S. Map 1/2,500, Wilts. XXXVI. 8 (1880 edn.).
26 *Bd. of Educ., List 21, 1908–38* (H.M.S.O.).
27 Wilts. co. council, *Sched. of Educ. Establishments* (1996), p. 8.
28 *Daily Telegraph*, 17 Dec. 1994.
29 *Endowed Char. Wilts.* (N. Div.), 32, 35–6; *W.A.M.* vi. 290; *Hist. Parl., Commons, 1558–1603*, 353.
30 Char. Com. file.
31 *Endowed Char. Wilts.* (N. Div.), 33.
32 Ibid. 36, 38–9.
33 W.R.O., L 2, Great Bedwyn.
34 Ibid. 2649/1.
35 Ibid. 2649/4; Char. Com. file.
36 *Endowed Char. Wilts.* (N. Div.), 40–1.
37 W.R.O., L 2, Great Bedwyn.
38 Char. Com. file.

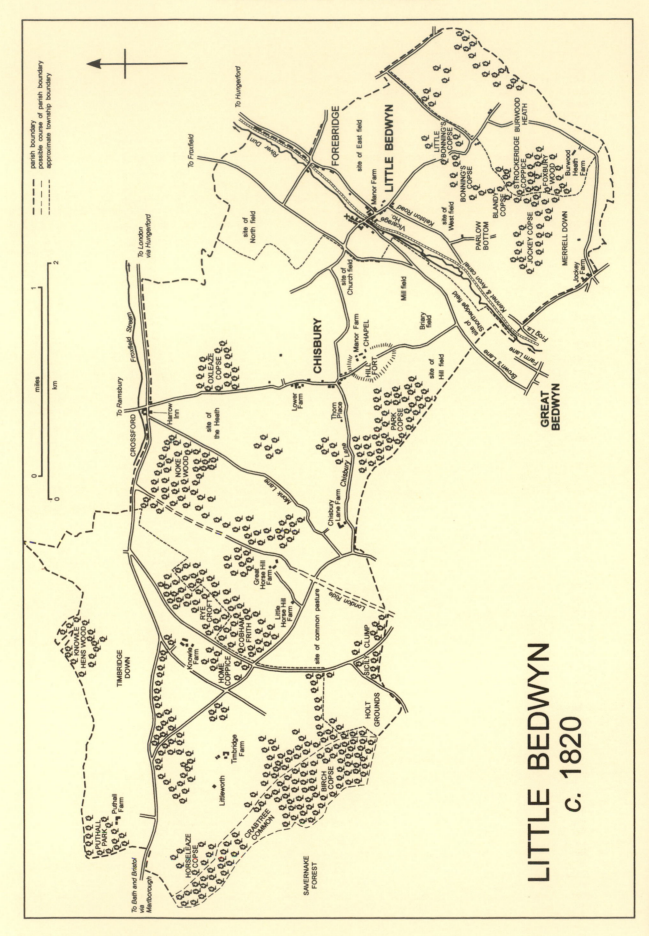

LITTLE BEDWYN
c. 1820

LITTLE BEDWYN

LITTLE BEDWYN parish,[39] lying ESE. of Marlborough and WSW. of Hungerford (Berks.), contains Little Bedwyn village, Chisbury village, and several outlying farmsteads. Most of it was apparently part of a large estate called Bedwyn held in the early Middle Ages by the kings of Wessex and of England: Chisbury was apparently separated from the estate in 778, Little Bedwyn in the 12th century or early 13th.[40] A church built at Little Bedwyn no later than the 12th century was dependent on Great Bedwyn church in the 15th; the inhabitants of Little Bedwyn had all rights in their church, which was a parish church in the 16th century.[41] The inhabitants of Chisbury may have been parishioners of Froxfield until the 13th century; after 1547, the year from which a church built at Chisbury in the earlier 13th century and dependent on Great Bedwyn church was no longer served,[42] they were parishioners of Little Bedwyn. The farmsteads west of Chisbury village, and those on Burwood heath south-east of Little Bedwyn village, were also part of Little Bedwyn parish from the 16th century.[43] In the early 19th century it was apparently uncertain whether the parish included at its west end c. 150 a. of Savernake forest;[44] the land was part of the parish in the 1880s.[45] From the 1880s to 1987 the parish measured 4,343 a. (1,758 ha.); it was reduced to 1,710 ha. by a transfer to Great Bedwyn in 1987.[46]

The boundary of an estate said to lie at Bedwyn and apparently the land of Chisbury was recited in 778. No point on it can be unequivocally identified with a point on the modern parish boundary. On the north the boundary of the estate, probably with land later part of Froxfield parish, was marked by prehistoric monuments, a barrow, and a possible site of pagan worship. On the south the boundary between Little Bedwyn and Great Bedwyn parish seems to follow roughly a line recorded in 778 and 968.[47] The modern boundary of Little Bedwyn follows ridges and dry valleys in several places. For a short stretch on the east it was marked by a road until, between the 1790s and 1812, it was transferred to the canal which was built beside the road. On the north it probably followed a stream flowing eastwards to Froxfield; by the early 19th century it was marked by the main road which runs beside the stream and along the dry valley above it.[48] Other roads mark the boundary in several other places.

Little Bedwyn is a parish of broken relief drained by the river Dun, formerly called the Bedwyn river or the Bedwyn brook, which flows north-eastwards across the south-east part of the parish;[49] the stream flowing eastwards to join the Dun at Froxfield, sometimes called the Froxfield stream, formerly flowed across the parish and cut the dry east–west valley followed by the main road. North of the dry valley chalk outcrops and, on the higher ground near the parish boundary, there are deposits of clay-with-flints. Between the dry valley and the Dun chalk outcrops on the lower slopes, and Reading Beds, London Clay, and Bagshot Beds outcrop on the higher. Gravel has been deposited along the valley, in several other places, and extensively south of Knowle Farm; clay-with-flints has been deposited east and west of Chisbury village and at the west end of the parish; deposits of plateau gravel lie within Chisbury hill fort. South-east of the Dun chalk outcrops on the lower slopes, and Reading Beds and London Clay outcrop on the higher. There is alluvium beside the Dun.[50] At 176 m. Chisbury hill fort is the highest point in the parish; where the Dun leaves it at c. 110 m. is the lowest. Little Bedwyn and Chisbury had open fields mainly on the chalk, Little Bedwyn's being on both sides of the Dun; there may have been small open fields in the west part of the parish in the Middle Ages, when the clay and sandy soils were apparently mainly pasture. The parish is well wooded, some of the woodland in the west being joined to that of Savernake forest.[51]

The population of the parish was 428 in 1801. Between then and 1841 it rose steadily to reach its peak at 597. For reasons which are obscure it fell from 591 to 496 between 1851 and 1861 and rose to 579 between 1861 and 1871. It had declined to 456 by 1901 and risen to 505 by 1911. Thereafter it declined steadily to reach 254 in 1981. Although it lost population by the boundary change of 1987 Little Bedwyn parish had 286 inhabitants in 1991.[52]

The road from London to Bath and Bristol probably crossed the north part of the parish in the 13th century in the valley cut by the Froxfield stream,[53] and it was on its present course in 1675.[54] It was turnpiked through the parish in 1726, disturnpiked in 1871.[55] Roads linking Little Bedwyn with Hungerford, via the London road, and with Great Bedwyn may have followed the Dun closely on each bank, that on the

39 This article was written in 1998. Maps used include O.S. Maps 6", Wilts. XXIX–XXX, XXXVI–XXXVII (1887–9 and later edns.); 1/25,000, SU 26/36 (1983 edn.).
40 Above, Great Bedwyn, manors [preamble]; below, manors (Little Bedwyn; Chisbury).
41 Below, church.   42 Ibid.; ibid. manors [tithes].
43 W.R.O., bishop's transcripts, bdle. 1.
44 Ibid. 1955/25; C. Greenwood, Map of Wilts. (1820).
45 O.S. Maps 6", Wilts. XXIX, XXXVI (1888–9 edns.).
46 Census, 1991; Statutory Instruments, 1987, no. 619, Kennet (Parishes) Order.
47 Arch. Jnl. lxxvi. 151–5; lxxvii. 75–6, 79–80; W.A.M. xli. 293–7; xlv. 525–6. In the 1st and 3rd sources unconvincing attempts are made to relate the 8th-cent. boundaries to modern par. boundaries; for comment on the chart. of 968, above, Great Bedwyn, manors [preamble], n. 28.
48 Arch. Jnl. lxxvi. 154–5; W.R.O. 1955/25; ibid. EA/68; below, this section [canal].
49 For the Dun, above, Great Bedwyn, intro.
50 Geol. Surv. Maps 1/50,000, drift, sheet 266 (1974 edn.); 1", drift, sheet 267 (1971 edn.).
51 Below, econ. hist.
52 V.C.H. Wilts. iv. 340; Census, 1961; 1971; 1981; 1991.
53 V.C.H. Wilts. iv. 255, 448.
54 J. Ogilby, Brit. (1675), pl. 10.
55 V.C.H. Wilts. iv. 257–8, 267; L.J. xxii. 664.

north-west bank leading to Farm Lane in Great Bedwyn, that on the south-east bank to Frog Lane in Great Bedwyn. By the late 18th century most of the road on the north-west bank had been diverted to higher ground, crossing a ridge from the London road at Froxfield and leading to Brown's Lane in Great Bedwyn. South-west of Little Bedwyn village part of that on the south-east bank had also been diverted to higher ground by then;[56] the new section of road was later called Kelston Road. Close to the river, footpaths and sections of road remained in use on both banks in 1998. A north–south road leading from Ramsbury towards Great Bedwyn crossed Chisbury hill fort; its crossing of the London road on the northern parish boundary, near where it crossed the Froxfield stream, had been given the name Crossford by 1773. Then and later the road was apparently of no more than local importance.[57] In the west part of the parish the courses of most lanes changed little between the early 18th century[58] and 1998. Chisbury Lane, leading west from Chisbury village, was so called in 1609.[59] Monk Lane, leading south-west from Crossford, has largely gone out of use,[60] a lane leading south-west from the London road near Knowle Farm was largely obliterated in the 20th century, and east of Knowle Farm another lane leading south-west from the London road was remade on a new straight course between 1820 and 1885.[61] To improve the route between Marlborough and Great Bedwyn a new straight section of road running south-east from the London road, and joining the existing road south of Knowle Farm, was made between 1773 and 1817.[62] London ride, a north-east and south-west avenue linking Tottenham House in Great Bedwyn to the London road, was made across the west part of the parish c. 1730.[63]

The Kennet & Avon canal was built beside the Dun in the late 1790s. In 1799 it was opened across the parish, in which there are two locks, and in 1810 was opened completely.[64] It was restored across the parish in the mid 1970s.[65]

The Berks. & Hants Extension Railway was built along the north-west side of the canal and opened across the parish in 1862. The line led from Reading to Devizes, from 1900 to Westbury, and from 1906 to Exeter. It has a station at Great Bedwyn.[66]

Hand axes used in the Palaeolithic period and artefacts of the Neolithic period and the Bronze Age were found near Knowle Farm in the west part of the parish; an implement of the Palaeolithic period, and Roman coins and other Roman

artefacts, were found at Chisbury.[67] Also at Chisbury the banks and ditches of a hill fort, probably constructed in the 1st century A.D., remain well defined.[68] South-east of the hill fort an ancient ditch lies north-west and south-east; a ditch leading south-west from the hill fort has been obliterated. There may have been other ancient ditches in the west part of the parish.[69] A bowl barrow seen south-east of the hill fort in the 18th century has not survived.[70]

The whole parish lay within Savernake forest, the part north of the London road only until 1228.[71] About 1302 part of the forest at a place called Little farm, probably what was later called Littleworth farm, was granted by the king and apparently assarted.[72] When new boundaries of the forest were adopted in 1330 the land at the west end of the parish about which there was uncertainty in the early 19th century remained within them; the rest of the parish was placed outside. On the grounds that they had been parts of the forest leased by the king, or were held in chief of him, Puthall, Timbridge, Littleworth, and Holt, all in the west part of the parish, were some of the places subject to the forest law although from 1330 outside the boundary.[73] Timbridge down and most of Puthall's land, held in chief, lay north of the London road and had been outside the forest since 1228.[74]

LITTLE BEDWYN. The church stands at the north end of the village on the north-west bank of the Dun. In the Middle Ages the demesne farmstead of Little Bedwyn manor, incorporating a manor house or a farmhouse, may have stood near the church, and the copyhold farmsteads of the manor were apparently built on either side of the Dun beside a north-west and south-east street. In the early 14th century the village probably consisted of little more than the church, the demesne farmstead of Little Bedwyn manor, a mill, and the farmsteads of seven customary tenants.[75]

In the mid 18th century a house which has sometimes been lived in by the lord of Little Bedwyn manor and sometimes by the lessee of the demesne farm,[76] later called Manor farm, was built south-east of the Dun on the north-east side of the street. In the late 18th century no manor house or farmhouse stood near the church, which by then had been linked to the street by a short lane later called Church Street. A large barn and other buildings of the demesne farm then stood on the south-east side of Church Street, other buildings on the north-west side.[77] The Dun had been bridged by 1773.[78] In 1792

56 W.R.O., EA/68; ibid. 9/3/387; cf. above, Great Bedwyn, intro. (Great Bedwyn: streets).
57 Andrews and Dury, Map (W.R.S. viii), pl. 12.
58 W.R.O. 1300/372, ff. 7, 20, 22, 36.
59 Ibid. 9/8/144, ct. 12 June 1609.
60 Cf. ibid. 1300/372, f. 7.
61 Ibid. f. 20; Greenwood, Map of Wilts.; O.S. Maps 6", Wilts. XXIX, XXXVI (1888–9 and later edns.).
62 Andrews and Dury, Map (W.R.S. viii), pl. 12; O.S. Map 1", sheet 14 (1817 edn.); W.R.O. 1300/372, f. 36.
63 W.R.O. 9/3/388; above, Great Bedwyn, manors (Tottenham).
64 K. R. Clew, Kennet & Avon Canal (1985), 60, 73; W.R.O. 1955/25.
65 Kennet and Avon Canal: a Leisure Strategy (pub. Brit. Waterways: copy in Wilts. local studies libr., Trowbridge), 7.
66 V.C.H. Wilts. iv. 286–7, 289.
67 Ibid. i (1), 82–3; W.A.M. lxxvii, 144–5.
68 V.C.H. Wilts. i (1), 267; i (2), 431, 436.
69 Ibid. i (1), 257; i (2), 479; W.A.M. lv. 119–21.
70 V.C.H. Wilts. i (1), 181.   71 Ibid. iv. 418, 451.
72 Cal. Pat. 1301–7, 59; for Littleworth farm, below, econ. hist. (Timbridge and Littleworth).
73 V.C.H. Wilts. iv. 399–400, 450–1; W.A.M. xlix. 415–17; W.R.O. 1300/47A; for the W. end of the par., above, this section.
74 V.C.H. Wilts. iv. 418, 451; W.R.O. 1300/372, ff. 22, 36; below, manors (Puthall; Timbridge).
75 Wilts. Inq. p.m. 1242–1326 (Index Libr.), 381.
76 e.g. W.A.M. xliii. 494; W.R.O., A 1/345/27; ibid. 9/8/146, ct. 21 Oct. 1767.   77 W.R.O., EA/68.
78 Andrews and Dury, Map (W.R.S. viii), pl. 12.

the village consisted of the church, a vicarage house, four farmsteads, and *c.* 15 houses and cottages.[79] Although each is bridged, the canal and the railway, built in the late 1790s and early 1860s respectively,[80] form a barrier between the north-west and south-east parts of the village, which was designated a conservation area in 1985.[81]

The house built in the mid 18th century is of red brick and in 1998 stood as a north-west range against which a south-east block, also of red brick, had been built *c.* 1800. In 1998 the house was called Manor House. The part of the newer block which forms the centre of its south-west front projects and has a Tuscan porch and a pediment in which there is a semicircular window. In the 18th century the garden of the house was walled, a summer house was built in the garden, and red-brick stables were built between the house and the Dun. Adjoining the stables a small 18th-century building, red-brick and on a circular plan, may have been a game larder. The farm buildings north-west of the Dun were demolished between 1841 and 1884, probably when the railway was built. A new barn, timber-framed, weatherboarded, and thatched, was built north-east of the stables between 1792 and 1841,[82] and north-east of it new farm buildings were erected in the 20th century.

Of the other farmsteads standing in 1792,[83] one north-west of the Dun and two south-east, the only building standing in 1998 was the farmhouse of that north-west: it is 17th-century, timber-framed, and thatched, and much of its walling has been clad with brick. North-west of the Dun a pair of red-brick and thatched cottages was built in the late 18th century or early 19th, and two of the buildings standing in Church Street in 1792 were replaced in the 19th century, one by a pair of cottages dated 1860.[84] South-east of the Dun a terrace incorporating two pairs of cottages was apparently built shortly before 1841,[85] and in Kelston Road a terrace of four estate cottages was built *c.* 1860. A house which may have been the vicarage house between *c.* 1845 and 1863 was enlarged in the later 19th century.

Little Bedwyn village remains small, although from the later 19th century buildings were erected on new sites at its edges. At the north-west end on high ground a new school and a new vicarage house were built in the later 19th century.[86] At the south-east end in Kelston Road a large house was built *c.* 1910,[87] three linked pairs of cottages were built as a crescent in 1936 and a fourth was built in 1961,[88] and four other houses were built in the 20th century. The eight

cottages[89] were built by trustees of S. W. Farmer (d. 1926) to house retired farm labourers. The trustees sold them to a housing association in 1996.[90] The site of a nonconformist chapel at the south-east end of the village was used for a house in the late 20th century,[91] and, each time further south-east, new farm buildings were erected in the mid 20th century and in 1971.[92]

At the junction of Kelston Road and the village street the Harrow inn, a building of red and blue bricks with a slate roof, took the name of an inn on the London road and was open in 1840.[93] It was closed in 1990, bought in 1991 by inhabitants of the village,[94] and open in 1998.

CHISBURY. A statement made in the 13th century that Chisbury took its name from, and was the site of a castle built by, Cissa in the late 7th century is almost certainly fantasy.[95] It has also been suggested that the hill fort at Chisbury was prepared as a fortress for defence by King Alfred (d. 899) against the Danes. The suggestion depends on the form of the name, 'Cissanbyrig', in a copy of a list of Alfred's fortresses and, especially because the name appears between Wilton and Shaftesbury (Dors.) in the list, it is more likely that the fortress was near Tisbury than at Chisbury.[96]

In the 14th century a manor house, Chisbury church, and farm buildings described in 1398 as old stood within the hill fort. The manor house incorporated a hall, with a high chamber at the west end and roofed with stone slates, a tower, containing a chapel and a chamber and roofed with lead, and a latrine roofed with tiles; it had a gatehouse and probably a moat.[97] The house standing within the hill fort in 1612, a building with a west front of three wide gabled bays with chimney stacks between the bays,[98] may have survived until the late 18th century, when a new house, later called Manor Farm and Chisbury Manor, was built on its site. The new house incorporates re-used materials, bears the date 1793 on the leadwork of a downpipe, and has a three-bayed south front and two short rear wings. It was much altered inside *c.* 1985, when fittings in mid 18th-century style were introduced. North of the house an outbuilding is possibly 17th-century and there is an 18th-century walled garden; east of the house old farm buildings were replaced *c.* 1985 by a house which incorporates an octagonal tower.[99] In 1998 the farm buildings within the hill fort stood near Chisbury church and were mostly 20th-century.

Chisbury had fewer than 10 households in 1428,[1] and in the 16th and 17th centuries included, apart from that within the hill fort, no

[79] W.R.O., EA/68; for successive vicarage hos., below, church.
[80] Above, this section.
[81] Inf. from Dept. of Planning and Highways, Co. Hall, Trowbridge.
[82] O.S. Map 6", Wilts. XXXVII (1887 edn.); W.R.O., tithe award; ibid. EA/68.
[83] W.R.O., EA/68.
[84] Ibid.; date on bldg.   [85] Cf. W.R.O., tithe award.
[86] Below, church; educ.
[87] W.R.O., G 8/760/14.
[88] Dates on bldgs.   [89] Below, plate 33.
[90] Inf. from Mr. D. Gauntlett, 4 Isles Ct., Ramsbury.

[91] Cf. O.S. Map 6", Wilts. XXXVII. NW. (1926 edn.); below, nonconf.
[92] Below, econ. hist. (Little Bedwyn).
[93] W.R.O., tithe award; cf. below, this section (other settlement).
[94] *Daily Telegraph*, 16 Aug. 1991.
[95] Above, Great Bedwyn, intro. (Great Bedwyn).
[96] *Medieval Arch*. viii. 74–9; xiii. 84–92; *V.C.H. Wilts.* ii, p. 15; xiii. 197.
[97] *Cal. Inq. Misc.* vi. 151; for Chisbury ch., below, church.   [98] W.R.O. 9/8/153H.
[99] Inf. from Mrs. L. Stafford-Deitsch, Chisbury Manor.
[1] *V.C.H. Wilts.* iv. 314.

more than about five farmsteads. One of the farmsteads in 1552 was Thorn Place,[2] which stood in Chisbury Lane. In 1719 there were six farmsteads, four on the west side of the Ramsbury road and two in the lane; seven houses and cottages stood near the junction of the road and the lane, and a house and two cottages stood on the edge of a common pasture east of the road.[3] The only building which undoubtedly survives from 1719 is a red-brick and thatched farmhouse of the late 17th century beside the Ramsbury road. It was apparently superseded by a new farmhouse and in 1998 was occupied as two cottages. The new house, later called Lower Farm, was built of red brick c. 1800. Three cottages and a range of what was three cottages,[4] all of red brick and thatch and incorporating timber framing, are apparently 18th-century, and a house on the site of Thorn Place is possibly of 18th-century origin. In the mid 19th century a pair of cottages and a farmhouse later converted to cottages were built at the junction of the Ramsbury road and Chisbury Lane, where a mission room was built in the later 19th century.[5] Of 15 houses built in the village in the 20th century six were council houses which had been built in Chisbury Lane by 1922,[6] two were estate cottages built on the east side of the Ramsbury road in the 1950s,[7] and two were built immediately south of the hill fort. Large farm buildings were erected on the east side of the Ramsbury road in the 20th century. In 1998 no building stood on the sites occupied in 1719 by a farmstead in Chisbury Lane and by the house and cottages east of the Ramsbury road. The village was designated a conservation area in 1993.[8]

OTHER SETTLEMENT. In the south-east part of the parish two farmsteads had been built by the mid 16th century on Burwood heath.[9] Pasture on the heath was inclosed c. 1570, and on or near the heath two or three new farmsteads may have been built soon afterwards.[10] In 1672 each of four livings said to lie on Burwood heath may have included a farmstead there.[11] In the later 18th century there were three farmsteads on or near the heath.[12] The sites of two were deserted in the 19th century.[13] At the third, Burwood (later Burridge) Heath Farm, a new house was built in 1909,[14] and by 1998 farm buildings had been converted for residence.

North-east of Little Bedwyn village a small farmstead stood in 1719[15] where by 1817 a hamlet had been given the name Forebridge.[16] In 1792 the hamlet consisted of four small houses and a building called a workhouse. Three of the houses survive and were probably built in the 18th century. One had been demolished by 1841; the workhouse, occupied as three tenements in 1841, had been demolished by 1884. Two new cottages were built at Forebridge between 1792 and 1841 and a house and five cottages between 1841 and 1884;[17] of all those only the house and a pair of much altered mid 19th-century cottages survived in 1998.

South of Little Bedwyn village a house stood on Merrell down in the 16th century[18] and from the 18th century.[19] About 1770 a house there was said to be new:[20] it may be that, 18th-century and of red brick and thatch, which stood there in 1998.[21] On the parish boundary nearby the Horse and Jockey was an inn in 1773.[22] The buildings on its site were those of a farmstead from 1788 or earlier.[23] The farm buildings had been removed by 1884,[24] and in the 20th century the house, built in the 18th century, probably the former inn, and much enlarged, was occupied as three cottages.[25] Also south of Little Bedwyn village a pair of cottages and farm buildings were built in Parlow bottom in the mid 19th century. The cottages, of red brick with lancet-style windows, were occupied as a house in 1998. South-west of the village a pair of cottages was built beside the Great Bedwyn road in the mid 19th century.[26]

In the west part of the parish, west of Chisbury's land, settlements apparently stood on eight sites in the Middle Ages. Some possibly had their own open fields and may have consisted of several farmsteads; others may have been planted as single isolated farmsteads. They all stood near the edge of the woodland of Savernake forest, probably on land brought into cultivation later than that of Little Bedwyn and Chisbury. Two of the sites had been deserted by the 16th century, when there was apparently no more than a single farmstead at all but one of the others.[27]

Chisbury Lane Farm has stood at the west end of Chisbury Lane from 1719 or earlier;[28] in 1998 it consisted of a 19th-century house bearing a date stone for 1629, and mainly 20th-century farm buildings. North-west of it Upper Horsehall Hill Farm, formerly Great Horse Hill Farm, was built on high ground. A farmhouse of 18th-century origin and altered in the later 19th century, a smaller house, of red brick and thatch

2 W.R.O. 9/1/95, pp. 45–53; 9/8/147.
3 Ibid. 9/8/149; 1300/372, ff. 7, 10.
4 Cf. O.S. Map 1/2,500, Wilts. XXXVII. 1 (1880 edn.).
5 Below, church.
6 O.S. Map 1/2,500, Wilts. XXXVII. 1 (1924 edn.).
7 Cf. ibid. 1/25,000, SU 26 (1961 edn.); below, manors (Chisbury).
8 Inf. from Dept. of Planning and Highways, Co. Hall, Trowbridge.
9 W.R.O. 9/1/95, pp. 50, 53.
10 Below, econ. hist. (Little Bedwyn; Burwood heath).
11 W.R.O. 9/4/88.
12 Ibid. EA/68; Andrews and Dury, Map (W.R.S. viii), pl. 12.
13 O.S. Map 6", Wilts. XXXVII. NW. (1900 edn.); W.R.O., tithe award.
14 Date on bldg.   15 W.R.O. 1300/372, f. 18.

16 O.S. Map 1", sheet 14 (1817 edn.).
17 Ibid. 6", Wilts. XXXVII (1887 edn.); W.R.O., EA/68; ibid. tithe award; for the workhouse, cf. below, local govt.
18 W.R.O. 9/5/28.
19 Ibid. 1064/19, deed, Goddard to Streat, 1700.
20 Ibid. 9/4/88.
21 No ho. on Merrell down was marked on a map of 1792: ibid. EA/68.
22 Andrews and Dury, Map (W.R.S. viii), pl. 12.
23 W.R.O. 79B/11, lease, Tucker to Hawkins, 1788.
24 O.S. Map 6", Wilts. XXXVII (1887 edn.).
25 Ibid. 1/2,500, Wilts. XXXVII. 5 (1924 edn.); W.R.O. 1010/22.
26 O.S. Map 6", Wilts. XXXVII (1887 edn.); W.R.O., tithe award.
27 Below, this section; econ. hist. (except Little Bedwyn; Burwood heath).   28 W.R.O. 1300/372, f. 7.

and apparently 18th-century, and farm buildings stood on the site in 1998. On lower ground south-west of that site a timber-framed and thatched house, Lower Horsehall Hill Cottage, formerly Little Horse Hill Farm, was built as a farmhouse in the 17th century[29] and was standing in 1998. Near the parish boundary west of Chisbury Lane Farm a farmstead called Holt had apparently been deserted by 1552.[30]

Knowle was a settlement in the 13th century;[31] c. 1311 it probably consisted of no more than a demesne farmstead and the homes of six cottars,[32] and, apart from the farmhouse, there was no domestic building on the site in 1716.[33] A small chapel was built at the farmstead in the 14th century. The farmhouse, called Knowle House in 1998, was rebuilt in 1733 for Edward Savage,[34] who held Knowle farm by a lease on lives.[35] Knowle House is of red and grey brick and has a north-west entrance front of five bays with a central pediment; it contains an oak staircase of high quality, and several rooms retain panelling of c. 1733; a south-east service wing was built in the 19th century. In 1998 the chapel stood immediately south-east of the house, and vestiges of a garden which lay immediately south-west of the house in the 18th century[36] could still be seen. The farm buildings, north-east of the house, were mainly 20th-century, and a later 20th-century bungalow stood near them. North of the farmstead a pair of cottages was built in the 19th century[37] where the track to the farmstead left the London road.

Puthall was almost certainly the small village of which in the Middle Ages the buildings stood on a site adjoining the present Puthall Farm to the north and east.[38] The name Puttan ealh was in use in the 8th century;[39] Puthall was a settlement in the 12th.[40] There may have been no more than a single farmstead there in the later 14th century,[41] as there was in the early 16th century[42] and later.[43] The farmhouse standing in 1998 was built on a three-roomed plan in the 17th century; it had a large internal chimney stack and a lobby entrance. In the early 19th century it was extended eastwards and refitted. The farm buildings stand east of the house, include part of a 19th-century farmyard, and are otherwise 20th-century. South of the farmstead a pair of cottages was built in the 19th century where the track to the farmstead left the London road,[44] and a bungalow was built beside the track in the later 20th century.

Timbridge was apparently a small settlement in the early 14th century,[45] and in the early 18th consisted of two small farmsteads. One of the farmhouses was rebuilt in the mid 18th century and, as Timbridge Farm,[46] was standing in 1998. The house has a three-bayed east front of brick with Venetian windows on the first floor. It was extended westwards by a low dairy built in the 18th century or early 19th and by a large new kitchen, built in the early 19th century, in which substantial timbers worked in the 16th or 17th century were re-used. In 1998 a small 19th-century stable yard, extensive 20th-century farm buildings, and a pair of cottages built in 1958[47] stood east of the house. On the site of the second farmstead, a little north of Timbridge Farm, there was no more than a pair of cottages in the late 19th century; the cottages were demolished in the later 20th century.[48]

Henset, first mentioned in the early 12th century,[49] was probably a small village, on the site of which a farmstead may have stood in the 14th century.[50] Its land was apparently that north of the London road and east of Timbridge down.[51] The site of the settlement, which was deserted, is unknown.[52] A farmstead called Littleworth standing west of Timbridge Farm in the 18th century[53] may have originated as one built on part of Savernake forest assarted c. 1302.[54] Buildings stood on the site of the farmstead until the early 20th century.[55]

Beside the London road a house or cottage called the Harrow was built c. 1765;[56] it was presumably the thatched house on the east side of the Ramsbury road standing in 1998. Also beside the London road a red-brick house was built immediately west of the Ramsbury road c. 1800; the house, the outbuildings of which stood on the north side of the road in Froxfield parish, was open as the Harrow inn in 1812.[57] By 1841 it had become a farmhouse and its outbuildings had been converted to farm buildings.[58] In 1998 the house remained the only part of Harrow Farm in Little Bedwyn parish. West of Harrow Farm the Golden Arrow café, a bungalow, a petrol station, and a commercial garage were built together on the north side of the London road c. 1930: in 1998 the wooden tea room built in 1930,[59] two bungalows, and a petrol station stood on the site.

In the west part of the parish two pairs of ornamental cottages were built beside the Great Bedwyn road in the 19th century. Voronzoff

29 Cf. ibid.; ibid. 9/8/149.
30 Ibid. 9/1/95, p. 52.
31 Crown Pleas, 1249 (W.R.S. xvi), p. 218; Feet of F. 1272–1327 (W.R.S. i), p. 36.
32 Wilts. Inq. p.m. 1242–1326 (Index Libr.), 382.
33 W.R.O. 1300/372, f. 20.
34 ES/1733 on rainwater hopper.   35 W.R.O. 9/5/39.
36 Andrews and Dury, Map (W.R.S. viii), pl. 12.
37 Cf. O.S. Map 1/2,500, Wilts. XXIX. 16 (1886 edn.).
38 The site has been ascribed to Henset on O.S. Maps: e.g. 1/25,000, SU 26/36 (1983 edn.).
39 Arch. Jnl. lxxvi. 153.
40 Pipe R. 1191 & 92 (P.R.S. N.S. ii), 281; Cur. Reg. R. i. 424.
41 W.R.O. 1300/20.
42 Longleat Mun., Seymour papers, xii, f. 309.
43 e.g. W.R.O. 1300/372, ff. 22–3.
44 Cf. O.S. Map 1/2,500, Wilts. XXIX. 15 (1886 edn.).
45 Wilts. Inq. p.m. 1242–1326 (Index Libr.), 313; Cal.

Close, 1323–7, 389–90.
46 W.R.O. 1300/372, ff. 36–7; Savernake estate map, c. 1820 (copy in W.R.O.).
47 Date on bldg.
48 O.S. Maps 1/2,500, Wilts. XXIX. 16 (1886 edn.); 1/25,000, SU 26 (1961 edn.).
49 Reg. Regum Anglo-Norm. ii, no. 1204A.
50 P.R.O., C 260/132, no. 1.
51 Cat. Anct. D. ii, C 2891.
52 It was probably not that indicated on O.S. maps: above, this section [Puthall].
53 Andrews and Dury, Map (W.R.S. viii), pl. 12.
54 Above, this section [Savernake forest].
55 O.S. Maps 6", Wilts. XXIX. SE. (1900, 1925 edns.).
56 W.R.O. 9/8/150–1.
57 Ibid. 9/8/154; 1955/25.
58 Ibid. tithe award; Froxfield tithe award.
59 Ibid. G 8/505/1; G 8/760/111; G 8/760/130.

Gate, of patterned polychrome brickwork incorporating the date 1856, with fretted bargeboards, and with stone details in Gothic style at the doorway and windows, was built beside the London road.

MANORS AND OTHER ESTATES. Little Bedwyn was probably part of the estate called Bedwyn which passed with the crown almost certainly from the 8th century. The estate was held by Abingdon abbey (Berks., later Oxon.) from 968 to 975, and from 978 again passed with the crown. When the estate was granted by Henry I to his marshal John FitzGilbert, probably c. 1130,[60] Little Bedwyn may not have been part of it. In 1154–5 Little Bedwyn was apparently held by Walter Waleran, and by 1156 it had apparently been resumed by the Crown. Little Bedwyn manor had been infeudated or subinfeudated by c. 1211:[61] in the 14th century it was sometimes said to be held in chief, sometimes of John FitzGilbert's successors in title.[62]

LITTLE BEDWYN manor was held c. 1211 by John Russel; 1 yardland at Little Bedwyn held by Russel for the service of providing two bushels of wine for the king[63] presumably became part of the manor. Russel (d. 1220 × 1224) had a son Ralph (fl. 1239), and Ralph Russel (d. c. 1278), presumably another, held Little Bedwyn manor in 1275 as ½ knight's fee.[64] The manor passed, probably at that Ralph's death, to his son William Russel (d. c. 1311). William was succeeded by his son Theobald.[65]

About 1325–6 Theobald Russel sold 1 carucate, probably part of Little Bedwyn manor, to William Musard[66] (d. 1330). The rest of the manor was also acquired by Musard, and it descended to his son William.[67] By 1332 the second of those estates had possibly been acquired by William Braybrook,[68] and it was probably that, described as Little Bedwyn manor, in 1348 settled by Braybrook on himself and his wife Margery and on the marriage of his son William to Elizabeth Musard.[69] The land sold c. 1325–6 apparently passed in turn to the younger William Musard and to Elizabeth Musard, his sister or daughter. Elizabeth and the younger William Braybrook had three daughters, Margery, the wife of Thomas Hansworth,

John Short, and John Sydele, Alice, the wife of John Shaw and Richard Rock, and Olive. After William's death Elizabeth married John Scot.[70]

The estate settled in 1348 was held from Elizabeth Scot's death in 1391 by John Scot (fl. 1397) with reversion to Alice Shaw,[71] and it descended on Richard Rock's death in 1428 to Alice's daughter Anne Rock, the wife of Richard Axsmith.[72] In 1438 the Axsmiths sold it to Nicholas Wootton[73] (d. 1454), whose heirs were his daughter Agnes, the wife of William York, and his granddaughter Emmote Mills;[74] the estate was apparently assigned to Emmote, from 1458 or earlier the wife of Henry Organ.[75] The land conveyed c. 1325–6 was held from Elizabeth Scot's death by John Scot, who in 1397, in exchange for a pension for life, gave up his interest to Margery Sydele and to Olive Braybrook's daughter Joan, the wife of John Staplehill[76] (d. 1436). Joan's estate at Little Bedwyn descended to John Staplehill, John's son and probably hers;[77] in 1454 John sold it to William York,[78] and it later belonged to Henry Organ. On Organ's death in 1499 that estate and his wife's, each described as a third of Little Bedwyn manor, passed to his and Emmote's son Richard[79] (d. 1506), who was succeeded by his son John[80] (d. 1559). From 1559 the two thirds was held for life by John's daughter-in-law Jane[81] (fl. 1615), who, apparently before 1573, married Nicholas Luttrell.[82] The reversion was held jointly by John's daughters Margery, the wife of John Larder, Alice (d. 1586), the wife of Robert Harrison, Bridget, the wife of Giles Saunders, Mary, the wife of Robert Morgan, and later of William Stourton, and Philippe (d. s.p. 1563), who married George Morton.[83] Stephen Biggs (d. by 1620) acquired Bridget's interest in 1597, Alice's from her son Richard Harrison in 1598, and probably Margery's, in each case presumably by purchase. In 1620 John Booth sold three quarters of the two thirds, formerly held by Biggs, to Nicholas Hyde (knighted 1627, d. 1631) and his brother Sir Laurence (d. 1642):[84] in 1646 four of Sir Laurence's sons sold his portion of Little Bedwyn manor to Francis Goddard.[85] In 1596 Mary Stourton's interest in the two thirds passed at her death to her grandson Christopher Morgan, whose uncle William Morgan sold it to Nicholas Hyde in 1615.[86] At his death Sir Nicholas's portion of Little Bed-

60 Above, Great Bedwyn, manors [preamble], where, in n. 28, there is comment on the chart. of 968.
61 *Red Bk. Exch.* (Rolls Ser.), ii. 484, 649, 664.
62 e.g. *Wilts. Inq. p.m. 1242–1326* (Index Libr.), 324; *Cal. Fine R. 1327–37*, 177; for FitzGilbert's successors, above, Great Bedwyn, manors (Wexcombe).
63 *Red Bk. Exch.* (Rolls Ser.), ii. 484, 488.
64 *Rot. Hund.* (Rec. Com.), ii (1), 259; J. Hutchins, *Hist. Dors.* ii. 189–90; *Ex. e Rot. Fin.* (Rec. Com.), i. 121; *Cal. Fine R. 1272–1307*, 99.
65 *Wilts. Inq. p.m. 1242–1326* (Index Libr.), 381–2; Hutchins, *Dors.* 190; I. J. Sanders, *Eng. Baronies*, 68; cf. *Cal. Inq. p.m.* iii, pp. 264–5.
66 *Cal. Pat. 1324–7*, 158; *Abbrev. Rot. Orig.* (Rec. Com.), i. 293.
67 *Cal. Fine R. 1327–37*, 177; *Abbrev. Rot. Orig.* (Rec. Com.), ii. 35.
68 *Tax List, 1332* (W.R.S. xlv), 125.
69 *Feet of F. 1327–77* (W.R.S. xxix), p. 89.
70 Ibid.; *Cal. Inq. p.m.* xvii, pp. 233–4; P.R.O., C 139/32, nos. 14, 20.

71 *Cal. Inq. p.m.* xvii, pp. 233–4; *Feet of F. 1377–1509* (W.R.S. xli), p. 41.   72 P.R.O., C 139/32, no. 14.
73 *Feet of F. 1377–1509* (W.R.S. xli), p. 110.
74 P.R.O., C 139/154, no. 27.
75 *Cal. Close, 1454–61*, 315–16.
76 *Cal. Inq. p.m.* xvii, pp. 233–4; *Feet of F. 1377–1509* (W.R.S. xli), p. 41.   77 P.R.O., C 139/79, no. 8.
78 *Feet of F. 1377–1509* (W.R.S. xli), p. 131.
79 *Cal. Inq. p.m. Hen. VII*, ii, p. 185.
80 Ibid. iii, p. 433.
81 P.R.O., C 142/124, no. 197.
82 Hutchins, *Dors.* i. 414; W.R.O. 9/27/51, view 10 Mar. 1573; ibid. A 1/200/1, rot. 19.
83 P.R.O., C 142/124, no. 197; C 142/140, no. 198; C 142/215, no. 244.
84 Ibid. CP 25/2/242/39 & 40 Eliz. I Mich.; CP 25/2/242/40 & 41 Eliz. I Mich.; CP 43/149, Carte rott. 1–2; for the Hydes, Hoare, *Mod. Wilts.* Dunworth, pedigree at p. 131; *Wilts. Inq. p.m. 1625–49* (Index Libr.), 381–2.
85 W.R.O. 1064/19, deed, Hyde to Goddard, 1646.
86 Ibid. A 1/200/1, rot. 19; P.R.O., C 142/247, no. 96.

wyn manor passed with Hinton Daubnay manor in Catherington (Hants) to his son Laurence, who sold it in portions in 1665.[87]

The estate in Little Bedwyn held from 1397 by Margery Sydele passed on John Sydele's death in 1428 to her daughter Christine Short, the wife of Henry Parker.[88] Its descent from 1428 is obscure until 1540, when it was held by John Goddard (d. 1545) of Upper Upham in Aldbourne. It descended to John's son John[89] (d. c. 1567) and with Standen Hussey manor in Hungerford in turn to that John's son Thomas (d. 1610) and Thomas's son Francis Goddard, who bought Sir Laurence Hyde's portion of Little Bedwyn manor in 1646. Francis Goddard (d. 1652) was succeeded by his son Edward (d. 1684), and Edward by his son Francis,[90] who between 1695 and 1700 sold his part of that manor in portions.[91]

The demesne of Little Bedwyn manor was bought from Francis Goddard by Thomas Streat in 1700.[92] As Manor farm, and later as Little Bedwyn manor, it descended with a freehold on Burwood heath which belonged to Thomas's father Thomas (d. 1686) and with a holding bought by the elder Thomas from Laurence Hyde in 1665.[93] From Thomas Streat (will proved 1736) the estate passed to his son the Revd. Richard Streat (d. 1767), who by purchases in the period 1742–60 added to it holdings with land in Little Bedwyn and apparently on Burwood heath. Richard Streat's estate passed to his sisters Susannah Streat (d. 1770) and Elizabeth Kent (d. 1781) as coheirs. From Elizabeth it passed to her daughter Martha (d. unmarried 1784), and it descended to Martha's son William Kent (d. 1786) and in turn to William's son William (d. c. 1804) and daughter Elizabeth Kent.[94] The estate, 589 a. including land on Burwood heath, was sold by Elizabeth to Anthony Guy c. 1809.[95]

Of the portions of Little Bedwyn manor sold in the later 17th century 2 yardlands belonged to Stephen Blandy in 1711 and 1728,[96] to a Mrs. Blandy c. 1770,[97] and in the 1780s and 1790s, when the estate consisted of c. 135 a., to Martha and Mary Blandy, spinsters. The land was apparently bought from a Miss Blandy by Anthony Guy c. 1811.[98]

From c. 1811 all but c. 100 a. of Little Bedwyn's land was owned by Anthony Guy. In each case presumably by sale it passed from Guy

to John Pain c. 1825, from Pain to the Revd. Thomas Tragett c. 1829, and from Tragett to Sir William Curtis, Bt., c. 1840.[99] In 1858 Sir William sold it to R. C. L. Bevan[1] (d. 1890). It passed with Fosbury manor to Bevan's son F. A. Bevan,[2] who between 1899 and 1903 sold it to S. W. Farmer (d. 1926), the tenant of Manor farm.[3] In 1927 Farmer's executors sold Little Bedwyn manor to his half-brother's son E. B. Gauntlett (d. 1958), who, by purchase in 1930, added to it Jockey Green farm, 157 a. including 101 a. in Great Bedwyn, and Foxbury wood and Strockeridge coppice, a total of 42 a. About 1970 Gauntlett's trustees sold the estate, 922 a.,[4] to Paul Wansbrough, who in 1986 sold it to Mr. R. H. Tucker, the owner in 1998.[5]

Some of Little Bedwyn's land was part of Chisbury manor:[6] as lord of that manor Charles Brudenell-Bruce, marquess of Ailesbury, owned c. 41 a. of it in 1841,[7] and he or a successor acquired other land later. In 1930 George, marquess of Ailesbury, sold 56 a. of Little Bedwyn's land as part of Jockey Green farm, most of which lay in Great Bedwyn. The farm was bought by E. B. Gauntlett and added to Little Bedwyn manor, of which its land remained part in 1998.[8]

Burwood, presumably the land later called *BURWOOD* heath, was given by the king to his servant Jordan c. 1178.[9] About 1189 it passed to Stephen Chamber (d. c. 1189) and was held by his relict Gillian, also relict of Alan de Neville, until c. 1193.[10] In the earlier 14th century Burwood may have been part of Chisbury manor[11] as Burwood heath was in the 16th century, when much of it lay as common pasture. In the 1570s, soon after the pasture was inclosed, divided, and allotted, much of the heath was sold by John Cook, the lord of Chisbury manor, in portions;[12] some of it remained part of the manor.[13]

Burwood (later Burridge) Heath farm originated as a close, estimated at 60 a., bought c. 1577 by John Organ *alias* Taylor, who sold it to John Hunt of Ham in 1580.[14] The farm belonged to William Hunt in 1745, when it was of 72 a. In 1766 Hunt's brother and heir John sold it to Thomas Brudenell, Lord Bruce,[15] who, as lord of Chisbury manor, already owned some of Burwood heath. Lord Bruce's land on the heath descended with the manor to his successors as owners of Tottenham House, who acquired other parts of the heath.[16] In 1929 George,

87   *V.C.H. Hants*, iii. 96–7; W.R.O. 79B/11, deeds, Hyde to Streat, 1665; Hyde to Bushell, 1665; Hyde to Dore, 1665.
88   P.R.O., C 139/32, no. 20.
89   *Land. Gent.* (1937), 899; P.R.O., REQ 2/201/42.
90   *V.C.H. Berks.* iv. 196.
91   W.R.O. 110/16, deed, Goddard to Smith, 1695; 1064/19, deeds, Goddard to New, 1695; Goddard to Streat, 1700; P.R.O., C 5/595/109.
92   W.R.O. 1064/19, deed, Goddard to Streat, 1700.
93   Ibid. 79B/11, deed, Hyde to Streat, 1665; 79B/11, will of Thomas Streat, 1684; ibid. bishop's transcripts, bdle. 1; for Burwood heath, below, this section.
94   P.R.O., PROB 11/679, ff. 289–91; W.R.O. 79B/12; 315/27/5; 1955/25; ibid. A 1/345/27.
95   W.R.O. 315/28/1; ibid. A 1/345/27.
96   Ibid. 9/5/20; 488/10, lease, Blandy to Swaite, 1711.
97   Ibid. 9/4/88.
98   Ibid. A 1/345/27; ibid. EA/68.
99   Ibid. A 1/345/27; ibid. EA/68; ibid. tithe award.
1   *W.A.M.* vi. 274.

2   Below, Fosbury, manor.
3   *Kelly's Dir. Wilts.* (1899, 1903); *W.A.M.* xliii. 494.
4   W.R.O. 9/1/521; 1010/22; Princ. Regy. Fam. Div., will of S. W. Farmer, 1926; will of E. B. Gauntlett, 1959; for the farm, below, this section; for the woodland, ibid. (Burwood).
5   W.A.S. Libr., sale cat. xxxiv, no. 36; inf. from Mr. R. H. Tucker, Manor Ho.
6   e.g. W.R.O. 1300/372, f. 8; for Chisbury manor, below, this section.
7   W.R.O., tithe award.   8   Above, this section.
9   *Pipe R.* 1178 (P.R.S. xxvii), 28.
10   *Pipe R.* 1189 (Rec. Com.), 171; *Pipe R.* 1190 (P.R.S. N.S. i), 117; 1193 (P.R.S. N.S. iii), 78; *V.C.H. Wilts.* xv. 97.
11   B.L. Harl. Ch. 48 I. 22; Harl. Roll C. 13A.
12   W.R.O. 9/1/95, p. 54; 9/5/8; 9/8/5; for Chisbury manor, below, this section; for the pasture, ibid. econ. hist.
13   W.R.O. 1300/372, ff. 8, 17–18.
14   Ibid. 9/5/18; *Cal. Pat.* 1575–8, p. 265.
15   W.R.O. 9/5/11–12.   16   e.g. ibid. tithe award.

marquess of Ailesbury, owned *c.* 190 a. of it, which he offered for sale. The buyer of Burridge Heath farm, 271 a. including 123 a. in Shalbourne, sold it to A. S. Knight, who offered it for sale in 1930.[17] The farm was probably bought then by W. E. Rootes (knighted 1942, cr. Baron Rootes 1959, d. 1964), who apparently owned it in 1933, as he did later, as part of his estate based at Stype Grange in Shalbourne;[18] it remained part of the Stype Grange estate and in 1998 belonged to Mrs. V. L. Duffield. Foxbury wood and Strockeridge coppice, a total of 42 a., were sold by Lord Ailesbury to E. B. Gauntlett in 1930, were added to Little Bedwyn manor, and remained part of it in 1998.[19]

Part of Burwood heath devised by Thomas Streat (d. 1686) to his son Thomas[20] was probably bought from John Cook in the 1570s. The younger Thomas merged it with the demesne of Little Bedwyn manor, which he bought in 1700.[21] Part of the heath bought by Ralph Ardley *alias* Early from Cook in 1575[22] was estimated at 45 a. in 1640 and descended in the Ardley *alias* Early family until *c.* 1730 or later.[23] It was apparently bought in 1760 by the Revd. Richard Streat[24] and added to Little Bedwyn manor, which in 1841 included 120 a. of Burwood heath.[25] Most of that land descended with Little Bedwyn manor until the earlier 20th century[26] and belonged to Mrs. Duffield as part of the Stype Grange estate in 1998.[27]

A fourth part of Burwood heath was sold by John Cook to Henry Clifton *c.* 1570[28] and was assessed at 60 a. in 1640. It descended in the Clifton family until 1696 or later[29] and had apparently been sold in portions by *c.* 1730.[30]

The land of Chisbury was apparently that, assessed at 13 *manentes* and said to lie at Bedwyn, given by King Cynewulf to his thegn Bica in 778.[31] *CHISBURY* was held by Edric in 1066, by Gilbert of Breteuil in 1086.[32]

The overlordship of Chisbury manor was held in 1243 by Baldwin de Reviers, earl of Devon and lord of the Isle of Wight (d. 1245), presumably passed to his son Baldwin, earl of Devon (d. 1262), and was held in 1275 by that Baldwin's heir, his sister Isabel de Forz, countess of Aumale and of Devon. Walter

Marshal, earl of Pembroke, was the mesne lord in 1243, and his heirs were mesne lords in 1275.[33]

Gilbert de Columbers held Chisbury manor in 1167,[34] Michael de Columbers apparently held it in 1210,[35] and Matthew de Columbers held it from 1243 or earlier.[36] On Matthew's death *c.* 1272–3 the manor passed to his brother Michael, who conveyed it, apparently in fee, to John Havering. Probably *c.* 1279 Havering conveyed it to John Cobham (d. 1300). Matthew's relict Maud held a third of the manor as dower[37] and in 1285, when she married his son Henry, surrendered it to Cobham. The manor descended to Henry[38] (from 1313 Lord Cobham, d. 1339) and in the direct line to John, Lord Cobham (d. 1355), and John, Lord Cobham (d. 1408). It was among Lord Cobham's estates which were forfeited to the Crown in 1398 and recovered *c.* 1400.[39] It passed in 1408 to his granddaughter Joan Hawkberk, Baroness Cobham, who in 1408 married Sir John Oldcastle (d. 1417), a leader of the Lollards, and afterwards married Sir John Harpeden. At her death in 1434 Chisbury manor passed to her daughter Joan Braybrook, Baroness Cobham, wife of Sir Thomas Brooke,[40] and at hers *c.* 1443 it passed to her son Edward Brooke, Lord Cobham (d. 1464). It descended in the direct line to John, Lord Cobham (d. 1512), Thomas, Lord Cobham (d. 1529), and George, Lord Cobham (d. 1558).[41] In circumstances which are obscure it was transferred from Lord Cobham to Edward Seymour, duke of Somerset, *c.* 1552;[42] in 1552 it passed to the Crown on the execution and attainder of Somerset and was granted to John Dudley, duke of Northumberland; in 1553 it passed to the Crown on the execution and attainder of Northumberland.[43] The manor was presumably restored to Lord Cobham *c.* 1553,[44] and in 1567 it was sold by his son William, Lord Cobham (d. 1597), to John Cook for a rent charge of £27.[45] The rent charge descended to William's son Henry, Lord Cobham, on the attainder of whom it passed to the Crown in 1603.[46]

In the 16th century Chisbury manor included to the south-east Burwood heath, to the west farms called Holt, Horse Hill, and Monks (later Chisbury Lane), and to the north land at Rudge in Froxfield.[47] In the 1570s John Cook sold part of it, mainly land on Burwood heath and at Rudge, in portions.[48] In 1586 he sold the main

[17] W.R.O. 9/1/521; 1010/21.
[18] Ibid. G 8/505/1; G 8/505/3; *Who Was Who, 1961–70,* 975–6.
[19] W.R.O. 9/1/521; 1010/22; inf. from Mr. Tucker; local inf.
[20] W.R.O. 79B/11, will of Thomas Streat, 1684.
[21] Above, this section (Little Bedwyn).
[22] W.R.O. 9/8/5.
[23] Ibid. 9/1/101; 9/1/161, rot. 15; 9/8/147; 192/24B; 212B/3774.
[24] Ibid. 79B/12, sched. of deeds.
[25] Ibid. tithe award.
[26] Cf. ibid. 1010/35.
[27] Local inf.
[28] *Cal. Pat.* 1569–72, p. 314.
[29] *Wilts. Inq. p.m.* 1625–49 (Index Libr.), 142–3; W.R.O. 9/1/160; 9/1/165; 9/8/144; 9/8/147; 192/24B.
[30] W.R.O. 9/1/101.
[31] Finberg, *Early Wessex Chart.* p. 71; *Arch. Jnl.* lxxvi. 151–5; cf. above, Great Bedwyn, manors [preamble].
[32] *V.C.H. Wilts.* ii, p. 147.
[33] *Cur. Reg. R.* xvii, pp. 285–6; *Rot. Hund.* (Rec. Com.), ii (1), 260; *Complete Peerage,* iv. 318–23.
[34] *Pipe R.* 1167 (P.R.S. xi), 129.
[35] P.R.O., CP 25/1/250/3, no. 33.
[36] *Cur. Reg. R.* xvii, pp. 285–6.
[37] *Colln. Topog. et Geneal.* vii. 148; P.R.O., JUST 1/1006, rot. 2; B.L. Harl. Roll C. 28; for Cobham and his successors, *Complete Peerage,* iii. 343–9.
[38] *Feet of F.* 1272–1327 (W.R.S. i), pp. 25–6; *Cal. Pat.* 1281–92, 178.
[39] *Cal. Inq. Misc.* vi. 149; cf. *Complete Peerage,* iii. 344.
[40] P.R.O., C 139/65, no. 37, rot. 8.
[41] e.g. ibid. E 326/7063; B.L. Harl. Ch. 46 H. 35.
[42] W.R.O. 9/1/95, p. 43.
[43] *Complete Peerage,* ix. 722–6; xii (1), 59–64; *Cal. Pat.* 1550–3, 368–70; P.R.O., E 318/32/1820.
[44] Cf. *Complete Peerage,* iii. 348.
[45] W.R.O. 9/8/2.
[46] Ibid. 9/8/23.
[47] Ibid. 9/1/95, pp. 43–55; for the holdings to the W., cf. below, econ. hist. (Chisbury).
[48] *Cal. Pat.* 1569–72, p. 314; 1572–5, p. 68; 1575–8, p. 265; W.R.O. 9/8/5; 79B/11, deed, Cook to Ardley, 1575; for Burwood heath, above, this section; for Rudge, below, Froxfield, manors.

part to William Read[49] (d. 1593), and as Chisbury manor that part descended to Read's son Edward.[50] In 1602 Edward Read sold the manor to Edward Seymour, earl of Hertford,[51] who bought the rent charge from the Crown in 1605.[52] With Tottenham Lodge and Tottenham House in Great Bedwyn the manor thereafter descended in the Seymour, Bruce, Brudenell, and Brudenell-Bruce families to George Brudenell-Bruce, marquess of Ailesbury, who in 1950 sold all of it except its woodland to the Crown, the owner in 1998.[53]

In 1119 the king gave *HENSET* to St. Maurice's cathedral, Angers (Maine et Loire). It belonged to the cathedral *c.* 1167, but not *c.* 1211, when with Teteridge in Froxfield it was held by William May and Thomas de Landon.[54] It was acquired by Peter des Roches, bishop of Winchester (d. 1238), as an endowment of Netley abbey (Hants), which was founded in 1239. The abbey gave it to the king in an exchange in 1241.[55] In 1308–9 an estate called Henset was held by John le Dun,[56] who settled it on himself for life and on Stephen of Brigmerston and his wife Joan.[57] At John's death in 1332 it passed to Stephen's daughter Isabel, the wife of Nicholas of Wylye,[58] and in 1334 Nicholas and Isabel conveyed it to Roger Normand.[59] It passed from Roger (d. 1349) to his grandson Giles Normand[60] (d. 1361), whose heir was his cousin Margaret Chamberlain. The estate was apparently acquired *c.* 1364 by John Eastbury[61] (d. 1374), and in 1416 it was held for life by John's son Thomas. By 1416 the reversion had been acquired by John Lovel, Lord Lovel, the lord of Axford manor in Ramsbury, who in that year conveyed it with that of Knowle manor to Sir William Sturmy (d. 1427).[62] Henset's land was apparently later part of Knowle farm.[63]

KNOWLE was bought by William Russel (d. *c.* 1311), the lord of Little Bedwyn manor, from Ralph de la Knowle in 1291, and it passed with the manor to William's son Theobald.[64] By 1345, when Theobald's relict Eleanor was claiming a third of it as dower, Knowle manor had been acquired by Sir Thomas Seymour[65] (d. 1358).[66]

Sir Thomas conveyed it to Sir John Stock in fee tail with remainder to Sir John's brother Hugh in fee tail and reversion to Sir Thomas.[67] In 1398 and 1416 Knowle manor was held for life by Hugh's relict Parnel Stock.[68] The reversion was acquired by John Lovel, Lord Lovel (d. 1408), the lord of Axford manor, and it passed to his son John, Lord Lovel,[69] who in 1416 sold it with that of Henset to Sir William Sturmy (d. 1427).[70] Knowle manor, to which the land of Henset was apparently added,[71] passed to William Sturmy (d. by 1482), to his son John[72] (fl. 1497),[73] and to John's son Thomas (fl. 1512).[74] By 1544 it had passed to Margaret, the daughter and heir of a Sturmy, presumably Thomas, and the wife of Roger Hereford,[75] and in 1548 the Herefords sold it to Edward Seymour, duke of Somerset.[76] The manor passed to the Crown on Somerset's execution and attainder in 1552, and in 1553 it was assigned to his son Sir Edward Seymour (cr. earl of Hertford 1559, d. 1621).[77] As Knowle farm, 524 a. in 1841,[78] it descended with Tottenham Lodge and Tottenham House, from 1602 also with Chisbury manor.[79] In 1950 George, marquess of Ailesbury, sold all of it except its woodland to the Crown, the owner in 1998.[80]

About 1166 the overlordship of *PUTHALL* was transferred from John the marshal, who then held what was formerly the king's estate called Bedwyn and was a minor and the king's ward, to the keeper of the king's castle at Marlborough.[81] The lordship in demesne of Puthall descended from Robert of Puthall to his son Richard and to Richard's son William of Puthall (fl. 1201).[82] In 1229 it was the subject of litigation between Muriel, relict of William de Ros, and Reynold de Whitchurch, and between Reynold and Hugh de Ros, Muriel's son and formerly Reynold's ward. Muriel, then the wife of Roger Wallis, surrendered her claim to dower in the estate to Geoffrey Bingham and his wife Muriel in 1259,[83] and in 1260 the Binghams conveyed the estate to Harvey Boreham.[84] In 1310 the estate was held by William de Lillebonne,[85] who in 1318–19 conveyed it to Henry Tyeys, Lord Tyeys (d. 1322), and his wife

49   W.R.O. 9/8/8.   50   P.R.O., C 142/236, no. 46.
51   W.R.O. 9/8/16.   52   Ibid. 9/8/23.
53   Above, Great Bedwyn, manors (Tottenham); inf. from the agent for the Crown Estate Com., 42 High Street, Marlborough; for the woodland, below, this section.
54   *Reg. Regum Anglo-Norm.* ii, no. 1204A; *Pipe R.* 1167 (P.R.S. xi), 129; *Red Bk. Exch.* (Rolls Ser.), ii. 484, 489; cf. below, Froxfield, manors (Teteridge).
55   *Cal. Chart. R.* 1226–57, 260–1; *V.C.H. Hants,* ii. 146.
56   *Abbrev. Rot. Orig.* (Rec. Com.), i. 163.
57   *Feet of F.* 1272–1327 (W.R.S. i), p. 124.
58   *V.C.H. Hants,* iv. 392; *Cal. Inq. p.m.* vii. 333–4.
59   *Feet of F.* 1327–77 (W.R.S. xxix), p. 43.
60   *Cal. Inq. p.m.* ix, pp. 231–2.
61   Ibid. xi, pp. 206–8; *Feet of F.* 1327–77 (W.R.S. xxix), p. 147.
62   *Feet of F.* 1377–1509 (W.R.S. xli), p. 74; *V.C.H. Wilts.* xii. 31, 49; P.R.O., C 139/28, no. 22.
63   Cf. W.R.O., tithe award; above, intro. (other settlement).
64   *Feet of F.* 1272–1327 (W.R.S. i), pp. 36–7; *Wilts. Inq. p.m.* 1242–1326 (Index Libr.), 381–2.
65   P.R.O., CP 40/344, rot. 600d.
66   *Cal. Inq. p.m.* x, pp. 345–7.
67   *Cal. Pat.* 1361–4, 68; *Cal. Inq. Misc.* iii, p. 170.
68   *Cal. Inq. Misc.* vi, p. 151; *Feet of F.* 1377–1509

(W.R.S. xli), p. 74.
69   *Cal. Inq. p.m.* xix, pp. 143, 146; *V.C.H. Wilts.* xii. 49.
70   *Feet of F.* 1377–1509 (W.R.S. xli), p. 74; P.R.O., C 139/28, no. 22.   71   Above, this section (Henset).
72   *Cat. Anct. D.* i, B 1778.
73   P.R.O., E 210/5034.
74   Ibid. E 326/5881.
75   Ibid. CP 25/2/46/323, no. 45; Burke, *Commoners* (1833–8), iii. 345.
76   P.R.O., CP 25/2/65/531, no. 46.
77   Ibid. E 328/117; *Complete Peerage,* vi. 505–6; xii (1), 59–64.
78   W.R.O., tithe award.
79   Above, Great Bedwyn, manors (Tottenham); this section (Chisbury).
80   Inf. from the agent for the Crown Estate Com.; for the woodland, below, this section.
81   *Cur. Reg. R.* i. 424; *Complete Peerage,* x, App. G, 95–6; *Pipe R.* 1191 & 92 (P.R.S. N.S. ii), 281; 1194 (P.R.S. N.S. v), 201; above, Great Bedwyn, manors (preamble; Wexcombe).
82   *Cur. Reg. R.* i. 424.
83   *Cal. Pat.* 1225–32, 305; *Cur. Reg. R.* xiii, p. 322; *Civil Pleas, 1249* (W.R.S. xxvi), p. 67; P.R.O., CP 25/1/251/19, no. 22.
84   P.R.O., CP 25/1/251/20, no. 8.
85   *Feet of F.* 1272–1327 (W.R.S. i), pp. 77–8.

Margaret. In 1322 it was forfeited because of Henry's contrariance, and in 1325 was restored to Margaret.[86] About 1370 Henry Sturmy granted it to Easton priory,[87] which held it until the Dissolution.[88] The estate was granted in 1536 as part of Easton Druce manor to Edward Seymour, Viscount Beauchamp (cr. earl of Hertford 1537, duke of Somerset 1547). On Somerset's execution and attainder in 1552 it passed by Act to his son Sir Edward[89] and as Puthall farm, 201 a. in 1841,[90] it descended as part of that manor, from 1553 with Tottenham Lodge and later with Tottenham House, from 1602 also with Chisbury manor.[91] In 1950 George, marquess of Ailesbury, sold all of it except the woodland to the Crown, the owner in 1998.[92]

A small estate called *TIMBRIDGE*, which may have consisted mainly of Timbridge down, was held in chief at his death c. 1305 by Henry Sturmy, lord of Burbage Sturmy manor.[93] Thereafter it descended with that manor, from 1553 also with Tottenham Lodge, later with Tottenham House, and from 1602 also with Chisbury manor.[94] As Timbridge farm, 291 a., it belonged to Charles Brudenell-Bruce, marquess of Ailesbury, in 1841;[95] in 1950 George, marquess of Ailesbury, sold it to the Crown, the owner in 1998.[96]

The land which may have been added to the west end of the parish between the early 19th century and the 1880s, c. 150 a.,[97] was part, and belonged to the owner, of Savernake forest. In 1939 George, marquess of Ailesbury, leased it with the woodland of Chisbury manor, Knowle farm, and Puthall farm, a total of 662 a., for 999 years to the Forestry Commission.[98] The reversion descended in the Brudenell-Bruce family with Tottenham House and in 1998 belonged to David Brudenell-Bruce, earl of Cardigan.[99]

In the Middle Ages the church at Little Bedwyn and that at Chisbury were chapels of Great Bedwyn church.[1] All tithes arising from the land of Little Bedwyn village and from Henset, Knowle, Puthall, and Timbridge were among the revenues of Great Bedwyn church, which was given to Salisbury cathedral in 1091 and used to endow Bedwyn prebend in the

cathedral.[2] As part of the prebend they were acquired by Edward Seymour, earl of Hertford, in 1544 and by St. George's chapel, Windsor, in 1547. From 1603 those tithes were held on lease by Edward, earl of Hertford (d. 1621), and his successors as owners of Tottenham Lodge and Tottenham House.[3]

The tithes arising from the land of Chisbury village were taken by the rector of Froxfield in the earlier 13th century, thereafter by St. Denis's priory, Southampton. In 1246–7 the priory successfully resisted the prebendary of Bedwyn's claim to the tithes which arose from the demesne of Chisbury manor,[4] and those tithes passed to the Crown at the dissolution of the priory in 1536.[5] In 1543 the Crown granted them to Christopher Willoughby,[6] who probably conveyed them to Sir Edward Baynton (d. 1544) and his wife Isabel.[7] About 1550 Isabel conveyed them to William Stumpe,[8] to whom she was related by marriage. Stumpe (d. 1552) settled them on himself, his wife Catherine (d. 1556), and his son William,[9] who in 1576 sold them to John Cook, the lord of Chisbury manor. From 1576 the tithes from the demesne descended with the manor.[10] The tithes arising from the rest of Chisbury's land, and presumably from Burwood heath and the farms called Holt, Horse Hill, and Chisbury Lane, were held in 1535 by the chaplain serving Chisbury church. They were held then and later for 6s. 8d. a year paid to St. Denis's priory and its successors as owners of the tithes from the demesne.[11] In 1547 they passed to the Crown under the Act by which chantries were dissolved,[12] and the Crown held them until 1613, when it granted them to Francis Morris.[13] In 1615 Morris sold them to Edward, earl of Hertford,[14] the lord of Chisbury manor and already the owner of the tithes from its demesne. From 1615 all the tithes arising from Chisbury descended with Chisbury manor and with the lease of the tithes from the rest of the parish.[15]

By 1672 small tithes from most of the parish, and great tithes from most of Little Bedwyn's land and some of Chisbury's, had been assigned to the vicar of Little Bedwyn. The rest of the tithes continued to descend with Tottenham Lodge and Tottenham House and with Chis-

86 *Cal. Close*, 1323–7, 389–90; *Complete Peerage*, xii (2), 103–5.
87 *Cal. Pat.* 1370–4, 145; W.R.O. 1300/20.
88 *Valor Eccl.* (Rec. Com.), ii. 148.
89 *L. & P. Hen. VIII*, x, pp. 526–7; *Complete Peerage*, xii (1), 59–65; Longleat Mun., Seymour papers, xii, f. 309; below, Easton, manors (Easton Druce).
90 W.R.O., tithe award.
91 Above, Great Bedwyn, manors (Tottenham); this section (Chisbury); below, Easton, manors (Easton Druce).
92 Inf. from the agent for the Crown Estate Com.; for the woodland, below, this section.
93 *Wilts. Inq. p.m.* 1242–1326 (Index Libr.), 312–14.
94 Above, Great Bedwyn, manors (Tottenham); this section (Chisbury); below, Burbage, manors (Burbage Sturmy); cf. W.R.O. 1300/36; 1300/43.
95 W.R.O., tithe award.
96 Inf. from the agent for the Crown Estate Com.
97 Above, intro.
98 W.R.O. 9/33/5; for the descent of Savernake forest, below, Savernake, estates.
99 Above, Great Bedwyn, manors (Tottenham); inf. from the earl of Cardigan, Savernake Lodge, Savernake.
1 Below, church.

2 *Reg. St. Osmund* (Rolls Ser.), i. 203; *Chandler's Reg.* (W.R.S. xxxix), p. 33; *Cal. Pat.* 1547–8, 149; above, Great Bedwyn, manors (Prebendal); for Henset, cf. ibid. this section.
3 Above, Great Bedwyn, manors (Prebendal), where more inf. is given.
4 *Sar. Chart. and Doc.* (Rolls Ser.), pp. 310–12; *Chandler's Reg.* (W.R.S. xxxix), p. 32; P.R.O., E 135/21/26; cf. below, church [Chisbury].
5 *V.C.H. Hants*, ii. 163; P.R.O., SC 6/Hen. VIII/3326, rot. 6.
6 W.R.O. 9/8/22.
7 *L. & P. Hen. VIII*, xviii (2), p. 281; *Hist. Parl., Commons*, 1509–58, i. 403.
8 *Cal. Pat.* 1549–51, 356.
9 *W.N. & Q.* viii. 336, 391–3, 482–4.
10 W.R.O. 9/8/6; above, this section (Chisbury).
11 *Valor Eccl.* (Rec. Com.), ii. 150; P.R.O., E 301/58, no. 66; ibid. SC 6/Hen. VIII/3326, rot. 6; cf. above, this section (Chisbury).
12 P.R.O., E 301/58, no. 66; W.R.O. 9/8/10.
13 P.R.O., C 66/1985, no. 1.
14 W.R.O. 9/8/24.
15 Above, this section.

bury manor to Thomas Bruce, earl of Ailesbury, to whom the freehold of those formerly part of Bedwyn prebend was transferred in 1790.[16] By a deed of 1840 Lord Ailesbury's son Charles, marquess of Ailesbury, who owned nearly all the land of the parish apart from Little Bedwyn manor, merged the land of Knowle (including that of Henset), Puthall, and Timbridge, and nearly all of Chisbury's, a total of 3,203 a., with the great tithes arising from it. By the same deed Lord Ailesbury merged the tithes of wool and lambs from an additional 125 a. with that land, which he also owned. Lord Ailesbury's tithes arising from land owned by others, all tithes from 33 a. and tithes of wool and lambs from 872 a., were valued at £33 10s. in 1840 and commuted in 1842.[17]

ECONOMIC HISTORY. LITTLE BEDWYN.

In 1086 Little Bedwyn's land was probably part of the king's estate called Bedwyn.[18] In 1311 the demesne of Little Bedwyn manor included 128 a. of arable, 6 a. of meadows, and 12 a. of pasture; on the manor there were seven customary tenants, two yardlanders and five ⅓-yardlanders, each of whom presumably had a small farmstead in the village, and there were nine freeholders, the size and location of whose holdings are obscure.[19]

In the early 16th century and later Little Bedwyn had three open fields. North field, 190 a., lay north of the village and north-west of the Dun, East field, 134 a., lay east of the village and south-east of the Dun, and West later South field lay south of the village and south-east of the Dun. By 1570 c. 50 a. south-west of West field had been inclosed: it was apparently demesne and may formerly have been part of West field, later 149 a. Merrell down, probably c. 125 a. excluding the woodland which stood on it, was a common pasture lying along the southern boundary of the parish. Little Bedwyn had meadow land beside the Dun north-east and south-west of the village. Its woodland stood on Merrell down and apparently between East and West fields and Burwood heath.[20] From the 14th century most of the land and feeding rights were probably demesne of Little Bedwyn manor, and until the 18th century the only other holdings likely to have been worked from Little Bedwyn village of which there is evidence were small.[21]

By the mid 17th century, and possibly by the early 16th, some of the woodland between West field and Burwood heath had apparently been cleared for agriculture. In 1659 a holding with 30 a. in Little Bedwyn's open fields had five closes there;[22] its farmstead may have been that which in the 18th century stood on high ground 1 km. south-east of the village.[23] Much of Merrell down was also inclosed, an inclosure said in 1674 to have been recent;[24] the centre part, 52 a., south of the woodland, remained a common pasture.[25]

In the 18th century there were four farmsteads in Little Bedwyn village. The largest stood near the church in 1792 and consisted of the farm buildings on the demesne, later called Manor farm; south-east of it on the north-east side of the village street stood the farmstead from which a holding of 2 yardlands was probably worked in the early 18th century. In addition a small farm was worked from Forebridge, and in 1788 Jockey farm included buildings on the site of the Horse and Jockey inn. The open fields and Merrell down were inclosed in 1792 by Act. Of 525 a. allotted, 291 a. was in respect of Manor farm, and 109 a. in respect of a farm worked from the buildings on the north-east side of the street.[26]

By 1841 the farm for which 109 a. was allotted in 1792 had been added to Manor farm and most of its buildings demolished; some of the closes near Burwood heath which were farmland in 1659 had apparently been added to Manor farm; others, and the one surviving building of the farmstead there, had apparently become part of Burwood Heath farm. In 1841 Manor farm, 820 a., also included the land and buildings of Jockey farm, a barn at Parlow bottom, and 120 a. at the north-east end of Burwood heath; from the mid 19th century its principal buildings, Manor Farm, stood south-east of the Dun. A farm with 112 a., including a farmstead south-west of the church, 43 a. formerly in North field, land in Chisbury, and land on Burwood heath, was then the only other one with buildings on Little Bedwyn's land. The 43 a. was later added to Manor farm. As it was later, 27 a. of Merrell down allotted in 1792 may have been part of Jockey Green farm in 1841, and 29 a. east of it was added to the farm later; the buildings of Jockey Green farm stood in Great Bedwyn parish.[27]

About 1875 Manor farm was leased to S. W. Farmer,[28] who lived at Manor House until his death in 1926. Farmer, from 1885 in partnership with Frank Stratton, acquired much land, including Manor farm, Chisbury, and especially in the Vale of Pewsey, and farmed it profitably by introducing dairying on what were otherwise sheep-and-corn farms and by supplying milk for the London market. At their apogee Farmer and Stratton owned or leased c. 25,000 a. on which c. 2,000 cows were kept. In 1910 Manor farm, Little Bedwyn, had c. 830 a.[29] In the earlier 20th

[16] W.R.O. 9/4/88; above, Great Bedwyn, manors (Prebendal).

[17] W.R.O., tithe award; cf. above, this section.

[18] Above, manors; for what was on the estate, ibid. Great Bedwyn, econ. hist. [preamble].

[19] *Wilts. Inq. p.m. 1242–1326* (Index Libr.), 381–2.

[20] S. R. Ranson, *Verney Papers* (cat. for Claydon Ho. trust), p. 423; P.R.O., CP 43/149, Carte rott. 1–2; W.R.O. 212B/135; ibid. EA/68; for the meadow land, cf. ibid. 9/8/153H; for the woodland, below, this section.

[21] e.g. W.R.O. 9/5/35.

[22] Ibid. 79B/11, lease, Goddard to Checker, 1685; 110/16, deed, Grey to Bush, 1508; 212B/135; 212B/143.

[23] Ibid. EA/68; *Andrews and Dury, Map* (W.R.S. viii), pl. 12.

[24] W.R.O. 79B/11, deed, Tanner to Bushell, 1674.

[25] Ibid. EA/68.

[26] Ibid.; ibid. 79B/11, lease, Tucker to Hawkins, 1788; 488/10, lease, Blandy to Swaite, 1711; 1300/372, ff. 8, 17–18; for the Horse and Jockey, above, intro. (other settlement).

[27] W.R.O., tithe award; ibid. Inland Revenue, val. reg. 56; ibid. 9/1/521; 1010/22; above, intro. (Little Bedwyn); for Jockey Green farm, above, Great Bedwyn, econ. hist. (Brail); for Burwood Heath farm, below, this section.

[28] W.R.O., A 1/345/27.

[29] Ibid. Inland Revenue, val. reg. 56; *V.C.H. Wilts.* iv. 106–7; *W.A.M.* xliii. 494–5.

century the land at the north-east end of Bur-wood heath was separated from it, in 1930 Jockey Green farm, 157 a. including 101 a. in Great Bedwyn, was added to it,[30] and in the mid 20th century a new dairy was built a little south-east of Little Bedwyn village.[31] Farmer's successor as owner and occupier, E. B. Gauntlett, also held Chisbury Manor farm, which adjoined Manor farm.[32]

In 1970 Manor farm was an arable and dairy farm of, excluding woodland, 722 a.; pigs were, or had been, kept in buildings at Parlow bottom.[33] A new dairy was built south-east of the village in 1971, young stock was kept at the old dairy, and Manor Farm was used to store grain and house machinery.[34] In 1998 Manor farm, 920 a., was still an arable and dairy farm.[35]

In the 18th century there was c. 25 a. of woodland in three coppices on Merrell down;[36] that woodland was later called Jockey copse. In the early 19th century Blandy copse, 3 a., Bonning's copse, 19 a., and Little Bonning's copse, 7 a., stood between Burwood heath and what was East and West fields. To link Jockey copse to Foxbury wood on Burwood heath and to Little Bedwyn's other woodland, trees were planted on an additional 11 a. before 1841 and 10 a. between 1841 and 1879; 3 a. was planted north-east of Little Bonning's copse between 1899 and 1922, and 9 a. south-east of Jockey copse in the mid 20th century.[37]

A water mill stood on Little Bedwyn manor in the early 14th century,[38] presumably on the Dun c. 400 m. south-west of Little Bedwyn church where a mill stood in the 17th century.[39] The mill was part of a holding of the manor sold by Laurence Hyde to Thomas Streat in 1665.[40] It was last mentioned in 1727[41] and had been demolished by 1773.[42]

A wool stapler, Thomas Greenaway, lived at Little Bedwyn in 1719 and 1750.[43] There was a brickworks on Merrell down from c. 1850 to the mid 20th century. Bricks were made by members of the Hawkins family, later by C. W. Hawkins & Sons.[44]

BURWOOD HEATH. Its name in the 12th century suggests that Burwood,[45] presumably the land later called Burwood heath, was then woodland, and some or all of it was wooded in the 13th century.[46] By the later 16th century two farmsteads had been built; the tenants held c. 30 a. in closes, presumably in the middle of the heath and near the farmsteads, and much land lay as

pasture which was common and presumably for them to share.[47] There is no evidence of open fields on Burwood heath. The common pasture was inclosed, divided, and allotted by agreement c. 1570[48] and one or two additional farmsteads may have been built soon afterwards.[49]

On the south-west part of the heath Burwood Heath Farm was built, probably on a 60-a. close allotted c. 1570.[50] In 1745 Burwood Heath farm was accounted 72 a., including 12 a. of Little Bedwyn's land.[51] In the earlier 18th century 52 a. in the middle of the heath lay in 13 closes, most of which were part of farms worked from elsewhere.[52] By 1841 most of the 52 a. and other land had been added to Burwood Heath farm, then 148 a. The north-east part of the heath, 120 a., was worked as part of Manor farm, Little Bedwyn, probably from the earlier 18th century.[53]

In 1867 Burwood (later Burridge) Heath farm had 156 a., including 32 a. in Shalbourne.[54] In 1929, when it was a mixed farm with 81 a. of arable, it had 271 a., including 124 a. in Shalbourne and 24 a. of woodland on Burwood heath.[55] The 120 a. of Burwood heath was detached from Manor farm in the earlier 20th century,[56] and in 1998 the north-easternmost 34 a. of it was used as paddocks for horses stabled at Stype Wood Stud in Shalbourne. In 1998 only c. 100 a. of Burwood heath was agricultural land, nearly all of which was arable.

Some of Burwood heath may not have been cleared of woodland, and in 1792 Swaite's coppice (later Foxbury wood) and Strockeridge coppice, each c. 10 a., and several smaller coppices stood at the south-west end.[57] Additional woodland was planted in the 19th century, and in 1884 Foxbury wood and Strockeridge coppice totalled 42 a. and adjoined woodland of Little Bedwyn. East of Foxbury wood Burridge Heath plantation was then 24 a., and at the north-east end of the heath four copses totalled 35 a.[58] All 101 a. of woodland was standing in 1998.

CHISBURY. In 1086 Chisbury had land for 9 ploughteams. There were 4 teams and 7 *servi* on the demesne, and 12 *villani*, 3 bordars, and 14 coscets had 5 teams. There were 15 a. of meadow and 45 square furlongs of pasture.[59]

In the 13th century the lord of the manor had a park at Chisbury, probably the land, west of the hill fort and bounded north by Chisbury Lane and south-west by the parish boundary, on which Park copse later stood. In 1261 the king

30 Cf. above, manors (Little Bedwyn; Burwood).
31 O.S. Maps 6", Wilts. XXXVII. NW. (1926 edn.); 1/25,000, SU 26 (1961 edn.).
32 W.R.O., G 8/505/1; above, manors (Little Bedwyn).
33 W.R.O. 1010/22.
34 W.A.S. Libr., sale cat. xxxiv, no. 36.
35 Inf. from Mr. R. H. Tucker, Manor Ho.
36 W.R.O., EA/68.
37 Ibid. tithe award; O.S. Maps 1/2,500, Wilts. XXXVII. 5 (1880 edn.); 6", Wilts. XXXVII. NW. (1900, 1926 edns.); 1/25,000, SU 26 (1961 edn.).
38 *Wilts. Inq. p.m.* 1242–1326 (Index Libr.), 381.
39 W.R.O. 9/8/153H.
40 Ibid. 79B/11, deed, Hyde to Streat, 1665.
41 Ibid. 79B/11, will of Thomas Streat, 1727.
42 Cf. *Andrews and Dury, Map* (W.R.S. viii), pl. 12.
43 W.R.O. 9/5/40; 315/27/4.

44 Ibid. 1010/22; *Kelly's Dir. Wilts.* (1848 and later edns.).
45 *Pipe R.* 1178 (P.R.S. xxvii), 28.
46 *V.C.H. Wilts.* iv. 418; *W.A.M.* xlix. 433.
47 W.R.O. 9/1/95, pp. 50, 53–4.
48 Ibid. 9/5/8; 9/8/5; 79B/11, deed, Cook to Ardley, 1575.
49 Ibid. 9/4/88.
50 Ibid. 9/5/8; 9/5/12.
51 Ibid. 9/5/11.
52 Ibid. 1300/372, ff. 8, 17–18.
53 Ibid. tithe award; above, manors (Burwood).
54 W.R.O. 9/1/110.
55 Ibid. 9/1/521.
56 Cf. above, manors (Burwood).
57 W.R.O., EA/68.
58 O.S. Map 6", Wilts. XXXVII (1887 edn.).
59 *V.C.H. Wilts.* ii, p. 147.

licensed the lord to take 4 bucks and 4 does from Savernake forest to stock it.[60] In 1364 the demesne of the manor was said to have enough pasture for 800 sheep.[61] The demesne farmstead stood within the hill fort. In 1398 there were 361 sheep on the demesne, the arable was poorly cultivated, and the farm buildings were said to be old and to need repair.[62]

Open fields lay south and east of the hill fort, and extensive pasture called the Heath lay north of it. By the mid 16th century three demesne fields had been separated from three other open fields, and a several demesne pasture, c. 235 a., had been separated from a common pasture west of it. The three demesne fields, Briary, 34 a., Church, 25 a., and Mill, 36 a., were those which lay nearest to Chisbury village on its south-east and east. That they were formerly open is shown by the survival in each of them of three strips belonging to the prebendary of Bedwyn.[63]

From the mid 16th century or earlier the demesne of Chisbury manor lay north–south across the parish as a farm virtually both compact and several. It included the park, the pasture of which was estimated at 40 a. in 1552, and was worked from the farmstead within the hill fort. Beside the Dun and detached from the rest of the farm lay meadow land which in 1612 was assessed at 13 a. and said to be watered. Immediately north-east of the hill fort there was a warren in which rabbits were probably kept in the early 17th century. In 1552 and 1612 the farm was mainly pasture. In 1719 it had 610 a. including 472 a. of arable, 23 a. of meadow of which 18 a. lay beside the Dun, 9 a. of pasture, and 98 a. of woodland. The arable included the warren, 11 a.[64] In 1807–8 the farm, later called Chisbury Manor farm, had 538 a. including 476 a. of arable, 40 a. of meadow and pasture of which 12 a. was watered meadow, and 23 a. of woodland.[65]

In the mid 16th century there were apparently five or six copyholds of Chisbury manor with farmsteads in the village. Most of the farmsteads probably stood beside the Ramsbury road a little north of the hill fort; by then one called Thorn Place had been built in Chisbury Lane, and another stood in the lane in 1719. From the mid 16th century or earlier Chisbury's open fields were shared mainly by the tenants of those farmsteads. Hill field, 42 a., lay south of the hill fort, Church field, 64 a., near Little Bedwyn village, and Shorthedge or Shortridge field, 26 a., south-east of Chisbury village between Briary field and the Dun. Chisbury manor included land in the open fields of Froxfield, Oakhill and Rudge (both in Froxfield parish), and Little Bedwyn, and some of that land was held by the tenants of the farmsteads at Chisbury. The tenants had a common pasture consisting of a heath, c. 111 a. on the west side of the Ramsbury

road, and a green, 9 a. immediately east of the farmsteads beside that road. The tenants also had c. 200 a. in closes south of Noke wood and in the angle of the Ramsbury road and Chisbury Lane.[66] In 1602 Thorn Place farm was accounted 156 a.: of its nominal 73 a. in open fields only 23 a. lay in Chisbury's.[67] In 1719 three farms, of 107 a., 27 a., and 21 a., had buildings beside the Ramsbury road; 84 a. of their land lay in closes, 63 a. in Chisbury's open fields, and 8 a. in other open fields. Thorn Place farm, 180 a., included the 23 a. in Chisbury's open fields and 48 a. in others; the other farm worked from Chisbury Lane had 49 a. including 11 a. in Chisbury's and 8 a. in other open fields. The five farms had feeding in common for 700 sheep on the heath.[68] The open fields and common pasture were inclosed in 1722 by agreement. Holdings not based in Chisbury included 35 a. of the fields; of 50 a. of pasture allotted to the lord of the manor for permitting the inclosure,[69] 23 a. was added to Manor farm, Little Bedwyn, and 27 a. to Knowle farm.[70] In the early 19th century 67 a. beside the London road north of the village became part of Harrow farm, the farmhouse of which stands in Little Bedwyn parish, the farmyard in Froxfield parish. The land of Thorn Place farm was apparently distributed among other farms, and in 1841 Lower farm, worked from buildings beside the Ramsbury road, had 377 a.[71]

On three sites west of Chisbury village farmsteads were built on land, part of Chisbury manor in the 16th century, probably brought into cultivation later than Chisbury's and possibly assarted from Savernake forest. There is evidence from the 16th century that some of the land was cultivated in open fields; if it was, it is almost certain that more than one farmstead was built on each site. By the 16th century the land worked from each site lay in a single several farm: in 1552 Monks (later Chisbury Lane) farm had 152 a. including 40 a. said to be inclosed in Monk field, Horse Hill farm had 93 a. including 60 a. said to be inclosed in Horse Hill fields, and Holt farm had 137 a. including 60 a. said to be inclosed from the common field. Holt farm then had a toft and apparently no farmhouse.[72] The farms shared a common pasture, 146 a., west of Chisbury Lane Farm. In the 17th century, when all the farms were in the same ownership, the tenant of Knowle farm and presumably the tenant of a farm based at Timbridge also kept animals on the common: in 1640 the tenant of Knowle farm was entitled to keep sheep there three days a week. By 1602 the toft and some land of Holt farm had been added to Horse Hill farm, then 123 a.[73] In 1702 Great Horse Hill farm had 133 a., and Little Horse Hill farm, with buildings on lower land south-west of Great Horse Hill Farm, had 75 a.[74] The common pasture was inclosed by agreement in 1703: 41

60   *Close R.* 1259–61, 355; *Cal. Close,* 1288–96, 230; P.R.O., SC 1/22/199; W.R.O. 1300/372, f. 7.
61   B.L. Harl. Ch. 48 E. 23.
62   *Cal. Inq. Misc.* vi. 151.
63   W.R.O. 9/1/95, ff. 43–55; 9/8/153H; 1300/372, ff. 7, 9.
64   Ibid. 9/1/95, ff. 43–4; 9/8/29; 9/8/153H; 1300/372, ff. 7, 9.   65   Ibid. 9/1/107, ff. 1–3.
66   Ibid. 9/1/95, ff. 45–54; 1300/372, ff. 7–8, 10–13.
67   Ibid. 9/8/147.

68   Ibid. 1300/372, ff. 7–8, 10–13.
69   Ibid. 9/8/27–8.
70   Ibid. 9/1/101.   71   Ibid. tithe award.
72   Ibid. 9/1/95, pp. 47–8, 52; for Holt, cf. *W.A.M.* xliv. 417.
73   W.R.O. 9/8/26; 9/8/147; above, manors (Chisbury; Knowle; Timbridge).
74   W.R.O. 9/8/149; for the bldgs., cf. 1300/372, ff. 7, 9–10.

a. was allotted to Chisbury Lane farm, 57 a. to Great Horse Hill farm, and 20 a. to Little Horse Hill farm. In 1719 those farms were accounted 237 a., 233 a., and 98 a. respectively; they included 450 a. of arable, all the former common pasture having been ploughed by then.[75] Chisbury Lane farm increased from 224 a. in 1801 to 288 a. in 1807–8 and 398 a. in 1841,[76] presumably by the transfer to it of land of the other farms.

Chisbury Manor farm was probably the largest of Chisbury's farms throughout the 19th century. In 1910, when the tenant was S. W. Farmer, it had 466 a.; then and until the mid 20th century it was worked in conjunction with Manor farm, Little Bedwyn. In 1910 Lower farm had 264 a., Chisbury Lane farm 150 a., and Great Horse Hill farm 120 a.; 187 a. of Chisbury's land was part of Harrow farm, and 130 a., including part of the former Holt farm, was worked from Burbage parish as part of Warren farm.[77] In the 1930s the land in Little Bedwyn parish which lay in those farms was about half arable and half pasture,[78] and it was almost certainly used partly for dairy farming. In 1998 the land of Manor farm, 446 a., was mainly arable; it was worked in conjunction with Bewley farm, an arable and beef farm based in Great Bedwyn parish which itself included c. 90 a. in Little Bedwyn parish. The buildings of Manor farm on the hill fort and 67 a. on and around the hill fort were then used as a stud farm. In 1998 Lower farm was an arable farm of 512 a., the tenant of which also held 70 a. south of the London road formerly part of Harrow farm. Chisbury Lane farm, 267 a., was a dairy farm, and Warren farm, also a dairy farm, included c. 50 a. in the parish. The rest of Harrow farm, north of the London road and including c. 40 a. in Little Bedwyn parish, was worked in conjunction with Knowle farm.[79]

Chisbury had 40 a. of wood in 1086.[80] Later it was well wooded. In 1260 the lord of Chisbury manor was licensed to inclose as part of his park woodland which, although outside the regard and far from the covert, was then within Savernake forest,[81] presumably the woodland later called Park copse; woods called Frith and Noke were also standing in the 13th century.[82] In 1552 trees stood in the park and there were woods called Cobham, Noke, and Oxleaze.[83] In 1612 Oxleaze copse was accounted 16 a. and Park copse 50 a.[84] In 1719 Chisbury manor included 332 a. of woodland: the largest woods were Cobham frith, 69 a., Noke wood, 60 a., Park copse, 42 a., and Oxleaze copse, 18 a., and there was 36 a. of woodland near Great Horse Hill Farm. Cobham frith adjoined woodland of Knowle.[85] At the south end of the common pasture inclosed in 1703 Sicily clump, c. 45 a., had been planted by c. 1820, and at the north end 9 a. of woodland adjoining Cobham frith was planted in the mid 20th century. Oxleaze copse was grubbed up between c. 1820 and c. 1880; the other woodland was standing in 1998.[86]

Chisbury had two mills in 1086.[87] A mill was part of Chisbury manor in the 16th and 17th centuries. It stood on the Dun near Great Bedwyn village and in 1590, when it was called Cop mill or Little Bedwyn mill, consisted of a mill and mill house under one roof.[88] There may have been no mill on the site in the earlier 18th century:[89] one belonging to the owner of Manor farm, Little Bedwyn, stood there in 1762 and 1792.[90] The supply of water to the mill may have been reduced in the late 1790s by the construction of the Kennet & Avon canal, which was fed from head streams of the Dun.[91] The mill, standing in 1802,[92] had apparently been demolished by 1812, when the land on which it stood bore the name Burnt Mill field.[93]

In the early 18th century a brickworks stood on the green east of the Ramsbury road.[94]

HENSET AND KNOWLE. Henset's land was probably that, c. 200 a., north of Knowle Farm and the London road and east of Timbridge down.[95] References to Henset field suggest that in the 13th century it included open-field arable.[96] In the 14th century a holding consisting of a farmstead, 1 carucate, 1 a. of meadow, 2 a. of pasture, and 12 a. of wood may have comprised all Henset's land.[97] The woodland may have been Knowle Hens wood, 20 a., which was standing in 1716 and 1998 and adjoined Hens wood in Ramsbury. There is no evidence of a farmstead standing after the 14th century on what was probably Henset's land, and that land was part of Knowle farm in the 18th century.[98]

Knowle farm was possibly assarted from Savernake forest. Knowle Farm is the only farmstead known to have stood on it, and there is no evidence that any part of it was open field or common pasture. About 1311 it consisted of the farmstead, 120 a. of arable, 6 a. of pasture, and 8 a. of wood,[99] and it was leased as a single farm in the 16th century.[1] In 1640 the farmer was allowed to feed sheep three days a week on

---

75 W.R.O. 9/8/26; 1300/372, ff. 7, 9–11.
76 Ibid. 9/1/107, ff. 28–9; 9/8/103; ibid. tithe award.
77 Ibid. Inland Revenue, val. reg. 56; ibid. G 8/516/2; Kelly's Dir. Wilts. (1911); for Farmer, above, this section (Little Bedwyn); for Warren farm, below, Burbage, econ. hist. (Durley).
78 [1st] Land Util. Surv. Map, sheet 112.
79 Inf. from the agent for the Crown Estate Com., 42 High Street, Marlborough; for Bewley farm, above, Great Bedwyn, econ. hist. (Great Bedwyn: agric.); for Knowle farm, below, this section.
80 V.C.H. Wilts. ii, p. 147.
81 Cal. Chart. R. 1257–1300, 28; for the park, above, this section.   82 V.C.H. Wilts. iv. 418–19.
83 W.R.O. 9/1/95, pp. 54–5.   84 Ibid. 9/8/153H.
85 Ibid. 1300/372, ff. 7, 9–11, 20.
86 Ibid. 9/8/26; O.S. Maps 6", Wilts. XXX (1887 edn.);

XXXVI. NE. (1926 edn.); 1/25,000, SU 26 (1961 edn.); Savernake estate map, c. 1820 (copy in W.R.O.); for the pasture, above, this section.
87 V.C.H. Wilts. ii, p. 147.
88 W.R.O. 9/1/95, p. 51; 9/8/147; cf. 1300/372, ff. 8, 17.
89 Cf. ibid. 9/1/101; 1300/372, ff. 8, 17–18.
90 Ibid. 9/3/386–7; ibid. EA/68.
91 Above, intro.; Great Bedwyn, intro. [canal].
92 W.R.O. 9/5/16.
93 Ibid. 1955/25.
94 Ibid. 9/8/28; 1300/372, ff. 7, 9.
95 Cat. Anct. D. ii, C 2891.
96 Ibid.; Crown Pleas, 1249 (W.R.S. xvi), p. 218.
97 P.R.O., C 260/132, no. 1.
98 W.R.O. 1300/372, ff. 20–1.
99 Wilts. Inq. p.m. 1242–1326 (Index Libr.), 382.
1 P.R.O., REQ 2/20/64; ibid. STAC 4/4/14.

the common pasture west of Chisbury Lane Farm,[2] and 8 a. of the pasture was allotted for the farm at inclosure in 1703.[3] In 1716 Knowle farm had 489 a., including 348 a. of arable, 13 a. of meadows, 21 a. of pasture, and 95 a. of woods. Its land north of the London road, 182 a. of arable and Knowle Hens wood, was probably Henset's.[4] In 1722 a 27-a. allotment of Chisbury heath was added to the farm,[5] 524 a. in 1841.[6] In 1910 Knowle farm had 406 a., 112 a. having been transferred to Warren farm, Burbage.[7] Without its woodland it was an arable and beef farm of 272 a. in 1998. It was then worked in conjunction with Harrow farm, 250 a. north of the London road including c. 210 a. in Froxfield parish.[8]

In 1716 the woodland of Knowle farm included, in addition to Knowle Hens wood, Rye croft, 26 a. adjoining Cobham frith in Chisbury, Home coppice, 14 a. immediately south-west of the farmstead, 20 a. of the woodland later called Birch copse, and a copse of 7 a. and one of 5 a.;[9] 18 a. of additional woodland was planted to adjoin the south-west end of Home coppice between c. 1820 and 1886, and an additional copse of 19 a. adjoining that and the 5-a. copse was planted between 1886 and 1899.[10] All that woodland except the copse of 7 a. was standing in 1998.

In the earlier 20th century gravel was extracted commercially from a pit near Knowle Farm. The land had been returned to agriculture by the late 20th century.[11]

PUTHALL. Puthall's land was possibly assarted from Savernake forest, and most of it was probably agricultural in the earlier 13th century,[12] but whether it included open fields and common pasture in the Middle Ages is uncertain. Its north-west corner, where woodland was said in the 16th century to stand in Puthall park,[13] was presumably imparked.

In the earlier 16th century all Puthall's land apparently lay in Puthall farm, 174 a., which was several and probably compact. The farm had six closes of arable, 82 a., three closes of pasture, 59 a., 1 a. of meadow, and 31 a. of woodland.[14] From the mid 16th century or earlier the farm was held with 30 a. in four adjoining closes in Mildenhall parish.[15] In 1634 it consisted of its farmstead, 3 a. of home closes, 107 a. of arable, 80 a. of

pasture, 12 a. of meadows, 8 a. of woodland, and the herbage of 32 a. of woodland. The farmer had the first cut of hay from 2 a. of meadow at Stitchcombe in Mildenhall and feeding for horses, cattle, and 400 sheep in Savernake forest.[16] The area of the forest designated for the sheep of Puthall farm was possibly c. 100 a.; it apparently lay immediately south-west of the farm but never became part of it.[17]

In 1717 Puthall farm was a compact farm of 314 a. of which c. 56 a. lay in Mildenhall: it included 192 a. of arable, 44 a. of pasture, 19 a. of meadows, and 25 a. of wood.[18] In 1867 it had 316 a. including 258 a. of arable,[19] and in 1996 it was an arable farm of 297 a.[20]

Puthall had woodland in 1300,[21] presumably that standing in Puthall park in the earlier 16th century, when it was accounted 20 a. About 1536 Little Frith copse was estimated at 10 a.,[22] and in 1634 there was another 8 a. of woodland.[23] In 1717 Puthall park and woodland adjoining it totalled 34 a., Little Frith copse and woodland adjoining it totalled 22 a., and Horseleaze copse, later linked to Little Frith copse by other woodland, was 11 a.[24] By c. 1820 Little Frith copse had been enlarged to c. 47 a.[25] Puthall Park wood, Little Frith copse, and Horseleaze copse, c. 92 a., were all standing in 1998.

TIMBRIDGE AND LITTLEWORTH. There were possibly small open fields at Timbridge in the early 14th century, when a holding was assessed at 1 yardland, two customary tenants had small holdings there, and downland was pasture.[26] Later evidence shows that Timbridge down, 59 a., lay north of the London road.[27]

Two farmsteads stood at Timbridge in the Middle Ages and until the 18th century.[28] In the 17th century each was part of a mainly several farm.[29] One of the farms presumably included the right to feed animals on the common pasture west of Chisbury Lane Farm, and 20 a. was allotted to it when the common was inclosed in 1703. In 1719 one farm had 109 a., including Timbridge down which was then arable, and the other had 61 a., including the 20-a. allotment: 159 a. of the 170 a. was arable.[30] In the later 18th century the smaller farm was held by the tenant of Chisbury Lane farm.[31]

By 1812 the two farms based at Timbridge, and Littleworth farm which lay west of them,

2 W.R.O. 9/8/147.
3 Ibid. 9/8/26; for the common pasture, above, this section (Chisbury).
4 W.R.O. 1300/372, ff. 20–1.
5 Ibid. 9/8/67; for the heath, above, this section (Chisbury).
6 W.R.O., tithe award.
7 Ibid. Inland Revenue, val. reg. 56.
8 Inf. from the agent from the Crown Estate Com.
9 W.R.O. 1300/372, ff. 20–1.
10 O.S. Maps 6", Wilts. XXXVI (1888 edn.); XXXVI. NE. (1900 edn.); Savernake estate map, c. 1820 (copy in W.R.O.).
11 W.A.M. lxxvii. 27; O.S. Maps 6", Wilts. XXIX. SE. (1900, 1925 edns.).
12 Cur. Reg. R. xiii, p. 322.
13 Longleat Mun., Seymour papers, xii, f. 309.
14 Ibid.
15 Alnwick Castle Mun. X.II.11, box 1, lease, Hertford to Hyde, 1559.
16 Ibid. X.II.11, box 6, survey, 1634, f. 9; for the

woodland, below, this section.
17 W.R.O. 1300/1840; for the feeding of sheep in the forest, e.g. above, Great Bedwyn, econ. hist. (Great Bedwyn: agric.); below, Burbage, econ. hist. (Durley).
18 W.R.O. 1300/372, ff. 22–3.
19 Ibid. 9/1/110.
20 Inf. from the agent for the Crown Estate Com.
21 V.C.H. Wilts. iv. 450.
22 Longleat Mun., Seymour papers, xii, f. 309.
23 Alnwick Castle Mun. X.II.11, box 6, survey, 1634, f. 9.
24 W.R.O. 1300/372, ff. 22–3.
25 Savernake estate map, c. 1820 (copy in W.R.O.).
26 Wilts. Inq. p.m. 1242–1326 (Index Libr.), 312–13; Cal. Close, 1323–7, 389–90.
27 W.R.O. 1300/372, ff. 36–7.
28 Ibid.; ibid. 1300/47A.
29 Ibid. 9/5/38; 9/8/147.
30 Ibid. 9/8/26; 1300/372, ff. 36–7; for the common pasture, above, this section (Chisbury).
31 W.R.O. 9/8/143; 9/8/150.

had been merged as Timbridge farm, 276 a. including 213 a. of arable.[32] Timbridge farm had 291 a. in 1841,[33] 150 a. in 1910,[34] and 267 a. in 1998, when it was an arable and dairy farm.[35]

From the 18th century to the 20th no more than a few acres of Timbridge's land was wooded.[36]

Littleworth farm was probably the land called Little farm apparently assarted from Savernake forest c. 1302.[37] By 1786 its land, apparently c. 100 a., seems to have been added to the larger of the farms based at Timbridge,[38] and the land was part of Timbridge farm in 1812.[39] The farmstead had been largely demolished by c. 1820.[40]

The land which may have been added to the west end of the parish in the 19th century included Crabtree common, then a pasture of c. 20 a., and 130 a. of woodland including part of Birch copse.[41] All but c. 5 a. of Crabtree common was woodland in 1998.

LOCAL GOVERNMENT

No lord exercised leet jurisdiction in respect of a manor in Little Bedwyn parish. In the 16th century Little Bedwyn, Chisbury, Henset, and Puthall were each a tithing of Kinwardstone hundred.[42] Henset tithing included Timbridge.[43] It had been merged with Puthall tithing by 1760:[44] the composite tithing, which continued to be represented at the hundred court by two tithingmen, included Knowle and Rudge in Froxfield parish.[45]

A court of Little Bedwyn manor was held in the earlier 14th century.[46] In the 16th a court was held jointly by the owners of portions of the manor.[47]

Records of the court baron of Chisbury manor survive from 1602. The court was usually held once a year, proceeded on the presentments of the homage, reported the death of tenants, and witnessed transfers of copyholds. In the 17th century it also concerned itself with rights of way, the condition of buildings, gates, and boundaries, and the use of common pasture. In 1604 the unlicensed killing of hares on the manor was reported; in 1678 the court chose two overseers of the open fields and a grass hayward to oversee the use of the common pasture. Minor agrarian malpractices continued to be presented occasionally until 1771. Thereafter the court did little more than to

record that the tenants of the manor had paid their quitrents.[48]

A court was apparently held at Henset in the 14th century.[49]

The parish spent £177 on poor relief in 1775–6, an average of £216 in the three years to Easter 1785, and £407 in 1802–3, when 62 adults and 56 children were relieved regularly and 29 people occasionally and the poor rate was slightly above average for the hundred. A building called a workhouse stood at Forebridge in 1792, but all relief in 1802–3 was outdoor.[50] In 1812–13, when the population of the parish was c. 450, 44 adults were relieved regularly and 178 occasionally at a total cost of £964. Thereafter expenditure fell: between 1813–14 and 1833–4 it exceeded £600 only twice,[51] and in the three years to Easter 1835 it averaged £349. Little Bedwyn joined Hungerford poor-law union in 1835[52] and became part of Kennet district in 1974.[53]

CHURCH

Little Bedwyn church had been built by 1158,[54] Chisbury church by the earlier 13th century.[55] In the Middle Ages each church was dependent on Great Bedwyn church as a chapel, the rector of Great Bedwyn church was the prebendary of Bedwyn, and the whole of what became Little Bedwyn parish was in the peculiar over which the prebendary, and his successors as owners of the Prebendal manor in Great Bedwyn, exercised archidiaconal jurisdiction. From the early 15th century or earlier the chaplain of Little Bedwyn was authorized to administer all sacraments and sacramentals in Little Bedwyn church, which had a graveyard,[56] and in 1554, when the bishop collated a perpetual vicar, the church was expressly said to be a parish church.[57] Chisbury church was served until 1547,[58] not thereafter. Where the inhabitants of Chisbury and the other settlements in the parish, apart from Little Bedwyn, were baptized, married, and buried in the Middle Ages is uncertain. From the 16th century or earlier Little Bedwyn's was their parish church.[59] In 1864 the west third of Little Bedwyn parish was assigned to the church of St. Katharine, Savernake Forest, as part of its district.[60] In 1982 the vicarages of Little Bedwyn, Great Bedwyn, and Savernake Forest were united.[61]

32 W.R.O. 9/1/109; for Littleworth farm, below, this section.
33 W.R.O., tithe award.
34 Ibid. Inland Revenue, val. reg. 56.
35 Inf. from the agent for the Crown Estate Com.
36 Cf. O.S. Maps 6", Wilts. XXIX, XXXVI (1888–9 and later edns.); W.R.O. 1300/372, ff. 36–7.
37 Cal. Pat. 1301–7, 59; cf. W.R.O. 1300/372, ff. 36–7.
38 W.R.O. 1300/360.
39 Ibid. 9/1/109.
40 Savernake estate map, c. 1820 (copy in W.R.O.).
41 Ibid.; above, intro.
42 First Pembroke Survey, ed. Straton, i. 190–2.
43 W.R.O. 9/5/38.
44 Ibid. 9/5/7.
45 Ibid. 9/8/12; ibid. A 1/345/29; ibid. EA/119.
46 Wilts. Inq. p.m. 1327–77 (Index Libr.), 127.
47 P.R.O., REQ 2/201/42.
48 W.R.O. 9/1/137, rott. 12d.–13; 9/1/139, rot. 9; 9/1/160–1; 9/1/165; 9/1/170–5; 9/1/177–82; 9/1/184–5; 9/1/187–9; 9/1/191–203; 9/1/204, pp. 291–305; 9/8/144–6;

192/24B.
49 Cal. Close, 1323–7, 389–90; Wilts. Inq. p.m. 1327–77 (Index Libr.), 313.
50 Poor Law Abstract, 1804, 564–5; W.R.O., EA/68.
51 V.C.H. Wilts. iv. 340; Poor Law Abstract, 1818, 498–9; Poor Rate Returns, 1816–21, 188; 1822–4, 228; 1825–9, 218; 1830–4, 212.
52 Poor Law Com. 1st Rep. App. D, 242.
53 O.S. Map 1/100,000, admin. areas, Wilts. (1974 edn.).
54 Reg. St. Osmund (Rolls Ser.), i. 203.
55 Below, this section [Chisbury].
56 Chandler's Reg. (W.R.S. xxxix), pp. 31, 33; Reg. Martival (Cant. & York Soc.), ii (1), 77–8; W.R.O., D 21, passim; above, Great Bedwyn, churches, where there is more inf. about the jurisdiction.
57 W.R.O., D 1/2/16, f. (2nd foliation) 53.
58 P.R.O., E 301/58, no. 66; for how it was served, below, this section [Chisbury].
59 W.R.O., bishop's transcripts, bdle. 1.
60 Ibid. D 377/9; Lond. Gaz. 12 Apr. 1864, pp. 2018–21.
61 Ch. Com. file, NB 34/156B/2.

In the Middle Ages the chaplain who served Little Bedwyn church was appointed by the prebendary of Bedwyn.[62] From 1543, when the prebend was dissolved, the patronage passed as part of the Prebendal manor.[63] In 1554, when the manor was held, as land concealed from the Crown, by Sir Edward Seymour (cr. earl of Hertford 1559), a ward of the Crown, the bishop collated by lapse.[64] From 1567 the advowson of the vicarage passed as part of the manor, and with Tottenham Lodge and Tottenham House in Great Bedwyn, in the Seymour, Bruce, Brudenell, and Brudenell-Bruce families. Assignees of Lord Hertford presented in 1562 while the manor remained concealed from the Crown, Robert Blake presented in 1583, presumably by grant of a turn, and Sir William Pynsent, Bt., presented by grant of a turn in 1693.[65] George Brudenell-Bruce, marquess of Ailesbury, who sold the land of the Prebendal manor to the Crown in 1950, transferred the advowson of Little Bedwyn vicarage to the bishop of Salisbury in 1953. The bishop was appointed patron of the united benefice formed in 1982.[66]

Little Bedwyn vicarage, valued at £9 6s. 8d. in 1535[67] and £280 c. 1830,[68] was of below average wealth for the diocese. By 1672 corn tithes from some of Chisbury's land, corn and hay tithes from Burwood heath and most of Little Bedwyn's land, some tithes of wood, and small tithes from the whole parish except the demesne of Chisbury manor had been assigned to the vicar. Those tithes were valued at £257 in 1840 and commuted in 1842. In 1672 the vicar had a house and a meadow held instead of some tithes of hay. In 1841 he had a house and 1 a. of meadow.[69] The vicarage house stood on a site north-west of, and close to, which the Kennet & Avon canal was built in the 1790s and the Berks. & Hants Extension Railway in 1862.[70] After 1841 the vicar moved to a house, later called the White House, on an adjoining site, and the glebe house which was altered and repaired in 1845[71] was probably the new one. That house was sold in 1863, when a new vicarage house was built[72] on higher ground north-west of the canal and the railway. That new house was enlarged in 1873 and 1882[73] and sold in 1949.[74]

A church was standing at Chisbury in the earlier 13th century.[75] It was presumably built by the lord of Chisbury manor, who was probably the patron of Froxfield rectory then, as he was later. In the earlier 13th century the rector of Froxfield received the tithes from Chisbury and presumably served the church, and before 1246 he gave the tithes, and presumably the duty of serving the church, to St. Denis's priory, Southampton. By 1246, the year in which the prebendary of Bedwyn claimed the tithes from the demesne of Chisbury manor on the grounds that Chisbury was part of Great Bedwyn parish, the priory had probably appointed a chaplain to serve Chisbury church and assigned the tithes arising from the rest of Chisbury to him. In 1247 the tithes from the demesne were confirmed to the priory in exchange for a small payment by the priory to the prebendary. That payment, and the requirement, of which there is later evidence, that the priest serving Chisbury church should attend Great Bedwyn church at major festivals, presumably marked the dependence of the church at Chisbury on that at Great Bedwyn. In 1259 the rector of Froxfield unsuccessfully claimed that the priory's tenure of Chisbury church was temporary and that it should revert to him.[76] Thereafter the church was served by chaplains appointed by the priory.[77] There was an incumbent chaplain in the early 15th century, the church was sometimes unserved in the late 15th century,[78] and the bishop collated by lapse in 1496.[79] In 1518 the prior granted the patronage for a turn to John Man,[80] who in 1535 and 1543 was himself the chaplain and, for a rent of 6s. 8d., held the tithes except those arising from the demesne of Chisbury manor.[81] The church, called St. Martin's in 1496,[82] was served until 1547, when the chaplain's tithes passed to the Crown by Act.[83] It was later used as a barn[84] and in 1998 was quasi-ruinous.[85] It is rectangular and of rubble with ashlar dressings; in 1998 old rendering survived inside and outside, and scars of a screen between the chancel and the nave could be seen on that inside. To judge from the cusped lancets in the nave, the church was built in the earlier 13th century; in each of its three walls the chancel has a two-light window of the later 13th century. The north doorway survives from the 13th century, the south doorway is 19th-century, and the roof, which incorporates some of the old timbers, was largely reconstructed in the 19th century.

A chapel was built at Knowle Farm in the 14th century. It is not known how or for how long it was served. In 1998 it survived as an outbuilding of Knowle House.

In the Middle Ages 1 a. was given for a light in Little Bedwyn church.[86] Goods taken from the church in Edward VI's reign had not been

62 *Chandler's Reg.* (W.R.S. xxxix), p. 33.
63 For the descent of the manor, above, Great Bedwyn, manors (Prebendal).
64 W.R.O., D 1/2/16, f. (2nd foliation) 53.
65 Ibid. D 5/1/2, ff. 10, 17, 24v., 62, 78v., 92, 103, 124, 148, 151, 163v.; above, Great Bedwyn, manors (Tottenham).
66 Ch. Com. files, NB 34/156B/1–2.
67 *Valor Eccl.* (Rec. Com.), ii. 150.
68 *Rep. Com. Eccl. Revenues*, 824–5.
69 W.R.O. 9/4/88; ibid. tithe award.
70 Ibid. EA/68; for the canal and the railway, above, intro.
71 W.R.O., D 1/11/153A; D 5/3/2; ibid. tithe award.
72 Ibid. D 1/11/155.
73 Ibid. D 1/11/217; D 1/11/219; D 1/11/279.
74 Inf. from Ch. Com.
75 For its archit., below, this section.
76 *Sar. Chart. and Doc.* (Rolls Ser.), pp. 310–12; *Chandler's Reg.* (W.R.S. xxxix), p. 102; P.R.O., E 135/21/26; above, manors (Chisbury); below, Froxfield, church.
77 B.L. Harl. Ch. 44 I. 51.
78 *Chandler's Reg.* (W.R.S. xxxix), p. 31.
79 W.R.O., D 1/2/13, f. 22v.
80 B.L. Harl. Ch. 44 I. 51.
81 *Valor Eccl.* (Rec. Com.), ii. 150; P.R.O., SC 6/Hen. VIII/3326, rot. 6; W.R.O. 9/8/22.
82 Phillipps, *Wilts. Inst.* i. 178; cf. *Valor Eccl.* (Rec. Com.), ii. 150.
83 P.R.O., E 301/58, no. 66; W.R.O. 9/8/10.
84 Aubrey, *Topog. Colln.* ed. Jackson, 381; *W.A.M.* li. 231–2.
85 Above, *frontispiece*.
86 P.R.O., E 301/58, no. 124.

THE NORTH ARCADE OF THE CHURCH

restored by 1556.[87] Nathaniel Saunders, vicar from 1638, had been deprived by 1656 and was restored in 1660 or soon after.[88] A curate who lived at Froxfield served both Little Bedwyn and Froxfield in 1783.[89] At Little Bedwyn in 1812 one service was held each Sunday and a communion service was held four times a year; there were 20 communicants.[90] In 1832, when there was still only one service each Sunday, the church was being served by a curate who lived in the vicarage house.[91] There were two services each Sunday in 1851.[92] In 1864 the two services were held with an average congregation of 70, excluding children, and there were additional services in Lent and Advent, at great festivals, and on 1 January. Communion services were held at the great festivals with c. 20 communicants and on the first Sunday in each month with c. 13.[93] A mission room was built at Chisbury in the later 19th century. Services were probably held in it until the earlier 20th.[94] From 1953 to 1958 the vicarage was held in plurality with that of Great Bedwyn, from 1958 to 1965 with that of Froxfield, and from 1965 with those of Great Bedwyn and Savernake Forest.[95]

By 1922 S. W. Farmer (d. 1926) had given £650 stock to maintain Little Bedwyn's churchyard. The income, £26, was mostly used for that purpose, partly to repair the church.[96] By will proved c. 1946 Amy Makeham gave £570 stock for repairs to the church.[97] Nothing was known of either charity in 1998.

The church of *ST. MICHAEL*, so called in 1405,[98] is of flint rubble and ashlar and consists of a chancel with north vestry, an aisled and clerestoried nave with south porch, and a west tower with stone spire. The nave, which is narrow, and the arcades were built c. 1200. The south has pointed arches and the north round arches, but the capitals suggest that the arcades are contemporary with each other. To judge from its arch, the tower was built in the later 13th century. The chancel and the aisles were apparently rebuilt c. 1400. In the 15th century the porch was built, the tower was rebuilt, and the spire was added. The roof of the north aisle is of c. 1500;[99] the chancel and the nave were reroofed in 1841.[1] In 1868 the church was extensively restored, and the vestry was built, to designs by T. H. Wyatt; new seating was provided and the outside of the church was renovated.[2] The spire was dismantled and rebuilt in 1963 after being struck by lightning.[3]

In the early 15th century the church had two silver-gilt chalices each with a paten.[4] In 1553 a chalice of 11 oz. was left in the parish and 2½ oz. of plate was taken for the king. A chalice with paten cover, hallmarked for 1681, was bought in 1682, was the only silver held for the church in 1812, and belonged to the parish in 1998. A 19th-century paten which had been given by 1891, and a chalice and paten given in 1951, also belonged to the parish in 1998.[5]

There were four bells in the church in 1553. The treble and the tenor were replaced by bells cast by John Wallis in 1581, the other two by a

87 W.R.O., D 1/43/2, f. 13.
88 *Subscription Bk. 1620–40* (W.R.S. xxxii), p. 67; *Walker Revised*, ed. Matthews, 380.
89 *Vis. Queries, 1783* (W.R.S. xxvii), pp. 106–7.
90 *W.A.M.* xli. 131.
91 Ch. Com. file, NB 34/156B/1.
92 P.R.O., HO 129/121/2/4/8.
93 W.R.O., D 1/56/7.
94 O.S. Maps 1/2,500, Wilts. XXXVII. 1 (1880 and later edns.).
95 Ch. Com. files, NB 34/156B/1–2.

96 W.R.O., L 2, Little Bedwyn.
97 Ch. Com. file, NB 34/202.
98 *Chandler's Reg.* (W.R.S. xxxix), p. 33.
99 Description based partly on J. Buckler, watercolours in W.A.S. Libr., vol. iv. 2; vol. viii. 48.
1 W.R.O. 1955/17.
2 Ibid. 1955/16.
3 Ibid. 1955/19.
4 *Chandler's Reg.* (W.R.S. xxxix), p. 64.
5 Nightingale, *Wilts. Plate*, 164–5; *W.A.M.* xli. 131; inf. from Mrs. E. S. Bishop, Chisbury Cottage.

bell cast in 1605, probably by Robert Beconsall, and a bell cast by William Purdue in 1663. The treble was replaced by a bell cast by Mears & Stainbank in 1869; the tenor was recast by Mears & Stainbank in 1887.[6] The two 17th-century bells and the two 19th-century bells hung in the church in 1998.[7]

The registers begin in 1722. Except for baptisms 1727–30, marriages 1727–9, and burials 1729–40 they are complete.[8]

NONCONFORMITY. A meeting house at Little Bedwyn for dissenters was certified in 1840, another, possibly for Primitive Methodists, was certified in 1843, and a chapel for Primitive Methodists was built in 1846.[9] Afternoon and evening services were held in the chapel each Sunday in 1851.[10] It was probably closed in the mid 20th century.[11]

A cottage at Chisbury was certified in 1828 for meetings of Wesleyan Methodists.[12] In 1851 a meeting was held on Sunday evenings, and on Census Sunday it was attended by 21.[13] Meetings were held in 1864[14] and are not known to have been held later.

EDUCATION. There was no school in the parish in 1818,[15] in 1833 two schools had a total of 20 pupils,[16] and from 1835 to 1840 children from Little Bedwyn attended the National school at Great Bedwyn. A new school in Little Bedwyn was opened in 1841.[17] It was held in a rented house in 1846–7, when it was attended by 22 boys and 6 girls.[18] A new school, incorporating two classrooms and a house, was built in 1854. Until 1885 it was usually attended by children from Froxfield, who were among c. 80 pupils at the school in 1858 and 116 in 1878; in 1885, when a new school was opened at Froxfield, attendance at Little Bedwyn school fell from 102 to 55.[19] Average attendance was 56 in 1908, c. 90 between 1907 and 1910, a period in which there was no school at Froxfield, 54 in 1910–11, and 36 in 1926–7. The school had c. 116 pupils in the 1930s,[20] 30 in 1970. It was closed in 1971.[21]

Between 1894 and 1903 an evening school was held in winter.[22]

CHARITY FOR THE POOR. None known.

BURBAGE

BURBAGE parish[23] lies south of Savernake forest and at the east end of the Vale of Pewsey. It contains Burbage village, 9 km. SSE. of Marlborough, and Durley village, hamlets called Ram Alley and Stibb Green, and several other pockets of settlement. Burbage's land lies as a north–south strip comparable to the strips of other settlements in the Vale of Pewsey; Durley was planted on downland which was probably part of Burbage's land until assigned to the new village as its agricultural land.[24] About 1213 a gift to Burbage church of the tithes from assarts at Durley probably confirmed that Durley was in Burbage parish.[25]

The boundary between Burbage parish and Savernake forest, which was extra-parochial, seems to have run east–west immediately north of Durley village.[26] In the 18th century it was called into question. It was debated whether a warren, which lay north-east of the village, was inclosed in 1703, and was converted to farmland, lay on Durley's land or the forest's,[27] and the parish, to which paupers born in the forest were

returned, attempted to bring more of the forest within its boundaries in order to levy the poor rate on property in it.[28] The parishioners perambulated as far as Amity Oak, a point 3.5 km. north of Durley village.[29] The owner of the forest attempted to exclude all parts of the forest from the parish. Under an agreement between the parish and the owner proposed in 1786 part of the forest called Durley heath, the south-east part of which had been inclosed by the owner of the forest as a new part of the park of Tottenham House in Great Bedwyn, and other parts of the forest would have been excluded from the parish, the former warren included.[30] The proposal was apparently adopted, and in 1843 Burbage parish consisted of a main part, c. 3,038 a., and of the former warren, 145 a., which was separated from the main part by Durley heath and the park of Tottenham House.[31] By 1886 the heath, that part of the park, parts of the forest called Black Vault and Coal coppice, and c. 25 a. north of Leigh Hill copse had been added to the parish, thenceforth 1,624 ha. (4,012 a.).[32]

6   Walters, *Wilts. Bells*, 20, 22.
7   W.R.O. 1955/15, where different dates are given for the 19th-cent. bells; inf. from Mrs. Bishop.
8   W.R.O. 1955/1; 1955/3; 1955/25; transcripts for 1591–7 and several periods in the 17th cent. and early 18th are in W.R.O.
9   *Meeting Ho. Certs.* (W.R.S. xl), pp. 152, 158, 164.
10   P.R.O., HO 129/121/2/4/9.
11   Cf. O.S. Map 1/2,500, Wilts. XXXVII. 1 (1924 edn.).
12   *Meeting Ho. Certs.* (W.R.S. xl), p. 117.
13   P.R.O., HO 129/121/2/3/5.
14   W.R.O., D 1/56/7.   15   *Educ. of Poor Digest*, 1018.
16   *Educ. Enq. Abstract*, 1028.
17   P.R.O., ED 7/130, no. 169; W.R.O., F 8/600/2/31/1.
18   Nat. Soc. *Inquiry, 1846–7*, Wilts. 2–3.
19   *Acct. of Wilts. Schs.* 6, 24; W.R.O., F 8/600/16/1/24/1; below, Froxfield, educ.

20   *Bd. of Educ., List 21* (H.M.S.O.); below, Froxfield, educ.   21   W.R.O., F 8/600/1/26/1.
22   Ibid. F 8/500/16/2/1.
23   This article was written in 1995. Maps used include O.S. Maps 1", sheet 14 (1817 edn.); 1/25,000, SU 25/35 (1994 edn.); SU 26/36 (1983 edn.); 6", Wilts. XXXVI, XLII (1888 and later edns.).
24   Cf. below, econ. hist.
25   *Reg. St. Osmund* (Rolls Ser.), i. 250–2; W.R.O. 9/7/1.
26   W.R.O. 1300/360; 1300/1840A.
27   Ibid. 1300/333; below, econ. hist. (Durley).
28   W.R.O. 1300/1847.
29   Ibid. 1955/25.
30   Ibid. 1300/1847; below, econ. hist. (Durley).
31   W.R.O., tithe award.
32   O.S. Map 6", Wilts. XXXVI (1888 edn.); for the place names, W.R.O. 1300/360.

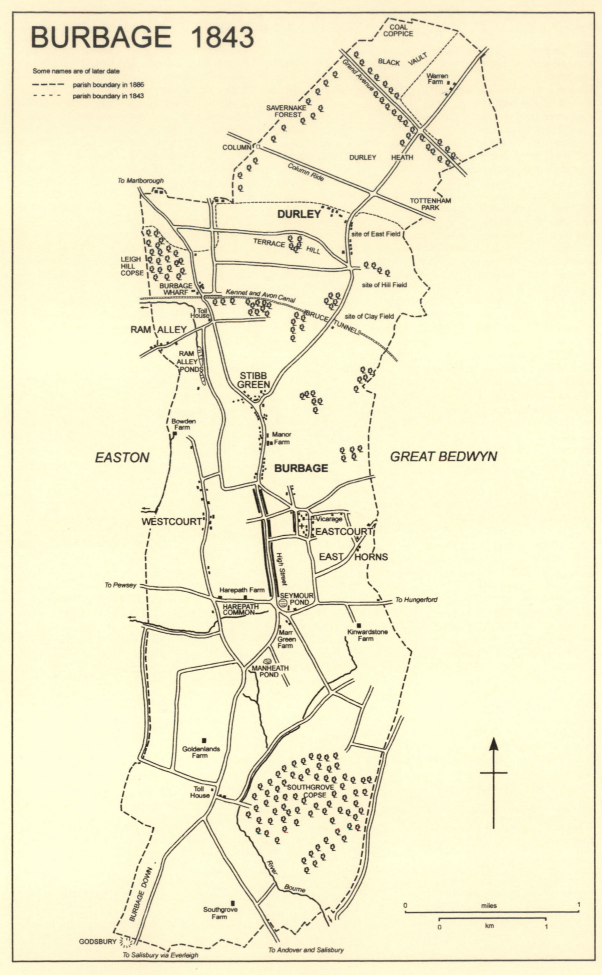

BURBAGE 1843

Some names are of later date

－ ‧ － ‧ － parish boundary in 1886

－ － － － parish boundary in 1843

COAL COPPICE

BLACK VAULT

Warren Farm

Grand Avenue

SAVERNAKE FOREST

COLUMN

DURLEY HEATH

Column Ride

TOTTENHAM PARK

To Marlborough

DURLEY

site of East Field

TERRACE HILL

LEIGH HILL COPSE

site of Hill Field

BURBAGE WHARF

Kennet and Avon Canal

Toll House

BRUCE TUNNEL

site of Clay Field

RAM ALLEY

RAM ALLEY PONDS

STIBB GREEN

Bowden Farm

Manor Farm

EASTON

BURBAGE

GREAT BEDWYN

WESTCOURT

Vicarage

EASTCOURT

EAST HORNS

To Pewsey

Harepath Farm

High Street

SEYMOUR POND

To Hungerford

HAREPATH COMMON

Marr Green Farm

Kinwardstone Farm

MANHEATH POND

Goldenlands Farm

Toll House

SOUTHGROVE COPSE

River Bourne

BURBAGE DOWN

Southgrove Farm

0 miles 1

0 km 1

GODSBURY

To Salisbury via Everleigh

To Andover and Salisbury

The area was increased to 1,743 ha. in 1987 when a small part of Burbage was transferred to Great Bedwyn, and small parts of Great Bedwyn, Easton, Grafton, and Savernake were transferred to Burbage.[33]

Part of the boundary of an estate called Burbage was defined in the 10th century. Few of the features on it can be plotted on a modern map, but a track on the south-east or south-west, and a prehistoric enclosure now called Godsbury on the south, marked the boundary of the estate, and later a track on the south-east and Godsbury marked the parish boundary. The north part of the west boundary of the parish was marked by the pale of Brimslade park in Savernake parish and possibly followed the line of a deer fence which was on the boundary in the 10th century.[34] The rest of the parish's west boundary is generally straight; for a short distance it follows a stream.

To the north the parish is crossed by the southern scarp of the Marlborough Downs, there called Terrace Hill, and to the south-west by the scarp at the north-east edge of Salisbury Plain. At both ends of it chalk outcrops; north of Durley village, Reading Beds and Bagshot Sands also outcrop, there are extensive deposits of clay-with-flints, and gravel has been deposited in a valley now dry. In the south-west the land is highest, at 205 m., on the boundary at Godsbury, and in the north it reaches 200 m. on Terrace Hill. A broad band of Upper Greensand outcrops across the middle of the parish. The river Bourne and head streams of the Christchurch Avon rise on the greensand, and there are low points at c. 140 m. where they cross respectively the south and west boundaries of the parish.[35] Sheep-and-corn husbandry was for long practised on the land of both Burbage and Durley, and open fields covered much of the greensand and, both to the north and south, much of the chalk.[36]

The parish had 107 poll-tax payers in 1377.[37] The population, 1,008 in 1801, rose from 1,195 to 1,448 between 1821 and 1831. It reached its peak of 1,603 in 1861, when men building a railway line were temporarily resident. It declined steadily from 1861 and was at a low point of 989 in 1951.[38] It increased in the later 20th century, when new houses were built; it was 1,319 in 1981 and, after the boundary changes of 1987, 1,434 in 1991.[39]

The course of the Roman road between Cirencester and Winchester via Mildenhall crosses the north-east corner of the parish.[40] A Marlborough–Winchester road via Ludgershall was important in the early 13th century and probably passed through Burbage.[41] Its most likely course is that now followed by High Street. In the 16th century the northern part of the direct course of a main Marlborough–Salisbury road west of Burbage was blocked, and Salisbury traffic seems to have been diverted on to the road from Marlborough through Burbage village and a road across the south-west part of the parish. In the later 17th century the road from Marlborough, of which High Street was part, forked c. 2 km. south of the village into branches to Salisbury and to Ludgershall, Andover, and Winchester; it seems that the Salisbury branch was then more important. North of Marlborough the road led from Chipping Campden (Glos.).[42] In 1736 the inhabitants of Burbage were presented for not repairing the Marlborough road and its Salisbury branch, but not its Andover branch,[43] and in 1762 the road from Marlborough to Burbage, and the Salisbury branch from Burbage to Everleigh, were turnpiked. The Andover branch was turnpiked in 1835 as part of a road to Salisbury along the Bourne valley. Two toll houses were built, one north of Burbage village before 1773, one south of the village between 1773 and 1817; only the southern was standing in 1995. The Marlborough road and both its branches were disturnpiked in 1876.[44] The Marlborough–Salisbury road via the Bourne valley remained an important route in 1995, and in 1991 was diverted to a new course west of High Street.[45] Use of the branch to Salisbury via Everleigh may have declined after 1835, and c. 1900 the road was closed south of Everleigh to allow for military training;[46] in Burbage the branch survived as a rough track in 1995. An east–west road across the parish links several villages east of Pewsey. On its original course it may have linked them from centre to centre, but in 1773 its course lay at the south end of Burbage village and at the north end of the villages west of Burbage.[47] East of Burbage it was declared a main road in 1886[48] and grew in importance as a Hungerford–Salisbury route in the 20th century. In 1991 a roundabout was built at its junction with the Marlborough–Salisbury road.[49] Across the part of Durley heath which lay in the park of Tottenham House a new road was made, probably c. 1820, to link Durley village and Warren Farm.[50] North of Burbage village a new east–west road was built soon after 1862 to link the Marlborough road to Savernake station.[51]

33 Statutory Instruments, 1987, no. 619, Kennet (Parishes) Order.
34 Arch. Jnl. lxxvi. 218; lxxvii. 62–5, 77–9; for Brimslade park, below, Savernake, intro.; econ. hist.
35 Geol. Surv. Maps 1", drift, sheets 267 (1971 edn.); 282 (1985 edn.); 1/50,000, drift, sheets 266 (1974 edn.); 283 (1975 edn.).   36 Below, econ. hist.
37 V.C.H. Wilts. iv. 309.
38 Ibid. 323, 342; for the railway, below, this section.
39 Census, 1981; 1991; for the boundary, above, this section; for the housing, below, this section (Burbage).
40 I. D. Margary, Rom. Roads in Brit. (1973), pp. 98–9.
41 Archaeologia, xxii. 132, 138, 140–1, 147–9, 152, 155–7, 159.
42 J. Ogilby, Brit. (1675), pl. 85; below, Easton, intro. [roads].
43 Q. Sess. 1736 (W.R.S. xi), p. 126.
44 V.C.H. Wilts. iv. 257, 262, 270; L.J. xxx. 205; Andrews and Dury, Map (W.R.S. viii), pl. 12; O.S. Map 1", sheet 14 (1817 edn.).   45 Wilts. Cuttings, xxxii. 62.
46 V.C.H. Wilts. xv. 63, 65.
47 Andrews and Dury, Map (W.R.S. viii), pl. 12; cf. below, Easton, intro. [roads]; Milton Lilbourne, intro. [roads]. The name of Harepath common, which lay beside the road, may be spurious: cf. Arch. Jnl. lxxxv. 90.
48 W.R.O., A 1/110/1886/E.
49 Wilts. Cuttings, xxxii. 62.
50 Cf. C. Greenwood, Map of Wilts. (1820); O.S. Map 1", sheet 14 (1817 edn.); W.R.O. 1300/360; Savernake estate map, c. 1820 (copy in W.R.O.); for Warren Farm, below, this section (other settlement).
51 K. Robertson and D. Abbott, Marlborough Branch: Railways of Savernake and Marlborough, 30; O.S. Map 6", Wilts. XXXVI (1888 edn.); for the station, below, this section.

The Kennet & Avon canal was opened across the parish in 1809 and completely in 1810. It passes through the Bruce tunnel, 502 yd. long, said to have been built instead of a deep cutting at the request of Thomas Bruce, earl of Ailesbury, the owner of the surrounding land. Burbage wharf was built in the west part of the parish.[52] The canal was reopened across the parish in 1988.[53]

The Berks. & Hants Extension Railway, linking Reading and Devizes, was opened across the parish in 1862 as part of the G.W.R. network. It runs beside the canal, east of the Bruce tunnel on the north bank, west of it on the south bank. Savernake station, for passengers, was built where the line passed under the road from Stibb Green to Durley, and Burbage station, for goods, was built near Burbage wharf. In 1864 a branch line to Marlborough was built from a junction a little west of Savernake station, and from 1883 it and the main line east of it were used by trains running between Swindon and Andover. In 1898 a new line for Swindon–Andover trains via Marlborough was built a little north of the existing main and branch lines across the parish; a second station called Savernake, 150 m. north-east of the first, was built on the new line. From 1923, when the G.W.R., which owned the lines built in 1862 and 1864, and the Midland & South Western Junction Railway, which owned the line built in 1898, merged, there was a single stationmaster for the two passenger stations; from 1924 that built in 1862 was called Savernake Low Level, that built in 1898 Savernake High Level. Most of the line built in 1864 was closed in 1933, from when that built in 1898 was operated as two single lines. Burbage station was closed in 1941, and Savernake High Level station was closed to passengers in 1958 and entirely in 1959. The line to Marlborough was closed to passengers in 1961, from when Savernake Low Level was again called Savernake station, and entirely in 1964. Savernake station was closed to freight in 1964 and entirely in 1966. The line built in 1862 was part of a main London–Exeter line from 1906[54] and remained so in 1995.

Artefacts from the Neolithic period and the Bronze Age have been found in the parish. Iron-Age sherds associated with Godsbury, and goods from a Romano-British grave, have been found in the south part.[55]

The whole parish lay within Savernake forest. In 1330 the parish as it was until the 18th century was disafforested except for Southgrove copse, which stands in the south part of the parish and was thereafter a detached part of the forest.[56]

Between the 1720s and 1740s two straight rides, leading towards Marlborough from Tot-

tenham House and later called the Grand Avenue and Column ride, were made across Durley heath. The south-east part of the heath was inclosed in the park of Tottenham House c. 1768, a column was built in Column ride in 1781, and, presumably c. 1820, gates were erected across the Grand Avenue where it crossed the new road between Durley and Warren Farm.[57]

BURBAGE. The present Burbage village embraces three north–south lines of old settlement, Eastcourt, Westcourt, and High Street.

Westcourt was probably the site of a manor house in the earlier Middle Ages.[58] Nothing remains of a manor house, but two ponds, c. 1574 stocked with carp, bream, tench, and roach and called Stibb ponds, may have been associated with one.[59] The ponds were presumably those lying north-west of Stibb Green and called Ram Alley ponds in 1773.[60] In 1995 there was one large pond on the site of Ram Alley ponds. In the north–south lane called Westcourt a 17th-century house, thatched and timber-framed, then stood on the west side and there were a few 18th-century houses of brick and thatch. At the south end of the lane and on the east side a house of brick and slate has a five-bayed west front and a central portico, of stone and with Tuscan columns; the house was extended to the south in the 19th century, when it may have been used as a school.[61] A house and a terrace of three estate cottages were built in the lane in the 1950s.[62]

The line of settlement which in the 20th century was given the name High Street was much more populous than Westcourt in the 18th century[63] and, being on the course of a main road, is likely to have been so long before; it was often called Burbage village to the exclusion of Eastcourt and Westcourt.[64] In 1995 the street, which especially at the north end has sunk between greensand banks, contained c. 30 thatched houses and cottages of the 17th century or later. Many of those buildings are timber-framed, some of the timber framing being concealed by later brickwork. A large house of brick and thatch on the west side of the street is dated 1712. Buildings of the 19th century included, both on the west side, an ornamental estate house dated 1846 and Barn House dated 1852. In the early 20th century a nonconformist chapel was built on the east side of the street at the north end,[65] c. 1925 a terrace of eight red-brick cottages was built on the west side at the middle,[66] and 12 council houses were built c. 1936 on the east side at the south end.[67] On both sides of the street new houses were built in the later 20th century between the old. High

52 V.C.H. Wilts. iv. 273–4; K. R. Clew, Kennet & Avon Canal (1985), 54, 71; below, manors (Burbage Sturmy).
53 Inf from the curator, Kennet & Avon Canal trust, Crouch Lane, Devizes.
54 V.C.H. Wilts. iv. 286–7, 289–90, 292; xii. 163; Robertson and Abbott, Marlborough Branch, 27–9, 48, 78–9; Clinker's Reg. Closed Passenger Sta. 1830–1977 (1978 edn.), 120, 172.
55 V.C.H. Wilts. i (1), 52–3.
56 Ibid. iv. 399–400, 448, 450–1; above, this section.
57 W.R.O. 1300/360; above, Great Bedwyn, manors

(Tottenham); this section [roads].
58 Below, manors (Burbage Sturmy).
59 W.R.O. 9/6/757, p. 31.
60 Andrews and Dury, Map (W.R.S. viii), pl. 12.
61 Below, educ.
62 Dates on bldgs.
63 Andrews and Dury, Map (W.R.S. viii), pl. 12.
64 e.g. O.S. Map 6", Wilts. XXXVI (1888 edn.).
65 Below, nonconf.
66 Cf. O.S. Map 6", Wilts. XXXVI. SE. (1926 edn.).
67 W.R.O., G 10/600/1; G 10/613/3.

Street is part of a conservation area designated in 1993.[68]

Eastcourt may have originated on land given to Burbage church, which stands there presumably on the site of the church standing in 1086.[69] The vicarage house was built north of the church.[70] In a north–south street west of the church and separated from it by a small green there is a row of 17th- and 18th-century cottages, thatched and partly timber-framed, and in a parallel street on the east side of the churchyard there are several cottages of similar dates and materials. At the south end of the west street schools were built in the 19th century.[71] A few new houses were built in the eastern street in the later 20th century. Eastcourt was designated a conservation area in 1985.[72]

Between 1843 and 1886 a group of houses, cottages, and other buildings was erected SSE. of the church and given the name East Sands, a name later transferred to the lane beside which they stood.[73] The land between East Sands and the church, crossed by Eastcourt Road, and between East Sands and High Street was built on in the 20th century. In Eastcourt Road 14 council houses were built in 1926–7.[74] About 62 council houses and bungalows were built between c. 1950 and c. 1974, mostly west of Eastcourt Road,[75] and from c. 1970 over 100 private houses and bungalows were built between Eastcourt Road and High Street and c. 10 others in East Sands. Other private houses were being built east of High Street at its south end in 1995.[76] Small private estates were also built on both sides of High Street at the north end in the later 20th century.

In the 1820s there were two inns in High Street, the Cleaver and the White Hart, both in the north part of the street and on the east side. The Cleaver, at the north end,[77] was called the Star and Cleaver c. 1850 and had been closed by 1859.[78] The White Hart was rebuilt in 1928[79] and was open in 1995. South of the White Hart and also on the east side of the street the New inn had been opened by c. 1875;[80] as the Bullfinch it remained open in 1995. At East Sands the Red Lion beerhouse was open in 1880 and 1939; the building housed a restaurant in 1995.[81] A village hall has stood in Burbage from the 1920s, at first in High Street,[82] later in Eastcourt Road, and a British Legion club has been open in Eastcourt Road from 1950 or earlier.[83] A friendly society with members from Burbage and Easton was based in Burbage in the later 19th century and the earlier 20th. It had 260 members in 1898.[84]

DURLEY. The village stands north of Terrace Hill on high ground which was probably colonized from Burbage.[85] In 1773 it consisted of buildings standing beside a north–south street and of buildings standing west of the street along the south edge of Durley heath.[86] In 1843 there were c. 12 houses and cottages and, at the south end of the village, a farmstead incorporating a house on the east side of the street and other buildings on the west.[87] The farmhouse, of 18th-century origin and called Sturmy House in 1995, was enlarged in the 19th century. Immediately north of it Durley House was built in the late 19th century on the site of a house of that name standing in 1786,[88] and all the other buildings beside the street were either much altered or rebuilt in the mid or later 19th century, several in red brick decorated with yellow bricks arranged in diamond patterns.[89] West of the street a thatched house of c. 1800 survives, and other cottages and a house, each of the mid 19th century, stand there.

RAM ALLEY is a hamlet on Burbage's border with Easton and Savernake parishes. It bore its present name in 1632,[90] when it probably consisted of several cottages on the waste.[91] There were apparently eight cottages or houses there in 1773[92] and in 1843 at Ram Alley a late 17th- or early 18th-century cottage, a pair of cottages of c. 1800, a tenement housing five families and of c. 1800, and another cottage stood in Burbage parish.[93] The first three of those buildings were standing in 1995, when Ram Alley consisted of seven cottages or houses in Burbage, Easton, and Savernake; a 19th-century cottage on the site of the fourth may have been built after 1843.

STIBB GREEN stands where the road to Durley forks from the Marlborough road north of Burbage village, and it apparently originated as a group of cottages built on the waste around the triangular green at the fork. By 1843 the settlement had extended a short distance along each of the Durley and Marlborough roads.[94] The oldest house to survive in the hamlet is of brick and thatch and stands at the south end on the east side of the green: it was probably built not long before 1711, when it incorporated an inn called the Duke of Somerset's Arms. The inn, called the King's Arms from 1716 or earlier, was closed apparently soon after 1859.[95] Several

68 Inf. from Dept. of Planning and Highways, Co. Hall, Trowbridge.
69 Below, church.   70 W.R.O., tithe award.
71 Below, educ.
72 Inf. from Dept. of Planning and Highways, Co. Hall, Trowbridge.
73 O.S. Map 6", Wilts. XXXVI (1888 and later edns.); W.R.O., tithe award.
74 W.R.O., G 10/600/1; G 10/613/3.
75 Ibid. G 10/613/3.
76 Ibid. A 1/355/455/1; A 1/355/465/1.
77 Ibid. A 1/326/3; ibid. tithe award.
78 Kelly's Dir. Wilts. (1848 and later edns.).
79 Inf. in White Hart.
80 Kelly's Dir. Wilts. (1875 and later edns.); O.S. Map 6", Wilts. XXXVI (1888 edn.).
81 Kelly's Dir. Wilts. (1880, 1939); Sun. Telegraph, 23

Apr. 1995.
82 Kelly's Dir. Wilts. (1923).
83 W.R.O., G 10/505/1.
84 Kelly's Dir. Wilts. (1875 and later edns.).
85 Cf. below, econ. hist.
86 Andrews and Dury, Map (W.R.S. viii), pl. 12; W.R.O. 1300/360.
87 W.R.O., tithe award; ibid. 2027H, map of Savernake, 1843.
88 Ibid. 1300/360.
89 Below, plates 28, 39.
90 W.R.O. 9/1/151, rot. 3.
91 Cf. below, Easton, intro.; Savernake, intro.
92 Andrews and Dury, Map (W.R.S. viii), pl. 12.
93 W.R.O., tithe award.
94 Ibid.
95 Ibid.; ibid. 9/6/133; 9/6/136; ibid. A 1/326/3; Kelly's Dir. Wilts. (1848 and later edns.).

other houses at Stibb Green are of brick and thatch and were built in the later 18th century or the early 19th. The Three Horse Shoes on the west side of the green was a beerhouse in the late 19th century[96] and was open as a public house in 1995. A pair of estate cottages was built at the north-east corner of the green in 1843, a block of four on the east side of the green in 1845.[97] To the south, building beside the Marlborough road in the 19th and 20th centuries linked Stibb Green and the north end of High Street, and, to the north-west, bungalows extended the hamlet further along the Marlborough road in the 20th. Stibb Green was, with High Street, part of a conservation area designated in 1993.[98]

OTHER SETTLEMENT. East of Burbage village three buildings beside a lane collectively bore the name East Horns, possibly a mistake for East Sands, in 1773.[99] Two small houses of the 17th or 18th century and a 19th-century house stood there in 1995. North of Burbage village red-brick buildings, including a wharfinger's house, were erected in a small group beside the canal at Burbage wharf. North-east of Stibb Green a hotel, open in 1995, was built near Savernake station between 1862 and 1886.[1]

Of the farmsteads built outside Burbage village and the hamlets in the parish Bowden Farm, which stood in 1773 near the boundary with Easton north of Westcourt,[2] was probably the first. The farmhouse was rebuilt in brick in the 19th century. Six other farmsteads were built in the earlier 19th century. Manor Farm, including a farmhouse and large farm buildings, was built on the east side of the Marlborough road between Stibb Green and the north end of High Street. Marr Green Farm, of brick and thatch, Goldenlands Farm, and Southgrove Farm were built off the Salisbury and Andover roads, Harepath Farm was built on the site of cottages beside the Pewsey road, and Kinwardstone Farm was built off the Hungerford road.[3] New Barn Farm was built north of the site of Savernake station between 1843 and 1886.[4] All except Marr Green Farm and Goldenlands Farm were in use as farmsteads in 1995, the buildings of Southgrove Farm being particularly extensive. A house and farm buildings were erected in Southgrove copse in the later 20th century.

On the former warren north-east of Durley village three large houses were built shortly before 1820.[5] Each is rendered, has brick dressings, and stands on the north-west side of the new road from Durley. The middle one was built as the farmhouse of Warren Farm,[6] which also has model farm buildings of red brick. Warren Lodge was built of stone south-west of the group c. 1860. By 1886 the buildings collectively were called the Warren.[7] South-east of the Warren and on the boundary with Great Bedwyn a house for the vicar of St. Katharine's church, which stands in Great Bedwyn parish, was built in Burbage parish in 1879–80.[8]

MANORS AND OTHER ESTATES. King Edgar (d. 975) allegedly gave 22 *cassati* at Burbage to Abingdon abbey (Berks., later Oxon.) in 961, and Burbage's land was part of a large estate called Bedwyn given by Edgar to the abbey in 968.[9] On Edgar's death Burbage was taken from the abbey by force and assigned to his younger son Ethelred, king from 978.[10] By 1066 it had been granted away by the king, and in 1086 its land lay in four estates.[11]

An estate of 2½ hides, the later manor called *BURBAGE STURMY* or *WESTCOURT*, was held by Alvric the huntsman in 1066. Richard Sturmy held it in 1086, when William held it of him.[12] The manor was sometimes said to be held by the serjeanty of keeping Savernake forest, and later owners of it were hereditary wardens of the forest. Henry Sturmy held the manor c. 1130.[13] Henry Sturmy, possibly another, held the forest and perhaps the manor in 1156 and 1162.[14] The manor was held by Geoffrey Sturmy (d. 1198–9), who was deprived of it briefly c. 1197 for his opposition to Richard I, and passed to his son Henry[15] (d. c. 1226). From Henry Sturmy the manor, which from the earlier 13th century was held with Durley, descended in the direct line to Geoffrey[16] (d. c. 1254), Henry[17] (d. c. 1296), Henry[18] (d. c. 1305), Henry[19] (d. c. 1338), and Henry Sturmy[20] (d. 1381). The last Henry, who in 1359 was granted free warren in his demesne lands at Burbage, was succeeded by his nephew Sir William Sturmy[21] (d. 1427). From Sir William the manor descended to his grandson Sir John Seymour[22] (d. 1464). It descended to Sir John's grandson John Seymour[23]

96 O.S. Map 1/2,500, Wilts. XXXVI. 11 (1900 edn.).
97 Dates on bldgs.
98 Inf. from Dept. of Planning and Highways, Co. Hall, Trowbridge.
99 *Andrews and Dury, Map* (W.R.S. viii), pl. 12.
1 O.S. Map 6", Wilts. XXXVI (1888 edn.); above, this section [railways].
2 *Andrews and Dury, Map* (W.R.S. viii), pl. 12.
3 Cf. ibid.; Greenwood, *Map of Wilts.*; O.S. Map 1", sheet 14 (1817 edn.); W.R.O., tithe award.
4 O.S. Map 6", Wilts. XXXVI (1888 edn.); W.R.O., tithe award.
5 Cf. Greenwood, *Map of Wilts.*; O.S. Map 1", sheet 14 (1817 edn.); Savernake estate map, c. 1820 (copy in W.R.O.).
6 W.R.O., tithe award.
7 O.S. Map 6", Wilts. XXXVI (1888 edn.).
8 Above, Great Bedwyn, churches (St. Katharine).
9 Finberg, *Early Wessex Chart.* pp. 94, 96; *Arch. Jnl.* lxxvii. 62–5, 75–80. The authenticity of the chart. of 961 is doubted in P. H. Sawyer, *Anglo-Saxon Chart.* (revised S. E.

Kelly; priv. circulated 1996), no. 688; for comment on the chart. of 968, above, Great Bedwyn, manors [preamble], n. 28.
10 *Eng. Hist. Doc.* i, ed. D. Whitelock (1979), pp. 582–4.
11 Below, this section.
12 *V.C.H. Wilts.* ii, p. 165; iv. 392.
13 Ibid. iv. 420, 438–40; *Pipe R.* 1130 (H.M.S.O. facsimile), 17; cf. below, this section.
14 *Pipe R.* 1156–8 (Rec. Com.), 58; 1162 (P.R.S. v), 12.
15 *Bk. of Fees*, i. 3, 13; *Red Bk. Exch.* (Rolls Ser.), ii. 487.
16 *Rot. Litt. Claus.* (Rec. Com.), ii. 162; *Bk. of Fees*, i. 586; below, this section (Durley).
17 *Ex. e Rot. Fin.* (Rolls Ser.), ii. 182.
18 *Cal. Inq. p.m.* iii, pp. 171–2.
19 Ibid. iv, p. 210.
20 Ibid. viii, p. 101.
21 Ibid. xv, pp. 202–3; *Cal. Chart. R.* 1341–1417, 164.
22 P.R.O., C 139/28, no. 22.
23 Ibid. C 140/14, no. 32.

(d. 1491) and passed in the direct line to Sir John Seymour[24] (d. 1536) and Sir Edward Seymour (cr. Viscount Beauchamp 1536, earl of Hertford 1537, duke of Somerset 1547).[25] On Somerset's execution and attainder in 1552 Burbage Sturmy manor passed by Act to his son Sir Edward[26] (cr. earl of Hertford 1559, d. 1621), a minor until 1558.[27] The manor, with other manors and estates in the parish, descended from 1553 to the 20th century in the Seymour, Bruce, Brudenell, and Brudenell-Bruce families with Tottenham Lodge and Tottenham House in Great Bedwyn.[28]

A manor house, in which c. 1213 Henry Sturmy was licensed to have an oratory, almost certainly stood on Burbage Sturmy manor.[29] There is no evidence that the house survived the Middle Ages.[30]

An estate of 2½ hides at Burbage was held by Edric in 1066, was held of Humphrey Lisle by Blacheman in 1086,[31] and was apparently the origin of two manors. The overlordship presumably passed to Adelize Lisle and in the Dunstanville family, possibly like estates at Bathampton in Steeple Langford, and Walter de Dunstanville (d. 1270) was overlord of ½ knight's fee at Burbage in 1242–3.[32]

What became *BURBAGE SAVAGE* manor, probably part of what Edric held in 1066, was apparently the estate conveyed by Sir Thomas Savage to Pain de Chaworth in 1274.[33] Burbage Savage manor later belonged to Sir William Sturmy (d. 1427), who in 1425–6 conveyed it to Robert Erley in tail male. The manor passed to Robert's grandson Richard Erley[34] (d. s.p. 1502), on whose death Sir John Seymour (d. 1536), the heir of Sir William Sturmy, entered on the manor as reversioner. Despite a challenge to Seymour's title by Richard Erley's nephew William Chafin in 1535, from 1502 the manor descended like Burbage Sturmy manor.[35]

A manor later called *BURBAGE DARELL*, probably the other part of what Edric held in 1066, was held in 1242–3 as 1 knight's fee by Thomas Savage, allegedly of Walter Marshal, earl of Pembroke.[36] The manor passed to James Savage, to whom Thomas granted a carucate for life in 1250, and in 1262 James conveyed it for life to Philip Basset (d. 1271) and his wife Ela, countess of Warwick (d. 1298).[37] The reversion

was acquired by Hugh Chastulon, who in 1286 conveyed it to Gilbert de Clare, earl of Gloucester and of Hertford[38] (d. 1295). Gilbert's relict Joan (d. 1307) entered on the manor in 1298.[39] From then to 1660 the manor descended like Wexcombe manor in Great Bedwyn,[40] apart from the period 1392–1438 when Burbage Darell manor was held in dower by Anne (d. 1438), the relict of Thomas de Stafford, earl of Stafford (d. 1392), from c. 1398 to 1403 the wife of Thomas's brother Edmund, earl of Stafford, and later the wife of William Bourgchier, count of Eu.[41] From 1553 Burbage Darell manor also passed with Burbage Sturmy manor, as it did after 1660.[42]

In 1066 Alric, and in 1086 Ralph de Halvile, held 2 hides and 1 yardland at Burbage.[43] The estate was presumably that at Burbage acquired by William Brewer (d. 1226) before 1194, the year in which it was held by the Crown, for reasons which are obscure, as an escheat.[44] The king granted woodland at Burbage to Brewer in 1199, a grant confirmed in 1200 when the right to hunt on his land was also granted to Brewer.[45] Other land at Burbage was held by John de Palerne, whose son Henry conveyed it to Brewer c. 1200.[46] William Brewer gave the rent from his land at Burbage to the priory which he founded at Mottisfont (Hants),[47] and by 1227 his son William had apparently given the land. In 1228–9 the priory's title was challenged, apparently unsuccessfully, by John de Neville, who claimed that the land had descended to him from his great-great-grandfather Alan de Neville (fl. before 1189).[48] The estate, part of which was later called *MOTSON'S* farm, was kept by Mottisfont priory until the Dissolution. In 1536 the Crown granted it to William Sandys, Lord Sandys (d. 1540), and his wife Margery (d. 1539). The estate passed with the title to William's son Thomas (d. 1560), and to Thomas's grandson William,[49] who seems to have sold it in portions. In 1599 Edward, earl of Hertford, bought Motson's coppice, 22 a. later Leigh Hill copse, from William, Lord Sandys,[50] and that, and almost certainly other parts of Lord Sandys's estate, afterwards descended with Burbage Sturmy manor.[51] Motson's farm, accounted 70 a., was acquired by Thomas Hooper and Richard Hooper, who together sold it to Robert Hitchcock in 1627.[52] It was sold by Hitchcock

[24] *Cal. Inq. p.m. Hen. VII*, i, pp. 327–8.
[25] *Complete Peerage*, xii (1), 59–64; P.R.O., C 142/115, no. 69.
[26] P.R.O., E 328/117.
[27] *Complete Peerage*, vi. 505–7.
[28] Above, Great Bedwyn, manors (Tottenham); e.g. *Wilts. Inq. p.m. 1625–49* (Index Libr.), 20–31; W.R.O., tithe award; below, this section.
[29] *Reg. St. Osmund* (Rolls Ser.), i. 250–2.
[30] For ponds which may have been associated with it, above, intro. (Burbage).
[31] *V.C.H. Wilts.* ii, p. 143.
[32] Ibid. xv. 194; *Bk. of Fees*, ii. 713.
[33] P.R.O., DL 25/2316.
[34] W.R.O. 9/6/12–14; above, this section (Burbage Sturmy).
[35] *Cal. Inq. p.m. Hen. VII*, ii, p. 327; *Wilts. Pedigrees* (Harl. Soc. cv/cvi), 36–7, where Ric. is said to be Wm.'s grandfather; W.R.O. 9/6/18; above, this section (Burbage Sturmy).
[36] *Bk. of Fees*, ii. 745.
[37] *Complete Peerage*, xii (2), 365; *Rot. Hund.* (Rec. Com.),

ii (1), 259; P.R.O., CP 25/1/251/17, no. 6; CP 25/1/251/20, no. 25.
[38] *Feet of F. 1272–1327* (W.R.S. i), p. 28.
[39] *Wilts. Inq. p.m. 1242–1326* (Index Libr.), 339–41; *Complete Peerage*, v. 707–10.
[40] Above, Great Bedwyn, manors (Wexcombe).
[41] *Cal. Close, 1392–6*, 39–40; *Cal. Inq. p.m.* xviii, p. 269; *Complete Peerage*, xii (1), 180–1.
[42] Above, this section (Burbage Sturmy).
[43] *V.C.H. Wilts.* ii, p. 166.
[44] *Pipe R. 1194* (P.R.S. n.s. v), 19; *D.N.B.*
[45] *Cartae Antiquae* (Pipe R. Soc. n.s. xvii), pp. 124–5.
[46] *Pipe R. 1200* (P.R.S. n.s. xii), 161.
[47] *V.C.H. Hants*, ii. 172; Dugdale, *Mon.* vi. 481.
[48] *Cal. Chart. R.* i. 41; *Cur. Reg. R.* xiii, pp. 201, 356, 370, 514; xiv, p. 261.
[49] *L. & P. Hen. VIII*, xi, p. 87; for the Sandyses, *Complete Peerage*, xi. 441–6.
[50] *V.C.H. Wilts.* iv. 420; W.R.O. 9/6/5.
[51] Above, this section (Burbage Sturmy).
[52] W.R.O. 9/6/117.

to William Hitchcock in 1650,[53] by William Hitchcock to Richard Shipreeve in 1664,[54] and by Shipreeve's son William to John Horner in 1683.[55] At Horner's death in 1714[56] the farm passed to his daughter-in-law Rebecca Horner (fl. 1726).[57] In 1739 Rebecca's son Walter Horner sold it to Anthony Bathe[58] (d. c. 1769),[59] whose son Anthony sold it in 1792 to Thomas Bruce, earl of Ailesbury;[60] it was added to Lord Ailesbury's other estates in the parish.[61]

John de Mohun (d. c. 1279) was overlord of an estate in Burbage, possibly part of that held by his great-great-grandfather William Brewer (d. 1226). In 1275 John's tenant in demesne was Alan of Walton, who may have held the estate, then assessed as ½ knight's fee,[62] as an heir of William de Reyny.[63] The estate descended to Stephen of Walton, who in 1338 settled it on himself with remainder to Alan of Walton and Alan's wife Isabel.[64] Before 1405 John of Walton conveyed it to Sir William Sturmy[65] and it afterwards descended with Burbage Sturmy manor.[66]

From 1792 Thomas Bruce, earl of Ailesbury, owned nearly all Burbage's land.[67] About 1929 George Brudenell-Bruce, marquess of Ailesbury, sold the farmland south of the Hungerford and Pewsey roads as Goldenlands farm, 375 a., Southgrove farm, 639 a., and Kinwardstone farm, c. 296 a.[68] Goldenlands farm was bought by W. Colebrook, Southgrove farm by T. Curnick; in 1995 Mr. T. W. Curnick owned both farms.[69] Kinwardstone farm was bought by H. C. Norris; Mr. and Mrs. R. B. Denny owned it in 1995.[70] In 1950 Lord Ailesbury sold most of Burbage's other land, c. 1,000 a., to the Crown; nearly all that land belonged to the Crown in 1995, when it lay in Manor, Harepath, and Bowden farms, all based in Burbage parish, and in Wolfhall farm based in Great Bedwyn parish.[71] About 125 a. on Terrace Hill continued to descend with Tottenham House, and in 1980 Lord Ailesbury's grandson Michael Brudenell-Bruce, marquess of Ailesbury, sold it as New Barn farm to Mr. P. D. Blanchard, the owner in 1995.[72]

In 1255 SOUTHGROVE copse, which Robert le Moyne had previously held by ser-

jeanty, was in the king's hands.[73] As a detached part of Savernake forest it was held by the Crown for most of the period 1255–1544.[74] In 1544 it was granted to Edward, earl of Hertford,[75] later duke of Somerset. In 1552 it was forfeited to the Crown on Somerset's attainder and granted to William Herbert, earl of Pembroke.[76] It passed with the earldom of Pembroke[77] until 1683, when Philip, earl of Pembroke and of Montgomery, sold it to Thomas Kingston,[78] and from 1699, when Kingston sold it to Thomas, earl of Pembroke and of Montgomery.[79] In 1783 Henry, earl of Pembroke and of Montgomery, sold Southgrove copse to Thomas, earl of Ailesbury,[80] who added it to his other estates in the parish. About 1929 George, marquess of Ailesbury, sold the wood, then 232 a., to H. A. Twyford.[81] The Crown bought 100 a. of the wood in 1957 and owned it in 1995. The rest, c. 120 a., belonged to Mr. T. W. Curnick in 1995, having previously belonged to his father W. R. Curnick.[82]

St. Denis's priory, Southampton, held a small estate in Burbage from 1291 or earlier[83] until the Dissolution.[84] In 1399 Sir John Lovell gave land in Burbage to St. Margaret's priory, Marlborough.[85] It was retained by the priory and was worth 26s. 8d. at the Dissolution.[86] The Hospitallers also held a small estate in Burbage at the Dissolution.[87]

The land of DURLEY, probably colonized from Burbage, almost certainly belonged c. 1213 to Henry Sturmy (d. c. 1226).[88] It descended with, and remained or became part of, Burbage Sturmy manor; from the 16th century it also descended with Tottenham Lodge and later with Tottenham House.[89] Of the land north-east of it which had been added to the parish by 1886,[90] in 1939 George Brudenell-Bruce, marquess of Ailesbury, leased c. 130 a. of woodland on Durley heath and Black Vault to the Forestry Commission for 999 years,[91] and in 1950 sold Coal coppice, the rest of Black Vault, and the former Durley warren, c. 215 a. in all, to the Crown; the land sold in 1950 belonged to the Crown in 1995 as part of Warren farm. In 1950 Lord Ailesbury also sold the southern part of Durley's former open fields, c. 95 a., to the

53 W.R.O. 9/6/119.
54 Ibid. 9/6/122.
55 Ibid. 9/6/125.
56 Ibid. wills, cons. Sar., John Horner, 1714.
57 Ibid. 9/6/129; 9/6/141.
58 Ibid. 9/6/146.
59 Ibid. 9/6/148.   60 Ibid. 9/6/153.
61 Above, this section.
62 Complete Peerage, ix. 19–24; Rot. Hund. (Rec. Com.), ii (1), 260; Cal. Inq. p.m. ii, p. 174; above, this section (Motson's).
63 Cal. Inq. p.m. ii, p. 353.
64 Feet of F. 1327–77 (W.R.S. xxix), p. 53.
65 Cal. Close, 1402–5, 498, 504.
66 Above, this section (Burbage Sturmy).
67 Ibid. this section; below, this section (Southgrove).
68 W.R.O. 9/1/521.
69 Inf. from Mrs. I. S. Curnick, Southgrove Farm.
70 Inf. from Mr. and Mrs. R. B. Denny, Kinwardstone Farm.
71 Inf. from the agent for the Crown Estate Com., 42 High Street, Marlborough.
72 Above, Great Bedwyn, manors (Tottenham); inf. from Mr. D. Shorey, Messrs. Herbert Mallam Gowers, W. Way

Ho., Elms Parade, Oxf.
73 Rot. Hund. (Rec. Com.), ii (1), 231.
74 V.C.H. Wilts. iv. 448, 451; below, Savernake, estates.
75 L. & P. Hen. VIII, xix (2), pp. 313–14.
76 Cal. Pat. 1550–3, 358; Complete Peerage, xii (1), 59–64.
77 For the earls of Pembroke, Complete Peerage, x. 405–26.
78 W.R.O. 2057, deed, Pembroke to Kingston, 1683.
79 Ibid. 2057, deed, Kingston to Pembroke, 1699.
80 Ibid. 9/18/6–7.
81 W.A.S. Libr., sale cat. xxviiiB, 17A–B.
82 Inf. from the Head Forester, Forest Enterprise, Postern Hill, Marlborough.
83 Tax. Eccl. (Rec. Com.), 192.
84 P.R.O., SC 6/Hen. VIII/3326, rot. 6.
85 Cal. Pat. 1396–9, 560.
86 Valor Eccl. (Rec. Com.), ii. 148.
87 P.R.O., SC 6/Hen. VIII/7262, rot. 6.
88 Reg. St. Osmund (Rolls Ser.), i. 250–2; cf. above, intro. (Durley); below, econ. hist.
89 e.g. W.R.O. 1300/16; 1300/43; 1300/360; above, Great Bedwyn, manors (Tottenham).
90 Cf. above, intro.
91 W.R.O. 9/33/5.

Crown; in 1995 the Crown owned it as part of Manor farm, Burbage.[92] The reversion of the woodland and the rest of Durley's land continued to descend with Tottenham House, the park of which then included the rest of Durley heath and the northern part of Durley's former open fields, a total of *c*. 300 a. In 1975 Michael, marquess of Ailesbury, sold *c*. 73 a.; the reversion of the woodland and the park of Tottenham House belonged to his son David, earl of Cardigan, in 1995.[93]

Burbage church was held by Viel the priest in 1086.[94] Between 1103 and 1139 it was bought by Roger, bishop of Salisbury, and given by him to the cathedral.[95] By *c*. 1150 a prebend, later called the prebend of Hurstbourne and Burbage, had been endowed with the *RECTORY* estate,[96] which in 1341 included 1 carucate and all the tithes from Burbage parish.[97] Part of the estate was later assigned to the vicar of Burbage,[98] and in 1840 the prebendary held 40 a. and most of the tithes of the parish. The tithes were then valued at £678 and in 1843 were commuted.[99] In 1847, on the death of the last prebendary, the estate passed to the Ecclesiastical Commissioners, who in 1868 sold the land to George Brudenell-Bruce, marquess of Ailesbury (d. 1878).[1]

ECONOMIC HISTORY. Burbage. In 1086 Burbage had land for 6½ ploughteams, and 6 teams were there. Only 1½ hide, on which there was 1 team, is known to have been demesne land; the other teams were held by 5 *villani*, 7 coscets, 1 bordar, and 2 *servi*. Meadow on one of the four estates was accounted 2 arpens.[2]

In the Middle Ages Burbage apparently had extensive open fields, probably 1,000–1,500 a. In the early Middle Ages *c*. 230 a. of downland to the north was probably taken from it to provide the agricultural land of Durley, and thereafter Burbage had little downland pasture. In the 16th century there were probably some five open fields on the greensand east and west of the village, there were two fields on the chalk north of the village, and there were three main fields, South Clay, East Clay, and West Clay, on the chalk in the south part of the parish. In the south-west corner of the parish Burbage down, estimated at 22 a. *c*. 1574, and north of the village Leigh Hill, 20 a., were upland pastures on which sheep were fed in common. On the greensand there were extensive lowland pastures used in common. North of the village they included Bitham common, estimated at 80 a., which was for cattle in summer and sheep in winter, and

Nether heath, 25 a., which was for cattle and sheep throughout the year; south of the village Harepath and Marr Green common was estimated at 3 a. and Short Heath common at 4 a.; other common pastures were estimated at 30 a., 24 a., and 18 a. By *c*. 1574 *c*. 40 a. of East Sands field, probably open field east of the village, had been converted to a common pasture for cattle. Four ponds were used in common, including Stibb ponds which earlier may have been associated with a manor house at Westcourt. Southmere, later Seymour, pond, at the south end of what was later called High Street, contained eels and carp *c*. 1574; in 1995, newly relined and restored, it lay within a small enclosure. Manheath pond south of it, which *c*. 1574 contained fry of carp, was drained between 1843 and 1886.[3]

Burbage Sturmy, Burbage Savage, and Burbage Darell manors all had demesne and customary lands in the open fields.[4] In 1305 the demesne of Burbage Sturmy manor included arable estimated at 320 a. and meadow at 11 a.; 10 customary tenants each held a messuage and 10 a., 4 freeholders had similar holdings, and 5 other freeholders had a total of 8½ yardlands and 5 a.[5] The demesne was in hand in the earlier 14th century and there were exchanges of stock with other manors of the lord. In 1312–13 there was sown on the demesne 42 a. of wheat, 34 a. of rye, 27 a. of barley, 11½ a. of dredge, and 7 a. of oats; 17 oxen were kept but only 28 wethers and 48 ewes.[6] By the early 15th century the demesne had been leased in portions; land at Westcourt was leased to the prior of Easton, whose demesne land at Easton it presumably adjoined.[7] In 1307 on what became Burbage Darell manor the demesne included an estimated 150 a. of arable, 4 a. of meadow, a several pasture worth 6*s*. 8*d*. for sheep, and a several pasture worth 10*s*. for oxen; each of eight ½-yardlanders worked on the demesne for two half days and one full day a year.[8] In 1314 the demesne was said to include 169 a. of arable, 10 a. of meadow, and 110 a. of pasture; there were 18 free tenants, 9 tenants each holding ½ yardland in villeinage, and 17 cottars.[9] The demesne had been leased by the earlier 15th century.[10] In the later 16th century the three manors included *c*. 28 copyholds with *c*. 600 a., and 9 yardlands were held freely. Most of the copyhold land was in the open fields. Most of the demesne of Burbage Savage manor was a farm of 169 a., of which 50 a. lay in closes and 60 a. of its open-field arable lay as one parcel; at Westcourt another 52 a. of demesne had been added to a copyhold. Of the demesne of Burbage Darell manor 57 a. had been added to copyholds as bourdland.[11]

92   Inf. from the agent for the Crown Estate Com.; for the open fields, below, econ. hist. (Durley).
93   *Debrett's Peerage and Baronetage* (1995), 14–16; inf. from Mr. Shorey; the earl of Cardigan, Savernake Lodge, Savernake.   94   *V.C.H. Wilts.* ii, p. 119.
95   *Sar. Chart. and Doc.* (Rolls Ser.), p. 10.
96   Ibid. p. 9; Le Neve, *Fasti, 1066–1300, Salisbury*, 78; for the claims of Salisbury cath. and the prebendary to Hurstbourne ch., *W.A.M.* xc. 91–8.
97   *Inq. Non.* (Rec. Com.), 173.
98   Below, church.   99   W.R.O., tithe award.
1   Le Neve, *Fasti, 1541–1857, Salisbury*, 53; *Alum. Cantab. 1752–1900*, iii. 496; Ch. Com. file 3433.

2   *V.C.H. Wilts.* ii, pp. 119, 143, 165–6.
3   *Andrews and Dury, Map* (W.R.S. viii), pl. 12; O.S. Map 6", Wilts. XLII (1888 edn.); W.R.O. 9/6/757; ibid. tithe award; for Stibb ponds, above, intro. (Burbage); for Durley, below, this section.
4   W.R.O. 9/6/757.
5   *Wilts. Inq. p.m.* 1242–1326 (Index Libr.), 312–14.
6   W.R.O. 9/6/754.
7   Ibid. 9/6/756; below, Easton, econ. hist.
8   *Wilts. Inq. p.m.* 1242–1326 (Index Libr.), 340–1.
9   Ibid. 404–5.
10   B.L. Add. Roll 28000.
11   W.R.O. 9/6/757.

Apart from the home closes in the village,[12] the first inclosure of Burbage's land seems to have been at Westcourt, where c. 1450 the demesne land held by the prior of Easton lay in closes.[13] It adjoined a warren and inclosed pasture associated with the house in Easton later owned by the lord of Burbage Sturmy manor and was in hand in the late 16th century.[14] A few small inclosures east of Burbage village may also have been made by the early 15th century,[15] and by c. 1574 some of the meadow land had been inclosed.[16] Some of the open fields on the greensand, probably lying east and west of the village, and Leigh Hill and the pasture formerly part of East Sands field were inclosed, divided, and allotted c. 1596,[17] but proposals in the 17th century to inclose other common pasture were disputed and not carried out.[18] The remaining open fields, 922 a., were inclosed with 76 a. of common meadow and 139 a. of common pasture in 1721; most of the 922 a. lay on the chalk in the south part of the parish, but on Terrace Hill it included Great Leigh field, 185 a., and Little Leigh field, 15 a.[19] Other common pastures, called the Marsh and Lower Heath, had been inclosed by c. 1730.[20] The remaining common pasture, Burbage down, Burbage or Stibb common north-west of the village, Marr Green common, Harepath common, and Short Heath common, a total of c. 213 a., was inclosed in 1824 by Act.[21]

Burbage was among the villages on the periphery of Savernake forest for each of which a particular part of the forest was designated for their sheep to feed on in common. In the 18th century Burbage's designated area, c. 200 a., lay north of Leigh Hill copse; most of it could be fed on only in winter. Cattle kept on farms in Burbage in winter could be fed in the forest at large in summer.[22] The rights to feed cattle and sheep in the forest were extinguished presumably in the later 18th century and earlier 19th when copyholds fell in hand. All had apparently been extinguished by 1874.[23]

By c. 1840 most of Burbage's land had been arranged into mainly compact farms, for which new farmsteads had recently been built outside the village. Two farms, one with a farmstead at Stibb Green, had apparently been merged as Manor farm, 325 a.; Southgrove farm had 316 a., Goldenlands farm 231 a., Kinwardstone farm 200 a., and Harepath farm 122 a. A farm of c. 207 a. with a farmstead in High Street had been

added to Durley farm; Bowden farm had 125 a. in Burbage and, as it had later, probably c. 150 a. in Easton; north-east of Burbage village 128 a. was worked from Great Bedwyn as part of Wolfhall farm. There remained several farms, each of 50–100 a., with their buildings in the village. All the farms were predominantly arable.[24] Later in the 19th century the larger farms grew in size, probably as the smaller ones were added to them. Goldenlands farm had 299 a. in 1867, when it was worked from Easton as part of Easton farm. Manor farm was c. 450 a. in 1867, when the tenant, W. H. Gale,[25] hired agricultural machinery to neighbouring farmers.[26] In the late 19th century large flocks of sheep were kept, and cereal growing, dairy farming, and pig keeping all increased.[27] S. W. Farmer and W. B. Gauntlett introduced intensive dairy farming on Southgrove farm in the early 20th century. Cereal growing declined after 1916,[28] and in the early 1930s most of Burbage's land was meadow or permanent pasture.[29] By 1995 nearly all the land had been restored to arable. Southgrove farm, which from c. 1987 included Goldenlands farm, was in 1995 an arable and poultry farm of c. 1,600 a., some of which lay in Easton and West Grafton.[30] Harepath farm, c. 300 a., was entirely arable.[31] Kinwardstone farm, 334 a. including 38 a. outside the parish, and Bowden farm, c. 335 a. including c. 150 a. in Easton, were mainly arable; cattle for beef were kept on Kinwardstone farm, and potatoes were grown on c. 100 a. of Bowden farm.[32] Manor farm, 640 a. including c. 100 a. of Durley's former open fields, was worked in conjunction with New Barn farm, c. 125 a.; mixed farming was practised on it.[33] Wolfhall farm's land in Burbage, c. 100 a., was used for arable and dairy farming.[34]

Racehorses were trained at Westcourt in the 20th century.[35] By 1981 the stables had been converted to kennels for the Tedworth hunt;[36] the hunt's kennels remained there in 1995.

There was woodland assessed at 20 square furlongs at Burbage in 1086.[37] In 1568 Southgrove copse was fenced and contained 180 a. in four coppices, one of which, Hazelditch, 60 a., was planted with ash, hazel, willow, maple, and oak.[38] Southgrove copse and Leigh Hill copse were the only extensively wooded parts of Burbage's land in 1773. About 37 a. of Southgrove copse was grubbed up and converted to meadow, probably between 1773 and c. 1840. Southgrove

12 e.g. W.R.O. 9/6/757.
13 Ibid. 9/6/756.
14 Ibid. 192/53; below, Easton, manors; econ. hist.
15 Chandler's Reg. (W.R.S. xxxix), p. 34.
16 W.R.O. 9/6/757.
17 P.R.O., C 2/Eliz. I/B 26/54.
18 Ibid. C 2/Chas. I/B 162/116; C 5/323/3; C 78/527, no. 19.
19 W.R.O. 9/6/3.
20 Ibid. 9/1/99.
21 Ibid. EA/128.
22 Ibid. 1300/360; 1300/1840A.   23 Ibid. 529/245.
24 Ibid. tithe award; above, intro. (other settlement); below, Easton, econ. hist.; for Wolfhall farm, above, Great Bedwyn, econ. hist. (Wolfhall); for Durley farm, below, this section (Durley).
25 W.R.O. 9/1/110.
26 Rep. Com. Children and Women in Agric. [4202–I], p. 242, H.C. (1868–9), xiii.

27 P.R.O., MAF 68/493, sheet 9; MAF 68/1633, sheet 12.
28 Ibid. MAF 68/2203, sheet 6; MAF 68/2773, sheet 11; V.C.H. Wilts. iv. 106–7; W.R.O., Inland Revenue, val. reg. 59; ibid. G 10/510/23.
29 [1st] Land Util. Surv. Map, sheet 112.
30 Inf. from Mrs. I. S. Curnick, Southgrove Farm; Mrs. H. Constanduros, 3 Westcourt, Burbage.
31 Inf. from Mr. A. R. Gordon, Harepath Farm.
32 Inf. from Mr. R. B. Denny, Kinwardstone Farm; Mrs. M. Rowland, Bowden Farm.
33 Inf. from Mrs. P. D. Blanchard, Manor Farm; below, this section (Durley).
34 Inf. from the agent for the Crown Estate Com.
35 Kelly's Dir. Wilts. (1903 and later edns.); O.S. Map 6", Wilts. SU 26 SW. (1961 edn.).
36 O.S. Map 1/10,000, SU 26 SW. (1982 edn.).
37 V.C.H. Wilts. ii, pp. 143, 166.
38 First Pembroke Survey, ed. Straton, i. 186.

copse measured 194 a., Leigh Hill copse 28 a., c. 1840.[39] The woods covered the same area in 1995, c. 100 a. of Southgrove copse having been replanted in the 1960s.[40]

There was a miller at Burbage in 1349.[41] A horse mill stood there in 1574.[42]

At Burbage wharf coal, timber, bricks, and other goods carried on the Kennet & Avon canal were loaded or unloaded, presumably from 1810 when the canal was opened. A revolving wooden crane built at the wharf in 1831 was restored in the period 1972–8. A firm of coal and timber merchants was based there in the mid 19th century,[43] and from 1874 to the early 1970s members of the Fall family were in business there as wharfingers, coal and corn merchants, and wholesalers of animal foodstuffs and fertilizers. Until the 1940s they kept steam engines there and used them in ploughing and threshing under contract to local farmers.[44]

A malthouse was built in the parish c. 1762;[45] there was a malthouse at Westcourt c. 1840[46] and one at Kinwardstone Farm in 1867.[47] Bricks and tiles were made in the parish in the 19th century.[48] In the 1920s and 1930s Vines & Pinneger, agricultural auctioneers and valuers, were based at Burbage; at Savernake Low Level station the firm held monthly livestock auctions and separate monthly auctions of calves.[49] In 1995 W. Mundy & Sons supplied coal and building materials from a depot in East Sands and employed 19 people.[50] There was an office of the Crown Estate Commission at Burbage wharf in 1995.[51]

DURLEY. The land of Durley, c. 230 a.,[52] is downland. Before Durley village was planted on it most of it was probably rough pasture used by the men of Burbage.[53] Afterwards most of it was worked as open fields.[54] Some of the land was demesne and some was held customarily. Early 18th-century evidence suggests that the farmsteads stood in the north–south street of the present Durley village.[55] The demesne had been leased by the early 15th century;[56] in 1441 there were six customary holdings with farmsteads probably in Durley, c. 1574 there were seven,[57] and in 1729 there were 11 holdings with land in the open fields.[58]

Three of Durley's open fields lay east of the Durley–Burbage road and covered 124 a.: they were, from north to south, East field, c. 33 a., Hill field, c. 46 a., and Clay field, 45 a. A field probably called Sands field, c. 41 a.,[59] probably lay west of the village street; it was inclosed, divided, and allotted shortly before 1574.[60] The others were inclosed by private agreement in 1729,[61] and by 1786 all or most of East field had been added to the park of Tottenham House. The land west of the street, c. 95 a., lay in 20 closes in 1786.[62] Durley seems to have had very little woodland.[63]

About 1840 most of the former open fields, including the land west of the street, lay in Durley farm, 454 a., which also included land in Burbage and buildings at the south end of Durley village and in Burbage village.[64] Durley farm was later divided and its buildings at Durley were demolished. In 1995 most of its former open-field land east of the Durley–Burbage road was arable and in Manor farm, Burbage.[65]

Like those of Burbage the men of Durley had the right to feed cattle in Savernake forest at large in summer. They also had the right to feed sheep the whole year on their designated area of the forest: that area lay north and north-east of Durley village and included Durley heath, c. 400 a.,[66] and two warrens in which rabbits were preserved from the early 17th century or earlier. A smaller warren had been inclosed by a pale by 1609. A lodge stood in each warren, and in the early 17th century a tenant held both for a render of 1,520 rabbits. From 1623 or earlier rabbits were apparently preserved only in the great warren.[67] In 1703 the warren, 145 a., was inclosed and divided by private agreement; to replace their feeding rights the men of Durley received allotments totalling 130 a., for which they were thereafter required to pay a yearly rent of 6s. an acre. The lodges, all the trees, and 15 a. were allotted to the owner of the forest.[68] The south-east part of Durley heath, c. 150 a., was inclosed in 1768 and added to the park of Tottenham House. To compensate for the loss of feeding rights the owner of the forest extended Durley's designated area northwards.[69] The rights of the men of Durley to feed animals in the forest, like those of the men of Burbage, were presumably extinguished in the later 18th century and earlier 19th.[70]

North-west of the former warren parts of the forest called Black Vault and Coal coppice had apparently been inclosed by 1673 and 1786 respectively. Trees had been cleared from Coal coppice by 1786.[71] In the early 19th century Warren Farm was built and 135 a. of the former

39   Andrews and Dury, Map (W.R.S. viii), pl. 12; W.R.O., tithe award.
40   Inf. from the Head Forester, Forest Enterprise, Postern Hill, Marlborough.
41   W.A.M. xxxiii. 396.
42   W.R.O. 9/6/757.
43   Kelly's Dir. Wilts. (1848 and later edns.); Harrod's Dir. Wilts. (1865); Dept. of Environment, list of bldgs. of hist. interest (1987); above, intro. [canal].
44   Folk Life, xxxi. 77–87.
45   W.R.O. 9/6/767.
46   Ibid. tithe award.
47   Ibid. 9/1/110.
48   Kelly's Dir. Wilts. (1855 and later edns.).
49   Ibid. (1927, 1939); Mkts. and Fairs (H.M.S.O. 1929), iv (E. and S. Mkts.), 201.
50   Wilts. co. council, Dir. of Employers (1995).
51   For the Crown estate in Burbage, above, manors.
52   Cf. below, this section.

53   Cf. above, this section (Burbage).
54   Below, this section.
55   W.R.O. 9/6/4.
56   Ibid. 9/1/112–13.
57   Ibid. 9/6/756–7.
58   Ibid. 9/6/4.
59   Ibid.; ibid. tithe award.
60   Ibid. 9/6/757.
61   Ibid. 9/6/4.
62   Ibid. 1300/360.
63   e.g. Andrews and Dury, Map (W.R.S. viii), pl. 12.
64   W.R.O., tithe award.
65   Inf. from the agent for the Crown Estate Com.
66   W.R.O. 1300/360; 1300/1840A.
67   Ibid. 9/22/12; 9/22/19; 9/22/37; 9/22/42; 9/22/64.
68   Ibid. 9/6/1.
69   Ibid. 1300/360; 1300/1840A.
70   Above, this section (Burbage).
71   Ibid. 9/22/42; 1300/360.

warren, and probably Black Vault, which was then meadow land, Coal coppice, which was then apparently arable, and other land were worked from it.[72] In the 20th century Warren farm included land in Great Bedwyn and Little Bedwyn parishes;[73] in 1995 it was a dairy farm of 492 a., of which c. 215 a. lay in Burbage parish.[74]

In the 19th century c. 180 a. of Durley and Durley heath lay in the park of Tottenham House.[75] Trees beside the Grand Avenue, between Black Vault and Durley heath, were presumably planted in the earlier 18th century, and a belt standing along the north-west boundary of Durley heath in 1786 was presumably planted after 1764.[76] In the late 19th century the rest of the heath seems to have been added to the park informally, and woodland in the north-west part of it and in the angle of the Grand Avenue and the belt increased to c. 130 a.[77] The woodland was used for commercial forestry from 1939.[78] In 1995 on the rest of the park in Burbage parish, c. 300 a., sheep were grazed on all but c. 50 a. which was arable.[79]

LOCAL GOVERNMENT. Between 1263 and 1266 and in 1271–2 the meetings of the court of Burbage Sturmy manor were roughly quarterly. The chief business of the court was to demand payment from the tenants for the use of the lord's pasture.[80] The court of the manor which came to be called Burbage Darell also met several times a year in the Middle Ages, and records of meetings held between 1358 and 1374 and in 1455 survive. In 1367 the court met at Stibb Green and settled a dispute between tenants. In 1362 and 1374 it was presented that neifs had left the manor without licence.[81] Although from the mid 16th century Burbage Sturmy, Burbage Savage, and Burbage Darell manors were in the same ownership,[82] a separate court continued to be held for each manor and to proceed on the presentments of the relevant homage. In the later 16th century and earlier 17th each court usually met twice a year and on the same days as the other two. From the later 17th century the meetings were usually annual and usually in the autumn. Each court dealt with all aspects of copyhold tenure and the regulation of common husbandry. In the 18th century the

courts frequently ordered that the gates to the common pastures of Burbage should be repaired. From the later 18th century each court was held less regularly, less often, and only when copyhold business required it. No court was held after 1817.[83]

The parish spent £146 on poor relief in 1757, £333 in 1775–6, and £536 in 1802–3. It had a smallpox house in 1761, and from c. 1774 a workhouse in which paupers were employed in spinning and laundering. Most poor relief, however, remained outdoor, and in 1794 the parish bought 74 wheels for paupers to use in their own homes to spin hemp. In 1802–3, when the population of the parish was c. 1,008, 83 paupers were relieved regularly and 30 occasionally.[84] Expenditure on the poor reached a peak in 1812–13, when the parish spent £1,139 on relieving 46 regularly and 173 occasionally.[85] In 1824 the parish was housing 12 paupers and their families in buildings at Ram Alley, Stibb Green, and Westcourt.[86] Expenditure on the poor reached a low point of £425 in 1828[87] and averaged £657 in the period 1833–5. The parish became part of Pewsey poor-law union in 1835.[88] It was included in Kennet district in 1974.[89]

CHURCH. A church stood at Burbage in 1086.[90] By 1139 it had been given to Salisbury cathedral and by c. 1150 a prebend had been endowed with its revenues.[91] Although a man was described in 1281 as the vicar of Burbage,[92] the church was probably served by a chaplain appointed by the prebendary[93] until, apparently, between 1341 and 1405, a vicarage was ordained.[94] In 1864 the Warren and land at the north-east end of Burbage parish were transferred from the ecclesiastical parish of Burbage to that of St. Katharine, Savernake Forest.[95] The vicarage of Burbage was united to the vicarage of Savernake (Christchurch) in 1973, and in 1975 most of Savernake Christchurch ecclesiastical parish was added to Burbage ecclesiastical parish;[96] the united benefice became part of Wexcombe benefice in 1979.[97]

The prebendary of Hurstbourne and Burbage exercised archidiaconal jurisdiction in the parish until 1847[98] and presented vicars to the dean of Salisbury for institution.[99] The bishop collated for an unknown reason in 1434,[1] and the relict

72 W.R.O., tithe award; Little Bedwyn tithe award; Savernake estate map, c. 1820 (copy in W.R.O.); above, intro. (other settlement).
73 e.g. W.R.O., Inland Revenue, val. reg. 56, 59.
74 Inf. from the agent for the Crown Estate Com.
75 O.S. Map 6", Wilts. XXXVI (1888 edn.); W.R.O. 1300/360.
76 W.R.O. 1300/360; above, Great Bedwyn, manors (Tottenham).
77 Cf. O.S. Map 6", Wilts. XXXVI (1888 and later edns.).
78 Cf. W.R.O. 9/33/5.
79 Inf. from the earl of Cardigan, Savernake Lodge, Savernake.
80 P.R.O., SC 2/183/56, rott. 1–5.
81 W.R.O. 9/6/749; 192/4.
82 Above, manors.
83 W.R.O. 9/1/134–5; 9/1/137; 9/1/139–41; 9/1/169–204; 9/6/750–3.
84 Ibid. 831/11–13; Poor Law Abstract, 1804, 564–5.
85 Poor Law Abstract, 1818, 498–9.

86 W.R.O. 831/15.
87 Poor Rate Returns, 1825–9, 219.
88 Poor Law Com. 2nd Rep. App. D, 560.
89 O.S. Map 1/100,000, admin. areas, Wilts. (1974 edn.).
90 V.C.H. Wilts. ii, p. 119.
91 Above, manors (Rectory).
92 Gaol Delivery, 1275–1306 (W.R.S. xxxiii), pp. 66–7.
93 Tax. Eccl. (Rec. Com.), 182.
94 Inq. Non. (Rec. Com.), 173; Chandler's Reg. (W.R.S. xxxix), p. 34.
95 Lond. Gaz. 12 Apr. 1864, pp. 2018–21; for St. Katharine's ch., above, Great Bedwyn, churches.
96 Ch. Com. file, NB 34/371B/2.
97 Inf. from Ch. Com.
98 Le Neve, Fasti, 1541–1857, Salisbury, 53; Cathedrals Act, 3 & 4 Vic. c. 113; e.g. W.R.O., D 7/5/6, Burbage, 1735; D 11/2/1–6.
99 Chandler's Reg. (W.R.S. xxxix), p. 155; Rep. Com. Eccl. Revenues, 826–7; P.R.O., IND 1/17007, f. 523 and v.; IND 1/17013, f. 425v.; W.R.O., D 5/9/4; ibid. 130/49A/6.
1 Phillipps, Wilts. Inst. i. 125.

of the prebendary who died in 1661 presented in 1662.[2] In 1847 the advowson passed by Act to the bishop of Salisbury,[3] who from 1973 to 1979 shared the patronage of the united benefice[4] and from 1979 sat on the board of patronage for Wexcombe benefice.[5]

The vicarage, worth £7 3s. in 1535[6] and £257 c. 1830,[7] was of average value for the diocese. By 1405 it had been endowed with some great tithes, and all the small tithes, from the parish.[8] The tithes were valued at £363 in 1840 and commuted in 1843.[9] The vicar's glebe was accounted 4 a. in 1615,[10] was increased to 8 a. at inclosures in the 18th century and early 19th,[11] and measured 4 a. in 1995.[12] The vicarage house was ruinous in 1650.[13] It was presumably replaced in the later 17th century or restored: in the early 19th century the vicarage house, which stood north of the church, was old and thatched and had low rooms.[14] That house was replaced in 1853 by a new house built on the same site in coursed brick and flint to designs by T. H. Wyatt.[15] The house built in 1853 was sold in 1969[16] and replaced as the Vicarage by a new house built north-west of it.

In the early 15th century the church was rich in service books and vestments, which included a set made of red cloth of gold.[17] Charges made against the vicar in 1412 included immorality.[18] Hugh Nash, vicar from c. 1644 to c. 1662, was ejected in 1646 and restored in 1660.[19] Curates frequently assisted the vicar or served the cure in the 18th and 19th centuries.[20] In 1832 the curate lived in the vicarage house and held two services each Sunday.[21] Two services were held each Sunday in 1850–1, when the average congregation was c. 150.[22] During the incumbency of Thomas Stanton, vicar 1852–75, a canon of Salisbury from 1859 and archdeacon of Wiltshire 1868–74,[23] the church, the vicarage house, and the parish school were rebuilt.[24] In 1864 Stanton held two well attended services each Sunday and preached at both, and he held other services in Lent and on Christmas day, Good Friday, and Ascension day. About 30 communicants attended the monthly celebration of communion, and c. 50 the additional celebrations on Christmas day and on Easter, Whit, and Trinity Sundays.[25] The vicarage of Burbage was held in plurality with the vicarage of Savernake from 1970.[26]

The income from 3 a. on Leigh Hill was given, possibly by Philip Pearce (d. 1805), for repairs to the church. The land was sold c. 1921, and the income of the Leigh Hill charity in 1962 was only £2. In 1973, after two gifts of capital, the income was £52.[27]

ALL SAINTS' church, so called c. 1213,[28] was largely rebuilt c. 1853.[29] Of the old church the tower, which incorporated a west porch, was 14th-century, the chancel mostly 14th-century, the south aisle 15th-century, and the south porch 16th-century.[30] The west end of the roof of the south aisle was elevated in 1702, when a gallery was built.[31] The new church was built of patterned flint and stone to designs by T. H. Wyatt.[32] It consists of a chancel, to which a south chapel was added c. 1876,[33] an aisled and clerestoried nave with south porch, and a west tower with west porch: the tower and its porch are those of the old church.

The church had two chalices and two patens in 1405.[34] In 1553 a chalice of 10½ oz. was left and 11 oz. of plate was taken for the king. A chalice, a paten, and a flagon, hallmarked respectively for 1624, 1719, and 1733, were held in 1995.[35] There were three bells in the church in 1553. A ring of five cast by John Wallis was hung, presumably in 1607, the date of four of the bells. The tenor, dated 1606, was recast in 1851 by J. Warner & Sons. The ring remained in the church in 1995.[36] The registers survive from 1561 and are complete.[37]

NONCONFORMITY. A few papists may have lived at Burbage in the 1660s.[38]

Thomas Taylor, the intruder in Burbage vicarage 1646–60, was a Presbyterian.[39] There were Baptists at Burbage in 1663, and a Baptist conventicle which met there in 1669 was led by Edward Delamaine.[40] In 1676, however, there was no dissenter in the parish,[41] and the meeting houses certified in 1697, 1704, and 1714,[42] may not have been open long.

In 1821 Wesleyan Methodists certified a house at Ram Alley and in 1822 a chapel at Eastcourt.[43] Three services at the chapel on

2 Le Neve, *Fasti, 1541–1857, Salisbury*, 51–2; P.R.O., IND 1/17007, f. 523.
3 Cathedrals Act, 3 & 4 Vic. c. 113.
4 Ch. Com. file, NB 34/371B/2.
5 Inf. from Ch. Com.
6 *Valor Eccl.* (Rec. Com.), ii. 150.
7 *Rep. Com. Eccl. Revenues*, 826–7.
8 *Chandler's Reg.* (W.R.S. xxxix), p. 34.
9 W.R.O., tithe award.
10 Ibid. D 5/10/1, Burbage, 2.
11 Ibid. EA/128; ibid. 9/6/3; idid. tithe award.
12 Inf. from Ch. Com.
13 *W.A.M.* xli. 31–2.
14 Ch. Com. file 13897; W.R.O., tithe award.
15 Ch. Com. file 920; date on bldg.; below, plate 29.
16 Inf. from Ch. Com.
17 *Chandler's Reg.* (W.R.S. xxxix), p. 63.
18 Ibid. p. 119.
19 *Walker Revised*, ed. Matthews, 378; *W.A.M.* xlv. 478.
20 W.R.O., D 7/5/6; D 11/2/1; D 11/2/4–6; Ch. Com. file 920.
21 Ch. Com. file, NB 34/371B/1.
22 P.R.O., HO 129/261/2/5/9.

23 *Alum. Oxon. 1715–1886*, iv. 1344.
24 Above, this section; below, this section; educ.
25 W.R.O., D 1/56/7.
26 Ch. Com. file, NB 34/371B/2.
27 *Endowed Char. Wilts.* (S. Div.), 83; Char. Com. file; W.R.O., tithe award.
28 *Reg. St. Osmund* (Rolls Ser.), i. 251.
29 W.R.O., D 1/61/8/7.
30 J. Buckler, watercolour in W.A.S. Libr., vol. iv. 3; below, plate 5.
31 W.R.O., D 5/33/2.   32 Ibid. D 1/61/8/7.
33 Ibid. D 1/61/27/13.
34 *Chandler's Reg.* (W.R.S. xxxix), p. 63.
35 Nightingale, *Wilts. Plate*, 165; inf. from the vicar.
36 Walters, *Wilts. Bells*, 44; inf. from the vicar.
37 W.R.O. 1678/1–9.
38 Williams, *Cath. Recusancy* (Cath. Rec. Soc.), 296–7, 310, 317, 332.
39 *V.C.H. Wilts*. iii. 106; xv. 153; above, church.
40 *V.C.H. Wilts*. iii. 114 n., 115.
41 *Compton Census*, ed. Whiteman, 112.
42 *Meeting Ho. Certs.* (W.R.S. xl), pp. 6, 13, 17.
43 Ibid. pp. 95, 97; W.R.O., tithe award.

Census Sunday in 1851 had congregations averaging 119.[44] The chapel was closed in 1906, when a new one was opened in High Street.[45] In 1995 services were still held in the chapel in High Street. Primitive Methodists certified a house in 1838, and dissenters certified a cottage at Ram Alley and another house in respectively 1842 and 1850.[46]

EDUCATION.

A schoolmaster lived at Durley in 1717.[47]

A school was built at Eastcourt in 1806[48] and was endowed with £10 a year by Philip Pearce (d. 1805).[49] It was attended by 45 children in 1818,[50] and by 80 in 1833, when the attendance of 40 was paid for partly by Pearce's charity.[51] As a National school it had 106 pupils in 1846–7.[52] It was rebuilt in 1854,[53] and in 1858 had 140–60 pupils.[54] A separate building for the younger children was erected in 1861.[55] The schools were attended by 179 on return day in 1871.[56] By will proved 1872 Robert Highett added £5 a year to the endowment.[57] In the 20th century the number of pupils attending the schools increased: average attendance was c. 190 in 1906[58] and c. 226 between 1932 and 1936.[59] The schools were closed in 1989, when a new one was opened. The new school, between Eastcourt and High Street, was for children aged 5–11 and had 127 on the roll in 1995.[60]

Other schools in the parish were attended by a total of 80 children in 1818,[61] and in 1833 there was a girls' day school and a school begun in 1827 and attended by 24 children.[62] None of the three evening schools held in 1864 flourished,[63] and attendance was poor at another held in the period 1893–1901 to teach boys arithmetic, carpentry, geography, and other subjects.[64]

A private boarding and day school was open at Eastcourt in the 1840s and 1850s, and a similar school at Westcourt from the 1870s to the 1890s.[65]

CHARITIES FOR THE POOR.

A gift of £20 a year from the earls of Ailesbury to the poor of Great Bedwyn and Burbage in the 18th century was voluntary and by 1834 had been discontinued. Payments to the second poor of the parish of 7s. a year by Henry Deacon, of 3s. a year by John Baynton, and of 3s. a year by Mary Baynton were all given by will and were said to have been made from 1730, 1740, and 1776 respectively; all three charities had been lost by 1834. A payment of 10s. a year for poor widows, said to have been made from 1679, was given under the will of John Bushell. Until the 1920s 1s. a year was given to each of 10 widows.[66] The charity was afterwards lost.

Philip Pearce (d. 1805) by will gave the income from £2,000, except £10 a year reserved for the school, to the second poor of the parish. In the earlier 19th century c. £90 a year was spent on flour, and in the early 20th allowances to be spent with local tradesmen were given; in 1902 an allowance of 2s. 2d. each was given to 434.[67] In 1928 £43 was spent on groceries and coal for 428 people. Cash was distributed in the 1950s and later; in 1979 c. £2 was given to each of 19 people.[68]

By will proved 1872 Ralph Highett gave the income from £250 to buy coal for paupers; 44 people received 3 cwt. each in 1900.[69] Coal was still distributed in the 1920s, but later small gifts of cash were made.[70] From c. 1990 the income of the charity, £43 a year, was apparently allowed to accumulate.[71]

Thomas Stanton, vicar of Burbage, by will proved 1875 gave the income from £200 to buy food, blankets, and cloaks for paupers. In the early 20th century only blankets were given, to 14 people in 1900[72] and to 11 in 1926. In 1948 doles of 5s. were given to 19 people.[73] The charity's income, £26 in 1993, was allowed to accumulate from c. 1990.[74]

BUTTERMERE

BUTTERMERE[75] lies c. 7 km. south of Hungerford (Berks.) on Wiltshire's boundary with Berkshire and Hampshire; the parish, which contains Buttermere village and Henley hamlet, measures 608 ha. (1,501 a.). The parish church stands near the centre of Buttermere's land, the boundaries of which were given in the mid 9th century;[76] Henley's land, forming the parish's south-west tail, may have been added to Buttermere's to form the parish in the 11th century, when apparently both were held by St. Swithun's priory, Winchester.[77]

44 P.R.O., HO 129/261/2/5/10.
45 O.S. Map 6", Wilts. XXXVI. SE. (1900, 1926 edns.); W.R.O., G 10/760/33.
46 Meeting Ho. Certs. (W.R.S. xl), pp. 146, 155, 167.
47 P.R.O., E 134/4 Geo. I Mich./24.
48 Ibid. ED 7/130, no. 49; W.R.O., tithe award.
49 Endowed Char. Wilts. (S. Div.), 83.
50 Educ. of Poor Digest, 1020.
51 Educ. Enq. Abstract, 1031.
52 Nat. Soc. Inquiry, 1846–7, Wilts. 4–5.
53 W.R.O. 782/19.   54 Acct. of Wilts. Schs. 11.
55 Kelly's Dir. Wilts. (1903); O.S. Map 6", Wilts. XXXVI (1888 edn.).
56 Returns relating to Elem. Educ. 424–5.
57 Endowed Char. Wilts. (S. Div.), 85.
58 Return of Non-Provided Schs. 20, 39.
59 Bd. of Educ., List 21, 1932 (H.M.S.O.), 406; 1936, 423.   60 Inf. from the vicar.
61 Educ. of Poor Digest, 1020.

62 Educ. Enq. Abstract, 1031.
63 W.R.O., D 1/56/7.
64 Ibid. F 8/500/45/3/1.
65 Kelly's Dir. Wilts. (1848 and later edns.).
66 Char. Don. H.C. 511 (1816), xvi (2), 1350–1; Endowed Char. Wilts. (S. Div.), 82–3; W.R.O., L 2, Burbage.
67 Endowed Char. Wilts. (S. Div.), 83, 85; for Pearce's educational charity, above, educ.
68 W.R.O., L 2, Burbage; Char. Com. file.
69 Endowed Char. Wilts. (S. Div.), 85.
70 W.R.O., L 2, Burbage.   71 Char. Com. file.
72 Endowed Char. Wilts. (S. Div.), 86.
73 W.R.O., L 2, Burbage.
74 Char. Com. file.
75 This article was written in 1994–5. Maps used include O.S. Maps 6", Wilts. XXXVII, XLIII (1882–7 and later edns.); 1/25,000, SU 25/35 (1994 edn.); SU 26/36 (1983 edn.); 1", sheet 12 (1817 edn.).
76 Arch. Jnl. lxxvi. 183–7.   77 Below, manors.

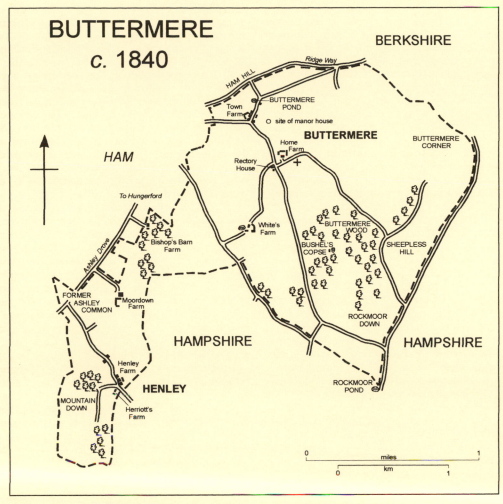

BUTTERMERE
c. 1840

On the north the parish boundary is marked by a ridge way, and on the east the boundary with Hampshire, from 1895 partly with Berkshire, follows another ridge and was marked by another road. Until boundary changes of 1895 Wiltshire, Berkshire, and Hampshire met at Buttermere Corner.[78] Another part of the parish's boundary with Hampshire is also marked by a road across high ground. On the east the boundary of the tail follows a dry valley; on the west it crossed land possibly used in common by men of Ham and Henley and may have been given its indentations at inclosure in the later 17th century.[79]

Chalk outcrops over the whole parish, and on the highest ground is overlain by large areas of clay-with-flints.[80] The parish is on the dip slope of downland, the highest land, at 287 m., being in the extreme north, the lowest, at 155 m., at the south-east corner of the tail. The relief is broken and every valley is dry. In the north part of the parish Buttermere probably had open fields on all sides of the village, and it had upland pastures near the parish boundary north-east, east, and south-east of the

village. On the chalk in the tail Henley almost certainly had open fields and probably had a common pasture for sheep, and there was a common pasture on the high land north-west of the hamlet. Parts of the clay-with-flints are wooded.[81]

In 1377 Buttermere had 6 poll-tax payers and was one of the least populous places in Wiltshire.[82] In the 19th century the population of the parish was remarkably constant, not exceeding 138 or falling below 121. From 130 in 1901 it declined steadily to 39 in 1971. It was 51 in 1981, 43 in 1991.[83]

No main road crosses the parish. The ridge way on the northern parish boundary, leading east to Basingstoke (Hants), went out of use as a thoroughfare in the 19th century.[84] Ashley Drove along the western parish boundary leads to and from Hungerford. For traffic from Buttermere village to reach it more directly a new road, later called Woodcote Road, leading west from the north end of the village, was made between 1773 and 1808.[85]

The whole parish was part of Savernake forest until 1330.[86]

78 V.C.H. Berks. iv. 157.
79 Cf. below, econ. hist.
80 Geol. Surv. Maps 1", drift, sheet 267 (1971 edn.); 1/50,000, drift, sheet 283 (1975 edn.).
81 Below, econ. hist.
82 V.C.H. Wilts. iv. 309, 312.

83 Ibid. 342; Census, 1961; 1971; 1981; 1991.
84 O.S. Maps 1", sheet 12 (1817 edn.); 6", Wilts. XXXVII (1887 edn.).
85 Andrews and Dury, Map (W.R.S. viii), pl. 12; B.L. Maps, O.S.D. 78.
86 V.C.H. Wilts. iv. 399–400, 448, 451.

BUTTERMERE is a hill-top village standing on the clay on generally level ground above the escarpment called Ham Hill. It almost certainly stood on its present site in the mid 9th century: its name was in use then and was taken from a pond (or mere), possibly the embanked pond on the clay at the north end of the present village which may have been its early source of water.[87] In the 18th century the village was small and consisted of two groups of buildings,[88] in the lane between which a new pond was made in the mid 19th century.[89]

In the later 18th century the group of buildings to the south-east consisted of the church, the rectory house, and a farmstead later called Home or Manor Farm and in the late 20th century called Grange Farm.[90] Earthworks west of the church suggest that a manor house may have stood there.[91] A school was built near the rectory house in the later 19th century.[92] The farmhouse of Grange Farm was rebuilt in the later 19th century; in 1995 most of its extensive buildings were of the later 20th century. Large farm buildings north of the rectory house were also erected in the later 20th century.

In the later 18th century the group of buildings to the north-west included a manor house, a farmstead, and presumably several cottages. The manor house, standing in 1773,[93] had been demolished by 1808.[94] West of its site Town Farm includes a house built on a three-roomed plan in the 17th century. Its farm buildings were disused in 1995. Of the six cottages standing c. 1840[95] none survives. In the lane north of Town Farm, called Downs Lane in 1995, a brick house was built in the mid 19th century; south of Town Farm a pair of cottages was built in the same period,[96] and two bungalows were built in Downs Lane in the later 20th century.

About 750 m. south-west of the church a farmstead called White's, later Manor, Farm was standing in 1773.[97] The farmhouse was rebuilt in the later 19th century. About 900 m. south of the church a range of flint and brick cottages was built in the mid 19th century. The cottages were later called Newtown, and in the later 20th century were converted to a house called Ballyack. A gamekeeper's cottage built in the woods east of Newtown in the earlier 19th century was replaced by a bungalow in the 20th.[98]

HENLEY. The hamlet stands at the parish boundary around a pond in an otherwise dry valley. In 1773 it comprised two farmsteads and, on the south-west side of the lane north-west of them, a pair of cottages. The two farmhouses and, in single occupancy, the cottages, were standing in 1995. Henley Farm, called Herriott's Farm c. 1840, is a timber-framed house of the 17th century. Its walls were rebuilt in flint and brick in the 18th and 19th centuries. Henley Lodge, called Henley Farm c. 1840,[99] and the cottages are also timber-framed and 17th-century. In the 19th and 20th centuries farm buildings were renewed on the Wiltshire side of the boundary, and a few buildings were added on the Hampshire side.

On high ground north of the hamlet Moordown Farm, called the Folly in 1773,[1] was built in the 17th century. Originally timber-framed, its walls were rebuilt in rubble and brick in the 18th century, possibly c. 1786,[2] and the 19th. Bishop's Barn Farm, incorporating a house, was built north of Moordown Farm between 1773 and 1808.[3] The house was extended c. 1938.[4]

MANOR AND OTHER ESTATES. Between 862 and 867 either King Ethelbert or King Ethelred granted to Wulfhere 6 cassati, including what became *BUTTERMERE* manor.[5] Wulfhere was outlawed 877 × 883 and forfeited his lands.[6] Buttermere was later held by Wulfgar, possibly Wulfhere's grandson, who between 933 and 948 devised 2 hides of his estate there to Byrhtsige.[7] Later the whole estate belonged to St. Swithun's priory, Winchester: land at Buttermere apparently passed to the priory when, between 1016 and 1035, Wlwric became a monk there, and between 1070 and 1087 the king confirmed land at Buttermere to it.[8] In 1110 the priory granted Buttermere manor to Walter of Combe for a fee-farm rent of £3 a year,[9] a rent paid by the lords of the manor to the priory until the Dissolution and to the dean and chapter of Winchester until the 18th century[10] or later.

In the late 12th century Robert held the manor. William of Buttermere held it from 1199 or earlier[11] to 1228–9 or later.[12] William Buggy held it in 1242–3,[13] and Henry Buggy held it in 1259.[14] William de St. Martin held it in 1275, when Walter Northwich held it of him.[15] In 1379, when they granted a rent of 8 marks from

87 *P.N. Wilts.* (E.P.N.S.), 339; O. G. S. Crawford, *Arch. in the Field*, 124.
88 *Andrews and Dury, Map* (W.R.S. viii), pl. 12; J. Rocque, *Topog. Surv. Berks.* (1761), sheet V.
89 O.S. Map 6", Wilts. XXXVII (1887 edn.); W.R.O., tithe award.
90 *Andrews and Dury, Map* (W.R.S. viii), pl. 12; Rocque, *Topog. Surv. Berks.* (1761), sheet V; *Kelly's Dir. Wilts.* (1899 and later edns.); O.S. Map 1/25,000, SU 26/36 (1983 edn.); W.R.O. 2250/1, abstr. of title.
91 B.L. Maps, O.S.D. 78.   92 Below, educ.
93 *Andrews and Dury, Map* (W.R.S. viii), pl. 12.
94 B.L. Maps, O.S.D. 78.
95 W.R.O., tithe award.
96 Ibid.; O.S. Map 6", Wilts. XXXVII (1887 edn.).
97 *Andrews and Dury, Map* (W.R.S. viii), pl. 12.
98 O.S. Map 6", Wilts. XLIII (1882 and later edns.); W.R.O., tithe award; J. H. Chandler, 'Hist. Buttermere' (TS. in possession of Dr. Chandler, Jupe's Sch., E. Knoyle), cap. 7.

99 *Andrews and Dury, Map* (W.R.S. viii), pl. 12; W.R.O., tithe award.
1 *Andrews and Dury, Map* (W.R.S. viii), pl. 12.
2 Date on ho.
3 *Andrews and Dury, Map* (W.R.S. viii), pl. 12; B.L. Maps, O.S.D. 78.
4 W.R.O., G 8/760/338.
5 Finberg, *Early Wessex Chart.* p. 75.
6 *V.C.H. Wilts.* ii, p. 7.
7 Ibid. p. 8; Finberg, *Early Wessex Chart.* p. 85.
8 *Reg. Regum Anglo-Norm.* i, no. 268.
9 Ibid. ii, no. 948.
10 e.g. K. A. Hanna, 'Winchester Cath. Custumal' (Southampton Univ. Coll. M.A. thesis, 1954), 352; D. & C. Winton. Mun., W 52/76; P.R.O., C 11/2055/12.
11 P.R.O., CP 25/1/250/2, no. 3.
12 *Cur. Reg. R.* xiii, pp. 269, 341.
13 *Bk. of Fees*, ii. 714.
14 *Close R. 1259–61*, 150.
15 *Rot. Hund.* (Rec. Com.), ii (1), 260.

it to Michael Skilling, the manor was held by Peter Besiles and his wife Mabel and apparently of them by Richard Thorold.[16] It was later held in fee by Hugh Thorold, who by 1390 had granted it for life to Isabel, wife of Lambert Farmer; under a grant of that year[17] Farmer acquired the reversion and c. 1403 died seised of the manor.[18] John Franks, clerk of parliament 1414–23 and Master of the Rolls from 1423, held the manor in fee in 1411,[19] and in 1417 he bought from Michael Skilling's son John the rent of 8 marks.[20] About 1433 Franks sold the manor to Thomas Chaucy.[21] By 1447 Chaucy had conveyed it to William Ludlow,[22] presumably the William Ludlow who died in 1478.[23]

Buttermere manor passed from William Ludlow to his son William, who was succeeded by his son Thomas (fl. 1504 × 1515).[24] In 1571 John Ludlow (d. 1614) settled the manor for life on Catherine Dallyson. He devised it to William Curll[25] (d. 1617),[26] and it descended to Curll's son Edward[27] (d. 1621). It was held by Edward's relict Mary and passed in turn to his son John[28] (d. c. 1661),[29] John's son Walter (d. c. 1686), and Walter's relict Frances (d. by 1698). Walter's son Walter[30] sold the manor in 1719 to Nicholas Terrell (d. 1727).[31] It descended to Terrell's son Nicholas (d. s.p. 1736–7),[32] who was succeeded by a kinsman, Sir Charles Crispe, Bt. (d. 1740). Sir Charles's heir was his niece Mary Crispe (d. 1751),[33] who devised the manor to her husband the Revd. George Stonehouse.[34] About 1790 Stonehouse sold it to William Southby, c. 1796 Southby sold it to James Lockhart,[35] and in 1803 Lockhart conveyed it to his son John (d. 1835), who took the name Wastie instead of Lockhart in 1832. Wastie devised the manor to his nephew James Lockhart, who sold it in portions c. 1861.[36]

Lockhart sold White's (later Manor) farm, 626 a., to M. H. Marsh[37] (d. 1881). Marsh's trustees sold it in 1889 to H. O. Kidman, and Kidman sold it in 1909 to William Wiles.[38] A. D. Hart owned it from c. 1926 to c. 1934. His successor C. MacPherson sold it c. 1947. Mr. J. J. Hosier owned Manor farm from c. 1966 and in 1994.[39]

Lockhart sold Home and Town farms, 551 a., to J. T. Gough (d. 1868), who was succeeded by his brother James (d. 1890). James's trustees sold the farms in 1892 to his son Henry,[40] who sold them c. 1910 to Henry a'Barrow[41] (d. 1934). A'Barrow's son Maurice sold the farms c. 1951 to Douglas and Iris Waters. Members of the Waters family owned the land as Grange farm in 1994.[42]

The land of HENLEY belonged to St. Swithun's priory, Winchester, in the mid 13th century as part of the priory's manor of Ham,[43] and it may have been part of it in the mid 10th century when Wulfgar devised Ham to his wife Aeffe for life with remainder to the Old minster at Winchester.[44] As part of Ham manor Henley passed from the priory to the dean and chapter of Winchester in 1541 and to the Ecclesiastical Commissioners in 1861.[45] Henley farm, 70 a., was enfranchised for H. D. Woodman (d. 1915) in 1862,[46] and Herriott's farm was probably enfranchised for a member of the Herriott family. As Henley farm, 169 a., both farms were owned in 1910 by John Herriott[47] and in 1994 by members of the Herriott family.[48] Bishop's Barn farm, 59 a., was enfranchised for John Canning (fl. 1863),[49] whose executors owned it in 1910.[50] It was part of White's farm c. 1934,[51] and c. 1947 belonged to J. Alexander.[52] It has not been traced further. In 1914 the Ecclesiastical Commissioners sold Moordown farm, 59 a., to S. W. Farmer[53] as part of an estate based in Ham. As part of that estate Farmer sold it in 1920 to S. R. Brown,[54] who offered it for sale in 1928.[55] It was part of White's farm c. 1934 and was later sold to W. Hine.[56] Mr. R. Hine owned it in 1994.[57]

Three estates at Buttermere in 1086 have not been traced further. Waleran the huntsman and of him Azelin held 1 hide and 1 yardland held by eight thegns in 1066, Anschitil held ½ yardland held by Godwin in 1066, and Ernulf of Hesdin held 5 a.[58]

16 *Feet of F. 1377–1509* (W.R.S. xli), pp. 2–3.
17 *Cal. Close, 1389–92*, 292.
18 *Cal. Pat. 1401–5*, 153.
19 Ibid. 1408–13, 250; A. B. Emden, *Biog. Reg. Univ. Oxf. to 1500*, ii. 721.
20 *Feet of F. 1377–1509* (W.R.S. xli), p. 77.
21 *Cal. Close, 1429–35*, 253; P.R.O., C 88/115, no. 85.
22 *Cal. Close, 1441–7*, 464–5.
23 *V.C.H. Wilts.* xi. 57.
24 P.R.O., C 1/331, no. 18; C 1/334, no. 55.
25 Ibid. CP 25/2/239/13 Eliz. I Trin.; ibid. PROB 11/123, ff. 264v.–266v.; *V.C.H. Hants*, iv. 610.
26 R. Clutterbuck, *Hist. Herts.* ii. 370.
27 P.R.O., PROB 11/131, f. 343 and v.
28 Ibid. PROB 11/137, ff. 215v.–216v.; W.R.O. 212A/27/21/1, deed, Curll to Wilcox, 1639.
29 *W.A.M.* xlix. 113.
30 P.R.O., C 5/150/44; C 5/593/14.
31 W.R.O. 212A/27/21/1, deed, Curll to Terrell, 1719; ibid. bishop's transcripts, bdle. 2.
32 P.R.O., PROB 6/113, f. 7.
33 Ibid. PROB 11/623, ff. 224v.–226; G.E.C. *Baronetage*, iv. 12.
34 P.R.O., PROB 11/799, ff. 222v.–223v.
35 Ibid. CP 25/2/1447/30 Geo. III Mich.; W.R.O., A 1/345/67.
36 W. P. W. Phillimore and E. A. Fry, *Changes of Name*,

335; W.R.O. 2250/1, abstr. of title.
37 W.R.O. 211/15/26–7; 2250/1, sale cat. 1861.
38 Ch. Com. deed 326420.
39 Chandler, 'Hist. Buttermere', cap. 6; inf. from Mrs. S. Hosier, Manor Farm.
40 W.R.O. 2250/1, abstr. of title; copy will of J. T. Gough; partic. of estate, 1869; deed, 1892.
41 Ibid. Inland Revenue, val. reg. 60; *Kelly's Dir. Wilts.* (1911).
42 Chandler, 'Hist. Buttermere', cap. 6; local inf.
43 Hanna, 'Winchester Cath. Custumal', 344–51.
44 Finberg, *Early Wessex Chart.* p. 85.
45 *V.C.H. Wilts.* xi. 152–3.
46 Ch. Com. files 19108; 26571.
47 W.R.O., Inland Revenue, val. reg. 60.
48 Inf. from Mrs. M. Herriott, Henley Farm.
49 D. & C. Winton. Mun., W 52/83.
50 W.R.O., Inland Revenue, val. reg. 60.
51 Ibid. G 8/516/1.
52 Ibid. G 8/516/4.
53 Ch. Com. file 26556.
54 *V.C.H. Wilts.* xi. 153; W.R.O. 1932/1; ibid. tithe award, altered apportionment.
55 D. & C. Winton. Mun., W 52/83.
56 W.R.O., G 8/516/1; G 8/516/4.
57 Inf. from Mr. R. Hine, Moordown Farm.
58 *V.C.H. Wilts.* ii, pp. 139, 151, 166.

ECONOMIC HISTORY. BUTTERMERE. Waleran's, Anschitil's, and Ernulf's were the only estates in Buttermere to be separately surveyed in 1086, when they were said to consist of land for 2 ploughteams, land for 2 oxen, and 5 a.[59]

Sheep-and-corn husbandry in common was probably practised at Buttermere, and 17th-century evidence suggests that open fields may have been called East, West, and Church. Sheepless (otherwise Sheep Leaze) Hill south-east of the village was presumably a common pasture for sheep, and Rockmoor down south of it and downland at the parish boundary east of the village may have been for cattle and sheep. Both arable and pasture had evidently been inclosed by 1686.[60]

Between 1624 and 1686 the demesne farm of Buttermere manor was possibly divided into Home farm and Town farm, and Town Farm may have been built as a new farmstead in that period.[61] About 1700 there were four other farms, two of c. 92 a. each, one of c. 31 a., and one of 12 a.[62] All four had apparently been united as White's by c. 1730, when that farm, Home, and Town were roughly the same size as each other.[63] Town and White's were held by the same tenant in the period 1791–1800, and c. 1827 part of Home farm, including the farmstead, was added to Town farm and the rest to White's.[64] About 1840 Town and Home farm, mainly to the north-east, was 550 a., White's, mainly to the south-west, c. 547 a. More than two thirds of each was arable. All but one of the arable fields were of less than 50 a. Each farm had downland pasture, Town and Home at the parish boundary north-east of the church, White's on Sheepless Hill and Rockmoor down.[65]

In the late 19th century the amount of arable at Buttermere declined, and in the earlier 20th there was more grassland than arable. Sheep farming declined and dairy farming increased. In the 1930s most of the arable lay in an arc along the northern parish boundary and there was some near Buttermere wood. There was rough grazing on Sheepless Hill and Rockmoor down. Town and Home (then called Manor, later Grange) was presumably an arable and sheep farm, White's (later called Manor) presumably a dairy farm.[66] In 1994 Grange remained an arable and sheep farm; Manor, c. 700 a. including Bishop's Barn farm and land in Ham, was entirely arable;[67] the late 20th-century farm buildings north of the rectory house were used for cattle rearing.

In the late 17th century and early 18th Buttermere had c. 24 a. or more of coppiced wood.[68] Between 1773 and 1817 Buttermere wood, c. 72 a., and Bushel's copse, c. 14 a., were planted,[69] and c. 1840 they and other coppices totalled c. 95 a.[70] In 1994 those woods, and several others mainly planted in the 20th century, totalled c. 130 a.[71]

HENLEY. In the mid 13th century all Henley's land, c. 300 a., was held by copy of Ham manor. Four holdings were based at Henley hamlet, those of a yardlander with 30 a., a ½-yardlander with 15 a., and two cottagers with 10 a. each; two were allegedly based at Moordown, those of a yardlander with 30 a. and a ½-yardlander with 15 a. The arable of all six almost certainly lay at Henley and in open fields; the tenants probably shared Mountain down, 46 a. south-west of the hamlet, as a common pasture for sheep, and they had pasture rights on Ashley common north-west of the hamlet. The tenants all had obligations comparable to those of the manor's customary tenants with holdings based at Ham: they owed a wide variety of labour services, the yardlanders twice as many as the ½-yardlanders, and they had to serve as officers of the manor. The service was presumably done at Ham.[72] In 1649 there were three holdings of 1 yardland, one of ½ yardland. Nearly all the arable had been inclosed by then,[73] Ashley common was inclosed in the later 17th century,[74] and Mountain down had been inclosed by the earlier 19th century.[75]

There were still four holdings in the earlier 19th century. About 1840 Bishop's Barn farm and Moordown farm each had c. 59 a., Henley farm had 70 a., Herriott's farm 95 a. All four were mainly arable; no field was as large as 25 a., and Mountain down had by then been ploughed. Herriott's farm was then worked by a farmer with much land in Ham,[76] and in the later 19th century Henley, Bishop's Barn, and Moordown were all worked with land in Ham.[77] In the 1930s there was arable west of the hamlet but most of Henley's land was grassland.[78] In 1994 Henley farm, a mixed farm of 169 a., included Herriott's and was worked with land in Hampshire;[79] Moordown farm, c. 250 a., was arable.[80]

About 1840 there was 5 a. of woodland near Bishop's Barn Farm, 3 a. west of Henley hamlet, and 5 a. south of it.[81] The 3 a. had been cleared by 1879[82] but most of the other woodland was standing in 1994.

59 V.C.H. Wilts. ii, pp. 139, 151, 166.
60 P.R.O., C 5/97/120; C 5/593/14; W.R.O., tithe award.
61 P.R.O., C 5/97/120; ibid. STAC 8/94/18; above, intro. (Buttermere).
62 P.R.O., C 5/593/14; W.R.O. 212A/27/21/1, deeds, Curll to Wilmott, 1703; Curll to Terrell, 1719.
63 P.R.O., C 11/2055/12.
64 Chandler, 'Hist. Buttermere', cap. 6.
65 W.R.O., tithe award.
66 P.R.O., MAF 68/493, sheet 9; MAF 68/1633, sheet 12; MAF 68/2773, sheet 12; MAF 68/3319, sheet 11; [1st] Land Util. Surv. Map, sheet 112.
67 Inf. from Mrs. S. Hosier, Manor Farm; for Bishop's Barn farm, below, this section (Henley).
68 P.R.O., C 5/97/120; C 5/634/29; W.R.O. 212A/27/21/1, deed, Curll to Terrell, 1719.
69 Andrews and Dury, Map (W.R.S. viii), pl. 12; O.S. Map 1", sheet 12 (1817 edn.).   70 W.R.O., tithe award.
71 O.S. Maps 6", Wilts. XXXVII. SE. (1926 edn.); XLIII. NE. (1926 edn.); 1/10,000, SU 35 NE., NW. (1982 edn.); SU 36 SE. (1976 edn.); SU 36 SW. (1975 edn.).
72 Hanna, 'Winchester Cath. Custumal', 341–51; W.R.O., tithe award.
73 D. & C. Winton. Mun., W 52/76, ff. 99–108.
74 Ibid. estate bk. 8.   75 W.R.O., tithe award.
76 Ibid.; Ham tithe award.
77 V.C.H. Wilts. xi. 154, 156; Ch. Com. file 26571.
78 [1st] Land Util. Surv. Map, sheet 112.
79 Inf. from Mrs. M. Herriott, Henley Farm.
80 Inf. from Mr. R. Hine, Moordown Farm.
81 W.R.O., tithe award.
82 O.S. Map 6", Wilts. XLIII (1882 edn.).

LOCAL GOVERNMENT. In 1775–6 the parish spent £66 on the poor, in the period 1783–5 an average of £83. Although in 1802–3 £102 was raised by the poor rate, only £68 was spent; 3 children received regular relief, 8 adults occasional relief. On average in the three years to Easter 1815 £75 was spent on relieving 8 adults regularly and 3 occasionally.[83] At £48 expenditure on the poor was lowest in 1816 and at £157 highest in 1832.[84] Buttermere became part of Hungerford poor-law union in 1835,[85] and was included in Kennet district in 1974.[86]

CHURCH. Buttermere church was standing in 1268.[87] The rectory was united in 1912 with the vicarage of Combe (Berks., formerly Hants).[88] That union was dissolved in 1933, when the rectory was united with Ham rectory.[89] Shalbourne vicarage was added in 1956,[90] Buttermere and Ham parishes were united in 1958,[91] and in 1979 the united benefice became part of Wexcombe benefice.[92]

In 1284 St. Swithun's priory confirmed the bishop of Winchester's right to collate rectors of Buttermere.[93] The bishop thereafter collated except in 1594 and 1626 when the Crown presented because the see was vacant.[94] The advowson was transferred in 1869 to the bishop of Oxford,[95] and in 1905 to St. George's chapel, Windsor.[96] The chapel had the right to present at alternate vacancies from 1933[97] and at two of every three vacancies from 1956;[98] from 1979 it had a seat on the board of patronage for Wexcombe benefice.[99]

The rectory was worth £4 6s. 8d. in 1291,[1] £10 10s. 7d. in 1535,[2] and £229 c. 1830.[3] A pension of 9s. being paid to Poughley priory (Berks.) in 1291[4] apparently lapsed. The rector took all tithes from the whole parish: they were valued at £299 in 1843 and commuted. The glebe, c. 2 a.[5] until c. 4 a. near the rectory house was bought in 1914,[6] was sold c. 1933.[7] The rectory house was burned down before 1668.[8] The small cottage which had been built by 1671 to replace it[9] was in poor condition in the 19th

century.[10] A new red-brick rectory house was built on the site of the cottage in 1876[11] and sold in 1933.[12]

In 1304–5 the rector was licensed to study canon law at Oxford for three years,[13] and in 1307 his successor was also licensed to study for three years.[14] Other early 14th-century rectors were also in minor orders.[15] William Rede, rector 1361–5, became bishop of Chichester in 1368.[16] In 1412 the rector was licensed to hold a second benefice,[17] and in 1560 the rector held two benefices.[18] Curates served the church in 1620 and 1623.[19] Joseph Nixon, rector 1637–79, was in 1647 accused of intemperance; he employed sequestered ministers to serve the cure, was ejected c. 1655, and was restored in 1660. Three intruders served successively from 1656 to 1658.[20] From 1660 Nixon was also rector of West Shefford (Berks.),[21] and a curate served Buttermere in 1668.[22] Thomas Baker, rector 1772–89, was also vicar of Combe, where he lived. At Buttermere in 1783 he held two services each Sunday and one on Christmas day. Few attended his quarterly celebrations of communion.[23] In 1812, when the church was served by a curate who lived outside the parish, only one service was held each Sunday.[24] Curates also served Buttermere during the incumbency of Nathaniel Dodson, rector 1818–67 and a pluralist.[25] In 1851 the curate lived in Combe and his service each Sunday at Buttermere, held alternately morning and afternoon, was attended by 55 people.[26] The pattern of Sunday services was the same in 1864, when a congregation of c. 38 attended. A Good Friday service was then attended by 50–60, and there were c. 10 communicants.[27]

The church of ST. JAMES, so called in 1763,[28] was wholly rebuilt in 1855–6.[29] The old church, standing in the 13th century,[30] was built of flint and had an undivided chancel and nave, a north porch, and a western bell turret of timber.[31] The windows in the north wall were replaced in the 14th century, and the porch was built in the 18th.[32] The new church, built of rubble with freestone dressings to designs by R.

83 *Poor Law Abstract, 1804*, 564–5; *1818*, 498–9.
84 *Poor Rate Returns, 1816–21*, 188; *1822–4*, 228; *1825–9*, 219; *1830–4*, 212.
85 *Poor Law Com. 1st Rep.* App. D, 242.
86 O.S. Map 1/100,000, admin. areas, Wilts. (1974 edn.).
87 P.R.O., JUST 1/998, rot. 34d.
88 Ch. Com. file 42391.
89 *Lond. Gaz.* 15 Aug. 1933, pp. 5411–13.
90 Ibid. 11 Sept. 1956, p. 5168.
91 Ibid. 31 Jan. 1958, p. 683.
92 Inf. from Ch. Com.
93 *Reg. Pontoise* (Cant. & York Soc.), ii (1), 431.
94 Phillipps, *Wilts. Inst.* (index in *W.A.M.* xxviii. 215).
95 *Lond. Gaz.* 4 June 1852, pp. 1578, 1580; *Handbk. Brit. Chronology* (1986), ed. E. B. Fryde and others, 278.
96 Ch. Com. file 101186.
97 *Lond. Gaz.* 15 Aug. 1933, pp. 5411–13.
98 Ibid. 11 Sept. 1956, p. 5168.
99 Inf. from Ch. Com.
1 *Tax. Eccl.* (Rec. Com.), 192.
2 *Valor Eccl.* (Rec. Com.), ii. 151.
3 *Rep. Com. Eccl. Revenues*, 826–7.
4 *Tax. Eccl.* (Rec. Com.), 192.
5 W.R.O., D 1/24/32/1; D 1/24/32/3; ibid. tithe award; Ch. Com. file 40041.	6 Ch. Com. deed 326420.
7 Ibid. file 101186.
8 W.R.O., D 1/54/3/1/35.

9 Ibid. D 1/24/32/1.
10 *W.A.M.* xli. 132; *Rep. Com. Eccl. Revenues*, 826–7; Ch. Com. file 40041.	11 W.R.O., D 1/11/232.
12 Ch. Com. file 101186; ibid. file, PG 1432.
13 *Reg. Ghent* (Cant. & York Soc.), ii. 870.
14 Ibid. ii. 693.
15 Ibid. ii. 748, 831–2, 895, 901; *Reg. Martival* (Cant. & York Soc.), i. 162.
16 Phillipps, *Wilts. Inst.* i. 54, 59; *D.N.B.*
17 *Cal. Papal Reg.* vi. 307.
18 W.R.O., D 1/43/3, f. 56.
19 Ibid. bishop's transcripts, bdle. 1.
20 *Walker Revised*, ed. Matthews, 378.
21 *Alum. Oxon. 1500–1714*, iii. 1072.
22 W.R.O., D 1/54/3/1/35.
23 Phillipps, *Wilts. Inst.* ii. 95; *Vis. Queries, 1783* (W.R.S. xxvii), p. 50.	24 *W.A.M.* xli. 132.
25 *Rep. Com. Eccl. Revenues*, 826–7; *Alum. Oxon. 1715–1886*, i. 376.
26 P.R.O., HO 129/121/1/6/10.
27 W.R.O., D 1/56/7.
28 J. Ecton, *Thesaurus* (1763), 405.
29 W.R.O., D 1/60/5/51; D 1/61/9/1.
30 Above, this section.
31 *W.A.M.* xli. 132.
32 J. Buckler, watercolour in W.A.S. Libr., vol. iv. 4; below, plate 7.

J. Withers, has the same plan as the old except that it was given a small central timber spirelet instead of a western turret.[33] The spirelet was removed in 1946, when the bell was hung on the outside of the west wall. A new spirelet was built in 1991, but the bell was not moved.[34]

In 1553 a chalice of 5 oz. was kept for the parish and 14 oz. of plate was taken for the king. A chalice with cover in use in 1783 and 1812 was replaced c. 1856 by the chalice and paten held in 1994.[35] There were two bells in the old church,[36] an undated one in the new.[37] Registrations of baptisms begin in 1720, of burials in 1721, and of marriages in 1722; they are apparently complete.[38]

NONCONFORMITY. About 1864 a few inhabitants of Buttermere were Primitive Methodists and met in a house which was apparently in the parish.[39] There is no other evidence of nonconformity in the parish.

EDUCATION. There was a school attended by 13 children c. 1846,[40] perhaps that in which a woman taught 10–15 in 1859.[41] There was no school in the parish in 1864, when children went to school at Fosbury in Tidcombe,[42] or in 1871, when they went to school at Fosbury or Ham.[43] Buttermere school, opened in 1872,[44] was attended by c. 27 children in 1906–7, by c. 38 in 1938,[45] and by only c. 9 when it closed in 1944.[46]

CHARITY FOR THE POOR. None known.

CHILTON FOLIAT

CHILTON FOLIAT village stands on the river Kennet 3 km. north-west of Hungerford (Berks.).[47] Its church served a parish which by 1341 had embraced lands which were in 1086, and remained, in Berkshire.[48] The Wiltshire part of the parish, 2,202 a. (891 ha.), contained Chilton Foliat village and East Soley and West Soley hamlets. The Berkshire part, 1,292 a. (523 ha.), contained Leverton village and settlements called Calcot and Hayward; it was transferred to Hungerford parish in 1895.[49] This article deals with the history of the whole parish, 3,494 a. (1,414 ha.).

Chilton Foliat, Calcot, and Leverton were settlements beside the Kennet each with a strip of land running north to downland, and Chilton Foliat also had land south of the river. Their boundaries were generally straight,[50] and together they formed an almost square parish. Between 1086 and the early 13th century Chilton Foliat's downland was apparently assigned as agricultural land to a new settlement called Soley, and Leverton's likewise to Hayward.[51] A hamlet called Cakewood, possibly planted in the same period, was said in the earlier 15th century to stand in Chilton Foliat parish and Berkshire and to contain five messuages. It was not mentioned after 1439[52] and its precise site is unknown: it presumably stood south of the Kennet near either the river or Cake wood and, if so, the attribution of it to Berkshire seems

incorrect. It had apparently been deserted by the 16th century.[53] The suffix in the name Chilton Foliat is the surname of the lords of the manor in the 12th and 13th centuries[54] and was in use in 1221.[55]

Across the parish the county boundary follows the Kennet north-west and south-east and a dry tributary valley for much of its length north–south. Where it coincides with the parish boundary it remains on the Kennet on the south-east and follows the dry valley there called Wiltshire bottom on the north-west. In addition to where it coincides with the county boundary the parish boundary responds to relief on the south by following the contours on Furze Hill, following a dry valley, and crossing a summit. Elsewhere it was marked by few natural or prominent man-made features. The east part was little changed after 984, when it was recorded as part of Leverton's boundary.[56]

Nearly all the parish lies on chalk; a small area of Reading Beds outcrops north of Chilton Foliat village. Much of the northern part of the parish is overlain by clay-with-flints, there are extensive deposits of alluvium beside the Kennet, and between the alluvium and the clay and across the northern part of the parish in the deep dry valley called Old Hayward bottom and Wiltshire bottom there are extensive deposits of gravel. South of the Kennet clay-with-flints lies in the south-west corner of the parish.[57] The

33 W.R.O., D 1/60/5/51; D 1/61/9/1.
34 Inf. in church.
35 Nightingale, *Wilts. Plate*, 165–6; *W.A.M.* xli. 132; W.R.O., D 1/24/32/3; inf. from the team rector, Shalbourne.
36 *W.A.M.* xli. 132; W.R.O., D 1/24/32/3.
37 Walters, *Wilts. Bells*, 44; inf. from the team rector.
38 W.R.O. 508/1–3; 1022/2–3; bishop's transcripts for c. 18 years in the 17th cent. and for 1709–16 are in W.R.O.
39 Ibid. D 1/56/7.
40 Nat. Soc. *Inquiry, 1846–7*, Wilts. 4–5.
41 *Acct. of Wilts. Schs.* 11.
42 W.R.O., D 1/56/7; for Fosbury sch., which stood in Shalbourne par., below, Fosbury, educ.
43 *Returns relating to Elem. Educ.* 418–19.
44 *Return of Non-Provided Schs.* 20.
45 *Bd. of Educ., List 21, 1908* (H.M.S.O.), 501; *1938*, 421.
46 W.R.O., F 8/500/47/1/1; Chandler, 'Hist. But-

termere', cap. 5.
47 This article was written in 1995. Maps used include O.S. Maps 6", Berks. XXXIII (1882 edn.); Wilts. XXIV, XXX (1887 and later edns.); 1/25,000, SU 26/36 (1983 edn.); SU 27/37 (1985 edn.); 1/50,000, sheet 174 (1981 edn.).
48 *V.C.H. Berks.* i. 340, 345; *Inq. Non.* (Rec. Com.), 173.
49 W.R.O., F 2/200/2/2.
50 For the approximate boundaries, map on p. 90.
51 Below, manors (Leverton; Hayward); econ. hist. (Chilton Foliat; Soley; Leverton; Hayward).
52 *Cal. Inq. p.m.* xx, p. 251; P.R.O., C 139/94, no. 54, rot. 30.
53 Below, econ. hist. (Chilton Foliat).
54 Ibid. manors (Chilton Foliat).
55 *Pat. R.* 1216–25, 288.
56 *P.N. Berks.* (E.P.N.S.), iii. 673–4.
57 Geol. Surv. Map 1", sheet 267 (1947 edn.).

Kennet flows west–east across the parish at *c.* 100 m. The land rises steeply south of it to 169 m. in the south-west corner, more gradually to the north where it is broken by many dry valleys. The highest land, at 187 m., is on the parish boundary at the north-west corner, where the terrain is generally flat. There was much meadow land, and there were open fields in all parts of the parish. The clay favours woodland and the north-east and south-west corners are well wooded.[58] Several parts of the parish were imparked.[59]

The parish was lived in by 120 adult males in 1676.[60] The population numbered 616 in 1801. Between 1811 and 1821 it increased by 25 per cent to reach its peak of 777; it remained over 700 until 1851 and had fallen to 525 by 1891. In the 19th century about four fifths of the inhabitants lived in Wiltshire, and *c.* 130 lived in the Berkshire part of the parish when it was transferred to Hungerford in 1895. The population of the reduced parish fluctuated: it was 409 in 1901, 336 in 1921, 372 in 1931,[61] 286 in 1971, and 299 in 1991.[62]

In the 17th century a subsidiary course of the road from London to Bath and Bristol followed the north bank of the Kennet, bypassed Hungerford, crossed Chilton Foliat parish, and linked Chilton Foliat village to Ramsbury and Marlborough.[63] In Chilton Foliat village it was called High Street in 1704,[64] east of it later Leverton Lane. On the south bank of the Kennet a parallel road across the parish linked Hungerford and Littlecote House in Ramsbury. Chilton Foliat village was linked to that road by a short north–south road which crossed the river at the east end of the street. A bridge had been built at the crossing by 1773;[65] the present bridge, triple-arched, red-brick, and 18th-century, was widened in 1936.[66] In the 19th and 20th centuries the road from Hungerford, the road across the bridge, and the road through Chilton Foliat village were increasingly used by London–Swindon traffic; from 1946, when part of it was widened, that line of roads was part of a trunk road to Swindon, Gloucester, and Hereford,[67] diverging from the London–Bristol road at Hungerford. Its importance diminished in 1971, when the London and south Wales motorway was opened,[68] and it was distrunked in 1977.[69] Several roughly parallel roads linked the northern parts of the parish to the Marlborough road; three of them met a road through Old Hayward

bottom, by which Chilton Foliat and Leverton were linked to Lambourn (Berks.), and one crossed first the Marlborough road a little west of the church and then the Kennet.[70] At inclosure in 1813 that leading from East Soley and crossing the Kennet was closed north of the Marlborough road, where it ran near Chilton House; south of the Marlborough road it survives as a footpath. Also in 1813 another road from East Soley was closed north of Chilton Park Farm and about then a new road, which remains in use as Stag Hill, was built to link East Soley and Chilton Foliat. Only one of the roads, that for which a new south section was made west of Chilton House in 1813,[71] has not been tarmacadamed.

Artefacts of the Neolithic period and the Bronze Age have been found north-west of the church, and one of the late Bronze Age has been found at Leverton.[72]

The Berkshire part of the parish lay in the forest of Berkshire until 1227.[73]

In 1769 Dorothy Bethell gave a fire engine and £100 stock to pay for repairs to it and for men to be trained to use it.[74] A new building to house the fire engine was erected in 1831,[75] and in the early 20th century the income from the stock, *c.* £3 a year, was being used as the donor intended.[76] Under a Scheme of 1934 the fire engine was given to Swindon Museum, and in 1995 it was housed at Coate Agricultural Museum.[77] In the 1950s the charity's income was used to buy fire extinguishers,[78] later for general charitable purposes.[79]

CHILTON FOLIAT. The village stands along both sides of the Marlborough road and was designated a conservation area in 1974.[80] On the north side of the road the rectory house stands immediately east of the church, and the manor house which was standing in the Middle Ages probably stood immediately west of the church. The old manor house was almost certainly the house demolished in the 1750s immediately before its replacement, Chilton House, was built on a site, probably that behind its own, on rising ground north-west of the church.[81]

In the 17th century and the mid 18th there were probably as many buildings west of the church as east,[82] in the early 19th century there were many more east than west,[83] and in 1995 no building clearly earlier than 1700 survived west. A house of brick and thatch, apparently

58 Below, econ. hist.
59 Ibid. manors (Chilton Lodge); econ. hist. (Chilton Foliat; Calcot).
60 *Compton Census*, ed. Whiteman, 126.
61 *V.C.H. Berks.* ii. 238; *V.C.H. Wilts.* iv. 344.
62 *Census*, 1971; 1991.
63 J. Ogilby, *Brit.* (1675), pl. 10.
64 Som. R.O., DD/PO 6B, deed, Smith to Spanswick, 1704.
65 *Andrews and Dury, Map* (W.R.S. viii), pl. 12.
66 Date on bridge.
67 *V.C.H. Wilts.* v. 291; Ch. Com. file 528291.
68 W.R.O., F 1/250/6/1 (1971–2).
69 Statutory Instruments, 1977, no. 387, Hungerford–Hereford Trunk Road Order.
70 *Andrews and Dury, Map* (W.R.S. viii), pls. 12, 15; J. Rocque, *Topog. Surv. Berks.* (1761), sheet V.
71 W.R.O. 735/43; 2454/12; for the two hos., below, this section (Chilton Foliat); manors (Chilton Ho.).

72 *W.A.M.* xxxiii. 232; lxxxii. 183; *V.C.H. Wilts.* i (1), 56.
73 *V.C.H. Berks.* ii. 341–2; *Cal. Chart. R.* 1226–57, 39.
74 *Endowed Char. Wilts.* (N. Div.), 227.
75 W.R.O. 735/41.
76 Ibid. L 2, Chilton Foliat; *Endowed Char. Wilts.* (N. Div.), 228.
77 W.R.O. 2281/1; inf. from the Curator, Swindon Museum.
78 W.R.O., L 2, Chilton Foliat (Hawkins).
79 Char. Com. file; below, charities.
80 Inf. from Dept. of Planning and Highways, Co. Hall, Trowbridge.
81 Below, manors (Chilton Ho.); for the rectory ho., ibid. church; cf. W.R.O. 735/43.
82 Ogilby, *Brit.* (1675), pl. 10; Rocque, *Topog. Surv. Berks.* (1761), sheet V; *Andrews and Dury, Map* (W.R.S. viii), pl. 12.
83 W.R.O. 735/43.

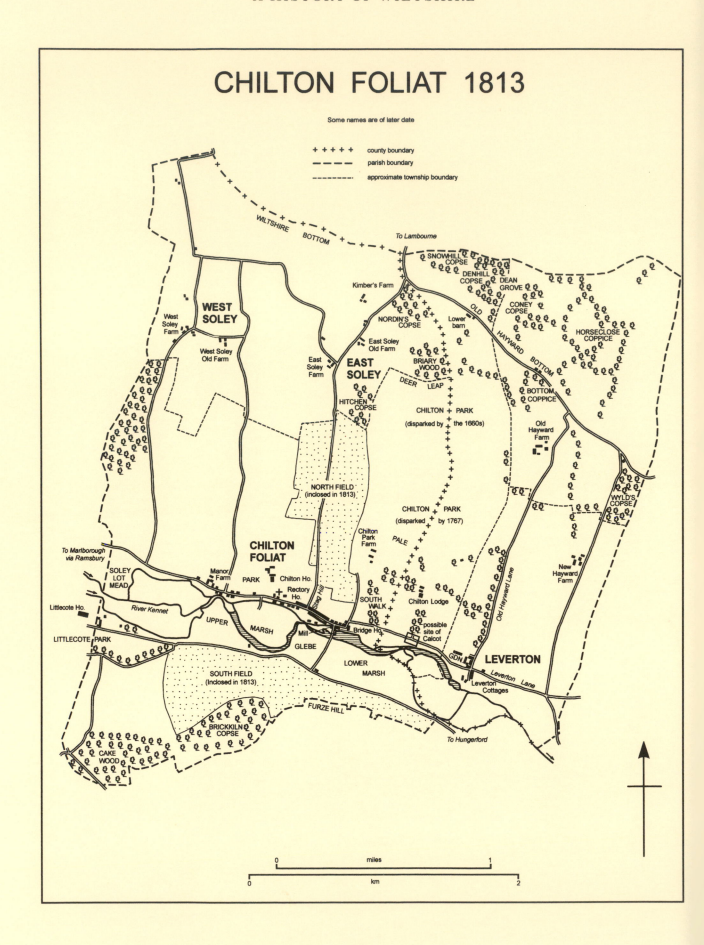

CHILTON FOLIAT 1813

Some names are of later date

+ + + + + county boundary
– – – – – parish boundary
–·–·–·– approximate township boundary

WILTSHIRE BOTTOM

To Lambourne

SNOWHILL COPSE

DENHILL COPSE

DEAN GROVE

Kimber's Farm

NORDIN'S COPSE

CONEY COPSE

WEST SOLEY

West Soley Farm

Lower barn

HORSECLOSE COPPICE

West Soley Old Farm

East Soley Old Farm

East Soley Farm

EAST SOLEY

BRIARY WOOD

DEER LEAP

HITCHEN COPSE

BOTTOM COPPICE

CHILTON + PARK

(disparked by the 1660s)

Old Hayward Farm

NORTH FIELD (inclosed in 1813)

CHILTON + PARK

(disparked by 1767)

WYLD'S COPSE

Chilton Park Farm

PALE

To Marlborough via Ramsbury

CHILTON FOLIAT

SOLEY LOT MEAD

Manor Farm

PARK

Chilton Ho.

Stag Hill

New Hayward Farm

Rectory Ho.

Littlecote Ho.

River Kennet

SOUTH WALK

Chilton Lodge

LITTLECOTE PARK

UPPER MARSH

Mill

Bridge Ho.

possible site of Calcot

GLEBE

LOWER MARSH

GDN

LEVERTON

Leverton Lane

Leverton Cottages

SOUTH FIELD (inclosed in 1813)

FURZE HILL

To Hungerford

BRICKKILN COPSE

CAKE WOOD

miles

0   1

0   km   2

18th-century but perhaps older, stands on the south side of the road a short distance west of the church. Further west Manor Farm was built in the later 18th century and before 1791[84] on what was probably a virgin site. In the early 19th century the farmhouse, which has a three-bayed south front of red and grey brick, was extended northwards by a block of similar size to form a square. A farm building contemporary with the first part of the house and converted for residence stands nearby. A pair of flint and thatched cottages was built west of Manor Farm in 1898;[85] two pairs of council houses were built east of it in 1925–6.[86]

From the church east to where the road across the bridge joins the street at the mill most of the cottages now have red-brick fronts of the 18th century, many with decoration of black or grey brick. Older gable walls of flint rubble survive in some, and several bear signs of earlier timber framing and of having been raised to two storeys from one storey and attics; a few unreconstructed timber-framed and thatched cottages of the 17th century survive. Modern houses have also been built of red brick and have tiled roofs. On the north side of the street a red-brick house of c. 1700 has a four-bayed south entrance front, with a heavy dentilled cornice, and gables incorporating patterned brickwork. Nearby on the north side and at right angles to each other a terrace of four cottages, two of the 17th century and two of the 18th, and a terrace of three 18th-century cottages are called the Square. Also on the north side a nonconformist chapel, a school,[87] and a church room were built in the 19th century and a commercial garage was built in the 20th. The church room was built in 1895[88] and by will Dame Dinah Pearce (d. 1918) gave the income from £300 to maintain it; in 1994 the income was used as the donor intended.[89] Red-brick buildings of a former tannery[90] and two 19th-century houses stood on the south side of the street in 1995. Also on the south side 9 old people's bungalows were built, 5 in 1959[91] and 4 in 1974,[92] and 7 private houses were built in the early 1980s.[93]

East of the mill Bridge House[94] was built in the 18th century of red brick. Its principal feature is its south elevation in which there is a tall round-headed window in each of five regular bays; there is a sixth bay to the east. The windows were constructed to light two first-floor rooms, one of three bays and one of two. On the ground floor the five bays were taken up by a central hall, entered by a door below the central

window of the five, and a room on each side of it: each has a low ceiling. A two-storeyed north corridor incorporating a stair turret serves the principal rooms and gives access to the minor ones at the east end. Between the service corridor and outbuildings on the south side of Leverton Lane a narrow yard was approached through a wide arch. The building, easily reached from Hungerford and several country mansions, may have been erected to provide assembly rooms or, facing a reach of the Kennet which was dammed to form a narrow lake, as a fishing lodge. The decoration and fittings of the principal rooms suggest that it was erected in the mid 18th century, probably in 1766, the date on rainwater heads. It was apparently in use as a house in the early 19th century[95] and was restored and altered in the mid 20th, when a new west entrance was made and the ground-floor rooms were rearranged to allow for it.[96] South of the mill on the west side of the Hungerford road a red-brick and thatched cottage was built in the 19th century.

Beside Stag Hill, built c. 1813,[97] a pair of cottages had been constructed on the east side near Chilton Foliat village by c. 1880,[98] and the village grew along the road in the 20th century. Also on the east side a house and three bungalows were built in the mid 20th century,[99] 8 council houses in 1950, and 20 private houses in the late 1980s and the 1990s. On the west side 8 council houses were built in the 1930s, 10 council houses and bungalows were built in 1954–5,[1] and a school was built later.[2]

There was an inn in the village in 1620[3] and an inn called the Red Lion possibly stood there in 1679.[4] An inn called the Wheatsheaf standing in 1767 and 1773 had been demolished by 1792.[5] The Stag's Head was open in 1813,[6] gave a name to Stag Hill which was built immediately east of it, and was closed c. 1955.[7] A new Wheatsheaf had been opened by 1815;[8] as a red-brick and thatched building of the 18th century it remained open in 1995. The New inn was open in the 1840s and 1850s.[9]

A farmhouse said in 1767 to be newly built[10] is presumably that built in the 18th century of red brick c. 100 m. east of Chilton Foliat bridge and in Leverton Lane; it had possibly been converted to cottages by c. 1813 and had been by 1883.[11] Between 1814 and c. 1880 a short new section of the lane was built to avoid a sharp bend at the farmhouse, a pair of ornamental red-brick cottages was built on the north side of the new lane, and a block in vernacular style and consisting of a house and four cottages was built

84 W.R.O. 2027, map of Chilton Foliat, 1791.
85 Date on bldg.
86 W.R.O., G 8/600/1.
87 Below, nonconf.; educ.
88 Date on bldg.
89 W.R.O., L 2, Chilton Foliat; Char. Com. files.
90 Below, econ. hist. (Chilton Foliat).
91 W.R.O., G 8/602/1.
92 Inf. from Chief Executive, Sarsen Housing Assoc., Old Browfort, Bath Road, Devizes.
93 W.R.O. 2281/4, deed, 1984.
94 Below, plate 26.   95 W.R.O. 735/43.
96 Country Life, 30 Apr. 1964.
97 Above, this section [roads].
98 O.S. Map 6", Wilts. XXX (1887 edn.).
99 W.R.O., G 8/760/137; cf. O.S. Map 6", Wilts. XXX.

NE. (1925 edn.).
1 W.R.O., G 8/600/1; G 8/602/1.
2 Below, educ.
3 Early-Stuart Tradesmen (W.R.S. xv), p. 22.
4 W.R.O. 735/20.
5 Coroners' Bills, 1752–96 (W.R.S. xxxvi), pp. 31–2; Som. R.O., DD/PO 5D; DD/PO 5E, deed, Smith to Bigg, 1773.
6 W.R.O. 735/43.
7 Wilts. Cuttings, xxi. 229.
8 Reading Univ. Libr., BER 36/5/317.
9 Kelly's Dir. Wilts. (1848 and later edns.); Som. R.O., DD/POt 41, sched. of purchases.
10 Reading Univ. Libr., BER 36/5/204.
11 O.S. Map 1/2,500, Wilts. XXX. 11 (1887 edn.); W.R.O. 735/43.

on the south side.[12] In 1995 a pair of early 20th-century brick, flint, and stone piers stood beside the lane.

Land east of Chilton Foliat village has been imparked probably since the Middle Ages, and a lodge stood in the park presumably on the site of Chilton Park Farm north-east of the village on the Wiltshire side of the county boundary. The house called Chilton Lodge on that site was enlarged in the later 17th century and demolished in the late 18th, when a new Chilton Lodge was built on the Berkshire side of the boundary.[13] A new red-brick farmhouse was built on the site of the old Chilton Lodge, possibly *c.* 1800.[14] It was demolished *c.* 1939 and replaced by Chilton Park Farm, a large neo-Georgian house of red brick with stone dressings, built in 1939–40 to designs by W. A. Forsyth.[15] A large timber-framed 18th-century barn stands north of the house.

East of the village a small farmstead on the south side of Leverton Lane was demolished probably *c.* 1800;[16] on the north side of the lane a lodge cottage for Chilton Lodge was built probably between 1890 and 1898.[17] South of the Kennet and west of the village outbuildings of Littlecote House stand in the parish, and in the mid 19th century a lodge was built 550 m. east of the parish boundary where the road from Hungerford becomes the main drive of the house. South of the road most of a 19th-century farmstead was demolished in the later 20th century.[18]

SOLEY. In the Middle Ages, when it had open fields,[19] Soley may have been a small nucleated settlement. About 1240 it was called a hamlet.[20] East and West Soley were separate settlements in the later 16th century[21] and each may have consisted then, as it did in the later 18th century, of several farmsteads loosely grouped.[22] Since the later 18th century Straight Soley and Crooked Soley have been alternative names for East Soley and West Soley respectively.[23]

In the later 18th century three farmsteads stood at East Soley.[24] The farmhouse of only one, East Soley Farm, the southernmost, survives. It bears a reset date stone MS 1658, is partly timber-framed, and has been largely re-

built in brick. Large new farm buildings were erected in the 20th century. The northernmost farmstead, Kimber's Farm, was demolished between 1813 and *c.* 1880.[25] That between East Soley Farm and Kimber's Farm was called East Soley Old Farm in 1995. In the 19th century the farmhouse was replaced by a new red-brick one; in the later 20th most of the farm buildings were demolished[26] and an indoor riding school was built. Between East Soley Old Farm and Kimber's Farm two cottages standing in 1791 were demolished between 1898 and 1922, and north of East Soley Farm a trio of cottages standing in 1791[27] was rebuilt in the later 19th century.

In the later 18th century five farmsteads stood at West Soley. One, that in the north-west corner of the parish, was demolished between 1813 and 1830;[28] another, that between those later called West Soley Farm and West Soley Old Farm, was demolished between *c.* 1880 and 1898.[29] North of West Soley Farm a trio of red-brick cottages built in 1900[30] marks the site of a third, demolished between 1830 and *c.* 1880.[31] West Soley Farm is an 18th-century house near which stands an 18th-century cottage of brick, flint, and thatch; a large 20th-century barn and former farm buildings of red brick stand nearby. A house of flint and brick, formerly two cottages[32] and possibly 18th-century, survives at West Soley Old Farm; in the late 20th century large stud farm buildings replaced the other buildings at the site.[33]

CALCOT. In 1086 and the earlier 14th century, when it was assessed separately for taxation,[34] Calcot was probably a small riverside settlement. It stood between Chilton Foliat and Leverton,[35] its precise site is unknown, and there is no evidence that it survived the Middle Ages. Between 1340 and the mid 16th century most of its land was taken into Chilton park, and a new Chilton Lodge was built on that land probably in the late 1790s.[36] Some of Calcot's land to the east remained farmland worked from Leverton or Old Hayward Farm,[37] some to the north farmland worked from East Soley and Old Hayward Farm.[38] On that to the north Lower barn was standing in Old Hayward bottom *c.* 1754.[39] A farmhouse was built at the site *c.* 1814.[40] The

[12] O.S. Map 6", Wilts. XXX (1887 edn.); W.R.O. 248/188.
[13] Below, manors (Chilton Lodge); econ. hist. (Chilton Foliat; Calcot).
[14] W.A.S. Libr., sale cat. vi, no. 45; W.R.O. 735/43; below, manors (Chilton Lodge).
[15] W.R.O., G 8/760/369; inf. from Mr. G. J. Ward, Chilton Park Farm.
[16] Reading Univ. Libr., BER 36/5/284; Som. R.O., DD/POt 156, Morgan's farm; cf. below, manors (Chilton Lodge).
[17] O.S. Map 6", Wilts. XXX. SE. (1900 edn.); cf. below, manors (Chilton Lodge).
[18] O.S. Maps 6", Wilts. XXX (1887 and later edns.); 1/25,000, SU 36 (1961 edn.); W.R.O. 735/43.
[19] Below, econ. hist. (Soley).
[20] *Cart. St. Frideswide*, ii (Oxf. Hist. Soc. xxxi), p. 361.
[21] P.R.O., IND 1/16943, f. 83v.; ibid. REQ 2/64/72.
[22] *Andrews and Dury, Map* (W.R.S. viii), pls. 12, 15; W.R.O. 2027, map of Chilton Foliat, 1791.
[23] *Coroners' Bills, 1752–96* (W.R.S. xxxvi), p. 83; W.R.O. 735/43.
[24] W.R.O. 2027, map of Chilton Foliat, 1791; cf. ibid.

735/43.
[25] Ibid. 735/43; O.S. Map 6", Wilts. XXX (1887 edn.).
[26] Cf. O.S. Map 1/25,000, SU 37 (1960 edn.).
[27] Ibid. 6", Wilts. XXX. NE. (1900, 1925 edns.); W.R.O. 735/43; 2027, map of Chilton Foliat, 1791.
[28] O.S. Map 1", sheet 13 (1830 edn.); W.R.O. 735/43; 2027, map of Chilton Foliat, 1791.
[29] O.S. Maps 6", Wilts. XXX (1887 edn.); XXX. NW. (1900 edn.).   [30] Date on bldg.
[31] O.S. Maps 1", sheet 13 (1830 edn.); 6", Wilts. XXX (1887 edn.).
[32] Cf. ibid. 1/2,500, Wilts. XXX. 2 (1885 and later edns.).
[33] Cf. ibid. 1/25,000, SU 37 (1960 edn.).
[34] *V.C.H. Berks.* i. 345; R. E. Glasscock, *Lay Subsidies of 1334*, 10.
[35] P.R.O., CP 25/1/251/14, no. 10; CP 40/1348, Carte rott. 8d.–9d.; Reading Univ. Libr., BER 36/5/204.
[36] Below, manors (Chilton Lodge); econ. hist. (Calcot).
[37] Reading Univ. Libr., BER 36/5/7; BER 36/5/10.
[38] Ibid. BER 36/5/19; W.R.O. 248/188; 2027, map of Chilton Foliat, 1791.
[39] Rocque, *Topog. Surv. Berks.* (1761), sheet V.
[40] W.R.O. 248/188; 735/43.

barn had been demolished by 1878; the farm-house and a pair of cottages built between 1878 and 1898[41] remained in 1995.

LEVERTON. The village stood beside Leverton Lane and in the Middle Ages may have consisted of *c*. 13 small farmsteads,[42] possibly some in each of the quadrants at the crossing of Old Hayward Lane, running north–south between the downs and the Kennet, and Leverton Lane. From the later 17th century much of Leverton's land was worked from outside the village,[43] which was small in the mid 18th.[44] The last farmsteads to survive were one in the north-east quadrant demolished between 1814 and 1878 and one in the south-west quadrant demolished between 1898 and 1909;[45] in the north-west quadrant a surviving timber-framed and thatched cottage, encased in brick and rendered, was built on the waste[46] possibly in the 17th century.

Between 1767 and 1813 the farmstead called New Hayward Farm was built on the downs north-east of the village, the park of Chilton Lodge was extended eastwards to Old Hayward Lane and extensive walled kitchen gardens and a farmyard were built in the north-west quadrant of the crossroads, and a terrace of six red-brick and thatched estate cottages, later called Lever-ton Cottages, was built in the south-east quadrant.[47] New Hayward Farm, of which the farmhouse is of red brick with a three-bayed south entrance front and a rear service wing extended several times in the 19th century, had been built by 1791;[48] the other building was probably of the late 1790s.[49]

Each time in a style to match the first six, Leverton Cottages[50] was extended to eight between 1814 and 1878 and to 10 between 1898 and 1909. A gardener's house west of the walled gardens was built in the mid 19th century. Between 1878 and 1898 a pair of houses in vernacular style was built at the entrance to the farmyard from Old Hayward Lane, and in the north-east quadrant of the crossroads Leverton Manor, a large house of red brick, gabled and partly hung with tiles, was built *c*. 1900. In the late 19th century three cottages were built at New Hayward Farm;[51] in the later 20th they were replaced by a bungalow, farm buildings were converted for residence, two houses were built, and extensive new farm buildings were erected.[52]

HAYWARD. Like Soley, Hayward may have been a settlement of several small farmsteads in the Middle Ages, when it had open fields. From the 16th century there is unlikely to have been more than a single farmstead,[53] that later called Old Hayward Farm. In the mid 18th century the farmstead was very large,[54] and in the early 19th it incorporated some large buildings.[55] It ceased to be used for agriculture in 1988.[56] The surviving farmhouse incorporates a house of one storey and attics, on a three-roomed plan, and probably timber-framed and 17th-century. The outer walls of that house were rebuilt in brick and flint at several dates. The house had been extended eastwards by the later 18th century, and was extended northwards in the late 18th century or early 19th, north-westwards in the mid 19th century, and further eastwards *c*. 1990.

In the later 18th century or early 19th, respectively north and east of Old Hayward Farm, two gamekeeper's lodges and a barn were built in Old Hayward bottom. A cottage was built near the barn *c*. 1814.[57] By 1878 the lodges had been replaced by kennels and a kennelman's house.[58] The house was being restored in 1995. A new cottage for a gamekeeper was built of brick, flint, and thatch near Old Hayward Farm in 1903.[59]

MANORS AND OTHER ESTATES. In 1066 Earl Harold held what became *CHILTON FOLIAT* manor. In 1086 Rainbald held it of Miles Crispin[60] (d. 1107),[61] who also held Wallingford castle (Berks., later Oxon.). The manor became part of the honor of Wallingford, and those holding the castle remained overlords.[62]

The lordship in demesne may have been held by Ralph de St. German (possibly Ralph Foliot) in 1156,[63] and was probably held by Robert Foliot *c*. 1167.[64] The manor, which in the late 12th century or early 13th included Soley, passed to Ralph Foliot and from him to his brother Henry (d. by 1236). Henry's heir was his son Sampson[65] (fl. 1281),[66] who in 1249 was granted free warren in the demesne.[67] Joan (fl. 1282), the wife of Henry Tyeys (d. 1282), was probably Sampson's daughter, and by 1289 his estates had passed to his grandson, and Henry's son, Henry Tyeys (from 1289 Lord Tyeys, d. 1307).[68] Chilton Foliat manor was held as dower from 1307 by Henry's relict Hawise, who *c*. 1309 leased it to his son Henry, Lord Tyeys. In 1322

41 O.S. Maps 6", Berks. XXXIII (1882 edn.); XXXIII. NE. (1900 edn.).
42 Reading Univ. Libr., BER 36/5/19; BER 36/5/204.
43 Below, econ. hist. (Leverton).
44 Rocque, *Topog. Surv. Berks.* (1761), sheet V.
45 O.S. Maps 6", Berks. XXXIII (1882 and later edns.); W.R.O. 248/188.
46 W.R.O. 248/188.
47 Ibid. 735/43; Reading Univ. Libr., BER 36/5/204; below, manors (Chilton Lodge); econ. hist. (Calcot); for Leverton Cottages, below, plate 34.
48 W.R.O. 2027, map of Chilton Foliat, 1791.
49 Cf. below, manors (Chilton Lodge).
50 Ibid. plate 34.
51 O.S. Maps 6", Berks. XXXIII (1882 and later edns.); W.R.O. 248/188.
52 Cf. O.S. Map 1/25,000, SU 37 (1960 edn.).
53 Above, this section (Soley); below, econ. hist. (Hayward).
54 Rocque, *Topog. Surv. Berks.* (1761), sheet V.

55 W.R.O. 248/188.
56 Inf. from Mr. Ward.
57 Rocque, *Topog. Surv. Berks.* (1761), sheet V; W.R.O. 248/188; 735/43.
58 O.S. Map 6", Berks. XXXIII (1882 edn.).
59 W.A.S. Libr., sale cat. vi, no. 45.
60 *V.C.H. Wilts.* ii, p. 146.
61 I. J. Sanders, *Eng. Baronies*, 93.
62 e.g. *Red Bk. Exch.* (Rolls Ser.), ii. 485; below, local govt.; for an acct. of the castle and honor, *V.C.H. Berks.* iii. 523–32.
63 *Red Bk. Exch.* (Rolls Ser.), ii. 664; cf. *Cart. St. Frideswide*, ii (Oxf. Hist. Soc. xxxi), p. 221.
64 *Pipe R.* 1167 (P.R.S. xi), 130.
65 *Cart. St. Frideswide*, ii, pp. 359–61; *Bk. of Fees*, i. 423.
66 *Cal. Pat.* 1272–81, 441.
67 *Cal. Chart. R.* 1226–57, 342.
68 *Complete Peerage*, xii (2), 102–3; P.R.O., JUST 1/1006, rot. 51d.

Henry was attainted and executed[69] and the king granted the manor to Hugh le Despenser when he created him earl of Winchester.[70] Hawise petitioned parliament for its return but died before the petition was heard.[71] In 1326 the king resumed the manor on Despenser's execution[72] and restored it to the younger Lord Tyeys's sister Alice (d. 1347), the relict of Sir Warin de Lisle,[73] from whom that Lord Tyeys's relict Margaret (d. 1349), the wife of Thomas de Monthermer, claimed a third of it as dower.[74] Alice was succeeded by her son Sir Gerard de Lisle (from 1357 Lord Lisle, d. 1360), whose relict Elizabeth (d. 1362), the wife of Richard Pembridge, held Chilton Foliat manor for life. The manor passed to Gerard's son Warin, Lord Lisle, who at his death in 1382 also held Calcot manor and Leverton manor.[75] The three manors were held by Warin's relict Joan (d. 1392) for life. They passed in 1392 to his daughter Margaret (d. 1392), the wife of Thomas Berkeley, Lord Berkeley (d. 1417),[76] in 1417 to Margaret's daughter Elizabeth (d. 1422), the wife of Richard de Beauchamp, earl of Warwick (d. 1439),[77] and soon after 1439 to one of Elizabeth's three daughters Eleanor, the relict of Thomas de Ros, Lord Ros, the wife of Edmund Beaufort (cr. earl of Dorset 1442 and marquess of Dorset 1443, earl of Somerset from 1444, cr. duke of Somerset 1448, d. 1455), and later possibly the wife of Walter Rokesley.[78] Eleanor's sons Thomas de Ros, Lord Ros, and Henry Beaufort, duke of Somerset, were attainted in 1461 and executed in 1464, and her grandson Edmund de Ros, Lord Ros, and her son Edmund Beaufort were thus disinherited.[79] From 1467, when Eleanor died, until 1505 her estates seem to have been held by her seven daughters, their husbands, and their heirs as coparceners.[80] Eleanor's grandson Henry Stafford, duke of Buckingham, evidently entered on Chilton Foliat, Calcot, and Leverton manors. Henry was executed and attainted in 1483, an Act of 1485 restored his lands to his son Edward, duke of Buckingham,[81] and Edward was later among the coparceners.[82] The estates of Thomas, Lord Ros (d. 1464), were restored to Edmund, Lord Ros (d. 1508), by Act in 1485, when Edmund was a lunatic,

but were retained by the Crown during pleasure.[83] In 1505 the Crown resumed the three manors in Chilton Foliat parish as concealed lands, and from 1519 they were held as dower by successive queens consort.[84]

In 1546 the king sold Chilton Foliat manor, Chilton park, in which most of Calcot manor had apparently been subsumed, and Leverton manor to Sir Edward Darell of Littlecote House.[85] Nearly half the purchase money, £500, had not been paid when Darell died in 1549 leaving his son and heir William a ward of the king.[86] Presumably soon after 1549 Henry Manners, earl of Rutland, maintaining the right of his great-granduncle Edmund, Lord Ros, successfully claimed the estate against Darell and the Crown,[87] and in 1563 he died seised of it.[88] Between 1572 and 1574 Henry's son Edward, earl of Rutland, sold Chilton Foliat manor in c. 8 portions. The largest was bought in 1574 by Thomas Rosewell,[89] who between 1575 and 1578 sold that in c. 15 portions.[90] Many small estates thereafter descended separately, but by the early 19th century all except c. 150 a. of the parish had been agglomerated in the three principal estates.[91]

William Darell bought land south of the Kennet and near Littlecote House from Lord Rutland in 1572,[92] and, probably c. 1578, from Rosewell a rump of Chilton Foliat manor, almost certainly the manorial rights and the demesne farm; by 1587 he had bought two holdings at Soley.[93] As Chilton Foliat manor Darell's estate passed at his death in 1589 to Sir Francis Walsingham (d. 1590), to whom he had sold the reversion in that year.[94] Part of it, evidently the land near Littlecote House, the manorial rights, and the land at Soley, was settled on Walsingham's wife Ursula and later sold to Sir John Popham (d. 1607), the owner of Littlecote House, probably in 1591 by Ursula and Walsingham's daughter Frances and her husband Robert Devereux, earl of Essex.[95] That reduced manor passed with Littlecote House until the 20th century. It descended in the direct line to Sir Francis Popham (d. 1644), Alexander (d. 1669), Sir Francis (d. 1674), and Alexander (d. 1705), who was succeeded by his uncle

69 Complete Peerage, xii (2), 103–4; Cal. Inq. p.m. iv, p. 27; vii, p. 24.
70 Cal. Chart. R. 1300–26, 443–4. 71 Rot. Parl. i. 412.
72 Complete Peerage, xii (2), 754; Cal. Fine R. 1319–27, 427.
73 Complete Peerage, viii. 49; P.R.O., E 142/33, rot. 5.
74 Complete Peerage, xii (2), 104–5; P.R.O., CP 40/279, rot. 174d.
75 Complete Peerage, viii. 49–52; Cal. Inq. p.m. x, p. 473; xi, p. 318.
76 Complete Peerage, ii. 130–1; viii. 53–4; Cal. Inq. p.m. xv, pp. 316–17; xvii, pp. 38–9.
77 Complete Peerage, viii. 54; Cal. Inq. p.m. xx, p. 250.
78 Complete Peerage, viii. 54–5; xi. 104–5; xii (1), 49–53; Feet of F. 1377–1509 (W.R.S. xli), p. 124.
79 Complete Peerage, xi. 105–7; xii (1), 53–8; Rot. Parl. vi. 310–11.
80 Cal. Inq. p.m. Hen. VII, iii, p. 26; Complete Peerage, ii. 389–90, 422; vi. 605; ix. 720; xi. 24, 105, 107.
81 Complete Peerage, ii. 389–90; P.R.O., SC 1/44, no. 75.
82 Cal. Inq. p.m. Hen. VII, iii, p. 26.
83 Complete Peerage, xi. 106–7; Rot. Parl. vi. 452–4.
84 Cal. Inq. p.m. Hen. VII, iii, p. 26; L. & P. Hen. VIII, iii (1), pp. 153–4; vii (1), p. 147; xiv (2), p. 224; xv, p. 52; xvi, p. 240; xix (1), p. 83; P.R.O., SC 6/Hen. VIII/345, rot.

7; SC 6/Hen. VIII/6882.
85 P.R.O., E 318/9/353; for Calcot, above, intro.; below, econ. hist.; for Chilton park and Leverton manor, below, this section (Chilton Lodge); for Littlecote, V.C.H. Wilts. xii. 28.
86 P.R.O., C 142/92, no. 111; ibid. E 321/32/42.
87 Ibid. REQ 2/64/72; ibid. SP 46/45, no. 224; Complete Peerage, xi. 107–8; for a similar claim by Lord Rutland to Draycot Foliat, W.A.M. xxxi. 51–68.
88 P.R.O., C 142/155, no. 168.
89 Ibid. C 146/9100; ibid. CP 25/2/239/15 Eliz. I Trin.; CP 25/2/239/16 Eliz. I East.; CP 25/2/260/16 & 17 Eliz. I Mich.; CP 40/1354, Carte rott. 9d.–10.
90 Ibid. CP 40/1348, Carte rott. 7–9, 30d.; CP 40/1354, Carte rott. 9–11; ibid. IND 1/16943, ff. 82v., 83v.
91 W.R.O. 735/43; below, this section.
92 P.R.O., C 146/9100.
93 Ibid. C 2/Eliz. I/G 13/59; ibid. CP 43/28, Carte rot. 3 and d.; ibid. SP 46/45, no. 224.
94 V.C.H. Wilts. xii. 49; E. A. Webb, G. W. Miller, J. Beckwith, Hist. Chislehurst, 362; W.R.O. 1883/96/1.
95 V.C.H. Wilts. xii. 28, 49; P.R.O., C 2/Eliz. I/W 6/41; C 3/378/10; ibid. CP 25/2/241/33 Eliz. I East.; for the other part, below, this section (Chilton Ho.).

Alexander Popham (d. 1705), and again passed in the direct line to Francis (d. 1735), Edward (d. 1772), and Francis (d. 1780), from the death of whose widow Dorothy Popham c. 1797 it passed to her husband's reputed son Francis Popham (d. s.p. 1804). In 1800 Francis sold 102 a. to John Pearse, who added it to the Chilton Lodge estate, and in 1813 Francis's successor E. W. Leyborne-Popham owned 902 a. in the parish.[96] Between 1813 and 1879 Leyborne-Popham's estate was more than doubled in size.[97] After his death in 1843 most of it was held with Littlecote House by his son Francis (d. 1880), a smaller part by his son E. W. Leyborne-Popham (d. s.p. 1881). Francis's son F. W. Leyborne-Popham (d. s.p. 1907) inherited both parts[98] and in 1896 sold Manor farm and farms at West Soley, a total of c. 565 a., to V. J. Watney.[99] Francis was succeeded by his brother H. F. A. Leyborne-Popham, who bought Watney's land after 1910. In 1929 Leyborne-Popham sold all his land in Chilton Foliat, c. 1,830 a., to Sir Ernest Wills, Bt., as part of the Littlecote estate.[1] Wills (d. 1958) was succeeded by his son G. S. Wills (d. 1979), who in 1965 gave the estate to his son (David) Seton Wills (Bt. from 1983), the owner of c. 560 a. in the south-west part of the parish in 1995.[2] In 1956 Sir Ernest sold Briary wood and c. 60 a. east of Chilton Foliat bridge to E. J. S. Ward, and in 1979 Sir Seton sold 71 a. north of Chilton Park Farm to Mr. G. J. Ward:[3] the lands sold were added to the Chilton Lodge estate.[4] In 1978 Sir Seton sold West Soley farm, 532 a. including c. 150 a. outside the parish, to R. A. Pearce, who in 1981 sold 135 a., thereafter West Soley Stud farm, to Mr. Justin Hayward, and in 1982 sold 82 a. to Mr. A. T. Pearce, the owner of that land in 1995, and 312 a., including the land outside the parish, to Mr. P. A. C. L. Oppenheim. In 1995 Miss Sandy Pflueger owned West Soley Stud farm and most of Oppenheim's land in the parish. In 1978 Sir Seton sold Manor farm, 310 a., to Mrs. V. M. Pearce and East Soley farm, 264 a., to her son Mr. A. T. Pearce. In 1995 all that land, the 82 a. bought in 1982, and 60 a. outside the parish belonged to Mr. Pearce as East Soley farm, c. 725 a.[5] In 1986 Sir Seton sold c. 43 a. with Littlecote House to Mr. P. J. de Savary, the owner in 1995.[6]

An estate consisting of the medieval manor house of Chilton Foliat, or its site, and what was apparently a large inclosed demesne farm and former park[7] were the nucleus of the *CHILTON HOUSE* estate. It seems that in 1590 Sir Francis Walsingham conveyed the estate to his secretary Francis Mylles (d. 1618)[8] and that it passed to Mylles's daughter Philippa, whose husband, the courtier John Packer (d. 1649), held it in 1623. It descended to Philippa's son John Packer,[9] and in 1689, when it included land at Soley, John sold the estate to Lovelace Bigg[10] (d. 1725).[11] It passed in turn to Bigg's sons Henry (d. 1740), from 1730 warden of Winchester College, Thomas (will proved 1761), and the Revd. Walter Bigg (d. 1772), and it descended to Walter's son Lovelace (from 1789 Lovelace Bigg Wither).[12] It was enlarged several times.[13] In 1792 Bigg Wither sold it to the Revd. John Craven[14] (d. 1804),[15] who also enlarged it.[16] In 1813 Craven's son and heir Fulwar owned 756 a. in the parish.[17] In 1834 he sold the estate, 877 a., to E. W. Leyborne-Popham, who added it to the Littlecote estate.[18]

Members of the Foliot and Tyeys families may have lived at Chilton Foliat, where Alice de Lisle imparked and, she said in 1334, her ancestors were buried.[19] A manor house mentioned in 1546[20] probably stood immediately west of the church. It was almost certainly the house lived in by Thomas Bigg and demolished c. 1754. Chilton House was built, evidently between 1755 and 1758 and probably immediately north of the old house's site,[21] was lived in by the Biggs and Cravens,[22] and was demolished in 1965.[23] It was a large three-storeyed red-brick building with an entrance through a canted bay at the south-west corner. The principal front was to the south, there were lower service wings to the north, and the roof pattern suggests that the original building had been enlarged. North of it there stood a large farm courtyard,[24] some buildings of which were converted for residence after 1965, and east of the rectory house lay a kitchen garden walled in red brick.[25]

In the late 12th century or early 13th Ralph Foliot granted a small estate in Soley to Roger Foliot; later and before c. 1210 Henry Foliot confirmed that estate to Roger's brother Richard and gave 1 yardland in Chilton Foliat to him,

96　*V.C.H. Wilts.* xii. 28–9; W.R.O. 735/43; Reading Univ. Libr., BER 36/5/284; for the Chilton Lodge estate, below, this section.
97　Som. R.O., DD/POt 41, sched. of purchases.
98　*V.C.H. Wilts.* xii. 29; Burke, *Land. Gent.* (1937), 1831; W.R.O. 211/16/3; ibid. A 1/345/98.
99　Som. R.O., DD/PO 99.
1　*V.C.H. Wilts.* xii. 29; W.R.O., Inland Revenue, val. reg. 54; inf. from Sir (David) Seton Wills, Bt., Eastridge Ho., Ramsbury.
2　Inf. from Sir Seton Wills.
3　W.R.O. 2281/4, abstr. of title.
4　Below, this section (Chilton Lodge).
5　W.R.O. 2281/4, abstr. of title; inf. from Mr. A. T. Pearce, E. Soley Farmhouse.
6　Inf. from Sir Seton Wills.
7　Cf. W.R.O. 2027, map of Chilton Foliat, 1791; above, intro. (Chilton Foliat); below, econ. hist. (Chilton Foliat).
8　D. S. Smith, *On Footings from the Past*, 243, 298–9; Webb, *Chislehurst*, 131.
9　Smith, op. cit. 108, 242; *D.N.B.*
10　Som. R.O., DD/PO 5A, deed, Packer to Bigg, 1689.

11　Mon. in church.
12　Burke, *Land. Gent.* (1846), ii. 1621; *V.C.H. Hants*, ii. 366; Som. R.O., DD/PO 5D; P.R.O., PROB 11/864, ff. 149v.–151.
13　Som. R.O., DD/PO 5E, deeds, Spier to Bigg, 1772; Smith to Bigg, 1773; Smith to Bigg, 1785; DD/PO 6B, mortgage, 1710.
14　Som. R.O., DD/PO 5D.
15　Burke, *Peerage* (1959), 566.
16　Som. R.O., DD/POt 13–14.
17　Burke, *Peerage* (1959), 566; W.R.O. 735/43.
18　Som. R.O., DD/POt 41, sched. of purchases; above, this section (Chilton Foliat).
19　*Cal. Chart. R.* 1327–41, 357; *Cal. Papal Reg.* ii. 410.
20　P.R.O., E 318/9/353.
21　Ibid. PROB 11/864, ff. 149v.–151; above, intro. (Chilton Foliat).
22　e.g. *Andrews and Dury, Map* (W.R.S. viii), pl. 12; W.R.O. 735/43.
23　R. Strong, *Destruction of the Country Ho.* 190.
24　Air photo. in church.
25　Local inf.

and Richard granted both estates to St. Frides-wide's priory, Oxford.[26] The land was absorbed into the priory's adjoining manor of Eddington or Hidden, mainly in Hunger-ford.[27] On each occasion as part of that manor the land at Soley, c. 43 a. presumably with pasture rights, passed to the Crown at the dissolution of the priory in 1524, in 1525 was granted to Cardinal Wolsey for Cardinal College, Oxford, in 1532 was granted to King Henry VIII's College, Oxford, from 1545 was held by the Crown, and in 1599 was sold to trustees of Sir John Popham. From 1599 it apparently descended with the reduced Chilton Foliat manor.[28]

An estate said to be of c. 200 a. at Soley was held by William Bird and passed to the Crown on his attainder in 1540. Between 1546 and 1551 it was held by royal officials, presumably for their service, and in 1551 was granted to the Lady Elizabeth,[29] from 1558 Elizabeth I. In 1562 the queen sold the estate to Gilbert Sherrington and Thomas Blackwell,[30] presumably specula-tors or trustees, who immediately conveyed it to John Langley. In 1567 Langley sold it to Henry Parvis. It passed to Henry's son Jewell, and in 1594 his relict Jane conveyed her life interest to Jewell.[31] The estate was afterwards acquired by Thomas Smith and combined with his other estate at Soley.[32]

In 1575 Henry Smith bought an estate in West Soley from Thomas Rosewell.[33] It de-scended to his son Thomas, who by the early 17th century had acquired several other free-holds at Soley, including others formerly part of Chilton Foliat manor. Thomas Smith (d. 1637) settled his estate at Soley on the mar-riage of his daughter Mary (d. by 1654) and Charles Seymour (from 1664 Lord Seymour, d. 1665). It descended to Mary's daughter Frances, the wife of Sir George Hungerford,[34] and, apparently between 1707 and 1710, the Hungerfords sold it to William Lewis le Grand.[35] The estate passed to Edward le Grand, who, apparently before 1773, sold it to Lovelace Bigg (later Bigg Wither) or one of his predecessors:[36] it became part of the Chilton House estate.[37]

In 1066 Brictuard held *CALCOT*. William I gave it to William, count of Évreux (d. 1118), and William gave it to a conventual priory of the abbey of St. Evroul which in 1108 he founded at Noyon-sur-Andelle (now Charleval, Eure).[38] The priory held the manor in demesne until 1243; thereafter it was overlord.[39]

In 1243 Noyon priory sold Calcot manor to Alan of Farnham, whose heir was his daughter Gillian, the wife of Gilbert of Elsfield and later of John de St. Helen. On the evidence of jurors who in 1275 testified that Alan had acquired the manor by forcing two freeholders (sokemen of the king) from the land, the king claimed it from John and Gillian in 1280, but in 1282 Alan's right to it was proved. By 1289 John and Gillian had settled the manor on Gillian's grandson Alan Elsfield,[40] and in 1305 John Elsfield con-veyed it to his own son Gilbert.[41] In 1316–17 Gilbert conveyed it to Henry, Lord Tyeys, and Henry's wife Margaret for life. In 1322, on Tyeys's attainder and execution, the life interest passed to the Crown; in 1325 it was restored to Margaret (d. 1349), who as Margaret de Monthermer,[42] held the manor in 1341.[43] Warin, Lord Lisle, held it in fee at his death in 1382.[44] It thereafter descended with Chilton Foliat manor and by the 16th century had apparently been merged with it.[45]

Much of the land of Calcot manor and land of Chilton Foliat manor were the components of Chilton park,[46] in which there was a lodge,[47] and the nucleus of the *CHILTON LODGE* estate. In 1574 Edward, earl of Rutland, sold Chilton park, with Leverton manor, to Anthony Hinton (d. 1599),[48] the owner of Hayward manor.[49] Anthony's composite Chilton Lodge estate, to which Eddington manor had been added by 1623,[50] descended to his son (Sir) Thomas (d. 1635) and to Sir Thomas's son (Sir) Anthony,[51] who in 1639 sold it to Thomas Hussey[52] (d. 1657–8).[53] In 1663 Thomas's son William, relict Catherine, the wife of Sir Robert Mason, execu-tors, and trustees sold it to the lawyer, politician, and diarist Sir Bulstrode Whitelocke (d. 1675).[54] It descended to Sir Bulstrode's son Samuel (d. 1690)[55] and in the direct line to Samuel (d.

[26] *Cart. St. Frideswide*, ii (Oxf. Hist. Soc. xxxi), pp. 359–61.
[27] Ibid. p. 356; cf. *V.C.H. Berks*. iv. 192.
[28] *V.C.H. Berks*. iv. 192; *V.C.H. Oxon*. iii. 228–31; N. F. Hidden, *Manor of Hidden* (copy in Wilts. local studies libr., Trowbridge), 61, 83, 85; above, this section (Chilton Foliat).
[29] *L. & P. Hen. VIII*, xxi (1), p. 74; *Cal. Pat.* 1550–3, 92; *L.J.* i. 162; P.R.O., C 1/1297, nos. 52–3; ibid. E 305/20/G 37; E 318/32/1784.
[30] *Cal. Pat.* 1560–3, 297–8; P.R.O., E 318/47/2504, rot. 12.
[31] Alnwick Castle Mun. X.II.11, box 22, deeds, Black-well to Langley, 1562; Langley to Parvis, 1567; Parvis to Parvis, 1594.
[32] W.R.O. 1081/111; below, this section.
[33] P.R.O., IND 1/16943, f. 83v.
[34] Ibid. C 2/Jas. I/S 31/62; *Wilts. Inq. p.m.* 1625–49 (Index Libr.), 266–8; Burke, *Peerage* (1924), 2077; W.R.O. 1081/111; Alnwick Castle Mun. X.II.11, box 22, deeds, Rosewell to Mundy, 1576; Mundy to Kember, 1621.
[35] W.R.O. 39/20, deed, Popham to Blake, 1707; Som. R.O., DD/PO 6B, mortgage, 1710.
[36] Som. R.O., DD/PO 5E, deed, Smith to Bigg, 1773; DD/PO 6B, mortgage, 1710.
[37] Above, this section (Chilton House).
[38] *V.C.H. Berks*. i. 345; *Cal. Doc. France*, ed. Round, p.

220; *Eccl. Hist. Orderic Vitalis*, ed. M. Chibnal, iii, p. xx; vi, p. 149 n.
[39] *Cal. Inq. p.m.* xv, pp. 316–17; P.R.O., KB 27/58, rot. 9d.
[40] *Rot. Hund.* (Rec. Com.), i. 19; *V.C.H. Berks*. iv. 83; P.R.O., KB 27/58, rot. 9d.; KB 27/119, rot. 2d.
[41] P.R.O., CP 25/1/9/37, no. 13.
[42] Ibid. CP 40/279, rot. 174d.; *Cal. Close*, 1323–7, 282; *Complete Peerage*, xii (2), 104–5.
[43] *Inq. Non.* (Rec. Com.), 173.
[44] *Cal. Inq. p.m.* xv, p. 316.
[45] Above, this section (Chilton Foliat).
[46] Below, econ. hist. (Chilton Foliat; Calcot).
[47] Ibid. this section.
[48] Reading Univ. Libr., BER 36/5/7; P.R.O., C 142/257, no. 85; for Leverton manor, below, this section (Leverton).
[49] Below, this section (Hayward).
[50] *V.C.H. Berks*. iv. 192.
[51] *Wilts. Inq. p.m.* 1625–49 (Index Libr.), 278–90; P.R.O., C 142/257, no. 85.
[52] Reading Univ. Libr., BER 36/5/14.
[53] P.R.O., PROB 11/273, ff. 1–5.
[54] Reading Univ. Libr., BER 36/5/19; for Whitelocke's life, *Diary of Bulstrode Whitelocke*, ed. R. Spalding.
[55] R. Spalding, *Contemporaries of Bulstrode Whitelocke*, 448–50; Reading Univ. Libr., BER 36/5/24.

1743)[56] and John Whitelocke, who in 1767 sold it to J. Z. Holwell, a survivor of the Black Hole of Calcutta.[57] In 1771 Holwell sold the estate to Gen. Richard Smith,[58] who in 1785 sold it to John Macnamara.[59] In 1788 Macnamara sold it to the mortgagees William Morland and Thomas Hammersley, bankers of Pall Mall, and in 1789 Hammersley released his interest to Morland.[60] In 1796 Morland sold the estate to John Pearse, a director of the Bank of England and from 1818 to 1832 M.P. for Devizes,[61] who in 1813 owned 1,488 a. in the parish.[62] In 1834 Pearse sold the estate to the Revd. Sir William Cooper, Bt.[63] (will proved 1835).[64] It was devised by Sir William to his wife Isabella[65] (d. 1855) and by Isabella to her and Sir William's grandson William Honywood,[66] who sold it in 1890 to Sir William Pearce, Bt. (d. 1907). Pearce devised it for sale after the death of his wife Caroline (d. 1907),[67] and his executors sold it in 1908 to H. W. Henderson. In 1909 the estate was bought from Henderson by (Sir) John Ward (d. 1938) and his wife Jean (d. 1962). It passed in 1938 to the Wards' son E. J. S. Ward (d. 1990) and in 1967 to E. J. S. Ward's son Mr. G. J. Ward, the owner in 1995.[68]

A lodge in Chilton park in 1546[69] and part of the Chilton Lodge estate from 1574[70] presumably stood on or near the site of Chilton Park Farm, where Chilton Lodge stood until the late 18th century.[71] Chilton Lodge, almost certainly the house called Chilton Park lived in by Sir Thomas Hinton in the 1620s and 1630s[72] and by Thomas Hussey in the 1640s,[73] was enlarged by Sir Bulstrode Whitelocke in the 1660s: work was done on the drawing room in 1664 and the house was much extended in 1667–8 when a new hall and bedrooms were built.[74] Until 1785 or later the house was lived in by Whitelocke's successors as owners of the estate.[75] It is unlikely to have been rebuilt before 1789, probably the year in which it was demolished.[76] In that year, when William Morland became sole owner of the estate,[77] the foundations of a new house, which Morland commissioned (Sir) John Soane to build, were being set out.[78] The new house was probably on the site of the old,[79] and its form was dictated by Morland's instruction to Soane to re-use materials from demolished buildings, presumably those of the old house. It was a villa with a two-storeyed centre and short single-storeyed wings.[80] It was demolished, probably before 1800, and was replaced by a new and much larger Chilton Lodge built for John Pearse, the owner of the estate from 1796: the house called Chilton Lodge in which Pearse lived in 1800 was probably the new one.[81] Two other houses afterwards occupied the site of the old Chilton Lodge.[82] The new Chilton Lodge was designed by William Pilkington[83] and was built south-east of the site of Chilton Park Farm and in what was then or soon afterwards the centre of the park.[84] It was built with a south front and a west front each of five bays, the south incorporating a full-height Corinthian portico, with an east front of seven bays, and with a large north stable court.[85] A large north-west pavilion was built between 1890 and 1892 for Sir William Pearce to designs by Sir Arthur Blomfield[86] and was demolished c. 1963. A porte cochère removed from the east side of the house c. 1963[87] may also have been designed by Blomfield.

In the 1660s and probably near the house Sir Bulstrode Whitelocke laid out new walled gardens, one with a terraced walk; a pond for trout was dug,[88] possibly the pond which lay in 1814 on the county boundary east of the site of the house.[89] Formal gardens survived south-west of the house in the later 18th century,[90] when there was also a haha.[91] The park was estimated at 360 a. in 1663,[92] but later in the 1660s pales were taken down,[93] and later there was a smaller paled park stocked with deer.[94] In the 17th century an avenue called the South walk led from the house to Leverton Lane.[95] In the mid 18th century there was also an avenue which led east from the house, and from the east end of that avenue another, parallel to the South walk, which led to Leverton Lane.[96] Most of the park, however, was then used for agriculture, and in 1767 only 24 a.

---

56   Spalding, *Contemporaries*, 450; Reading Univ. Libr., BER 36/5/52–3.
57   *D.N.B.*; Reading Univ. Libr., BER 36/5/204.
58   Reading Univ. Libr., BER 36/5/209.
59   Ibid. BER 36/5/226.
60   Ibid. BER 36/5/235.
61   Ibid. BER 36/5/256; *Hist. Parl., Commons*, 1790–1820, iv. 739–40.
62   W.R.O. 735/43.
63   Reading Univ. Libr., BER 36/5/353.
64   G.E.C. *Baronetage*, ii. 447.
65   Lond. Metro. Archives, Acc. 775/6.
66   E. Walford, *Co. Fams. U.K.* (1872), 501; *V.C.H. Berks.* iv. 193.
67   Princ. Regy. Fam. Div., will of Sir Wm. Pearce, 1907; will of Lady (Caroline) Pearce, 1908.
68   *V.C.H. Berks.* iv. 193: Chas. Crutchley, named ibid., was an executor of Sir Wm. Pearce; inf. from Mr. G. J. Ward, Chilton Park Farm; for the Wards, Burke, *Peerage* (1967), 793.
69   P.R.O., E 318/9/353.
70   Reading Univ. Libr., BER 36/5/7.
71   *Andrews and Dury, Map* (W.R.S. viii), pl. 12; below, this section.
72   Reading Univ. Libr., BER 36/5/11–12.
73   Ibid. BER 36/5/14.
74   *Diary of Bulstrode Whitelocke*, 685, 716–17, 719–21, 731.

75   e.g. *Andrews and Dury, Map* (W.R.S. viii), pl. 12; Reading Univ. Libr., BER 36/5/24; BER 36/5/52; BER 36/5/204; W.R.O. 894/3.
76   Below, this para.
77   Above, this section (Chilton Lodge).
78   Soane Mus., Lond., ledger bk., 1789.
79   W.R.O. 2027, map of Chilton Foliat, 1791.
80   J. Soane, *Sketches in Archit.* pls. xvii–xix.
81   Reading Univ. Libr., BER 36/5/284; above, this section (Chilton Lodge).
82   Above, intro. (Chilton Foliat).
83   J. Britton and E. Brayley, *Beauties of Eng. and Wales*, xv (2), 695.   84   For the park, below, this section.
85   Below, plate 19.
86   Wilts. Cuttings, xvi. 260; W.A.S. Libr., sale cat. vi, no. 45; above, this section (Chilton Lodge).
87   Inf. from Mr. Ward.
88   *Diary of Bulstrode Whitelocke*, 694, 699, 701, 703, 705, 707–8, 710.
89   W.R.O. 248/188.
90   *Andrews and Dury, Map* (W.R.S. viii), pl. 12.
91   Som. R.O., DD/POt 16, lease, Popham to Morland, 1789.
92   Reading Univ. Libr., BER 36/5/19.
93   *Diary of Bulstrode Whitelocke*, 697, 711.
94   Reading Univ. Libr., BER 36/5/24.
95   *Diary of Bulstrode Whitelocke*, 703.
96   J. Rocque, *Topog. Surv. Berks.* (1761), sheet V.

and woodland were held with Chilton Lodge.[97] Land near Chilton Lodge was again imparked c. 1777,[98] and between then and 1813 the park was extended eastwards. The Chilton Lodge built for John Pearse stands in the centre of the extended park,[99] which is therefore likely to have been extended between 1796 and 1800.[1] The principal avenues of the 18th century, but not the South walk, have survived and in 1995 framed the landscape south-west of the house. The features of the extension probably of the late 18th century, including an eastern boundary plantation and across the centre a curving belt of woodland called the Shrubbery,[2] are less regular.

In 1666 a new gate was erected at the bottom of the South walk, and gate piers erected in 1667 may have stood at that entrance.[3] From c. 1800 the main entrance to the park was presumably where the eastern avenue met Leverton Lane:[4] west of that avenue the lodge and entrance gates standing in Leverton Lane in 1995 were of the late 19th century.[5] A farmyard and the walls of a kitchen garden of c. 4 a. stand in the south-east corner of the park: they were apparently built in the late 18th century, and the size of the garden suggests that they are contemporary with Pearse's house. The kitchen garden was restored in the 1980s.[6]

The northernmost part of Calcot manor, not in Chilton park, was apparently added to an estate at Soley and, 70 a., was among the lands sold by Francis Popham to John Pearse in 1800.[7] The other part not in the park, c. 50 a. evidently lying east of the park, was sold by Lord Rutland to Anthony Hinton in 1574.[8]

In 984 *LEVERTON*, then described as 8 *mansae* beside the Kennet formerly held by Etheric, a villein (*rusticus*), was granted by King Ethelred to Bryhtric. King Edward allegedly granted or confirmed it to Abingdon abbey (Berks., later Oxon.) in 1050,[9] and in 1066 it was held of the abbey by Blacheman, a priest. On Blacheman's flight from England with King Harold's mother in 1068 William I confiscated the estate, and the abbey recovered it from him only, it was said, after much difficulty. Hezelin held Leverton of the abbey in 1086,[10] as did

Gueres de Palence probably in the 12th century,[11] and the abbey remained overlord in the 15th century.[12]

Leverton manor evidently descended from Robert de Wancey to Geoffrey de Wancey (fl. c. 1160–70), to William de Wancey (fl. c. 1180–90), and in turn to William de Wancey (fl. c. 1220–30) and his son Geoffrey. What was apparently the northern part of it was granted away by the second William[13] and became a separate manor.[14] The second Geoffrey held the reduced Leverton manor in 1242–3,[15] Stephen de Hamville held it in 1292,[16] and Alan Hamville held it in 1341.[17] In 1343 Alan granted it to James Hussey for James's life, a grant ratified by Alan's son Thomas,[18] and by 1373 Warin, Lord Lisle, had acquired it in fee.[19] The manor thereafter descended with Chilton Foliat manor and from 1574 was part of the Chilton Lodge estate.[20]

Land granted to Littlemore priory (Oxon.) by William de Wancey in the earlier 13th century[21] became *HAYWARD* manor. The priory held the manor in 1242–3[22] and until its dissolution in 1525. In 1526 the manor was granted to Cardinal Wolsey for the endowment of Cardinal College[23] and, when the college was refounded in 1532 as King Henry VIII's College, was granted to the new college. In 1545 it was among the college's estates surrendered to the king,[24] who in 1546 gave it by exchange to his physician George Owen.[25] In 1547 Owen sold the manor to Sir John Williams, the treasurer of the court of Augmentations, who in 1551 sold it to Owen Oglethorpe. In 1552 Oglethorpe sold it to Thomas Hinton[26] (d. 1567). It descended to Hinton's son Anthony[27] and since 1574 has been part of the Chilton Lodge estate.[28]

At its dissolution in 1525 Poughley priory in Chaddleworth (Berks.) owned land, probably no more than 1 a., at Leverton. As part of the priory's manor of Bagnor, in Speen (Berks.), in 1526 the land was granted to Cardinal Wolsey for Cardinal College, in 1529 resumed by the king, in 1531 granted to Westminster abbey, and in 1542 transferred to the dean and chapter of Westminster. It was held of the dean and chapter by copy, measured 1 a. c. 1870, and was enfranchised in 1890.[29]

97 Reading Univ. Libr., BER 36/5/204.
98 Som. R.O., DD/POt 16, lease, Popham to Morland, 1789; DD/POt 156, Morgan's farm.
99 W.R.O. 735/43.
1 Cf. above, this section.
2 W.R.O. 735/43.
3 *Diary of Bulstrode Whitelocke*, 703, 722.
4 W.R.O. 735/43.
5 O.S. Maps 6", Wilts. XXX (1887 edn.); XXX. SE. (1900 edn.).
6 J. Davies, *Victorian Kitchen Gdn.*
7 Reading Univ. Libr., BER 36/5/284; W.R.O. 735/43; 2027, map of Chilton Foliat, 1791; above, this section (Chilton Foliat).
8 Reading Univ. Libr., BER 36/5/7; BER 36/5/19.
9 *Early Chart. Thames Valley*, ed. M. Gelling, pp. 61, 66; the authenticity of the chart. is doubted in P. H. Sawyer, *Anglo-Saxon Chart.* (revised S. E. Kelly; priv. circulated 1996), no. 1020.
10 *V.C.H. Berks.* i. 340; *Chron. Mon. Abingdon* (Rolls Ser.), i. 483–4; ii. 283; F. Barlow, *Feud. Kingdom of Eng.* 89.
11 *Chron. Mon. Abingdon* (Rolls Ser.), ii. 4.
12 P.R.O., C 140/24, no. 20, rot. 18.
13 *Cal. Chart. Bodl.* ed. W. H. Turner and H. O. Coxe,

295.
14 Below, this section (Hayward).
15 *Bk. of Fees*, ii. 843.
16 P.R.O., CP 25/1/9/34, no. 4.
17 *Inq. Non.* (Rec. Com.), 173.
18 *Cal. Close, 1343–6*, 248–9.
19 Ibid. 1369–74, 557, 580–1.
20 Reading Univ. Libr., BER 36/5/7; above, this section (Chilton Foliat; Chilton Lodge).
21 *Cal. Chart. Bodl.* ed. Turner and Coxe, 295.
22 *Bk. of Fees*, ii. 846.
23 *L. & P. Hen. VIII*, iv (1), pp. 848–9; *V.C.H. Oxon.* ii. 77.
24 *L. & P. Hen. VIII*, v, p. 587; *V.C.H. Oxon.* iii. 231; P.R.O., SC 6/Hen. VIII/2931, rot. 4.
25 P.R.O., E 305/9/E 52.
26 *D.N.B.* (s.v. Williams); Reading Univ. Libr., BER 36/5/2.
27 *V.C.H. Wilts.* ix. 177.
28 e.g. P.R.O., C 142/257, no. 85; for the Chilton Lodge estate, above, this section.
29 *V.C.H. Berks.* ii. 86; iv. 103; *V.C.H. Oxon.* iii. 231; *L. & P. Hen. VIII*, v, p. 286; xvii, pp. 392, 394; Ch. Com. file 44313; ibid. 70923.

ECONOMIC HISTORY. Chilton Foliat. In 1086 Chilton Foliat had enough land for 12 ploughteams, but only 7 teams were there: on 6½ hides of demesne there were 2 *servi* and 2 teams, and 7 *villani* and 10 coscets had 5 teams. There were 2 square furlongs of both meadow and pasture; the woodland measured 1 league by 2 furlongs.[30] The demesne, evidently under-stocked with teams, apparently included a large area of uncultivated downland,[31] presumably that used to found the settlements at Soley and Cakewood and to provide them with agricultural land. By the early 13th century Chilton Foliat's land had been divided into two, probably three, agricultural units: to the north Soley had *c.* 800 a., to the south-west Cakewood probably had 100–200 a., and Chilton Foliat was left with *c.* 1,200–1,300 a.[32] Cakewood's open fields, probably *c.* 100 a., were shared by five tenants each holding 1 yardland;[33] the hamlet had apparently been deserted by the 16th century, from when the land was used in severalty.[34]

By the early 14th century some of Chilton Foliat's land had been imparked.[35] The imparking may have been contemporary with a grant of free warren over the demesne land made in 1249,[36] and the park may have been the square, of *c.* 350–400 a. with the church and the manor house in the south-east corner, bounded by Soley's land, North field, the Marlborough road, and the western parish boundary.[37] The agricultural land of the demesne, 130 a. of arable and 20 a. of meadow, was scanty in 1307.[38] The park reverted to common pasture in winter,[39] and by 1327, when the demesne included 380 a. of arable, 31 a. of meadow, and pasture worth 6s. 8d., it may again have been cultivated.[40] There is no later evidence of common rights over that square, which thereafter seems to have been the land of an inclosed demesne farm.[41] It was apparently used for sport in the 17th century,[42] and in the early 19th century included near Chilton House 25 a. called a park.[43] On the east, parts of the square may have been added to other farms in the 1570s.[44] All the remaining agricultural land was presumably worked from buildings at Chilton House until, in the later 18th century and before 1791, Manor Farm was built on the north side of the Marlborough road and to the west.[45] Between Manor Farm and the Kennet 19 a. of inclosed meadows was part of the farm.[46]

In 1336 a licence was granted for 400 a. at Chilton Foliat to be imparked,[47] and by 1341 a carucate had been inclosed as a park in which game was preserved.[48] The land imparked *c.* 1340 was probably the strip between North field and the county boundary: there were deer in the park in 1483,[49] the park keeper was paid 2d. a day in 1539,[50] and a lodge stood on it in 1546 presumably on the site of Chilton Park Farm.[51] By the 16th century much of Calcot's land, a similar strip on the other side of the county boundary, had been added to the park, 360 a. around Chilton Lodge in the 17th century.[52]

In the early 13th century there may have been meadow beside the Kennet watered and used in common,[53] and *c.* 1550 the tenants of Chilton Foliat manor claimed the hay of, and winter pasture in, Chilton mead, 37 a., a claim denied by the lord of the manor.[54] The claim seems to have failed: west of Upper marsh the meadows, *c.* 60 a. excluding Soley Lot mead,[55] were later used in severalty as demesne, and the rector had 11 a. of inclosed meadow east of Upper marsh.[56] From 1572 Lord's mead, 40 a., 60 a. of woodland, Cakewood field, and Cakewood closes, a total of *c.* 290 a. in the south-west corner of the parish and near Littlecote House, were held in severalty as part of the house's parkland, of a home farm, or of a tenanted farm based in Ramsbury.[57]

On Chilton Foliat manor in 1327 there were 4 free tenants and 44 bond tenants and cottars,[58] some of whom presumably lived at Soley; 32 tenants claimed the rights in Chilton mead *c.* 1550.[59] The land at Chilton Foliat divided among holdings which until the 1570s were customary consisted of two open fields, North, 141 a. in a strip running north from the east part of the village, and South, 144 a., lying east–west south of the Kennet, and of two commonable marshes beside the Kennet, Upper, 30 a. south-west of the village, and Lower, 47 a. south-east of the village.[60] In the later 17th century 4 a. of North field was inclosed and added to the Chilton Lodge park.[61] Most of the copyholds were sold separately in the 1570s.[62] The holdings based at Chilton Foliat, consisting of land in both the open fields and of pasture rights for cattle in the marshes, were evidently small, without meadow land, and with pasture for sheep only in the open fields.[63] In the 1570s some

---

30 *V.C.H. Wilts.* ii, p. 146.
31 For other suggestions, ibid. p. 51.
32 W.R.O. 735/17; for Soley, below, this section (Soley); for the approximate boundary between Chilton Foliat and Soley, map on p. 90; for Cakewood, below, this section.
33 P.R.O., C 139/94, no. 54, rot. 30.
34 Below, this section.   35 P.R.O., SC 6/1145/12, rot. 1.
36 *Cal. Chart. R.* 1226–57, 342.
37 For the location of N. field, map on p. 90.
38 *Wilts. Inq. p.m.* 1242–1326 (Index Libr.), 350.
39 P.R.O., SC 6/1145/12, rot. 1.
40 *Wilts. Inq. p.m.* 1327–77 (Index Libr.), 7–8.
41 e.g. P.R.O., C 2/Eliz. I/G 13/59.
42 *Wilts. Inq. p.m.* 1625–49 (Index Libr.), 354.
43 Som. R.O., DD/PO 96.
44 Cf. W.R.O. 2027, map of Chilton Foliat, 1791; above, manors (Chilton Foliat); below, this section.
45 W.R.O. 2027, map of Chilton Foliat, 1791; above, intro. (Chilton Foliat).
46 W.R.O. 735/43; 2027, map of Chilton Foliat, 1791.
47 *Cal. Chart. R.* 1327–41, 357.

48 *Inq. Non.* (Rec. Com.), 172–3.
49 P.R.O., SC 1/44, no. 75.
50 *L. & P. Hen. VIII*, xiv (2), p. 224.
51 P.R.O., E 318/9/353; above, manors (Chilton Lodge).
52 Reading Univ. Libr., BER 36/5/19; below, this section (Calcot), where the later hist. of the park is given.
53 *Cart. St. Frideswide,* ii (Oxf. Hist. Soc. xxxi), p. 359.
54 P.R.O., REQ 2/11/163.
55 For Upper marsh, below, this section; for Soley Lot mead, ibid. (Soley).
56 W.R.O. 735/43; 2027, map of Chilton Foliat, 1791.
57 P.R.O., C 146/9100; cf. W.R.O. 735/43.
58 *Wilts. Inq. p.m.* 1327–77 (Index Libr.), 8.
59 P.R.O., REQ 2/11/163.
60 W.R.O. 735/43; cf. above, manors (Chilton Foliat).
61 *Diary of Bulstrode Whitelocke*, ed. R. Spalding, 708; Reading Univ. Libr., BER 36/5/52.
62 Above, manors (Chilton Foliat).
63 e.g. W.R.O. 212B/1720; Som. R.O., DD/POt 12, deed, Chunn to Bodkin, 1681; DD/POt 13, deed, Bennett to Gregory, 1731.

of them may have had part of the demesne farm added to them, and in 1772 the largest known, 44 a., included 14 a. of inclosed arable, 7 a. in 4 parcels in North field, 19 a. in 9 parcels in South field, 3 a. of inclosed grassland, and feeding for 9 cows in the marshes.[64] Most were presumably worked from small farmsteads in the street, but in 1777 Morgan's farm included, besides 11 a. in the open fields, a farmstead in Leverton Lane and 13 a. in closes near Chilton Lodge.[65] The closes of Morgan's farm were absorbed by the Chilton Lodge park,[66] and by the early 19th century most of the small farms had been acquired by the owners of Littlecote House, Chilton House, and Chilton Lodge.[67]

In 1813 the open fields and the marshes were inclosed by Act and land was exchanged. South of the Kennet the Lower marsh was to be converted to water meadow, and South field was added to the roughly 290 a. in the south-west corner and worked from outside the parish. North of the Kennet the Upper marsh was added to Manor farm, separate farms may have been worked from Chilton House and Manor Farm, and 77 a. may have been worked from a farmstead in the street.[68] By 1835 Chilton House farm had been added to Manor farm, c. 400 a., which was held by the tenant of an adjoining farm based at West Soley, and the farm based in the street had been increased to 107 a.[69] In the later 19th century a stud farm, 164 a. in 1896, was based north of the street at the east end,[70] and land south of the Kennet was worked from Littlecote Home Farm, which had been built on the former South field by c. 1880.[71]

In 1929 south of the Kennet 35 a. was held with Littlecote House, Littlecote Home farm measured 159 a., and Littlecote Park farm, based in Ramsbury, included 116 a. in Chilton Foliat; north of the Kennet, Manor farm measured 273 a. and Chilton Stud farm 178 a.[72] In the 1920s and 1930s Manor farm and West Soley farm were held together.[73] In 1961 south of the Kennet Littlecote Park farm included 124 a., 75 a. of grassland was held with Littlecote House or let for grazing, and Littlecote Home farm, 75 a., was mainly arable. North of the Kennet and all mainly arable, Manor farm, 180 a., and Chilton Stud farm, 245 a., were worked with East Soley farm and West Soley farm respectively.[74] In 1995 south of the Kennet c. 225 a. of arable was in hand as part of the Eastridge (formerly Littlecote) estate, and c. 20 a. of grassland was held with Littlecote House.[75] North of the Kennet most of the land was arable: that east of Stag Hill was worked from New Hayward Farm, 178 a. west of Stag Hill was in hand as part of the Eastridge estate, and the remainder was part of East Soley farm.[76]

Three coppices in the south-west corner of the parish in 1572 probably included the east part of Cake wood and the west part of Brickkiln copse:[77] in 1813 and 1995 c. 50 a. of each of those woods was in Chilton Foliat.[78] Cake wood, held by the Ministry of Agriculture and Fisheries from 1953[79] and by the Forestry Commission in 1995, was replanted with beech and Norway spruce in the early 1960s.[80] Woods beside the western boundary of the parish adjoining Foxbury wood in Ramsbury were standing in the later 18th century[81] and probably much earlier. They measured c. 46 a. in 1813,[82] 42 a. in 1922[83] and 1995, when they were called Daffy copse. A belt of trees had been planted around 27 a. of parkland near Littlecote House by 1773,[84] and in the 20th century two coppices, each of c. 4 a., were planted east of Daffy copse.[85]

There were two mills at Chilton Foliat in 1086,[86] and a water mill, presumably for grain, and a fulling mill, presumably driven by water, stood on Chilton Foliat manor in the early 14th century.[87] A fulling mill remained on the manor until the 17th century.[88] The corn mill was rebuilt in the 17th century[89] and, with an attached miller's house, in the early 19th: it remained in use until the 1930s.[90]

A tanner may have lived at Chilton Foliat in the earlier 15th century,[91] and there was a tannery in the village from 1620 or earlier. In 1680 it was used by a collar maker,[92] and from 1704 or earlier it stood on the south side of the street.[93] The tannery remained in use until c. 1850:[94] the buildings which survived in 1995 were apparently of c. 1800. There was a malthouse in the village from the early 18th century to the later 19th; it stood on the south side of the street in the early 19th century.[95] In the 19th century premises in the street were used for a wide variety of trades to serve local needs.[96]

64 Som. R.O., DD/PO 5E, deed, Spier to Bigg, 1772; W.R.O. 2027, map of Chilton Foliat, 1791.
65 Som. R.O., DD/POt 156, Morgan's farm.
66 Ibid. DD/POt 16, lease, Popham to Morland, 1789.
67 W.R.O. 753/43.
68 Ibid.; Som. R.O., DD/POt 156, land in Chilton Foliat.
69 W.R.O. 735/17; 735/29.
70 Ibid. 735/21; O.S. Map 6", Wilts. XXX (1887 edn.); W.A.S. Libr., sale cat. i, no. 23.
71 O.S. Map 6", Wilts. XXX (1887 edn.).
72 W.R.O. 2281/4, abstr. of title.
73 Kelly's Dir. Wilts. (1920 and later edns.).
74 W.R.O. 2281/4, abstr. of title; below, this section (Soley).
75 Inf. from Sir Seton Wills, Eastridge Ho., Ramsbury.
76 Ibid.; inf. from Mr. G. J. Ward, Chilton Park Farm; Mr. A. T. Pearce, E. Soley Farmhouse; below, this section (Soley; Leverton).
77 P.R.O., C 146/9100.
78 W.R.O. 735/43.
79 Ibid. 2281/4, abstr. of title.
80 Inf. from the Head Forester, Forest Enterprise, Postern Hill, Marlborough.
81 Andrews and Dury, Map (W.R.S. viii), pl. 12.

82 W.R.O. 735/43.
83 O.S. Maps 1/2,500, Wilts. XXX. 2 (1924 edn.); XXX. 6 (1924 edn.).
84 Andrews and Dury, Map (W.R.S. viii), pl. 12; W.R.O. 735/43.
85 O.S. Maps 6", Wilts. XXX. NW. (1925 edn.); 1/25,000, SU 37 (1960 edn.); SU 27/37 (1985 edn.).
86 V.C.H. Wilts. ii, p. 146.
87 Wilts. Inq. p.m. 1242–1326 (Index Libr.), 350; 1327–77 (Index Libr.), 8; P.R.O., SC 6/1145/12, rot. 1.
88 Som. R.O., DD/POt 42, lease, Popham to Plaisteed, 1621.
89 W.R.O. 212B/1722.
90 Kelly's Dir. Wilts. (1931, 1935).
91 P.R.O., SC 2/212/2, rot. 3d.
92 Early-Stuart Tradesmen (W.R.S. xv), p. 22; Som. R.O., DD/POt 12, deed, Chunn to Bodkin, 1681.
93 Som. R.O., DD/PO 6B, deed, Smith to Spanswick, 1704; W.R.O. 735/43.
94 Kelly's Dir. Wilts. (1848, 1855).
95 Harrod's Dir. Wilts. (1865); Som. R.O., DD/POt 12, deed, Bennett to Bodkin, 1713; W.R.O. 735/43.
96 Kelly's Dir. Wilts. (1848 and later edns.).

SOLEY. Almost certainly between 1086 and 1200 what was apparently uncultivated downland, c. 800 a., was presumably assigned to Soley as agricultural land.[97] Soley had open fields called East and West, a common pasture called the Heath on which sheep were fed, and, beside the Kennet and detached from its other land, a common meadow in which plots were divided by merestones and assigned by lot.[98] In the 16th century and probably earlier much of the land was in copyholds of Chilton Foliat manor.[99]

Soley's open fields were inclosed between 1585 and 1603, probably c. 1600. The Heath had possibly been inclosed by 1585, when a holding included Heath close, 4 a., and had been divided, allotted, and inclosed by 1600.[1] Soley Lot mead, 17 a., was inclosed by Act in 1813.[2]

In 1791 there were three farmsteads at East Soley, five at West Soley: one farm consisted of 127 a. in 21 closes and of half a lot in Soley Lot mead, and one based at East Soley included Lower barn and c. 56 a. of Calcot's land in Old Hayward bottom.[3] About 1813 there were farms of 169 a., 108 a., and 92 a. based at East Soley, of 135 a., 133 a., and 62 a. based at West Soley; all were predominantly arable.[4] By 1835 the farms had been reduced to four based at the sites later called East Soley Farm, East Soley Old Farm, West Soley Farm, and West Soley Old Farm. One of the farms based at West Soley, of 148 a. and probably that based at West Soley Old Farm, was held by the tenant of Manor farm, Chilton Foliat; the others were of 220 a., 217 a., and 209 a.[5]

In 1896 two farms, of 218 a. and 191 a., were based at East Soley and one of 376 a. was based at West Soley Farm.[6] The two East Soley farms were held as one from 1910 or earlier, and in the 1920s and 1930s West Soley farm was held with Manor farm.[7] In the 1960s East Soley farm measured 608 a. including Manor farm; West Soley farm, 384 a., was held with Chilton Stud farm and land at Thrup in Ramsbury, a total of 786 a.; both were mainly arable,[8] and their fields were greatly enlarged in the later 20th century. East Soley farm, including Manor farm, 82 a. formerly in West Soley farm, and 60 a. outside the parish, a total of c. 725 a., was still mainly arable in 1995. West Soley farm, without Chilton Stud farm from 1978, was reduced to 312 a. in 1982 and

afterwards split up. A 135-a. stud farm based at West Soley Old Farm was started in 1981 and later enlarged; extensive new buildings were erected c. 1990, and in 1995 the farm measured c. 200 a. From c. 1990 the Raffin Stud, based at Thrup, had c. 48 a. in the north-west corner of Chilton Foliat parish.[9]

In 1773 the only woodland at Soley was Nordin's copse, 14 a. north-east of East Soley.[10] By 1791 Briary wood, 14 a., and Hitchen copse, 10 a., had been planted respectively east and south-east of East Soley,[11] and between c. 1880 and 1898 Queen's coppice, 17 a., was planted south of West Soley. Nordin's copse and the south half of Hitchen copse were grubbed up between 1813 and c. 1880.[12] The other woodland was standing in 1995.

CALCOT AND CHILTON PARK. Calcot's land was not extensive. In 1086 it was sufficient for 2 teams and was assessed at 1 hide; the demesne had 1 team on it, 3 *villani* and 4 bordars shared 1 team, and there were 5 a. of meadow.[13] The land lay as a strip of c. 300 a. along the east side of the county boundary and north of the Kennet, with Leverton's land east of it and Chilton Foliat's west.[14] Until 1341 or later Calcot manor probably comprised demesne and customary land in open fields, and meadow and pasture used in common.[15] About 1340 a strip of land probably on the west side of the county boundary and bounded to the north by Soley was imparked,[16] and by 1439, when Calcot manor was said to include 120 a. of arable, 70 a. of pasture, and 6 a. of woodland, either a comparable strip of its land or its woodland had been encompassed by Chilton park.[17] By the 16th century Calcot village had almost certainly ceased to exist[18] and, except for two closes called Calcot, 39 a., part of Leverton farm in 1574, and presumably east of the park, and for c. 70 a. north of the park, all its land had been encompassed by Chilton park.[19] The two closes, 59 a. in 1663,[20] seem to have been taken into the park when it was enlarged eastwards, probably in the late 1790s.[21] The land north of the park was probably worked from East Soley in the late 16th century,[22] as it was until the late 18th. A farmhouse was built on it c. 1814, when as Dunnels farm it was probably of c. 70 a. and mainly arable.[23] In the mid 19th century Dunnels farm

97   Cf. above, this section (Chilton Foliat); for the approximate boundary of Soley's land, map on p. 90.
98   W.R.O. 735/43; ibid. D 1/24/43/2; Alnwick Castle Mun. X.II.11, box 22, deeds, Reynolds to Smith, 1605; Smith to Mundy, 1618.
99   P.R.O., CP 25/2/239/15 Eliz. I Trin.; CP 25/2/260/16 & 17 Eliz. I Mich.; CP 40/1348, Carte rott. 8–9; CP 40/1354, Carte rott. 9d.–10; ibid. IND 1/16943, f. 83v.
1   Ibid. E 311/28, no. 316; Alnwick Castle Mun. X.II.11, box 22, deed, Reynolds to Smith, 1605; X.II.11, box 23, deeds, Mundy to Smith, 1600; Smith to Seymour, 1632.
2   W.R.O. 735/43.
3   Ibid. 2027, map of Chilton Foliat, 1791; Som. R.O., DD/POt 16, lease, Popham to Pontin, 1788; Reading Univ. Libr., BER 36/5/284.
4   Som. R.O., DD/POt 156, land in Chilton Foliat; W.R.O. 735/43.
5   W.R.O. 735/17; 735/29; 735/43.
6   W.A.S. Libr., sale cat. i, no. 23.
7   *Kelly's Dir. Wilts.* (1920 and later edns.); W.R.O., Inland Revenue, val. reg. 54.

8   W.R.O. 2281/4, abstr. of title.
9   Inf. from Mr. Pearce, and sale cats. of 1981 and 1982 in his possession.
10   *Andrews and Dury, Map* (W.R.S. viii), pls. 12, 15; W.R.O. 735/43.
11   W.R.O. 735/43; 2027, map of Chilton Foliat, 1791.
12   Ibid. 735/43; O.S. Maps 6", Wilts. XXX (1887 edn.); XXX. NW. (1900 edn.).
13   *V.C.H. Berks.* i. 345.
14   For its approximate boundaries, map on p. 90.
15   *Inq. Non.* (Rec. Com.), 173.
16   Above, this section (Chilton Foliat).
17   P.R.O., C 139/94, no. 54, rot. 30.
18   Above, intro. (Calcot).
19   Reading Univ. Libr., BER 36/5/7.
20   Ibid. BER 36/5/19.
21   Below, this section.
22   Alnwick Castle Mun. X.II.11, box 23, deed, Smith to Seymour, 1632.
23   Reading Univ. Libr., BER 36/5/284; W.R.O. 248/188; 735/43; 2027, map of Chilton Foliat, 1791.

was 74 a.,[24] in the later 19th 143 a.[25] By 1908 it had been absorbed by Old Hayward farm[26] and its land was later in hand as part of the Chilton Lodge estate and worked from New Hayward Farm.[27]

Chilton park, 315 a. in 1619,[28] 360 a. in 1663,[29] was divided from Chilton Foliat's North field to the west by pales;[30] a deer leap which existed in the early 19th century marked what in the 16th was the park's boundary with Soley to the north.[31] In the 1660s pales were taken down and the northern part of the park, 137 a., was added to Hayward farm and presumably converted to agriculture; in the small park which remained deer were hunted and partridges shot.[32] In the 18th century much of the small park was also used for agriculture. In 1767 only 24 a. and woodland were held with Chilton Lodge, and Chilton Park farm, 252 a., was worked from a farmhouse then said to be new;[33] the farmhouse was probably that which stands c. 100 m. east of Chilton Foliat bridge.[34] Land near Chilton Lodge was imparked c. 1777[35] and, to surround the new Chilton Lodge, the park was extended eastwards probably in the late 1790s.[36] Since c. 1800 the rectangular park, 160 a., has been bounded on the south by Leverton Lane and on the east by Old Hayward Lane. Its northern boundary runs east from the site of the old Chilton Lodge at its north-east corner and was marked by a pale in the earlier 19th century. In 1813 Chilton Park farm, 186 a. including 154 a. of arable, lay between that pale and the land which was presumably converted to agriculture in the 1660s; it was worked from a new farmhouse which had replaced the old Chilton Lodge. Model farm buildings which had been erected in the south-east corner of the park by 1813[37] incorporated a dairy. Chilton Park farm, 182 a., included 7 a. of water meadow and 37 a. of pasture in 1908.[38] By 1938 it had been brought in hand as part of the Chilton Lodge estate and in 1995 was used for arable and dairy farming.[39] In 1995 cattle were kept in Chilton park but the model farm buildings had no agricultural use.

In 1086 Calcot had woodland enough only for fencing.[40] Dean grove was standing in 1577.[41] Denhill copse, adjoining it, and Snowhill copse were standing c. 1754.[42] The woods measured 7

a., 14 a., and 7 a. respectively in 1813:[43] none had changed much in area by 1995. There was little woodland in the park in the 18th century although there were avenues in several parts of it. The Shrubbery, 8 a. of woodland, and a belt of trees beside Old Hayward Lane were planted in the new part of the park probably in the late 1790s,[44] and Tower wood, 29 a., was planted NNE. of Chilton Lodge mainly between c. 1880 and 1898.[45]

A mill stood at Calcot in 1086,[46] in 1243, when it was intended to raise the dams of the pond and build a fulling mill,[47] and in 1305.[48] No later mill has been traced.

LEVERTON. In 1086 Leverton was assessed at 4½ hides. It had enough land for 4 teams but only 3 were there, 1 on the demesne and 2 shared by 4 *villani* and 3 bordars; 2 *servi* there probably worked on the demesne.[49] Like Chilton Foliat's, Leverton's demesne seems to have been under-stocked with teams and may also have included uncultivated downland to the north. Downland separated from Leverton manor in the earlier 13th century apparently became Hayward's agricultural land,[50] c. 500 a.; Leverton was left with c. 500 a. in the south-east corner of the parish.[51]

Cultivation in open fields probably continued at Leverton until the 18th century,[52] and meadow land may have been used in common in the 17th;[53] the other grassland had evidently been inclosed by the 16th century. In 1574 the demesne farm of Leverton manor included c. 120 a. in the open fields, the first cut of 7 a. of meadow, and c. 80 a. of inclosed meadow and pasture including the two closes called Calcot, and a copyhold included 16 a. in the open fields and 6 a. of inclosed grassland.[54] The copyholds, of which there were c. 13, were worked from farmsteads in Leverton village,[55] and the demesne was almost certainly worked from a farmstead there.

Leverton had c. 45 a. of meadows and in 1665, when 32 a. was held with Chilton Lodge, a new weir was built for watering some or all of them. By 1663 most of the demesne had been added to Hayward farm.[56] All the arable had possibly been inclosed by 1738, when an apparently recent inclosure of 5 a. of East field was men-

24 W.R.O. 735/17.
25 Reading Univ. Libr., BER 36/13/1.
26 W.A.S. Libr., sale cat. vi, no. 45.
27 Inf. from Mr. G. J. Ward, Chilton Park Farm; below, this section (Leverton).
28 Reading Univ. Libr., BER 36/5/10.
29 Ibid. BER 36/5/19.
30 Som. R.O., DD/POt 12, deed, Chunn to Bodkin, 1681.
31 Ibid. DD/POt 42, lease, Horner to Smith, 1594; W.R.O. 248/188.
32 *Diary of Bulstrode Whitelocke*, 685–6, 697, 711, 821; Reading Univ. Libr., BER 36/5/24; for Hayward farm, below, this section (Hayward).
33 Reading Univ. Libr., BER 36/5/204.
34 Cf. above, intro. (Chilton Foliat).
35 Som. R.O., DD/POt 16, lease, Popham to Morland, 1789; DD/POt 156, Morgan's farm.
36 W.R.O. 735/43; above, manors (Chilton Lodge).
37 W.R.O. 248/188; 735/43; cf. *Andrews and Dury, Map* (W.R.S. viii), pl. 12.
38 W.A.S. Libr., sale cat. vi, no. 45.
39 Inf. from Mr. Ward.

40 *V.C.H. Berks.* i. 345.
41 P.R.O., CP 40/1348, Carte rot. 8.
42 J. Rocque, *Topog. Surv. Berks.* (1761), sheet V.
43 W.R.O. 735/43.
44 Ibid. 249/188; *Andrews and Dury, Map* (W.R.S. viii), pl. 12.
45 O.S. Maps 6", Wilts. XXX (1887 edn.); XXX. NE. (1900 edn.).
46 *V.C.H. Berks.* i. 345.
47 P.R.O., CP 25/1/251/14, no. 10.
48 Ibid. CP 25/1/9/37, no. 13.
49 *V.C.H. Berks.* i. 340.
50 Above, manors (Leverton; Hayward); this section (Chilton Foliat).
51 For the approximate boundaries, map on p. 90; for Hayward, below, this section.
52 Below, this section.
53 *Wilts. Inq. p.m.* 1625–49 (Index Libr.), 279.
54 Reading Univ. Libr., BER 36/5/7; for Calcot closes, above, this section (Calcot).
55 Reading Univ. Libr., BER 36/5/19; W.R.O. 735/43.
56 *Diary of Bulstrode Whitelocke*, 699; Reading Univ. Libr., BER 36/5/19; W.R.O. 735/43.

tioned,[57] and evidently had been by 1767. In 1767 the copyholds included 117 a. lying north and east of the village. Between 1767 and 1791 New Hayward Farm was built on the north part of Leverton's land, and in 1813 a long and narrow farm of 443 a., including land in the north-east corner of the parish, was worked from it; 390 a. of the farm was arable.[58] A strip of c. 60 a. on the west side of Old Hayward Lane was taken into Chilton park when it was extended probably in the late 1790s,[59] and in the early 19th century only Leverton farm, 68 a., and a smaller farm were worked from farmsteads in the village.[60] About 1884 New Hayward farm measured 470 a., Leverton farm 73 a.[61] By 1909 the farm buildings in the village had been demolished; the land of Leverton farm was then worked from buildings east of the village as Upper Eddington farm, 66 a. In 1909 New Hayward farm measured 381 a. including 60 a. of grassland.[62] It was in hand from 1967, and in the later 20th century New Hayward Farm became the base from which all the agricultural land of the Chilton Lodge estate was worked. Extensive farm buildings were erected and in 1995 an arable and dairy farm of c. 2,300 a. was worked from them.[63]

In 1086 Leverton had woodland for 2 swine.[64] Most of it probably stood on the downland assigned to Hayward. Downs copse, 15 a., was the only woodland in the mid 18th century and had been grubbed up by 1814.[65] Some of the wood planted in Chilton park probably in the late 1790s[66] was on Leverton's land and, adjoining the north-east corner of the park, Park plantation, 19 a., was grown between c. 1880 and 1898.[67]

A mill stood at Leverton in 1086 and 1292,[68] and a water mill stood there in 1343 and the earlier 15th century.[69] There was a malthouse in the village in the later 18th century.[70]

HAYWARD. The 500 a. in the north-east corner of the parish may have been rough pasture until separated from Leverton manor in the early 13th century.[71] Open fields were laid out, sheep and cattle were fed in common, and, as meadow land apparently was to Soley in similar circumstances, Hayward mead, 16 a. beside the Kennet,

was probably assigned to Hayward at the separation. Hayward manor evidently included a demesne farm and customary tenants,[72] but in the 16th century or earlier apparently all the land was brought into Hayward farm and common husbandry thus eliminated.[73] By 1663, when it was 620 a., Hayward farm had been extended southwards by the addition of most of the demesne of Leverton manor,[74] and in 1664 it was extended westwards by the addition of the 137 a. of Calcot and Chilton Foliat until then the northern part of Chilton Foliat park.[75] In 1767 it was a several farm of c. 807 a. with land in c. 31 fields and with 30 a. of watered meadow. Between 1767 and 1791 much of its land was transferred to New Hayward farm.[76] As Old Hayward farm it measured 398 a., including 334 a. of arable, in 1813.[77] In the mid 19th century it measured 436 a.,[78] in the later 19th 356 a.[79] Old Hayward farm had absorbed Dunnels farm by 1908, when it was a mainly arable farm of 433 a.[80] It was brought in hand as part of the Chilton Lodge estate in the 1970s, and in 1995 its land was worked from New Hayward Farm and devoted to arable and dairying.[81]

Hayward has long been well wooded. In 1663 Coney copse, Horseclose coppice, Bottom coppice, and Wyld's copse were all standing;[82] in 1813 they measured 16 a., 17 a., 10 a., and 19 a. respectively. In 1663 there may also have been some smaller coppices and some belts of trees linking some of the coppices, as there were in 1813.[83] In the 19th century Bottom coppice was enlarged to c. 30 a., partly by merger with other woodland, and between c. 1880 and 1898 Horseclose coppice was increased to c. 50 a. and c. 3 a. of woodland was planted to adjoin Briary wood in Soley.[84] In the later 20th century c. 10 a. of Wyld's copse was grubbed up,[85] and in 1995 there was c. 110 a. of woodland at Hayward.

LOCAL GOVERNMENT. Chilton Foliat tithing, which excluded the Berkshire part of the parish and in the 17th century or earlier included East and West Soley,[86] attended the view of frankpledge held for the honor of Wallingford, despite the claim by Henry, Lord Tyeys, in 1289 to have the assize of bread and of ale in Chilton

57 Reading Univ. Libr., BER 36/5/167.
58 Ibid. BER 36/5/204; W.R.O. 735/43; 2027, map of Chilton Foliat, 1791.
59 W.R.O. 735/43; for model farm bldgs. erected at Leverton, above, this section (Calcot).
60 Som. R.O., DD/POt 156, land in Chilton Foliat; W.R.O. 735/43.
61 Reading Univ. Libr., BER 36/13/1.
62 O.S. Map 6", Berks. XXXIII. SE. (1925 edn.); W.A.S. Libr., sale cat. vi, no. 45; above, intro. (Leverton).
63 Inf. from Mr. Ward.
64 V.C.H. Berks. i. 340.
65 Rocque, Topog. Surv. Berks. (1761), sheet V; W.R.O. 248/188; 735/43.
66 Above, this section (Calcot).
67 O.S. Maps 6", Wilts. XXX (1887 edn.); XXX. NE. (1900 edn.).
68 V.C.H. Berks. i. 340; P.R.O., CP 25/1/9/34, no. 4.
69 Cal. Close, 1343-6, 248-9; P.R.O., C 138/28, no. 58, rot. 10; C 139/94, no. 54, rot. 30.
70 Reading Univ. Libr., BER 36/5/167; BER 36/5/204.
71 Above, this section (Leverton); for the approximate boundaries of Hayward's land, map on p. 90.

72 Inq. Non. (Rec. Com.), 173; P.R.O., E 315/19, no. 125; Reading Univ. Libr., BER 36/5/5; BER 36/5/19; W.R.O. 735/43; above, this section (Soley).
73 Cal. Chart. Bodl. ed. W. H. Turner and H. O. Coxe, 296; P.R.O., CP 40/1138, Carte rot. 9; ibid. E 315/19, no. 125; Reading Univ. Libr., BER 36/5/2.
74 Reading Univ. Libr., BER 36/5/19.
75 Diary of Bulstrode Whitelocke, 685; above, this section (Calcot).
76 Reading Univ. Libr., BER 36/5/204; above, this section (Leverton).
77 W.R.O. 735/43.   78 Ibid. 735/17.
79 Reading Univ. Libr., BER 36/13/1.
80 W.A.S. Libr., sale cat. vi, no. 45; for Dunnels, above, this section (Calcot).
81 Inf. from Mr. Ward.
82 Reading Univ. Libr., BER 36/5/19.
83 W.R.O. 248/188; 735/43.
84 Ibid. 735/43; O.S. Maps 6", Wilts. XXX (1887 edn.); XXX. NE. (1900 edn.).
85 O.S. Maps 1/25,000, SU 37 (1960 edn.); SU 27/37 (1985 edn.).
86 e.g. W.R.O. 735/20.

Foliat.[87] St. Frideswide's priory's tenants in Chilton Foliat and Soley, however, attended the priory's biannual court, probably a view, of Eddington manor,[88] and in the mid 13th century Alan of Farnham caused his men of Calcot to withdraw their suit from Kintbury hundred.[89] In the 15th century the tithingman of Chilton Foliat presented at the view held for the honor of Wallingford at Ogbourne St. George: brewers who broke the assize were the offenders most frequently amerced.[90] About 1520 Chilton Foliat withdrew its suit at the command of Queen Catherine, the lord of the manor.[91] A court leet was held for Chilton Foliat in the 18th and 19th centuries[92] but none of its records is extant. A court of Chilton Foliat manor was held from the 14th century to the 16th.[93] There was little if any copyhold business to be done after the sale of the manor in portions in the period 1572–8;[94] other business was presumably done at the court leet.

As parts of different counties Chilton Foliat tithing and Calcot and Leverton tithing, which included Hayward, levied separate poor rates. In the 17th century it seems that they elected separate pairs of overseers, but that the Chilton Foliat overseers, who received payments from the Leverton overseers, relieved the poor of the whole parish.[95] In the early 19th century, when two thirds of the expenditure was met from Chilton Foliat tithing, the rates were still collected separately but there was only one pair of overseers.[96]

In 1666–7 £14 8s. was spent on poor relief, in the 1670s an average of c. £32 was spent, and in the 1680s and 1690s, for example at £77 in 1686–7 and £65 in 1692–3, expenditure was sometimes higher. In the 17th century most money was spent on weekly doles, rents were paid, and fuel, food, and clothing were bought. In the earlier 18th the cost of extraordinary items sometimes exceeded that of doles: in 1724–5 £16 was spent on extraordinaries, including clothing, fuel, funerals, and a pair of spectacles, £14 on doles for c. 5 paupers, and £10 on rents.[97] In 1775–6 £302 was spent on poor relief, in the early 1780s an average of £395. In 1802–3, when the poor rate was above average for Kinwardstone hundred, £422 was spent on relieving 72 adults and 76 children regularly and 45 people occasionally.[98] Expenditure rose rapidly in the early 19th century and, probably c. 1804, the

parish acquired a poorhouse or workhouse and began to employ a salaried assistant overseer, who was also the resident governor of the poorhouse: in 1810–11, when c. 48 received weekly payments, £841 was spent.[99] In 1812–13 £1,333 was spent and 63 were relieved regularly and 30 occasionally. Nine of the 31 relieved regularly in 1814–15 lived in the poorhouse.[1] From c. 1818 expenditure decreased and in the 1820s it averaged £750.[2] The poorhouse remained open and the overseers continued to give doles and to pay for clothing, footwear, and other necessities. There were c. 12 in the poorhouse in 1827.[3] Expenditure was slightly higher in the 1830s;[4] the poorhouse remained open until the parish joined Hungerford poor-law union in 1835.[5]

The parish became part of Hungerford rural district in 1872. From 1895 the Wiltshire part lay in Ramsbury rural district,[6] from 1974 in Kennet district. The Berkshire part lay in Newbury district from 1974.[7]

In 1813 the vestry ordered a lockup to be built: no physical evidence of one survives.[8] Stocks standing in Leverton village were renewed in 1994.[9]

CHURCH. Chilton Foliat church was probably standing in the 12th century.[10] The rectory was added to Whitton benefice in 1976.[11] The Berkshire part of the parish was exempted from the transfer of Berkshire from Salisbury diocese to Oxford diocese in 1836[12] and, although transferred to Hungerford civil parish in 1895,[13] remains part of Chilton Foliat ecclesiastical parish.[14]

From the earlier 14th century or earlier to the 1570s the advowson of the rectory belonged to the lord of Chilton Foliat manor.[15] Sir Gilbert Talbot presented in 1386 and 1389,[16] possibly as a feoffee of Joan de Lisle, and in 1487 Thomas Warren presented by grant of a turn. Edward Burgh, Lord Burgh, a grandson of Eleanor, duchess of Somerset (d. 1467), and a coparcener of the manor, presented in 1496, and Margaret, countess of Richmond, Henry VII's mother, presented in 1499 by Edward's grant. The Crown, which resumed the manor in 1505, presented in 1507, 1508, and 1509, and the queen, who held the manor as dower, presented in 1521.[17] After the death of Henry, earl of Rutland, the lord of Chilton Foliat manor, in

[87] P.R.O., JUST 1/1006, rot. 51d.; below, this section; cf. *Wilts. Inq. p.m.* 1242–1326 (Index Libr.), 350.
[88] *Cart. St. Frideswide,* ii (Oxf. Hist. Soc. xxxi), p. 356.
[89] *Rot. Hund.* (Rec. Com.), i. 19.
[90] P.R.O., SC 2/212/2, rot. 3d.; SC 2/212/9, rot. 2.
[91] Ibid. SC 2/212/14; SC 2/212/18, rot. 7d.; above, manors (Chilton Foliat).
[92] W.A.S. Libr., J. Wilkinson, par. hist. colln. no. 95; Som. R.O., DD/POt 123.
[93] *Wilts. Inq. p.m.* 1242–1326 (Index Libr.), 350; P.R.O., C 139/94, no. 54, rot. 19; ibid. REQ 2/64/72.
[94] Above, manors (Chilton Foliat).
[95] W.R.O. 735/19–20; Reading Univ. Libr., BER 36/5/5; Som. R.O., DD/PO 25.
[96] W.R.O. 735/28; 735/33.
[97] Ibid. 735/19–20; 735/31.
[98] *Poor Law Abstract, 1804,* 564–5.
[99] Ibid.; W.R.O. 735/33; 735/37.
[1] *Poor Law Abstract, 1818,* 498–9.
[2] *Poor Rate Returns, 1816–21,* 188; *1822–4,* 228; *1825–9,* 219; *1830–4,* 212.

[3] W.R.O. 1814/7.
[4] *Poor Rate Returns, 1830–4,* 212.
[5] *Poor Law Com. 1st Rep.* App. D, 242; W.R.O. 1814/7.
[6] *V.C.H. Wilts.* iv. 336; for the date 1895, cf. above, intro.
[7] O.S. Maps 1/100,000, admin. areas, Wilts. (1974 edn.); 1/50,000, sheet 174 (1981 edn.).
[8] W.R.O. 735/37.
[9] Plaque on stocks.
[10] Below, this section [archit.].
[11] *V.C.H. Wilts.* xii. 42.
[12] Ibid. iii. 55; W.R.O., D 1/48/5, f. 73.
[13] Above, intro.
[14] Inf. from Mr. G. J. Ward, Chilton Park Farm.
[15] Phillipps, *Wilts. Inst.* (index in *W.A.M.* xxviii. 216); above, manors (Chilton Foliat).
[16] Phillipps, *Wilts. Inst.* i. 71, 73; the presentation of 1386 is wrongly referred to as one for a chantry: cf. below, this section.
[17] Phillipps, *Wilts. Inst.* i. 170, 178, 180, 185–7, 195; *Complete Peerage,* ii. 422; above, manors (Chilton Foliat).

1563 John James and Alexander Rosewell disputed the right to present by Henry's grant of a turn:[18] in 1566 the bishop collated by lapse, and the Crown presented in 1567, while Henry's son Edward, earl of Rutland, was a minor.[19] The advowson was bought from Edward by Thomas Rosewell in 1574.[20] In 1578 it was conveyed by Alexander Rosewell to Peter Rosewell[21] (d. 1579), whose son and heir James was a minor until 1587.[22] By 1589 the advowson had apparently been acquired by William Darell, and it presumably passed with the rump of Chilton Foliat manor to Sir John Popham,[23] who presented in 1598. It thereafter descended with the manor and Littlecote House, on the sale of which in 1929 it was kept by H. F. A. Leyborne-Popham[24] (d. 1943). It passed to Leyborne-Popham's nephew E. T. Buller, from 1943 E. T. Buller Leyborne-Popham (d. 1973). Buller Leyborne-Popham's executors held the advowson until 1976,[25] but no successor to his title was a member of the board of patronage set up for Whitton benefice in that year.[26]

At £9 in 1291[27] and at £14 8s. 8½d. in 1535[28] the church was highly valued, at £994 c. 1830 very highly valued.[29] The rector was entitled to all tithes from the whole parish;[30] in 1811 nearly all of them were valued at £919 and commuted.[31] There was c. 10 a. of glebe in 1608 and c. 1700.[32] At inclosure in 1813 the rector's inclosed land was increased from 13 a. to 30 a. by allotments to replace a few acres in the open fields, feeding rights in common, and some tithes.[33] The rector sold 19 a. in 1928, 11 a. in 1967.[34] The rectory house of the late 16th century or early 17th was probably timber-framed. Of its central range and two cross wings only parts of the west wing survive, but almost the complete plan is marked out by existing walls.[35] Early in the 17th century a south range, of flint rubble with dressings of ashlar and brick, was added to the front of the east wing. The main south front was rebuilt in brick in the earlier 18th century and a north staircase block was added between the main range and the kitchen range to the west. Later in that century a canted bay was added to the south of the early 17th-century range, the side windows of which were blocked. Then or early in the 19th century the space between the wings

at the back was filled and service rooms were added on the west of the house. Extensive alterations to the inside in the later 20th century were partly in 18th-century style. The house was sold in 1963,[36] when a new rectory house was built.[37]

Two chantries had been founded in the church by 1334, when Alice de Lisle was licensed to exhume the corpses of her brother, Henry, Lord Tyeys, and of her husband, Sir Warin de Lisle, and rebury them at Chilton Foliat.[38] There were chantry chaplains from 1335 to 1397 or later: in 1397 there were two, as presumably there had been since 1335. Walter of Salford presented a chaplain in 1335, the bishop presented in 1351, when the rectory may have been vacant, and in 1384, and the rector presented at seven other times. Richard Fanelore, rector from 1389, presented his own successor as chaplain.[39] No chaplain is known to have been appointed in the 15th century and a chapel in the parish church, presumably that in which both chantries were served, was demolished between 1549 and 1556.[40]

Until the Dissolution a light in the church was paid for with the income, 2s. in 1548, from ½ a. of meadow and 1 a. in open fields.[41] Richard Fanelore, rector 1389–97 and formerly one of the chantry chaplains, seems to have lived in the parish and to have managed the glebe farm directly.[42] Thomas Balgay, rector from c. 1530 to 1566,[43] was employing a curate in 1553.[44] In 1577 the church had a Bible, Erasmus's *Paraphrases*, three books of homilies, and other books.[45] Robert Collard was rector from 1598 to 1648.[46] The ministers in the Interregnum were Thomas Hounsell (d. 1658) and James Hounsell, probably his son, who was a commissioner for ejecting scandalous and negligent ministers.[47] James was himself ejected at the Restoration but continued to preach at Chilton Lodge until 1670. In the later 17th century the rector was often assisted by a curate. Grindall Sheafe, rector from 1662, is said to have sent a spy to a conventicle, at which James Hounsell preached, held at Chilton Lodge in 1666.[48] Timothy Topping, rector 1680–1708, was also rector of Thruxton (Hants).[49] Edward Popham, rector 1779–1815, was also vicar of Lacock, where he lived in

18 P.R.O., C 3/99/18; above, manors (Chilton Foliat).
19 Phillipps, *Wilts. Inst.* i. 222–3; *Complete Peerage*, xi. 257.
20 P.R.O., CP 25/2/260/16 & 17 Eliz. I Mich.
21 Ibid. CP 40/1354, Carte rot. 11d.
22 Ibid. C 142/187, no. 107.
23 Ibid. CP 25/2/241/31 Eliz. I Trin.; above, manors (Chilton Foliat).
24 Phillipps, *Wilts. Inst.* ii. 1, 25, 36, 49, 53, 71, 89; *Clergy List* (1870 and later edns.); *Crockford* (1907 and later edns.); W.R.O., D 1/48/4, p. 42; above, manors (Chilton Foliat).
25 F. W. Popham, *W. Country Fam.* 70; *Sar. Dioc. Dir.* (1948 and later edns.); Burke, *Land. Gent.* (1965), i. 97.
26 Ch. Com. file, NB 34/378C.
27 *Tax. Eccl.* (Rec. Com.), 189.
28 *Valor Eccl.* (Rec. Com.), ii. 152.
29 *Rep. Com. Eccl. Revenues*, 828–9.
30 W.R.O., D 1/24/43/2.
31 Ibid. 735/43.
32 Ibid. D 1/24/43/1–2.
33 Ibid. 735/43.
34 Ch. Com. file 91133; ibid. deed 596703.
35 Cf. W.R.O., D 1/11/310.

36 Ch. Com. deed 584966.
37 W.R.O. 2395/7.
38 *Cal. Papal Reg.* ii. 410.
39 Phillipps, *Wilts. Inst.* i. 31, 36, 38, 43, 49–50, 64, 69; *Reg. Waltham* (Cant. & York Soc.), pp. 62, 64–5; W.R.O., D 1/2/6, f. 18.
40 W.R.O., D 1/43/2, f. 14; for the date 1549, cf. P.R.O., C 142/92, no. 111.
41 P.R.O., E 301/58, no. 125.
42 Phillipps, *Wilts. Inst.* i. 73; *Reg. Waltham* (Cant. & York Soc.), pp. 62, 64–5; W.R.O., D 1/2/6, f. 18.
43 *L. & P. Hen. VIII*, iv (3), p. 2857; Phillipps, *Wilts. Inst.* i. 222.
44 W.R.O., D 1/43/1, f. 141v.
45 Ibid. 735/19, f. 4.
46 Phillipps, *Wilts. Inst.* ii. 1; *Topog. and Geneal.* iii. 584.
47 *Calamy Revised*, ed. Matthews, 279; *V.C.H. Wilts.* iii. 102.
48 *Diary of Bulstrode Whitelocke*, ed. R. Spalding, 675, 706, 744, 761, 769–70, 796; Phillipps, *Wilts. Inst.* ii. 25; W.R.O. 735/19, ff. 48, 55; ibid. D 1/54/3/1, f. 3C.
49 Phillipps, *Wilts. Inst.* ii. 36; *Topog. and Geneal.* iii. 586; W.R.O., D 1/48/1, f. 18; D 1/48/2, f. 18.

1783:[50] in 1812 he lived in Chilton Foliat rectory house.[51] Each Sunday in 1783 at Chilton Foliat the curate held two services, at one of which he preached. He held additional services at Christmas, on Good Friday, and, if he wished, on Fridays in Lent, and he held communion four times a year with c. 40 communicants. Each Sunday in Lent the schoolchildren were examined in the catechism. The curate was Edward Meyrick, who kept a school at Hungerford and later at Ramsbury; in 1812 the curate was his son Arthur, who kept the school at Ramsbury from 1811.[52] John Leyborne-Popham, rector 1835–72, lived in the rectory house and usually employed an assistant curate. Attendance at the two services on Census Sunday in 1851, 260 in the morning, 220 in the afternoon, was about the average for 1850–1. In 1864 there was a service in the church every day, morning prayers on weekdays and two services each Sunday. Communion was celebrated c. 25 times: c. 90 attended each celebration at the great festivals, 20–40 the others. Leyborne-Popham favoured the teaching of the catechism, in which children were still examined in Lent.[53] From 1966 to 1975 the living was held in plurality with Froxfield vicarage. The incumbent lived at Chilton Foliat,[54] as did the team rector of Whitton benefice in 1995.

By 1577 a stall of bees and 1 a. had been given to the church.[55] The land was presumably the 1 a. later held by the rector's churchwarden[56] and sold in 1933.[57]

The church of ST. MARY, so called in 1763,[58] is built of flint, ashlar, and rubble and is partly rendered. It consists of a chancel with north vestry, a nave with south aisle and south porch, and a west tower. The nave is long, has a thick north wall, and was probably built in the 12th century; there are reset fragments of 12th-century billet moulding above the windows in the upper stage of the tower. The aisle may have been built in the 13th century, and an early 14th-century window survives in the north wall of the nave. A mid 14th-century window survives in the north wall of the chancel near its east end: its position suggests either that the chancel was lengthened or rebuilt at that date, or that the chapel which was demolished in the mid 16th century[59] stood on that side of the chancel at its west end. The tower may be 15th-century. Three windows made in the north wall of the nave in the 15th century[60] were replaced

in the 19th. The arcade, aisle, and tower were among the parts of the church affected by an extensive reconstruction of c. 1629 paid for by John Packer.[61] A new roof for the nave, a screen for the chancel, and box pews were apparently constructed then, and a gallery was erected in 1694.[62] In 1845, to designs by Benjamin Ferrey, the aisle was replaced by a wider one, the vestry was built, and an east window was made;[63] about then the nave roof was extensively restored, the box pews were replaced by open pews facing east,[64] and the gallery was rebuilt. A reredos in Jacobean style was fitted in 1926 and added to in 1931–2.[65] A neo-classical mausoleum for members of the Pearse family was built before 1814, almost certainly in the early 19th century, to designs by William Pilkington;[66] in 1995 it stood in the churchyard north of the chancel.

A 6½-oz. chalice was kept in 1553 when 4½ oz. of plate was taken for the king. A chalice and stand given in 1699, two chalices given in 1796, and a paten were replaced in 1862 by a chalice, a paten, a flagon, an almsdish, and a spoon, all of silver-gilt.[67] The church retains the plate given in 1862.[68]

Three bells hung in the church in 1553 and 1834.[69] A plan of 1699 to recast the bells as a large bell and a sanctus bell was presumably ineffective.[70] The ring was increased to five in 1844, when a treble and a second cast by Thomas Mears at London were added to a bell of 1663 cast by William Purdue at Salisbury, a tenor of 1742 cast by Henry Bagley probably at Witney (Oxon.), and a bell of 1771 cast by Robert Wells at Aldbourne.[71] Those five bells hung in the church in 1995,[72] having been repaired and rehung in 1932–3[73] and 1962.[74]

The parish registers are complete from 1575; registrations of baptisms begin c. 1569.[75]

NONCONFORMITY. Sir Bulstrode Whitelocke, who lived at Chilton Lodge 1663–75, supported Independency. He attended Chilton Foliat church regularly and, often on a Sunday on which he went to church, held conventicles at his house. Those preaching at the conventicles included James Hounsell, the minister ejected from Chilton Foliat at the Restoration, George Cokayn, Whitelocke himself, and James Pearson, a member of Whitelocke's household.[76] In 1672 a room in the house was

50 Phillipps, *Wilts. Inst.* ii. 89; *Vis. Queries, 1783* (W.R.S. xxvii), p. 135; *Alum. Oxon. 1715–1886*, iii. 1131.
51 *W.A.M.* xli. 132.
52 Ibid.; *Vis. Queries, 1783* (W.R.S. xxvii), pp. 60–1; *V.C.H. Wilts.* xii. 46.
53 *Alum. Oxon. 1715–1886*, iii. 1132; *Kelly's Dir. Wilts.* (1848 and later edns.); W.R.O., D 1/48/5, f. 73; D 1/56/7; P.R.O., HO 129/121/2/10/17.
54 *Crockford* (1967–8 and later edns.); W.R.O. 2395/7.
55 W.R.O. 735/19, f. 4.
56 *Endowed Char. Wilts.* (N. Div.), 227.
57 W.R.O. 2281/4, abstr. of title.
58 J. Ecton, *Thesaurus* (1763), 405.
59 W.R.O., D 1/43/2, f. 14.
60 J. Buckler, watercolour in W.A.S. Libr., vol. iv. 2.
61 Hist. MSS. Com. 15, *10th Rep. VI, Braye*, p. 174; *Diary of the Marches of the Royal Army* (Camd. Soc. [1st ser.], lxxiv), 153.
62 W.R.O. 735/20.

63 Pevsner, *Wilts.* (2nd edn.), 166; *Topog. and Geneal.* iii. 580.
64 W.R.O., D 1/61/17/17.
65 Ibid. D 1/61/70/16; D 1/61/73/43; ibid. 735/46.
66 J. Britton and E. Brayley, *Beauties of Eng. and Wales*, xv (2), 694; cf. above, manors (Chilton Lodge).
67 Nightingale, *Wilts. Plate*, 155; for the date 1699, *W.A.M.* xli. 132; W.R.O. 735/5.
68 Inf. from Mr. Ward.
69 *W.A.M.* xii. 363; *Topog. and Geneal.* iii. 579.
70 W.R.O. 735/20.
71 Walters, *Wilts. Bells*, 55, 301.
72 Inf. from Mr. Ward.
73 W.R.O., D 1/61/76/28; ibid. 735/53.
74 Ibid. 2395/7.
75 Ibid. 735/1–12; 2395/1–3.
76 *Diary of Bulstrode Whitelocke*, 672 sqq.; for Hounsell, cf. above, church; for Cokayn, Spalding, *Contemporaries of Bulstrode Whitelocke*, 51–6; *D.N.B.*; for Pearson, Spalding, *Contemporaries*, 245–6.

licensed as a Congregational meeting place, and at the first meeting after the licence was received Cokayn and Pearson preached to a congregation including strangers from Hungerford and Ramsbury. Whitelocke claimed that at one of the meetings in 1674 Cokayn preached to a congregation of c. 300.[77] The meetings almost certainly ceased on Whitelocke's death: in 1676 there was said to be no more than two nonconformists among the adult males of the parish[78] and in 1683 there was possibly no more than a reputed Quaker.[79] A Quaker and eight members of his family lived in the parish in 1783.[80]

In 1794 a house was certified for meetings of Methodists, and in 1796 a medium-sized red-brick Methodist chapel was built. In 1820 a licence was also granted for Methodists to meet in a courtyard, and a meeting house for Independents was certified in 1832.[81] The one service in the Methodist chapel on Census Sunday in 1851 was attended by 58,[82] and the rector said in 1864 that there were only c. 24 Wesleyans or Independents in the parish.[83] The chapel was enlarged in 1932[84] and was closed between 1988 and 1994.[85]

EDUCATION. In 1770 Roger Spanswick and his wife Elizabeth, according to the wish of Elizabeth's aunt Sarah Smith, gave the income from £600 stock to pay for 16 poor children of the parish to be taught. From 1771 a schoolmaster was given £16 a year to teach boys the elements and to pay a woman to teach girls reading, household work, and plainwork: surplus income was to be spent on books.[86] At his request £100 stock of the estate of the Revd. Walter Bigg (d. 1772) was added to the endowment by his administrator in 1772.[87] The school was to be open from the later of 7 a.m. or sunrise, on four days of the week to 5 p.m. and to noon on two. It was to be closed on Sundays and on seven other days of the year, including the king's birthday. It is likely that the master also accepted private boarding pupils[88] and that he held the charity school in his own house.[89] In 1783 the children were being taught the catechism at the school, the conduct of which, according to the curate, himself a schoolmaster, had recently improved.[90] The schoolmaster was being paid £20 a year in the early 19th century.[91] In 1816 he refused to teach, and the school was closed, because all the trustees holding the endowment

had died; the school was reopened in 1817 when Chancery appointed new trustees. In 1818 a mistress received £20 for teaching 8 boys and 8 girls, and there were another 12–14 pupils in her school; c. 40 children were taught at two other schools in the parish, and 40 attended a National school recently opened at Hungerford.[92] In 1833 there were still three schools in the parish with a total of 41 pupils, and c. 16 children still attended Hungerford National school.[93]

A National school in Chilton Foliat was opened in 1835[94] and, on the north side of the street, a new building for it was erected in 1847.[95] In 1857 that school had 60–70 pupils, and 20–30 children were taught in two dame schools.[96] There were 66 pupils at the National school on return day in 1871,[97] 87 on the roll and two teachers in 1902.[98] Average attendance fell from 81 in 1906[99] with some fluctuations to 56 in 1937–8.[1] The income from Spanswick's charity, £18 in 1904, was given to the school.[2] In 1970 a new primary school was built in Stag Hill and the old one closed.[3] The school had 99 pupils on the roll in 1995.[4]

CHARITIES FOR THE POOR. In the later 16th century two or three small sums of money, from one of which the rector was to give 2s. 6d. a year for clothing, were held as stock for the poor,[5] but apparently no eleemosynary charity endured.

By will proved 1856 Sarah Hawkins gave the interest from £179 for clothes, food, or fuel to be given to the poor yearly. In the earlier 20th century the income, c. £5 a year, was spent on coal, small amounts of which were given to many parishioners: in 1910, for example, 80 cwt. was shared among 60. In the mid 20th century small gifts of money were made instead: 3s. was given to each of 32 elderly people in 1955.[6] Money from the Ellen Wilson Fund[7] was added to the charity's income from 1961, and in the 1960s coal was again distributed.[8]

Dame Dinah Pearce (d. 1918) gave by will £200 stock for the sick and poor of Chilton Foliat parish: the gift was on condition that the trustees maintained her son's and his wife's tomb at Chilton Foliat.[9] In the early 1920s most of the income was spent on weekly doles of 1s. for 3–4 pensioners; later it was given to a general fund for the sick and poor.[10]

In the 1990s Chilton Foliat parish council

[77] Diary of Bulstrode Whitelocke, 795, 825; Meeting Ho. Certs. (W.R.S. xl), p. 172.
[78] Compton Census, ed. Whiteman, 126.
[79] W.R.O., D 1/54/10/2.
[80] Vis. Queries, 1783 (W.R.S. xxvii), p. 60.
[81] Meeting Ho. Certs. (W.R.S. xl), pp. 42, 44–5, 91, 129; the chapel is misidentified as Baptist in V.C.H. Wilts. iii. 137: cf. W.R.O., D 1/2/29, (2nd foliation) f. 7.
[82] P.R.O., HO 129/121/2/10/18.
[83] W.R.O., D 1/56/7.
[84] Ibid. G 8/760/153; date on bldg.
[85] W.R.O. 2193/27.
[86] Ibid. 1814/3.
[87] Char. Don. H.C. 511 (1816), xvi (2), 1352–3; Educ. of Poor Digest, 1022; Som. R.O., DD/PO 5E, admin. of Wal. Bigg.
[88] W.R.O. 1814/5.
[89] Endowed Char. Wilts. (N. Div.), 227.
[90] Vis. Queries, 1783 (W.R.S. xxvii), p. 61.
[91] W.R.O. 1814/4.

[92] Ibid. 1814/6; Educ. of Poor Digest, 21, 1022.
[93] Educ. Enq. Abstract, 20, 1032.
[94] Return of Non-Provided Schs. 36.
[95] Kelly's Dir. Wilts. (1885).
[96] Acct. of Wilts. Schs. 14.
[97] Returns relating to Elem. Educ. 418–19.
[98] W.R.O., F 8/220/1.
[99] Return of Non-Provided Schs. 36.
[1] Bd. of Educ., List 21, 1906–38 (H.M.S.O.).
[2] Endowed Char. Wilts. (N. Div.), 228.
[3] W.R.O., F 8/600/64/1/27/1.
[4] Wilts. co. council, Sched. of Educ. Establishments (1995), p. 2.
[5] W.R.O. 735/19, ff. 4, 9, 12v.
[6] Ibid. L 2, Chilton Foliat (Hawkins); Endowed Char. Wilts. (N. Div.), 229.
[7] Below, this section.
[8] W.R.O. 2281/2.   [9] Char. Com. file.
[10] W.R.O., L 2, Chilton Foliat (Pearce).

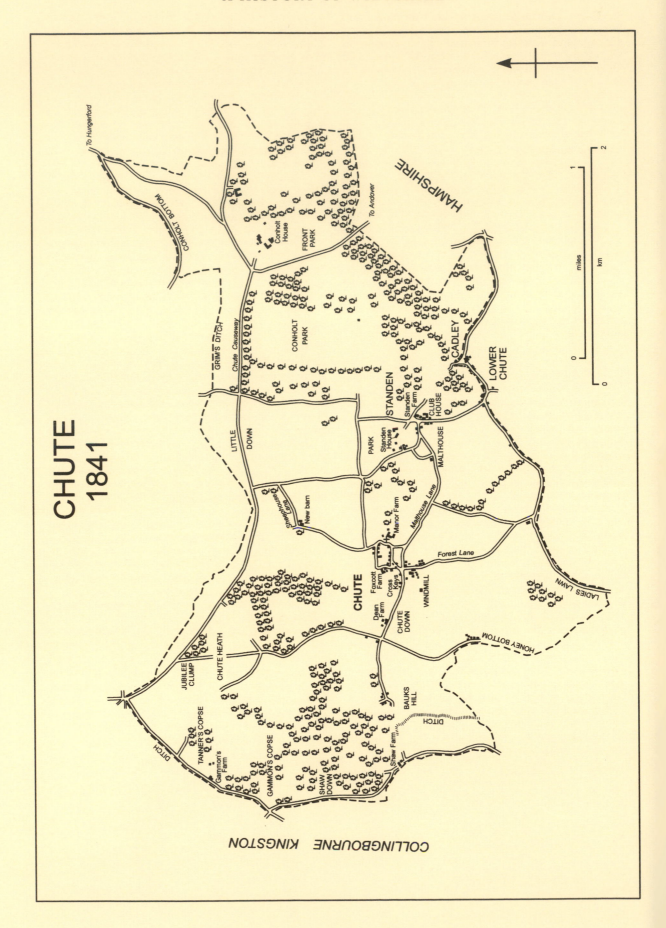

CHUTE
1841

managed Hawkins's and Pearce's eleemosynary charities, Bethell's fire-engine charity, Dame Dinah Pearce's church-room charity, and two charities for the general benefit of the parish, the Ellen Wilson Memorial Fund set up by S. G.

Chamberlain in 1959 and the Dora, Lady Romilly, Fund set up by William Romilly, Lord Romilly, in 1962. In 1994 the income from all the charities was £446: £168 was spent on gifts distributed to old people at Christmas.[11]

CHUTE

CHUTE parish,[12] 1,318 ha. (3,256 a.), lies c. 10 km. north-west of Andover (Hants). It contained villages and hamlets named Chute, Cadley, Lower Chute, Conholt, Shaw, and Standen: in the 20th century the epithet Upper was added to the name Chute and, to distinguish them from eponymous settlements elsewhere in Wiltshire, the word Chute was added as a prefix to the names Cadley and Standen. The names as they were c. 1900 are used throughout this article.[13]

From the 14th century the parish was bordered by Chute forest on the north, south, and east. On the north the boundary followed a probably prehistoric ditch, the bottom of a deep dry valley, and, for a short distance, a Roman road. On the south it ignored relief; it was apparently marked by a road in the 14th century and was in the 17th century and later; to the west it was settled in 1809 by commissioners under an Act of 1808. On the east the parish boundary is Wiltshire's boundary with Hampshire; that the county boundary was apparently less intricate in the 14th century than it was in the 19th suggests that part of Chute forest was transferred to the parish from Hampshire after 1330. On the west the parish boundary follows a prehistoric ditch for c. 1 km. and, further south, two dry valleys.[14]

Chalk outcrops over the whole parish, in which no stream runs. The land falls from north to south and is broken by, mainly north–south, ridges and dry valleys. The only flat land is the highest, that along the northern boundary where it reaches 255 m. and clay-with-flints overlies the chalk. Gravel has been deposited in Conholt bottom, the deep valley followed by the northern boundary. The lowest land in the parish is at c. 125 m. at its southernmost point.[15] In the Middle Ages Chute, probably Conholt and Standen, and possibly Shaw had open fields. Extensive common pasture lay in the west part of the parish, and woodland stood in most parts.[16]

There were apparently 129 poll-tax payers in the parish in 1377.[17] In 1801 the population numbered 389. It rose steadily to reach its peak of 571 in 1851 and declined steadily to reach 388 in 1891. From 410 in 1911 it had declined to 301

by 1931, and from 329 in 1951[18] to 275 by 1961. The population numbered 309 in 1991.[19]

The Roman road between Cirencester and Winchester deviates south-westwards from its otherwise straight course to avoid broken relief: part of the straight course and much of the deviation cross Chute parish[20] and were in use as roads in 1997. Some of the straight course in the parish was a section of a road between Hungerford (Berks.) and Andover; the rest went out of use when, before the later 18th century, the land which it crossed west of Conholt House was imparked.[21] The deviation, on the high ground near the parish's northern boundary, was called the Causeway or Causeway Lane in 1841,[22] Chute Causeway in 1997. A new section of the Andover road was made between 1820 and 1841 to take traffic away from Conholt House.[23] No road across the parish was turnpiked, and no major road crossed it in 1997. The pattern of lanes, most of which ran north–south with the relief, changed little between the later 18th century and the late 20th. Sheephouse Lane, leading north from Chute village, was apparently made between 1773 and 1817.[24] An east–west road linking Chute and Standen was called Malthouse Lane in 1841[25] and later.

Four barrows in the parish have been identified, all in the west part. The ditch which marks the north part of the parish's western boundary is older than the Roman road; Grim's ditch, which marks the northern boundary, is probably prehistoric, and there is another prehistoric ditch near the western boundary. Two prehistoric field systems in the south-west part of the parish have been identified.[26]

The whole parish lay in Chute forest in the 13th century. It was disafforested in 1330.[27]

CHUTE. In the Middle Ages Chute village probably consisted of the church, the demesne farmstead of Chute manor immediately east of it, a vicarage house north-west of it, and the farmsteads of the customary holdings of the manor in a short lane west of it. There was apparently a small green at the west end of the lane.[28]

[11] Char. Com. files; for the fire engine and church room, above, intro.
[12] This article was written in 1997.
[13] Maps used include O.S. Maps 6", Wilts. XLIII, XLIX (1882–3 and later edns.); 1/25,000, SU 25/35 (1994 edn.); 1", sheets 12, 14 (1817 edns.).
[14] V.C.H. Wilts. iv. 452–3; P.R.O., MR 342; W.R.O. 304/1; for the ditches and the Rom. road, below, this section.
[15] Geol. Surv. Map 1/50,000, drift, sheet 283 (1975 edn.).
[16] Below, econ. hist.
[17] V.C.H. Wilts. iv. 309, where the attribution of Standen to Hungerford par. seems incorrect.
[18] Ibid. 345.

[19] Census, 1961; 1991.
[20] I. D. Margary, Rom. Roads in Brit. (1973), pp. 98–9.
[21] Andrews and Dury, Map (W.R.S. viii), pl. 9; for Conholt Ho. and its park, below, manors (Conholt).
[22] W.R.O., tithe award.
[23] Ibid.; C. Greenwood, Map of Wilts. (1820).
[24] Andrews and Dury, Map (W.R.S. viii), pl. 9; O.S. Map 1", sheet 12 (1817 edn.).
[25] W.R.O., tithe award.
[26] V.C.H. Wilts. i (1), 139, 166, 254, 275; W.A.M. lviii. 37; inf. from Arch. section, Co. Hall, Trowbridge.
[27] V.C.H. Wilts. iv. 399–400, 425, 452–3.
[28] Cf. W.R.O., tithe award; below, econ. hist. (Chute).

Manor Farm, the demesne farmhouse, was apparently large in the later 18th century, when it had a small formal garden east of it.[29] In 1897 it was called Chute Manor and was apparently a house built in the late 17th century and altered in the earlier or mid 19th; it had a canted entrance bay in the middle of its main front.[30] It was demolished in the mid 20th century.[31] In 1997 modern farm buildings and large buildings of brick and flint stood east of the church. In 1841 a small farmstead, including a house later called Parsonage Farm, stood near the vicarage house;[32] the house, apparently 18th-century, was standing in 1997, when the farm buildings included some apparently of the 19th century and some of the 20th. An 18th-century thatched cottage stood nearby. In 1841 only two farmsteads stood west of the church. The farm buildings of one of them, Foxcott Farm, which stood north of the green at the end of the lane, had been demolished by 1879,[33] and the farmhouse, possibly 18th-century, had been converted to a pair of cottages by the late 19th century.[34] A thatched house of the 18th century, two large 19th-century houses, one of brick and flint, and a 20th-century house stood in the lane in 1997. A building on the east part of the green was replaced by a pair of cottages built in 1904.[35]

South-west of the church cottages were built from the 18th century or earlier on waste ground from which a lane later called Forest Lane led southwards. In 1841 c. 25 cottages stood there,[36] and a nonconformist chapel was built in the later 19th century.[37] Several cottages built of rubble and thatch in the 18th century or earlier survived in 1997. Other cottages were replaced in the 20th century.

At its west end Malthouse Lane bifurcates: one branch leads north to the church, the other west along the north edge of the waste ground on which the cottages stood in 1841. On the south side of the west branch a thatched house was built, probably in the 18th century, and a brick and flint house was built in the 19th; west of those houses and on the north side of the lane the Cross Keys was probably built in the early 19th century and was open as a public house from 1822[38] or earlier and in 1997.

The two parts of Chute village were linked by 20th-century building between the west branch of Malthouse Lane and the lane leading west from the church. The rural district council built 4 houses there in 1930,[39] 4 houses in 1950,[40] and 2 bungalows later, and 17 private houses were built in the 1990s. In 1975 the village was designated a conservation area.[41]

CADLEY AND LOWER CHUTE. Two small settlements, mainly of cottages built on common pasture, had grown up along the southern boundary of the parish by the 18th century, and by the later 18th century buildings had been erected beside the road linking them. Other buildings were later erected on the small allotments into which the common was divided in 1820.[42] Several of the buildings of each settlement, and those on the south side of the road, stood in Chute Forest parish.

At Cadley, north-east of Lower Chute, the cottages were built around a steeply sloping triangular green, on which in the 19th and 20th centuries there was a pond.[43] Around the green in 1841 there stood 13 cottages and houses, two of which were each divided into three tenements.[44] The cottages and houses standing in 1997 included several built of brick and flint between the 17th century and the early 19th and a pair of estate cottages built in the 1930s. In the later 18th century and earlier 19th a small group of cottages north of the green was apparently called Hatchett; the cottages had been demolished by 1841.[45]

At Lower Chute 10 cottages and houses, one divided into four tenements, were standing in 1841.[46] Those surviving in 1997 included an 18th-century house with walls of chalk, flint, and timber, a thatched cottage of the 18th century or earlier, and a possibly 17th-century house, of a single storey and attics and with a thatched roof, open in 1901 or earlier and in 1997 as the Hatchet public house.[47] The building divided into four tenements was replaced by a house built in 1879 and open as the Star public house from the 1880s until 1939[48] or later.

Several buildings were standing on both sides of the road between Cadley and Lower Chute in 1773.[49] A nonconformist chapel astride the boundary with Chute Forest was built in the mid 19th century.[50] The cottages and houses standing in 1997 included a mid 18th-century house of knapped flint with brick dressings and a thatched roof, three thatched cottages apparently of the 18th century or earlier, and several 20th-century houses and bungalows.

The north-east and south-west line of settlement was extended in both those directions in the 20th century. To the north-east Home Farm, incorporating a house, farm buildings, and a pair and a trio of cottages, was built c. 1905. To the south-west a British Legion club had been built by 1923[51] and eight houses and bungalows were built. The club was later enlarged and was open in 1997. The south-west extension embraced an

29   *Andrews and Dury, Map* (W.R.S. viii), pl. 9; W.R.O., tithe award.
30   W.R.O. 2715/7, sale cat. of Conholt Park estate.
31   O.S. Maps 6", Wilts. XLIX. NW. (1926 edn.); 1/25,000, SU 35 (1958 edn.); local inf.
32   W.R.O., tithe award; for the vicarage ho., below, church.
33   O.S. Map 6", Wilts. XLIX (1883 edn.); W.R.O., tithe award.
34   O.S. Map 1/2,500, Wilts. XLIX. 2 (1900 edn.).
35   Ibid.; ibid. (1924 edn.); date on bldg.
36   W.R.O., tithe award.   37   Below, nonconf.
38   W.R.O., A 1/326/3.   39   Ibid. G 10/603/2.
40   Ibid. G 10/505/1.
41   Inf. from Dept. of Planning and Highways, Co. Hall, Trowbridge.

42   *Andrews and Dury, Map* (W.R.S. viii), pl. 9; W.R.O. 304/1; ibid. tithe award.
43   O.S. Maps 6", Wilts. XLIX (1883 and later edns.).
44   W.R.O., tithe award; Chute Forest tithe award.
45   *Andrews and Dury, Map* (W.R.S. viii), pl. 9; *Meeting Ho. Certs.* (W.R.S. xl), p. 146; W.R.O., tithe award.
46   W.R.O., tithe award; Chute Forest tithe award.
47   Ibid. 2715/5, sale cat., 1901.
48   Ibid. tithe award; *Kelly's Dir. Wilts.* (1889 and later edns.); O.S. Map 1/2,500, Wilts. XLIX. 2 (1900 edn.); date on bldg.
49   *Andrews and Dury, Map* (W.R.S. viii), pl. 9.
50   Below, nonconf.
51   *Kelly's Dir. Wilts.* (1903, 1907); O.S. Maps 1/2,500, Wilts. XLIX. 2 (1900, 1924 edns.).

apparently 18th-century thatched cottage and a pair of mid 19th-century cottages.[52]

The combined settlement, except the two extensions, was designated a conservation area in 1994.[53]

CONHOLT may have been a small village in the 13th century, when Conholt manor included 17 customary tenants.[54] The site of such a village has not been identified, and by the 16th century there may have been no more than four farmsteads on Conholt's land.[55] By the later 18th century much of the land had been imparked, and Conholt House, which is of 17th-century origin, its outbuildings immediately north of it, and a barn in the park were apparently the only buildings standing on it.[56] The barn had been demolished by 1817,[57] and between 1820 and 1841 a new farmyard, later called Middle Conholt Farm, was built north-east of Conholt House.[58] Between 1879 and 1899 two pairs of cottages were built, one beside the Andover road and one at Middle Conholt Farm.[59] Beside Chute Causeway a pair of cottages was built between 1899 and 1923[60] and later demolished. At Middle Conholt Farm in the 20th century two pairs of cottages were built and farm buildings were renewed.

SHAW. In the Middle Ages Shaw was probably a small settlement in the deep valley followed by the west boundary of the parish where a farmstead called Shaw Farm stood alone in 1773.[61] The farmhouse was destroyed by fire in the 1940s[62] and the last building was removed from the site in the late 20th century.[63]

STANDEN. On a site where three valleys meet Standen was probably a small village in the Middle Ages. In the 17th century Standen Farm and a timber-framed and thatched house of that century, both of which survive, were standing on that site, and on high ground to the north-west Standen House is also of 17th-century origin.[64] A thatched lodge west of Standen House was built in the 18th century and was standing in 1997. In 1841 all those buildings, a few other houses, and a club room or school constituted the village.[65] Standen Farm, called the Dower House in 1997, is a brick and flint house of four bays on an L plan. An early 17th-century chimney stack stands between the two east bays; the west part of the house is

mostly 18th-century. Extensions of the 20th century include one which links the house to a former outbuilding with a queen-strut roof. A friendly society met in the club room, which was called the Adelphi in 1815.[66] In the 19th century a weatherboarded granary, apparently other farm buildings, and a brick and flint house were built south of Standen Farm, and in the 20th century new farm buildings were erected there.

A little west of Standen the site of a malthouse was used for a school built in the mid 19th century and converted to a village hall after 1978.[67]

OTHER SETTLEMENT. Away from the villages and hamlets most settlement in the parish has been in the west part. In a valley west of Chute village a farmstead on the site of Dean Farm may have been standing in the 16th century.[68] Dean Farm is a farmhouse built in the early 18th century with walls of knapped flint, a thatched roof, and a five-bayed south front. A rear wing was added in the 18th century; most of the farm buildings were removed in the mid 20th.[69] South of Dean Farm and in the same valley, there called Honey bottom, a group of five or six cottages had been built by 1773;[70] one enlarged and apparently of the 18th century stood there in 1997. Another group of cottages built by 1773 stood on Bauks hill west of Dean Farm; six buildings divided into 10 tenements stood there in 1841,[71] none in 1997.

On high ground in the north-west part of the parish a house called Gammon's had been built by 1773,[72] and in 1841 a barn stood on the parish boundary nearby;[73] the house was demolished in the mid 20th century.[74] In 1997 Gammon's Farm, consisting of a house and farm buildings all of the 20th century, stood on the site of the barn. In the 19th century two other farmsteads were built on high ground. A farmyard called New Barn, of which two brick and flint buildings survived in 1997, was built north of Chute village between 1820 and 1841; a pair of cottages between 1841 and 1879, and a house in the 20th century, were added. New Zealand Farm was built 600 m. east of Gammon's Farm between 1841 and 1879.[75] In the mid 20th century Chantry Farm was built south of New Zealand Farm, buildings called the Rutherfords Stud were erected north-west

[52] O.S. Map 6", Wilts. XLIX (1883 edn.); W.R.O., tithe award.
[53] Inf. from Dept. of Planning and Highways, Co. Hall, Trowbridge.
[54] *Custumals of Battle Abbey* (Camd. Soc. N.S. xli), 69–70.
[55] Below, manors (Conholt); econ. hist. (Conholt).
[56] *Andrews and Dury, Map* (W.R.S. viii), pl. 9; for Conholt Ho., below, manors (Conholt).
[57] O.S. Map 1", sheet 12 (1817 edn.).
[58] Greenwood, *Map of Wilts.*; W.R.O., tithe award.
[59] O.S. Maps 6", Wilts. XLIII (1882 edn.); 1/2,500, XLIII. 15 (1900 edn.).
[60] Ibid. 1/2,500, Wilts. XLIII. 14 (1900, 1924 edns.).
[61] *Andrews and Dury, Map* (W.R.S. viii), pl. 9; cf. below, manors (Shaw); econ. hist. (Shaw).
[62] Inf. from Mr. M. Sykes, Chute Farms Ltd.
[63] O.S. Map 1/25,000, SU 25/35 (1994 edn.); air photo.

in possession of Arch. section, Co. Hall, Trowbridge.
[64] For Standen Ho., below, manors (Standen).
[65] W.R.O., tithe award.
[66] P.R.O., FS 4/55, Wilts. no. 4.
[67] W.R.O., tithe award; below, educ.
[68] W.R.O. 9/11/18; Dept. of Environment, list of bldgs. of hist. interest (1988).
[69] O.S. Maps 6", Wilts. XLIX. NW. (1926 edn.); 1/25,000, SU 25 (1958 edn.).
[70] *Andrews and Dury, Map* (W.R.S. viii), pl. 9.
[71] Ibid.; W.R.O., tithe award.
[72] *Andrews and Dury, Map* (W.R.S. viii), pl. 9.
[73] W.R.O., tithe award.
[74] O.S. Maps 6", Wilts. XLIII. SW. (1926 edn.); 1/25,000, SU 25 (1958 edn.).
[75] Greenwood, *Map of Wilts.*; O.S. Map 6", Wilts. XLIII (1882 edn.); W.R.O., tithe award.

of Dean Farm, and Collis Farm was built south-east of Chute village.[76]

MANORS AND OTHER ESTATES. In 1066 St. Peter's abbey, Winchester, held the land of Chute as part of its estate called Collingbourne. The land was part of an estate, held of the abbey and assessed at 10 hides and ½ yardland, which became heritable between 1066 and 1086.[77] The overlordship of Chute manor belonged to the abbey, otherwise called the New minster and from 1109 called Hyde abbey, until the Dissolution.[78]

The estate assessed at 10 hides and ½ yardland consisted of what became *CHUTE* manor and what became Collingbourne Valence manor in Collingbourne Kingston.[79] In 1086 it was held by Croc the huntsman,[80] and it presumably descended to his son Rainald, to Matthew Croke (fl. 1156), and with the manor of Crux Easton (Hants) to Matthew Croke (fl. 1163, d. by 1200), whose son Ellis (d. 1215) held Chute manor.[81] The manor passed to Ellis's daughter Avice (d. c. 1259), the wife of Michael de Columbers (d. 1235), and to Avice's son Matthew de Columbers[82] (d. c. 1272–3), whose heir was his brother Michael. It apparently passed to Michael and to his daughter Nichole, the wife of John de Lisle (d. 1304), whose son Sir John de Lisle (d. c. 1331) held it in 1329. The manor descended in the direct line to Bartholomew[83] (d. 1345), Sir John[84] (d. 1370), John[85] (d. 1407), John[86] (d. 1429), Sir John[87] (d. c. 1471), Sir Nicholas[88] (will proved 1506), and Sir John Lisle (d. s.p., will proved 1524). On Sir John's death Chute manor apparently passed with the manor of Thruxton (Hants) to his sister Eleanor, the wife of John Kingston, and, after the death of Eleanor's sons John Kingston and Nicholas Kingston, to her daughter Mary (d. s.p. 1539), the wife of Sir Thomas Lisle (d. 1542).[89] Sir Thomas held Chute manor in 1539.[90] On his death the manor apparently reverted, as Thruxton manor did, to Sir Nicholas Lisle's grandnephew Thomas Philpot (d. 1586), who held it in 1576. It descended in the direct line to Sir George[91] (d. 1622), Sir John[92] (d. 1634), and Henry Philpot (fl. 1651), whose relict Mary Philpot held it in 1684.[93]

By 1691 Chute manor had been acquired by Thomas Arundell[94] (Lord Arundell from 1694, d. 1712). It passed in the direct line to Henry, Lord Arundell (d. 1726), Henry, Lord Arundell (d. 1746), Henry, Lord Arundell (d. 1756), and Henry, Lord Arundell, who in 1778 sold it to John Freeman.[95] On Freeman's death in 1794 it passed to his son Strickland.[96] In each case presumably by sale it passed c. 1809 from Strickland Freeman to George Smith and c. 1814 from Smith to Evelyn Medows,[97] the owner of Conholt manor. Chute manor descended with Conholt manor from c. 1814 to 1897, when Manor farm, 836 a., apparently comprised most of it.[98]

Manor farm may have been bought c. 1897 by E. B. Maton; by 1903 it had been bought by Freville Cookson (d. 1909), the owner of an estate at Standen.[99] Cookson's executors owned Manor farm in 1923.[1] In 1926 a diminished Manor farm was bought by Ulric Hopton; it passed to his son John (d. 1969), whose relict Mrs. J. Hopton held the farm, 200 a., in 1997.[2] Part of Manor farm was bought c. 1924 by J. R. Hamilton, who also owned New Zealand farm, and, with New Zealand farm, c. 220 a. of Manor farm south-west of Chute village became part of the Chantry estate and remained so in 1998. Other parts of Manor farm had been added to Dean farm by 1985 and were part of it in 1997.[3]

Although it had alienated what became Chute manor, Hyde abbey retained c. 2 yardlands at Chute which in the earlier 13th century was held customarily of it. The land, the tenant of most of which was then Hugh of the dean,[4] is likely to have been that later called *DEAN* farm and possibly held freely by members of the Corderoy family from the mid 14th century. The farm probably descended in the Corderoy family with land at Conholt and from c. 1549 with the Chantry estate. William Corderoy sold it to John Foyle (d. 1648), probably in 1624. From 1635 it descended with the Chantry estate. Foyle was succeeded by his grandson John Foyle (d. 1671) and he by his sons Robert (d. 1689) and Edward (d. 1719) in turn. From Edward the composite estate descended in the direct line to Edward (d. 1736), Gorges (d. 1801), and George Foyle (d. 1839),[5] who owned 613 a. in the parish.[6] The

76 O.S. Maps 6", Wilts. XLIII. SW. (1926 edn.); XLIX. NW. (1926 edn.); 1/25,000, SU 25 (1958 edn.); SU 35 (1958 edn.); 1/10,000, SU 25 SE. (1978 edn.).
77 *V.C.H. Wilts.* ii, p. 127.
78 *V.C.H. Hants*, ii. 116–17; *Bk. of Fees*, ii. 747; *Feud. Aids*, v. 263; P.R.O., SC 6/Hen. VIII/3341, rot. 52d.
79 Cf. *Close R.* 1234–7, 74; for Collingbourne Valence manor, below, Collingbourne Kingston, manors.
80 *V.C.H. Wilts.* ii, p. 127.
81 Ibid. iv. 425; *V.C.H. Hants*, iv. 312; *Close R.* 1234–7, 73–4.
82 *Close R.* 1234–7, 73–4; *Wilts. Inq. p.m.* 1242–1326 (Index Libr.), 30; *V.C.H. Wilts.* iv. 425.
83 *V.C.H. Hants*, iv. 312, 353; *Wilts. Inq. p.m.* 1327–77 (Index Libr.), 70; *Colln. Topog. et Geneal.* vii. 148; P.R.O., C 143/204, no. 19.
84 *Wilts. Inq. p.m.* 1327–77 (Index Libr.), 168–9.
85 Ibid. 364–5. 86 *V.C.H. Hants*, iv. 388.
87 P.R.O., C 139/39, no. 42, rot. 4.
88 Ibid. C 140/39, no. 59, rot. 8.
89 *V.C.H. Hants*, iv. 388.
90 P.R.O., SC 6/Hen. VIII/3341, rot. 52d.
91 Ibid. CP 25/2/260/18 & 19 Eliz. I Mich.; ibid. E 134/33 & 34 Eliz. I Mich./10; *V.C.H. Hants*, iii. 407; iv.

388.
92 P.R.O., C 142/402, no. 129.
93 Ibid. CP 25/2/512/18 Chas. I Trin.; CP 25/2/763/36 Chas. II East.; *V.C.H. Hants*, iv. 388; W.R.O. 212B/1863.
94 W.R.O. 564/1.
95 *Complete Peerage*, i. 265–6; P.R.O., KB 122/426, rot. 344. 96 P.R.O., PROB 11/1249, ff. 243v.–245.
97 W.R.O., A 1/345/111.
98 Ibid. 2715/7, sale cat. of Conholt Park estate; below, this section (Conholt).
99 *Kelly's Dir. Wilts.* (1899, 1903); below, this section (Standen). 1 W.R.O., G 10/500/19.
2 Inf. from Mrs. J. Hopton, Chute Manor.
3 F. Sykes, *Humus and the Farmer*, end maps; W.R.O., G 10/500/20; ibid. tithe award; below, this section (Dean; Chantry); inf. from Viscount Eccles, Dean Farm; Mr. M. Sykes, Chute Farms Ltd.
4 B.L. Harl. MS. 1761, f. 145 and v.; P.R.O., CP 25/1/251/13, no. 69.
5 G. Gibbon, 'Foyles of Chute and Cholderton' (TS. in Wilts. local studies libr., Trowbridge), 4, 35, 37–8; below, this section (Chantry; Conholt).
6 W.R.O., tithe award.

estate passed to George's daughter Mary Anne, the wife of the Revd. Charles Randolph, and to her son C. F. Randolph (fl. 1910). About 1910 it was acquired by E. S. Latham, presumably by purchase.[7] It belonged to Samuel Cohen in 1917, to Thomas Pile in 1920, when it consisted of Dean farm, c. 320 a., and New Zealand farm.[8] Dean farm, 166 a., was held by Mrs. J. L. Pile in 1929,[9] by J. Thompson in 1935.[10] In 1938 it was bought by David Eccles (cr. Baron Eccles 1962, Viscount Eccles 1964), who added other land to it. In 1985 Lord Eccles conveyed Dean farm, c. 285 a., to his son the Hon. John Eccles, the owner in 1997.[11]

By 1542 the land of a chantry in Chute church had been sold by the chaplain to Thomas Wroth, probably the patron, and John Cork.[12] It passed to the Crown as the estate of a chantry dissolved without licence,[13] and in 1549 it was accounted 80 a. and granted to John Barwick and Robert Freke, agents or speculators[14] who conveyed it to Thomas Corderoy.[15] The *CHANTRY* estate descended in the Corderoy family with most of Conholt's land to William Corderoy, who sold it in 1635 to John Foyle[16] (d. 1648). From 1635 it descended with Dean farm.[17] The composite estate was divided in the early 1920s when c. 435 a. of it was sold as New Zealand farm. J. R. Hamilton owned that farm, to which c. 220 a. of Manor farm was added, from 1924 or earlier to 1931 or later.[18] About 1936 Eleanor, Lady Yarrow, sold it to Friend Sykes (d. 1965). Other land was added to it and in 1997 Sykes's nephew Mr. Michael Sykes owned 770 a. as the Chantry estate, including c. 80 a. in Tidcombe and Fosbury parish.[19]

What became *CONHOLT* manor was held in 1066 by St. Peter's abbey, Winchester, as part of its estate called Collingbourne.[20] In the earlier 13th century the manor was transferred from Hyde abbey,[21] which remained overlord until the Dissolution,[22] to Battle abbey (Suss.), which held it from 1243 or earlier to 1307 or later.[23] The manor was held at her death in 1353 by Anstice, daughter of William Harding and wife of William de Lillebonne and of Sir Robert Bilkemore, and it passed at Sir Robert's death in 1361 to her grandson Sir John Lillebonne.[24] By 1535 it had been divided into three portions,

held by Thomas Corderoy, Brian Fauntleroy, and John Benger.[25] One portion descended from Corderoy (will proved 1547) to his son Thomas,[26] and one from Brian to Henry Fauntleroy. In 1570 Corderoy bought Fauntleroy's;[27] Benger's portion has not been traced.

Most of Conholt's land presumably passed from the younger Thomas Corderoy in turn to his sons Edward (d. 1587) and William (d. 1623), and William's son William[28] probably sold it to Francis Lucy in 1632.[29] Lucy (fl. 1682)[30] owned the estate in 1660,[31] and it apparently passed to his daughter Constance, the wife of Sir Philip Medows (d. 1718). It descended to Sir Philip's, and presumably Constance's, son Sir Philip Medows (d. 1757), to that Sir Philip's son Sir Sydney (d. 1792), and to Sir Sydney's nephew Evelyn Medows (d. *s.p.* 1826), who added Chute manor to it.[32] Under Sir Sydney's will the estate passed in 1826 to his grandnephew Henry Manvers Pierrepont (d. 1851), who held 2,063 a. in the parish in 1841, and in 1851 to Henry's brother Philip (d. 1864).[33] Under Evelyn's will the estate reverted in 1864 to W. H. Norie (d. c. 1896), who took the surname Medows, and in 1897 members of W. H. Medows's family sold it, excluding Manor farm, Chute, to George Knowles.[34] In 1904 Knowles sold Conholt House and c. 1,100 a. in the east part of the parish to E. A. Wigan[35] (d. 1942), under whose will they passed to Henrietta Gaskell[36] (d. 1991). In 1992 the estate was bought, and in 1998 owned, by a company owned by Mr. Paul van Vlissingen's family.[37]

The oldest part of Conholt House, the principal house on the estate, was the main part of a house built in the late 17th century. The 17th-century house, double-pile, of brick, of nine bays, and probably of two storeys, lay north-east and south-west; brick vaulting in its basement suggests that it was a small country house rather than a farmhouse. It had central chimney stacks, rooms with corner fireplaces, and a staircase in the centre of the north-west front, which was probably the entrance front. The main part of Conholt House was built c. 1795.[38] It lies east–west and runs eastwards from the south-west end of the 17th-century house, to which it was linked by an entrance hall. The new block is of two storeys, taller than those of the 17th-century house, has a main south front,

[7] Ibid. Inland Revenue, val. reg. 60; *V.C.H. Hants*, iv. 373; *Kelly's Dir. Wilts.* (1911).
[8] W.R.O., G 10/500/17–18.
[9] Ibid. G 10/500/22.
[10] Ibid. G 10/505/1.
[11] Ibid.; *Who's Who* (1997), 579; inf. from Viscount Eccles.   [12] P.R.O., E 301/59, no. 34; below, church.
[13] *W.A.M.* xii. 377.
[14] *Cal. Pat.* 1549–51, 139–41; P.R.O., E 318/25/1423.
[15] Gibbon, 'Foyles of Chute and Cholderton', 37.
[16] P.R.O., CP 25/2/510/11 Chas. I Mich.; below, this section (Conholt).
[17] Above, this section (Dean).
[18] *Kelly's Dir. Wilts.* (1931); W.R.O., G 10/500/18–19; above, this section (Chute).
[19] Inf. from Mr. Sykes; for the land in Tidcombe and Fosbury par., below, Hippenscombe, manors (Blagden).
[20] *V.C.H. Wilts.* ii, p. 127.
[21] B.L. Harl. MS. 1761, f. 147.
[22] *Wilts. Inq. p.m.* 1327–77 (Index Libr.), 232; P.R.O., SC 6/Hen. VIII/3341, rot. 52d.
[23] *Bk. of Fees*, ii. 705; P.R.O., SC 2/153/67.

[24] *Wilts. Inq. p.m.* 1327–77 (Index Libr.), 231–3, 274–6; below, Milton Lilbourne, manors (Milton Lilbourne).
[25] P.R.O., SC 6/Hen. VIII/3341, rot. 52d.
[26] *Wilts. Pedigrees* (Harl. Soc. cv/cvi), 40.
[27] P.R.O., CP 25/2/239/12 Eliz. I Trin.
[28] *Wilts. Pedigrees* (Harl. Soc. cv/cvi), 40.
[29] *Cal. S.P. Dom.* 1631–3, 371.
[30] Burke, *Commoners* (1833–8), iii. 99.
[31] P.R.O., CP 25/2/760/12 Chas. II Mich.
[32] Ibid. CP 25/2/889/11 Wm. III Hil.; Burke, *Peerage* (1915), 1351–2; W.R.O., A 1/345/111; above, this section (Chute).
[33] Burke, *Peerage* (1915), 1352; W.R.O. 2715/10, notes from doc. lent by Sir Arthur Hareford; ibid. tithe award.
[34] *Kelly's Dir. Wilts.* (1895); W.R.O. 2715/1, deed, Norie to Knowles, 1897; 2715/10, notes from doc. lent by Hareford; above, this section (Chute).
[35] W.R.O. 2715/1, deed, Knowles to Wigan, 1904.
[36] Ibid. 2715/2, deed, Gedge to Gaskell, 1945.
[37] Ibid. 2715/23; inf. from Mr. P. van Vlissingen, Conholt Ho.
[38] W.R.O. 2715/10, statement of facts, 1839.

and contains a drawing room, a dining room, and a library. The five south-westernmost bays of the older house were raised by one storey and refenestrated, and a corridor was made the length of the house south-east of the chimney stack, presumably when the new block was built. In 1826 G. A. Underwood of Bath designed improvements to the house; some of the main features he proposed were incorporated in designs by J. H. Langdon which were executed soon afterwards.[39] The south front was refaced with buff brick and given new window surrounds; on the north side a cantilevered staircase and a canted two-storeyed projection were built. The entrance hall between the two ranges was slightly altered, and a semicircular porch of Ionic columns was added to it as a west entrance. New plasterwork was done in the drawing room and the dining room and plain neoclassical fireplaces were inserted in the first-floor rooms of the 18th-century block. Later in the 19th century a single-storeyed east bay was added, c. 1928 the roof of the house was replaced by one incorporating an attic storey, c. 1957 the north-easternmost bay of the older part of the house and a service building were demolished, and in the later 1990s a covered swimming pool was built immediately north of the house.[40]

In the late 18th century a large riding school and stables were built immediately north-west of the house. The riding school was demolished in 1896;[41] the stables, L-shaped in plan, were standing in 1997, and in the 20th century cottages were built against them to form a court. East of the house the walls of a kitchen garden had been built by 1841; they and a late 19th-century orchid house were standing in 1997. North of the house farm buildings had been erected by 1841;[42] those on the site in 1997 were mostly 20th-century.

A park for Conholt House was probably made in the late 17th century or early 18th. In 1773 a park of c. 47 a., the Front park, lay south of the house, and Conholt park, c. 350 a., lay west of the Andover road and of the house. In Conholt park there were straight walks through a plantation west of the house, a formal garden west of that, and a main roughly north–south avenue to the south. The formality of those features suggests that they were designed c. 1700. In 1841 the main avenue still led through woodland west of the house; the walks and the garden may not have survived until then.[43] In 1997 the Front park remained pasture, and several avenues,

which were poorly preserved until 1992, survived in Conholt park. Many trees were planted in Conholt park between 1992 and 1997, when the park was used partly for farming.[44]

From 1539, when it was held by Thomas Sotwell, or earlier a holding of land at Conholt called *EASTCOURT*[45] descended in the Sotwell family with an estate at Standen and until 1628 with a farm at West Grafton in Great Bedwyn.[46] In 1705 it belonged to Sir Philip Medows,[47] and it was thereafter part of the Conholt estate.[48]

In 1086 the land of *SHAW* was probably part of the estate of St. Peter's abbey, Winchester, called Collingbourne. The abbey's estate included Sunton in Collingbourne Kingston,[49] and later each of two manors called Sunton included land of Shaw. Hugh Thorold, the lord of one of them, held some in 1394,[50] and John Benger, the lord of the other, held some in 1447.[51] Benger's manor descended from 1548 in the Seymour, Bruce, Brudenell, and Brudenell-Bruce families with Tottenham Lodge and Tottenham House in Great Bedwyn,[52] and land called Gammon's was held by Edward Seymour, earl of Hertford (d. 1621).[53] Thorold's manor had been acquired by Thomas Bruce, earl of Ailesbury, by 1780, and thereafter it descended with Tottenham House.[54] In 1929 George Brudenell-Bruce, marquess of Ailesbury, owned 179 a. in Chute parish and sold 108 a. as Shaw farm and 71 a. as part of Gammon's farm, 288 a., which lay mainly in Collingbourne Kingston parish.[55] About 1964 the land of both farms was bought by Mr. M. K. B. Colvin, who sold it in 1975 to Mr. J. R. Crook. In 1997 Mr. Crook owned the land as Gammon's farm, 425 a.[56]

In the 16th century the land of *STANDEN* apparently lay in two estates. One belonged to Thomas Sotwell in 1539[57] and descended with a farm in West Grafton to Richard Sotwell (d. 1628).[58] Richard's heir was his son John.[59] By 1705 the estate in Standen had possibly been acquired by Sir Philip Medows, as Eastcourt had;[60] in 1773 the estate, as Standen farm, c. 175 a., was part of Sir Sydney Medows's Conholt estate,[61] and, apart from the farmstead and c. 75 a. apparently sold separately c. 1897, it remained part of the Conholt estate in 1997.[62]

In the later 16th century an estate at Standen

---

39 Plans in possession of Mr. van Vlissingen.
40 Inf. from Mr. van Vlissingen.
41 O.S. Maps 6", Wilts. XLIII (1882 edn.); XLIII. SE. (1901 edn.); W.R.O. 2715/10, notes by the duke of Wellington, 1929. 42 W.R.O., tithe award.
43 Ibid.; *Andrews and Dury, Map* (W.R.S. viii), pl. 9, where Conholt park is called Chute park.
44 Inf. from Mr. van Vlissingen.
45 P.R.O., SC 6/Hen. VIII/3341, rot. 52d.
46 Ibid. C 3/352/31; ibid. PROB 11/91, ff. 367–8; above, Great Bedwyn, manors (Sotwell's); below, this section (Standen). 47 W.R.O. 564/1.
48 e.g. ibid. tithe award; *Andrews and Dury, Map* (W.R.S. viii), pl. 9.
49 *V.C.H. Wilts.* ii, p. 127; below, Collingbourne Kingston, manors; the Shaw identified in *V.C.H. Wilts.* ii, pp. 153–4 as that in Chute par. was probably that in Overton: ibid.

xi. 190–1.
50 *Feet of F. 1377–1509* (W.R.S. xli), p. 36.
51 W.R.O. 9/11/6.
52 Above, Great Bedwyn, manors (Tottenham); below, Collingbourne Kingston, manors (Sunton).
53 P.R.O., C 2/Jas. I/F 4/2.
54 Below, Collingbourne Kingston, manors (Sunton).
55 W.R.O. 9/1/521.
56 Inf. from Mr. J. R. Crook, Gammon's Farm.
57 P.R.O., SC 6/Hen. VIII/3341, rot. 52d.
58 Ibid. C 3/352/31; ibid. PROB 11/91, ff. 367–8; above, Great Bedwyn, manors (Sotwell's).
59 *Wilts. Pedigrees* (Harl. Soc. cv/cvi), 185–6.
60 Above, this section (Eastcourt).
61 W.R.O. 1195/18, survey, 1773; ibid. tithe award.
62 Ibid. 2715/7, sale cat. of Conholt Park estate; inf. from Mr. van Vlissingen; above, this section (Conholt).

belonged to Nicholas Bacon[63] (will proved 1599); it passed to his daughter Joan, the wife of William Noyes, who held it at her death in 1622 leaving as heir her son William Noyes.[64] The estate, on which Standen House was built, was sequestrated from John Fisher in 1648[65] and held by him or a namesake in the 1690s;[66] Thomas son of John Fisher held it in 1717.[67] From 1773 or earlier it was owned by Philip Pulse (d. 1824). Pulse was succeeded by his nephew S. E. Scroggs (d. 1845), from whom the estate, which included Standen House and 149 a. in the parish, had passed to S. M. Scroggs by 1841. It later passed to W. S. Scroggs, who held it until *c.* 1876. The estate was acquired *c.* 1876 by Henry Hancock (d. 1880), whose relict held it until 1882 or later.[68] Between 1895 and 1899 it was bought by Freville Cookson (d. 1909),[69] who apparently bought Standen Farm and *c.* 75 a. from members of the Medows family, the owners of the Conholt estate, *c.* 1897. Cookson's executors held *c.* 215 a. at Standen until 1920 or later.[70] From 1924 or earlier to 1931 or later the estate belonged to C. F. W. Lang.[71] In 1997 Standen farm, including *c.* 200 a. in Chute parish, but not Standen House, belonged to Mr. G. B. Lambert.[72]

Standen House incorporates what was probably an east–west range of a late 17th-century house. To that range a parallel red-brick range was added on the north in the mid 18th century, and in the later 18th century a bow window of full height was added on the gabled east wall of the new range. The old range was extensively altered in the earlier 19th century. It was raised to three storeys, embellished with a pediment, and became the centre of an extended range of nine bays; the two storeys of the extensions occupied the height of the central three. The south façade is of grey brick and has blocked surrounds to the windows and a bowed central porch. A north-west wing, with a ballroom or billiard room on the ground floor, was built between 1879 and 1899.[73] In 1986–7 projecting service additions were demolished, much of the inside of the house was restored, and new fittings, including a staircase in late 17th-century style, were introduced.[74] A group of farm buildings stood south-west of the house in 1841 and until the mid or later 20th century.[75] A stable block north of the house was demolished in 1940.[76]

Chute church was apparently given to Salisbury cathedral and was an endowment of the prebend of Chisenbury and Chute founded in the cathedral. The prebend had probably been founded by *c.* 1150; the prebendary is known to have held Chute church in 1343.[77] In 1405 the *PREBENDAL* estate in Chute consisted of 26 a. and all tithes of grain and of coppices.[78] In 1840 it was transferred to the Ecclesiastical Commissioners. In 1841 it included 29 a. and the tithes were valued at £350 and commuted.[79]

ECONOMIC HISTORY. It appears that Chute, Conholt, Shaw, and Standen each had a strip of land lying north–south across the parish, and each seems to have had open fields and, mainly on the higher ground to the north, common pasture.

CHUTE. The village had open fields called East, West, and Middle[80] and five or six main common pastures. At the north-west end of the parish Chute heath, 200 a., lay on high flat land; almost immediately west of the village lay Chute down, 44 a.; south of the village Honey bottom, 23 a., and Ladies Lawn, 34 a., lay along the parish boundary. West of Chute down, Bauks hill, 128 a., was a common pasture shared in the later 16th century between William Corderoy, the owner of the Chantry estate and probably of Dean farm, and Edward Seymour, earl of Hertford, either as owner of Collingbourne Kingston manor or of part or all of Shaw. In 1594, when Corderoy gave up his right to feed animals in Lord Hertford's woodland in Collingbourne Kingston parish, Lord Hertford gave up his right to common pasture east of the prehistoric ditch which crosses Bauks hill north–south.[81] Commonable land called Thickett, probably pasture, apparently lay east of Forest Lane south of the village.[82] The men of Chute had rights of herbage and mast in Chute forest in the 13th century.[83] Pasture rights there were apparently retained until *c.* 1639, when the forest was inclosed.[84]

About 1331 the demesne of Chute manor was said to include 400 a. of arable and 30 a. of pasture.[85] In the later 16th century the demesne farm, later called Manor farm, and the six copyholds of the manor presumably each had a farmstead in Chute village.[86] Then and possibly earlier Dean farm was apparently worked from the farmstead west of the village.[87]

The commonable land called Thickett had been inclosed by 1658,[88] and by 1698 the

[63] W.R.O. 2667/11/19.
[64] *V.C.H. Wilts.* xi. 173; *Wilts. Inq. p.m.* 1625–49 (Index Libr.), 124–6.
[65] *Cal. Cttee. for Compounding,* ii. 1162.
[66] W.R.O. 564/1.   [67] Ibid. 2210/3.
[68] Ibid. 627/7; 1195/18, survey, 1773; ibid. A 1/345/111; ibid. tithe award; below, Milton Lilbourne, manors (Rectory).   [69] *Kelly's Dir. Wilts.* (1895, 1899).
[70] W.R.O. 2715/7, sale cat. of Conholt Park estate; ibid. G 10/500/18.
[71] Ibid. G 10/500/19; *Kelly's Dir. Wilts.* (1931).
[72] Inf. from Mr. G. B. Lambert, Standen Farm.
[73] Cf. O.S. Maps 6", Wilts. XLIX (1883 edn.); XLIX. NW. (1901 edn.).
[74] Inf. from Mr. A. Andrews, Standen Ho.
[75] O.S. Maps 6", Wilts. XLIX (1883 and later edns.); W.R.O., tithe award.

[76] Inf. from Mr. Andrews.
[77] Le Neve, *Fasti, 1066–1300, Salisbury,* p. 62; *Cal. Papal Pets.* i. 17.
[78] *Chandler's Reg.* (W.R.S. xxxix), p. 27.
[79] Le Neve, *Fasti, 1541–1857, Salisbury,* pp. ix, 36; W.R.O., tithe award.
[80] P.R.O., C 2/Jas. I/S 9/24; W.R.O. 2667/11/138.
[81] W.R.O. 304/1; 382/1.
[82] Ibid. 130/6, deed Orom to Dudman, 1658; ibid. tithe award.
[83] P.R.O., CP 25/1/251/13, no. 69.
[84] Ibid. E 134/33 & 34 Eliz. I Mich./10; below, Chute Forest, econ. hist.
[85] *Wilts. Inq. p.m.* 1327–77 (Index Libr.), 70.
[86] For the copyholds, W.R.O. 2667/11/19.
[87] Above, intro. (other settlement); manors (Dean).
[88] W.R.O. 130/6, deed, Orom to Dudman, 1658.

demesne in the open fields had apparently been inclosed.[89] A proposal of *c.* 1708 to inclose the rest of the open fields[90] may have been deferred: the fields were apparently open in 1717[91] and had been inclosed by 1774.[92] In the early 18th century some woodland was cleared to provide arable closes,[93] 128 a. of woodland was leased in 1743 with a licence for 123 a. of it to be grubbed up and laid in closes for agriculture, and other woodland may have been converted to agriculture in the 18th century.[94]

In 1774 Manor farm had 197 a.; it and four other holdings of Chute manor, of 113 a., 92 a., 23 a., and 14 a., included farm buildings and the right to feed animals on the common pastures. Three holdings with 226 a. apparently consisted of former woodland.[95] By 1809 most of the manor's agricultural land had been consolidated into Manor farm, 348 a., and Foxcott farm, 254 a., each of which included pasture rights.[96] The common pastures were inclosed in 1820 by Act.[97]

In 1841 Dean farm had 500 a., Manor farm 470 a., and Foxcott farm 281 a. including New barn. The lessee of Manor farm also held Foxcott farm. The three farms had 742 a. of arable and 359 a. of downland pasture. A farm of 24 a. was worked from Chute village, and one of 79 a., including Ladies Lawn and 32 a. of arable converted from woodland in the 18th century, was worked from Lower Chute.[98]

Between 1841 and 1879 New Zealand Farm was built at the north end of Dean farm,[99] and from the early 20th century a separate farm was worked from it. Manor farm had 836 a., including Foxcott farm, in 1897 and 820 a. in 1912.[1] From the 1920s Dean farm and New Zealand farm grew and Manor farm shrank. In 1929 additional buildings called Chantry Farm were erected on New Zealand farm, *c.* 655 a. including woodland, which from *c.* 1936 was worked by Friend Sykes.[2] In the 1940s what was later called Chantry farm was of *c.* 770 a., including *c.* 80 a. in Tidcombe and Fosbury parish. Sykes improved it by an intensive programme of grazing and leys to produce, without artificial fertilizers, a rich soil and high crop yields from formerly unproductive land. Racehorses were bred in the mid 20th century and pigs and dairy and beef cattle were kept. In 1997 the farm was worked with Dean farm, *c.* 285 a., and land outside the parish and was used for producing seeds from wheat, barley, and other crops and

for keeping sheep;[3] Manor farm, 200 a., was used for arable and sheep farming.[4]

In the 18th century apparently *c.* 200 a. of woodland of Chute manor, much of it standing south-west of Chute village, was grubbed up.[5] In 1841 *c.* 62 a. of woodland stood in adjoining copses north-west of the village; Jubilee clump, 6 a., stood north of them, several copses, *c.* 70 a., stood west of them, and a copse of 9 a. adjoined Ladies Lawn.[6] All that woodland was standing in 1997 except a 13-a. copse to the west, which had been grubbed up by 1879, and Jubilee clump, which was grubbed up between 1899 and 1923.[7]

A mill, presumably a windmill, possibly stood at Chute in 1305,[8] and a windmill stood on Chute manor *c.* 1331[9] and in 1763.[10] In 1773 the windmill stood south-west of Chute village.[11] It was demolished in the 1930s.[12]

CONHOLT. There is no evidence that Hyde abbey or Battle abbey, the owners of it in the 13th century, held land at Conholt in demesne, and the holdings of the customary tenants were small. In the early 13th century 10 tenants held 6½ yardlands, and in the late 13th century 15 held 7½ yardlands; they owed no labour service and therefore paid higher rents.[13] In 1361 three tenants held a total of 5 yardlands.[14] Open fields probably lay where land was later parkland, and the steep south side of Conholt bottom, and perhaps the high flat land above it, were possibly common pastures.

In the mid 16th century each of the four holdings of Conholt's land in separate ownership may have been a farm.[15] Eastcourt barn, later standing 1 km. south-west of Conholt House, possibly marked the site of one of the farmsteads.[16]

In 1773 much of Conholt's land lay in the Front park, *c.* 47 a., and Conholt park, *c.* 350 a.[17] In 1809 a herd of 294 deer was kept, presumably in Conholt park, and parkland was mown to provide its winter fodder.[18] In 1841, apart from 4 a. of arable in Conholt park, the land of both parks was pasture and woodland.[19] Deer were kept until the 1850s, and in the later 19th century, when Henry Wellesley, duke of Wellington, was the tenant, the parks were used for shooting birds.[20]

In 1841 the 4 a. of arable in Conholt park, 60 a. of arable south of Conholt park, 16 a. of

89   W.R.O. 708/1, deed, Arundell to Earle, 1698.
90   Gibbon, 'Foyles of Chute and Cholderton', 16.
91   W.R.O. 2210/3.
92   Ibid. 1195/18, survey, 1774.
93   Ibid. 708/2, deed, Arundell to Collins, 1705.
94   Ibid. 1195/18, survey, 1774; 2667/11/138; cf. ibid. tithe award.
95   Ibid. 1195/18, survey, 1774; 2667/11/138.
96   Ibid. 1195/18, survey, 1809.   97   Ibid. 304/1.
98   Ibid. tithe award.
99   Ibid.; O.S. Map 6", Wilts. XLIII (1882 edn.).
1   W.R.O. 2715/7, sale cat. of Conholt Park estate; ibid. G 10/500/16.
2   Above, manors (Chute; Dean; Chantry); inf. from Mr. M. Sykes, Chute Farms Ltd.
3   F. Sykes, *Humus and the Farmer*, 4–5; inf. from Mr. Sykes; for the land in Tidcombe and Fosbury par., below, Hippenscombe, econ. hist. (Blagden).
4   Inf. from Mrs. J. Hopton, Chute Manor.

5   Above, this section; W.R.O. 1195/18, survey, 1774; ibid. tithe award.
6   W.R.O., tithe award.
7   O.S. Map 6", Wilts. XLIII (1882 and later edns.).
8   *Gaol Delivery, 1275–1306* (W.R.S. xxxiii), p. 118.
9   *Wilts. Inq. p.m.* 1327–77 (Index Libr.), 70.
10   W.R.O. 2667/11/138.
11   *Andrews and Dury, Map* (W.R.S. viii), pl. 9.
12   W.R.O. 1650/25.
13   *Custumals of Battle Abbey* (Camd. Soc. N.S. xli), 69–71; B.L. Harl. MS. 1761, f. 147.
14   *Wilts. Inq. p.m.* 1327–77 (Index Libr.), 276.
15   P.R.O., SC 6/Hen. VIII/3341, rot. 52d.
16   *Andrews and Dury, Map* (W.R.S. viii), pl. 9.
17   Above, manors (Conholt).
18   W.R.O. 2715/6.
19   Ibid. tithe award.
20   Ibid. 2715/7, sale cat. of Conholt Park estate; 2715/10, notes by the duke of Wellington, 1929.

pasture east of the Front park, and 8 a. of arable and 20 a. of meadow and pasture between Conholt House and the Andover road north of it were apparently the lands of a home farm worked from farm buildings immediately north of Conholt House. A farm of 400 a., consisting of land north of Chute Causeway and of the Andover road, and of land east of the Front park, was worked then from the farmyard built since 1820 and later called Middle Conholt Farm; the farm included 47 a. of Little down, which earlier was probably a common pasture of Standen, and had c. 290 a. of arable.[21] In 1897 the home farm had some of the land north of Chute Causeway and included 235 a. of arable, of which 91 a. lay in Tangley (Hants). Middle Conholt farm then had 287 a. including 158 a. of arable and 106 a. of down.[22]

Home Farm was built south of Conholt park c. 1905,[23] and the use of buildings near Conholt House for farming presumably declined from then. The two parks were apparently used for farming in the earlier 20th century. In 1912 Home farm had 418 a., apparently including Conholt park, and Middle Conholt farm had 517 a. in Chute parish, probably including the land north of Chute Causeway; one or both included some of Standen's land.[24] In 1997 the land of those two farms was in hand as part of an estate of c. 2,000 a., including land in Hampshire, much of which had not been intensively farmed in the mid and later 20th century. In 1997 a third of the estate, including half of Conholt park, was arable and worked from Middle Conholt Farm; on the grassland, which included the Front park, bison, a herd of 30 Highland cattle, and wild boar were kept, sheep were fed for part of the year, and wild flowers were preserved; the woodland was used for sport.[25]

In 1841 there was 100 a. of woodland in Conholt park, 2 a. in the Front park, c. 57 a. east of the Front park, 6 a. east of Conholt House, and 8 a. south of Conholt park.[26] Nearly all of it was standing in 1997, as were two small copses planted in Conholt park, one in the late 19th century and one in the early 20th.[27] Many trees were planted between 1992 and 1997.[28]

SHAW. The strip of land occupied by Shaw farm and Gammon's farm in the 18th century[29] possibly included open fields and common pastures in the Middle Ages. The men of Shaw apparently had the right to feed animals on the whole of Bauks hill until 1594, when the north–south ditch crossing the hill was adopted as a boundary to divide the pasture and they were

apparently confined to the western part,[30] c. 40 a. Along the west boundary of the parish Shaw down, 18 a., was also a common pasture which, with the whole of Bauks hill, was inclosed in 1820 by Act.[31]

In 1774 Shaw farm had 77 a. and Gammon's farm 70 a.;[32] in 1841 they had 102 a. and 54 a. respectively, and the tenant of Gammon's also held 91 a. in Collingbourne Kingston parish.[33] In 1929 Shaw farm had 108 a.; Gammon's farm, 288 a., then included c. 71 a. in Chute parish, 11 a. in Tidcombe, and 206 a. in Collingbourne Kingston.[34] The two farms had been merged by c. 1964. The farmstead of Shaw farm was demolished, and in 1997 the land was worked as Gammon's farm from modern farm buildings on the parish boundary. Gammon's farm, then 425 a., included 320 a. of arable, 55 a. of permanent pasture on which cattle were kept, and 50 a. of woodland.[35]

In 1841 there was 21 a. of woodland in belts between Shaw Farm and Gammon's Farm, Gammon's copse south of Gammon's Farm was of 9 a., and Tanner's copse east of Gammon's Farm was of 10 a.[36] Some of the belts, the two copses, and c. 5 a. of additional woodland planted on Shaw down were standing in 1997.

STANDEN apparently had a north–south strip of land between Chute's and Conholt's. Little down, 85 a., was a common pasture on the high flat land north of the village and was probably Standen's. Between Little down and the village Standen probably had open fields called Great Town field and Little Town field, and it apparently had a common pasture called Hoe, c. 150 a., south of the village.[37] By the 18th century all the land had been inclosed except Little down and c. 10 a. of Hoe lying along the south boundary of the parish.[38] The common pastures were inclosed by Act in 1820, that along the south boundary, on which cottages had already been built, being divided into small allotments.[39]

In 1773 Standen farm apparently had c. 175 a.; 119 a. was held with Standen House and may have been worked as a farm with 43 a. of Chute's land.[40] In 1841 Standen farm had 251 a. including c. 181 a. of arable and, lying south of Chute Causeway, 34 a. of Little down. The 126 a. then held with Standen House included 66 a. of arable, 35 a. of pasture, and 21 a. of wood and was apparently a home farm; the pasture included a park of 25 a. north of the house. Manor farm, Chute, included 58 a. of Hoe and 24 a. of the Town fields, and what was later called Middle Conholt farm included 47 a. of Little down north of Chute Causeway.[41]

In 1897 Standen farm, 305 a., was mainly

21 Ibid. tithe award; Greenwood, *Map of Wilts.*; for Standen, below, this section.
22 W.R.O. 2715/7, sale cat. of Conholt Park estate.
23 Above, intro. (Cadley and Lower Chute).
24 W.R.O., G 10/500/16; for Standen, below, this section.
25 Inf. from Mr. P. van Vlissingen, Conholt Ho.
26 W.R.O., tithe award.
27 O.S. Maps 6", Wilts. XLIII (1882 edn.); XLIII. SE. (1901 edn.); XLIII. SW. (1900, 1926 edns.).
28 Inf. from Mr. van Vlissingen.
29 *Andrews and Dury, Map* (W.R.S. viii), pl. 9; W.R.O.

1195/18, survey, 1774.
30 W.R.O. 382/1.
31 Ibid. 304/1; ibid. tithe award.
32 Ibid. 1195/18, survey, 1774.
33 Ibid. tithe award; Collingbourne Kingston tithe award.
34 Ibid. 9/1/521.
35 Inf. from Mr. J. R. Crook, Gammon's Farm.
36 W.R.O., tithe award.
37 Ibid.; ibid. 304/1.
38 Ibid. 1195/18, survey, 1773.
39 Ibid. 304/1; above, intro. (Cadley and Lower Chute).
40 W.R.O. 1195/18, surveys, 1773–4.
41 Ibid. tithe award.

arable. It was divided about then: c. 230 a. north of the village, part of the Conholt estate, was probably added either to Home farm, the buildings of which were at Cadley from c. 1905, or to Middle Conholt farm, or divided between them. In 1997 that land north of the village, still part of the Conholt estate, was mainly arable.[42] About 1897 Standen Farm and c. 75 a. south of the village were added to the 137-a. home farm worked from buildings adjacent to Standen House.[43] The buildings near the house later went out of agricultural use, and in 1997 Standen farm, with buildings immediately south of the farmhouse, was an arable farm of c. 400 a., including c. 200 a. in Chute Forest parish, on which wheat and barley were the main crops.[44]

In 1841 three adjoining copses totalling 10 a. stood east of Standen village, a copse of 8 a. stood south-east of it, and there were smaller areas of woodland including two adjoining belts, 7 a., south-west of the village which may have marked the boundary of Hoe. Nearly all that woodland was standing in 1997, two copses each of c. 5 a. were planted north of the village in the 20th century, and 5 a. of Little down south of Chute Causeway which was furze in 1841[45] was woodland in 1997.

A malthouse standing in the parish in 1773 was presumably that which stood west of Standen village in 1841.[46] That malthouse had fallen into disrepair by the 1850s.[47]

LOCAL GOVERNMENT. Records of the court baron of Chute manor exist for 1676, 1691–1711, and 1721–35. In most years the court was held once, and most of its business was conveyancing. The homage frequently presented the customs of the manor and sometimes that they had been infringed, and occasionally it presented that buildings and the pound needed repair and that misdemeanours, such as encroaching on the waste, had been committed.[48]

In 1282–3 Battle abbey's tenants at Conholt were required to attend its view of frankpledge held at Bromham.[49] From 1293 to 1307 they attended the abbey's view at Brightwalton (Berks.), at which the tithingman of Conholt presented misdemeanours, such as the unlicensed felling of trees, and failure to observe the assize of ale. A suit concerning the right to hold customary land at Conholt came before the court in 1293.[50]

In 1775–6 the parish spent £104 on the poor, in the three years to Easter 1785 an average of £129, and in 1802–3 £271. In 1802–3 the poor rate was below the average for the hundred, 22 adults and 27 children were relieved regularly, and 8 adults were relieved occasionally. In 1812–13, when 9 adults were relieved regularly and 71 occasionally, £609 was spent.[51] At £791 spending reached a peak in 1817–18; it fluctuated between £497 and £338 in the 1820s, and, for reasons which are not clear, it rose to £601 in 1829–30 and fell to £297 in 1832–3.[52] The parish joined Andover poor-law union in 1835[53] and was transferred to Pewsey union in 1879.[54] It became part of Kennet district in 1974.[55]

CHURCH. Chute church was first mentioned in 1320[56] and may have been standing long before. In 1343 it was an endowment of the prebend of Chisenbury and Chute, which had been founded in Salisbury cathedral by c. 1150, and the parish was in the peculiar jurisdiction of the prebendary, triennially inhibited by the dean of the cathedral. In 1343 the church may have been served by a chaplain appointed by the prebendary.[57] A vicarage had been ordained by 1386.[58] In 1924 it was united to the vicarage of Chute Forest,[59] and in 1954 the two parishes were united.[60] The united benefice became part of Wexcombe benefice in 1979.[61]

The king presented the vicar in 1386.[62] By 1554 and until 1838 candidates for the vicarage were presented to the dean, usually by the prebendary. In 1580 Edward Corderoy presented, probably by grant of a turn, in 1618 Thomas Leech presented by grant of a turn, and in 1789 the prebendary was admitted to the vicarage on his own petition.[63] In 1840 the advowson was transferred by Act to the bishop of Salisbury,[64] and in 1891 by exchange to the dean and chapter of Winchester.[65] From 1924 to 1979 the dean and chapter were entitled to present at two of every three vacancies of the united benefice,[66] and from 1979 were on the board of patronage for Wexcombe benefice.[67]

Chute vicarage was of moderate value. In 1535 the vicar's income was £11,[68] between 1829 and 1831 c. £244.[69] In 1405 he was entitled to all tithes from the whole parish except those of grain and coppices.[70] In 1841 the tithes were valued at £302 and commuted. The vicar had

42 W.R.O. 2715/7, sale cat. of Conholt Park estate; inf. from Mr. van Vlissingen; for the Conholt estate, above, this section (Conholt).
43 W.R.O., Inland Revenue, val. reg. 60; above, manors (Standen).
44 Inf. from Mr. G. B. Lambert, Standen Farm.
45 Cf. O.S. Maps 6", Wilts. XLIII. SW. (1900, 1926 edns.); W.R.O., tithe award.
46 W.R.O. 1195/18, survey, 1773; ibid. tithe award; cf. Andrews and Dury, Map (W.R.S. viii), pl. 9.
47 W.R.O. 1650/25.
48 Ibid. 564/1; 2667/14/36; 2667/14/38.
49 Custumals of Battle Abbey (Camd. Soc. N.S. xli), 71.
50 Sel. Pleas in Manorial Cts. (Selden Soc. ii), 165–6, 169; P.R.O., SC 2/153/67.
51 Poor Law Abstract, 1804, 564–5; 1818, 498–9.
52 Poor Rate Returns, 1816–21, 188; 1822–4, 228; 1825–9, 219; 1830–4, 212.
53 Poor Law Com. 1st Rep. App. D, 248.
54 V.C.H. Wilts. iv. 331.
55 O.S. Map 1/100,000, admin. areas, Wilts. (1974 edn.).
56 Cal. Pat. 1317–21, 450.
57 Cal. Papal Pets. i. 17; Le Neve, Fasti, 1066–1300, Salisbury, p. 62; W.R.O., D 7, passim.
58 Cal. Pat. 1385–9, 133.
59 Lond. Gaz. 9 Dec. 1924, pp. 8971–2.
60 W.R.O. 1916/2.
61 Inf. from Ch. Com.
62 Cal. Pat. 1385–9, 133.
63 Chandler's Reg. (W.R.S. xxxix), p. 146; W.R.O., D 5/1/2.
64 Le Neve, Fasti, 1541–1857, Salisbury, 36; V.C.H. Wilts. iii. 201.
65 Lond. Gaz. 26 June 1891, pp. 3374–5.
66 Ibid. 9 Dec. 1924, pp. 8971–2.
67 Inf. from Ch. Com.
68 Valor Eccl. (Rec. Com.), ii. 151.
69 Rep. Com. Eccl. Revenues, 830–1.
70 Chandler's Reg. (W.R.S. xxxix), p. 27.

no glebe apart from his house. The house lived in by the vicar in 1841[71] was probably built in the earlier 19th century, was enlarged in 1860,[72] and was sold in 1977.[73]

A chantry was founded in Chute church, probably by Ralph of Barford (d. c. 1327) whose endowment of it was licensed by the king in 1320.[74] The chantry, in honour of the Assumption of the Virgin and probably with an altar in the south transept,[75] was called the Haldeway chantry in the later 14th century.[76] It was served by a chaplain presented to the prebendary of Chisenbury and Chute for institution. Ralph of Barford was presumably the patron c. 1320, and the patronage seems to have passed like Barford manor in Downton to Sir John Wroth (d. 1407), who was patron in 1405.[77] It may later have descended in the Wroth family like Newton Wroth manor in North Petherton (Som.) to Thomas Wroth (fl. c. 1542).[78] With an estate consisting in 1405 of a house, 1½ carucate, 3 a. of meadow, 3 a. of wood, and 5s. rent the chantry was well endowed,[79] and it was worth £3 13s. 4d. in 1535. It was dissolved at the Reformation, apparently between 1535[80] and 1542.[81]

In 1611 Richard Horwood, the vicar from 1602, was accused of allowing laymen to conduct funerals;[82] he was also accused of sexual immorality, gambling, and litigiousness.[83] Two services were held on Census Sunday in 1851: in the morning the congregation numbered 246, in the afternoon 185.[84] In 1864 two services were held each Sunday, others on Good Friday, Ascension day, Christmas day, and Wednesdays in Lent; congregations averaged c. 150. Communion was celebrated at Christmas, Easter, and Whitsun, on Trinity Sunday, and on the first Sunday of each month; 15–18 communicants attended the celebrations.[85] From 1903 to 1924 the vicarage was held in plurality with that of Chute Forest.[86]

In 1891 Mary Scroggs gave 1 a., the income from which was to be spent on religious education. In 1905 the income, c. £1 10s., was given to the Sunday school.[87] In 1997 the charity was considered lost.[88]

The church of ST. NICHOLAS, so called in 1405,[89] was almost completely rebuilt in the period 1868–72.[90] The old church, the walls of which were stuccoed on the outside, consisted of a chancel and a nave with south transept, south porch, and west timber bell turret. Some windows seem to have been 15th-century; the east window was apparently 18th-century.[91] The church was rebuilt to designs by J. L. Pearson.[92] The walls were faced with knapped flint and supported by prominent red-brick buttresses, and the windows were replaced by new ones in 13th-century style. A vestry was built on the north side of the chancel, and the porch and the bell turret were replaced by a new south porch from which a tower with a slated broached spire rose. The chancel roof incorporates trussed rafters, the nave roof emphatic arched braces. A 14th-century piscina was reset in the chancel.

In the early 15th century there was a silver chalice and paten in the church.[93] In 1553 a chalice weighing 9 oz. was left in the parish and 11 oz. of plate was taken for the king. A new chalice and paten was made and given to the parish in 1710. In 1891 and 1997 the parish held the chalice and paten of 1710, a salver hallmarked for 1726, and a flagon hallmarked for 1863.[94]

Two bells hung in the church in 1553. They were replaced by one of 1582 cast by John Wallis and one of 1681 cast by Clement Tosier.[95] One of those bells, and six transferred from Chute Forest church in 1976, hung in the church in 1997.[96]

Registrations of baptisms, marriages, and burials begin in 1581 and are complete.[97]

NONCONFORMITY. Several parishioners presented between 1611 and 1632 for failing to attend church or the celebration of communion may have been popish recusants,[98] and a recusant lived in the parish in the late 17th century.[99]

In 1816 a house in the parish was certified as a dissenters' meeting house. Methodists certified meeting houses in the parish in 1818, 1823, and 1838, two of the houses being at Hatchett near Cadley; they built a chapel between Cadley and Lower Chute in 1844.[1] Two services were held in the chapel on Census Sunday in 1851; 58 attended in the afternoon, 76 in the evening.[2] It was closed in 1990.[3] A small chapel for Primitive Methodists was built of corrugated iron at Chute in 1879 and closed in 1927.[4] A meeting house at Hatchett for Baptists was certified in 1825, and two houses at Chute were certified for Particular Baptists, one in 1835 and one in 1836.[5]

EDUCATION. There were two schools in Chute parish in 1818, one with 30 pupils and

71 W.R.O., tithe award.
72 Ibid. D 1/11/147.   73 Ibid. D 365/3/14.
74 Cal. Pat. 1317–21, 450; V.C.H. Wilts. xi. 53.
75 Chandler's Reg. (W.R.S. xxxix), pp. 27, 90; for the parts of the church, below, this section [archit.].
76 Cal. Papal Reg. iii. 477; Phillipps, Wilts. Inst. i. 74.
77 Chandler's Reg. (W.R.S. xxxix), p. 27; V.C.H. Wilts. xi. 53.
78 V.C.H. Som. vi. 287; above, manors (Chantry).
79 Chandler's Reg. (W.R.S. xxxix), p. 27.
80 Valor Eccl. (Rec. Com.), ii. 150.
81 P.R.O., E 301/59, no. 34.
82 W.R.O., D 5/1/2, f. 24v.; D 7/5/2.
83 P.R.O., STAC 8/104/1.
84 Ibid. HO 129/118/4/2/2.
85 W.R.O., D 1/56/7.
86 Ibid. D 1/2/45, pp. 490, 511–12; Clergy List (1905, 1914).   87 Endowed Char. Wilts. (S. Div.), 98.
88 Inf. from Mrs. A. W. Cherrington, Tantanoola, Chute

Forest.
89 Chandler's Reg. (W.R.S. xxxix), p. 27.
90 W.R.O., D 1/61/20/12; ibid. 627/22.
91 J. Buckler, watercolour in W.A.S. Libr., vol. iv. 5.
92 A. Quiney, J. L. Pearson, 247; W.R.O., D 1/61/20/12; ibid. 627/22.
93 Chandler's Reg. (W.R.S. xxxix), p. 60.
94 Nightingale, Wilts. Plate, 166; inf. from Mr. J. Burden, Fairview, Hatchett Hill, Lower Chute.
95 Walters, Wilts. Bells, 58.
96 W.R.O. 627/20; inf. from Mr. Burden.
97 W.R.O. 627/1–3.   98 Ibid. D 7/5/2.
99 Williams, Cath. Recusancy (Cath. Rec. Soc.), 230.
1   Meeting Ho. Certs. (W.R.S. xl), pp. 78, 87, 101, 146, 159.
2   P.R.O., HO 129/118/4/2/3.
3   Inf. from Mrs. J. Buchanan, Chute Cadley.
4   W.R.O. 1650/25.
5   Meeting Ho. Certs. (W.R.S. xl), pp. 107, 139, 142.

the other a dame school with 6,[6] and there were two schools with 48 pupils in 1835.[7] From 1841 or earlier a room at Standen was used partly for a school,[8] which was affiliated to the National society. In 1846–7 the school had 72 pupils, in 1858 c. 70. A new school was built between Chute and Standen in 1858;[9] it was attended by pupils from Chute Forest parish in addition to those from Chute. It had 48 pupils in 1871,[10] and an average attendance of 82 in 1908–9 and of 76 in 1937–8.[11] Until 1902 the school received the income from 1 a. given by Mary Scroggs for religious education.[12] It was closed in 1978.[13]

CHARITIES FOR THE POOR. Gorges Foyle

(d. 1801) gave by will the income from £100 for clothes or other help to be given to paupers of Chute parish, and by will proved 1829 Charlotte Poore gave £100 for blankets for the second poor of the parish. From 1831 the income of both charities was used to buy blankets for the poor.[14] George Foyle (d. 1839) gave by will £200 to the poor, and Mary Scroggs (d. 1900) gave by will the income from £200 to buy coal for the poor. In 1905 the income from all four charities, £15, was spent on blankets and coal.[15] Coal was given in the 1930s and 1940s, cash later.[16] By a Scheme of 1979 the charities were united as Chute Relief in Need charity.[17] In the 1990s the income, c. £32 a year, was usually allowed to accumulate. The last gift to have been made before 1997 was in 1992.[18]

CHUTE FOREST

CHUTE FOREST parish adjoins Hampshire c. 5 km. north-west of Andover.[19] Its land, which formed a rough quadrilateral, was the demesne wood of the Wiltshire part of Chute forest until it was disafforested in 1639,[20] and it was extra-parochial. Its inhabitants relieved their own poor from c. 1780[21] and it was a civil parish in the 19th century.[22] A church was built in 1870–1, and from 1875, when the church was consecrated and the civil parish was assigned to it as a district,[23] Chute Forest was also an ecclesiastical parish. Between 1820 and 1839 an eastern projection of c. 150 a. at the south end of its east side, which was the Hampshire part of Chute forest in the earlier 17th century, was added to, or acknowledged to be part of, the parish,[24] presumably because the overseers of Chute Forest began to relieve paupers living on it. Thereafter the parish measured 1,973 a. (798 ha.) until 1987, when it was increased to 825 ha. by a transfer of land to it from Ludgershall.[25]

The boundary of the parish as it was in 1820, most of which, as the boundary of Chute forest, was recited in 1300 and 1330, was from the early 17th century or earlier almost entirely marked by roads on its north and east sides, and mainly by roads on the other two sides.[26] On the east the boundary follows the bottom of a dry valley, as it does for a short distance on the west; elsewhere it ignores relief.

Chalk outcrops over the whole parish, across which no stream flows. The land falls from north to south and is broken by north–south dry valleys, one of which, called Cadley bottom in the north and Soper's bottom in the south, is straight and runs across the middle of the parish. There are deposits of clay-with-flints on the ridges between Soper's bottom and Long bottom, west of Long bottom, and in the eastern projection, and of gravel in Soper's bottom and the valley east of it. The land reaches 185 m. on the northern boundary, 107 m. on the southern.[27] In the Middle Ages much of the parish was presumably woodland;[28] in the earlier 17th century much of it was farmland.[29] From the 18th century to the 20th, although there was a park and some woodland, c. 85 per cent of the parish was farmland, and in the earlier 19th century mainly arable.[30]

Chute Forest had 99 inhabitants in 1801, 144 in 1821. The population had fallen to 110 by 1831, after which it rose steadily to reach its peak of 188 in 1871. It had fallen to 119 by 1891, risen to 152 by 1911, fallen to 98 by 1951,[31] and risen to 145 by 1981. The parish, which was slightly enlarged in 1987, had 146 inhabitants in 1991.[32]

No major road crosses the parish, access to which, as a royal forest, may for long have been

6 *Educ. of Poor Digest*, 1023.
7 *Educ. Enq. Abstract*, 1033.
8 W.R.O., tithe award.
9 Ibid. 782/31; Nat. Soc. *Inquiry, 1846–7*, Wilts. 4–5; *Acct. of Wilts. Schs.* 15.
10 *Returns relating to Elem. Educ.* 418–19.
11 *Bd. of Educ., List 21, 1910* (H.M.S.O.), 505; *1938*, 422.
12 *Endowed Char. Wilts.* (S. Div.), 98; above, church.
13 W.R.O., list of primary schs. closed since 1946.
14 *Endowed Char. Wilts.* (S. Div.), 95–6, where the name of each donor is misprinted; above, manors (Dean); cf. *V.C.H. Hants*, iv. 376; *V.C.H. Wilts.* xv. 98.
15 *Endowed Char. Wilts.* (S. Div.), 97–8; below, Milton Lilbourne, manors (Rectory).
16 W.R.O. 1650/8–9; ibid. L 2, Chute.
17 Char. Com. file.
18 Inf. from Mrs. Cherrington.
19 This article was written in 1998. Maps used include O.S. Maps 6", Wilts. XLIX (1883 and later edns.); 1/25,000, SU 25/35 (1994 edn.).

20 *V.C.H. Wilts.* iv. 425, 427, 452–3; P.R.O., MR 342.
21 *Poor Law Abstract, 1804*, 564–5.
22 e.g. P.R.O., HO 107/1683; ibid. RG 9/716; RG 10/1244.
23 W.R.O. 1916/7; below, church.
24 C. Greenwood, *Map of Wilts.* (1820); P.R.O., MR 342; W.R.O., tithe award.
25 *Census*, 1981; 1991; Statutory Instruments, 1987, no. 619, Kennet (Parishes) Order.
26 Greenwood, *Map of Wilts.*; *V.C.H. Wilts.* iv. 452; P.R.O., MR 342.
27 Geol. Surv. Map 1/50,000, drift, sheet 283 (1975 edn.).   28 Cf. *V.C.H. Wilts.* iv. 425.
29 P.R.O., C 5/14/30; ibid. E 126/5, ff. 116v.–117; ibid. MR 342.
30 *Andrews and Dury, Map* (W.R.S. viii), pl. 9; O.S. Maps 6", Wilts. XLIX (1883 and later edns.); W.R.O., tithe award; below, econ. hist.
31 *V.C.H. Wilts.* iv. 345.
32 *Census*, 1981; 1991; above, this section.

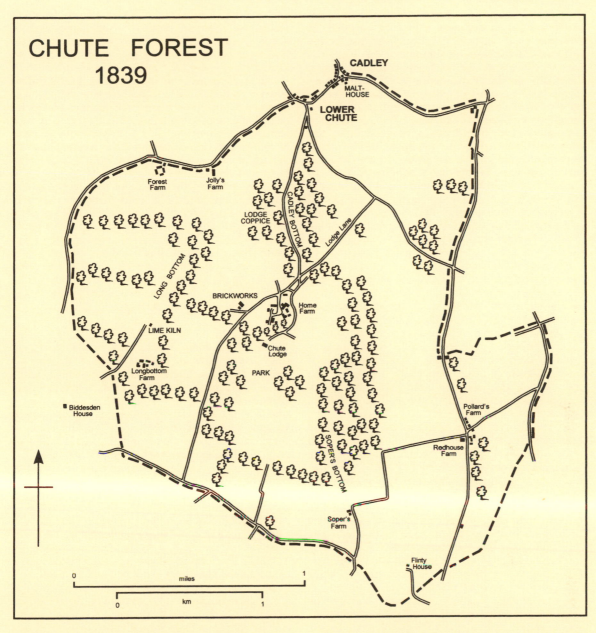

CHUTE FOREST 1839

restricted, and roads ran along its boundaries.[33] None was of more than local importance. In the later 18th century a north–south road across the parish ran through Cadley bottom and Soper's bottom; where it ran across the park in the centre of the parish it had been partly obliterated by the 19th century,[34] but its course remained a public bridleway in the late 20th. Also in the later 18th century a road crossed the north-east part of the parish, and between that and the road along the south boundary a road led across the parish to serve the mansion called Chute Lodge;[35] both were public roads in the late 20th century. That serving the mansion, which also served Chute Forest village in the 20th century,[36] was called Lodge Lane on the north-east; its south-west end skirted the park.

A hoard of early Iron-Age coins found in the north-east part is the only evidence of prehistoric activity in the parish.[37]

A lodge in the Wiltshire part of Chute forest in 1501[38] probably stood near its centre. A house called Chute Lodge standing in the centre of the forest in 1632[39] was presumably that lodge or a successor built on or near its site, and a new Chute Lodge built in the later 18th century stands on or near the site of that standing in 1632.[40] Outbuildings stood north of the new Chute Lodge; in 1839, when some of them were used for farming, they apparently included a gardener's cottage. A farmstead, also standing north of the house in 1839,[41] was possibly built in the early 19th century and was later called Home Farm; the farmhouse had a main north-

33   Above, this section.
34   *Andrews and Dury, Map* (W.R.S. viii), pl. 9; O.S. Map 6", Wilts. XLIX (1883 edn.); W.R.O., tithe award; for the park, below, estates (Chute Lodge).
35   *Andrews and Dury, Map* (W.R.S. viii), pl. 9; for Chute

Lodge, below, estates (Chute Lodge).
36   For the village, below, this section.
37   *V.C.H. Wilts.* i (1), 57.   38   *Cal. Pat.* 1494–1509, 265.
39   P.R.O., MR 342.   40   Below, estates (Chute Lodge).
41   W.R.O., tithe award.

west front of red brick and other walls of flint and brick. A church was built further north in the later 19th century[42] and that, Chute Lodge and its outbuildings, and Home Farm were the only buildings at the centre of the parish until the 20th century. One of the outbuildings was converted to a pair of cottages, possibly in the 19th century, and another was apparently converted to a house in the 20th.[43] At Home Farm large new farm buildings were erected in the later 20th century: they and most of the other farm buildings were demolished in the 1990s,[44] and in 1998 the farmhouse was being rebuilt. In the early 20th century two pairs of cottages were built beside Lodge Lane,[45] farm buildings and c. 15 other houses were built later, and in the later 20th century the village was given the name Chute Forest.[46] From c. 1942 to c. 1950 Chute Lodge was used as a Borstal institution.[47]

Most other settlement in Chute Forest parish has been beside the roads on its periphery. On the northern boundary at Cadley and Lower Chute, hamlets which grew up on common pasture mainly in Chute parish, five cottages and houses of the 17th and 18th centuries, four of them thatched, and five 20th-century houses stand in Chute Forest parish.[48] A little south of Lower Chute a lodge was built between 1839 and 1879 beside the old road through Cadley bottom.[49] South-west of Lower Chute, Jolly's House had been built by 1731,[50] and Jolly's Farm and Forest Farm had been built by 1773.[51] The farmhouse of Jolly's Farm, of flint with brick dressings, was apparently built in the earlier 18th century and may be Jolly's House; that of Forest Farm was replaced in the late 19th century by Forest House, a large, three-storeyed, house of red brick and flint. In the extreme north-east corner of the parish a small farmstead built between 1820 and 1839 was demolished in the mid 20th century.[52]

Beside the road which marked the south part of the parish's eastern boundary until the earlier 19th century two farmsteads were built. Pollard's Farm, called Forest Farm or Mockbeggared in 1773,[53] incorporates an apparently earlier 18th-century house of flint, brick, and thatch. Redhouse Farm, including a brick and flint farmhouse, was built between 1820 and 1839.[54] In the 20th century farm buildings were erected on both sites and three bungalows were built; a new farmstead, incorporating a late

20th-century house, was built 250 m. west of Redhouse Farm. South of the farmsteads a cottage, which belonged to the parish in 1839, had been built on the verge beside the road by 1773.[55]

Near the southern boundary a house called Flingly, later Flinty, standing in 1773,[56] was apparently built in the 18th century; two pairs of cottages were built beside it in the mid 19th century.[57] North-west of Flinty House a small farmstead called Soper's had been built by 1773;[58] the farmhouse was demolished between 1923 and 1942.[59]

In the south-west corner of the parish Longbottom Farm, the farmstead of the home farm of the estate on which Biddesden House in Ludgershall stood, was apparently built shortly before 1820.[60] The farmhouse, which had a main south front of three bays striped in brick and flint, was extended eastwards and westwards in the mid 20th century and much altered in the 1990s. West of the house two estate houses were built in the mid 20th century.

ESTATES. The Crown owned Chute forest until 1639, when it granted it at fee farm to Sir Henry Ludlow, Edward Manning, and Henry Kelsey.[61] The forest was inclosed and divided, apparently about then, and parts of it were presumably allotted to the lords of manors in villages around it in exchange for the right of their tenants to feed animals on it.[62] The existence in the earlier 19th century of severally owned small fields, mainly near the south boundary of the parish,[63] suggests that allotments were also made to replace cottagers' rights in the forest.

What came to be called the *CHUTE LODGE* estate, including a lodge, agricultural land accounted 286 a., and woodland, was apparently acquired by Edward Manning c. 1639 and passed to Richard Manning. In 1650, after Richard's death, his representatives sold the estate to John Collins[64] (knighted 1681, d. 1711), apparently a non-juror.[65] By 1691 the estate had been bought by Sir William Scroggs (d. 1695), who by his nuncupative will gave it to his wife Anne (d. 1746) for the good of her and her children.[66] It passed to William Scroggs (d. 1756), who had sons William and Edward,[67] and c. 1760 was bought by John Freeman.[68] The estate passed

42 Below, church.
43 Cf. W.R.O., tithe award.
44 Cf. O.S. Maps 1/25,000, SU 35 (1958 edn.); SU 25/35 (1994 edn.).
45 Ibid. 6", Wilts. XLIX. NW. (1926 edn.).
46 Ibid. 1/25,000, SU 35 (1958 edn.); SU 25/35 (1994 edn.).
47 W.R.O. 1650/25, pp. 9–10.
48 For more about the hamlets, above, Chute, intro. (Cadley and Lower Chute).
49 O.S. Map 6", Wilts. XLIX (1883 edn.); W.R.O., tithe award.
50 W.R.O. 212B/1874.
51 *Andrews and Dury, Map* (W.R.S. viii), pl. 9.
52 Greenwood, *Map of Wilts.*; O.S. Maps 6", Wilts. XLIX. NE. (1926 edn.); 1/25,000, SU 35 (1958 edn.); W.R.O., tithe award.
53 *Andrews and Dury, Map* (W.R.S. viii), pl. 9.
54 Greenwood, *Map of Wilts.*; W.R.O., tithe award.
55 *Andrews and Dury, Map* (W.R.S. viii), pl. 9; W.R.O.,

tithe award.
56 *Andrews and Dury, Map* (W.R.S. viii), pl. 9.
57 O.S. Map 1/2,500, Wilts. XLIX. 11 (1880 edn.); W.R.O., tithe award.
58 *Andrews and Dury, Map* (W.R.S. viii), pl. 9.
59 O.S. Maps 1/2,500, Wilts. XLIX. 10 (1942 edn.); 6", Wilts. XLIX. SW. (1926 edn.).
60 Ibid. 1", sheet 14 (1817 edn.); Greenwood, *Map of Wilts.*; for Biddesden Ho., *V.C.H. Wilts.* xv. 134.
61 *V.C.H. Wilts.* iv. 427.
62 Below, this section; econ. hist.; cf. Braydon forest: *V.C.H. Wilts.* xiv. 37.
63 W.R.O., tithe award.
64 P.R.O., C 5/14/30.
65 *Hist. Parl., Commons*, 1660–90, ii. 107–8.
66 *D.N.B.*; P.R.O., PROB 11/424, f. 250 and v.; W.R.O., Ch. Com., chapter, 93/9.
67 *Colln. Topog. et Geneal.* viii. 199; P.R.O., C 78/1954, no. 4.
68 W.R.O., Ch. Com., chapter, 93/18–19.

1. GREAT BEDWYN: St. Mary's church from the south-east *c.* 1850

2. GREAT BEDWYN: the north arcade of St. Mary's church *c.* 1850

3. PEWSEY: St. John the Baptist's church from the north-east in 1806

4. COLLINGBOURNE KINGSTON: St. Mary's church from the south-west in 1806

5. BURBAGE: All Saints' church from the south-east in 1806

6. FROXFIELD: All Saints' church from the south-east in 1806

7. BUTTERMERE: St. James's church from the north-west in 1806

8. EASTON: Holy Trinity church from the north-east in 1806

12. WOOTTON RIVERS: Manor Farmhouse from the south-east in 1982

13. PEWSEY: houses at the south end of East Sharcott Street from the south-east in 1998

14. PEWSEY: Ball Cottage at Ball in 1998

15. PEWSEY: Court House in Church Street from the north-west in 1998

16. GREAT BEDWYN: air view of Tottenham House and its park from the south-east in 1948

17. GREAT BEDWYN: the south-east front of Tottenham House in 1806

18. GREAT BEDWYN: the north-west front of Tottenham House in 1998

19. CHILTON FOLIAT: Chilton Lodge from the south-east in 1998

20. CHUTE FOREST: Chute Lodge from the south in 1967

21. TIDCOMBE: the south front of Tidcombe Manor in 1998

22. MILTON LILBOURNE: the south front of Fyfield Manor in 1961

23. MILTON LILBOURNE: the east front of Milton Lilbourne Manor in 1982

31. FROXFIELD: the south front of Froxfield almshouse in 1998

32. FROXFIELD: the quadrangle and chapel of Froxfield almshouse from the west in 1998

33. LITTLE BEDWYN: the Farmer Homes in Kelston Road in 1998

34. CHILTON FOLIAT: Leverton Cottages at Leverton in 1998

35. GREAT BEDWYN: Railway Terrace, off Brook Street, in 1998

36. GREAT BEDWYN: Wilton windmill in 1976

37. PEWSEY: the Kennet & Avon canal from the west at Pewsey wharf *c.* 1965

38. PEWSEY: the church of the Holy Family in Broadfields *c.* 1965

39. Burbage: cottages at Durley from the south in 1907

40. Milton Lilbourne: part of Milton Lilbourne village street from the north *c*. 1955

41. Pewsey: Market Place from the east in 1929

42. Pewsey: North Street from the south *c*. 1900

43. Pewsey: High Street from the west *c*. 1955

44. GREAT BEDWYN: the market house demolished in 1870

45. GREAT BEDWYN: air view of Great Bedwyn village from the south in 1973

on Freeman's death in 1794 to his son Strick-land,[69] who sold it to William Fowle c. 1805.[70] In 1839 Fowle (d. 1840) owned Chute Lodge, 724 a. around it, and an additional 184 a. in Chute Forest parish.[71] He devised that estate to his son the Revd. Henry Fowle (d. 1865),[72] who was succeeded in it by his brother T. E. Fowle (d. 1877). The Chute Lodge estate passed from T. E. Fowle to his son W. H. Fowle, who c. 1906 sold Chute Lodge, the land around it, and 100 a. of the other land to Alexander Grant-Meek.[73] In 1908 Grant-Meek sold the estate to Isabella, the wife of Lord John Joicey-Cecil,[74] in 1927 Lady Joicey-Cecil sold it to W. A. Adinsell, and in 1928 Adinsell owned 902 a. in the parish. In 1942 Adinsell sold his estate there to the Crown.[75] About 1950 the Crown sold the estate to a speculator, from whom John Cherrington bought Home farm, c. 550 a. In 1962 Cher-rington sold the farm to his son Mr. Rowan Cherrington,[76] who sold it in 1996. In 1998 the farm belonged to members of the Guinness family as part of the estate centred on Biddesden House.[77]

A house called Chute Lodge was standing in 1632 and was lived in by Sir John Collins in 1650; a chapel was consecrated in it in 1674.[78] It was replaced by a new Chute Lodge,[79] built on or near its site c. 1768 for John Freeman to designs by Sir Robert Taylor. The new house was one of several compact country houses designed by Taylor in the 1760s for men who were connected with the West India Company.[80] It was built of red brick with stone dressings, as a rectangle of seven bays by five, and with a tall basement faced in rusticated stone, a piano nobile, and, except above the north-east and north-west corner bays, an attic storey crowned with a wide bracketed cornice. The north front, of five bays, incorporates the main entrance, which was reached by a pair of curved flights of steps, in the central bay of the piano nobile; the three central bays were surmounted by a pedi-ment above the cornice.[81] On each of the other three fronts there was a canted bay, that on the south being of full height, those on the east and west of two storeys. Exterior details, especially the vermiculated surrounds to the main win-dows, are of high quality. Inside the house the piano nobile has a hall, an octagonal saloon, a dining room, and a library around an oval staircase leading to the attic storey and lit from above. Delicate neoclassical plasterwork, chim-ney pieces, and doorcases survive in situ. The only access from the piano nobile to the base-ment was a staircase in the north-west angle of the house. The kitchen, below the dining room, is a double-height room sunk into a sub-base-ment. In the 19th century the north front of the house was altered: the two corner bays were raised by an attic storey, and a level stone balustrade was added to each; the flights of steps to the entrance were replaced by a terrace con-nected to the ground by a straight flight of steps at each end. The alterations may have been those made to the house in 1866 to designs by J. L. Pearson.[82] The house was greatly enlarged in the period 1906–8 by the construction of new bed-rooms in the roof, in which dormer windows were made, and by the building of an east wing. The wing, on an L plan, is almost as large as, and was built in a style and with materials sympathetic to, the original house. In the mid 20th century the house, especially the wing, was altered for use as a Borstal institution and after-wards as a school; by the early 1980s it had been divided into five dwellings.[83]

The house built c. 1768 was approached from the north by a drive leading through a small plantation. About 150 m. north of the house a walled garden lay east of the plantation, and outbuildings stood north of the garden; all that survived of them in 1998 were 18th-century gate piers and part of the garden wall. The house stood in a park of c. 150 a. crossed by the road through Cadley bottom and Soper's bottom, and a long north–south plantation stood east of the road.[84] Between 1773 and 1795 the park was altered in the style of Lancelot Brown[85] and, presumably at the same time, it was apparently enlarged in all directions. Belts of trees standing in 1839, and, with Lodge coppice, enclosing c. 440 a., probably marked the boundaries of an enlarged park, in which other belts stood in the south-east part; through the main north–south and east–west belts there were rides. A new main drive, screened from the farm buildings west of it by trees, was made north-east of the house, the plantation north of the house was enlarged as a wilderness, and land immediately south of the house was enclosed by a semicircular haha. Further south of the house two circular planta-tions were made in the park. The road through Soper's bottom was apparently closed. In 1839 a long drive led from the house southwards across the park: where it left the park a lodge was built between then and 1879, and where it met the road along the south boundary of the parish gate piers survived in 1998. The semicir-cle within the haha was planted with trees

[69] W.R.O., A 1/345/112; P.R.O., PROB 11/1249, ff. 243v.–245.

[70] J. Britton, *Beauties of Wilts.* iii. 351; W.R.O., Ch. Com., chapter, 93/25–6.

[71] W.R.O., tithe award; memorial in Chute ch.; below, this section (Forest).

[72] *Alum. Oxon. 1715–1886*, ii. 485; P.R.O., PROB 11/1932, ff. 146–152v.

[73] *V.C.H. Wilts.* x. 36; *Kelly's Dir. Wilts.* (1907); W.A.S. Libr., sale cat. xxiv, no. 7; W.R.O. 211/15/27–8.

[74] W.R.O. 1650/25, p. 9; ibid. Inland Revenue, val. reg. 60.

[75] Ibid. 1650/25, p. 9; ibid. G 10/500/25.

[76] Ibid. 1650/25, pp. 9–10; J. Cherrington, *On the Smell of an Oily Rag*, 173, 177.

[77] Inf. from Mrs. A. W. Cherrington, Tantanoola; for the Biddesden estate, *V.C.H. Wilts.* xv. 134; below, this section.

[78] *W.N. & Q.* iii. 474; P.R.O., MR 342; W.R.O. 212B/1861.

[79] Above, plate 20.

[80] *Country Life*, 13 July 1967; M. Binney, *Sir Rob. Taylor*, 34.

[81] Binney, *Taylor*, 51.

[82] A. Quiney, *J. L. Pearson*, 247.

[83] W.R.O. 1650/25.

[84] Ibid. tithe award; *Andrews and Dury, Map* (W.R.S. viii), pl. 9.

[85] Binney, *Taylor*, 51, where the design of the alterations is attributed to Brown and William Emes. Brown and Emes are unlikely to have worked at Chute Lodge together: cf. R. Desmond, *Dict. Brit. Botanists*, 233.

between 1839 and 1879. In 1839 and later only *c*. 110 a. around and south of the house was preserved as a park; except for the woodland, the rest of the enlarged park was used for agriculture. In the 20th century the wilderness and the semicircle within the haha were cleared of trees, and belts of trees south and south-east of the house were grubbed up.[86]

Land in the south-west part of the parish, near Biddesden House, was probably allotted to the lord of Biddesden manor when Chute forest was inclosed, apparently *c*. 1639.[87] In 1780 the children of Thomas Humphreys, jointly lord of Biddesden manor, held an estate in the parish, and in 1839 J. H. Everett, the lord of that manor, held 240 a. in the south-west part.[88] That land, as Home later *LONGBOTTOM* farm, continued to pass with Biddesden manor and, with Home farm, Chute Forest, in 1998 belonged to members of the Guinness family.[89]

Land in the east part of the parish belonged in 1780 to John Freeman, the lord of Chute manor and the owner of Chute Lodge. It passed to his son Strickland, who sold it *c*. 1805 to Thomas Everett, the lord of Biddesden manor.[90] It passed with that manor to Everett's son J. H. Everett, who in 1839 held it as *REDHOUSE* farm and Forest later *POLLARD'S* farm, a total of 348 a. About 1868 J. H. Everett's son Henry Everett sold the two farms to T. E. Fowle,[91] the owner of Chute Lodge. They passed with Chute Lodge until *c*. 1927, when they were apparently sold by Lady Joicey-Cecil. Redhouse farm, 273 a., belonged to A. E. Potter in 1928.[92] It was later bought by Mr. M. K. B. Colvin, who in 1993 sold 160 a. of it to Mr. and Mrs. A. J. Hutchinson, the owners of that land in 1998, and himself owned *c*. 70 a. in Chute Forest in 1998.[93] The descent of Pollard's farm from *c*. 1927 has not been traced.

In the north-west part of the parish Jolly's House, and probably the land later called *FOREST* farm on which Forest House and Jolly's Farm stood, belonged in 1731 to Richard Earle,[94] whose estate may have passed successively to his sons Charles (d. *c*. 1758) and John, and by 1770 had passed to his daughter Elizabeth (d. unmarried 1780). Elizabeth Earle settled the estate in turn on Edward Poore (d. 1780 after her) and his daughter Charlotte Poore[95] (will proved 1829), a descendant of the lessee of Jolly's House

in 1731, who devised it to Sir Edward Poore, Bt. By 1831 it had passed, presumably by sale, to William Fowle[96] (d. 1840), who held 184 a. in the north-west part of the parish as Forest farm in 1839. That land descended with Chute Lodge. About 1906 W. H. Fowle (d. 1942) sold 100 a. of it with Chute Lodge.[97] He retained Forest House and 83 a. apparently until his death.[98] In 1998 Mr. G. B. Lambert owned *c*. 200 a. in the north-west part of the parish as part of Standen farm based in Chute parish.[99]

Land in the north-east part of the parish was owned by Evelyn Medows, the owner of Conholt House in Chute parish, from 1801 or earlier. In 1839 his successor Henry Manvers Pierrepont owned 69 a. there,[1] most of which passed with Conholt's land until *c*. 1897.[2] Its descent has not been traced further.

From 1780 or earlier to 1880 or later 31 a. in the west part of Chute Forest parish descended in the Holt and Pollen families with the manor of Fyfield (Hants).[3]

A charity endowed by Henry Rogers (will proved 1672) to relieve poverty in Fyfield and Thruxton (Hants) bought 30 a. in Chute Forest *c*. 1813.[4] It sold it *c*. 1964.[5]

In the later 19th century or early 20th 50 a. in the parish was bought by an almshouse at Ewelme (Oxon.).[6] The almshouse owned the land in 1998.[7]

The tithes of Chute forest were taken by Salisbury cathedral, probably from the 12th century as tithes from other forests in Wiltshire were.[8] In the early 19th century the dean and canons were entitled to all tithes from the whole parish. In 1839 the tithes were valued at £460 and commuted.[9]

ECONOMIC HISTORY. Although Chute forest was not disafforested until granted by the Crown in 1639,[10] the part of it north-east of the lodge which in 1632 stood near the centre of what became Chute Forest parish was apparently used for agriculture by the lessees before then. In 1642 corn was grown over much of the former forest, and in 1650 *c*. 286 a. of agricultural land in nine closes was held with Chute Lodge.[11] By 1665 allotments of land had replaced rights to feed animals on the former forest: most allotments were small,

86 O.S. Maps 6", Wilts. XLIX (1883 and later edns.); W.R.O., tithe award.
87 Above, this section.
88 W.R.O., A 1/345/112; ibid. tithe award; for the descent of Biddesden manor, *V.C.H. Wilts.* xv. 133–4.
89 *V.C.H. Wilts.* xv. 134; inf. from Mrs. Cherrington; above, this section.
90 *V.C.H. Wilts.* xv. 134; W.R.O., A 1/345/112; above, Chute, manors (Chute); this section (Chute Lodge).
91 *V.C.H. Wilts.* xv. 134; W.R.O. 211/15/28–9; ibid. tithe award.
92 W.R.O., G 10/500/23–5; W.A.S. Libr., sale cat. xxiv, no. 7; above, this section (Chute Lodge).
93 Inf. from Mrs. A. J. Hutchinson, Woodland Grange; Colvin Farms Estate Off., Tangley, Hants.
94 W.R.O. 212B/1874.
95 Ibid. 9/11/49–50; 9/11/52; *W.N. & Q.* vii. 33; memorial in Chute ch.
96 *V.C.H. Wilts.* xv. 98; W.R.O. 212B/1874; ibid. A 1/345/112.
97 *V.C.H. Wilts.* x. 36; W.A.S. Libr., sale cat. xxiv, no.

7; W.R.O., tithe award; above, this section (Chute Lodge).
98 *Kelly's Dir. Wilts.* (1939); W.R.O., G 10/500/23; G 10/505/1.
99 Inf. from Mr. G. B. Lambert, Standen Farm, Chute.
1 W.R.O., A 1/345/112; ibid. tithe award; above, Chute, manors (Conholt).
2 W.R.O. 2715/7, sale cat. of Conholt Park estate.
3 *V.C.H. Hants.* iv. 367; W.R.O., A 1/345/112; ibid. tithe award.
4 *V.C.H. Hants.* iv. 368; W.R.O., A 1/345/112; ibid. tithe award.
5 Inf. from Mr. J. Futcher, Blake's Farm, Redenham, Hants.
6 W.R.O., A 1/345/112; ibid. Inland Revenue, val. reg. 60.
7 Inf. from Mr. A. Robson, Messrs. Sidleys, 24A Mkt. Square, Bicester, Oxon.
8 *Close R.* 1231–4, 21; W.R.O., Ch. Com., chapter, 93/1–34.
9 W.R.O., tithe award.   10 Above, estates.
11 P.R.O., C 5/14/30; ibid. E 126/5, ff. 116v.–117; ibid. MR 342.

especially in the south where one consisting of a close of 1¾ a. in respect of a tenement and 10 a. in Appleshaw (Hants) may not have been untypical.[12]

By 1773 five or more farmsteads had been built beside the roads on the periphery of the parish; Forest Farm and Jolly's Farm stood in the north-west, Soper's, Flinty, and Pollard's in the south-east. Longbottom Farm and Redhouse Farm were built in the earlier 19th century.[13] In 1839 Chute Forest had c. 1,494 a. of arable and c. 169 a. of meadows and pastures. Along the southern boundary many of the allotments made before 1665 remained small rectangular fields. In the centre of the parish the owner of Chute Lodge kept in hand 428 a., of which 408 a. lay around Chute Lodge and was bounded south, east, and west by belts of trees. The 428 a. included 155 a. of arable, the park of Chute Lodge and other pasture, c. 150 a., and woodland, and the agricultural land was worked from buildings north of Chute Lodge. The farmstead later called Home Farm also stood in the centre of the parish north of Chute Lodge: in 1839 it was part of a mainly arable farm of 294 a. lying in the north-east part of the parish. In the south-west part of the parish Longbottom Farm and 240 a., of which 222 a. was arable, were then kept in hand by the owner of Biddesden House. Of the other farms in Chute Forest parish Forest had 184 a. and included Jolly's Farm, Pollard's had 202 a., Redhouse had 146 a., and Soper's had 31 a.[14]

In the later 19th century land in the parish was converted from arable to pasture, and on farms worked from the parish fewer sheep and more cattle were kept.[15] In the 1930s and 1990s the parish was mainly arable.[16] In 1910 woodland and 186 a., probably all parkland, were held with Chute Lodge. Home farm had 445 a., Redhouse farm 205 a., Pollard's farm 118 a., Jolly's farm 76 a., and Soper's farm 66 a.; 129 a. in the parish was worked from Cadley. Longbottom Farm and 250 a. were part of the home farm of the Biddesden estate, and other land, mainly in the south and east, was worked from outside the parish.[17] In 1928 Home farm had 417 a., Redhouse farm 273 a.[18]

Most of the buildings of Home farm were demolished in the 1990s,[19] and in 1998 three sets of farm buildings in the south-east corner, on and near the sites of Redhouse Farm and Pollard's Farm, were the only ones in the parish. The land formerly worked from Longbottom Farm, Home farm, Forest farm, and much of what had been the park of Chute Lodge were worked from outside the parish and were mainly arable. North-west of Home Farm large houses for poultry were built in the later 20th century.[20]

In the Middle Ages what became Chute Forest parish was the king's demesne wood,[21] and much of it was presumably covered with trees. In the earlier 17th century the woodland in what became the parish stood as five coppices, 484 a., in the north and west parts, and trees grew on much of the land in the south. Most of the woodland was grubbed up, possibly in the 17th century,[22] and in 1839 there was 146 a. of woodland in the parish. The largest wood in 1839 was Lodge coppice, 18 a. north of Chute Lodge, a remnant of a wood of that name accounted 92 a. in 1650. Most of the other woodland in 1839 stood immediately north-west of Chute Lodge, in the belts along the boundary of the land held with Chute Lodge, in circular plantations in the park, and in north-south linear plantations in the park and east of Lodge coppice.[23] The woodland immediately north-west of the house was removed in the mid 20th century; the southern boundary belt, the south part of the eastern boundary belt, and the linear plantations in the south-east part of the park were removed in the later 20th century.[24]

A malthouse standing in 1785[25] was probably at Cadley. In 1839 a malthouse stood there, a brickworks 300 m. north-west of Chute Lodge, and a lime kiln 850 m. west of Chute Lodge.[26] The brickworks apparently remained in use until the late 19th century.[27]

LOCAL GOVERNMENT. Chute Forest was extra-parochial and paupers born there were presumably unrelieved until, c. 1780, the inhabitants began to relieve them. In the three years to Easter 1785 Chute Forest spent an average of £56 to relieve its poor. In 1802-3 it spent £101 on regular relief for 15 adults and 22 children and occasional relief for 3 people.[28] At £235 spending was high in 1812-13, when 9 adults were relieved regularly and 6 occasionally, and at £113 low in 1813-14, when there were still 9 adults receiving regular relief and 4 received occasional relief. Between 1813-14 and 1823-4 spending exceeded £200 in only one year, between 1823-4 and 1833-4 in all years but one. It reached a peak of £311 in 1829-30.[29] Chute Forest joined Andover poor-law union in 1835[30] and was transferred to Pewsey union in 1879.[31] The parish became part of Kennet district in 1974.[32]

---

12 W.R.O. 130/6, deed, Fay to Lewes, 1665; cf. ibid. tithe award.   13 Above, intro.

14 W.R.O., tithe award.

15 P.R.O., MAF 68/151, sheet 15; MAF 68/493, sheet 10; MAF 68/1063, sheet 3; MAF 68/1633, no. 12.

16 [1st] Land Util. Surv. Map, sheets 112, 122.

17 O.S. Maps 6", Wilts. XLIX. NW. (1901, 1926 edns.); W.R.O., Inland Revenue, val. reg. 60.

18 W.R.O., G 10/500/25.

19 Above, intro.

20 Cf. O.S. Map 1/25,000, SU 35 (1958 edn.).

21 V.C.H. Wilts. iv. 425.

22 P.R.O., MR 342; cf. above, this section.

23 P.R.O., C 5/14/30; ibid. MR 342; W.R.O., tithe award.

24 O.S. Maps 6", Wilts. XLIX. NW. (1926 edn.); 1/25,000, SU 35 (1958 edn.); SU 25/35 (1994 edn.).

25 W.R.O. 130/6, copy will of Major Bailey, 1785.

26 Ibid. tithe award.

27 O.S. Maps 6", Wilts. XLIX (1883 and later edns.).

28 Poor Law Abstract, 1804, 564-5.

29 Ibid. 1818, 498-9; Poor Rate Returns, 1816-21, 188; 1822-4, 228; 1825-9, 219; 1830-4, 212.

30 Poor Law Com. 1st Rep. App. D, 248.

31 V.C.H. Wilts. iv. 331.

32 O.S. Map 1/100,000, admin. areas, Wilts. (1974 edn.).

CHURCH. Chute Forest church was built in 1870–1.[33] In 1875 it was consecrated,[34] a district was assigned to it,[35] and an incumbent called a vicar was licensed.[36] In 1924 the vicarage was united with Chute vicarage[37] and in 1954 the two parishes were united.[38] Chute Forest church was closed in 1972, and in 1974 it passed to the care of the Redundant Churches Fund, later the Churches Conservation Trust.[39] In 1979 the united benefice became part of Wexcombe benefice.[40]

In 1875 the incumbent was nominated by T. E. Fowle (d. 1877), the owner of Chute Lodge.[41] The patronage passed in turn to his relict Sarah Fowle (d. 1901) and son W. H. Fowle (d. 1942), who from 1924 shared the patronage of the united benefice. From 1942 the share was held by W. H. Fowle's son W. T. Fowle (d. 1968).[42] No member of the Fowle family sat on the board of patronage for Wexcombe benefice.[43]

The incumbency was endowed in 1875 by the Ecclesiastical Commissioners, who gave their tithe rent charge on 594 a. of the parish, and by T. E. Fowle.[44] No house was built for the incumbent, who from 1889 or earlier lived outside the parish. From 1903 the vicarage was held in plurality with Chute vicarage, and the incumbent lived in the vicarage house at Chute; from 1924 that house was lived in by the incumbent of the united benefice.[45]

The church of *ST. MARY* was built to designs by J. L. Pearson.[46] It is of patterned brick and flint and consists of a chancel with north vestry and south transept and a nave with north and south aisles, each with an east chapel, and south-west porch; above the transept there is a tower with a pyramidal spire. The chancel and the nave are undivided and each of two bays. Their roof is of trussed timber divided into bays by brick diaphragm arches; the vestry has a wagon roof. Inside the church the walls, piers, and arches are of brick, the reredos, pulpit, and font are of stone, and the seats are wooden.[47]

In 1875 T. E. Fowle gave a rent charge of £5 as a repair fund for the church.[48] In the 1920s insurance and occasional repairs were paid for from the fund.[49]

Two chalices, two patens, and a flagon, all of silver gilt, were given in 1875.[50] The church had six bells, all cast by Mears & Stainbank in 1871;[51] they were rehung in Chute church in 1976.[52]

NONCONFORMITY. A Methodist chapel straddling the boundary with Chute parish was built between Cadley and Lower Chute in 1844 and closed in 1990.[53]

EDUCATION. The children of inhabitants of Chute Forest attended schools in other parishes.[54] Chute Lodge was used as Staddles preparatory school from *c.* 1951 to 1970.[55]

CHARITY FOR THE POOR. None known.

COLLINGBOURNE KINGSTON

COLLINGBOURNE KINGSTON[56] is a large parish on the eastern edge of Salisbury Plain and *c.* 14 km. SSE. of Marlborough. It contained four small villages, Collingbourne Kingston, Aughton, Brunton, and Sunton, and part of Cadley hamlet. In 1934 the parish was reduced from 7,401 a. (2,995 ha.) to 2,915 ha. when Sunton and the part of Cadley were transferred to Collingbourne Ducis,[57] and in 1987 it was reduced to 2,018 ha. when its south-east and south-west parts were also transferred to Collingbourne Ducis.[58]

The parish lies mainly in the upper Bourne valley, and the name Collingbourne, referring to the Bourne as the stream of Cola's people, suggests that it was an area of early settlement.[59]

Each of the four villages stands beside the river, bears a Saxon name, and had a strip of land extending from the river to downland. To distinguish the two villages called Collingbourne suffixes were added to the name, and until the 14th century Collingbourne Kingston was called Collingbourne Abbot's: the earlier suffix refers to Hyde abbey, Winchester, the owner of the principal manor, and the later was possibly adopted under the misapprehension that the Collingbourne referred to in Domesday Book as the king's was not Collingbourne Ducis. Aughton took its name from Aeffe, the owner of it in the mid 10th century. The name Sunton, formerly Southampton, apparently refers to where the village stood on the abbey's estate called Collingbourne.[60]

33 A. Quiney, *J. L. Pearson*, 247; W.R.O. 1916/1.
34 W.R.O., D 1/60/11/24.   35 Ibid. 1916/7.
36 Ibid. D 1/2/41, p. 422; *Crockford* (1877).
37 *Lond. Gaz.* 9 Dec. 1924, pp. 8971–2.
38 W.R.O. 1916/2.
39 Ibid. 1916/10.   40 Inf. from Ch. Com.
41 W.R.O., D 1/2/41, p. 422; above, estates (Chute Lodge).
42 *Lond. Gaz.* 9 Dec. 1924, pp. 8971–2; *Clergy List* (1889 and later edns.); *Crockford* (1930 and later edns.); W.R.O. 1916/1; 1916/3.
43 Inf. from Ch. Com.
44 *Lond. Gaz.* 23 July 1875, p. 3721; W.R.O. 1916/7.
45 *Kelly's Dir. Wilts.* (1889 and later edns.); *Clergy List* (1914); W.R.O., D 1/2/45, pp. 490, 511–12.
46 Quiney, *Pearson*, 247.   47 Above, plate 10.
48 *Endowed Char. Wilts.* (S. Div.), 99.

49 W.R.O., L 2, Chute.
50 Nightingale, *Wilts. Plate*, 166.
51 Walters, *Wilts. Bells*, 59.   52 W.R.O. 627/20.
53 Above, Chute, nonconf.
54 e.g. *Returns relating to Elem. Educ.* 418–19.
55 W.R.O. 1650/25, p. 10.
56 This article was written in 1994–5. Maps used include O.S. Maps 1", sheet 14 (1817 edn.); 1/25,000, SU 25/35 (1994 edn.); 6", Wilts. XLII–XLIII, XLVIII–XLIX (1882–8 and later edns.).
57 *V.C.H. Wilts.* iv. 345.
58 Statutory Instruments, 1987, no. 619, Kennet (Parishes) Order.
59 *V.C.H. Wilts.* i (2), 479–80.
60 Ibid. ii, p. 118; *P.N. Wilts.* (E.P.N.S.), 342, 344–5; below, manors (Collingbourne Kingston; Aughton; Sunton); econ. hist.

In several places the parish boundary follows ridges and dry valleys, and on the south it is marked by a road. The north-west part had been defined by c. 933, when points on it included Oldhat barrow, a stone which gave its name to Falstone pond, and a prehistoric earthwork now called Godsbury.[61] Falstone pond had been dug on the boundary by 1773;[62] a new pond replaced it in the earlier 20th century.[63] Prehistoric ditches mark the boundary on the north-east and south-west.

The whole parish lies on chalk. The Bourne, which frequently dries out, flows from north to south across the middle of it and has deposited gravel, and there is also gravel in two long tributary valleys, now dry, which reach the Bourne from east and west at Sunton. Clay-with-flints overlies the chalk on high ground in the east half of the parish.[64] The downland is highest, at over 200 m., in the north-east and north-west corners of the parish. The Bourne leaves the parish at c. 130 m. and there is land at a similar height in the south-east corner, which drains south-eastwards, and the south-west corner. The relief is sharper in the east half of the parish. Each of the villages had meadow land beside the river, and to the east and west there were large areas of open fields and downland pastures for sheep. Much of the clay was wooded.[65] Horses were trained on the eastern downs in the 20th century,[66] and much of Snail down in the south-west, and downland along the western boundary of the parish, were used for military training from c. 1937.[67]

The parish had 164 poll-tax payers in 1377[68] and was highly assessed for taxation in the 16th century and earlier 17th; 93 inhabitants contributed to a subsidy in 1642, the highest number for any parish in the hundred except Great Bedwyn.[69] The population was 731 in 1801 and reached its peak of 933 in 1841, when Collingbourne Kingston village had 239 inhabitants, Aughton 166, Brunton 234, and Sunton 291. It had fallen to 696 by 1881, increased to 748 by 1911, and fallen to 585 by 1931. It was 440 in 1951, c. 166 inhabitants of Sunton and Cadley having been transferred to Collingbourne Ducis in 1934.[70] Collingbourne Kingston parish had 397 inhabitants in 1961, 441 in 1981, and, after the boundary changes of 1987, 454 in 1991.[71]

A Marlborough–Winchester road via Ludgershall and Andover (Hants) was important in the earlier Middle Ages[72] and presumably followed the Bourne through Collingbourne Kingston parish. Two other main roads crossed the parish, one between Oxford and Salisbury via Hungerford (Berks.) across the eastern downs, and one between Chipping Campden (Glos.) and Salisbury via Marlborough across the western: both were important in the later 17th century.[73] The Marlborough–Andover road branched southwards from the Marlborough–Salisbury road a little north of Collingbourne Kingston parish, and a little south of the parish a road linking the villages of the Bourne valley to Salisbury diverged from the Marlborough–Andover road.[74] In 1762 the north part of the Marlborough–Salisbury road, including the section through Collingbourne Kingston parish, was turnpiked, in 1772 the Hungerford road was turnpiked, and in 1835 the Bourne valley road was turnpiked from the junction north of the parish to complete Swindon–Salisbury and Swindon–Andover turnpike roads. The Hungerford road was disturnpiked in 1866, the other two in 1876.[75] The Salisbury road across Collingbourne Kingston's western downs may have declined in use after 1835 and was closed south of the parish c. 1900.[76] In the 20th century the Bourne valley route through the parish remained the main road from Swindon to Salisbury and Andover, and in 1995 the old Salisbury road (called the old Marlborough road) and the Hungerford road were still in use across the parish's downland. Of the east–west tracks linking them to the villages in the parish only Chick's Lane along the southern boundary has been tarmacadamed as a public road.

The Swindon, Marlborough & Andover Railway, from 1884 part of the Midland & South Western Junction Railway, was built beside the Bourne and opened in 1882. Cadley station in Collingbourne Ducis parish stood a little south of Sunton village. A halt immediately north-east of Collingbourne Kingston church was opened in 1932.[77] The line was closed in 1961.[78]

The parish provides much evidence of prehistoric activity. There is a long barrow east of Brunton village, and there are several barrows on the western downs including two, Oldhat barrow and another, on the parish boundary. A group of barrows forms a cemetery on Snail down.[79] The parish boundary crosses field systems of c. 100 a. on the east and of 200 a. or more on the north-east, and there are smaller field systems east of Sunton village, on the western downs, and on Snail down.[80] Several prehistoric ditches on Snail down are part of a system converging on an Iron-Age fort on Sidbury Hill in North Tidworth and may have been associated with cattle ranching.[81] Godsbury, on the boundary with Burbage, is an Iron-Age

61 W.A.M. lxiv. 60–4; for the date, P. H. Sawyer, Anglo-Saxon Chart. (revised S. E. Kelly; priv. circulated 1996), no. 379.
62 Andrews and Dury, Map (W.R.S. viii), pl. 9.
63 O.S. Map 1/2,500, Wilts. XLII. 10 (1900 and later edns.).
64 Geol. Surv. Maps 1", drift, sheet 282 (1985 edn.); 1/50,000, drift, sheet 283 (1975 edn.).
65 Below, econ. hist.
66 Ibid. (Sunton).
67 Inf. from Defence Land Agent, Durrington.
68 V.C.H. Wilts. iv. 309.
69 Taxation Lists (W.R.S. x), 11, 79; P.R.O., E 179/197/152; E 179/198/328; E 179/199/371; E 179/199/384;

E 179/199/411.
70 V.C.H. Wilts. iv. 345; P.R.O., HO 107/1180/8, ff. 4v.–27v.
71 Census, 1961; 1981; 1991; above, this section.
72 e.g. Archaeologia, xxii. 132, 138, 140–1.
73 J. Ogilby, Brit. (1675), pls. 83, 85.
74 Andrews and Dury, Map (W.R.S. viii), pls. 9, 12.
75 V.C.H. Wilts. iv. 257, 260, 262, 270; L.J. xxx. 205.
76 V.C.H. Wilts. xv. 63, 65.
77 Ibid. iv. 289–91.
78 Ibid. xi. 108.
79 Ibid. i (1), 60, 140, 168–9, 209, 217, 223.
80 Ibid. 275.
81 Ibid. 254–5; i (2), 402–3.

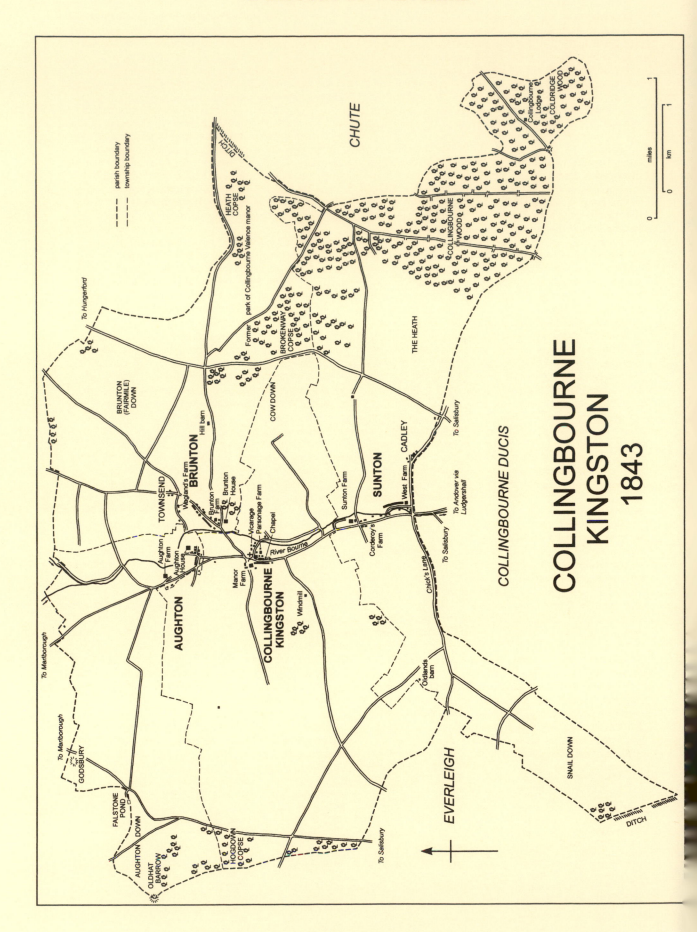

COLLINGBOURNE KINGSTON 1843

enclosure of 1½ a.; an enclosure of similar date and size lies on Aughton down and one of similar size on Fairmile down. A 10-a. enclosure lies on Snail down, and a possibly Romano-British one of 3½ a. lies *c.* 1 km. west of Aughton village.[82] A Pagan-Saxon cemetery east of Sunton village contained 33 inhumations.[83]

The whole parish was in Chute forest until 1330.[84]

COLLINGBOURNE KINGSTON is a nucleated village bisected by the Marlborough–Andover road, with the church, the vicarage house, and Manor Farm standing close to each other. West of the road the house called Manor Farm forms the north side of a large square farmyard. It comprises two parallel east–west ranges: the northern range, partly timber-framed, was built in the 17th century and extended eastwards in brick in the 18th, and the southern was built of yellow brick in the 19th century. On the west side of the farmyard a north–south barn was built in the later 16th century and extended northwards in the later 17th or the 18th. An 18th-century cart shed forms part of the south side of the farmyard. South of the church Parsonage Farm incorporates at its north-east corner fragments of a 17th-century house of flint with stone quoins. It was refaced and extended southwards in the early 18th century, and extended westwards in two stages in the 19th. Also south of the church the Old House was built in the mid 18th century with a principal north front of five bays and was extended westwards in the later 18th century. After a fire in 1976 a single-storeyed lean-to on the south side was raised to two storeys and new panelling in 18th-century style was fitted in the house.[85]

Most of the older cottages and small houses to survive in the village are timber-framed with daub and plaster infilling and have thatched roofs. Some are of one storey, some of one storey and attics. On the east side of the road Norrie Cottage, with heavy timber and evidence of substantial bracing, may be medieval. Some 18th-century cottages have walls of chalk block and brick arranged in horizontal bands. There are a few 19th-century cottages in the village, which in 1974 was designated a conservation area.[86]

The Falcon inn, which stood in Collingbourne Kingston village in the early 18th century, had been renamed the Chequers by 1722.[87] The Chequers remained open in 1773.[88] On the west side of the main road an inn was built of red brick in the early 19th century. It was called the Cleaver in 1822, 1843,[89] 1899–1911, and in the later 20th century, and was open under that name in 1995. It was called the Collingbourne Kingston inn from the 1840s to

the 1890s and the Kingston hotel in the earlier 20th century. On the east side of the road the Windmill was open from the 1850s[90] to the later 20th century.

In the 19th century a new vicarage house and a school were built at the north end of the village, respectively east and west of the main road, and at the south end a nonconformist chapel was built east of the road.[91] In the 20th century the village was extended further south by new detached houses built mainly on the west side of the road. On the downs west of the village Croft barn was built in the mid 19th century and other farm buildings, including Summerdown Farm near the old Marlborough road, in the mid and later 20th century.[92]

AUGHTON. The old part of the village stands at a staggered crossroads: the north–south element, from which lanes led east to the river and west to Aughton's open fields and downland, may be an old course of the Marlborough–Andover road, which was apparently diverted to higher ground to the west. Several timber-framed and thatched houses of the 17th and 18th centuries survive at the crossroads. Aughton House, in the north-east angle, was built in the 17th century as a small timber-framed house of one storey and attics; its southern part was replaced by a two-storeyed red-brick range in the 19th century.

A short distance north of the village Aughton Farm was built in the mid 18th century on the north-east side of what may then have been the main road. Of red brick with a thatched roof, it had a main north–south range with principal rooms north and south of a stair hall, in which early 17th-century panelling has been reset, and a single-storeyed lean-to on the east. An extension, possibly also of one storey, was built at the south end. The extension was rebuilt with, or raised to, two storeys in 1829,[93] and the house was reroofed with tiles in the 20th century.[94] On the waste beside the present main road a few cottages were standing near Aughton Farm in 1843:[95] none survived in 1995. Alborough House and a pair of cottages were built in the mid 20th century on the west side of the road.

At the southern edge of the village council houses and bungalows, a total of 38, were built as Ham Close and Cuckoo Pen Close in the 1930s and 1960s.[96]

BRUNTON. Settlement at Brunton was in a village street, which was designated a conservation area in 1994.[97] From the north-east end of the street a lane led west to Aughton via a ford in the Bourne,[98] and from the south-west end a lane led south, with the Bourne flowing along it, and west to Collingbourne Kingston village.[99]

82 *V.C.H. Wilts.* i (1), 264. 83 *W.A.M.* lxx/lxxi. 61–2.
84 *V.C.H. Wilts.* iv. 399–400, 425, 452–3.
85 Inf. from Mrs. W. de Mole, Old Ho.
86 Inf. from Dept. of Planning and Highways, Co. Hall, Trowbridge.
87 W.R.O. 1331/1, deed, Eeles to Chandler, 1722.
88 Ibid. 9/10/260, p. 1.
89 Ibid. A 1/326/3; ibid. tithe award.
90 *Kelly's Dir. Wilts.* (1848 and later edns.).
91 Below, church; nonconf.; educ.

92 O.S. Maps 6", Wilts. XLII (1888 and later edns.); W.R.O., tithe award; below, econ. hist. (Collingbourne Kingston). 93 Date on ho.
94 W.R.O. 1008/8. 95 Ibid. tithe award.
96 Ibid. G 10/603/2; G 10/613/2–3; G 10/760/170.
97 Inf. from Dept. of Planning and Highways, Co. Hall, Trowbridge.
98 Cf. O.S. Map 6", Wilts. SU 25 NW. (1961 edn.).
99 *Andrews and Dury, Map* (W.R.S. viii), pl. 9, where the village names Aughton and Brunton are transposed.

To link Brunton and Collingbourne Kingston a three-arched red-brick bridge and a new north-east and south-west section of lane were built in 1810.[1] Buildings stood on both sides of the Aughton lane in 1773,[2] fewer buildings later. A small group of cottages north of the junction of the street and the Aughton lane was called Townsend in 1798.[3] In 1843 there were four farmsteads at Brunton, one in the Aughton lane and three in the street;[4] later they were all superseded by farmsteads built outside the village.[5] On a steep slope north-east of Townsend strip lynchets, apparently made between 1817 and 1843 for allotments,[6] survived in 1995.

In the Aughton lane only a much altered house called Waglands Farm survived in 1995, and at Townsend only a timber-framed and thatched cottage. Cottages to survive in the street included a few, timber-framed and thatched, of the 17th century and a few built in each of the following centuries. Six council houses were built in the street in the 1920s and 1930s,[7] and a few private houses were built in the later 20th century. At the south-west end of the street Brunton House on the south-east side was built in 1692 for William Vince (d. 1697).[8] It has a regular west front of seven bays, chiefly of brick and with a central Tuscan porch, and has other elevations of banded brick and flint with alterations in brick. It was rectangular, with a central hall and staircase and a room at each corner on each of its two floors: the original staircase survived in 1995. About 1840 the east half of the south front was extended southwards and a new chimney stack was built against the east wall. East of the kitchen, which was in the north-east corner of the house, additional service rooms were built mostly in the 19th century. Terraced gardens were made east of the house, and from the upper terrace an avenue of yew trees led across a small park which had been made south of the house by c. 1773:[9] traces of the terraces survived in 1995. At the farmstead north of Brunton House a red-brick farmhouse was built in the earlier 19th century.

In the mid 19th century two new farmsteads, each incorporating cottages, were built outside the village, New Buildings, later Spicey Buildings, north of Waglands Farm, and Tinkerbarn to the east: both were standing in 1995. Hill barn, standing east of the village in 1843, and Johnson's barn, built north-east of the village in the mid 19th century, were demolished in the 20th century.[10]

SUNTON. Settlement at Sunton was on both sides of a north–south street which was part of the Marlborough–Andover road and along the middle of which the Bourne flowed; in 1773 there were more buildings on the east side than the west.[11] The main road curved to east and west, and in 1835 a new straight section was built to cut across the curves and to bypass Sunton village, which lies to the east of the new section.[12] In 1995 the east side of the street was lined by c. 15 timber-framed and thatched cottages of the 18th century or earlier, and a few such buildings survived between the Bourne and the new road; a ford remained at the north end of the street. At the south end West Farm was built, apparently as a timber-framed house on a three-roomed plan, in the later 18th century. About 1800 it was encased in brick and enlarged to the west by two gabled wings which were linked by a passage; in the 19th century a gabled extension was built on the north side. West of that house the King's Arms was open in 1773[13] and 1855:[14] unsuccessful attempts to enforce its closure as a house of ill repute were made in 1815.[15] The village is part of a conservation area designated in 1974.[16]

A short distance north of Sunton village a farmhouse may have been built in the early 17th century. Sunton Farm was built there in the mid 18th century and incorporates a fireplace and a chimney stack which may have been those of such a predecessor. Sunton Farm was built as an L-shaped house with a stair turret in the north-east angle. The east–west range has a principal south front of seven bays with a central doorway; in 1995 it was a garden front. Original panelling survives in the rooms on both floors at the east end of that range. Reset early 17th-century panelling in the ground-floor room at its west end, like the fireplace and chimney stack, which that room shares with the north service wing, may survive from an earlier house, the plan of which may have influenced the irregular arrangement of the windows on the south front of Sunton Farm. Between Sunton Farm and the village Corderoy's (later Cawdrey's) Farm is an 18th-century farmhouse of flint with red-brick dressings: in 1835 the new section of the main road east of it replaced the old section west of it.[17] East of Cawdrey's Farm and of the new section of road stand two thatched cottages apparently of the 17th century or early 18th, each partly timber-framed and partly of flint and brick.

A large house called Highfield Lodge was built on the west side of the new section of road between 1843 and c. 1880,[18] and from the 1950s private houses were built on that side between Cawdrey's Farm and Highfield Lodge. South of Highfield Lodge an estate of c. 17 private houses was built as Bourne Rise in the angle of the main road and Chick's Lane in the early 1970s.

Cadley, so called in the later 18th century,

1 W.R.O., A 1/316/36.
2 Andrews and Dury, Map (W.R.S. viii), pl. 9.
3 W.R.O., tithe award; ibid. 9/12/26.
4 Ibid. tithe award.   5 Below, this section.
6 O.S. Map 1", sheet 14 (1817 edn.); W.R.O., tithe award.
7 P.R.O., G 10/603/2.
8 Reset date stone with initials on ho.; below, manors (Brunton).
9 Andrews and Dury, Map (W.R.S. viii), pl. 9.
10 O.S. Maps 6", Wilts. XLII (1888 and later edns.);

W.R.O., tithe award.
11 Andrews and Dury, Map (W.R.S. viii), pl. 9.
12 Cf. O.S. Map 1", sheet 14 (1817 edn.); W.R.O., tithe award; above, this section [roads].
13 W.R.O. 9/10/260, p. 6.
14 Kelly's Dir. Wilts. (1855).   15 W.R.O. 9/1/484.
16 Inf. from Dept. of Planning and Highways, Co. Hall, Trowbridge.
17 Cf. W.R.O. 9/11/149.
18 Ibid. tithe award; O.S. Map 6", Wilts. XLII (1888 edn.).

was a small group of cottages standing on the waste at a road junction on the parish boundary 500 m. east of Sunton village.[19] The cottages on the north side of the east–west road stood in Collingbourne Kingston parish. Several apparently of the late 18th century or early 19th[20] survived in 1995; several were burned down c. 1914.[21] On the north side of the road between Cadley and Sunton two pairs of estate cottages were built in the mid 19th century[22] and private houses and an estate of 22 council houses were built in the mid and later 20th.

West of Sunton village Oldlands barn was standing in 1773.[23] Extensive farm buildings were erected a short distance south-east of its site in the 20th century. East of the village Herridge Farm was built between 1843 and 1878:[24] it was used for racing stables in the 20th century.[25] Collingbourne Lodge was standing in Coldridge wood in the south-east corner of the parish in 1773.[26] It was used by a gamekeeper in 1843[27] and was demolished in the late 19th century.[28]

MANORS AND OTHER ESTATES. In 1066 St. Peter's abbey, Winchester, otherwise called the New minster and from 1109 called Hyde abbey, held a 50-hide estate called Collingbourne, which almost certainly included Aughton, Brunton, and Sunton but excluded Collingbourne Ducis. Most of it was the later manor of *COLLINGBOURNE KINGSTON* or *COLLINGBOURNE ABBOT'S*. The abbey, founded in 901,[29] claimed to have held the estate from 903[30] and held the manor until the Dissolution.[31]

In 1544 the Crown granted Collingbourne Kingston manor to Edward Seymour, earl of Hertford[32] (cr. duke of Somerset 1547), and in 1552 took it back when Somerset was executed and attainted. In 1553 the manor was assigned by Act to Seymour's son Sir Edward (cr. earl of Hertford 1559),[33] and from then to c. 1929 it descended in the Seymour, Bruce, Brudenell, and Brudenell-Bruce families with Tottenham Lodge and Tottenham House in Great Bedwyn.[34] In 1843 the manor included 1,692 a. in the Collingbourne Kingston part of the parish.[35]

About 1929 George Brudenell-Bruce, marquess of Ailesbury, sold Manor farm, 1,117 a., to Alfred May.[36] In 1982 the farm, until then owned by A. May & Sons, was divided between R. J. May, who in 1995 owned c. 550 a. as Manor farm, and R. G. May & Sons, a partnership which in 1995 owned c. 550 a. as Summerdown farm.[37] About 1929 Lord Ailesbury sold the remaining Collingbourne Kingston land of the manor as part of Parsonage farm, 900 a., to J. S. Ruttle, who sold it in 1930 to I. C. Crook (d. 1969). The farm passed to Crook's grandson, Mr. J. R. Crook, who with members of his family owned it in 1995.[38]

Between 1532 and 1544 Margaret Chadderton held land in Collingbourne Kingston. *CHAD-DERTON'S* farm descended to her son Edmund Chadderton (d. 1545),[39] whose son William probably sold it, as he did Manton manor in Preshute, to Thomas Michelborne (d. 1582) in 1571. Chadderton's passed in turn to Thomas's sons Edward, Laurence (d. 1611), who held it in 1595, and Thomas,[40] who sold it in 1623 to James Jennings.[41] It passed to James Jennings (d. 1684) and to Robert Jennings (d. 1738). Robert demised the farm to his brother William (d. 1740), and it passed to William's son James (d. 1746 or 1747) and to James's son Robert.[42] In 1765 that Robert's brother James Jennings sold the farm, 164 a. and pasture rights, to Thomas Brudenell, Lord Bruce.[43] The estate was thereafter merged with Collingbourne Kingston manor.

The thegn Wulfgar was granted 10 *cassati* at *AUGHTON*, probably by King Athelstan c. 933. Between 933 and 948 Wulfgar devised the estate to his wife Aeffe for life with remainder to the New minster (later Hyde abbey) at Winchester.[44] After Aeffe's death the estate was merged with Collingbourne Kingston manor, and it remained part of it until the earlier 20th century.[45] About 1929 George, marquess of Ailesbury, sold c. 400 a. to Alfred May[46] with Manor farm, Collingbourne Kingston: in 1995 part of that land was in Manor farm, part in Summerdown farm.[47] Also c. 1929 Lord Ailesbury sold most of the land of Aughton House farm, c. 200 a., apparently to A. J. Hosier[48] with

19 W.R.O. 9/11/149.
20 Cf. ibid. tithe award; *Andrews and Dury, Map* (W.R.S. viii), pl. 9.
21 P. V. C. Codgell, *Collingbourne Remembered: a Village Hist.* 245.
22 O.S. Map 6", Wilts. XLVIII (1883–8 edn.); W.R.O., tithe award.
23 *Andrews and Dury, Map* (W.R.S. viii), pl. 9.
24 O.S. Map 6", Wilts. XLII (1888 edn.); W.R.O., tithe award.
25 Below, econ. hist. (Sunton).
26 *Andrews and Dury, Map* (W.R.S. viii), pl. 9.
27 W.R.O., tithe award.
28 O.S. Maps 6", Wilts. XLIX (1883 edn.); XLIX. NW. (1901 edn.).
29 *V.C.H. Wilts.* ii, p. 127; xi. 109; *V.C.H. Hants.* ii. 116–17; cf. below, this section.
30 Finberg, *Early Wessex Chart.* p. 80.
31 P.R.O., SC 6/Hen. VIII/3341, rott. 52–3.
32 *L. & P. Hen. VIII*, xix (2), pp. 313–14.
33 *Complete Peerage*, vi. 504–7; xii (1), 59–64; P.R.O., E 328/117.
34 Above, Great Bedwyn, manors (Tottenham).

35 W.R.O., tithe award; for the manor's land in Aughton and Sunton, below, this section; in Brunton, ibid. econ. hist. (Brunton).
36 W.R.O. 9/1/521; Ch. Com. file 89163/1.
37 Inf. from Mrs. M. May, Manor Farm; Mr. C. May, Summerdown Farm.
38 W.R.O. 9/1/521; inf. from Mr. G. I. Crook, Aughton Farm.
39 *V.C.H. Wilts.* xiv. 110; P.R.O., C 1/967, nos. 8–9.
40 *V.C.H. Wilts.* xii. 172; P.R.O., PROB 11/65, ff. 192v.–193v.; W.R.O. 9/10/254, p. 42.
41 W.R.O. 9/10/11.
42 Ibid. wills, archd. Wilts., Jas. Jennings, 1684; cons. Sar., Rob. Jennings, 1738; ibid. 9/1/98; 9/1/204, p. 128; 666/1–2.   43 Ibid. 9/10/24; 9/10/26.
44 Finberg, *Early Wessex Chart.* pp. 82–3, 85; Sawyer, *Anglo-Saxon Chart.* (revised Kelly), no. 379.
45 W.R.O. 9/10/254, pp. 21, 31–2, 34, 36, 38; Hants R.O. 11M59/59591, pp. 18–21, 23; D. & C. Winton. Mun., box 114, val. 1815.
46 W.R.O. 9/1/521; inf. from Mrs. May.
47 Above, this section (Collingbourne Kingston).
48 W.R.O. 9/1/521; ibid. G 10/500/130.

Brunton farm, of which farm the land was part in 1995.[49]

By will proved 1670 Edward Pile gave *PILE'S* farm at Aughton to his nephew Robert Pile and grandnephew Edward Pile as joint tenants.[50] In 1763 Thomas Gilbert (d. 1771) owned the farm, which may earlier have belonged to John Gilbert. The farm, 305 a., descended from Thomas in the direct line to Thomas (d. 1807) and Thomas Gilbert (d. 1840),[51] whose devisees sold it in 1841 to Charles Brudenell-Bruce, marquess of Ailesbury.[52] It descended with Tottenham House to George, marquess of Ailesbury, who in 1929 sold it as Aughton farm, c. 331 a., to J. S. Ruttle.[53] In 1932 Ruttle sold it to P. B. Darnell,[54] in 1939 Darnell sold it to P. W. B. Roberts, and in 1947 Roberts sold it to R. I. J. Crook (d. 1982), whose son Mr. G. I. Crook owned it in 1995.[55]

An estate assessed at 10 hides and ½ yardland, part of the 50-hide estate held by St. Peter's abbey, Winchester, in 1066, had became heritable by 1086. It was held of the abbey and consisted of what became *COLLING-BOURNE VALENCE* manor, which comprised land east of the Bourne and in the 19th century lay in farms based at Brunton, and of what became Chute manor. Croc the huntsman held it in 1086,[56] it presumably descended in the Croke family,[57] and in 1201 Ellis Croke (d. 1215) held the manor later called Collingbourne Valence.[58] That manor descended to Ellis's daughter Avice, the wife of Michael de Columbers (d. 1235),[59] who sold it in 1245 to Henry III.[60] The king granted it in 1253 to his half-brother William de Valence,[61] to whom in 1256 he granted free warren in its demesne.[62] The manor passed from William, styled earl of Pembroke (d. 1296), to his son Aymer, who assigned it as dower to his mother Joan (d. 1307). From Aymer, from 1307 earl of Pembroke (d. *s.p.* 1324),[63] it descended to his nieces Elizabeth and Joan Comyn. In 1325 the manor was allotted to Elizabeth,[64] and she and her husband Richard Talbot held it in 1327.[65] In 1332 it was reallotted to Joan's son David of Strathbogie, earl of Atholl (d. 1335),[66] who immediately sold it to Sir Edmund Cornwall (d. *s.p.* 1373) and his wife Isabel. In 1373 it reverted to David's

heirs.[67] In 1376 it was allotted to his granddaughter Elizabeth of Strathbogie, who married Sir Thomas Percy, and in 1388 she sold it to her sister Philippe (d. 1395) and Philippe's husband John Halsham (d. 1415). Philippe's son Sir Hugh Halsham (d. *s.p.* 1442)[68] in 1438 settled the manor for life on Anne, the relict of his brother Richard and the wife of John Thornbury. From Anne (d. 1460) it passed to Richard's daughter Joan (d. 1495), the wife of John Lewknor (d. 1471).[69] The Lewknors settled the manor on themselves for life with remainder to Thomas Rogers (d. by 1479) and his son William.[70] It was later owned in turn by Thomas's son George (d. 1524), George's son Sir Edward,[71] Sir Edward's son Sir George (d. 1582), and Sir George's son Edward,[72] who sold it in portions.

The largest portion of Collingbourne Valence manor was sold by Edward Rogers to John Durrington in 1591. It apparently included manorial rights[73] and was the estate later called *BRUNTON* manor. Durrington (d. 1619) devised it in thirds, presumably undivided, to his daughters Anne, wife of Adrian Bower, Cecily, wife of William Bower, and Joan (d. 1637), wife of William Vince. Joan's share descended to her son William Vince[74] (d. 1657) and to William's son William (d. 1697).[75] Cecily's share passed to her son William Bower, and in 1673 William's relict Mary and son William sold it to William Vince.[76] The share of Anne (d. 1625) apparently passed to her son Adrian Bower (fl. 1638);[77] it has not been traced further and was probably acquired by the younger William Vince. Brunton manor passed from that William to his son William, whose administrators sold it in 1714 to Joseph Macham (d. 1752). It descended to Macham's son William, at whose death in 1789[78] it passed to his kinsman and heir-at-law John Delmé. In 1794 Delmé sold the manor to William Ludlow.[79] In 1803 Ludlow sold three fifths of it to William Stagg,[80] and in 1808 his assigns sold two fifths to Charles Tylee.[81] Charles Brudenell-Bruce, marquess of Ailesbury, bought Stagg's lands in 1824,[82] Tylee's in 1825,[83] and added them to land in Brunton which he already owned.[84]

A small part of Collingbourne Valence manor

49 Cf. below, this section (Collingbourne Valence).
50 Hants R.O. 33M57/55.
51 Ibid. 11M59/59591, p. 24; *Q. Sess. 1736* (W.R.S. xi), p. 141; W.R.O. 9/13/14; 9/13/16–18; 9/13/20.
52 W.R.O. 9/13/21.
53 Ibid. 1008/8; above, Great Bedwyn, manors (Tottenham). 54 Ch. Com. file 89163/1.
55 Ibid. 89163/3; inf. from Mr. G. I. Crook, Aughton Farm.
56 *V.C.H. Wilts.* ii, p. 127; for Chute manor, above, Chute.
57 For the descent, above, Chute, manors (Chute).
58 *V.C.H. Wilts.* iv. 425; *Cur. Reg. R.* i. 418.
59 *V.C.H. Wilts.* iv. 425; *Bk. of Fees*, ii. 714.
60 *Cal. Lib.* 1240–5, 302; *Close R.* 1242–7, 397.
61 *Cal. Chart. R.* 1226–57, 416.
62 *Cal. Pat.* 1247–58, 533.
63 *Cal. Close*, 1296–1302, 3; *Complete Peerage*, x. 377, 380–2, 387.
64 *Cal. Fine R.* 1319–27, 338; I. J. Sanders, *Eng. Baronies*, 132; *Complete Peerage*, i. 307.
65 P.R.O., C 143/190, no. 5.
66 *Cal. Close*, 1330–3, 455–7, 584–5; *Complete Peerage*, i. 306–8.
67 *Cal. Pat.* 1330–4, 326; *Wilts. Inq. p.m.* 1327–77 (Index Libr.), 394.
68 *Cal. Close*, 1374–7, 322; 1396–9, 26; *Cal. Pat.* 1385–9, 421; *Cal. Inq. p.m.* xvii, pp. 255–6; *Complete Peerage*, i. 308–9; P.R.O., C 138/13, no. 38.
69 *Cal. Pat.* 1436–41, 161; *Complete Peerage*, i. 308–9; D. G. C. Elwes and C. J. Robinson, *Castles, Mansions, and Manors of W. Suss.* 284; P.R.O., C 139/178, no. 53.
70 *Cal. Pat.* 1467–77, 177; 1476–85, 169.
71 *Som. Pedigrees* (Harl. Soc. xi), 128; P.R.O., C 142/41, no. 1. 72 P.R.O., C 142/197, no. 52.
73 W.R.O. 382, pp. 90–3; cf. 9/12/95.
74 *Wilts. Inq. p.m.* 1625–49 (Index Libr.), 253; P.R.O., C 142/375, no. 53.
75 *Colln. Topog. et Geneal.* vii. 178–9.
76 P.R.O., E 134/6 Anne Mich./31.
77 Ibid. C 142/375, no. 53; *Wilts. Inq. p.m.* 1625–49 (Index Libr.), 255–6.
78 *Colln. Topog. et Geneal.* vii. 177–80; W.R.O. 9/12/69.
79 W.R.O. 9/12/86; 9/12/107.
80 Ibid. 9/12/96–7.
81 Ibid. 9/12/102; 9/12/107. 82 Ibid. 9/12/106.
83 Ibid. 9/12/112.
84 Below, this section.

was sold by Edward Rogers to Thomas Smith, John Andrews, John Dean, and Salathiel Dean in 1612. It was divided into four small farms,[85] the lands of most of which apparently belonged to Charles, marquess of Ailesbury, in 1843.[86]

An estate in Brunton descended from Roger Bacon to his daughter Christine, who sold it in 1350 to Sir Edmund Cornwall (d. 1373).[87] Cornwall's feoffees conveyed it in 1380 to John Blanchard.[88] John's son Thomas sold it c. 1426 to William Darell,[89] who conveyed it in 1426 to Richard Halsham.[90] In 1485 Constantine Darell (will proved 1508) held what was later called *DORMER* manor, probably the same estate, and in 1528 his son Constantine sold it to (Sir) Michael Dormer[91] (d. 1545). The manor was sold by Sir Michael's son Geoffrey to Edward Seymour, duke of Somerset, in 1547,[92] thereafter descended with Collingbourne Kingston manor and with Tottenham Lodge and Tottenham House,[93] and in 1843 belonged to Charles, marquess of Ailesbury.[94]

Nearly all the land of Brunton belonged to Lord Ailesbury in 1843.[95] It descended with Tottenham House to George Brudenell-Bruce, marquess of Ailesbury,[96] who in 1929 sold Brunton farm, 1,476 a., to A. J. Hosier (d. 1963) and his brother Joshua.[97] Mr. N. H. Hosier owned the farm in 1995.[98]

Much of Sunton's land was held customarily as part of Collingbourne Kingston manor.[99]

An estate of 1 hide and ½ yardland conveyed by William son of Edmund to Gervase and his wife Maud in 1199[1] was presumably that of 6½ yardlands held freely of Hyde abbey by Thomas Gervase in 1232. The 6½ yardlands became one of two manors called *SUNTON* and was held after 1232 by Hugh Chaucy.[2] The manor descended in the Chaucy family. Thomas Chaucy conveyed it in 1444 to John Benger,[3] who in 1447 settled it on another John Benger and that John's wife Anne.[4] Later the manor passed from John Benger, possibly Anne's husband, to his brother George. In 1511 George Benger sold it to William Chaucy[5] (d. 1523),[6] from whom it passed to his daughter Joan, the wife of William Thornhill, and in 1548 William sold it to Edward, duke of Somerset.[7] Thereafter it descended with

Collingbourne Kingston manor and with Tottenham Lodge and Tottenham House.[8] Presumably including land in Sunton which had been part of Collingbourne Kingston manor, it was sold in 1930 as West farm, 654 a., by George, marquess of Ailesbury, to Marjorie Wroth (d. 1981), who added Corderoy's farm to it. In 1937 Marjorie and her husband, Leslie Wroth (d. 1965), sold the west part of West farm, c. 390 a. including most of Snail down, to the War Department, and the Ministry of Defence owned that land in 1994.[9] The rest of West farm, c. 380 a., was sold by the Wroths to W. E. & D. T. Cave in 1948 and bought in 1983 by Mr. R. D. Hendry, the owner in 1995.[10]

A freehold in Sunton was held by Henry of Bridport in the earlier 13th century. He conveyed it to Hyde abbey, from which Thorold held it in 1232 as ½ knight's fee.[11] As the second *SUNTON* manor Hugh Thorold held it in 1394,[12] and Hugh Thorold, presumably another, held it in 1448.[13] The manor may have been held by a member of the Hyde family in the mid and later 17th century,[14] had been acquired by Thomas Bruce, earl of Ailesbury, by 1780,[15] and thereafter descended with Tottenham House.[16] As Sunton farm and Herridge farm, each presumably including land in Sunton which had been part of Collingbourne Kingston manor, it was sold c. 1929 by George, marquess of Ailesbury. Sunton farm, 347 a., was bought by C. G. Fribbance;[17] later the farm was divided, and its land was held c. 1994 by Mr. D. Leigh, Mr. I. Leigh, and Mr. P. Walker.[18] Herridge farm, c. 435 a., was bought by A. G. Bendir;[19] in 1995 the farm, c. 200 a., was owned by Mr. Richard Hannon.[20]

Francis Corderoy (d. 1716) devised *CORDEROY'S* farm, 124 a. in 1809, to his nephew Edward Corderoy,[21] who in 1745 sold it to Charles Earle. On Charles's death c. 1758 the farm may have passed to his brother John, and it passed to his sister Elizabeth Earle (d. unmarried 1780), who settled it in turn on Edward Poore (d. 1780 after her) and his daughter Charlotte Poore.[22] In 1814 Charlotte sold the farm to Charles Brudenell-Bruce, earl of Ailesbury.[23] It thereafter descended with Tottenham House to George, marquess of Ailesbury, who

85 P.R.O., CP 25/2/370/9 Jas. I Hil.; W.R.O. 9/12/121.
86 W.R.O., tithe award.
87 Ibid. 9/12/1; for Cornwall, above, this section (Collingbourne Valence).
88 W.R.O. 9/12/4.
89 Ibid. 9/12/7–8.   90 Ibid. 9/12/10.
91 Ibid. 9/12/12–15; *Hist. Parl., Commons, 1439–1509*, 259.
92 W.R.O. 9/12/16–17; G. Baker, *Hist. Northants.* 620.
93 Above, Great Bedwyn, manors (Tottenham); this section (Collingbourne Kingston).
94 W.R.O., tithe award.
95 Ibid.
96 Above, Great Bedwyn, manors (Tottenham).
97 A. J. and F. H. Hosier, *Hosier's Farming System*, 37; W.R.O. 9/1/521.
98 Inf. from Mr. N. H. Hosier, Waglands Farm.
99 B.L. Harl. MS. 1761, ff. 145v.–146; W.R.O. 9/1/95.
1 *Feet of F. 1198–9* (Pipe R. Soc. xxiv), p. 130.
2 B.L. Harl. MS. 1761, ff. 145v.–146.
3 W.R.O. 9/11/3.
4 Ibid. 9/11/2; 9/11/6.
5 Ibid. 9/11/8–10.

6 *V.C.H. Wilts.* x. 40.
7 J. Hutchins, *Hist. Dors.* iv. 417; W.R.O. 9/11/11.
8 Above, Great Bedwyn, manors (Tottenham); this section (Collingbourne Kingston).
9 W.R.O. 9/1/521; Ch. Com. file 89163/1; inf. from the Chief Executive, Govt. Property Lawyers, Taunton; mon. in churchyard; for Corderoy's farm, below, this section.
10 Inf. from Mr. T. Cave, Shoddesden Grange, Andover, Hants; Mr. R. D. Hendry, Lower Ho. Farm, Everleigh.
11 B.L. Harl. MS. 1761, ff. 140, 145v.–146.
12 *Feet of F. 1377–1509* (W.R.S. xli), p. 36.
13 W.R.O., D 1/2/10, f. 58 and v.
14 *W.A.M.* xli. 33–5; W.R.O., D 1/24/56/1.
15 W.R.O., A 1/345/120.
16 Above, Great Bedwyn, manors (Tottenham).
17 W.R.O. 9/1/521; Ch. Com. file 89163/1.
18 Codgell, *Collingbourne Remembered*, 145.
19 W.A.S. Libr., sale cat. xxviiiB, nos. 17A–B.
20 Inf. from Mrs. M. May, Manor Farm.
21 W.R.O. 529/205; Hants R.O. 11M59/59591, pp. 6–7.
22 W.R.O. 9/11/49–50; 9/11/52; above, Chute Forest, estates (Forest).
23 W.R.O. 9/10/260, p. 1; 9/11/50; 9/11/52.

in 1930 sold the farm, *c.* 112 a., to Marjorie Wroth.[24] It was thereafter part of West farm.[25]

Woodland presumably in the south-east part of the parish was divided between the lords of Collingbourne Kingston and Collingbourne Valence manors in 1241,[26] and the extensive woodland east of Sunton[27] thereafter belonged to the lord of Collingbourne Kingston manor.[28] In 1935 George, marquess of Ailesbury, sold Collingbourne and Coldridge woods, *c.* 850 a., to the Forestry Commission, the owner of both in 1995.[29]

In 1448 Hyde abbey appropriated Collingbourne Kingston church and until the Dissolution held the *RECTORY* estate, which consisted of most of the great tithes of the parish and, at Collingbourne Kingston, of a house, some cottages, and 89 a.[30] The Crown granted the estate in 1541 to the dean and chapter of Winchester.[31] In 1843 the tithes were valued at £1,230 and commuted. In 1865 the dean and chapter sold Parsonage farm, 105 a., to the trustees of Matilda Assheton-Smith.[32] By 1910 the farm had been acquired by Henry Brudenell-Bruce, marquess of Ailesbury,[33] whose son George, marquess of Ailesbury, sold it *c.* 1929 as part of a much enlarged farm.[34]

ECONOMIC HISTORY. In 1086 the 50-hide estate called Collingbourne, which almost certainly included Aughton, Brunton, and Sunton, may not have been fully cultivated. There were 27 ploughteams on land for 32. Excluding the later Collingbourne Valence manor, there were in demesne 10 hides on which there were 4 teams and 13 *servi*, and 40 *villani* and 13 coscets had 15 teams. There was 2 a. of meadow, and both pasture and woodland measured 1 by ½ league.[35]

COLLINGBOURNE KINGSTON. The village's land, *c.* 2,140 a., lay mostly west of the Bourne.[36] In the 16th century open fields called West (later Middle), North, and South lay west of the river, and one called East field lay east of it. To the west lay extensive rough pasture for sheep; east of East field Cow down was used in common for cattle.[37]

There was a flock of 818 sheep on the demesne of Collingbourne Kingston manor in 1210.[38] At Collingbourne Kingston there were 9 yardlanders and 13 ½-yardlanders on the manor. Labour services owed by the yardlanders included ploughing, harrowing, washing and shearing the

lord's sheep, and carting wool to Winchester. Each yardlander provided a man to weed on the demesne for half a day, each mowed and carted hay, and at the harvest each owed various services, to perform some of which two men were provided for a day. The ½-yardlanders owed half the services of the yardlanders, and 3 coscets worked on the demesne from 1 August to 29 September. Customary tenants at Sunton may also have worked on the demesne at Collingbourne Kingston.[39]

In 1552 the demesne farm included 500 a. of arable, all in the open fields, 10 a. of inclosed meadow, and a several down of 60 a.; the farmer could keep 1,500 sheep and presumably had rights to feed them on other downland. Five copyholders had 221 a. of arable and pasture rights for 600 sheep and 31 cattle, all in common.[40] About 1600 all the arable remained open, but more of the downland was several. The demesne, later Manor farm, then had 427 a. in the open fields, 11 a. of inclosed meadow, and 320 a. of several downland pasture for sheep: 6 a. of the downland was used as additional meadow land. Parsonage farm included 90 a. in the open fields and a several meadow of 3 a. on the downs. Manor farm, Parsonage farm, and the copyholds shared 642 a. of downland pasture including Cow down, 300 a., Winter down, 160 a., Summer down, 30 a., and Thornhill down, 60 a.[41] Cow down, then 250 a., was divided and allotted under a private agreement of 1693. In that year Manor farm included 596 a. of arable, of which 360 a. was sown each year, mostly with barley, and a flock of 1,300 sheep.[42] About 1765 Chadderton's farm, based at a farmstead south of the church, had 101 a. in Collingbourne Kingston and 53 a. in Brunton with pasture rights in both places.[43]

By the early 19th century most of Collingbourne Kingston's lands and pasture rights had been concentrated in two large farms, Manor, 1,074 a., and a farm of 678 a.[44] In 1824 the four open fields, then 356 a., and the common pastures west of them, then 337 a., were inclosed by Act.[45] In 1843 Manor farm, 961 a., lay entirely west of the Bourne. Parsonage farm, in 1843 consisting of 104 a. east of the Bourne,[46] and the 678-a. farm were worked together from the later 18th century to the later 19th by members of the Mackrell family.[47] In 1843 the composite farm, 834 a., lay on both sides of the Bourne, being south of Manor farm on the west side;[48] it was afterwards known as Parsonage farm. In the earlier 20th century Manor, *c.* 1,074

24 W.R.O. 9/1/521; Ch. Com. file 89163/1; above, Great Bedwyn, manors (Tottenham).
25 Above, this section (Sunton).
26 B.L. Harl. MS. 1761, f. 144.
27 For the woodland, below, econ. hist. (Sunton).
28 e.g. P.R.O., E 318/13/574, rott. 1–3; W.R.O., tithe award.
29 Inf. from the Head Forester, Forest Enterprise, Postern Hill, Marlborough.
30 W.R.O., D 1/2/10, ff. 58v.–60; P.R.O., SC 6/Hen. VIII/3341, rot. 53d.; for the other great tithes, below, church. 31 *L. & P. Hen. VIII*, xvi, p. 417.
32 W.R.O., tithe award; Ch. Com. file 30196.
33 W.R.O., Inland Revenue, val. reg. 56.
34 Ibid. 9/1/521; inf. from Mr. G. I. Crook, Aughton Farm; above, this section (Collingbourne Kingston).

35 *V.C.H. Wilts.* ii, p. 127; cf. above, manors.
36 W.R.O., tithe award.
37 Ibid.; ibid. 9/10/254.
38 *Interdict Doc.* (P.R.S. n.s. xxxiv), 28.
39 B.L. Harl. MS. 1761, ff. 145–7; below, this section (Sunton).
40 W.R.O. 9/1/95.   41 Ibid. 9/10/254.
42 Ibid. 9/10/2; 382, pp. 130–6.
43 Ibid. 9/10/26; cf. above, manors (Chadderton's).
44 Hants R.O. 11M59/59591, pp. 12–16.
45 W.R.O., EA/128.
46 Ibid. tithe award.
47 Ibid. A 1/345/120; ibid. 9/1/110, p. 10; D. & C. Winton. Mun., box 114, val. of Collingbourne Kingston, 1815.
48 W.R.O., tithe award.

a., and Parsonage, c. 883 a., were the only farms based in Collingbourne Kingston village.[49] There was a dairy on Manor farm in 1929, when the farm included c. 500 a. of arable and c. 600 a. of grassland.[50] From 1929 c. 400 a. of Aughton's land was part of Manor farm, which was divided in 1982 to create Manor and Summerdown farms, each of c. 750 a. Both were arable farms in 1995, when Manor was still worked from the farmstead in the village and Summerdown was worked from new buildings near the old Marlborough road.[51] In 1995 Parsonage farm, c. 900 a., was worked in conjunction with Aughton farm and was devoted to dairying, arable, and beef; its farmstead in the village was little used, the farm being run instead from new buildings to the south-west.[52]

The only woodland on Collingbourne Kingston's land in 1773 was Hogdown copse west of the old Marlborough road.[53] It measured 16 a. in 1809.[54] In 1843 it and c. 20 a. of other plantations west of the road were among woods associated with a manor house at Everleigh.[55] They were standing in 1995, when they were within a military training area.[56]

A mill was standing on Collingbourne Kingston manor in 1232.[57] A windmill mentioned in 1341[58] may have been the predecessor of the tower mill which stood south-west of the village in 1773.[59] The mill was demolished in the later 19th century.[60]

AUGHTON. The open fields and common pastures of Aughton, c. 1,030 a. all west of the Bourne, were shared from the 16th century to the 18th between the demesne farm of Collingbourne Kingston manor, three freeholds of which the largest came to be called Pile's farm, and copyholders of Collingbourne Kingston manor with holdings based at Aughton.[61] In 1552 there were 6 copyholds, 1 of 3 yardlands, 2 of 2 yardlands, and 3 of 1 yardland. They included c. 318 a. of arable and rights to feed a total of c. 660 sheep. Several tenants were allowed to pasture more than the usual 60 sheep for a yardland.[62] About 1600 c. 136 a. of the open fields and feeding rights on the downs were in the demesne farm of Collingbourne Kingston (later Manor farm).[63]

In 1763 three of Aughton's four open fields, North, South, and Low, c. 720 a., were inclosed by private agreement. Brakeham field remained open and Aughton down remained in common

use. The largest farm was apparently Gilbert's, later Aughton, for which 238 a. of arable was allotted; 84 a. was allotted for Manor farm, and 89 a. for a copyhold, and there were several smaller farms.[64] In 1809 Aughton farm covered 305 a., and farms of 258 a., 187 a., 154 a., and 27 a. were also based at Aughton.[65] All presumably included pasture rights on the downland. Common husbandry ceased in 1824 when Brakeham field and Aughton down were inclosed by Act.[66] In 1843 Aughton farm was 412 a. and farms of 303 a. and 202 a. were based in the village. They included c. 613 a. of arable, 22 a. of meadow, and 252 a. of downland pasture.[67] Two of the three farms were badly managed c. 1867.[68] The three had changed little in size by 1929.[69] Later, Aughton farm, 336 a., was worked with Parsonage farm, Collingbourne Kingston, as it was in 1995, when it was devoted to dairying, arable, and beef. A farm of c. 400 a. was added to Manor farm and in 1982 divided between Manor and Summerdown farms; in 1995 that land was mainly arable.[70] The 202-a. farm of 1843 became Aughton House farm and was added to Brunton farm, a mixed farm in 1995.[71]

There was a malthouse at Aughton in 1843.[72]

BRUNTON. In 1086 there were 8 or perhaps 10 ploughteams at Brunton.[73] Of Brunton's land, c. 1,620 a., much was imparked in the 13th century. The lord of Collingbourne Valence manor probably held woodland east of Brunton in severalty from 1241,[74] and William de Valence, lord of the manor, imparked woodland c. 1253.[75] In 1254 the king gave him 5 bucks and 15 does to stock the park.[76] By 1256 a pale had been made, and a hedge planted, as boundaries, and a deer leap had been constructed; a ditch forming part of the boundary may have been the prehistoric one on the parish boundary east of Brunton.[77] William de Valence acquired c. 10 a. by exchange in 1257 and apparently used the land to extend the park southwards.[78] Later the park reverted to agriculture: it was probably the easternmost 400 a. of Brunton, which in 1843 lay inclosed as arable fields of 10–15 a. and bore c. 140 a. of woodland.[79]

West and north-west of the park Brunton had c. 250 a. of common downland pasture, in the 20th century called Fairmile down, and west of that c. 600 a. in open fields. In the 18th century there were four open fields, called Slough, Har-

49 Ibid. Inland Revenue, val. reg. 56; ibid. G 10/500/29–30.
50 Ibid. 9/1/521.
51 Inf. from Mrs. M. May, Manor Farm; Mr. C. May, Summerdown Farm.
52 Inf. from Mr. G. I. Crook, Aughton Farm.
53 *Andrews and Dury, Map* (W.R.S. viii), pl. 9.
54 Hants R.O. 11M59/59591, pp. 12–14.
55 W.R.O., tithe award; cf. *V.C.H. Wilts.* xi. 137–8; O.S. Maps 6", Wilts. XLII, XLVIII (1883–8 edns.).
56 *V.C.H. Wilts.* xi. 137; inf. from Defence Land Agent, Durrington; O.S. Map 1/25,000, SU 25/35 (1994 edn.).
57 B.L. Harl. MS. 1761, f. 147.
58 *Inq. Non.* (Rec. Com.), 173.
59 *Andrews and Dury, Map* (W.R.S. viii), pl. 9; M. Watts, *Wilts. Windmills*, 19.
60 O.S. Map 6", Wilts. XLII (1888 and later edns.); Watts, *Wilts. Windmills*, 20.
61 Above, manors (Aughton; Pile's); below, this section;

cf. W.R.O., tithe award; ibid. 9/1/95; 9/13/14.
62 W.R.O. 9/1/95, pp. 31–8.
63 Ibid. 9/10/254, p. 53.
64 Ibid. 9/13/14–15.
65 Hants R.O. 11M59/59591, pp. 18–24.
66 W.R.O., EA/128.
67 Ibid. tithe award.
68 Ibid. 9/1/110, pp. 1–3.   69 Ibid. 9/1/521.
70 Above, this section (Collingbourne Kingston).
71 Below, this section (Brunton).
72 W.R.O., tithe award.
73 *V.C.H. Wilts.* ii, p. 127.
74 B.L. Harl. MS. 1761, f. 144.
75 *Cal. Chart. R.* 1226–57, 416.
76 *Close R.* 1254–6, 17.
77 Ibid. 1251–3, 373; 1254–6, 23, 234, 329; *Cal. Pat.* 1247–58, 484; above, intro. [boundaries].
78 *Cal. Chart. R.* 1226–57, 465.
79 W.R.O., tithe award.

ley, Coombe, and Stonehill.[80] All that land was shared by Collingbourne Valence (later Brunton), Dormer, and Collingbourne Kingston manors and Chadderton's farm. Neither Collingbourne Valence nor Dormer is known to have had customary tenants; in 1232 Collingbourne Kingston manor's land was in four customary holdings, each of 1 yardland,[81] in 1552 in two holdings totalling 3 yardlands.[82] About 1765 Chadderton's farm, based in Collingbourne Kingston village, included in Brunton a close of 15 a., 38 a. in the open fields, and the right to downland pasture for 100 sheep.[83] Five main farms were based in Brunton in the later 18th century. In 1773 Dormer was 244 a. and the copyhold land of Collingbourne Kingston manor was a farm of c. 75 a.;[84] in 1794 Brunton manor included three farms, Brunton, 277 a., Heath, 106 a., and Brunton House, 270 a. In the former parkland, where it had a barn, Heath farm was apparently several,[85] but all the other farms included pasture rights on the downland.

The open fields and common pastures were inclosed under a private agreement of 1799. In 1843 there were four farms based in the village, Brunton, 774 a., Brunton House, 166 a., Ivy House, 347 a., and Waglands, 154 a. Between 1799 and 1843 a new farmstead in the village and Hill barn on former open-field land were built for Brunton farm, which included 111 a. of Collingbourne Kingston's Cow down. Heath farm, 91 a., was worked from outside the parish in 1843. The farms then had a total of c. 1,170 a. of arable.[86] Two more farmsteads were built outside the village in the mid 19th century.[87] In the early 20th century most of the farmland was in Brunton farm, c. 1,422 a., which with c. 200 a. in Aughton was worked by S. W. Farmer and W. B. Gauntlett, pioneers of intensive arable and dairy farming.[88] In the mid 20th century Brunton farm was worked in conjunction with Wexcombe farm in Grafton parish by A. J. Hosier and members of his family, who also farmed by new methods.[89] In 1995 Brunton farm, 1,650 a., was an arable, dairy, and beef farm.[90]

Of the woodland imparked c. 1253[91] and of c. 140 a. of woodland standing in 1843[92] only Brokenway copse, 19 a., and Heath copse, 10 a., were standing c. 1880.[93] Of woodland on Collingbourne Kingston manor c. 1600, c. 44 a. was said to stand in Brunton[94] and may have been part of the woodland in 1843 considered to be in Sunton.[95]

There were three mills on Collingbourne Valence manor in 1324,[96] but the site of none at Brunton is known.

SUNTON. Before inclosure Sunton had, east of the Bourne, East field and, further from the village, the Heath, a total of c. 815 a.; west of the Bourne it had West field and Snail down, a total of 785 a.; the rest of its roughly 2,520 a. was woodland to the east.[97] The agricultural land was shared by customary tenants of Collingbourne Kingston manor with holdings based in Sunton and by the two manors called Sunton, each of which may have consisted of a single farm, the later West and Sunton farms.[98]

In 1232 Collingbourne Kingston manor had 10 yardlanders at Sunton. Their labour services were the same as those of yardlanders holding at Collingbourne Kingston and may have been performed at Collingbourne Kingston.[99] In the late 16th century the 10 copyholds included 157 a. in East field, 226 a. in West field, and rights to feed 1,200 sheep and 120 cattle and horses on the Heath, Snail down, and a cow down. The largest holding included 74 a. of arable and feeding for 200 sheep and 20 cattle and horses, the smallest 22 a. of arable and feeding for 8 cattle and horses.[1]

In 1703 West farm measured 308 a. and included 180 a. of arable.[2] It had 370 a. in Sunton and 66 a. in Collingbourne Kingston in 1730, by when former copyhold land at Sunton may already have been added to it.[3] In the later 18th century there was 716 a. in the open fields shared among 11 holdings, which all had land on both sides of the Bourne. Sunton farm had 232 a. in the fields, West farm 190 a., the largest farm consisting of copyholds or former copyholds 159 a., and Corderoy's farm 25 a. There was already inclosed land called Herridge and Pransley. The Heath then measured c. 330 a., Snail down 271 a.[4] Common husbandry was eliminated and farms were enlarged as copyholds fell in hand and Sunton's land came into single ownership. In 1809 pasture rights were still part of Corderoy's farm, 124 a., and of one or more copyhold,[5] but in 1814 Corderoy's farm was bought by the owner of almost all the other land of Sunton,[6] and in 1815 the arable and pasture were worked in severalty. Sunton farm then measured 945 a. and lay mainly east of the Bourne, West farm had 608 a. mainly west of it. Each included a barn at the edge, respectively east and west, of the former open fields.[7] In 1843 Sunton farm, 925 a., included c. 600 a. of arable,

80 W.R.O. 9/12/26.   81 B.L. Harl. MS. 1761, f. 146.
82 W.R.O. 9/1/95, p. 36.
83 Ibid. 9/10/26.
84 Ibid. 9/10/260, pp. 4, 41; 9/12/26; 9/12/169.
85 Ibid. 9/12/86; *Andrews and Dury, Map* (W.R.S. viii), pl. 9.
86 W.R.O. 9/12/26; 9/12/95; ibid. tithe award.
87 Above, intro. (Brunton).
88 *W.A.M.* xliii. 494; W.R.O., G 10/500/130; ibid. Inland Revenue, val. reg. 56; for S. W. Farmer, *V.C.H. Wilts.* iv. 106–7; above, Little Bedwyn, econ. hist. (Little Bedwyn).
89 Hosier, *Hosier's Farming System*, 37; for the farming, above, Great Bedwyn, econ. hist. (Wexcombe).
90 Inf. from Mr. N. H. Hosier, Waglands Farm.
91 Above, this section.
92 W.R.O., tithe award.

93 O.S. Maps 6", Wilts. XLII–XLIII (1882–8 edns.).
94 W.R.O. 9/10/254, pp. 1–12.
95 Below, this section (Sunton).
96 *Cal. Inq. p.m.* vi, p. 328.
97 W.R.O. 9/10/254, pp. 13, 22–3, 26, 28–9; ibid. tithe award.   98 Above, manors.
99 B.L. Harl. MS. 1761, ff. 145v.–146; above, this section (Collingbourne Kingston).
1 W.R.O. 9/10/254, pp. 13, 15–17, 22–3, 26, 28–9, 35.
2 Ibid. 9/9/374, p. 46.
3 Ibid. 9/1/100, p. 77.
4 Ibid. 9/11/149; cf. ibid. tithe award.
5 Hants R.O. 11M59/59591, pp. 6–7.
6 Above, manors.
7 D. & C. Winton. Mun., box 114, survey of Collingbourne Kingston, 1815.

and West farm, 659 a., included *c.* 379 a. of arable.[8]

Between 1843 and 1878 the east part of Sunton farm apparently became a new farm, Herridge, worked from a farmstead at the north edge of the Heath.[9] Racehorses were trained on Herridge farm, 380 a., in the earlier 20th century.[10] In 1995, then *c.* 200 a., the farm was associated with stables in Everleigh and still used for training racehorses.[11] In 1910 Sunton, 334 a., and Corderoy's, 107 a., were separate farms held by a single tenant.[12] In 1973 Sunton farm was divided among other farms.[13] West farm, 622 a. in 1910,[14] was greatly reduced after 1937 when much of Snail down was taken for military training.[15] The farmstead in the village was given up, Oldlands piggery at the north-east edge of Snail down was built, and in 1995 the land was used as an arable and pig farm.[16]

In 1544 Collingbourne wood east of the Heath, *c.* 300 a., was managed by the lessee of the demesne of Collingbourne Kingston manor as woodward and stood divided into 14 coppices.[17] About 1600 *c.* 237 a. of woodland stood in 13 coppices and there were deer and a lodge,[18] and in the 18th century *c.* 407 a. stood in 14 coppices.[19] Collingbourne wood and Coldridge wood south-east of it measured 860 a. in 1843.[20] They belonged to the Forestry Commission from 1935, and from 1937 were replanted, mainly with beech trees. In 1994 there was a herd of roe deer, and the woodland was used for commercial forestry and leisure activities such as riding and pheasant shooting.[21]

A horse mill standing in the parish in 1341[22] was presumably that said to stand at Sunton *c.* 1600.[23] There is no later evidence of such a mill.

A weaver lived at Sunton in 1751.[24]

LOCAL GOVERNMENT. For the period 1522–1819 some records of the Collingbourne Kingston manor court survive. The court was attended by the lord of the manor's tenants at Aughton, Brunton, and Sunton in addition to those at Collingbourne Kingston; freeholders at Chute also attended it until the mid 17th century. Records of a few meetings of a separate court for the Sunton tenants survive for the period 1559–1819. In the 16th century the Collingbourne Kingston and Sunton courts were both held twice a year, more often when

copyhold business required it. Common husbandry at Sunton was regulated in 1577 and at Collingbourne Kingston in 1579, buildings in need of repair were noted, and the death of customary tenants was recorded. In 1578 it was presented that fruit trees were illegally grubbed up at Collingbourne Kingston, and in 1579 a Collingbourne Kingston tenant was presented for coursing illegally. From the 17th century the business of each court was concerned chiefly with copyholds and common husbandry, and in the 18th century each was apparently held once a year. A single set of presentments was normally made at Collingbourne Kingston court for the whole manor, but in 1727 separate presentments were made there for Brunton and Sunton.[25]

In 1775–6 £353 was spent on the poor, in the three years ending at Easter 1785 an average of £450. In 1802–3, when the poor rate was above the average for Kinwardstone hundred, £650 was spent on regular outdoor relief for 42 adults and 60 children and occasional relief for 30 people, in all nearly a fifth of the inhabitants.[26] A few paupers were housed in the vicarage house in 1812.[27] Relief was apparently more generous in 1812–13, when £1,747 was spent and 94 were relieved regularly and 12 occasionally, than in 1814–15, when £801 was spent and 71 were relieved regularly and 14 occasionally.[28] Only £422 was spent in 1816, but the cost of relief again increased, and £1,411 was spent in 1832.[29] The parish was included in Pewsey poor-law union in 1835[30] and in Kennet district in 1974.[31]

CHURCH. Collingbourne Kingston church was standing in the 12th century.[32] It was held by rectors until Hyde abbey appropriated it in 1448. A vicarage was ordained in 1246 and confirmed in 1448.[33] A proposal of 1650 to transfer the inhabitants of Sunton, except those of Sunton Farm, to Collingbourne Ducis parish[34] was void, but it foreshadowed the transfer of Sunton to Collingbourne Ducis in 1934.[35] The vicarage was united with Collingbourne Ducis rectory in 1963, Everleigh rectory was added in 1975,[36] and the united benefice became part of Wexcombe benefice in 1979.[37]

The abbot of Hyde presented all the known rectors. An unsuccessful challenge to his right to present was apparently made by the king in 1344. The rectors presented vicars from 1246 to

8   W.R.O., tithe award.
9   Ibid.; O.S. Map 6", Wilts. XLII (1888 edn.).
10 *Kelly's Dir. Wilts.* (1907, 1939); W.R.O., Inland Revenue, val. reg. 56.
11 Inf. from Mrs. May.
12 W.R.O., Inland Revenue, val. reg. 56.
13 Codgell, *Collingbourne Remembered*, 145.
14 W.R.O., Inland Revenue, val. reg. 56.
15 Inf. from Chief Executive, Govt. Property Lawyers, Taunton.
16 Inf. from Mr. R. D. Hendry, Lower Ho. Farm, Everleigh.
17 P.R.O., E 318/13/574, rott. 1–3.
18 W.R.O. 9/10/254, pp. 1–12, 46.
19 Ibid. 9/9/374, p. 35; 9/10/260, p. 75.
20 Ibid. tithe award.
21 Inf. from the Head Forester, Forest Enterprise, Postern Hill, Marlborough.
22 *Inq. Non.* (Rec. Com.), 173.

23 W.R.O. 9/10/254, p. 22.
24 Ibid. 9/1/204, p. 130.
25 Ibid. 9/1/134; 9/1/137; 9/1/139; 9/1/141–2; 9/1/158; 9/1/160–6; 9/1/168–80; 9/1/182–6; 9/1/188–200; 9/1/204; 9/9/368–9; 9/10/249–53; 9/12/179; Winch. Coll. Mun. 14905, rot. Cd.; 14907; 19646.
26 *Poor Law Abstract, 1804*, 566–7; *V.C.H. Wilts.* iv. 345.
27 *W.A.M.* xli. 133.
28 *Poor Law Abstract, 1818*, 498–9.
29 *Poor Rate Returns, 1816–21*, 188; *1822–4*, 228; *1825–9*, 219; *1830–4*, 212.
30 *Poor Law Com. 2nd Rep.* App. D, 560.
31 O.S. Map 1/100,000, admin. areas, Wilts. (1974 edn.).
32 Below, this section [archit.].
33 W.R.O., D 1/2/10, f. 58 and v.; B.L. Harl. MS. 1761, f. 148 and v.
34 *W.A.M.* xl. 298.
35 Above, intro.   36 *V.C.H. Wilts.* xi. 113.
37 Inf. from Ch. Com.

1448, except in 1333 when a nominee of the bishop of Salisbury presented, and the abbot of Hyde presented them from 1448 to the Dissolution. In 1541 the advowson of the vicarage was granted with the Rectory estate to the dean and chapter of Winchester and, except in 1573 when Roger Earth and his wife Elizabeth, relict of Thomas Pile, presented by grant of a turn, the dean and chapter thereafter presented vicars.[38] From 1963 the dean and chapter were entitled to present alternately, and from 1975 twice in every five turns. From 1979 they sat on the board of patronage for Wexcombe benefice.[39]

In 1291 the rectory was valued at £20, the vicarage at £4 13s. 4d.[40] The vicarage was worth £16 in 1535.[41] In 1655 it was augmented with £30 a year,[42] but later the augmentation from the dean and chapter of Winchester, the owners of the Rectory estate, was of £20.[43] The vicarage was worth £261 c. 1830.[44] The rector presumably took all tithes from the whole parish until 1246, when the great tithes from the glebe and small tithes from the whole parish were assigned to the vicar,[45] and took all tithes other than the vicar's until 1448. By then the vicar was receiving most of the wool tithes from the parish in addition to the tithes assigned in 1246,[46] and by the 17th century most of the lamb tithes.[47] In 1843 his tithes were valued at £320 and commuted.[48] The rector had 1 carucate and a meadow in 1341,[49] 89 a., a house, and some cottages in 1448.[50] The vicar had no glebe but a house, one having been assigned by the rector in 1246,[51] until 7 a. east of the church was bought in 1871.[52] That land was still held in 1994.[53] In 1783 the house was of stone, timber, and brick and contained a partly wainscotted parlour.[54] It was presumably the house south-east of the church extended northwards by the addition of a brick range of two storeys and attics c. 1812[55] and eastwards in 1860.[56] A large new red-brick house was built north-east of the church c. 1880 and the old house was demolished.[57] The new house was sold in 1964.[58]

Robert de Cardeville, treasurer of Salisbury cathedral, in 1254 gave up Collingbourne Kingston rectory to a Roman provided by the pope.[59] Robert of Worcester, rector 1296–1324, was in 1300–1 and 1304 licensed to study and in 1308 licensed to accompany the abbot of Hyde abroad.[60] The rectors from 1348 to 1382, and perhaps most rectors after 1246, were pluralists and probably non-resident.[61] From the 16th century most vicars were also pluralists, several incumbencies were long, and curates were often employed. The vicar 1538–73 employed a curate,[62] as did Bartholomew Parsons, vicar 1611–42, whose son Edmund was curate in 1630. Bartholomew was a local pluralist and published sermons including that preached at Sir Francis Pile's funeral in Collingbourne Kingston church in 1635.[63] Leonard Alexander, vicar from c. 1642 to 1661, was ejected in 1647 and John Norris was intruded.[64] In 1674 the vicar, Richard Boardman, a presbyterian, attempted to dismiss the churchwardens for refusing to buy the Book of Homilies, the Book of Common Prayer, and a Bible.[65] Several later vicars were minor canons of Winchester. They included Nicholas Westcombe, vicar 1770–1813,[66] who lived at Winchester. In 1783 his curate, who was the vicar of Milton Lilbourne, held a Sunday service alternately morning and afternoon, held services on Good Friday and Christmas day, and administered the sacrament to c. 30 communicants at Christmas, Easter, Whitsun, and Michaelmas.[67] The curate in 1812 lived at Burbage.[68] The vicar 1814–33 employed a curate who in 1832 lived in the vicarage house and held a Sunday service alternately morning and evening.[69] In 1850–1 c. 320 people attended each service.[70] C. H. Poore, vicar 1839–79,[71] employed no curate and apparently resided. In 1864 he held, and preached at, two services each Sunday. Weekday services were held on Christmas day, Wednesdays and Fridays in Lent, and every day in Holy Week; in Lent and Holy Week the congregation numbered c. 20. Poore administered the sacrament on Christmas day, Easter Sunday, and Trinity Sunday to 40–5 communicants and once every seven weeks to c. 30.[72]

The rent from 1 a. at Sunton and ½ a. at Aughton had been given to the church by the early 18th century, that from the 1 a. evidently by c. 1600.[73] The rent, £1 15s. in 1935–6 and £26 in 1994, was used for general church expenses.[74]

[38] Phillipps, *Wilts. Inst.* (index in *W.A.M.* xxviii. 217); *Cal. Pat.* 1343–5, 225; 1345–8, 150; *L. & P. Hen. VIII*, xvi, p. 417; *Wilts. Pedigrees* (Harl. Soc. cv/cvi), 151; for the Rectory estate, above, manors (Rectory).
[39] Ch. Com. file 96677; ibid. file, NB 34/371B/2; inf. from Ch. Com.
[40] *Tax. Eccl.* (Rec. Com.), 189.
[41] *Valor Eccl.* (Rec. Com.), ii. 150.
[42] *Cal. S.P. Dom.* 1655–6, 72.
[43] W.R.O., D 1/24/56/1; D 1/24/56/3.
[44] *Rep. Com. Eccl. Revenues*, 830–1.
[45] B.L. Harl. MS. 1761, f. 148 and v.
[46] W.R.O., D 1/2/10, f. 58 and v.
[47] Ibid. D 1/24/56/1. [48] Ibid. tithe award.
[49] *Inq. Non.* (Rec. Com.), 173.
[50] W.R.O., D 1/2/10, ff. 58v.–59.
[51] B.L. Harl. MS. 1761, f. 148.
[52] *Lond. Gaz.* 18 Aug. 1871, p. 3650.
[53] Ch. Com. file 97210.
[54] W.R.O., D 1/24/56/3.
[55] Ibid. D 1/11/17; ibid. tithe award.
[56] O.S. Map 6", Wilts. XLII (1888 edn.); D. & C. Winton. Mun., W39C/11, p. 174.
[57] O.S. Map 6", Wilts. XLII. SE. (1901 edn.); D. & C. Winton. Mun., W39C/12, p. 107.
[58] Ch. Com. file, NB 34/371B/2.

[59] *Cal. Papal Reg.* i. 288, 298.
[60] A. B. Emden, *Biog. Reg. Univ. Oxf. to 1500*, iii. 2086; Phillipps, *Wilts. Inst.* i. 22; *Reg. Ghent* (Cant. & York Soc.), ii. 842, 849, 866, 907–8; B.L. Harl. MS. 1761, f. 148v.
[61] Phillipps, *Wilts. Inst.* i. 43, 53, 66; *Cal. Papal Reg.* i. 282; *Reg. Langham* (Cant. & York Soc.), 27.
[62] Phillipps, *Wilts. Inst.* i. 207, 227; W.R.O., D 1/43/2, f. 14v.
[63] *D.N.B.* (Bart. Parsons); *Subscription Bk. 1620–40* (W.R.S. xxxii), p. 48; *Alum. Oxon. 1500–1714*, iii. 1122.
[64] *Walker Revised*, ed. Matthews, 369; *W.N. & Q.* viii. 508.
[65] F. R. Goodman, *Revd. Landlords and their Tenants*, 35; W.R.O., D 1/54/6/2/47.
[66] *Alum. Oxon. 1715–1886*, iv. 1528.
[67] *Vis. Queries, 1783* (W.R.S. xxvii), pp. 76–7.
[68] *W.A.M.* xli. 133.
[69] *Alum. Oxon. 1715–1886*, iii. 1014; Ch. Com. file, NB 34/371B/1. [70] P.R.O., HO 129/261/2/6/11.
[71] *Alum. Cantab. 1752–1900*, v. 156.
[72] W.R.O., D 1/56/7.
[73] *Endowed Char. Wilts.* (S. Div.), 113; W.R.O. 9/10/254, p. 41; 666/13.
[74] W.R.O., L 2, Collingbourne Kingston; inf. from Mr. R. May, Manor Farm.

The church, called St. John the Baptist's in 1344[75] but *ST. MARY'S* by 1763,[76] is built of rubble with freestone dressings and consists of a chancel, an aisled and clerestoried nave with south porch, and a west tower.[77] The present nave survives from the late 12th century, when the arcades were cut through it and the aisles were built. The chancel was rebuilt in the 13th century, the date of the surviving chancel arch, and again in the earlier 14th; in the mid 14th century a new window was made in its south wall. The clerestory was built presumably in the late 12th century, when the aisles were built, or in the 13th century, when the chancel was rebuilt. In the earlier 14th century the east bay of the north aisle was rebuilt, probably to provide for a chapel. In the 15th century the tower and the porch were built and, except the west window of the north one, all the windows of both aisles were renewed. In the earlier 18th century the windows of the clerestory were replaced, the roof of the nave was reconstructed, and a west gallery was erected.[78] At a restoration of the nave in 1861–2 under the direction of John Colson the gallery was removed, the chancel arch was repaired, and the clerestory windows were altered.[79]

Constantine Darell (will proved 1508) and his wife Joan (d. 1495)[80] were commemorated by a brass in the chancel. In the south-east corner of the chancel a large canopied monument of painted stone incorporates effigies of Thomas Pile (d. 1561), his son Sir Gabriel (d. 1626), and their wives.[81]

In 1553 the king's commissioners took 24 oz. of plate and left a 9-oz. chalice. In 1891 and 1994 a chalice and paten, both hallmarked for 1687, were held for the church.[82] There were four bells in 1553. They were replaced by four cast in 1614 by John Wallis, and the ring was increased to five by a tenor cast by Samuel Knight in 1695. The tenor was recast by John Taylor & Company of Loughborough (Leics.) in 1896, when the ring was increased to six by a treble cast at the same foundry.[83]

Registrations of baptisms and burials exist from 1653, of marriages from 1654. Those of baptisms and burials are lacking for 1744–5 and 1747–54, those of marriages for 1744–5 and 1747–53.[84]

NONCONFORMITY. Daniel Burgess, ejected from Collingbourne Ducis rectory for presbyterianism,[85] in 1669 preached at a conventicle held in a house in Collingbourne Kingston parish.[86] There was no dissenter in the parish in 1676.[87] A meeting house at Sunton was certified in 1697, and in 1815 and 1818 houses at Collingbourne Kingston were certified by Methodists.[88] In 1819 a chapel for Methodists was built at Collingbourne Kingston. It was attended by 143 in the morning, 274 in the afternoon, and 240 in the evening on Census Sunday in 1851.[89] In 1914 a new medium-sized red-brick chapel was built on the south side of the old,[90] which was later demolished. The chapel was closed in 1985.[91]

EDUCATION. A total of 83 children attended several small schools in the parish in 1818.[92] In 1833 there was a school for 15 girls and another for 40 children.[93] A new school was built in 1845. It was attended in 1846–7 by *c.* 90 children,[94] in 1858 by 80–90, including some from Collingbourne Ducis.[95] On return day in 1871 it was attended by 84.[96] Average attendance was 130 in 1913–14, 65 in 1926–7, and 135 in the years 1932–8.[97] The school was closed in 1978, when the 28 children on the roll were transferred to Collingbourne Ducis school.[98]

CHARITIES FOR THE POOR. When Collingbourne Kingston church was appropriated in 1448 the bishop of Salisbury required that 8s. a year from the Rectory estate should be given to the poor of the parish:[99] there is no evidence that it ever was.

By will proved 1878 Anne Clarke gave the income from £1,600, and by will proved 1890 Elizabeth Piper gave that from £1,000, to buy blankets and coal for old paupers. In 1904 the joint income, *c.* £74, was spent on blankets, coal, and small money doles for 81 people.[1] In 1922–3 coal was given to 22 and money to 21, in 1934–5 coal to 28 and money to 29.[2] In 1994 the income was *c.* £100 and 7 people each received £10.[3]

In 1895 John Mackrell gave the income from £200 to insure and maintain his family's memorial windows in Collingbourne Kingston church and to buy coal and other gifts for old and sick paupers. The income for the poor, *c.* £4, was usually given to a clothing club.[4] In 1994 £3 was given to a general fund for the church.[5]

75 *Cal. Pat.* 1343–5, 225.
76 J. Ecton, *Thesaurus* (1763), 405.
77 Above, plate 4.
78 Phillipps, *Wilts. Inst.* ii. 47, 67; W.R.O. 9/1/132; 666/13.
79 Wilts. Cuttings, xvi. 175; W.R.O., D 1/61/13/13; J. Buckler, watercolour in W.A.S. Libr., vol. iv. 6.
80 *Hist. Parl., Commons, 1439–1509*, 259; E. Kite, *Monumental Brasses of Wilts.* 38.
81 Cf. *Wilts. Pedigrees* (Harl. Soc. cv/cvi), 151.
82 Nightingale, *Wilts. Plate*, 167; inf. from Mr. S. Everett, the Rectory, Collingbourne Ducis.
83 Walters, *Wilts. Bells*, 62; inf. from Mr. Everett.
84 W.R.O. 666/1–5; bishop's transcripts for 1607–10, 1621–3, 1629–32, and 1751–2 are in W.R.O.
85 *V.C.H. Wilts.* xi. 114.
86 *Orig. Rec.* ed. G. L. Turner, ii. 1060.
87 *Compton Census*, ed. Whiteman, 126.
88 *Meeting Ho. Certs.* (W.R.S. xl), pp. 6, 76–7, 86.

89 P.R.O., HO 129/261/2/6/12.
90 Date on bldg.; cf. O.S. Maps 1/2,500, Wilts. XLII. 15 (1900, 1924 edns.).
91 Inf. from Meth. Church Property Div., Central Bldgs., Oldham Street, Manchester.
92 *Educ. of Poor Digest*, 1024.
93 *Educ. Enq. Abstract*, 1034.
94 Nat. Soc. *Inquiry, 1846–7*, Wilts. 4–5; P.R.O., ED 7/130, no. 83.
95 *Acct. of Wilts. Schs.* 66.
96 *Returns relating to Elem. Educ.* 424–5.
97 *Bd. of Educ., List 21, 1908–38* (H.M.S.O.).
98 W.R.O., F 8/500/78/1/5.
99 Ibid. D 1/2/10, ff. 59–60.
1 *Endowed Char. Wilts.* (S. Div.), 114–15.
2 W.R.O., L 2, Collingbourne Kingston.
3 Inf. from Mr. May.
4 *Endowed Char. Wilts.* (S. Div.), 116.
5 Inf. from Mr. May.

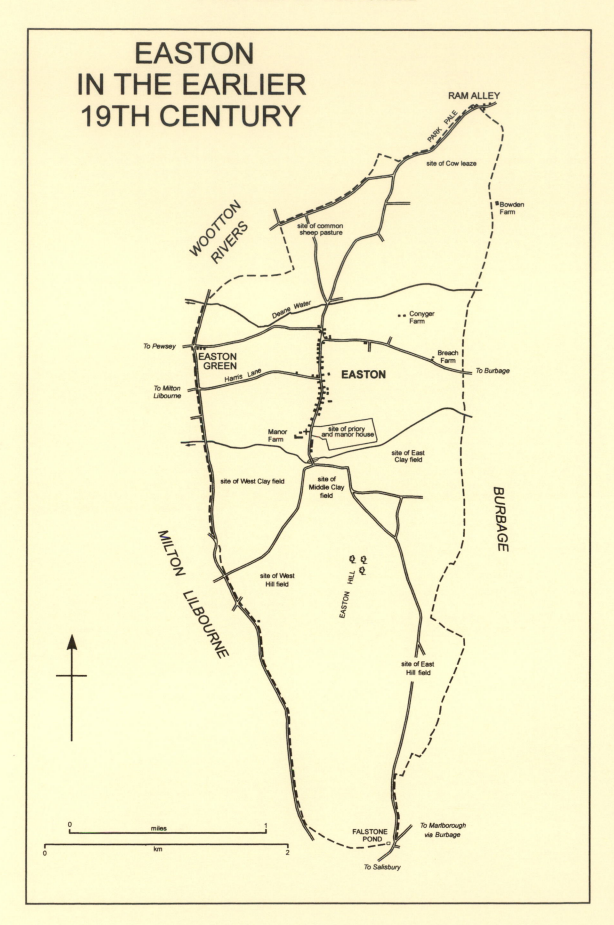

EASTON
IN THE EARLIER
19TH CENTURY

RAM ALLEY

PARK PALE

site of Cow leaze

Bowden Farm

WOOTTON RIVERS

site of common sheep pasture

Deane Water

Conyger Farm

To Pewsey

EASTON GREEN

Harris Lane

EASTON

Breach Farm

To Burbage

To Milton Lilbourne

Manor Farm

site of priory and manor house

site of East Clay field

site of West Clay field

site of Middle Clay field

BURBAGE

site of West Hill field

EASTON HILL

MILTON LILBOURNE

site of East Hill field

FALSTONE POND

To Marlborough via Burbage

0   miles   1

0   km   2

To Salisbury

EASTON

EASTON village stands 7 km. SSE. of Marlborough near the centre of a parish which measured 900 ha. (2,224 a.) until 1987,[6] when 3 ha. was transferred to Burbage.[7] The long and narrow parish lies north–south across the geological outcrops[8] at the north-east edge of Salisbury Plain, the scarp of which crosses the middle of it east–west. A ridge, Easton Hill, runs south from the scarp and forms a backbone in the south half of the parish.

Easton's name, the east tun, was presumably taken from its relationship to Pewsey, from which it was separated by a middle tun, Milton Lilbourne.[9] The village is the site of Easton priory, a house of friars of the Trinitarian order, to which the parish church was given, and the office of serving the parish church became a donative.[10] In 1838 John Ward, the vicar of Great Bedwyn, mistakenly described the donative as royal,[11] in the 1850s the village began to be called Easton Royal,[12] and by c. 1860 Ward's description had been accepted as accurate by the Wiltshire antiquarian the Revd. J. E. Jackson.[13] The suffix was apparently locally popular, and c. 1940 the Wiltshire historian H. C. Brentnall declared that Easton was Easton Royal to all but the official world.[14] In the late 20th century the local authorities still called the parish Easton, but by then Easton Royal had become the usual name of the village.[15]

The parish boundary was recited in 1634 and was not changed until 1987.[16] West of Easton Hill it follows a dry valley for c. 2 km., east of it another dry valley for c. 600 m. Where the two valleys meet at the south-eastern tip of the parish a stone marked the boundary c. 933,[17] in 1244,[18] and in 1634,[19] and it was apparently upright in 1675.[20] The stone gave its name to Falstone pond which had been dug by 1773[21] and lay on the boundary until, in the earlier 20th century, a new pond replaced it.[22] From 1773 or earlier a road has run the whole length of the boundary on the west.[23] Around the north part of the parish the boundary follows a dry valley for a short distance and in the extreme north is marked by a road. At the northern tip a pale beside the road separated Easton from Brimslade park in Saver-nake.[24] In 1908 the line of the Easton and Wootton Rivers boundary along the road was confirmed.[25]

The north half of the parish lies entirely on greensand, the south entirely on chalk. Across the north half two head streams of the Christchurch Avon flow from east to west, one south of the village, the other, Deane water, north; the highest land is at 173 m. in the north on the parish boundary, the lowest at 130 m. where the streams leave the parish; the fertile sandy soils are suitable for both arable and pasture, and there were open Welds on them until the 16th century and common pastures until the 17th. In the south half of the parish marly Lower Chalk outcrops between the village and Easton Hill and along the eastern slopes of the hill, and Middle and Upper Chalk outcrop elsewhere; the land rises steeply from the village to the summit of Easton Hill at 240 m., and descends more gently to the old Falstone pond at 159 m. There were open fields on the heavy soil of the Lower Chalk north of the scarp, on similar soil east of the hill, and on lighter soil west of the hill's summit. Easton Hill was for long a rough pasture for sheep.[26] A clump of trees standing on the summit and said to have been planted after 1747 was the only woodland in the parish in 1773.[27] About 1880 and in 1996 Easton clump on the summit was a circular plantation of 6 a.[28]

Easton had 66 poll-tax payers in 1377.[29] The statement that it had fewer than 10 households in 1428[30] is unlikely to be true. In 1801 the population was 391. It increased steadily to reach its peak of 532 in 1841, and declined steadily to 323 in 1881. From 1891 to 1931 it was between 332 and 304. From 256 in 1951 and 1961 it had fallen to 230 by 1981. The parish had 260 inhabitants in 1991.[31]

The Roman road from Mildenhall to Old Salisbury is likely to have run north–south on Easton Hill as a ridge way, and north of the hill Easton village may stand on or near its line.[32] In the earlier 13th century the village stood on a road which crossed the parish on the likely line of the Roman road and was probably the main Marlborough–Salisbury road.[33] The direct

---

6   This article was written in 1996. Maps used include O.S. Maps 6", Wilts. XXXVI, XLII (1888 and later edns.); 1/25,000, SU 05/15, SU 06/16 (1987 edns.); SU 25/35 (1994 edn.); SU 26/36 (1983 edn.).

7   Statutory Instruments, 1987, no. 619, Kennet (Parishes) Order.

8   Geol. Surv. Maps 1/50,000, drift, sheet 266 (1974 edn.); 1", drift, sheet 282 (1985 edn.).

9   P.N. Wilts. (E.P.N.S.), 345, 349.

10   V.C.H. Wilts. iii. 324–7; below, church.

11   Colln. Topog. et Geneal. v. 39.

12   e.g. W.A.M. ii. 346; Acct. of Wilts. Schs. 22; W.R.O., D 1/60/5/41.   13   Aubrey, Topog. Colln. ed. Jackson, 382.

14   W.A.M. xlix. 399.

15   Wilts. Gaz. and Herald, 8 Sept. 1977; Wilts. co. council, Local Govt. Areas, 1984 (map based on O.S. map); O.S. Map 1/10,000, SU 26 SW. (1982 edn.).

16   Alnwick Castle Mun. X.II.11, box 6, survey, 1634, pp. 1–2; above, this section.

17   Arch. Jnl. lxxvi. 218; W.A.M. lxiv. 61, 63; for the date,

P. H. Sawyer, Anglo-Saxon Chart. (revised S. E. Kelly; priv. circulated 1996), no. 379.

18   V.C.H. Wilts. iv. 448.

19   Alnwick Castle Mun. X.II.11, box 6, survey, 1634, p. 1.   20   J. Ogilby, Brit. (1675), pl. 85.

21   Andrews and Dury, Map (W.R.S. viii), pl. 9.

22   O.S. Maps 1/2,500, Wilts. XLII. 10 (1900 and later edns.).

23   Andrews and Dury, Map (W.R.S. viii), pl. 12.

24   O.S. Map 1/10,000, SU 26 SW. (1982 edn.).

25   W.R.O., F 2/200/3/1, no. 36.

26   Geol. Surv. Maps 1/50,000, drift, sheet 266 (1974 edn.); 1", drift, sheet 282 (1985 edn.); below, econ. hist.

27   Andrews and Dury, Map (W.R.S. viii), pl. 12; R. C. Hoare, Anct. Hist. Wilts. i. 190; Complete Peerage, i. 63.

28   O.S. Map 6", Wilts. XLII (1888 edn.).

29   V.C.H. Wilts. iv. 309.   30   Ibid. 314.

31   Ibid. 347; Census, 1961; 1981; 1991.

32   I. D. Margary, Rom. Roads in Brit. (1973), p. 99.

33   V.C.H. Wilts. iv. 448; below, this section.

course of a Marlborough–Salisbury road through Easton village was blocked in the 16th century when, between Marlborough and Easton, the west part of Savernake forest was inclosed as Savernake great park and Brimslade park,[34] and in the later 17th century the main Marlborough–Salisbury road, part of a road from Chipping Campden (Glos.), followed a more easterly course through Burbage village.[35] Across the downland in the south half of the parish in the 18th century roads led from the south end of the village south-east towards Collingbourne Kingston and south-west towards Upavon and West Everleigh (in Everleigh);[36] tracks and farm roads ran across it in the 19th and 20th centuries,[37] but no road has been tarmacadamed. In the north half of the parish east–west roads link the village with others standing below the scarp. West of the village Harris Lane, so called in 1759,[38] may be part of a direct Burbage–Pewsey road via Milton Lilbourne which crossed the middle of Easton village street. In the later 18th century and later Burbage–Pewsey traffic avoided Easton and Milton Lilbourne villages by using a road on higher ground to the north. In 1773 trees stood in the staggered crossing of that road and the north end of Easton village street.[39] To remove the stagger a short new section of road was built in the mid 20th century.[40]

The chalk upland in the south part of the parish was a site of prehistoric activity. There is evidence of Iron-Age and Roman settlement on and near the summit of Easton Hill, and there are several barrows further south.[41]

The east half of the parish was in Savernake forest until 1330.[42]

Easton is a street village and probably a planned settlement; its name suggests that it was colonized from Pewsey,[43] and its early church, which probably stood at or near the south end of the street,[44] may have been built after the farmsteads. The village was planted, or grew, along a road which was probably important in the earlier 13th century and long before.[45] To relieve poor travellers on the road Easton priory,[46] under construction in 1234,[47] was built at the south end of the street on its east side[48] and 60 paces from the parish church.[49]

Easton priory was severely damaged by fire in 1493 and almost certainly rebuilt.[50] In 1536 the

prior's house was said to have a defective roof but, presumably c. 40 years old, was probably not demolished when the priory was dissolved in that year.[51] It is likely to have been the house at Easton lived in by John Barwick, the receiver of Edward Seymour, duke of Somerset (d. 1552),[52] from 1544 to 1561 or longer,[53] and to have been demolished soon after a lease of it was surrendered in 1580.[54] A large manor house, probably built in the late 16th century, stood on the site until c. 1760.[55] The priory church, which had been the parish church since 1369, was demolished, presumably c. 1591, the year in which a new parish church was built on the west side of the street at the south end.[56]

A large demesne farm was based at buildings near the new church.[57] The farmhouse, Manor Farm, has an 18th-century north range of red brick and of two storeys and attics. A range of one storey and attics extending southwards from the west end was destroyed by fire in 1808[58] and replaced soon afterwards by a larger south block. In 1996 the farm buildings included a 19th-century open cart shed of timber. A house immediately north of the church and lived in by the vicar of Easton in the later 19th century and early 20th[59] was apparently timber-framed and built in the 17th century; it was altered and enlarged in brick in the later 19th century. Near the vicar's house and on the east side of the street a new school was built in the later 19th century.[60]

In the street, which, especially towards its north end, is sunken, there were apparently c. 23 small farmsteads c. 1600, each farmhouse having a close behind it.[61] It seems that all the farmhouses were replaced. In 1996 several of the 17th century survived and were mostly timber-framed and thatched. At the middle of the street on the east side Easton House, a tall red-brick house with a principal west front of three bays, was built in the later 18th century.[62] Home Farm, of grey brick with dressings of red brick, was built further north on the east side in 1843.[63] Nearly all of the 71 dwellings in the parish in 1735[64] and of the 76 in 1814 were in the street.[65] In 1996, including a few north of the crossroads, c. 25 timber-framed and thatched houses and cottages of the 17th and 18th centuries stood beside the street, and there were a few pairs of 19th-century cottages. In the 20th century c. 20 houses and bungalows have replaced older

34 Below, Savernake, intro. (roads; Brimslade); econ. hist.
35 Ogilby, *Brit.* (1675), pl. 85.
36 *Andrews and Dury, Map* (W.R.S. viii), pl. 12; W.R.O. 9/15/329.
37 O.S. Maps 6", Wilts. XLII (1888 and later edns.).
38 W.R.O. 9/15/195.
39 *Andrews and Dury, Map* (W.R.S. viii), pl. 12.
40 O.S. Maps 1", sheets 112 (1940 edn.); 167 (1960 edn.).
41 *V.C.H. Wilts.* i (1), 67–8, 173, 218; O.S. Map 1/10,000, SU 25 NW. (1982 edn.); inf. from Arch. section, Co. Hall, Trowbridge.
42 *V.C.H. Wilts.* iv. 399–400, 450–1.
43 Above, this section [place name]; for street villages almost certainly and possibly colonized from Pewsey, below, Milton Lilbourne, intro. (Milton Lilbourne); Pewsey, intro.
44 Below, this para.
45 Above, this section [roads].
46 *V.C.H. Wilts.* iii. 324.
47 *Close R.* 1231–4, 374.
48 Cf. air photo. in possession of Arch. section, Co. Hall,

Trowbridge.
49 W.R.O. 9/15/41.
50 Ibid. 9/15/54.
51 *V.C.H. Wilts.* iii. 327.
52 Hist. MSS. Com. 58, *Bath,* iv, p. 318.
53 *L. & P. Hen. VIII,* xix (1), pp. 382, 625; *Cal. Pat.* 1560–3, 81.
54 W.R.O. 9/15/63.
55 Ibid. 9/15/196; *Andrews and Dury, Map* (W.R.S. viii), pl. 12; below, manors.
56 Below, church [archit.].
57 Cf. ibid. econ. hist.
58 J. Buckler, watercolour in W.A.S. Libr., vol. iv. 7; W.R.O. 1300/3578.
59 O.S. Maps 6", Wilts. XLII (1888 and later edns.).
60 Below, educ.
61 W.R.O. 9/15/327.
62 A date of 1783 is given in H. H. Bashford, *Easton Royal,* 16.
63 Date on bldg.
64 W.R.O. 9/15/330.
65 Ibid. 9/15/336.

buildings or filled spaces on both sides of the street, most at the north end. In the late 18th century the Bleeding Horse was apparently an alehouse in the street;[66] at the north end a nonconformist chapel was built in the late 19th century[67] and a village hall c. 1935.[68] In 1773 there was a pond in the north part of the street on the west side, and there were others either side of a bridge across the stream at the south end.[69] The northern pond had been filled by 1886;[70] the southern two apparently dried up in the late 19th century[71] and were filled in 1955.[72] In 1975 the whole street was designated a conservation area.[73]

In Harris Lane a cottage of red brick and thatch was built c. 1800;[74] it was linked to the village in the 1950s when three pairs of council houses and a pair of old people's bungalows were built between it and the street.[75] From the crossroads the village was extended eastwards along the Burbage road by the building of five pairs of council houses between 1927 and 1936[76] and a pair in 1945;[77] afterwards 12 private houses were built along the road.

Outside the village a farmstead called Conyger, possibly on the site of an earlier lodge,[78] had been built by 1735,[79] and by 1773 Breach Farm had been built south-east of it, possibly on the site of a barn standing in 1735.[80] Conyger farmstead was greatly enlarged c. 1865;[81] the farmhouse had been demolished by c. 1970, when a bungalow was built at the farmstead.[82] Extensive farm buildings remained on the site in 1996. The site of Breach Farm is marked by a trio of mid 19th-century thatched cottages. West of the village, at a site called Easton Green in 1773,[83] a house was held by John Gammon in the earlier 17th century[84] and the Gammon of Bacon was an inn on the south side of the Pewsey road from 1736 or earlier.[85] Between 1848 and 1855 it was replaced by a new inn, the Bruce's Arms,[86] built on the opposite side of the road and open in 1996. On the south side of the road a pair of cottages was apparently altered in the late 19th century.[87] In the northern tip of the parish two cottages standing in 1634 and three in 1721–2 were part of Ram Alley,[88] a small settlement mainly in Burbage.[89] A pair of cottages was replaced by a house built in 1940;[90] the cottage which survives is timber-framed, thatched, and possibly early 18th-century. On the downs in the south of the parish farm buildings were erected west of Easton Hill between 1773 and 1814 and east between 1814 and 1867;[91] both groups were in use in 1996.

Michael Clark of Easton was said in 1649 to be a delinquent Royalist.[92] John Wildman, a republican, was arrested at Easton in 1655 while dictating a declaration against Cromwell.[93]

MANORS AND OTHER ESTATES. Easton may have been part of a large estate called Wootton which belonged to the king in 1086.[94] In the mid 12th century it belonged to John FitzGilbert (d. 1165), the king's marshal from c. 1130, who gave half of it to Bradenstoke priory.[95] The other half probably passed in turn to John's sons Gilbert FitzJohn (d. 1165–6) and John, and between 1174 and 1186 John, as John the marshal, gave it to the bishop of Hereford in an exchange.[96] Between c. 1196 and 1198 the bishop granted that half to Adam of Easton at fee farm for a rent of £10.[97] Adam's heir was his son Stephen of Tisbury, rector of Easton and of Tisbury, archdeacon of Wiltshire from c. 1226, and the founder of Easton priory, on whose death in 1246[98] the half passed in moieties to his nephew Geoffrey Sturmy and niece Felice, the wife of Sir William Druce.[99]

Felice Druce's quarter of Easton, later called EASTON DRUCE or EASTON PRIORY manor, was settled on her son Geoffrey (fl. 1275) in tail with remainder to his brother Hugh.[1] In 1321 Hugh's son Robert conveyed the estate to his cousin Robert Druce[2] (d. 1324 × 1328),[3] and from that Robert it passed to his son Sir John.[4] By 1344 it had been acquired by Walter Kingsettle[5] and his wife Lettice. In 1348–9 it was bought from the Kingsettles by Robert of Burbage, rector of Compton Chamberlayne, who under a licence of 1349 gave it to Easton priory: in exchange the priory was to assign two of its brethren to celebrate mass for Robert and his nominees and from Robert's death to give 1s. a year to each of seven new brethren to be received

66 Ibid. 9/15/333.
67 Below, nonconf.
68 W.R.O., G 10/505/1; Char. Com. file.
69 *Andrews and Dury, Map* (W.R.S. viii), pl. 12.
70 O.S. Map 6", Wilts. XXXVI (1888 edn.).
71 Ibid. XLII (1888 and later edns.).
72 Bashford, *Easton Royal*, 18.
73 Inf. from Dept. of Planning and Highways, Co. Hall, Trowbridge.
74 *Andrews and Dury, Map* (W.R.S. viii), pl. 12; O.S. Map 1", sheet 14 (1817 edn.).
75 W.R.O., G 10/505/1.
76 Ibid. G 10/600/1.
77 Ibid. G 10/505/1.
78 Ibid. 9/15/67.
79 Ibid. 9/15/330.
80 Ibid.; *Andrews and Dury, Map* (W.R.S. viii), pl. 12.
81 W.R.O. 9/1/110.
82 Ibid. 1268/6.
83 *Andrews and Dury, Map* (W.R.S. viii), pl. 12.
84 Alnwick Castle Mun. X.II.11, box 6, survey, 1634, p. 1.
85 Bashford, *Easton Royal*, 21; W.R.O. 9/15/163.
86 *Kelly's Dir. Wilts.* (1848, 1855).
87 O.S. Maps 1/2,500, Wilts. XXXVI. 14 (1887, 1900

edns.).
88 W.R.O. 9/15/140–1; 9/15/147; Alnwick Castle Mun. X.II.11, box 6, survey, 1634, pp. 46–7.
89 Above, Burbage, intro. (Ram Alley).
90 W.R.O., G 10/505/1.
91 Ibid. 9/1/110; 9/15/336; *Andrews and Dury, Map* (W.R.S. viii), pl. 12.
92 *Cal. Cttee. for Money*, ii. 1021.
93 *V.C.H. Wilts.* v. 148.
94 Ibid. ii, p. 118; below, Wootton Rivers, manors.
95 *Bradenstoke Cart.* (W.R.S. xxxv), p. 92; for the marshals, *Complete Peerage*, x, App. G, 93–7.
96 *Cal. Pat.* 1354–8, 197; *Handbook Brit. Chronology* (1986), ed. E. B. Fryde and others, 250.
97 *Handbook Brit. Chronology* (1986), 250; Le Neve, *Fasti, 1066–1300, Lincoln*, 36; P.R.O., E 326/10846.
98 *Bradenstoke Cart.* (W.R.S. xxxv), p. 91; Le Neve, *Fasti, 1066–1300, Salisbury*, 36; W.R.O. 9/15/7; 1300/30; below, church.
99 W.R.O. 9/15/16; 9/15/21; 1300/2.
1 Ibid. 9/15/21; *Rot. Hund.* (Rec. Com.), ii (1), 259.
2 *Cat. Anct. D.* iii, A 5826; W.R.O. 9/15/20.
3 *Cal. Pat.* 1321–4, 421; P.R.O., CP 40/274, rot. 81d.
4 P.R.O., CP 40/275, rot. 39d.; W.R.O. 9/15/25.
5 W.R.O. 9/15/28–30.

into the priory.[6] The estate belonged to the priory until 1536, when the priory was dissolved and the estate was granted to Sir Edward Seymour, Viscount Beauchamp[7] (cr. earl of Hertford 1537, duke of Somerset 1547), its patron and a descendant of its founder. Seymour held it until his execution and attainder in 1552,[8] when by Act it passed to his son Sir Edward[9] (a minor until 1558, cr. earl of Hertford 1559, d. 1621).[10]

At his death c. 1254 Geoffrey Sturmy's quarter of Easton, later called *EASTON WARREN* manor, descended to his son Henry (d. c. 1296).[11] It belonged to Philip Sturmy in 1324[12] and 1347[13] and to Henry Sturmy of Easton in 1349.[14] It was held by Richard Warren in 1428[15] and 1454,[16] and descended in the Warren family with Fyfield manor in Milton Lilbourne[17] until, between 1545 and 1550, the estate was bought from John Warren by Edward, earl of Hertford and from 1547 duke of Somerset.[18] On Somerset's attainder it was forfeited to the Crown, and in 1553 it was assigned by Act to his son Sir Edward.[19]

Bradenstoke priory kept its half of Easton until the Dissolution.[20] As *EASTON BRADENSTOKE* manor it was received by Edward, earl of Hertford, in 1541 in an exchange of land with the king.[21] Like Easton Warren manor it was forfeited to the Crown in 1552 and assigned to Sir Edward Seymour in 1553.[22]

From c. 1237 the *RECTORY* estate, consisting of 26 a., feeding rights for 40 sheep and 1 ram, and the tithes of the whole parish except those of corn, hay, and cheese from Bradenstoke priory's demesne land, belonged to Easton priory.[23] It passed with Easton Druce manor from c. 1349, and from 1553 all the tithes belonged to the owner of the land from which they arose.[24]

From c. 1237 the tithes excepted from the Rectory estate belonged to Bradenstoke priory and later owners of the land from which they arose.[25]

From 1553 to 1929 the whole parish, including all tithes from it, descended in the Seymour, Bruce, Brudenell, and Brudenell-Bruce families

with Tottenham Lodge and Tottenham House in Great Bedwyn.[26] Edward, earl of Hertford, was living at Easton in 1581,[27] and a new manor house was probably built about then on the site of Easton priory. From c. 1600 Lord Hertford also lived in a house at Amesbury,[28] but the manor house at Easton was kept in hand and lived in by him until 1621[29] and by his relatives until it was leased[30] in 1675. From 1693 the lease was held by Sir Edward Seymour, Bt. (d. 1740), who lived at Easton.[31] The house was demolished c. 1760.[32]

About 1929 George Brudenell-Bruce, marquess of Ailesbury, sold Manor farm, 754 a. in the west part of the parish, to J. S. Haines (d. 1937), from whom it descended with Lower farm, Milton Lilbourne, to his son J. S. Haines. Of Manor farm 130 a. passed with Lower farm and belonged to Mr. G. E. R. Osborne in 1996,[33] and 197 a. was sold to W. R. Curnick and in 1996 belonged to his son Mr. T. W. Curnick as part of Southgrove farm, Burbage.[34] The reduced Manor farm was sold by Haines to Robert de Pass in 1954, and in 1996, then 486 a., it belonged to de Pass's son Mr. M. A. R. de Pass.[35] In 1929 Lord Ailesbury sold Easton farm, 681 a. in the east part of the parish, to J. T. Cooper, whose grandson Mr. S. P. Cooper owned it in 1996.[36] Of land in the north part of the parish sold by Lord Ailesbury c. 1929 Conyger farm had 345 a. in 1971; the farm was bought then by Mr. J. C. Brook, the owner in 1996.[37] In 1950 Lord Ailesbury sold c. 150 a. at the north end of the parish to the Crown, which in 1996 owned it as part of Bowden farm based in Burbage.[38]

The bishop of Hereford kept the fee-farm rent of £10 until it was given to Elizabeth I in an exchange. Between 1651[39] and 1672 it was sold by trustees appointed by parliament, and in 1770 it was bought from William Morehead by Thomas Bruce, Lord Bruce,[40] the owner of Easton Druce and Easton Warren manors.[41]

ECONOMIC HISTORY. The lands of the three manors into which Easton was divided in

6   W.R.O. 9/15/31–5; 9/15/315.
7   *Valor Eccl.* (Rec. Com.), ii. 149; *V.C.H. Wilts.* iii. 327; *L. & P. Hen. VIII*, x, p. 526.
8   *Complete Peerage*, xii (1), 59–64; *V.C.H. Wilts.* iii. 324–7; above, Burbage, manors (Burbage Sturmy).
9   P.R.O., E 328/117.
10   *Complete Peerage*, vi. 505–6.
11   W.R.O. 1300/2; for the dates of d., above, Burbage, manors (Burbage Sturmy).
12   W.R.O. 9/15/25.
13   P.R.O., CP 40/345, rot. 135d.
14   W.R.O. 9/15/315.
15   *Feud. Aids*, v. 263.
16   W.R.O. 9/6/756.
17   Below, Milton Lilbourne, manors (Fyfield).
18   W.R.O. 9/15/317; 192/53, f. 4.
19   P.R.O., E 328/117.
20   *Valor Eccl.* (Rec. Com.), ii. 123.
21   P.R.O., E 305/4/C 18.
22   Ibid. E 328/117.
23   Ibid. E 315/398, f. 92; Longleat Mun., Seymour papers, xii, f. 311v.; below, church.
24   A statement of 1553 that the estate had been alienated by Seymour between 1540 and 1552 was apparently erroneous: cf. P.R.O., E 328/117; W.R.O. 192/53, f. 4v.; 1300/167.
25   Below, church; P.R.O., E 305/4/C 18.

26   Above, Great Bedwyn, manors (Tottenham).
27   Hist. MSS. Com. 58, *Bath*, iv, p. 192.
28   *V.C.H. Wilts.* xv. 32.
29   e.g. *Lieutenancy Papers* (W.R.S. xxiii), pp. 31, 139.
30   e.g. *Wilts. Inq. p.m.* 1625–49 (Index Libr.), 18, 26; *W.N. & Q.* ii. 588; W.R.O. 9/15/81.
31   *Complete Peerage*, xii (1), 83; W.R.O. 9/1/99, p. 22; 9/15/107.
32   *Andrews and Dury, Map* (W.R.S. viii), pl. 12; W.R.O. 9/15/196.
33   *W.A.M.* xlviii. 123; W.R.O. 9/1/521; inf. from Mr. G. E. R. Osborne, Lawn Farm, Milton Lilbourne; for the descent of Lower farm, below, Milton Lilbourne, manors (Lower).
34   Inf. from Mr. T. W. Curnick, Southgrove Farm, Burbage.
35   W.R.O. 2499/320/9; inf. from Mr. M. A. R. de Pass, Manor Farmhouse.
36   W.R.O. 9/1/521; inf. from Mr. S. P. Cooper, Easton Farm.
37   W.R.O. 9/1/521; 1268/6; inf. from Mr. J. C. Brook, Conygre Farm.
38   Inf. from the agent for the Crown Estate Com., 42 High Street, Marlborough.
39   P.R.O., E 308/4/35, rot. 87.
40   W.R.O. 9/15/56–9.
41   Above, this section.

the 12th and 13th centuries[42] were intermingled throughout the parish;[43] each manor consisted of demesne and customary land,[44] and later evidence suggests that the demesne in the parish was bisected in the mid 12th century and that one of the halves was bisected c. 1246.[45] The arable lay in open fields and c. 1200 there was apparently common pasture for cattle and pigs.[46] In the Middle Ages there were probably only two open fields, East and West, running north–south across the geological outcrops east and west of the village. Of all three manors both the demesne and the customary holdings apparently included arable in all parts of the fields, and they probably shared a common pasture for cattle in the north part of the parish and, on Easton Hill between the open fields, one for sheep in the south.[47]

By the 16th century some demesne land had been inclosed: Bowden close, 60 a. in the earlier 16th century[48] and presumably in the north-east corner of the parish,[49] had been inclosed by the mid 13th century,[50] In mead had been inclosed by the earlier 14th century,[51] and Easton Druce manor included other several pastures in the earlier 16th century. Also by the 16th century each open field had been divided into a Hill field, one on either side of Easton Hill, a Clay field, both on the Lower Chalk, and, one on either side of the village, a Sand field on the greensand; all but a small part of Easton Hill had been reserved for demesne sheep, and all the uninclosed pasture in the north for the copyholders' sheep and cattle.[52] At the Dissolution inclosed demesne of Easton Druce manor was held by Easton priory in hand, a demesne farm including a nominal 208 a. in the open fields and pasture for 240 sheep was held on lease, and the customary land of the manor was in eight copyholds which had small areas of meadow and inclosed pasture, a nominal 186 a. in the open fields, and feeding in common for 455 sheep and for cattle.[53] Bradenstoke priory apparently kept a directly managed flock at Easton in 1348–9,[54] and may have kept in hand the demesne pasture rights of Easton Bradenstoke manor after it had leased the demesne land.[55]

In the later 16th century the two fields on the greensand were inclosed and c. 130 a. of closes, called East Sands, West Sands, East Several, and West Several and mostly of 2–10 a., was added to copyholds. The copyholders' sheep stint, 80

to each yardland, was not reduced and, although it was customary to feed the demesne sheep on the open fields for only six days, most of the new closes were laid to grass. By 1579 the common pasture in the north part of the parish had been divided by hedges into two common pastures, one of c. 138 a. for sheep, and Cow leaze, c. 215 a.[56] The three demesne farms were merged[57] and inclosures east and north-east of the village, including some in Burbage parish, were held with the house standing on the site of the priory. A 50-a. rabbit warren on Bat field and Old land, presumably former arable, apparently lay north-east of the village,[58] and the Breach, a several demesne pasture, lay east of the warren.[59] In 1581 c. 8 a. of the downland open fields was inclosed as penning for sheep on the demesne.[60]

About 1600 the composite demesne farm, probably based partly in the buildings on the demesne of Easton Bradenstoke manor, formerly called the Black farm, may have been in hand. Of the three manors there were c. 23 copyholds averaging c. 30 a. They included c. 250 a. near the village and in closes of 2–12 a., rights to feed 1,832 sheep, and nominally c. 450 a. in the open fields.[61]

In the early 17th century, probably c. 1610, the sheep common and Cow leaze were inclosed and c. 54 closes were added to copyholds; another common pasture, West ridge, 37 a., was also inclosed.[62] In 1608, when it measured 150 a. and a lodge stood on it, the warren was leased for a rent of 500 pairs of rabbits.[63] In 1618 the Breach, 60 a., and part of In mead, a demesne meadow, were leased;[64] by 1634 the Breach had been divided into 3 closes. The preservation of rabbits had apparently ceased by 1625, when the warren was leased as 6 closes; also in 1625 demesne pastures called Longland and Oatleazes, a total of 42 a., were leased as 19 closes. In 1634 the demesne remaining in hand was 59 a. of meadow, 60 a. of lowland pasture, the rough pasture on Easton Hill, and nominally c. 340 a. in the open fields.[65] That farm, later Manor farm, was leased in 1637.[66]

In the early 18th century in the south half of the parish there were five open fields in which lay 628 a. of arable in 801 parcels with c. 48 a. of lynchets: on the downs to the south East Hill field measured 210 a., West Hill field 113 a.; to the north East Clay field measured 112 a., Middle Clay 100 a., and West Clay 93 a. Be-

42   Ibid. manors.
43   e.g. W.R.O. 9/15/318, ct. 8 Apr. 21 Eliz. I.
44   e.g. ibid. 9/15/315; 192/53, ff. 3v.–4, 6; *Sar. Chart. and Doc.* (Rolls Ser.), p. 302.
45   W.R.O. 9/15/327; above, manors.
46   W.R.O. 9/15/1; 9/15/25.
47   Ibid. 9/15/330–1; 9/15/339, n. about Easton farm; Longleat Mun., Seymour papers, xii, ff. 308–13.
48   P.R.O., C 1/786, no. 33; ibid. STAC 2/14, no. 154.
49   Cf. *Andrews and Dury, Map* (W.R.S. viii), pl. 12; Alnwick Castle Mun. X.II.11, box 6, survey, 1634, p. 2.
50   W.R.O. 9/15/20.
51   Ibid. 9/15/25.
52   Longleat Mun., Seymour papers, xii, ff. 308–13; cf. Alnwick Castle Mun. X.II.11, box 6, survey, 1634, pp. 11–54; W.R.O. 9/15/327.
53   Longleat Mun., Seymour papers, xii, ff. 308–13; P.R.O., C 1/786, no. 33; ibid. E 315/420, ff. 93v.–94.
54   W.R.O. 9/15/315.

55   P.R.O., SC 6/Hen. VIII/3985, rot. 59.
56   Alnwick Castle Mun. X.II.11, box 6, survey, 1634, pp. 2, 15–43; Longleat Mun., Seymour papers, xii, ff. 308–11; W.R.O. 9/1/122; 9/15/318–19; cf. 9/15/339, n. about Easton farm.
57   W.R.O. 192/53, ff. 3v.–4v.
58   Ibid. 9/15/67; 9/15/327; P.R.O., STAC 4/9/6; above, Burbage, econ. hist. (Burbage); for the ho., above, intro.; manors.
59   W.R.O. 9/15/69.
60   Ibid. 9/15/318, ct. 6 Oct. 23 Eliz. I.
61   Ibid. 9/15/327.
62   Ibid.; ibid. 192/24A, ff. 21, 37; Alnwick Castle Mun. X.II.11, box 6, survey, 1634, pp. 15–43.
63   W.R.O. 9/15/67.
64   Ibid. 9/15/69–70.
65   Alnwick Castle Mun. X.II.11, box 6, survey, 1634, pp. 6, 51–3.
66   W.R.O. 9/15/81; cf. 9/15/330.

tween East Hill field and West Hill field lay the farm down, 387 a., and *c*. 30 a. of tenantry down. The two downland fields were ploughed in alternate years; each of the three lowland fields was ploughed two years in three. Mainly in the north half of the parish there was 1,024 a. in 365 closes; *c*. 845 a. of that land was arable. Among the closes 24 called West Several included *c*. 60 a., 17 called East Several *c*. 35 a., 13 called Oatleaze *c*. 47 a., and 5 called Farm Oatleaze *c*. 55 a. On the former warren there were 18 closes called Conyger, *c*. 47 a., in one of which stood a farmhouse; the Breach, *c*. 54 a., had been divided into 12 closes, in one of which stood a barn. Manor farm, 782 a., included 264 a. of the open fields, 68 a. of inclosed arable, 44 a. of meadow, the 12-a. penning, and the farm down. There were *c*. 26 copyholds and leaseholds, varying from 82 a. to *c*. 15 a.; nearly all had more land in closes than in the open fields and most included feeding rights for sheep. Some of the holdings may have been worked with others but most farms seem to have been small, and all the farm buildings except those of Conyger farm and Breach farm stood in the village street.[67]

In 1773 the open fields were inclosed by private agreement. West Hill field, West Clay field, and part of Middle Clay field, a total of 305 a., were allotted for Manor farm, to which three small former copyholds had been added. The lands to the east were allotted as fields of 1–31 a. to the other holdings, of which there were *c*. 20. To compensate those holdings for the loss of feeding on the arable of Manor farm 130 a. of the farm's down was allotted for their use in common.[68] That and *c*. 22 a. of other downland apparently remained in common use until the mid 19th century.[69] In the late 18th century holdings were being enlarged and converted from lifehold to rack rent. By 1784 a farm had grown to 268 a., and four to 100–150 a., as holdings were agglomerated.[70]

In 1814 there was in the parish *c*. 1,500 a. of arable, 139 a. of meadow, 57 a. of permanent lowland pasture, and 461 a. of downland pasture. Manor farm measured 773 a. and included a farmyard on the former West Hill field. There were six other farms, of which the largest measured 236 a. and the smallest 77 a., and seven smaller holdings. All except Conyger farm, 77 a., were based in the street, and their lands were intermixed and inconvenient to use.[71] By 1867, when Manor farm measured 712 a., several farms had been merged as Easton farm, 860 a. including 299 a. in Burbage. Between 1867, when all eight farms based in the parish were

mainly arable,[72] and 1929 much land was laid to grass, and in the earlier 20th century the down-land pasture was used as gallops. In 1929 Manor, 754 a., and Easton, 681 a., were mixed farms; the others, of 313 a., 112 a., 55 a., and 38 a., were mainly dairy farms.[73]

At the north end of the parish *c*. 150 a. was probably worked from Burbage as part of Bow-den farm in the 19th century, as it was from 1910 or earlier and in 1996.[74] Manor farm was worked with Lower farm, Milton Lilbourne, from *c*. 1905 to 1954,[75] since when it has been a separate farm with land north of Easton Hill and west of the village; in 1996 it was a mixed farm of 486 a.[76] Most of the land in the south part of the parish taken from Manor farm[77] lay in the later 20th century as arable in large fields worked from Lawn Farm, Milton Lilbourne, and Southgrove Farm, Burbage.[78] In 1996 Easton farm, still 681 a., was an arable and beef farm.[79] In 1971 Conyger farm, 345 a., lay entirely on greensand in the north part of the parish. In the 1970s it was an arable, beef, and sheep farm; thereafter and in 1996, when it measured 381 a., it was an arable and sheep farm.[80]

A tailor and a weaver lived at Easton in 1352;[81] stone for building was quarried in the 16th and 17th centuries.[82] There was a malthouse in the village in the 18th century[83] and there were two in the earlier 19th.[84]

LOCAL GOVERNMENT. By 1289 Braden-stoke priory had made good its claim to enforce the assize of bread and of ale at Easton;[85] it held a view of frankpledge there twice a year in the mid 14th century[86] and apparently until the Dissolution.[87] The records of five meetings of the court of Easton Warren manor between 1263 and 1266 survive; misuse of pasture with sheep was reported in 1266 but little other business was done.[88] The records of two meetings of the court of Easton Druce manor in 1348–9 survive; the court heard pleas, recorded the death of tenants, witnessed admittances, and punished the misuse of pasture.[89]

Between 1541 and 1550 one court, called a view of frankpledge and manor court, was held for Easton Druce and Easton Bradenstoke man-ors, then in single ownership. A tithingman was chosen and the making of stocks required, but the court did little other leet business and dealt mainly with the transfer of copyholds, breaches of the rules of common husbandry, and the maintenance of hedges, ditches, and buildings.[90] From 1553 the three manors in the parish were

67 W.R.O. 9/15/330–1; 9/15/339, n. about Easton farm.
68 Ibid. 9/15/62.
69 Cf. ibid. 9/1/110; 9/15/336.
70 Ibid. 9/15/221; 9/15/333.
71 Ibid. 9/15/336.
72 Ibid. 9/1/110.
73 Ibid. 9/1/521; ibid. G 10/500/31.
74 Ibid. Inland Revenue, val. reg. 58–9; inf. from the agent for the Crown Estate Com., 42 High Street, Marlbor-ough; above, Burbage, econ. hist. (Burbage).
75 Below, Milton Lilbourne, econ. hist. (Milton Lil-bourne).
76 Inf. from Mr. M. A. R. de Pass, Manor Farmhouse.
77 Cf. above, manors.
78 Inf. from Mr. G. E. R. Osborne, Lawn Farm, Milton

Lilbourne; Mr. T. W. Curnick, Southgrove Farm, Burbage.
79 Inf. from Mr. S. P. Cooper, Easton Farm.
80 W.R.O. 1268/6; inf. from Mr. J. C. Brook, Conygre Farm.
81 *W.A.M.* xxxiii. 396.
82 Hist. MSS. Com. 58, *Bath*, iv. p. 335; *V.C.H. Wilts.* iv. 248.
83 W.R.O. 9/15/208; 9/15/330.
84 Ibid. 9/15/336.
85 P.R.O., JUST 1/1006, rot. 51d.
86 Ibid. CP 40/345, rot. 135d.
87 Ibid. SC 6/Hen. VIII/3985, rot. 59.
88 Ibid. SC 2/183/56, rott. 1–2, 4.
89 W.R.O. 9/15/315.
90 Ibid. 9/15/317; for the ownership, above, manors.

in single ownership,[91] and until *c.* 1580 a single court and, once a year, a single view were held for them all. The court, at which a single homage was sworn, acted as it had in the 1540s, but the view began to punish statutory offences such as the playing of unlawful games.[92]

From *c.* 1580 a separate court was held for each of the three manors, that for Easton Bradenstoke incorporating the view of frankpledge. Except for special meetings of the courts baron, the three courts met on the same day as each other and usually once a year, jurisdiction over the whole parish was exercised by the view, and until *c.* 1600 joint presentments were sometimes made by the three homages and sometimes by the jury and the three homages;[93] it was sometimes expressly stated that orders made by any one of the courts were to apply to the whole parish.[94]

At the view matters presented under leet jurisdiction in the late 16th century and early 17th included public nuisances, the condition of the stocks, affray, the playing of unlawful games, failure to practise archery, keep a rook net, wear statutory caps, and repair roads, and the unlawful building of cottages, carrying of a fowling piece, and accepting of inmates;[95] in the 1590s removal orders were made.[96] Very little was presented under leet jurisdiction after *c.* 1625.[97]

At the three manor courts private pleas were heard until the 1590s. The courts continued to be concerned with the definition and observance of agrarian custom and the condition of gates, boundaries, hedges, ditches, and buildings, but from the later 17th century presentments relating to such matters became fewer and conveyancing became the principal business. From *c.* 1730 to *c.* 1770 stereotyped presentments of some customs were recorded, but from *c.* 1770 the courts dealt only with tenurial business.[98]

The parish spent £103 on poor relief in 1775–6, an average of £117 a year in the early 1780s. It apparently had a workhouse which had been demolished by 1798. In 1802–3, when the poor rate was high and all relief was outdoor, the parish spent £304: 24 adults and 94 children were relieved regularly, 8 people occasionally.[99] Expenditure had risen to £701 by 1812–13, when 40 adults were relieved regularly and 25 occasionally; by 1814–15 it had been reduced to

£294 and the numbers to 22 and 15 respectively.[1] A tenement which the parish had built housed 7 paupers in 1814.[2] From 1814–15 to 1833–4 expenditure on poor relief averaged £389 a year. At £563 it was highest in 1818–19, at £249 lowest in 1815–16.[3] The parish joined Pewsey poor-law union in 1835[4] and became part of Kennet district in 1974.[5]

CHURCH. In 1086 on the king's large estate called Wootton there were two churches belonging to the abbey of Mont St. Michel (Manche), one of which may have stood at Easton.[6] Later Easton church may have belonged to the abbey of la Trinité du Mont, Rouen (Seine-Maritime), until, between 1193 and 1198, that abbey presented Adam of Easton's son Stephen, later Stephen of Tisbury (d. 1246), as rector.[7] Between 1199 and 1207 William Marshal, earl of Pembroke, whose father John FitzGilbert, the king's marshal, had granted half of Easton to Bradenstoke priory, incompatibly granted the church to the priory, and the priory prepared to present a rival rector.[8] Stephen's right to the church was examined and confirmed between 1218 and 1222,[9] but the patronage remained in dispute. Stephen claimed it by a grant of his patron, in the 1240s called the abbey of Sainte-Cathérine-du-Mont, which claimed it by a grant of a former marshal of England: Bradenstoke priory claimed it by grant of William, earl of Pembroke. The dispute was referred to the bishop of Salisbury for arbitration, and by 1237 it had been decided that Bradenstoke priory should have all the tithes of corn, hay, and cheese from its demesne land at Easton, that all other tithes arising at Easton should be kept by Easton church, and that the church should be given to the religious house founded at Easton by Stephen *c.* 1234. The decision was ratified in 1246.[10] From then the duty of serving the church was presumably given by the prior of Easton to a brother of the priory,[11] and from 1369 the parishioners worshipped in the priory church.[12]

The living remained a donative and from the dissolution of Easton priory in 1536 was held by curates, from 1868 by vicars, all nominated by the owner of the Rectory estate.[13] The parish was under the jurisdiction of the ordinary in the 16th and 17th centuries,[14] in the late 18th century and

91 Above, manors.
92 W.R.O. 9/15/318.
93 Ibid.; 9/15/319.
94 Ibid. 9/15/318, cts. 8 Apr. 21 Eliz. I; 27 Nov. 31 Eliz. I.
95 e.g. ibid. cts. 6 Oct. 23 Eliz. I; 13 Mar. 26 Eliz. I; ibid. 9/1/144, rott. 1–2; 9/15/319, cts. 30 Apr. 33 Eliz. I; 23 Nov. 35 Eliz. I; 3 Oct. 36 Eliz. I; 27 Apr. 38 Eliz. I; 2 May 40 Eliz. I; 20 Apr. 8 Jas. I; list of presentments, *c.* 1591.
96 e.g. ibid. 9/15/319, ct. 30 Apr. 33 Eliz. I.
97 Cf. ct. rec. listed below, n. 98.
98 W.R.O. 9/1/135; 9/1/137; 9/1/140–1; 9/1/144–57; 9/1/160–1; 9/1/163–5; 9/1/168–74; 9/1/176–80; 9/1/182–203; 9/15/318–23; 9/15/326; 192/24A–B.
99 Ibid. 9/15/233; *Poor Law Abstract, 1804*, 566–7.
1 *Poor Law Abstract, 1818*, 498–9.
2 W.R.O. 9/15/336.
3 *Poor Law Abstract, 1818*, 498–9; *Poor Rate Returns, 1816–21*, 188; *1822–4*, 228; *1825–9*, 219; *1830–4*, 212.
4 *Poor Law Com. 2nd Rep.* 560.

5 O.S. Map 1/100,000, admin. areas, Wilts. (1974 edn.).
6 *V.C.H. Wilts.* ii, p. 118; below, Wootton Rivers, manors.
7 Le Neve, *Fasti, 1066–1300, Salisbury*, 35–6; W.R.O. 9/15/5; 9/15/7; above, manors.
8 *Bradenstoke Cart.* (W.R.S. xxxv), p. 92; *Complete Peerage*, x, App. G, 93–7; above, manors.
9 W.R.O. 9/15/7.
10 Ibid. 9/15/8; *Sar. Chart. and Doc.* (Rolls Ser.), pp. 301–6, where the grant to the abbey was ascribed, apparently in error, to a marshal called Anselm, presumably Anselm Marshal, earl of Pembroke (d. 1245): cf. *Complete Peerage*, x. 376–7; for the foundation of Easton priory, above, intro.
11 Cf. *Sar. Chart. and Doc.* (Rolls Ser.), p. 303; P.R.O., STAC 2/14, no. 158.
12 Cf. below, this section [archit.].
13 e.g. Hist. MSS. Com. 58, *Bath*, iv. pp. 327, 331; W.R.O. 9/15/336; ibid. D 1/56/7; cf. Incumbents Act, 31 & 32 Vic. c. 117.
14 e.g. W.R.O., D 1/43/1, f. 140v.; D 1/54/3/1, no. 37.

early 19th claimed, apparently successfully, to be exempt from it and under the peculiar jurisdiction of the owner of the Rectory estate,[15] and again accepted the bishop's jurisdiction c. 1847.[16] In 1929 the vicarage was united to Milton Lilbourne vicarage, and in 1991 the united benefice was united to Pewsey rectory and Wootton Rivers rectory. George Brudenell-Bruce, marquess of Ailesbury, the owner of the Rectory estate, shared the patronage of the united benefice formed in 1929; in 1953 he transferred his share to the bishop of Salisbury, who became a member of the board of patronage for the united benefice formed in 1991.[17]

It seems that between the 1190s and the 1230s the rector took all tithes from the whole parish and held 26 a. in the open fields with feeding for sheep.[18] After the church was appropriated the minister had neither tithe nor glebe,[19] although in the earlier 17th century the owner of the Rectory estate allowed the curate to take some tithes.[20] In 1537 the curate's salary was £5,[21] in 1675 £30,[22] and in 1822 £60.[23] In 1928–9, the last year in which the owner of the Rectory estate paid it, the vicar's salary was £200.[24] In 1987 a house in the village was bought as a parsonage house.[25]

The foundation of a chantry in the parish church was confirmed in 1326: under an agreement of 1322 Easton priory, in exchange for land given to it by Robert Druce, the lord of Easton Druce manor, was to celebrate mass at an altar in honour of St. John the Baptist in a north chapel which Robert had added to the parish church by 1322. To maintain the chapel and provide lights in it Robert gave 12s. a year and a flock of 200 sheep to the parish church.[26]

About 1532 Henry Brian, the last prior of Easton, was said to have refused to allow services to be held for parishioners for more than two years, but in 1536–7, after the dissolution of the priory, he was himself serving the parish church as curate.[27] The parishioners complained in 1553 that quarterly sermons were not preached and an appropriate communion table had not been provided,[28] and in 1556 that church property had not been returned and prescribed ornaments were lacking.[29] Services were presumably adequate in 1634, when some parishioners of Burbage preferred them to those in their own church.[30] In 1662 the curate was found to have

slandered Henrietta, queen of Charles I.[31] Joseph Wall, curate 1693–1714 or longer, Charles Curtis, curate from 1766 to c. 1774, and John Swain, curate from c. 1776 to c. 1799, were each vicar of Milton Lilbourne, and Swain was also curate of Collingbourne Kingston.[32] David Llewellyn, curate 1839–68, probably lived in a house near the church. In 1864 he held a morning and an evening service each Sunday, both with a sermon, and held services on Christmas day, Ash Wednesday, the Wednesday in Holy Week, and Good Friday; he held communion four times a year with c. 20 communicants and catechized in the schoolroom.[33] From 1971 to 1986 the united benefice was held in plurality with Wootton Rivers rectory.[34]

The parish church, called St. Mary's in 1323,[35] was enlarged by the addition of the north chapel c. 1322.[36] In 1369 it was demolished, permission was given for its materials to be used to enlarge the priory church, and the parishioners were licensed to use the priory church as the parish church.[37] The church was badly damaged or destroyed in the fire of 1493[38] and apparently repaired or rebuilt. In 1536, 1553, and 1556 it was reported to be in poor condition.[39] In 1590 a monument to the owner's grandfather, Sir John Seymour (d. 1536), was taken from the church to Great Bedwyn church;[40] a new parish church at Easton was built in 1591,[41] and the old priory church was demolished presumably about then. The dedication of the new church, called *HOLY TRINITY* in 1763,[42] repeats that of the priory.[43] The church was built of rubble, much of it re-used ashlar, and consists of an undivided sanctuary and nave, with a south tower incorporating a vestry and with a north porch. The body of the church and the porch survive from 1591. A wall of a, presumably west, tower fell in or shortly before 1668.[44] By 1806 the tower had been taken down and replaced by a bell turret built above the west bay of the nave.[45] In 1852–3 the bell turret was removed, the nave was extended westwards by one bay, the south tower was built, and the church was generally restored.[46]

In 1553 a chalice of 7½ oz. was kept by the parish and 11½ oz. of silver was taken for the king. In 1891 and 1995 the parish had a chalice hallmarked for 1682 and a paten given in 1728.[47]

In 1536 the bells in the priory church be-

15 W.R.O., D 1/51/8; ibid. 9/15/336; *Colln. Topog. et Geneal.* v. 39; Ch. Com. file, NB 34/263B.
16 *W.A.M.* xxviii. 211.
17 Ch. Com. file, NB 34/263B; ibid. file 85777.
18 P.R.O., E 315/398, f. 92; Longleat Mun., Seymour papers, xii, f. 311v.; cf. above, this section.
19 Cf. W.R.O., D 1/24/82.
20 Ibid. 9/15/81.
21 Hist. MSS. Com. 58, *Bath*, iv, p. 331.
22 W.R.O. 9/15/328.
23 Bashford, *Easton Royal*, 20.
24 Ch. Com. file 53775/1.
25 Inf. from Ch. Com.
26 *Reg. Martival* (Cant. & York Soc.), ii. 519–23.
27 *V.C.H. Wilts.* iii. 327; Hist. MSS. Com. 58, *Bath*, iv, pp. 327, 331; P.R.O., STAC 2/14, no. 158.
28 W.R.O., D 1/43/1, f. 140v.
29 Ibid. D 1/43/2, f. 14v.
30 *V.C.H. Wilts.* iii. 37.
31 Hist. MSS. Com. 55, *Var. Colln.* i, p. 144.
32 *Vis. Queries, 1783* (W.R.S. xxvii), p. 159; W.R.O., D

1/9/1/3; D 1/48/3, f. 16; D 1/51/1; ibid. 615/2–3.
33 *Sar. Almanack* (1868–9); W.R.O., D 1/56/7; cf. O.S. Map 6", Wilts. XLII (1888 edn.); for the sch., below, educ.
34 *Crockford* (1971–2, 1987–8).
35 P.R.O., C 143/159, no. 8.
36 *Reg. Martival* (Cant. & York Soc.), ii. 519–23.
37 W.R.O. 9/15/41–3.
38 Ibid. 9/15/54; above, intro.
39 *V.C.H. Wilts.* iii. 327; W.R.O., D 1/43/1, f. 140v.; D 1/43/2, f. 14v.
40 Aubrey, *Topog. Colln.* ed. Jackson, 376.
41 J. Buckler, watercolour in W.A.S. Libr., vol. iv. 7; above, plate 8.
42 J. Ecton, *Thesaurus* (1763), 407.
43 *V.C.H. Wilts.* iii. 324.
44 W.R.O., D 1/54/3/1, no. 37.
45 Buckler, watercolour in W.A.S. Libr., vol. iv. 7.
46 Bashford, *Easton Royal*, 7–8.
47 Nightingale, *Wilts. Plate*, 167; inf. from Mrs. D. C. Strong, Hillwinds, Burbage Road.

longed to the parish;[48] there were three in 1553. The bells hung in the new church in 1591, presumably the same three, were replaced by a tenor cast by John Wallis in 1607, a bell cast by John Danton in 1633, and a treble cast by Robert Wells in 1764.[49] The treble was removed from the church in 1984 and not replaced; the other two bells hung in the church in 1995.[50]

The register was probably stolen when the church was robbed c. 1550, and in 1553 was not being kept.[51] Registers from 1580 are extant and complete, entries for 1580–1603 being transcripts.[52]

NONCONFORMITY. A papist may have lived at Easton in 1678 and 1681,[53] and members of the Batt family were Roman Catholics there in the later 18th century.[54]

Two protestant nonconformists lived at Easton in 1676.[55] A Methodist meeting house was described as a dwelling house in 1835, when it was certified,[56] and later as a chapel built in 1834. On Census Sunday in 1851 three meetings with an average attendance of 90 were held in it.[57] The building was in ruins in 1862, when the meeting, still well attended, was held in a converted farm building.[58] A new chapel, small and of red brick, was built in 1898–9.[59] It was closed in the mid 1950s.[60]

EDUCATION. In 1814 a school held in a large room in a house was possibly a boarding school with c. 40 pupils.[61] The parish received £8 a year from a charitable gift to support a school,[62] but it is not clear how it spent the money in 1814. The endowment probably supported the day school for 24 children kept in 1818[63] and a small school held in 1831,[64] but nothing more is known of it. In 1833 there was a National school with 20 pupils and an infants' school with 12.[65] A single school had 72 pupils in 1846–7,[66] 60–70 in 1859,[67] and 46 in 1871.[68] A new school was built in 1871: in the 1870s its pupils were aged from 2 to 11 and average attendance was c. 55.[69] Average attendance was 59 in 1902–3,[70] 51 in 1926–7, and 33 in 1937–8.[71] In 1995 there were 37 pupils on the roll.[72]

CHARITIES FOR THE POOR. William Francis (d. 1805) by will gave the interest from £500 to be distributed at Christmas among the industrious poor of the parish. From c. 1807 to c. 1822 money was distributed, from c. 1822 to c. 1829 coal, and from c. 1829 to c. 1833 sometimes coal and sometimes blankets. The charity's income was £22. J. T. Lawes (d. 1828) by will gave the interest from £100 to the industrious Anglican poor of the parish, gifts to be made with those of Francis's charity; the income was £4. In 1900 the income of the two charities was £23, and 2 cwt. of coal was given to each of 154 people.[73] From 1917 to the 1930s beneficiaries of Francis's charity usually received coal, those of Lawes's usually clothing. After the Second World War, when the income of the two charities was c. £24, most gifts were of money. In 1986 the charities were merged, in 1993 the capital was given away in sums of £25, and in 1994 the combined charity ceased to exist.[74]

FROXFIELD

FROXFIELD parish, 927 ha. (2,291 a.), adjoins Hungerford (Berks.) to the east and contains Froxfield village, Oakhill hamlet, and scattered settlement at Rudge.[75] Froxfield village is notable for a large red-brick almshouse built in the 1690s and 1770s.[76] Froxfield had c. 900 a., Oakhill c. 400 a., and Rudge c. 1,000 a.[77] Until the 13th century Chisbury, later in Little Bedwyn, may have been in the parish.[78] From the 13th century or earlier Oakhill was part of a composite manor with North Standen,[79] where there was a chapel:[80] North Standen became part of Hungerford parish and in 1896 was transferred to Berkshire,[81] but Oakhill was presumably already in Froxfield parish in the 13th century and remained so.

The parish boundary ignores relief and prominent man-made features for most of its

48 V.C.H. Wilts. iii. 327.
49 Walters, Wilts. Bells, 80.
50 Inf. from Mrs. Strong.
51 W.R.O., D 1/43/1, f. 140v.
52 Ibid. 615/1–5.
53 Williams, Cath. Recusancy (Cath. Rec. Soc.), 307.
54 W.R.O., D 1/9/1/3.
55 Compton Census, ed. Whiteman, 126.
56 Meeting Ho. Certs. (W.R.S. xl), p. 138.
57 P.R.O., HO 129/261/2/4/8.
58 W.A.S. Libr., J. Wilkinson, par. hist. colln. no. 113; Wilts. Cuttings, Biii, f. 2.
59 J. Pearce, Accts. and Recollections of Easton Royal, 67–8.
60 Inf. from Mrs. Strong.
61 W.R.O. 9/15/336.
62 Poor Law Abstract, 1818, 498–9.
63 Educ. of Poor Digest, 1026.
64 Lewis, Topog. Dict. Eng. (1831), ii. 105–6.
65 Educ. Enq. Abstract, 1036.
66 Nat. Soc. Inquiry, 1846–7, Wilts. 6–7.
67 Acct. of Wilts. Schs. 22.

68 Returns relating to Elem. Educ. 424–5.
69 Return of Public Elem. Schs. 1875–6 [C. 1882], pp. 282–3, H.C. (1877), lxvii; W.R.O., F 8/500/109/1/1–2; F 8/600/109/1/6/1.
70 W.R.O., F 8/220/1.
71 Bd. of Educ., List 21, 1927 (H.M.S.O.), 360; 1938, 423.
72 Wilts. co. council, Sched. of Educ. Establishments (1995), p. 4.
73 Endowed Char. Wilts. (S. Div.), 159–61; for the dates of d. Colln. Topog. et Geneal. v. 40; P.R.O., PROB 11/1427, ff. 110 sqq.
74 W.R.O., L 2, Easton; Char. Com. files.
75 This article was written in 1995. Maps used include O.S. Maps 6", Wilts. XXIX–XXX, XXXVII (1887–9 and later edns.); 1/25,000, SU 26/36 (1983 edn.); SU 27/37 (1985 edn.).   76 Below, charities.
77 W.R.O., EA/119; ibid. tithe award.
78 Above, Little Bedwyn, intro.; church; below, church.
79 Below, manors (Oakhill).
80 V.C.H. Berks. iv. 184.
81 V.C.H. Wilts. iv. 350.

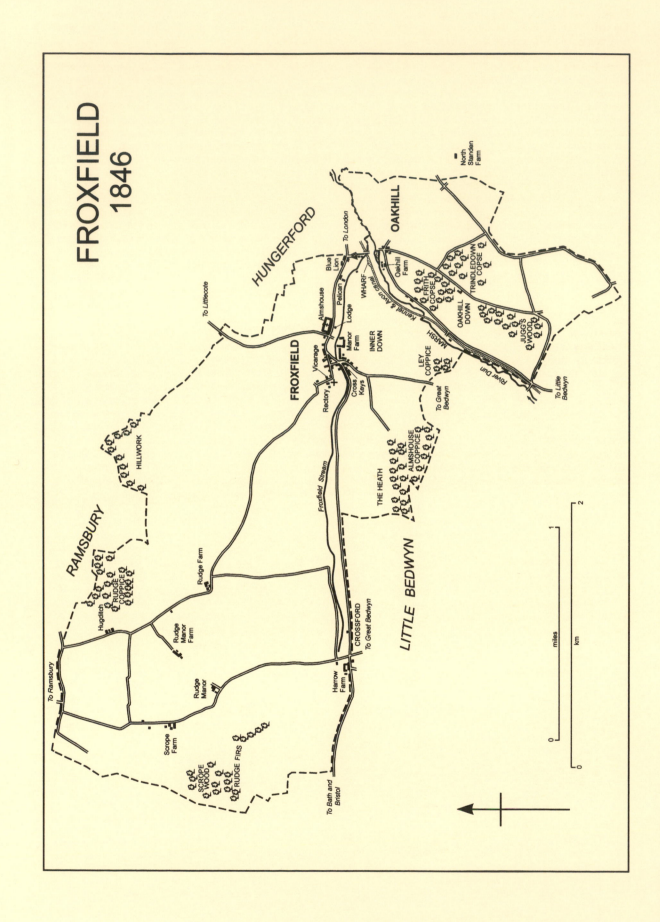

FROXFIELD
1846

length. The river Dun divided Froxfield and Oakhill[82] and for short distances east and south of Froxfield village was the parish boundary. To the south the parish boundary had been transferred from the river to a canal by 1812[83] although the river was not diverted when the canal was built.[84] For short distances south and west of Froxfield village the boundary follows dry valleys. In 778 an estate said to lie at Bedwyn, apparently the land of Chisbury, had on its boundary prehistoric monuments, a barrow, and a possible site of pagan worship; those features, west of Froxfield village, probably divided Chisbury from what was later Froxfield parish, and the boundary there may also have followed a stream.[85] A main road beside the stream marked the boundary there in the early 19th century[86] and later.

Chalk outcrops over the whole parish, in which there are many ridges and dry valleys. The highest land, at 180 m., is in the north-west corner; there and on land at 145 m. south-west of Froxfield village clay-with-flints overlies the chalk. The Dun crosses the parish in the south-east and leaves it at 105 m. A stream now rising in the south-west corner is sometimes called the Froxfield stream; it flows west–east across the parish and into the Dun at the boundary. The Froxfield stream has deposited gravel, the Dun alluvium.[87] Froxfield, Oakhill, and Rudge each had open fields, downland pasture used in common, meadows on the gravel or alluvium, and woodland.[88] It is likely that much woodland on the clay-with-flints in the north-west corner was cleared between the Middle Ages and the 18th century.[89] In the extreme north the highest land is also flat and was part of Ramsbury airfield from 1942 to 1955.[90]

The population of the parish was 492 in 1801 and at a peak of 625 in 1841, when 423 people lived at Froxfield, 131 at Oakhill, and 71 at Rudge. At Froxfield 85 of the 423 lived in the almshouse. The population was in decline from 1841 to 1921, when it was 285. It was 307 in 1931, between 266 and 293 in the period 1951–81, and, new housing having been built in the 1980s, 356 in 1991.[91]

The Roman road from London to Bath may have crossed the high ground in the north-west corner of the parish, but no trace of it survives.[92] The later road from London to Bath and Bristol probably crossed the parish in the 13th century in the valley cut by the Froxfield stream,[93] and it was on its present course through Froxfield

village in 1675.[94] It was turnpiked through Froxfield in 1726, disturnpiked in 1871.[95] In the west part of the parish it was crossed by a north–south road leading from Ramsbury towards Great Bedwyn, of no more than local importance in 1773[96] and between Ramsbury and Rudge no more than a footpath in the 19th and 20th centuries.[97] The crossroads, near where the Ramsbury road also crossed the Froxfield stream, had been given the name Crossford by 1773. The roads linking Froxfield village to Ramsbury and Great Bedwyn in 1995 were on the courses they followed in 1773, as were several roads at Oakhill.[98]

Beside and crossing the Dun the Kennet & Avon canal was opened through Froxfield parish in 1799 and completely in 1810. It had a wharf and three locks in the parish.[99] Through Froxfield the canal was restored in the mid 1970s.[1]

The Berks. & Hants Railway, opened from Reading to Hungerford in 1847, was extended across Froxfield parish along the north-west side of the canal in 1862. The line led to Devizes, from 1900 to Westbury, and from 1906 to Exeter. It had a station at Great Bedwyn.[2]

There were three bowl barrows in the south-west corner of the parish, possibly the ancient monuments referred to in the early recital of what was apparently Chisbury's boundary.[3] A Roman villa which stood on or near the Roman road from London to Bath was discovered in 1725; it had a tessellated pavement on which a human figure was depicted, and a bronze bowl made c. 150 A.D. and a stone statuette of Atys were found at the site.[4] It has been supposed that a cross erected at a site of pagan worship gave a name to Crossford.[5]

In the 12th and early 13th century the whole parish apparently lay in Savernake forest. From 1228 to 1330 the forest included only the part of the parish south of the London road, and from 1330 none of it.[6]

FROXFIELD. An estate called Froxfield was mentioned 801 × 805.[7] The village stands on gravel on both sides of the London road, which runs east–west. In 1773 and possibly in 1675 the road made two sharp bends in the village, and a bridge carried a short north–south section over the Froxfield stream. A road from Rudge joined the main road at the bend north of the stream, and a road to Great Bedwyn left it at the bend south of the stream.[8] About 1791 a short new north-east and south-west section of the main

82 P.R.O., DL 42/115, f. 18.
83 W.R.O. 1955/25; for the canal, below, this section.
84 W.R.O. 1644/34.
85 Arch. Jnl. lxxvi. 154–5; W.A.M. xlv. 525–6.
86 W.R.O. 1955/25.
87 Geol. Surv. Map 1", drift, sheet 267 (1971 edn.).
88 Below, econ. hist.
89 Cf. Andrews and Dury, Map (W.R.S. viii), pl. 12.
90 C. Ashworth, Action Stations, ix. 241–3; V.C.H. Wilts. xii. 17.
91 V.C.H. Wilts. iv. 319, 348; Census, 1961; 1971; 1981; 1991; for the housing, below, this section (Froxfield).
92 I. D. Margary, Rom. Roads in Brit. (1973), p. 135.
93 V.C.H. Wilts. iv. 255, 448.
94 J. Ogilby, Brit. (1675), pl. 10.
95 V.C.H. Wilts. iv. 257–8, 267; L.J. xxii. 664; W.R.O.,

A 1/205/10.
96 Andrews and Dury, Map (W.R.S. viii), pl. 12.
97 O.S. Maps 6", Wilts. XXX (1887 and later edns.).
98 Andrews and Dury, Map (W.R.S. viii), pl. 12.
99 V.C.H. Wilts. iv. 273–4.
1 Kennet and Avon Canal: a Leisure Strategy (pub. Brit. Waterways: copy in Wilts. local studies libr., Trowbridge), 7.
2 V.C.H. Wilts. iv. 283, 286–7, 289.
3 Ibid. i (1), 176.
4 Ibid. 71–2.
5 W.A.M. xlv. 525–6.
6 V.C.H. Wilts. iv. 399–400, 417–19, 448, 450–1.
7 Finberg, Early Wessex Chart. p. 72.
8 Ogilby, Brit. (1675), pl. 10; Andrews and Dury, Map (W.R.S. viii), pl. 12.

road was made to cut the north corner, and the bridge over the stream was lengthened; when buildings on the south side of the old east–west section north of the stream were removed[9] the triangle thus created became a village green.

In the 12th century the church was standing[10] beside the Rudge road at what was presumably then, and was in 1995, the west end of the village, and a house north of the church almost certainly stands on the site of the rector's house. It is likely that the road passed between the church and the house and that the course north and east of the house's garden which it followed in 1773 and 1995 was a diversion. The house, which belonged to the owners of the Rectory estate until 1909,[11] incorporates a 17th-century east–west range; to the west a truncated and timber-framed building, standing detached in 1995, is aligned with that range and may have been part of the house in the 17th century. In the later 17th century a tall brick cross wing was built to the north at the east end, and in the later 20th century the house was restored and architectural features of various periods were introduced. The vicarage house stood beside the Rudge road immediately east of the church and was replaced by a new vicarage house further north beside the new course of the road.[12] The demesne farmstead of Froxfield manor, including a farmhouse, stood east of the southern bend of the London road.[13] A new farmhouse in the west angle of the main road and a minor road to Littlecote in Ramsbury was built in 1849.[14] The village was extended south-westwards along the Great Bedwyn road apparently in the 17th century. It was extended eastwards in the 1670s, when the almshouse was built, and further east in the 18th century and the 20th.[15] Most of the village was designated a conservation area in 1993.[16]

Froxfield apparently prospered because of its position on the main road and from 1799 on the Kennet & Avon canal; railway transport may have undermined that prosperity and have partly caused the decline in the village's population from 1841.[17] In 1686 there was probably an inn in the village[18] and in the 18th century there were three. The Cross Keys, on the south side of the main road at its southern bend, may have been the oldest, and the brewhouse behind it gave the name Brewhouse Hill to the Great Bedwyn road.[19] The inn was repaired in 1758[20] and closed c. 1866.[21] The Blue Lion, on the north side of the main road at the eastern parish boundary, was said in 1718 to have been newly built.[22] In

1835 it was burned down,[23] by 1837 had been rebuilt, and c. 1862 was closed.[24] Architectural evidence suggests that the Pelican, east of the village on the south side of the main road, was newly built when first mentioned in the 1750s.[25] The Pelican remained an inn in 1995.

The copyhold farmsteads of Froxfield manor apparently stood beside the main road north of the bridge, now the north and west sides of the green.[26] On the north side of the green in 1995 stood a small farmhouse, apparently of 17th-century origin, with extensive mainly 20th-century farm buildings around it; also on the north side of the green part of what in 1846 was a house and malthouse[27] survived as three cottages; at the north-west corner of the green stood another small house of apparently 17th-century origin. Other buildings on the north side of the green in 1995 included a timber-framed and thatched cottage probably of the 17th century, a range of four cottages built in 1871,[28] and six small later 20th-century houses built on the site of the other part of the house and malthouse.[29] The site of a small farmstead on the west side of the green was used for a village hall built in 1949.[30]

South of the Froxfield stream cottages were built on the waste beside the Great Bedwyn road. Three, timber-framed, thatched, and apparently 17th-century, were standing in 1995, as were an early 19th-century house, an early 20th-century nonconformist chapel,[31] and four 20th-century houses and bungalows. On the verge of the main road west of its southern bend a timber-framed and thatched cottage was built on the south side in the 17th century, a range of three cottages on the north side in the 18th or early 19th, and a range of six cottages on the south side in 1843.[32] Further west a commercial garage and a large house were built in the 1920s or 1930s.[33]

East of the village in the earlier 19th century a group of some five cottages stood on the waste beside the parish boundary and the lane to Oakhill:[34] all were demolished, most presumably when in 1862 the railway was built[35] and the lane diverted. When the Blue Lion was closed it and its outbuildings were converted to seven cottages;[36] all were demolished when the main road was improved in 1968–9.[37] On the north side of the road, between the almshouse and those cottages, four council houses were built in 1927,[38] a police house c. 1938,[39] and eight council houses in 1959–60.[40] In the lane to Littlecote and near the almshouse a pair of estate cottages was

9   Andrews and Dury, Map (W.R.S. viii), pl. 12; W.R.O., EA/119; ibid. 2037/13.
10   Below, church [archit.].
11   Andrews and Dury, Map (W.R.S. viii), pl. 12; below, manors (Rectory); cf. W.R.O., tithe award; below, church.
12   W.R.O., D 1/61/1B, pp. 60–3; ibid. tithe award.
13   Ibid. 9/8/153H; ibid. EA/119; ibid. tithe award.
14   Ibid. 2037/14.
15   Below, this section; ibid. charities.
16   Inf. from Dept. of Planning and Highways, Co. Hall, Trowbridge.
17   Above, this section.   18   W.A.M. lxxxiv. 86.
19   W.R.O., tithe award; below, econ. hist. (Froxfield).
20   W.R.O. 2037/119, p. 15.
21   Harrod's Dir. Wilts. (1865); Kelly's Dir. Wilts. (1867).
22   W.R.O. 2037/109, lease, Pocock to Pethers, 1718.
23   Ibid. 2037/119, p. 82.

24   Ibid. 2037/14; Harrod's Dir. Wilts. (1865); Kelly's Dir. Wilts. (1859).
25   P.R.O., E 134/32 Geo. II Mich./7.
26   Cf. W.R.O., EA/119; ibid. 2037/119, pp. 55–7, 59–60, 62–5, 68–9.
27   Ibid. tithe award.   28   Ibid. 2037/152.
29   Cf. ibid. tithe award.
30   Ibid.; ibid. G 8/760/477; date on bldg.
31   Below, nonconf.   32   W.R.O. 2037/14.
33   Cf. O.S. Map 6", Wilts. XXX. SW. (1925 edn.).
34   W.R.O., EA/119; ibid. tithe award.
35   Above, this section.
36   O.S. Map 1/2,500, Wilts. XXX. 14 (1900 edn.); W.R.O. 2037/156; ibid. tithe award.
37   W.R.O., F 1/250/6/1.
38   Ibid. G 8/600/1.   39   Ibid. G 8/760/336.
40   Ibid. G 8/602/1.

built c. 1960,[41] and in 1986 a home for the elderly with 38 rooms for residents was built.[42]

In the mid 20th century new farm buildings were erected east of those of the demesne farmstead in the south-east part of the village. All the old buildings except a weatherboarded barn were demolished, and in 1979 an estate of 15 houses was built on their site.[43]

OAKHILL. In the 13th and 16th centuries Oakhill was possibly a village of a few small farmsteads and a water mill.[44] In 1612, 1773, and 1995 it consisted of a farmstead and cottages beside a lane to Little Bedwyn, and to the east cottages at the crossing of that and another lane.[45] A mill stood at the farmstead until the late 18th century or earlier 19th.[46] Oakhill Farm, of brick with a mansarded roof and a 19th-century extension, is apparently the house built at the farmstead c. 1750.[47] In 1910 c. 12 cottages stood at Oakhill.[48] Two pairs in the lane, early 19th-century and of red brick, were standing in 1995, as were, at the crossroads, two timber-framed and thatched 17th-century cottages, an early 19th-century cottage, and a pair of later 20th-century houses.

RUDGE. In the Middle Ages the farmsteads from which most of Rudge's open-field land was worked presumably stood, by analogy with Chisbury, on high ground north of the London road.[49] The farmsteads probably lay scattered in the 17th century, as they did in 1773, when there were five.[50] The northernmost, Hugditch, may have been a settlement site in the mid 13th century;[51] a thatched and timber-framed 17th-century house stood there in 1995. At Rudge Farm the farmhouse was replaced c. 1810 by a double-pile house, with a principal front of brick and other fronts of banded brick and flint, standing in 1995. At Rudge Manor Farm a timber-framed house of the 17th century, thatched and encased in brick, and an 18th-century cart shed were standing in 1995 among extensive farm buildings mainly of the 20th century. Rudge Manor, part of a farmstead south-west of Rudge Manor Farm,[52] was demolished in the mid 20th century; a cottage of c. 1870 and a pair of cottages of c. 1950 were standing at the site in 1995. Nearly all the buildings of Scrope Farm had been demolished by the early 1970s, when the farmhouse was largely rebuilt and a house was built in its grounds.[53]

OTHER SETTLEMENT. In the 13th century a settlement called Teteridge was said to stand in Froxfield parish and to have land beside the London road.[54] By analogy with Henset, a lost settlement in Little Bedwyn with which it was linked tenurially,[55] and with Puthall in Little Bedwyn, it may have stood north of the London road near the west boundary of the parish.[56] It was apparently deserted and there is no direct evidence of its site.

At Crossford a house open as the Harrow inn in 1812 was built in Little Bedwyn parish on the south side of the London road c. 1800. Its outbuildings stood on the north side of the road in Froxfield parish and from 1841 or earlier were used as farm buildings;[57] they were added to in the 19th century and the 20th. Nearby a pair of cottages standing in 1846[58] was replaced by a pair built in 1956.[59] East of Harrow Farm a turnpike cottage was standing in 1846[60] and was demolished in the later 19th century.[61]

Darrell's Farm, astride the parish boundary and incorporating buildings erected on Ramsbury airfield,[62] and two pairs of cottages nearby in Froxfield parish were all built in the mid 20th century.

MANORS AND OTHER ESTATES. Between 801 and 805 Byrhtelm gave *FROXFIELD* to Ealhmund, bishop of Winchester, and his see in an exchange.[63] There is no evidence that Froxfield belonged to the see later, and who held it between the 9th century and the 13th is obscure. The Froxfield which Aelfheah, ealdorman of Hampshire, devised to his nephew Aelfwine c. 970 was probably that in Hampshire.[64]

The overlordship of Froxfield manor was held as ½ knight's fee in 1242–3 by Baldwin de Reviers, earl of Devon and lord of the Isle of Wight (d. 1245), presumably passed to his son Baldwin, earl of Devon (d. 1262), and was held in 1275 by that Baldwin's heir, his sister Isabel de Forz, countess of Aumale and of Devon. In 1242–3 the manor was held of Baldwin by Walter Marshal, earl of Pembroke (d. 1245), and of Walter by Matthew de Columbers (d. c. 1272–3), the lord of Chisbury manor, whose heir was his brother Michael; in 1275 it was held of Isabel by Walter's heirs and of them by another Matthew de Columbers.[65] There is no evidence that Isabel's or Walter's successors later had an interest in Froxfield manor, the overlordship of

41 Inf. from Sir (David) Seton Wills, Bt., Eastridge Ho., Ramsbury.
42 W.R.O. 2037/161.
43 Local inf.
44 *Wilts. Inq. p.m. 1242–1326* (Index Libr.), 26–7; P.R.O., DL 42/108, ff. 86–8.
45 *Andrews and Dury, Map* (W.R.S. viii), pl. 12; W.R.O. 9/8/153H.
46 Below, econ. hist. (Oakhill).
47 P.R.O., E 134/32 Geo. II Mich./7.
48 W.R.O., Inland Revenue, val. reg. 54.
49 Cf. above, Little Bedwyn, intro. (Chisbury); below, econ. hist. (Rudge).
50 *Andrews and Dury, Map* (W.R.S. viii), pl. 12.
51 *Cat. Anct. D.* ii, C 2732.
52 W.R.O., tithe award.
53 Inf. from Sir Seton Wills.

54 *Cat. Anct. D.* ii, C 2645.
55 Below, manors (Teteridge).
56 Cf. above, Little Bedwyn, intro. (other settlement).
57 Ibid.
58 W.R.O., tithe award.
59 Date on bldg.
60 W.R.O., tithe award.
61 Ibid. A 1/205/10; O.S. Map 6", Wilts. XXX (1887 edn.).
62 Ashworth, *Action Stations*, ix. 243.
63 Finberg, *Early Wessex Chart.* p. 72.
64 D. Whitelock, *Anglo-Saxon Wills*, p. 23; cf. *V.C.H. Hants*, iii. 76.
65 *Bk. of Fees*, ii. 712; *Rot. Hund.* (Rec. Com.), ii (1), 260; *Complete Peerage*, iv. 318–23; x. 374–5; *Colln. Topog. et Geneal.* vii. 148; above, Little Bedwyn, manors (Chisbury).

which afterwards descended with Chisbury manor in the Cobham family. It has not been traced after 1389, the year in which John Cobham, Lord Cobham (d. 1408), was overlord.[66]

Richard de Columbers may have held Froxfield manor in 1212;[67] John de Columbers held it in demesne in 1242–3[68] and granted part of it to his son Nicholas in 1255;[69] William de Columbers held it in 1275.[70] In 1295 William's relict Joan, the wife of John de Popham, held the manor for life; her and William's daughter and heir Joan (d. *s.p.*), the relict of Richard de Popham, then conveyed the reversion to Michael of Droxford.[71] The manor passed to John Droxford (d. 1329), bishop of Bath and Wells from 1309, to whom in 1303 free warren in his demesne at Froxfield was granted.[72] John's was his brother Michael (d. by 1330), who had entered on the manor by 1328, and Michael's heir was his son John (d. 1341). Michael's title to the manor was challenged in 1328 by his brother-in-law Philip Croke, the nephew of the elder Joan de Columbers, and by Sir William Avenel, the husband of that Joan's niece Joan Croke, and Sir William entered on the manor by force. In 1330 Philip challenged the younger John Droxford's title but in 1332 confirmed it. The manor descended to that John's son Thomas. In 1341, however, Thomas's title was successfully challenged by Joan Croke, then the wife of William le Moyne,[73] and in 1344 the Moynes conveyed the manor, for a rent of 25 marks a year for their life, to Joan's son William Avenel.[74]

In 1377 Froxfield manor was conveyed between men who were probably trustees,[75] and in an exchange licensed in 1390[76] it was given by Sir William Sturmy to Easton priory.[77] The manor belonged to the priory until the Dissolution.[78] In 1536 it was granted to Sturmy's descendant Sir Edward Seymour, Viscount Beauchamp[79] (cr. earl of Hertford 1537, duke of Somerset 1547), on whose execution and attainder in 1552[80] it passed by Act to his son Sir Edward[81] (a minor until 1558, cr. earl of Hertford 1559, d. 1621).[82] From 1553 to 1675 it descended with Tottenham Lodge in Great Bedwyn successively to William, duke of Somerset

(d. 1660), William, duke of Somerset (d. 1671), and John, duke of Somerset (d. 1675),[83] and it passed like Pewsey manor to Sarah, duchess of Somerset (d. 1692).[84] By her will Sarah gave Froxfield manor and its profits from her death to Froxfield almshouse, which was founded under her will and opened *c.* 1694.[85]

In 1920 Froxfield almshouse sold Manor farm, *c.* 618 a.,[86] and in 1921–2 sold most of its other property in Froxfield.[87] The farm was bought by G. L. Bevan,[88] the tenant of Littlecote House in Ramsbury,[89] who sold it in 1922 to Sir Ernest Wills, Bt. (d. 1958), his successor as tenant and from 1929 the owner of the Littlecote estate.[90] Shortly after Sir Ernest's death the farm was sold to N. E. James and D. G. W. James, brothers who in 1965 sold *c.* 365 a. of it, that part north of the London road, to Sir Ernest's grandson (David) Seton Wills (Bt. from 1983), the owner of the Littlecote estate from that year. Sir Seton owned that land as part of the estate (from *c.* 1985 called the Eastridge estate) in 1995. The Jameses sold the rest of Manor farm, *c.* 255 a., to William Rootes, Lord Rootes, in 1965, since when that land has been part of the manor of North Standen and Oakhill.[91]

In 1242–3 *OAKHILL* was held of Matthew de Columbers and his overlords as Froxfield manor was,[92] and in 1248 and 1257 was held of William de St. Martin.[93] From the 13th century or earlier it was part of the manor of North Standen and Oakhill, North Standen later being in Hungerford parish.[94] Hugh de St. Martin probably held the composite manor in 1234,[95] and, if he was also Hugh of Standen, held both elements of it in demesne in 1242–3. Oakhill was then assessed at ½ knight's fee.[96] Hugh de St. Martin was succeeded *c.* 1247 by his son Peter,[97] who in 1248 granted the whole manor to Patrick de Chaworth, the overlord of the Standen part, and his heirs, either for 15 years with reversion to Peter or his heirs if by then Peter had issue by his wife Margery, or in perpetuity.[98] The inheritance passed to Patrick, who *c.* 1258 died holding the manor subject to the dower of Hugh's relict Joan and Peter's relict Margery[99] (fl. 1283).[1] Patrick's relict Hawise of London held the manor until her death *c.* 1274, when it

66 *Complete Peerage*, iii. 344–5; P.R.O., C 143/408, no. 9.
67 *Cur. Reg. R.* vi. 257. 68 *Bk. of Fees*, ii. 712.
69 *Cat. Anct. D.* ii, C 2732.
70 *Rot. Hund.* (Rec. Com.), ii (1), 260.
71 *Feet of F.* 1272–1327 (W.R.S. i), p. 41; P.R.O., CP 40/109, rot. 139d.; CP 40/283, rot. 2d.
72 *Cal. Chart. R.* 1300–26, 35; *Reg. Ghent* (Cant. & York Soc.), ii. 759; *D.N.B.*
73 *V.C.H. Hants*, iv. 312; P.R.O., CP 40/273, rot. 13d.; CP 40/275, rot. 305; CP 40/283, rot. 2d.; CP 40/292, Carte rot. 1; CP 40/328, rot. 214. In *Misc. Geneal. et Her.* (2nd ser.), ii. 314 Joan Croke is said to have been Phil. Croke's daughter.
74 *Feet of F.* 1327–77 (W.R.S. xxix), p. 73; *V.C.H. Hants*, iv. 312.
75 *Cal. Close*, 1377–81, 108.
76 *Cal. Pat.* 1388–92, 306. 77 W.R.O. 1300/17.
78 *Valor Eccl.* (Rec. Com.), ii. 149.
79 *L. & P. Hen. VIII*, x, p. 526; above, Burbage, manors (Burbage Sturmy).
80 *Complete Peerage*, xii (1), 59–64.
81 W.R.O. 1300/163; 1300/173–4.
82 *Complete Peerage*, vi. 505–6.
83 Above, Great Bedwyn, manors (Tottenham).

84 Below, Pewsey, manor (Pewsey).
85 *Endowed Char. Wilts.* (S. Div.), 980; P.R.O., C 78/1070, no. 1; for the almshouse, below, charities.
86 W.R.O. 2037/125; 2037/127.
87 Ibid. 2037/156–7.
88 Ibid. 2037/127.
89 *Kelly's Dir. Wilts.* (1920).
90 Ibid. (1923); *V.C.H. Wilts.* xii. 29; W.A.S. Libr., sale cat. xvii, no. 8; W.R.O. 1635/23.
91 W.R.O. 1008/35; 2281/4, abstr. of title; inf. from Sir (David) Seton Wills, Bt., Eastridge Ho., Ramsbury; below, this section (Oakhill).
92 *Bk. of Fees*, ii. 712; *Cur. Reg. R.* xvii, pp. 285–6, 482–3.
93 *Cal. Inq. p.m.* i, p. 114; P.R.O., DL 42/2, f. 186 and v., no. 14.
94 What follows in places corrects *V.C.H. Berks.* iv. 194–5.
95 P.R.O., DL 42/2, f. 188, no. 21.
96 *Bk. of Fees*, ii. 712, 716.
97 *Cal. Inq. p.m.* i, p. 22.
98 *V.C.H. Berks.* iv. 194; P.R.O., DL 42/2, f. 186 and v., no. 14.
99 *Cal. Inq. p.m.* i, p. 114.
1 Ibid. ii, p. 288.

passed to her son Sir Pain de Chaworth[2] (d. *c.* 1279). Sir Pain's heir was his brother Patrick[3] (d. *c.* 1283), whose relict Isabel (d. *c.* 1306), by 1286 the wife of Hugh le Despenser, Lord le Despenser, held it in dower.[4] About 1306 the manor passed to Patrick's daughter Maud (d. *c.* 1322), the wife of Henry of Lancaster (earl of Leicester from 1324, earl of Lancaster from 1326, d. 1345). It descended like Berwick St. James manor to Maud's son Henry, earl of Lancaster (cr. duke of Lancaster 1351), on whose death in 1361 it was assigned to his daughter Maud, the wife of William, duke of Bavaria. On the younger Maud's death in 1362 the manor passed to her sister Blanche, the wife of John of Gaunt, earl of Lancaster (cr. duke of Lancaster 1362, d. 1399), and as part of the duchy of Lancaster it was annexed to the Crown in 1399 at the accession of John's son as Henry IV.[5]

The manor of North Standen and Oakhill was granted in 1548 to Edward, duke of Somerset,[6] on whose attainder in 1552 the grant was annulled.[7] The Crown kept the manor until 1608, when it granted it to Sir Edward Phelips (d. 1614), John Seward, and Phelips's heirs.[8] By 1609 the manor had possibly been acquired by Edmund Hungerford,[9] who in 1656 sold it to Alexander Popham.[10] From 1656 to 1962 it was part of the Littlecote estate: it descended with Littlecote House, Chilton Foliat manor, and Rudge farm in the Popham, Leyborne-Popham, and Wills families.[11] In 1962 G. S. Wills sold it to William Rootes (from 1964 Lord Rootes, d. 1992), who in 1965 added part of Manor farm, Froxfield, to it. In 1992 the whole estate was bought by Mr. Philip Magor, the owner in 1995.[12]

Land at Rudge descended in the Chamberlain family in the 13th and 14th centuries. About 1268 Geoffrey Chamberlain successfully defended his and William Chamberlain's right to an estate there against William le Deepgate and Thomas le Savage.[13] The estate may have been held by (presumably the same) William Chamberlain (d. *c.* 1283), who was succeeded by his son William.[14] In 1318 it was held by John Chamberlain, the son of (presumably the younger) William,[15] and before 1330 passed to

John's brother William. In 1341 William's title was in doubt,[16] in 1348 apparently secure.[17] William Chamberlain (fl. 1376), that William's son and heir, in 1369 conveyed part of the estate to his brother Robert.[18] The whole was probably what was later called *RUDGE* farm. It was evidently acquired by a lord of Littlecote manor, possibly in the earlier 15th century by Thomas Calstone, whose right to an estate at Rudge was disputed by William Chamberlain and his wife Christine between 1408 and 1423. Jane Darell, relict of Sir George Darell (d. 1474), held land at Rudge in 1482.[19] Littlecote manor passed from Sir George to his son Sir Edward, who at his death in 1530 held what became Rudge farm.[20] The farm, 239 a. in 1831,[21] descended with the manor and Littlecote House, later also with Chilton Foliat manor and North Standen and Oakhill manor, in the Darell, Popham, Leyborne-Popham, and Wills families.[22] In 1976 Sir Seton Wills sold part of Rudge farm to G. W. Wilson, and in 1995 he owned 130 a. at Rudge as part of the Eastridge (formerly Littlecote) estate.[23]

Other land at Rudge was part of Chisbury manor.[24] In 1573 John Cook, the lord of the manor, sold an estate at Rudge later assessed at 3 yardlands to William George.[25] The estate apparently became the main part of *RUDGE MANOR* farm. In 1586 William George conveyed it to his brother John (d. 1611), from whom it passed in the direct line to John[26] (d. 1651) and Richard[27] (fl. 1696).[28] Richard George, presumably another, held the estate *c.* 1730,[29] and a Mrs. George held it in 1748.[30] By 1780 it had apparently been acquired by the Revd. John Gilmore (d. 1820): Gilmore owned Rudge Manor farm, which included two farmsteads and 225 a.[31] The farm passed to J. P. Gilmore, who sold it to Francis Leyborne-Popham in 1854.[32] It remained part of the Littlecote estate until 1976, when Sir Seton Wills sold it with other land at Rudge, a total of 479 a., to G. W. Wilson (d. 1984). In 1995 Wilson's son Mr. R. W. Wilson owned *c.* 550 a. at Rudge.[33]

In 1577 John Cook sold land at Rudge, later assessed at 2 yardlands and the main part of *SCROPE* farm, to John Organ *alias* Taylor.[34] It passed to Thomas Knapp, whose father Thomas

2 Ibid. p. 38; *Close R.* 1256–9, 348; P.R.O., DL 25/119; DL 25/2323.
3 *Cal. Inq. p.m.* ii, p. 182.
4 Ibid. p. 288; *Cal. Close,* 1279–88, 220; *Complete Peerage,* iv. 265.
5 *V.C.H. Wilts.* xv. 171; *Cal. Pat.* 1361–4, 50.
6 P.R.O., DL 42/23, ff. 30v.–32.
7 *Complete Peerage,* xii (1), 63–4; W.R.O. 1300/174.
8 *D.N.B.* (s.v. Phelips); P.R.O., C 66/1741, mm. 1–9.
9 Som. R.O., DD/POt 116, surrender, 12 June 7 Jas. I.
10 W.R.O. 39/15–16.
11 *V.C.H. Wilts.* xii. 28–9; above, Chilton Foliat, manors (Chilton Foliat); below, this section (Rudge).
12 *Who's Who, 1992,* 1606; *1993,* 1626; W.R.O. 2281/4, abstr. of title; inf. from Mr. C. H. H. Slater, Oakhill Farmhouse; above, this section (Froxfield).
13 P.R.O., JUST 1/998A, rot. 12d.
14 *Cal. Inq. p.m.* iii, p. 328.
15 *Cal. Close,* 1313–18, 589, 601.
16 *Cat. Anct. D.* i, C 1198; *Inq. Non.* (Rec. Com.), 172; *Extents for Debts* (W.R.S. xxviii), pp. 20–1.
17 *Cat. Anct. D.* i, C 655.
18 Ibid. ii, C 2463; *Feet of F.* 1327–77 (W.R.S. xxix), p.

147.
19 *Cat. Anct. D.* iii, C 3539; *V.C.H. Wilts.* xii. 28; P.R.O., SC 1/36/198.
20 P.R.O., WARD 9/129, f. 143.
21 Som. R.O., DD/PO 28.
22 *V.C.H. Wilts.* xii. 28–9, where details of the descent are given; above, Chilton Foliat, manors (Chilton Foliat); this section (Oakhill).
23 Inf. from Sir Seton Wills; for Wilson's estate, below, this section (Rudge Manor).
24 W.R.O. 9/1/95, pp. 43–55; for the descent of the manor, above, Little Bedwyn, manors (Chisbury).
25 *Cal. Pat.* 1572–5, p. 68; W.R.O. 9/8/8; 9/8/147.
26 P.R.O., C 142/330, no. 85.
27 W.R.O. 192/24B.
28 Ibid. 9/1/165, ct. 16 July 1696.
29 Ibid. 9/1/101.
30 Ibid. 9/1/117.
31 Ibid. A 1/345/185; ibid. tithe award; ibid. 1635/7.
32 Som. R.O., DD/POt 41, sched. of purchases.
33 W.R.O. 2281/4, abstr. of title; inf. from Mr. R. W. Wilson, Rudge Manor Farm.
34 *Cal. Pat.* 1575–8, p. 265; W.R.O. 9/8/8; 9/8/147.

bought other land in Rudge from Edward, earl of Hertford, the lord of Chisbury manor, in 1616. Before 1640 the younger Thomas sold an estate probably including his father's land to Sir Francis Seymour (cr. Baron Seymour 1641, d. 1664).[35] The estate apparently descended to Seymour's son Charles, Lord Seymour (d. 1665), and to Charles's daughter Frances, whose husband Sir George Hungerford held it in 1678.[36] By 1682 it had been acquired, presumably by purchase, by Sir James Long, Bt. (d. 1692), who bought land elsewhere from Sir George,[37] and it apparently passed like Draycot Cerne manor in turn to Sir James's grandsons Sir Robert Long, Bt. (d. 1692), Sir Giles Long, Bt. (d. 1697), and Sir James Long, Bt. (d. 1729).[38] Sir James devised the estate to his wife Henrietta (d. 1765), who devised it to their grandson Charles Long (d. 1783). It was held by Charles's relict Hannah, the wife of James Dawkins, and passed to his daughter Emma, the wife of William Scrope.[39] In the early 19th century Scrope farm was of c. 300 a.[40] In 1818 the Scropes sold 100 a., the south part of it, to Charles Brudenell-Bruce, earl of Ailesbury,[41] who added it to his other land at Rudge.[42] Also in 1818 the Scropes sold 203 a. to Francis Leyborne-Popham,[43] from 1843 the owner of the Littlecote estate,[44] with which that land passed. In 1949 c. 90 a. of the 203 a. was part of 111 a. in the north-west corner of the parish bought by the Crown to enlarge Ramsbury airfield. In 1954 the Crown sold c. 80 a. to G. W. Wilson,[45] who bought the rest of the 203 a. from Sir Seton Wills in 1976.[46]

Land at Rudge, later part of HARROW farm, remained part of Chisbury manor and from 1602 descended with Tottenham Lodge and Tottenham House in the Seymour, Bruce, Brudenell, and Brudenell-Bruce families.[47] Other land, including 100 a. of Scrope farm in 1818, was added to Harrow farm,[48] which in 1846 included 159 a. in Rudge and c. 67 a. in Chisbury.[49] In 1950 the farm was sold by George Brudenell-Bruce, marquess of Ailesbury, to the Crown, the owner in 1995.[50]

In 1119 the king gave TETERIDGE with Henset in Little Bedwyn to St. Maurice's cathedral, Angers (Maine et Loire). With Henset it belonged to William May and Thomas de Landon c. 1211,[51] was acquired by Peter des Roches, bishop of Winchester (d. 1238), as an endowment of Netley abbey (Hants), which was founded in 1239, and was given by the abbey to the king in an exchange in 1241.[52] It may have descended with Henset and, as Henset did, apparently belonged to the owner of Knowle farm in Little Bedwyn from the 15th century. From 1602 Knowle farm and Chisbury manor descended together,[53] and the land of Teteridge presumably became part of Harrow farm.

Easton priory appropriated Froxfield church between 1396 and 1403,[54] and held the RECTORY estate until the Dissolution.[55] The estate, consisting of a house, c. 35 a., pasture rights, and all the tithes from nearly all the parish,[56] was granted to Sir Edward Seymour, Viscount Beauchamp (later duke of Somerset), in 1536.[57] In 1547 Seymour gave it back to the king in an exchange and the king granted it to St. George's chapel, Windsor.[58] Except between 1643 and the Restoration[59] the chapel kept it until it passed to the Ecclesiastical Commissioners in 1867:[60] in 1651 the land was sold to Simon Cripps,[61] and in 1654 the tithes were granted to the almshouses of Windsor castle.[62] The tithes were valued at £742 in 1845 and commuted in 1846. Of the land, 51 a. after parliamentary inclosure,[63] 2 a. was annexed to Froxfield vicarage in 1910.[64] In 1909 a house and 49 a. were bought by Wiltshire county council,[65] which sold the house in 1910[66] and the remaining land, 48 a., in 1961.[67]

ECONOMIC HISTORY.

FROXFIELD. In the 16th century and probably throughout the Middle Ages there were two open fields at Froxfield. About 1536 East field was accounted c. 185 a., West field c. 175 a.[68] Both were apparently north of the London road. South of the road lay downland, woodland, and, beside the Dun, marsh. There was meadow land west of the village beside the Froxfield stream, other marsh east of the village.[69] The demesne of Froxfield

35 Complete Peerage, xi. 640–1; W.R.O. 9/5/21; 9/5/29A; 9/8/147.
36 Burke, Peerage (1924), 2077; W.R.O. 9/1/160.
37 P.R.O., C 112/53/2; W.R.O. 9/1/161, rot. 15.
38 V.C.H. Wilts. xiv. 77; W.R.O. 9/1/175, rot. 5.
39 Burke, Commoners (1833–8), iii. 218; W.R.O. 9/5/22; 1694/1, proposed exchange, 1807.
40 Som. R.O., DD/POt 41, sched. of purchases; W.R.O. 9/5/24.
41 W.R.O. 9/5/24; cf. ibid. tithe award.
42 Below, this section (Harrow).
43 Som. R.O., DD/POt 41, sched. of purchases.
44 V.C.H. Wilts. xii. 29.
45 W.R.O. 2281/4, abstr. of title; inf. from Mr. Wilson.
46 Inf. from Sir Seton Wills; for Wilson's estate, above, this section (Rudge Manor).
47 W.R.O. 1300/372, ff. 8, 10–16; above, Great Bedwyn, manors (Tottenham); Little Bedwyn, manors (Chisbury).
48 Above, this section (Scrope); cf. below, this section (Teteridge).
49 W.R.O., tithe award; Little Bedwyn tithe award.
50 Inf. from the agent for the Crown Estate Com., 42 High Street, Marlborough.
51 Reg. Regum Anglo-Norm. ii, no. 1204A; Red Bk. Exch. (Rolls Ser.), ii. 484, 489; cf. above, Little Bedwyn, manors (Henset).
52 Cal. Chart. R. 1226–57, 260–1; V.C.H. Hants, ii. 146.

53 Cat. Anct. D. i, B 1780; P.R.O., C 143/241, no. 4; ibid. CP 25/2/65/531, no. 46; above, Little Bedwyn, manors (Chisbury; Henset; Knowle).
54 Cal. Pat. 1388–92, 306; P.R.O., C 143/408, no. 9; cf. Phillipps, Wilts. Inst. i. 82, 89.
55 Valor Eccl. (Rec. Com.), ii. 149.
56 Longleat Mun., Seymour papers, xii, f. 292v.; W.R.O., tithe award.
57 L. & P. Hen. VIII, x, p. 526.
58 P.R.O., E 305/15/F 42–3.
59 V.C.H. Berks. iii. 26.
60 Lond. Gaz. 28 June 1867, pp. 3630–4; D. & C. Windsor Mun. XV. 39. 68–74P; ibid. Ch. Com., 117834–117849.
61 P.R.O., C 54/3608, no. 36.
62 Acts & Ords. of Interr. ed. Firth & Rait, ii. 1019–25.
63 W.R.O., tithe award; for inclosure, below, econ. hist. (Froxfield).
64 Ch. Com. survey bk., EE 5.
65 Ibid. deed 318402.
66 W.R.O., F 2/2200/1.
67 Ibid. F 9/101/36.
68 In this para. inf. for c. 1536 is from Longleat Mun., Seymour papers, xii, ff. 292–6; acreage of arable at that date is nominal.
69 Cf. W.R.O. 9/8/153H; ibid. EA/119; ibid. tithe award; for the woodland, below, this section.

manor then had 114 a. in the open fields, the copyholds 184 a., the Rectory estate *c.* 25 a., and a freehold, later assessed at 2 yardlands,[70] perhaps *c.* 40 a. There were seven copyholds, the largest of which had 36 a. in the fields, the smallest 13 a.: none had much meadow land or inclosed pasture. The downland south of the road was divided between demesne land, called the Heath and the Inner down, and a down on which in winter the copyholders and the owner of the Rectory estate could keep 500 sheep in common. The freeholder's sheep presumably pastured with the common flock, and on the open fields in summer the tenant of the demesne could keep 300 sheep with it. On the open fields and common downland and on the marsh, most of which was beside the Dun, the copyholders and the owner of the Rectory estate could keep 63 cattle or horses; the tenant of the demesne could keep such beasts on the open fields in summer, and on the Inner down and in Long mead after haymaking 6 beasts kept on the Rectory estate could be fed with his. Besides the open-field arable and the downland the demesne, 319 a., had 9 a. of meadow (including Long mead, 7 a.), 16 a. of several arable, Marsh close comprising 5 a. east of the village, and a several pasture called Hillwork comprising 60 a. north of the open fields.[71] Later the copyholders were said to feed cattle and horses on the Heath in winter.[72] Among the copyholders' obligations *c.* 1536 was work on the demesne for 37 days a year.

In the early 17th century the demesne was apparently divided into two farms,[73] on one of which *c.* 1654 the tenant kept only *c.* 160 sheep in winter, fewer in summer.[74] By 1683 the demesne may again have been a single farm, and the number of copyholds had evidently been reduced from seven to six.[75] The downland south of the London road, the marsh beside the Dun, and the marsh east of the village had been inclosed by 1779.[76] The marsh beside the Dun, *c.* 24 a., was apparently allotted to the freeholder, who also owned the land of Oakhill, and was added to Oakhill farm; part of it was converted to water meadow.[77] The Heath, 56 a., and the Inner down, 44 a., parts of the demesne farm, were converted to arable.[78] Part of the copyholders' down was planted with trees and the rest possibly ploughed; to replace the right to feed 100 sheep and 6 beasts there, and the feeding right on the Inner down, 9 a. was allotted to the owner of the Rectory estate.[79] About 1785 the

demesne, Manor farm, measured 347 a., including 299 a. of arable and 19 a. of water meadows; sainfoin was grown on 30 a. of the Inner down. The six copyholds, totalling 260 a. *c.* 1785, were brought in hand between 1796 and 1837.[80]

East and West fields, 441 a., were inclosed under an Act of 1818. The allotments may have been entered on by 1819 although the formal award was not made until 1823.[81] By allotment and exchange the freeholder, who also owned Littlecote manor and Rudge farm, acquired 112 a. in the north, including Hillwork; afterwards all that land lay in farms based in Rudge or Ramsbury.[82] Also by allotment and exchange the land of the Rectory estate, 51 a., was concentrated north-west of the church.[83] About 1846 only two farms were based at Froxfield: Manor farm was of 472 a., including a farmstead in the south-east part of the village, 428 a. of arable, and 10 a. of water meadow, and the other farm was of 215 a. including 177 a. of arable.[84] A new farmhouse away from the farmstead was built for Manor farm in 1849.[85] The two farms had been merged by 1901,[86] and in 1910, when the farmyard was improved and extended, Manor farm measured 662 a.[87]

From 1909 what had been the land of the Rectory estate became a small dairy farm: as Green farm, *c.* 70 a., it remained such in 1995.[88] Manor farm measured 618 a., including 542 a. of arable, in 1919;[89] it remained predominantly arable, although there were poultry houses and a small herd of cows on it in 1965.[90] From 1965 its land north of the London road, *c.* 365 a., was in hand as part of the Littlecote (later Eastridge) estate, and in 1995 it was devoted to arable farming. Its land south of the road was also mainly arable in 1995.[91]

About 1536 Froxfield had two main areas of woodland, Ley coppice and West wood, probably each of 15–20 a.[92] Almshouse coppice, 38 a. south-west of the village, had been planted by 1612.[93] In 1758 Ley coppice, south of the village, measured 27 a. and there was another coppice of 4 a.;[94] 8 a. along the parish boundary around the north part of Hillwork had been planted as part of Lawn coppice, part of the woodland of Littlecote House, by 1823.[95] In 1820 the lord of Froxfield manor granted a licence to grub up Ley coppice: 13 a. had been cleared of trees evidently by 1821, but the last 2 a. was not cleared until *c.* 1857.[96] North of the village six long and narrow coverts were planted between 1899 and 1922.[97] They, Almshouse coppice, the

70 W.R.O. 192/8.
71 For the locations, cf. ibid. EA/119; ibid. tithe award; ibid. 9/8/153H; 2037/119, p. 21.
72 Ibid. 1300/180.   73 Ibid.; ibid. 9/5/29.
74 P.R.O., E 134/1654 Mich./9.
75 D. & C. Windsor Mun. XV. 39. 75.
76 Ibid. Ch. Com. 120351.
77 W.R.O., tithe award; for the ownership of the freehold, cf. ibid. 192/8; ibid. EA/119.
78 Ibid. 2037/119, p. 21.
79 Cf. ibid. EA/119; Longleat Mun., Seymour papers, xii, f. 292v.
80 W.R.O. 2037/119, pp. 20–3, 55–7, 59–60, 62–5, 68–9.
81 Ibid. EA/119; D. & C. Windsor Mun., Ch. Com. 120142.
82 W.R.O., EA/119; ibid. tithe award; Som. R.O., DD/PO 99; above, manors (Rudge).

83 W.R.O., EA/119.
84 Ibid. tithe award.
85 Above, intro. (Froxfield).
86 W.R.O., L 2, Froxfield.
87 Ibid. Inland Revenue, val. reg. 54; ibid. 2037/176.
88 Local inf.; cf. above, manors (Rectory).
89 W.R.O. 2037/125.
90 Ibid. 1008/35.
91 Inf. from Sir (David) Seton Wills, Bt., Eastridge Ho., Ramsbury.
92 Longleat Mun., Seymour papers, xii, ff. 292v., 294v.
93 W.R.O. 9/8/153H.
94 Ibid. 2037/111, lease, Batson to Ivy, 1758; for the location, ibid. EA/119.
95 Ibid. EA/119; cf. *V.C.H. Wilts.* xii. 14.
96 *Endowed Char. Wilts.* (S. Div.), 987; W.R.O. 2037/14.
97 O.S. Maps 6", Wilts. XXX. SW. (1900, 1925 edns.).

part of Lawn coppice, and a coppice of *c.* 8 a. planted near the village in the later 20th century,[98] a total of *c.* 60 a., were standing in 1995.

In the later 18th century and earlier 19th Froxfield was apparently a minor centre for malting and brewing. There was a malthouse and brewery at the Cross Keys run by Thomas Noyes until *c.* 1771 and afterwards by his brother William, who by *c.* 1785 had expanded the business[99] and in 1793 sold it to William Newbury.[1] A new brewhouse fronting Brewhouse Hill was built in 1843.[2] Brown & Hillary were brewers and maltsters at Froxfield in 1830,[3] there were two maltsters in 1841,[4] and a malthouse was standing on the north side of the Green in 1846.[5]

Froxfield wharf on the Kennet & Avon canal was presumably used by local carriers in the 19th century,[6] but a shed standing in 1846 and 1878[7] is the only building known to have been erected there.

OAKHILL. The open fields and common pastures of Oakhill were part of North Standen and Oakhill manor from the 13th century, and presumably included both demesne and customary land. In 1257 the demesne of the composite manor included 225 a. of arable, 9 a. of meadow, a several pasture called Oakhill sufficient for 16 oxen, a marsh sufficient for 4 beasts, and pasture for 200 sheep; the eight customary holdings were small, including only 68 a. of arable, and between them the tenants had to work for 14 days and to plough 2½ a. Oakhill marsh, beside the Dun, was then held by the lord of Froxfield manor. It is likely that the demesne was worked from buildings in North Standen,[8] as it was later, and that some of the customary holdings were based at Oakhill.[9] In 1283 the demesne was roughly the size it was in 1257 but there were said to be 13 customary tenants each holding 1 yardland; the tenants' services included carrying writs.[10]

In 1552 the demesne arable of the manor was several, and most of it was almost certainly in the North Standen part of it. There were four copyholders. Their 3½ yardlands included 120 a. of arable, a 20-a. cow pasture, 7 a. of meadow, and 8 a. of several pasture; most of their land was almost certainly in Oakhill. The manor's 223 a. of common pasture, on which the lessee of the demesne could keep 300 sheep, the copyholders

90, included Oakhill down, 60 a. in the south part of Oakhill. The lessee could keep 30 cattle or horses, the copyholders 9;[11] in 1564 it was ruled that none might feed on Oakhill down. In 1562 there was apparently an exchange between the lessee of the demesne and the copyholders: the lessee gave up his pasture rights in Oakhill,[12] and from *c.* 1605 the demesne was a several farm mainly confined to North Standen.[13] From 1562 the open arable, marsh, common meadow, and common downland of Oakhill was apparently used mainly by the four copyholders, whose farmsteads may have stood at Oakhill. In 1591 the four could keep 44 cattle and *c.* 170 sheep, but the number of sheep they could keep was halved in alternate years. A few farms worked from Little Bedwyn parish included 10–20 a. of the open arable.[14]

The open fields of Oakhill were inclosed under an agreement of 1722,[15] and in the early 19th century all Oakhill's land lay in severalty and in either Oakhill farm, 210 a. in 1831, or North Standen farm. About 1846 Oakhill farm, 268 a., included 200 a. of arable, 17 a. of water meadow, 10 a. of marsh, and 33 a. of pasture on Oakhill down. North Standen farm then included 62 a. in Oakhill.[16] For a few years *c.* 1918 Oakhill farm, still 268 a., was held by A. J. Hosier and his brother Joshua.[17] It measured 277 a. in 1961,[18] and in the late 20th century was mainly arable.[19]

Trindledown copse was mentioned in the 13th century,[20] Frith copse in 1552, when both were estimated at 10 a.[21] They measured 15 a. and 13 a. respectively *c.* 1846,[22] 16 a. and 15 a. in 1995. Jugg's wood was standing in 1612[23] and was so called in 1720.[24] It measured 16 a. *c.* 1846,[25] 18 a. in 1995. In the later 20th century *c.* 12 a. of woodland was planted beside the eastern parish boundary.[26] Partridges and pheasants were kept on North Standen and Oakhill manor in the 16th century.[27]

Watercress beds of *c.* 1 a. were constructed on the Dun north-east of Oakhill Farm between 1883 and 1899;[28] they were used by growers with larger beds at Ramsbury[29] and went out of use in 1968.[30]

A mill on the demesne of North Standen and Oakhill manor in 1257[31] probably stood at Oakhill, where a demesne mill stood, and was to be rebuilt, in 1373.[32] In 1479–80 the mill stood idle while it was repaired and while the mill stream

98 O.S. Maps 1/25,000, SU 26 (1961 edn.); 1/10,000, SU 26 NE. (1982 edn.).
99 W.R.O. 118/93, accts. 1772; 2037/119, p. 26.
1 Ibid. 212A/36/7, deed, Noyes to Newbury, 1793.
2 Ibid. 2037/14; ibid. tithe award.
3 *Early Trade Dirs.* (W.R.S. xlvii), 62.
4 P.R.O., HO 107/1180.
5 W.R.O., tithe award. 6 Above, intro.
7 O.S. Map 6", Wilts. XXX (1887 edn.); W.R.O., tithe award.
8 *Wilts. Inq. p.m.* 1242–1326 (Index Libr.), 26–7.
9 Below, this section.
10 *Wilts. Inq. p.m.* 1242–1326 (Index Libr.), 145–6.
11 P.R.O., DL 3/44, f. 261; DL 42/108, ff. 86–8.
12 Som. R.O., DD/POt 116.
13 P.R.O., DL 44/700.
14 Ibid. DL 42/115, f. 18; W.R.O. 9/1/95, p. 53; 9/8/5; 79B/11; 1300/372, ff. 8, 17–18.
15 W.R.O. 9/5/19.
16 Ibid. tithe award; Som. R.O., DD/PO 28.

17 *W.A.M.* xlv. 388; W.R.O. 1635/21; for the Hosiers, above, Great Bedwyn, econ. hist. (Wexcombe).
18 W.R.O. 2281/4, abstr. of title.
19 Inf. from Sir Seton Wills.
20 *Wilts. Inq. p.m.* 1242–1326 (Index Libr.), 26.
21 P.R.O., DL 42/108, f. 88v.
22 W.R.O., tithe award.
23 Ibid. 9/8/153H.
24 Som. R.O., DD/POt 128.
25 W.R.O., tithe award.
26 O.S. Maps 1/25,000, SU 36 (1961 edn.); SU 26/36 (1983 edn.).
27 Som. R.O., DD/POt 116, view 30 Aug. 14 Eliz. I.
28 O.S. Maps 1/2,500, Wilts. XXX. 14 (1887, 1900 edns.).
29 *V.C.H. Wilts.* xii. 39; *W.A.M.* xlvi. 539–40.
30 Inf. from Miss M. Dixon, 32 Knowledge Crescent, Ramsbury.
31 *Wilts. Inq. p.m.* 1242–1326 (Index Libr.), 26.
32 *John of Gaunt's Reg.* i (Camd. 3rd ser. lvi), p. 133.

was scoured and two new stones were brought from St. Briavels castle (Glos.).[33] By 1528, when the lessee of the demesne of the manor agreed to build a new mill, it had apparently been demolished. The agreement was not kept,[34] but c. 1605 a new mill, with a new weir, two new hatches, a new channel, and a new pond, was built on the Dun on the site of the old. It was alleged that the new mill lessened the flow of water and trade to mills at Hungerford.[35] It was in use in 1758[36] and standing in 1793.[37] Water from the Dun was used to supply the Kennet & Avon canal,[38] and the mill had been demolished by 1846.[39]

RUDGE. Meadow land of Rudge lay beside the Froxfield stream, three open fields lay immediately north of the meadow land, and woodland and common pasture lay on higher ground further north.[40] There was possibly 250–350 a. of arable,[41] of which about a quarter was part of farms worked from Chisbury. In the early 18th century the fields were called West, Little, and Fisher.[42] By the 15th century some of the pasture and woodland had been inclosed and converted to arable,[43] and much had been inclosed by the mid 17th century. In 1565 a holding included 25 a. in the open fields and 15 a. in closes, and in 1641 a holding included 41 a. in the open fields and c. 50 a. in closes.[44]

Although in 1665 it was agreed to inclose the open fields and the common pasture called the Heath,[45] they were apparently not inclosed until between 1719 and 1741. In 1741 what was later Scrope farm included West field, 78 a., and 23 a. of the Heath. That farm, c. 286 a., then had 270 a. of arable in 18 closes;[46] in 1770 it had 328 a., of which 301 a. was arable.[47] In 1773 Rudge's five farmsteads were dispersed but not far from its centre.[48] In 1818 Scrope farm was divided,[49] and thereafter that part of its land in Rudge's south-west corner, with other land there, was worked as Harrow farm from a farmstead beside the London road; the farmhouse, on the south side of the road and in Little Bedwyn, was formerly the Harrow inn. About 1846 Rudge's land lay in Rudge Manor farm, 221 a., Scrope farm, 212 a., Rudge farm, 245 a., and Harrow farm, 159 a.; the farms included 733 a. of arable.[50]

There remained four farms in 1910, but Scrope and Rudge Manor, 511 a., were then and

later worked together.[51] Part of Rudge farm was added later, and in 1995 c. 550 a. of Rudge was worked with land in Ramsbury as Rudge Manor farm, an arable and beef farm of 770 a.[52] Also in 1995 Harrow farm, 322 a. including land in Little Bedwyn, was mainly arable,[53] and the rest of Rudge farm, c. 130 a., was in hand as part of the Eastridge (formerly Littlecote) estate and was arable.[54] Buildings in Froxfield parish were among those on the southern edge of Ramsbury airfield which after 1955 were converted for agricultural use and added to. As Darrell's Farm they were used for pig keeping in 1981 and 1995.[55]

Woodland was part of an estate at Rudge in the 14th century,[56] and in the 18th century there were small coppices on Scrope farm.[57] The 54 a. of woodland c. 1846 included Rudge coppice (25 a.) north-east of Rudge Manor Farm, and Scrope wood (11 a.) and Rudge firs (10 a.) south-west.[58] Those woods were standing in 1995.

A mill owned by the lord of Chisbury manor stood on the Froxfield stream 1 km. west of the church in 1589 and 1612.[59] It had apparently been demolished by 1694.[60]

LOCAL GOVERNMENT. There are records of Froxfield manor court for 1480–4, 1506, 1582–3, 1616–17, 1619, and 1715–1832. The court was held twice a year in the 15th century, once a year in the 16th and possibly the earlier 17th, every few years in the earlier 18th, and again once a year from c. 1750. In all those periods it transacted general manorial business: the death of tenants was reported, surrenders and admittances were witnessed, and matters such as encroachment on the waste, misuse of land worked in common, dilapidation of buildings, and unlicensed tree felling were dealt with. In the period 1480–4 the condition of hedges seems to have been of particular concern. In the 18th century some rules governing husbandry in common and some customs of the manor were repeatedly recorded.[61]

A view of frankpledge and a manor court were held for North Standen and Oakhill manor in the later 15th century, usually one or two of each a year. They may have transacted little business, and none was held in 1470–1, 1479–80, or 1492–3.[62] A view of frankpledge and court baron met

33 P.R.O., DL 29/690/11183.
34 Ibid. DL 3/44, f. 261; DL 29/700/11317.
35 Ibid. DL 4/54/15.
36 Ibid. E 134/32 Geo. II Mich./7; W.N. & Q. ii. 54.
37 W.R.O. 1644/34.
38 Above, Great Bedwyn, intro. [canal].
39 W.R.O., tithe award.
40 For the location of the open fields, ibid. 1300/372, ff. 7–8.
41 Cf. ibid. tithe award.
42 Ibid. 1300/372, ff. 7–8, 10–16.
43 Cat. Anct. D. vi, C 5058.
44 W.R.O. 9/5/27B; 9/5/29A.
45 Ibid. 9/1/132, pp. 255–7.
46 Ibid. 9/5/23, lease, Long to Pyke, 1741; 1300/372, ff. 8, 10–16.
47 Ibid. 9/5/23, survey, 1770.
48 Andrews and Dury, Map (W.R.S. viii), pl. 12.
49 Above, manors (Scrope).
50 W.R.O., tithe award; for Harrow farm and its bldgs., cf. above, intro. (other settlement); Little Bedwyn, intro.

(other settlement); econ. hist. (Chisbury; Knowle).
51 Kelly's Dir. Wilts. (1939); W.R.O., Inland Revenue, val. reg. 54.
52 Inf. from Mr. R. W. Wilson, Rudge Manor Farm.
53 Inf. from the agent for the Crown Estate Com., 42 High Street, Marlborough.
54 Inf. from Sir Seton Wills.
55 V.C.H. Wilts. xii. 38; inf. from Mr. F. Clothier, Park Farm, Ramsbury.
56 Extents for Debts (W.R.S. xxviii), p. 23.
57 W.R.O. 9/5/23, lease, Long to Pyke, 1741; survey, 1770.
58 Ibid. tithe award.
59 Ibid. 9/8/147; 9/9/153H.
60 Ibid. 9/8/49; cf. 1300/372, ff. 8, 18.
61 Ibid. 9/1/137, rot. 12; 9/1/139, rot. 9; 9/1/141, rot. 7 and d.; 9/5/73; 9/15/316; 192/8; 2037/129–30.
62 P.R.O., DL 29/688/11156; DL 29/689/11165; DL 29/689/11174; DL 29/690/11183; DL 29/690/11189; DL 29/691/11202; ibid. SC 6/1045/1.

twice in the period 1542–5: it punished and bound over the perpetrators of three assaults and ordered the construction of new stocks, but most business, such as the condition of boundaries, hedges, and gates and the use of common pastures, was agrarian.[63] In the period 1562–72 the court met four times, dealt with copyhold business, and recorded rules governing agriculture on the manor.[64]

The parish spent £164 on the poor in 1775–6 and an average of £128 in the three years to Easter 1785. The poor rate was high in 1802–3 when £355 was spent and 38 adults and 106 children, about a third of the population of the parish excluding the almshouse, were relieved regularly.[65] Expenditure had almost doubled by 1812–13, when it was £691 and 143 people were relieved, but was never as high again. It fluctuated between £297 and £561 in the period 1816–34.[66] The parish joined Hungerford poor-law union in 1835[67] and became part of Kennet district in 1974.[68]

CHURCH. Froxfield church was standing in the 12th century.[69] In the earlier 13th century the rector received all tithes from Chisbury and presumably served the church there. Before 1246 he gave the tithes, and presumably the duty of serving the church, to St. Denis's priory, Southampton. In 1259 the rector claimed that the priory's tenure of Chisbury church was temporary and that it should revert to him,[70] but the priory kept it.[71] Froxfield church was appropriated by Easton priory between 1396 and 1403,[72] and in 1403 a vicar was instituted.[73] In 1976 the vicarage was added to Whitton benefice.[74]

The overlord of Froxfield manor, Sir Henry Cobham, presented a rector in 1307 and in 1311. His right to present was challenged unsuccessfully by the lord of the manor, John Droxford, bishop of Bath and Wells, who presented a rival rector in 1311. The advowson descended in the Cobham family with the overlordship and with the lordship of Chisbury manor; for reasons that are obscure the bishop of Salisbury collated in 1348.[75] Between 1386 and 1390 John Cobham, Lord Cobham, sold the advowson to Sir William

Sturmy, who between 1396 and 1398 gave it to Easton priory.[76] From when the church was appropriated the advowson of the vicarage passed until 1867 with the Rectory estate, the owners of which, Easton priory, Edward, duke of Somerset, and St. George's chapel, Windsor, presented all the vicars except one: in 1454 the bishop collated by lapse. St. George's chapel kept the advowson when the estate passed to the Ecclesiastical Commissioners,[77] and in 1926 gave it to the Church Patronage society in an exchange.[78] From 1976 the Church Patronage trust had a seat on the board of patronage for Whitton benefice.[79]

In 1291 the rectory was worth £8 a year.[80] The vicarage, valued at £7 16s. 4d., was poor in 1535,[81] when the vicar's income was derived mainly from a pension of £7 6s. 8d. from the Rectory estate.[82] In 1625 St. George's chapel augmented the vicarage by £4 a year said to be for serving the cure.[83] From 1660 the pension was £17 6s. 8d.,[84] and from 1678 or earlier the chapel, and later the Ecclesiastical Commissioners, paid a total of £28 a year from the Rectory estate to the vicar.[85] The living was augmented in 1738 by £400 of which Queen Anne's Bounty gave half, in 1816 by a parliamentary grant of £1,400 by lot, in 1834 by a rent charge of £20 given by St. George's chapel, and in 1835 by £400 of which parliament gave half.[86] At £122 the vicar's income was still small c. 1830.[87] On the expiry of the lease of the great tithes the Ecclesiastical Commissioners augmented it in 1881.[88] The rector apparently took all tithes from nearly all the parish.[89] The vicar apparently took none.[90] The rector almost certainly had a house immediately north of the church[91] and in 1341 had arable estimated at 40 a. and a several pasture worth 19s. 4d.[92] The vicar's glebe consisted of no more than the vicarage house.[93] In 1674 the house was dilapidated and in danger of collapse,[94] and by 1680 the south part had fallen. The house was demolished in 1734, when a new house, with two rooms on each of two floors, two garrets, and a skilling, was built on higher ground in the north part of its garden.[95] About 1830 the new house was said to be unfit for residence,[96] and c. 1846 it was used as a pair of cottages.[97] A new, much larger, house was built

63 P.R.O., DL 30/127/1902, ff. 11–12, 15v.–16v.
64 Som. R.O., DD/POt 116.
65 *Poor Law Abstract, 1804*, 566–7; *V.C.H. Wilts.* iv. 348.
66 *Poor Law Abstract, 1818*, 498–9; *Poor Rate Returns, 1816–21*, 188; *1822–4*, 228; *1825–9*, 219; *1830–4*, 212.
67 *Poor Law Com. 1st Rep.* App. D, 242.
68 O.S. Map 1/100,000, admin. areas, Wilts. (1974 edn.).
69 Below, this section [archit.].
70 *Sar. Chart. and Doc.* (Rolls Ser.), pp. 310–12; P.R.O., E 135/21/26; above, Little Bedwyn, church.
71 *Tax. Eccl.* (Rec. Com.), 189.
72 Above, manors (Rectory).
73 Phillipps, *Wilts. Inst.* i. 89.
74 Ch. Com. file 34/378C.
75 *Reg. Ghent* (Cant. & York Soc.), ii. 692, 759–60; Phillipps, *Wilts. Inst.* i. 20, 43, 55, 68; above, manors (Froxfield); Little Bedwyn, manors (Chisbury).
76 *Cal. Pat.* 1388–92, 306; 1396–9, 333; Phillipps, *Wilts. Inst.* i. 82.
77 Phillipps, *Wilts. Inst.* (index in *W.A.M.* xxviii. 221); D. & C. Windsor Mun., livings bk., pp. 123–4; above, manors (Rectory).
78 Ch. Com. file 100594.

79 Ibid. 34/378C.   80 *Tax. Eccl.* (Rec. Com.), 189.
81 *Valor Eccl.* (Rec. Com.), ii. 150.
82 Hist. MSS. Com. 58, *Bath*, iv, p. 322.
83 *W.A.M.* xli. 35–6; D. & C. Windsor Mun. XI. C. 52; ibid. livings bk., p. 123.
84 D. & C. Windsor Mun. XV. 39. 73–74P; ibid. Ch. Com. 117834–49.
85 W.R.O., D 1/24/98/2; D 1/56/7; Ch. Com. survey bk., EE 5.
86 C. Hodgson, *Queen Anne's Bounty* (1845), p. cccxxxv; Ch. Com. file, F 1844.
87 *Rep. Com. Eccl. Revenues*, 834–5.
88 *Lond. Gaz.* 10 Mar. 1882, p. 1069; W.R.O. 1635/2.
89 *Inq. Non.* (Rec. Com.), 172; above, manors (Rectory).
90 e.g. W.R.O., tithe award.
91 Above, intro. (Froxfield).
92 *Inq. Non.* (Rec. Com.), 172; for the estate later, above, manors (Rectory).
93 W.R.O., D 1/24/98/2; ibid. tithe award.
94 Ibid. D 1/54/6/2, no. 30.
95 Ibid. D 1/48/1, f. 18; D 1/61/1B, pp. 60–3.
96 *Rep. Com. Eccl. Revenues*, 834–5.
97 W.R.O., tithe award.

in 1882–3; its west gable wall and the west part of its north wall are those of the house of 1734.[98] It was sold in 1967.[99]

John of Ogbourne, an acolyte when instituted as rector in 1311, was permitted to study at an English university for two years from his institution,[1] and Ellis Nethway, presented in 1394, was permitted to be non-resident and to lease the church for a year.[2] In 1553 the parishioners reported that the church had no pulpit,[3] in 1556 that goods belonging to the church were in private hands,[4] and in 1584 and 1585 that quarterly sermons were not preached. In 1584 the vicar's wife was among several who failed to receive the sacrament at Easter.[5] From the 17th century to the 20th vicars usually resided.[6] Geoffrey Godwin was vicar 1628–69.[7] His successor Thomas Foster composed and entered in the parish register a verse denigrating his parishioners for their ignorance; he rewrote it after a parishioner had blotted it out.[8] The vicarage house was not fit to be lived in,[9] Foster lived two miles away, and on Sundays no service was held in the morning and sometimes none before 5 p.m.[10] Thomas Brown, vicar 1773–88, lived at Stratford Tony, where he was rector. At Froxfield his curate, who also served Little Bedwyn, in 1783 held one service each Sunday, celebrated communion at the great festivals with 6–8 communicants, and lived in the vicarage house.[11] The vicar 1788–1827 was the mathematician and astronomer Lewis Evans, a contributor to the *Philosophical Magazine*. He had a private observatory at Woolwich, where he taught from 1799 to 1820, and in 1821 built an observatory incorporating a transit clock at the vicarage house at Froxfield.[12] He usually employed a curate at Froxfield: one, James Davidson, was in 1799 a proponent of a history of Wiltshire; another, John Gilmore, owned Rudge Manor farm.[13] In 1812 services were held with the same frequency as in 1783.[14] Lewis's successor, T. G. P. Atwood, lived in the house on the Rectory estate. In 1863–4 he held two services each Sunday and additional services on Christmas day and Good Friday, celebrated communion seven times, and catechized in the church. The congregation averaged c. 100 in the morning, c. 170 in the evening, and c. 250 on Christmas day and Good Friday; the church was considered too small.[15] The vicarage was held in plurality with that of

Little Bedwyn from 1958 to 1965, and with Chilton Foliat rectory from 1966 to 1975.[16]

Although the founder of Froxfield almshouse intended that the rector of Huish should be the chaplain of the almshouse,[17] the minister serving Froxfield church was usually the chaplain, acting either as a curate appointed by the rector of Huish or as an appointee of the trustees of the almshouse.[18]

The church of *ALL SAINTS*, so called in 1763,[19] is built of flint and sarsen rubble with freestone dressings and consists of a chancel with north vestry and organ chamber and a nave with south porch and west bell turret.[20] The nave, small and with thick walls, is 12th-century; the chancel was rebuilt in the 13th century. In the 14th century new windows were inserted in the north and south walls of the nave, and a new doorway was made in its north wall, and in the 15th century a new west window was inserted. A partly timber porch was apparently built in the 15th century.[21] At a restoration of 1891–2 to designs by Ewan Christian the porch was rebuilt, the roofs of the chancel and the nave were renewed, and a more elaborate bell turret was erected; the nave was reseated, and a west gallery was removed and its simple south window replaced by one in 15th-century style; the chancel arch was reconstructed, the chancel restored, and the vestry and organ chamber, in transeptal form, built to replace a small vestry north of the chancel.[22]

Froxfield retained an 11-oz. chalice in 1553 when 2 oz. of plate was taken for the king. In 1995 the parish had a richly ornamented Dutch or German chalice, dated 1619 and formerly gilt, and a paten hallmarked for 1854.[23]

The church had two bells in 1553.[24] The two in the church in 1671 were small and defective[25] and may both have been replaced in 1672. There hung in the church in 1995 a bell cast in 1672 by Henry Knight of Reading and an uninscribed bell possibly of similar date.[26]

The registers begin in 1561 and are complete, entries to c. 1609 being transcripts.[27]

NONCONFORMITY. Those in a small group which failed to receive the sacrament at Easter in 1584[28] may have been nonconformists. Froxfield had no nonconformist in 1676 and 1783.[29]

98 Ibid. 1635/2; ibid. D 1/11/278.
99 Ch. Com. deed 596148.
1 *Reg. Ghent* (Cant. & York Soc.), ii. 759–60, 902–3.
2 *Reg. Waltham* (Cant. & York Soc.), pp. 49, 105.
3 W.R.O., D 1/43/1, f. 141.
4 Ibid. D 1/43/2, f. 13.
5 Ibid. D 1/43/5, f. 18v.; D 1/43/6, f. 38Av.; cf. below, nonconf.
6 e.g. W.R.O., bishop's transcripts; *Kelly's Dir. Wilts.* (1848 and later edns.).
7 Phillipps, *Wilts. Inst.* ii. 14, 30.
8 W.R.O. 1635/1.
9 Above, this section.
10 W.R.O., D 1/54/4/1; D 1/54/6/2, no. 30.
11 Phillipps, *Wilts. Inst.* ii. 86, 94; *Vis. Queries, 1783* (W.R.S. xxvii), pp. 106–7.
12 *D.N.B.*; A. G. Barley, *Old Froxfield*, 18.
13 *Eng. Co. Hist.* ed. C. R. J. Currie and C. P. Lewis, 414; W.R.O., bishop's transcripts, bdles. 3–4; above, manors (Rudge Manor).
14 *W.A.M.* xli. 133.

15 W.R.O., tithe award; ibid. D 1/56/7.
16 *Crockford* (1961–2 and later edns.); Ch. Com. files, NB 34/156B/1–2.
17 *Endowed Char. Wilts.* (S. Div.), 981.
18 Barley, *Old Froxfield*, 28; *Harrod's Dir. Wilts.* (1865); W.R.O. 1300/6520; 2037/9; D. & C. Windsor Mun. XV. 39. 75.
19 J. Ecton, *Thesaurus* (1763), 406.
20 Above, plate 6.
21 J. Buckler, watercolour in W.A.S. Libr., vol. iv. 16; W.R.O., D 1/61/35, no. 9.
22 W.R.O., D 1/61/35, no. 9.
23 Nightingale, *Wilts. Plate*, 156; inf. from Mrs. S. Sutton, 4 Forge Cottages.
24 Walters, *Wilts. Bells*, 91.
25 W.R.O., D 1/54/4/1.
26 Walters, *Wilts. Bells*, 91; inf. from Mrs. Sutton.
27 W.R.O. 1635/1–8.
28 Ibid. D 1/43/5, f. 18v.
29 *Compton Census*, ed. Whiteman, 126; *Vis. Queries, 1783* (W.R.S. xxvii), p. 106.

Independents certified a meeting house at Froxfield in 1813, certified another in 1844,[30] and had a place of worship there in 1882.[31] In 1834 Wesleyan Methodists certified two houses for worship at Froxfield and in 1836 a house at Rudge.[32] A few Wesleyans who met in a cottage were said to be the only dissenters in the parish in 1864.[33] A small red-brick chapel for Primitive Methodists was built in Brewhouse Hill in 1909[34] and closed c. 1962.[35]

EDUCATION. In 1783 two dame schools were held in the parish, one in the almshouse.[36] In 1833 there were two day schools at which 13 boys and 22 girls were taught,[37] and in 1858, when most children went to school at Little Bedwyn, there was a dame school for a few young children.[38] There was no school in the parish in 1818, when some children went to one at Hungerford,[39] 1846–7,[40] and 1864, when the children went to Little Bedwyn.[41] A school in the parish, probably in Brewhouse Hill, had been opened by 1871, when 22 boys and 31 girls attended it on return day,[42] but in 1884 there was only an infants' school at Froxfield and children over six went to Little Bedwyn.[43] A school in Brewhouse Hill was rebuilt in 1885,[44] had an average attendance of 44 in 1906–7, and was closed in 1907.[45] A new school, designed by W. B. Medlicott and built near the church, was open from 1910 to 1963. Average attendance was 45 in 1910–11, 34 in 1937–8.[46]

CHARITIES FOR THE POOR. Robert Barber (d. by 1609) gave 2s. a year to be paid to the poor of Froxfield while his wife lived, and on her death 40s. or a cow as a stock. In 1611 William Fabian gave £3 as a stock for the poor. Both charities had been lost by 1786.[47]

Boys of Froxfield were eligible to benefit from the Broad Town charity, an apprenticing charity set up in the 1690s under the will of Sarah, duchess of Somerset.[48] In the late 20th century, when it was called the Broad Town trust, the charity helped young men entering employment or contributed to their education; in certain circumstances young women could be helped, and young people of Froxfield remained potential beneficiaries.[49]

FROXFIELD ALMSHOUSE. Sarah, duchess of Somerset, the wife of George Grimston (d.

1655), from 1661 to 1675 of John, duke of Somerset, and at her death in 1692 of Henry Hare, Lord Coleraine,[50] by her will directed her executors to found an almshouse at Froxfield and gave a site and money for it to be built and furnished. She prescribed a brick building which would enclose a quadrangle and have 30 houses each with a ground-floor room and a room above it. The occupants were to be 30 widows: half, 10 from Wiltshire, Somerset, or Berkshire and 5 from London or Westminster, were to be of clergymen, and half, 10 from manors (including Froxfield) which she owned and 5 from elsewhere in Wiltshire, Somerset, or Berkshire, were to be of laymen. A chapel was to be built in the court. The widows, who would qualify for residence if their inheritance was worth less than £20 a year, were to be given pensions and a cloth gown each year and the chaplain was either to be paid or to be presented as rector of Huish. In 1682 the duchess settled in trust land including Froxfield manor previously settled on the duke, herself, and the heirs or assigns of the survivor; by her will she gave the advowson of Huish to the trustees and directed them to endow the almshouse with that and the land. The income from the endowment was expected to rise and to become sufficient for the almshouse to be extended.[51]

Froxfield almshouse was built as the duchess prescribed by her executor Sir William Gregory. It was finished in 1694 or 1695 and widows were installed. The duchess's brother-in-law, Sir Samuel Grimston, Bt., the survivor of the trustees appointed in 1682, refused to convey the duchess's land to her executors, and after Gregory's death in 1696 his executors refused to transfer the income from it to the almshouse: by a decree of 1698 Chancery appointed local landowners as trustees of the almshouse, compelled the transfer of the endowment and its issues to them, and gave orders for the management of the almshouse.[52] Later questions of management and trusteeship were also referred to Chancery, which in 1729 sanctioned a body of 14 rules governing the duties of the trustees and the steward, the conduct of the widows, the performance of divine service in the chapel, and the locking of the outer door of the almshouse. The trustees nominated one of the widows as a matron to report on the behaviour of the other widows, carry a white wand, and receive £1 a year. Such nominations had ceased by the 1780s.[53]

30 Meeting Ho. Certs. (W.R.S. xl), pp. 72, 160.
31 Return of Churches, H.C. 401, p. 188 (1882), l.
32 Meeting Ho. Certs. (W.R.S. xl), pp. 135, 137, 142.
33 W.R.O., D 1/56/7.
34 Date on bldg.
35 Inf. from Miss M. Dixon, 32 Knowledge Crescent, Ramsbury.
36 Vis. Queries, 1783 (W.R.S. xxvii), p. 107.
37 Educ. Enq. Abstract, 1038.
38 Acct. of Wilts. Schs. 24.
39 Educ. of Poor Digest, 1027.
40 Nat. Soc. Inquiry, 1846–7, Wilts. 6–7.
41 W.R.O., D 1/56/7.
42 Returns relating to Elem. Educ. 418.
43 Ch. Com. file 65159.
44 Kelly's Dir. Wilts. (1895); O.S. Map 6″, Wilts. XXX.

SW. (1900 edn.); W.R.O., F 8/500/128/1/1.
45 Bd. of Educ., List 21, 1908 (H.M.S.O.), 503.
46 Ibid. 1910, 507; 1912, 550; 1938, 423; W.R.O., list of primary schs. closed since 1946; ibid. G 8/760/11.
47 Endowed Char. Wilts. (N. Div.), 482–3; W.R.O. 1635/1; cf. Char. Don. H.C. 511 (1816), xvi (2), 1352–3.
48 V.C.H. Wilts. ix. 42–3; for the duchess, below, this section.   49 Char. Com. file.
50 Complete Peerage, xii (1), 75–6.
51 W.R.O. 1300/290; 1300/299.
52 Complete Peerage, xii (1), 75; G.E.C. Baronetage, i. 106; P.R.O., C 78/1070, no. 1; for the finish, cf. W.R.O. 2037/119, prelim. p.; inscription on bldg.
53 J. Ward, Partics. relating to Som. Hosp. (copy in Wilts. local studies libr., Trowbridge), 21–7; P.R.O., C 78/1704, no. 3.

As expected, the almshouse's income grew in the 18th century, and in 1772–5 the building was enlarged to accommodate 50 widows.[54] As prescribed by the duchess, 5 of the additional 20 were to be from London or Westminster, 15 from any part of England except Wiltshire, Somerset, and Berkshire and anywhere more than 150 miles from London: 5 of the 20 were to be the widows of clergymen.[55] Pensions had increased from £6 in 1716 to £10 10s. in 1771 and, despite the enlargement of the almshouse, continued to increase. By the 1770s money was given instead of gowns. About 1833 each widow received £38 a year; the demand of laymen's widows for places was great and places for clergymen's widows were not easily filled, but the 50 places were occupied by the several categories in the prescribed numbers. The chaplain of the almshouse was then paid £50 a year, and salaries were paid to an apothecary, a receiver, a bailiff, a porter, and a chapel clerk.[56] From 1838 to 1851 the pensions were £40 a year.[57]

The almshouse's income declined in the later 19th century and earlier 20th. The pensions were reduced to £36 in 1851 and had fallen to £26 by 1882, from when accommodation was left vacant to avoid reducing them further.[58] As vacancies increased the occupants were not in the prescribed categories in the correct proportions, and in 1892 the trustees of the charities of St. John's and St. Margaret's parishes, Westminster, complained of under-representation for London and Westminster. After an inquiry by the Charity Commissioners in 1897, when only 16 widows lived in the almshouse, it was agreed that more from those areas should be installed. The inquiry found that the complicated system by which individual trustees in turn presented widows was open to objection. In 1907 there were 16 resident widows of whom 7 were of clergymen: 3 of the 16 were from London or Westminster, 3 from the duchess's manors.[59]

In the early 1920s the almshouse sold its lands and invested the proceeds.[60] In 1921–2 the number of resident widows was increased from 13 to 25 and the pensions were doubled to £52; a chaplain, a surgeon, a steward, a porter, and a matron were employed.[61] Under a Scheme of 1926 new rules were made for managing the almshouse, and the admittance of unmarried daughters of clergymen was permitted; under a Scheme of 1958 a matron, if appointed, was entitled to occupy one of the individual houses and the residents could be charged; and under a Scheme of 1966 any poor woman of 55 or more

could be admitted. In the later 20th century the charges, in 1986 £21 a week from each resident, and money given privately, by other charities, and by public bodies, were spent on maintaining and improving the almshouse.[62] There were 46 individual houses, one of which was reserved for guests, and 4 flats in 1995, when there was no resident matron. Each house then had a room and a kitchen on the ground floor, and a room and a bathroom on the first floor. There was a resident warden.[63]

As built in 1694 the two-storeyed almshouse[64] enclosed a square courtyard, in the centre of which stood the chapel. There was a house at each corner, between them there were seven houses on each side, and there was a narrow passage both east of the house at the north-west corner and west of the house at the north-east corner. The London road runs past the south side. Besides the 30 houses for widows, the slightly larger house at the centre of the south side was apparently a lodge, and that at the south-east corner was apparently used by the steward.[65] A cupola was erected in 1759,[66] presumably over the lodge. Between 1772 and 1775 the seven houses on the east side were demolished, what were apparently the lodge and the steward's room were converted for use by widows, and to the east 26 new houses and a lodge were built. The almshouse then enclosed a rectangular court: a row of nine houses was attached to the house at the old north-east corner, a narrow passage separated the row from the house at the new north-east corner, seven houses were built between that house and the steward's house at the new south-east corner, and eight houses were built between the steward's house and the new lodge, which linked the old and new parts of the south front. Facing the London road the lodge had a central pediment above an inscribed panel and a doorway with a segmental pediment. A cupola, possibly that of 1759, a weathervane dated 1772, and a clock were put up over the lodge. The grounds of the almshouse were walled. To the south the wall was low and outside it a terrace was made, from 1781 connected to the London road by steps; to the east and north the wall was higher and enclosed gardens.[67] In 1814, the year in which the new chapel was built, it was proposed that the lodge should be rendered; it was rebuilt in stone to harmonize with the chapel, presumably in that year when work was being done on it, and the inscription was engraved anew. In 1818 the steps were remade with parapet walls and an iron wicket.[68] On the south side of the almshouse wooden surrounds to the windows were

54 Endowed Char. Wilts. (S. Div.), 985; W.R.O. 2037/119, p. 15; for the date of the enlargement, cf. ibid. 2037/12.
55 W.R.O. 1300/299.
56 Endowed Char. Wilts. (S. Div.), 983–4, 986.
57 W.R.O. 2037/119, prelim. p.
58 Ibid.; Endowed Char. Wilts. (S. Div.), 996; A. T. Rix, Hist. Duchess of Som.'s Hosp. (copy in Wilts. local studies libr.), 8.
59 Endowed Char. Wilts. (S. Div), 996–7, 1000; for the system of presentment, W.R.O. 2037/7.
60 W.A.M. xlii. 354; V.C.H. Wilts. x. 63, 79; above, manors (Froxfield); below, Milton Lilbourne, manors (Lawn; Broomsgrove).

61 W.R.O., L 2 (Froxfield).
62 Rix, Hist. Duchess of Som.'s Hosp. 12, 15, 21; Wilts. Cuttings, xxvii. 240; W.R.O. 2037/97; 2037/99; 2037/102–3; Char. Com. file.
63 Inf. from Mr. R. T. Rowland, Friskie Place, Eastbury, Berks.
64 Above, plates 31–2.
65 Gent. Mag. lxxi (1), facing p. 306; W.R.O. 2037/86.
66 W.R.O. 2037/119, p. 15.
67 Ibid. p. 16; ibid. 2037/12; 2037/86; ibid. EA/119; Gent. Mag. lxxi (1), facing p. 306; Rix, Hist. Duchess of Som.'s Hosp. 8; J. Buckler, watercolour in W.A.S. Libr., vol. iv. 16.
68 W.R.O. 2037/13; 2037/119, prelim. p.; for the chapel, below, this section.

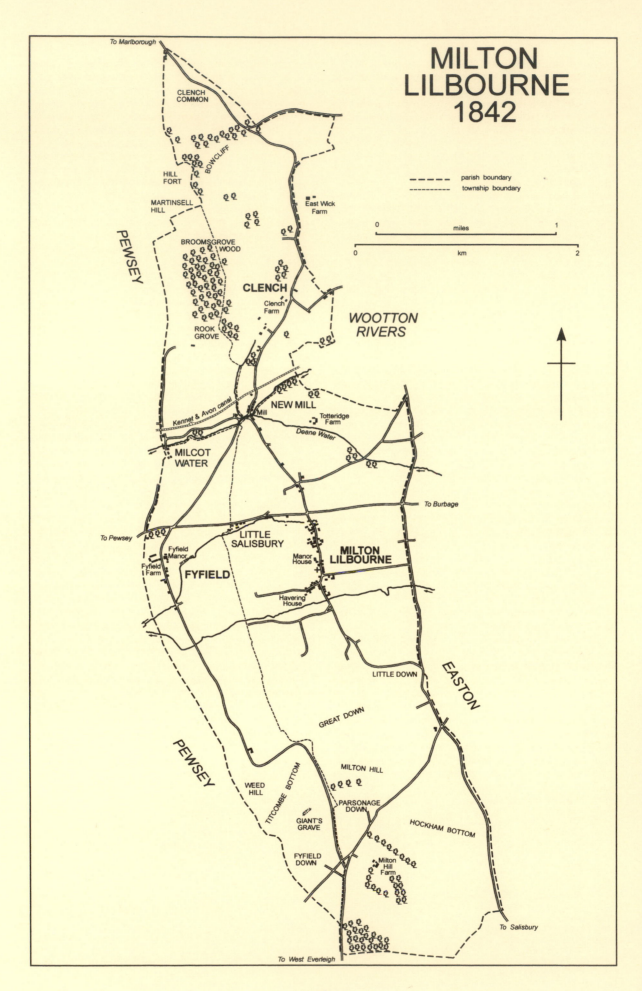

MILTON LILBOURNE 1842

parish boundary
township boundary

miles
0 · · · · · 1
km
0 · · · · · 2

To Marlborough

CLENCH
COMMON

BOWCLIFF

HILL
FORT

MARTINSELL
HILL

East Wick
Farm

BROOMSGROVE
WOOD

CLENCH

Clench
Farm

*WOOTTON
RIVERS*

PEWSEY

ROOK
GROVE

Kennet & Avon canal

Mill

NEW MILL

Totteridge
Farm

Deane Water

**MILCOT
WATER**

To Burbage

To Pewsey

Fyfield
Manor

**LITTLE
SALISBURY**

Manor
House

**MILTON
LILBOURNE**

Fyfield
Farm

FYFIELD

Havering
House

LITTLE DOWN

EASTON

PEWSEY

GREAT DOWN

MILTON HILL

WEED
HILL

TITCOMBE BOTTOM

PARSONAGE
DOWN

HOCKHAM BOTTOM

GIANT'S
GRAVE

FYFIELD
DOWN

Milton
Hill
Farm

To Salisbury

To West Everleigh

kept in the 17th-century range, stone ones in the 18th-century range, when the fenestration on that side was rearranged in the 19th century. On the south side of the London road and facing the lodge a small red-brick house was built for the porter c. 1833.[69] It was sold in 1965 and replaced by a warden's bungalow north of the almshouse.[70]

Although the rector of Huish may nominally have been chaplain, the chapel was usually served by the minister serving Froxfield church.[71] In 1729 it was ruled that there should be divine service in it every day and, with a sermon, twice on Sundays; the rule was not being observed in 1786,[72] and in 1907 services were thrice-weekly.[73] Services were held regularly in 1995. The chapel built between 1692 and 1695, from 1772–5 standing in the west part of the enlarged quadrangle,[74] was presumably of red brick and apparently in plain Gothic style;[75] it was demolished in 1813. A new chapel, designed by Thomas Baldwin and paid for by Charles Brudenell-Bruce, earl of Ailesbury, was built in the centre of the quadrangle in 1813–14.[76] It is of stone in neo-Gothic style and was restored in 1963.[77] It has a chalice and a paten each hallmarked for 1695.[78]

MILTON LILBOURNE

MILTON LILBOURNE parish lies south of Marlborough in the east part of the Vale of Pewsey.[79] It is long and narrow, measured 1,452 ha. (3,588 a.), reaches from the Marlborough Downs in the north to Salisbury Plain in the south, and contains the strips of land of four settlements, Milton Lilbourne and Fyfield to the south, Clench and Milcot to the north. In 1987, when the northern tip was transferred to Savernake parish and small areas were exchanged with Pewsey, Milton Lilbourne parish was reduced to 1,411 ha.[80]

The long and straight boundary which Milcot and Fyfield had with Pewsey in the 10th century has survived as the west boundary of Milton Lilbourne parish. The Iron-Age hill fort on Martinsell Hill, which lay east of Pewsey's boundary in the 10th century, was later part of Pewsey parish.[81] On the east the boundary between Milton Lilbourne and Easton is also straight and its whole length is marked by a road; its south part follows a dry valley for 1.5 km. On the extreme south the boundary with Collingbourne Kingston, marked by a barrow, had been defined by c. 933.[82] On the north-east Clench's boundary with Wootton Rivers is irregular: it was uncertain when, c. 1215 and c. 1327, tithes were disputed by the appropriator of Milton Lilbourne church and the rector of Wootton Rivers,[83] and the irregularity may be due partly to compromise.

The parish and each of the four strips of land within it lie north–south across the geological outcrops. The chalk of the Marlborough Downs and Salisbury Plain outcrops at the north and south ends of the parish respectively. To the north the scarp of the downs across the parish forms an arc and was called Bowcliff, the highest point of which is at 285 m.; north of Bowcliff there are deposits of clay-with-flints on Clench common, which declines gently to 206 m. at the north corner of the parish. To the south the highest point is at 238 m. on Milton Hill a little south of the scarp of the plain; south of the scarp the land slopes gently, is crossed by several dry valleys, and falls to 163 m. at the south-east corner of the parish. Between the scarps Lower Chalk outcrops to north and south, and in the centre, over about half the parish, Upper Greensand outcrops. The greensand is crossed east–west by four head streams of the Christchurch Avon, one of which is called Deane Water. The lowest point in the parish, at 115 m., is where the southernmost leaves it. In all four parts of the parish there were open fields on the greensand and the Lower Chalk, common pastures for sheep or cattle on the greensand, and rough pasture on the downs. Milton Lilbourne also had open fields on the downs.[84] Much of the parish is suitable for both arable and pasture: after inclosure there was usually more arable than pasture,[85] but in the earlier 20th century there was more pasture than arable.[86]

The parish, possibly excluding Clench, had 107 poll-tax payers in 1377;[87] it may have had no more than 362 inhabitants in 1676.[88] The population was 573 in 1801, 542 in 1811. It rose rapidly to reach a peak of 709 in 1841. By 1881 it had fallen to 599, by 1921 to 507,[89] and by

69 W.R.O. 2037/14.
70 Rix, *Hist. Duchess of Som.'s Hosp.* 21.
71 Above, church.
72 Ward, *Partics. relating to Som. Hosp.* 21, 23.
73 *Endowed Char. Wilts.* (S. Div.), 999.
74 *Gent. Mag.* lxxi (1), facing p. 306.
75 W.R.O. 2037/86.
76 Ibid. 2037/119, prelim. p.; ibid. D 1/60/1/14A; inscription on bldg.   77 Wilts. Cuttings, xxii. 114.
78 Nightingale, *Wilts. Plate*, 156; inf. from Mr. Rowland.
79 This article was written in 1996. Maps used include O.S. Maps 1", sheet 14 (1817 edn.); 1/25,000, SU 05/15, SU 06/16 (1987 edns.); SU 25/35 (1994 edn.); 6", Wilts. XXXVI, XLII (1888 and later edns.).
80 Statutory Instruments, 1987, no. 619, Kennet (Parishes) Order.
81 *Arch. Jnl.* lxxvi. 248–9; below, Pewsey, intro.

82 *Arch. Jnl.* lxxvi. 217–18; *W.A.M.* lxiv. 60–3; for the date, P. H. Sawyer, *Anglo-Saxon Chart.* (revised S. E. Kelly; priv. circulated 1996), no. 379.
83 *Letters of Innocent III*, ed. C. R. and M. G. Cheney, pp. 165–6; *Cart. Cirencester*, ii, ed. C. D. Ross, p. 433; *Reg. Martival* (Cant. & York Soc.), iv, p. 123.
84 Geol. Surv. Maps 1/50,000, drift, sheet 266 (1974 edn.); 1", drift, sheet 282 (1985 edn.); below, econ. hist.; for the name Bowcliff, cf. *V.C.H. Wilts.* iv. 421, 450; *W.A.M.* xlix. 406.   85 e.g. W.R.O., tithe award.
86 [1st] Land Util. Surv. Map, sheet 112.
87 *V.C.H. Wilts.* iv. 107; Clench was part of Bromham liberty and assessed for taxation as such in 1332: *Tax List, 1332* (W.R.S. xlv), 23; below, local govt.; cf. P.R.O., SC 2/208/16.
88 *Compton Census*, ed. Whiteman, 126.
89 *V.C.H. Wilts.* iv. 354.

1971 to 469. After the changes of 1987 to the parish boundary it was 484 in 1991.[90]

The parish lies on the east–west route linking the villages between Burbage and Pewsey. Surviving tracks suggest that an early road linked the villages from centre to centre, but by the later 18th century the present road, on higher ground and bypassing each village at its north end, had superseded it.[91] Milton Lilbourne village and Fyfield village each has a north–south street, but neither street forms part of a main road. A north–south road via Clench links both villages to Marlborough; the section across Bowcliff was apparently remade between 1773 and 1817,[92] and the section across Clench common was remade on a straight course in the mid 19th century.[93] From the south end of Milton Lilbourne village a road leads south and south-east to the downs, joins the road along the east boundary of the parish, and linked Milton Lilbourne to Salisbury via the Marlborough–Salisbury road and Everleigh. The Everleigh–Salisbury part of the road was closed c. 1900[94] and the road from Milton Lilbourne has been tarmacadamed for only 2 km. south of the village. A road also leads south from Fyfield village to the downs; the part south of the stream flowing from the south end of Milton Lilbourne village was declared a private road in 1823.[95] Other downland tracks included one from Easton to West Everleigh in Everleigh which in 1996 survived across Milton Lilbourne parish on the course it followed in 1773.[96] The Kennet & Avon canal, fully open from 1810, was built across the parish c. 1806–7;[97] it was restored in the early 1970s.[98] A little south of and parallel to it the Berks. & Hants Extension Railway was opened in 1862;[99] Pewsey was the nearest station.

In the north corner of the parish Neolithic and Bronze-Age artefacts were found on Clench common. On the chalk downland in the south part an artefact of the late Bronze Age was found and there are seven barrows in a group, other barrows, prehistoric earthworks, and a prehistoric field system. One of the barrows, Giant's grave, is an exceptionally large long barrow. On the greensand in the north part of the parish there was a Romano-British settlement; pottery from an earlier period and kilns have been found on the site.[1]

In 1237 the half of the parish north of Milton Lilbourne village and Fyfield village was defined as part of Savernake forest. All but Clench common was disafforested in 1330.[2] Clench common

was later part of Clench manor[3] and of the parish.

MILTON LILBOURNE. The village apparently takes the substantive part of its name, the middle tun, from its relationship to Easton, the east tun,[4] to the east and Pewsey to the west. The suffix is derived from Lillebonne, the surname of the lords of the principal manor from the 12th century to the 15th,[5] and was in use in 1249;[6] in the 18th century the diocese adopted the form Lilborne for the name of the benefice,[7] but the form Lilbourne, presumably derived by analogy with the many villages in Wiltshire which stand beside small streams, was frequently used in the 19th century,[8] was adopted by the Ordnance Survey,[9] and has become the normal form of the suffix in the 20th century.

Milton Lilbourne is a street village, its name implies that it was founded, or named, after Easton, and, like Easton, it may have been colonized from Pewsey.[10] The church, the vicarage house, and the principal manor house stand in the south part of the street on the west side.[11] Immediately south of the vicarage house an east–west lane crosses the street, and south of that three large houses were standing in 1773:[12] one beside the lane to the east was replaced by King Hall, that beside the lane to the west survives as Havering House and has given a name to Havering Lane,[13] and one has been demolished. Beside Havering Lane two thatched cottages standing in 1996 had probably been built by 1700. Beside the lane to the east King Hall Farmhouse, of red brick, was built c. 1750[14] and there are stables and farm buildings of red brick. South of the crossroads a school and Lower Farm were built in the later 19th century[15] and extensive farm buildings west of the street were erected in the mid 19th century and later[16] and demolished in 1996. Thatched farm buildings east of the street were converted for residence c. 1991.[17] Before the 19th century most of the farmsteads apparently stood in the north part of the street, where some eight farmhouses survived in 1996. On the east side the farmhouses included Upper Farm, built of red brick in the late 18th century with a three-bayed west front and extended in the 19th and 20th centuries, a timber-framed and thatched house of the 17th century, and an extended house, partly timber-framed and partly of brick, probably of 17th-century origin. On the west side two thatched farmhouses are apparently timber-

90 *Census*, 1971; 1991; above, this section.
91 *Andrews and Dury, Map* (W.R.S. viii), pl. 12.
92 Ibid.; O.S. Map 1", sheet 14 (1817 edn.).
93 O.S. Map 6", Wilts. XXXVI (1888 edn.); W.R.O., tithe award. 94 *V.C.H. Wilts.* xv. 63, 65.
95 W.R.O., EA/119.
96 *Andrews and Dury, Map* (W.R.S. viii), pls. 9, 12.
97 K. R. Clew, *Kennet & Avon Canal* (1985), 69, 73.
98 R. W. Squires, *Canals Revived*, 112.
99 *V.C.H. Wilts.* iv. 287.
1 Ibid. i (1), 89, 142, 169, 184, 215, 268, 277; i (2), 305; *W.A.M.* lxxii/lxxiii. 51; lxxx. 23–96.
2 *V.C.H. Wilts.* iv. 399–400, 418, 450–1; *W.A.M.* xlix. 394.
3 W.R.O. 9/21/19.
4 *P.N. Wilts.* (E.P.N.S.), 345, 349.
5 Below, manors (Milton Lilbourne).

6 *Crown Pleas, 1249* (W.R.S. xvi), p. 218.
7 W.R.O., D 1/48/4, p. 46; D 1/48/5, p. 93; D 1/56/7.
8 e.g. *Kelly's Dir. Wilts.* (1875 and later edns.).
9 O.S. Maps 6", Wilts. XXXVI, XLII (1888 edns.).
10 Cf. above, Easton, intro.; for street villages almost certainly colonized from Pewsey, below, Pewsey, intro.
11 The bldgs. are described below, manors (Milton under the hill); church.
12 *Andrews and Dury, Map* (W.R.S. viii), pl. 12.
13 The bldgs. are described below, manors (King Hall; Milton Havering).
14 P.R.O., PROB 11/963, f. 222; cf. below, manors (Rectory).
15 Below, manors (Lower); educ.
16 O.S. Maps 6", Wilts. XLII (1888 and later edns.); W.R.O., tithe award.
17 Inf. from Mr. G. E. R. Osborne, Lawn Farm.

framed, encased in brick, and 17th-century, a third farmhouse is of red brick and of the late 18th century, and Lawn Farm is a red-brick farmhouse built in 1867.[18] At the north end on the west side eight houses were built in Forge Close *c.* 1971,[19] and in the 1990s some farm buildings were converted for residence[20] and others replaced by several new houses. Near the church and on the east side of the street there are two 18th-century houses of brick, one thatched and the other with an extension of *c.* 1900, and a group of three thatched cottages incorporating timber framing and walls of red brick.[21] Several other cottages and small houses, none apparently built before the 17th century, also stand along the street. A memorial hall had been built south of the church by 1923:[22] it was replaced by a village hall built on the east side of the street in 1974.[23] The whole street, apart from Forge Close, was designated a conservation area in 1985.[24]

Several offshoots of Milton Lilbourne village grew in the 19th and 20th centuries. In the mid 19th century a lane parallel to and north of Havering Lane, and a north–south lane linking it to Havering Lane, were laid out west of the village, and several houses and cottages were built beside them.[25] In the square formed by those lanes, Havering Lane, and the village street 15 houses and 7 bungalows were built by the rural district council between 1947 and 1954;[26] a few other houses and bungalows were built beside the lanes in the 20th century, and 6 private houses were built in the square in the late 20th century. Also in the mid 19th century farm buildings were erected at the west end of Havering Lane;[27] between them and Havering House 7 houses were built in the 20th century, and in the late 20th century the farm buildings were replaced by extensive new ones.[28] In the north-west angle of the crossroads at the north end of the village street a parish room was built *c.* 1906.[29] It was removed in 1927 when eight council houses were built there;[30] afterwards a nonconformist chapel and several other houses were built in the north-west angle, and in the later 20th century a commercial garage was built in the south-west angle.[31]

Littleworth, so called in the later 19th century,[32] is a hamlet 300 m. north of the north end of Milton Lilbourne village street. A red-brick house of the 18th century was standing there in 1773.[33] Another red-brick house and two pairs of cottages, neither of which survives, had been built by 1842, and a nonconformist chapel and a third red-brick house were built there between 1843 and 1886.[34] A house and 11 bungalows were built at Little-worth in the 20th century.

West of the crossroads at the north end of the village street two pairs of thatched cottages were built on the verge of the Burbage–Pewsey road in the 17th or 18th century, and west of them a hamlet was called Little Salisbury in 1691 and later, but occasionally Newtown;[35] some nine cottages were standing at Little Salisbury in 1842,[36] and a beerhouse, the Three Horse Shoes, was opened there in the late 19th century.[37] The Three Horse Shoes, occupying a building partly of the 19th century and partly older, remained open in 1996, when other buildings at Little Salisbury included one which may have been built as a cottage in the 17th century and, standing on Fyfield's land, workshops and other buildings on the site of a small 19th-century farmstead.[38] East of the crossroads and on the south side of the Burbage road two pairs of council houses were built in 1938.[39]

A mill standing on Milton Lilbourne manor in the late 16th century and later gave the name New Mill to a nearby settlement in Clench.[40] On the site of Totteridge Farm east of the mill barns were standing in the earlier 18th century. A timber-framed farmhouse, Totteridge Farm, was built shortly before 1754,[41] given a new south front of red brick in the later 18th century, and extended east *c.* 1800 and west in the mid 20th century. Large and mainly 20th-century farm buildings stood at the farmstead in 1996. Milton Hill Farm was built on the downs south of Milton Lilbourne village shortly before 1724.[42] The farmhouse was replaced by a new house in the late 18th century, a pair of cottages built apparently in the mid 19th century was demolished when two new pairs were built in the mid 1940s,[43] and large farm buildings were erected in the 20th century.

CLENCH. Between East Wick in Wootton Rivers and West Wick in Pewsey the abbey of Battle (Suss.) held an estate called Wick, occasionally Bromham Wick, in Milton Lilbourne parish in the Middle Ages.[44] A settlement on the estate had apparently taken the name Clench by the 13th century.[45] The estate was called Wick Clench *c.* 1300,[46] and the names Clench *alias*

18 W.R.O. 2037/15, p. 2.
19 Ibid. A 1/355/445/2; A 1/355/450/2.
20 Inf. from Mr. Osborne.
21 Above, plate 40.
22 O.S. Map 6", Wilts. XLII. NW. (1926 edn.).
23 W.R.O. 1802/150/22.
24 Inf. from Dept. of Planning and Highways, Co. Hall, Trowbridge.
25 O.S. Maps 6", Wilts. XXXVI, XLII (1888 edns.); W.R.O., tithe award.
26 W.R.O., G 10/505/1.
27 Ibid. tithe award; O.S. Map 6", Wilts. XLII (1888 edn.).   28 Below, econ. hist. (Milton Lilbourne).
29 W.R.O., G 10/760/35.
30 Ibid. G 10/600/1.
31 O.S. Maps 1/25,000, SU 16 (1961 edn.); 1/10,000, SU 16 SE. (1983 edn.); below, nonconf.
32 O.S. Map 6", Wilts. XXXVI (1888 edn.).
33 *Andrews and Dury, Map* (W.R.S. viii), pl. 12.

34 O.S. Map 6", Wilts. XXXVI (1888 edn.); W.R.O., tithe award.
35 *Andrews and Dury, Map* (W.R.S. viii), pl. 12; W.R.O. 332/254, ct. 20 Oct. 1691.
36 W.R.O., tithe award.
37 *Kelly's Dir. Wilts.* (1867 and later edns.); O.S. Maps 6", Wilts. XXXVI (1888 edn.); XXXVI. SW. (1900 edn.).
38 Below, econ. hist. (Fyfield).
39 W.R.O., G 10/613/2.
40 Below, this section (Clench); econ. hist. (Milton Lilbourne).
41 W.R.O. 212B/5001; 212B/5021; 212B/5045.
42 Ibid. 130/49B/27.
43 Ibid. tithe award; ibid. G 10/505/1; G 10/760/395; O.S. Maps 6", Wilts. XLII (1888 and later edns.).
44 *Interdict Doc.* (Pipe R. Soc. N.S. xxxiv), 17, 28; P.R.O., SC 2/208/16, ct. St. Jas. 27 Edw. III.
45 *Cat. Anct. D.* i, B 1097; P.R.O., E 315/57, rot. 43.
46 *Cart. Cirencester*, ii, p. 453.

Abbot's Wick and Clench by Wick were in use in the earlier 16th century.[47] A tithing was usually called Clench and Wick in the later 16th century,[48] but Wick gradually lost currency as the name of an estate or settlement.[49]

In the Middle Ages four or five farmsteads stood at Clench,[50] which was possibly a linear settlement in the valley, now dry, in which Clench Farm stood in 1996. In the later 18th century and earlier 19th there were three farmsteads and a house on that line, and the road from Marlborough to Milton Lilbourne bypassed three of them on higher ground to the east.[51] All that survives of them is a timber-framed and thatched house of c. 1700 now called Brewers Cottages. The farmhouse at Clench Farm was rebuilt in the 19th century; in 1996 most of the extensive farm buildings were 20th century. North-east of Clench Farm a pair of cottages was built in 1870.[52]

Beside the Marlborough road a 17th-century cottage, timber-framed and thatched and now with walling of red brick, was built 70 m. north of New mill in Milton Lilbourne.[53] Between 1773 and 1814 five more cottages were built beside the road, and a wharf was built on the Kennet & Avon canal;[54] by 1822 the New inn had been opened in one of the cottages, and in 1842 the hamlet bore the name New Mill.[55] In the mid 19th century the inn was moved from a cottage on the east side of the road to a new house on the west side;[56] it was called the Liddiard Arms from the late 1930s[57] and was closed in the late 20th century.[58] Three of the cottages standing in 1814 were among eight dwellings at New Mill in 1996.[59] Between Clench and New Mill a pair of cottages for Broomsgrove farm was built c. 1845.[60]

Beside the road leading from Wootton Rivers to Clench three houses were standing in 1814.[61] Clench House at the parish boundary is a red-brick house of c. 1800; the other two houses have been greatly altered or rebuilt. In the late 20th century large farm buildings and a house were erected beside the road.

On Clench common two cottages standing in the extreme north corner of the parish in 1814,[62] three in 1842, had been replaced by two terraces each of four by 1886.[63] South-east of those a pair of cottages was built in 1955.[64]

FYFIELD. Fyfield's name refers to an assessment of its land, half as extensive as Milton Lilbourne's and held for ½ knight's fee, at 5 hides.[65] The name Milton suggests that Fyfield was settled after Milton Lilbourne and therefore that it was colonized from it.[66] Fyfield village stands along a street, but there is no evidence that the farmsteads or cottages were ever numerous.

Fyfield Manor has stood on the east side of the street since the Middle Ages,[67] and in the 16th century there may have been several farmsteads along the street.[68] The only farmsteads in the village in the early 19th century, and probably from the late 17th or earlier, were two on the west side of the street: in the early 19th century most of the farm buildings were at the northern one; the only farmhouse was at the southern.[69] Between 1842 and c. 1880 the farmhouse was replaced by Fyfield House,[70] a large house of red brick. Most of the farm buildings were demolished c. 1920:[71] a beast stall, timber-framed, thatched, and of the 18th century or earlier, stood on the site of the northern farmstead in 1996. The three cottages standing on the east side of the street in 1809 were standing in 1996 and all were thatched. The two pairs of cottages at the south end of the village and on the west side of the street in 1809[72] were demolished in the 20th century.[73] Apart from Fyfield House no house has been built in the village since 1809. In 1985 the village was designated a conservation area.[74]

Cottages on the waste of Fyfield manor were said in 1651 and later to stand at Milcot water.[75] They presumably stood south of the stream which was probably the boundary of Fyfield and Milcot where a hamlet took the name Milcot Water. In 1809 four cottages stood on the waste in a hollow lane near the stream.[76] The two cottages which stood on the site in 1996 were of timber framing and red brick and were possibly 18th-century. The name of the hamlet was corrupted to Milkhouse Water in the 19th century.[77]

Some of the land on which cottages were built at Little Salisbury was Fyfield manor's; a cottage stood on it in the early 19th century, other buildings later.[78] A trio, later a pair, of cottages north-west of Fyfield Manor was standing in

47 Longleat Mun., Seymour papers, xii, f. 162; P.R.O., SC 6/Hen. VIII/3675, rot. 24.
48 B.L. Add. MS. 37270.
49 Clench was wrongly identified with Clinghill in Bromham, and Wick with Wick Farm in Rowde, in *V.C.H. Wilts.* vii. 181–2, 184.   50 Below, econ. hist. (Clench).
51 *Andrews and Dury, Map* (W.R.S. viii), pl. 12; W.R.O. 2037/141.   52 Date on bldg.
53 Cf. below, econ. hist. (Milton Lilbourne).
54 *Andrews and Dury, Map* (W.R.S. viii), pl. 12; W.R.O. 2037/141.
55 W.R.O., A 1/326/3; ibid. tithe award.
56 Cf. O.S. Map 6", Wilts. XXXVI (1888 edn.).
57 *Kelly's Dir. Wilts.* (1935, 1939).
58 Cf. O.S. Map 1/10,000, SU 16 SE. (1983 edn.).
59 W.R.O. 2037/141.
60 Ibid. 2037/28; cf. below, this section (Milcot).
61 W.R.O. 2037/141.   62 Ibid.
63 Ibid. tithe award; O.S. Map 6", Wilts. XXXVI (1888 edn.).
64 W.R.O., G 10/505/1.
65 Ibid. tithe award; *P.N. Wilts.* (E.P.N.S.), 349; *Bk. of Fees*, ii. 714.
66 Above, this section (Milton Lilbourne).
67 Below, manors (Fyfield).
68 e.g. P.R.O., C 1/1200, no. 37; C 142/254, no. 81; ibid. CP 40/1360, rott. 17–20; ibid. REQ 2/37/59.
69 W.R.O. 135/11; 2037/169, deed, Keylway to Som., 1680; below, econ. hist. (Fyfield).
70 O.S. Map 6", Wilts. XLII (1888 edn.); W.R.O., tithe award.
71 O.S. Maps 6", Wilts. XLII. NW. (1901, 1926 edns.); cf. below, manors (Fyfield).
72 W.R.O. 135/11.
73 cf. O.S. Map 6", Wilts. XLII. NW. (1926 edn.).
74 Inf. from Dept. of Planning and Highways, Co. Hall, Trowbridge.
75 W.R.O. 332/161, leases, Ashe to Whitehart, 1651; Hungerford to Whitehart, 1720.
76 Ibid. 135/11.
77 Ibid. 1392, box 9, rent r. 1796–1817; 2037/146H; O.S. Map 6", Wilts. XLII (1888 edn.).
78 W.R.O. 135/11; ibid. tithe award; above, this section (Milton Lilbourne).

1809 and was part of a hamlet called Little Ann otherwise in Pewsey;[79] the cottages were demolished in 1963.[80]

MILCOT, so called in 1231,[81] apparently had no more than *c*. 275 a.[82] The settlement was not assessed for taxation separately in 1332[83] and did not survive. Two small farmsteads may have been all that stood at Milcot in the 16th century;[84] their sites are obscure, and by the 18th century Milcot's land was referred to as Fyfield's.[85] Broomsgrove Farm was built on it in 1845.[86] A pair of cottages was added there in 1943 and a bungalow *c*. 1950;[87] most of the farm buildings were replaced in the 20th century. A pair of timber-framed cottages,[88] cased in brick and converted to a house, stands south-east of Broomsgrove Farm and near New Mill.

North of the stream which probably divided Milcot and Fyfield and as part of Milkhouse Water a bungalow was built *c*. 1921,[89] a pair of council houses was built in 1935,[90] and a private house was built in the late 20th century.

MANORS AND OTHER ESTATES. As Stogursey (Som.) did, Milton Lilbourne may have belonged to William de Falaise (fl. 1086) and have passed to his daughter Emme, the wife of William de Curci (d. *c*. 1114). Emme's son William de Curci (d. 1125 × 1130) gave *MILTON LILBOURNE* manor for the service of 1 knight. The overlordship apparently passed as part of Stogursey honor to his son William de Curci (d. 1171), to that William's son William (d. 1194), to the youngest William's daughter Alice, the wife of Warin FitzGerald, and in turn to Alice's sons-in-law Fawkes de Breauté and Hugh Neville (d. 1234). Hugh's son John (d. 1246)[91] was overlord in 1242–3.[92] John's heir was his son Hugh (d. *s.p.* 1269), whose brother John (d. 1282) was overlord. That John's heir was his son Hugh (d. 1335), whose son and heir Sir John[93] was overlord in 1349[94] and claimed to be in 1359.[95] About 1353, however, when the tenant

in demesne was a minor, Ralph de Stafford, earl of Stafford, the lord of Wexcombe manor in Great Bedwyn and of Kinwardstone hundred, successfully claimed the overlordship,[96] which thereafter descended with Wexcombe manor and the hundred.[97]

In 1166 Milton Lilbourne manor was held in demesne by Walter de Lillebonne.[98] It passed in the direct line to William,[99] who held it evidently *c*. 1200,[1] and William, who held it in 1236.[2] Walter de Lillebonne held the manor in 1242–3[3] and he or a namesake in 1272[4] and 1278.[5] By 1282 the manor had passed to Walter's heir,[6] presumably William de Lillebonne (fl. 1318), who lived at Milton Lilbourne in 1286.[7] From that William it descended in the direct line to John (d. 1349) and (Sir) John, a minor until *c*. 1363.[8] In 1408 Sir John Lillebonne sold it to Edward Cowdray.[9]

Between 1412 and 1428 the manor passed from Edward Cowdray to Peter Cowdray;[10] it passed thereafter in the direct line to Edward and Peter Cowdray,[11] who held it in 1493.[12] It passed to the younger Peter's daughter Philippe, the wife of Robert Lard and John Strangways, and at her death in 1524 to her son Cowdray Strangways,[13] who held it in 1530.[14] It was acquired, presumably by purchase from Strangways, by Sir William Essex (d. 1548) and descended in the direct line to Thomas[15] (d. 1558), Thomas (d. 1575), and Thomas,[16] the last of whom sold it in portions.[17]

In 1578 the demesne of Milton Lilbourne manor was sold by Thomas Essex to Simon Gunter,[18] a lunatic in 1586,[19] and as Milton Lilbourne manor it passed to Simon's son Nicholas subject to successive beneficial leases to Nicholas's brothers Geoffrey and William.[20] In 1630 Nicholas sold the reversion to Sir Edward Clerk[21] (d. 1639), a master in Chancery. The reversion descended to Sir Edward's son Edward (d. 1664) and to Edward's son Thomas (d. 1714). About 1675 Thomas married Christian Gunter, to whose mother Grace Gunter (fl. 1663) a 90-year lease from 1595 had passed.

79 O.S. Map 6", Wilts. XLII (1888 edn.); W.R.O. 135/11; below, Pewsey, intro. (other settlement).
80 *Pewsey through the Ages*, iii (copy in Wilts. local studies libr., Trowbridge), 2.
81 W.R.O. 9/21/1.
82 Ibid. tithe award.
83 Cf. *Tax List, 1332* (W.R.S. xlv).
84 Longleat Mun., Seymour papers, xii, f. 163; W.R.O. 192/50, ff. 2–3.
85 W.R.O. 2037/138H.
86 Ibid. 2037/14; 2037/28.
87 B.L. Maps, 135, sale cat. of Broomsgrove estate, 1953.
88 Cf. W.R.O. 135/11.
89 Ibid. G 10/760/81.
90 Ibid. G 10/600/1.
91 *Red Bk. Exch.* (Rolls Ser.), i. 225; I. J. Sanders, *Eng. Baronies*, 143; *V.C.H. Som.* vi. 136, where more details are given.
92 *Bk. of Fees*, ii. 714.
93 Sanders, op. cit. 143; *Cal. Inq. p.m.* ii, p. 256; vii, p. 474.
94 *Cal. Inq. p.m.* x, p. 211.
95 *Feet of F.* 1327–77 (W.R.S. xxix), pp. 114–15.
96 *Cal. Inq. p.m.* x, pp. 156–8, 398; above, Kinwardstone hund.; Great Bedwyn, manors (Wexcombe).
97 e.g. *Cal. Inq. p.m.* xiii, p. 182; xvi, p. 161; xvii, pp. 106, 485; xviii, pp. 280–1; *Feud. Aids*, v. 263; P.R.O., C

139/180, no. 59, rot. 12.
98 *Red Bk. Exch.* (Rolls Ser.), i. 225.
99 *Stogursey Chart.* (Som. Rec. Soc. lxi), p. 8.
1 W.R.O. 9/15/3.
2 P.R.O., CP 25/1/250/9, no. 34.
3 *Bk. of Fees*, ii. 714.
4 P.R.O., CP 25/1/252/22, no. 29.
5 *Feet of F.* 1272–1327 (W.R.S. i), p. 10; *Cart. Cirencester*, iii, ed. M. Devine, p. 1057.
6 *Cal. Inq. p.m.* ii, p. 256.
7 Ibid. v, p. 50; *Cal. Close, 1323–7*, 389–90.
8 *Cal. Inq. p.m.* x, pp. 156–8, 211, 398.
9 *Feet of F.* 1377–1509 (W.R.S. xli), p. 60.
10 *Feud. Aids*, v. 263; vi. 537.
11 P.R.O., CP 40/906, rot. 454d.
12 *Cal. Inq. p.m. Hen. VII*, i, pp. 372–3.
13 P.R.O., C 142/41, no. 2.
14 *Extents for Debts* (W.R.S. xxviii), p. 52.
15 P.R.O., C 142/92, no. 120.
16 Ibid. CP 40/1250, Carte rott. 22d.–25; *V.C.H. Berks.* iv. 253.
17 Below, this section.
18 P.R.O., CP 40/1360, Carte rott. 17–20.
19 Ibid. C 142/210, no. 135.
20 Ibid. CP 25/2/241/28 & 29 Eliz. I Mich.; CP 25/2/242/37 & 38 Eliz. I Mich.; *Wilts. Pedigrees* (Harl. Soc. cv/cvi), 78.
21 P.R.O., CP 25/2/508/5 Chas. I Hil.

Thomas was succeeded by his son Edward Clerk,[22] who sold the estate in portions.[23]

In 1740 the northern half of Edward Clerk's estate, thereafter called the manor of *MILTON UNDER THE HILL*, was bought by John Webb (d. 1756). In 1754 Webb gave it to his son John Richmond Webb (d. 1805), who devised the estate, *c.* 275 a., to his sisters Ann Richmond Webb (d. 1808) and Elizabeth Richmond Webb (d. 1823) for life as tenants in common and afterwards to T. G. Villet (d. 1817).[24] In 1825 Villet's executors sold it in portions.[25]

About 1300 William de Lillebonne and his wife Joan were licensed to have an oratory in their manor house at Milton Lilbourne for life.[26] Milton Lilbourne Manor[27] consists of a main block built in the early 18th century and, on the south side of that, of a service wing which may incorporate part of a 17th-century house. In 1740 it was said to be in part newly erected.[28] The main block, of red brick with ashlar dressings, has a seven-bayed east front, the three central bays of which have elliptically headed windows and are capped by a segmental pediment. In 1825, when it was bought by Edmund Somerset, the inside of the house was in poor condition, having been damaged by fire.[29] About then the west front was altered, much of the interior refitted, and the roof reconstructed as a mansard. Later owners included the land agent George Ferris (d. 1929), who lived in it for *c.* 60 years.[30]

Of the land sold in 1825 by Villet's executors *TOTTERIDGE* farm, 170 a., was bought by T. B. Merriman[31] (d. 1867) and passed to his son E. B. Merriman[32] (d. 1915). E. B. Merriman's trustees sold the farm in 1944 to Frank Wells, whose son Mr. D. C. Wells owned it in 1996.[33]

The southern half of Edward Clerk's estate, *MILTON HILL* farm, 546 a. *c.* 1842, was probably sold by him *c.* 1740.[34] It was acquired by Sir John Astley, Bt. (d. 1771),[35] as part of whose estate based at Everleigh, and with an adjoining estate in Pewsey, it descended in the Astley family to Sir Francis Astley-Corbett, Bt. The farm was probably sold by Sir Francis *c.* 1918 to Alfred Cook[36] (d. 1923), who owned it in 1920. It belonged to Cook's nephew Abraham

Pocock from 1923 to 1939[37] or longer, and to A. W. Alexander in 1944.[38] In 1952 it was bought by Charles Sackville-West, Lord Sackville (d. 1962), who was succeeded in turn by his son Edward, Lord Sackville (d. 1965), and Edward's cousin Lionel Sackville-West, Lord Sackville. In 1992 Milton Hill farm was bought from the Sackville-West family by Mr. A. C. Brown, the owner in 1996.[39]

From *c.* 1578, when Thomas Essex apparently broke up the rest of Milton Lilbourne manor by selling the copyholds, several small or medium-sized estates descended separately. By the later 18th century much of their land had been accumulated in several sizeable estates, and some had almost certainly been added to the Rectory estate.[40]

What became *LAWN* farm was sold in 1680 by Thomas Keylway to Sarah, duchess of Somerset[41] (d. 1692), who by her will endowed Froxfield almshouse with it.[42] The almshouse owned the farm, 184 a. *c.* 1842,[43] until 1920. It then sold it to A. E. Jeeves,[44] the owner in 1939.[45] The farm was bought by R. S. Hudson (cr. Viscount Hudson 1952, d. 1957), from whose representatives it was bought in 1958 by J. F. Osborne. In 1996 it belonged with Lower farm to Osborne's son Mr. G. E. R. Osborne.[46]

Michael Ewen (d. 1782), clerk of the peace for Somerset and Wiltshire, held an estate, possibly from 1753 or earlier, and devised it for sale. In 1784 his executor sold it to William Coles[47] (d. 1798),[48] who bought another estate *c.* 1791. Coles devised the two estates to his wife Susanna (d. 1825) and after to John Coles. About 1826 they were acquired, presumably by purchase, by Thomas White.[49] About 1842 White held 246 a. in Milton Lilbourne.[50] George Duke (d. 1757) bought an estate which he devised to his wife Mary and, after her death, to his children Frances, Selenhah, and Edward.[51] In 1786 the estate belonged to Nathaniel Weekes, who apparently acquired it *c.* 1780 and sold it to William Coles *c.* 1791.[52] J. W. Stevens (d. 1787) held an estate which he devised to his wife Elizabeth. At her death in 1842 Elizabeth Stevens held 110 a. in Milton Lilbourne.[53] The lands of Ewen's, Duke's, and Stevens's estates

22 P.R.O., C 142/578, no. 23; ibid. CP 25/2/242/37 & 38 Eliz. I Mich.; *W.N. & Q.* viii. 95; W.R.O. 212B/4973; W.A.S. Libr., Wilts. Misc. MSS., vol. i, no. 6.
23 Below, this section.
24 *Topog. and Geneal.* iii. 350; W.R.O. 212B/4973; 212B/5045; 348/2, no. 28.
25 W.R.O. 212B/4973; 2863/1.
26 *Cart. Cirencester*, iii, pp. 1057–8.
27 Above, plate 23.   28 W.R.O. 212B/4973.
29 Ibid. 212B/5095; 2863/1.
30 *W.A.M.* xlv. 104–5; G. Ferris, *Hist. Milton Lilbourne* (copy in Wilts. local studies libr., Trowbridge), 4.
31 W.R.O. 212B/5095; 2863/1.
32 Princ. Regy. Fam. Div., will of T. B. Merriman, 1867.
33 Ibid. will of E. B. Merriman, 1915; inf. from Mrs. F. Price, Totteridge Farm.
34 W.R.O. 212B/4973; ibid. tithe award.
35 Ibid. 130/49B/38.
36 *V.C.H. Wilts.* xi. 137–8; below, Pewsey, manor [Kepnal and Southcott]; cf. W.R.O., tithe award; ibid. Inland Revenue, val. reg. 58.
37 *Pewsey through the Ages*, iii. 19, 23; *Kelly's Dir. Wilts.* (1939); W.R.O., G 10/500/62–3.
38 W.R.O., G 10/760/395–6.

39 Inf. from Mrs. P. Brown, Manor Ho. Farm, Bishop's Cannings.
40 e.g. P.R.O., C 142/281, no. 37; C 142/410, no. 22; ibid. CP 40/1360, Carte rott. 17–20; W.R.O. 149/104/2; below, this section.
41 W.R.O. 2037/169, deed, Keylway to Som., 1680.
42 *Endowed Char. Wilts.* (S. Div.), 980; for Sarah and Froxfield almshouse, above, Froxfield, charities.
43 W.R.O., tithe award.
44 Ibid. 2037/16.
45 *Kelly's Dir. Wilts.* (1939).
46 *Who Was Who, 1951–60*, 554; inf. from Mr. G. E. R. Osborne, Lawn Farm; below, this section (Lower).
47 *V.C.H. Wilts.* v. 174; *W.A.M.* iii. 132; W.R.O. 212B/4974.
48 W.R.O., bishop's transcripts, bdle. 3.
49 Ibid. A 1/345/299; ibid. 942/1; P.R.O., PROB 11/1303, f. 135.
50 W.R.O., tithe award.
51 *Musgrave's Obit.* ii (Harl. Soc. xlv), 224; P.R.O., PROB 11/828, f. 263 and v.
52 W.R.O., A 1/345/299; ibid. EA/20.
53 Ibid. 330/3, marriage settlement, 1818; deed, 1854; ibid. EA/20; ibid. tithe award.

south of the village, c. 200 a., were bought from Lovegrove Waldron by Daniel Haines in 1863. In 1879 Haines sold his estate, 217 a.,[54] as LOWER (later Sunnylands) farm apparently to one of Waldron's sons. It belonged to a Mr. Waldron until 1899 or later, and in 1905 to J. S. Haines[55] (d. 1937), who added the land of the Rectory estate south of the village and land in Fyfield to it. Lower farm descended to J. S. Haines's son J. S. Haines,[56] who in 1964 sold it to Mrs. B. Osborne. In 1996 it belonged with Lawn farm, a total of 1,100 a., to Mrs. Osborne's son Mr. G. E. R. Osborne.[57] Lower Farm is a red-brick house built by Daniel Haines c. 1863;[58] an east wing was added in the 20th century and extensive gardens were developed around the house from 1990.[59]

An estate given by William de Curci (d. 1125 × 1130) for ⅕ knight's fee and held c. 1166 by Goidlanus[60] may have been the estate in Milton Lilbourne held in 1199 by Peter son of Fulcher.[61] In 1242–3 John Fulcher held Peter's estate as ⅕ knight's fee; the overlord was Walter Marshal, earl of Pembroke.[62] The estate apparently passed to Sir Richard of Havering (d. c. 1267),[63] whose estate in Milton Lilbourne was the later MILTON HAVERING manor. The manor may have belonged to Robert Hungerford (d. 1352) in the 1320s[64] and to Walter Hungerford in 1349.[65] In 1368 Thomas Hungerford apparently gave it to Sir John de Lillebonne in an exchange.[66] From then until c. 1578 the manor passed with Milton Lilbourne manor,[67] and by 1372 Ralph, earl of Stafford, had established a claim to be overlord.[68] Thomas Essex sold a farm representing the manor to William Jones (d. 1610), probably c. 1578.[69] The estate passed with the Rectory estate to John Jones (d. 1611) and William Jones (d. 1632), who apparently sold it.[70] In 1663 it belonged to Edward Brown (d. 1693 or 1694), who devised it to his daughters Mary and Grace Brown.[71] It was held by Grace (fl. 1728) and her husband Edward Naish[72] (fl. 1736)[73] and by 1773 had descended to William Naish[74] (d. 1790), who devised it in trust for

sale.[75] By 1794 the estate had been bought by Edmund Somerset[76] (d. 1809), whose son Edmund (d. 1858) held 123 a. in Milton Lilbourne c. 1842.[77] The estate had been broken up by 1869.[78] The principal house on it c. 1842, Havering House, in 1996 incorporated a small house possibly of the late 17th century. In the mid 18th century a house of red brick with ashlar dressings and a principal north front of five bays was built to adjoin the small house on the north-west. In the early 20th century and to designs by Sir Herbert Baker[79] the south front of the enlarged house was extended westwards by a three-bayed block in 18th-century style and eastwards by a low range in the style of the original house. Further additions were made to the east later in the 20th century. West of the house an 18th-century walled garden was converted to an entrance court, and in 1996 the house stood in extensive formal gardens.

In 1198 Michael of Milton held a small estate in Milton Lilbourne by serjeanty;[80] William Michael or Michel held it 1210 × 1217,[81] Richard Michel in 1236.[82] The service was to keep two wolf hounds for the king.[83] John Michel held MICHEL'S, 2 yardlands, in 1275 and 1289.[84] At the death of a John Michel in 1319 the estate, then held for 13d. a year, passed to his son William[85] (d. 1330), and it descended in the direct line to Robert[86] (d. 1348), Simon[87] (d. 1401), and Thomas, a minor,[88] who was given seisin in 1417.[89] The estate may have belonged to a Thomas Michel in 1460.[90] It has not been traced further.

From 1321 or earlier the lord of Easton Druce manor in Easton held land in Milton Lilbourne.[91] From c. 1349 to the Dissolution ½ yardland in Milton Lilbourne belonged to Easton priory as part of that manor.[92]

In 1086 the estate called Wick held c. 1210 by Battle abbey may have been part of the king's large estate called Wootton,[93] and it was that later reputed CLENCH manor.[94] In the 13th century it lay in the abbey's liberty of Bromham[95]

54 Ibid. 374/130/77; ibid. EA/20; ibid. tithe award.
55 Ibid. 672/1; V.C.H. Wilts. xii. 31.
56 Wilts. Gaz. 3 June 1937; W.R.O., Inland Revenue, val. reg. 58 and map 42; ibid. tithe award; below, this section (Fyfield; Rectory).
57 Inf. from Mr. Osborne; above, this section (Lawn).
58 Ferris, Milton Lilbourne, 2.
59 Inf. from Mrs. B. Agate, Lower Farm.
60 Red Bk. Exch. (Rolls Ser.), i. 225; cf. above, this section (Milton Lilbourne).
61 Feet of F. 1198–9 (Pipe R. Soc. xxiv), p. 136.
62 Bk. of Fees, ii. 711, 745.
63 Cal. Inq. p.m. i, p. 203.
64 Ibid. x, p. 19; Feet of F. 1272–1327 (W.R.S. i), p. 103; Cal. Pat. 1327–30, 326.
65 P.R.O., C 143/293, no. 13.
66 Cal. Pat. 1367–70, 106.
67 Above, this section (Milton Lilbourne); cf. Feet of F. 1377–1509 (W.R.S. xli), p. 60; P.R.O., CP 40/1360, Carte rott. 17–20.
68 Cal. Inq. p.m. xiii, p. 182.
69 P.R.O., C 142/680, no. 30; ibid. CP 40/1360, Carte rott. 17–20.
70 Ibid. C 142/325, no. 187; Wilts. Inq. p.m. 1625–49 (Index Libr.), 120–4; below, this section (Rectory).
71 W.A.S. Libr., Wilts. Misc. MSS., vol. i, no. 6; W.R.O. 865/49, will of Edw. Brown.
72 W.R.O. 865/82.

73 Q. Sess. 1736 (W.R.S. xi), p. 142.
74 W.R.O. 332/276, poor rate, 1773.
75 Ibid. 616/3; ibid. wills, archd. Wilts., Wm. Naish, 1793.
76 Ibid. A 1/345/299.
77 Ibid. 2863/1; ibid. tithe award.
78 Princ. Regy. Fam. Div., will of John Somerset, 1892.
79 Dept. of Environment, list of bldgs. of hist. interest (1987).
80 Bk. of Fees, i. 12.
81 Red Bk. Exch. (Rolls Ser.), ii. 462, 487.
82 Bk. of Fees, i. 586.
83 J. H. Round, King's Serjeants, 295–6.
84 Rot. Hund. (Rec. Com.), ii (1), 259; P.R.O., JUST 1/1006, rot. 51.　　85 Cal. Inq. p.m. vi, p. 130.
86 Ibid. vii, p. 200.
87 Ibid. xi, p. 285.
88 Ibid. xviii, p. 231; xix, p. 55; xx, p. 98.
89 Cal. Fine R. 1413–22, 183.
90 Cal. Pat. 1452–61, 622.
91 Cat. Anct. D. iii, A 5826.
92 P.R.O., C 143/293, no. 13; Longleat Mun., Seymour papers, xii, ff. 310v.–311; above, Easton, manors (Easton Druce).
93 Interdict Doc. (Pipe R. Soc. N.S. xxxiv), 17; below, Wootton Rivers, manors.
94 For the identification, above, intro. (Clench).
95 Below, local govt.

and the abbey held it until the Dissolution. In 1538 Clench manor was granted by the king to Sir Edward Baynton[96] (d. 1544), from whom it passed with Bromham Battle manor in turn to his sons Andrew[97] (d. 1566) and Sir Edward[98] (d. 1593). From 1593 it descended in the direct line to Sir Henry (d. 1616), Sir Edward (d. 1657), Sir Edward (d. 1679), Henry (d. 1691), and John (d. *s.p.* 1716). John's heir was his sister Anne Rolt (d. 1734), whose heir was her son Edward, from 1762 Sir Edward Baynton-Rolt, Bt. (d. 1800). In 1803 Sir Edward's son Sir Andrew Baynton-Rolt, Bt., sold Clench manor to Thomas Bruce, earl of Ailesbury (d. 1814).[99] After an exchange of lands and inclosure of downland Thomas's son Charles Brudenell-Bruce, marquess of Ailesbury, owned 516 a. at Clench *c.* 1842.[1] That land descended in the Brudenell-Bruce family with Tottenham House in Great Bedwyn.[2] In 1921 George Brudenell-Bruce, marquess of Ailesbury, sold Clench farm, 156 a., to T. J. Dixon;[3] *c.* 1960 that land was bought by R. J. Butler (d. 1983), and in 1996 it belonged to his son Mr. R. C. Butler.[4] In 1939 Lord Ailesbury leased 110 a., most of Clench common, to the Forestry Commission for 999 years,[5] and he or a successor as owner of Tottenham House later sold the reversion of *c.* 95 a. of that land to the Crown. In 1950 Lord Ailesbury sold *c.* 250 a. at Clench to the Crown; in 1996 the Crown owned *c.* 345 a. there, *c.* 330 a. of it as part of East Wick farm based in Wootton Rivers parish.[6]

A freehold in Clench, 2 yardlands *c.* 1400,[7] was held by Vincent of Wick in the later 13th century[8] and descended in the Vynz family. It was held by John Vynz in 1329–30,[9] by him or a namesake in 1371–2,[10] and by a second or third John Vynz (d. *c.* 1400), who left as heir a son William.[11] John Vynz held it in 1419,[12] Alice Vynz in 1428,[13] and John Vynz in 1430.[14] By 1451 it had been acquired, presumably by purchase, by Sir John Seymour (d. 1464). Sir John also held ½ yardland in Clench which probably belonged to his grandfather Sir William Sturmy (d. 1427) and in the later 13th century belonged to Adam Robe.[15] Sir John's two holdings were presumably the two in Clench which in 1536 were part of Huish manor, then held by Sir

John's great-great-grandson Edward Seymour, Viscount Beauchamp (cr. earl of Hertford 1537, duke of Somerset 1547, d. 1552).[16] As part of Huish manor they descended in the Seymour family with Tottenham Lodge in Great Bedwyn;[17] they passed like Pewsey manor to Sarah, duchess of Somerset (d. 1692), who devised them to endow Froxfield almshouse.[18] About 1842, after the exchange of lands and inclosure, the almshouse owned 113 a. in Clench adjoining its land of Milcot.[19] The land was afterwards part of Broomsgrove farm.[20]

FYFIELD, like Milton Lilbourne, may have belonged to William de Falaise (fl. 1086) and have descended to his grandson William de Curci (d. 1125 × 1130).[21] It may have been an estate given by William for ½ knight's fee,[22] and the overlordship apparently descended like that of Milton Lilbourne manor to Alice de Curci. In 1242–3 Alice's daughter Margaret (d. 1252), the relict of Baldwin de Reviers and of Fawkes de Breauté, and Margaret's son Baldwin de Reviers, earl of Devon and lord of the Isle of Wight (d. 1245), were overlords; Isabel Mortimer held of Baldwin as a mesne lord.[23] The overlordship presumably passed to Baldwin's son Baldwin, earl of Devon (d. 1262), to his daughter Isabel de Forz, countess of Aumale and of Devon, and on Isabel's death in 1293 to Warin de Lisle (d. 1296), one of her heirs.[24] It was probably held by Warin's grandson John Lisle, Lord Lisle (d. 1355), and in 1368 was surrendered to the king by John's son Robert, Lord Lisle.[25] Presumably as part of the lordship of the Isle of Wight which was granted to him in 1385, William de Montagu, earl of Salisbury (d. 1397), held the overlordship,[26] and, despite a claim that it was held by Roger Mortimer, earl of March (d. 1398), a descendant of Isabel Mortimer,[27] it descended with the earldom of Salisbury.[28]

Warin of Fyfield possibly held Fyfield manor *c.* 1200.[29] His son William, otherwise called William Warren, held it for ½ knight's fee in 1235–6 and 1255.[30] Thomas Warren may have held it in 1337,[31] Edmund Warren in 1390.[32] Richard Warren (fl. 1454) held the manor in 1428;[33] Thomas Warren held it in 1474. The manor descended in the direct line from Thomas

96 P.R.O., C 66/679, mm. 41–2.
97 Ibid. C 142/72, no. 109.
98 *V.C.H. Wilts.* vii. 180–1, where there are more details for the period 1545–54.
99 Burke, *Commoners* (1833–8), iv. 685–6; *Complete Peerage*, i. 63; W.R.O. 9/21/16.
1 W.R.O. 9/21/19; 2037/140; ibid. tithe award.
2 Above, Great Bedwyn, manors (Tottenham).
3 W.A.S. Libr., sale cat. xvi, no. 8.
4 Inf. from Mr. R. C. Butler, E. Wick Farm, Wootton Rivers.
5 W.R.O. 9/33/5.
6 Inf. from the agent for the Crown Estate Com., 42 High Street, Marlborough.
7 P.R.O., SC 2/208/19, rott. 2–3.
8 Ibid. E 315/57, rot. 43.
9 *Cal. Inq. p.m.* vii, pp. 173–4.
10 P.R.O., SC 2/208/16.
11 Ibid. SC 2/208/19, rott. 2–3.
12 Ibid. SC 2/208/23.
13 Ibid. SC 2/208/24.
14 Ibid. E 315/56, f. 94.
15 Ibid.; ibid. E 315/57, rot. 43; ibid. SC 2/208/26; for Sturmy and the Seymours, above, Burbage, manors (Bur-

bage Sturmy).
16 Longleat Mun., Seymour papers, xii, ff. 162–3.
17 *V.C.H. Wilts.* x. 79; above, Great Bedwyn, manors (Tottenham).
18 *Endowed Char. Wilts.* (S. Div.), 980; below, Pewsey, manor (Pewsey).
19 W.R.O., tithe award; cf. below, this section (Milcot).
20 W.R.O. 2037/155; below, this section (Broomsgrove).
21 Above, this section (Milton Lilbourne).
22 *Red Bk. Exch.* (Rolls Ser.), i. 225.
23 Above, this section (Milton Lilbourne); *Bk. of Fees*, ii. 714, 745; Sanders, *Eng. Baronies*, 143–4; *Complete Peerage*, iv. 318–19.
24 *Complete Peerage*, iv. 319–23; viii. 71.
25 Ibid. viii. 71–7; *Cal. Close*, 1364–8, 498.
26 *Cal. Pat.* 1385–9, 16; *Cal. Inq. p.m.* xvii, p. 320.
27 *Cal. Inq. p.m.* xvii, p. 455; *Complete Peerage*, viii. 433–50; ix. 273–84.
28 e.g. *Cal. Inq. p.m.* xix, p. 233; xx, p. 72.
29 W.R.O. 9/15/3.
30 *Bk. of Fees*, i. 423; ii. 714, 745; *Close R.* 1254–6, 116.
31 *Cal. Inq. p.m.* xi, p. 126.
32 *Cal. Close*, 1389–92, 165.
33 *Feud. Aids*, v. 263; W.R.O. 9/6/756.

(d. 1493) to John[34] (d. 1527), John[35] (d. c. 1559), Anthony (d. by 1562), and William Warren (d. 1599). From 1562 or earlier it was held by Anthony's relict Alice, the wife of Thomas Michelborne (d. 1582). William Warren devised it to his sister Mary, the wife of Richard Venner,[36] and in 1613 Richard Warren, presumably Venner, sold it to Henry Cusse.[37]

Cusse mortgaged Fyfield manor to James Ashe and in 1648 sold it to James's son John. From John Ashe (d. by 1665) the manor descended in the direct line to James (d. 1671) and John, who sold it to Edward Ashe in 1682. In 1687 Edward conveyed it to his brother William Ashe of Heytesbury, and in 1688 Edward and William together sold it to Edmund Hungerford.[38]

The manor passed from Hungerford (d. 1713) to his son Henry (d. 1750). Under Henry's will it was held for life in turn by his wife Elizabeth (d. 1756) and his nephew Wadham Wyndham (d. 1768) and passed in turn to Wadham's son-in-law Charles Penruddocke (d. 1788) and Charles's son J. H. Penruddocke (d. s.p. 1841),[39] who at his death owned c. 629 a. in Fyfield.[40] Penruddocke's heir was his grandnephew Charles Penruddocke (d. 1899), whose son Charles[41] sold the manor in 1919.[42]

Fyfield Manor and 36 a. were bought in 1919 by W. MacC. Kirkpatrick,[43] who in 1924 sold the house and 107 a. to Louise Bishop,[44] the owner until c. 1942. From c. 1942 to 1957 the house belonged to Lord Hudson (d. 1957),[45] from 1958 to 1966 to Sir Anthony Eden (cr. earl of Avon 1961), and from 1966 to 1977 to the Hon. Charles Morrison.[46] In 1979 it was bought by Mr. D. K. Newbigging, in 1996 the owner of the house and c. 60 a.[47] Fyfield Manor[48] has external walls of red brick and is H-shaped in plan; its main range lies east–west and the north wings are longer than the south. Near the centre of the main range, and apparently surviving in situ from a late-medieval open hall, there is part of a post with a moulded capital on a pilaster below a mortice for a brace. At the east end of the range the two banks of purlins are moulded and 16th-century, but it is unclear whether they are contemporary with or later than the late-medieval post. There was a chapel in the house in 1577.[49] In the early 17th century the house was largely rebuilt and greatly enlarged: the west end of the main range, the north-west wing, the turret which forms the south-west wing, and the whole eastern cross wing are apparently of that date, and the principal south front was then encased with, or rebuilt in, brick and given a moulded string, a moulded cornice, and a row of brick gables which were probably decoratively shaped. In 1996 many features inside the house, including the staircase, survived from the early 17th century. In the 18th century sashed windows and a pedimented doorcase were made in the south front and the house was partly refitted; in the 19th century the gables were altered and bargeboards were added to them, and the house was reroofed with grey slate. In 1924 a narrow two-storeyed extension along the north front of the main range was built to improve access between the rooms of the house and to provide new service rooms.[50] A bath house, possibly associated with Fyfield Manor, had been built a little north of Milcot water by 1752; it stood very near the line of the Kennet & Avon canal[51] and was demolished probably c. 1806–7 when the canal was built.[52]

Fyfield farm, 568 a., was bought in 1919 by A. J. Hosier,[53] who sold it soon afterwards. By 1923 the southernmost 100 a. had been added to Milton Hill farm, a part of which it remained in 1996.[54] The rest of Fyfield farm, c. 450 a., was bought by F. Allen, who sold it in portions in 1921. A. J. Hosier bought 225 a. south of the village[55] and by 1922 had sold it to J. S. Haines. Since 1922 that land has been part of Lower farm, Milton Lilbourne.[56]

In the 16th century land in Fyfield was held customarily as part of Milton Lilbourne manor.[57] In 1578 it was in two copyholds which were apparently among the parts of the manor sold about then.[58] Another holding, a freehold of 3 yardlands, descended from John Benger (d. c. 1560) to his son William (d. 1571) and to William's son John (d. 1609).[59] All those three holdings were acquired by Thomas Keylway, who in 1680 sold his land in Fyfield, with what became Lawn farm in Milton Lilbourne, to Sarah, duchess of Somerset[60] (d. 1692). The duchess devised the land to endow Froxfield almshouse,[61] which, after land was given away by exchange at inclosure in 1823,[62] owned c. 95 a. at Fyfield. That land lay north of the village and adjoined the almshouse's land in Milcot:[63] it was afterwards part of Broomsgrove farm.[64]

34 Cal. Inq. p.m. Hen. VII, i, pp. 372–3.
35 P.R.O., C 142/46, no. 91.
36 Ibid. C 2/Eliz. I/B 9/46; C 2/Eliz. I/F 8/62; C 2/Eliz. I/W 26/35; C 3/122/8; ibid. PROB 11/93, ff. 327–328v.
37 Ibid. CP 25/2/370/10 Jas. I Trin.; CP 25/2/370/11 Jas. I Mich.
38 Hist. Parl., Commons, 1660–90, i. 555; W.R.O. 549/35–6.
39 Burke, Land. Gent. (1937), 1789–90; Topog. and Geneal. iii. 350–1; W.R.O. 332/168; 332/171B.
40 W.R.O., tithe award.
41 Burke, Land. Gent. (1937), 1790.
42 W.A.S. Libr., sale cat. xv, no. 8.
43 Wilts. Gaz. 25 Sept. 1919.
44 W.A.M. xlv. 274–5; W.R.O. 1627/1.
45 Country Life, 21 Sept. 1961; Who Was Who, 1951–60, 554; Wilts. Cuttings, xxi. 88; W.R.O., G 10/506/2.
46 Who Was Who, 1971–80, 32; Wilts. Cuttings, xxi. 195; xxviii. 142, 359.
47 Inf. from Mrs. C. Newbigging, Fyfield Manor.

48 Above, plate 22.   49 P.R.O., REQ 2/206/64.
50 Country Life, 30 Aug. 1930.
51 W.R.O. 2037/138H.
52 Cf. ibid. 135/11.
53 Wilts. Gaz. 25 Sept. 1919; W.A.M. xlvii. 435.
54 W.R.O., G 10/500/63; inf. from Mrs. P. Brown, Manor Ho. Farm, Bishop's Cannings.
55 W.A.S. Libr., sale cat. xvi, no. 4.
56 W.R.O., G 10/500/62; inf. from Mr. G. E. R. Osborne, Lawn Farm; above, this section (Lower).
57 P.R.O., CP 40/1250, Carte rott. 22d.–25.
58 Ibid. CP 40/1360, Carte rott. 17–20; above, this section (Milton Lilbourne).
59 P.R.O., C 3/11/72; C 142/254, no. 81; W.R.O. 493/1.
60 W.R.O. 332/286, survey, 1711; 2037/169, deed, Keylway to Som., 1680; above, this section (Lawn).
61 Endowed Char. Wilts. (S. Div.), 980.
62 W.R.O., EA/119.
63 Ibid. tithe award.
64 Below, this section (Broomsgrove).

King John gave land in *MILCOT* to Geoffrey de Hanville, who held it in 1231.[65] Holdings there were later parts of the manors of Fyfield,[66] Huish,[67] and Milton Lilbourne.[68] Those of Huish manor, like holdings in Clench, and those of Milton Lilbourne manor, like holdings in Milton Lilbourne and Fyfield, were assigned to Froxfield almshouse.[69] After 1823, when land was acquired at inclosure and by exchange from the lord of Fyfield manor, the almshouse owned 221 a. at Milcot, nearly all the land apart from Broomsgrove wood.[70] As *BROOMSGROVE* farm, 434 a. including land of Clench and Fyfield and, from 1877, including Broomsgrove wood, it sold it in 1920 to H. D. Cole[71] (d. 1953). Cole's son R. L. Cole sold the farm in 1953 to Andrew Veitch, whose son J. W. Veitch sold it in 1983 to Mr. Derek Baxter, the owner in 1996.[72]

The land of Milcot in Fyfield manor *c.* 1842 was mainly Broomsgrove wood, 41 a.[73] The wood was given to Froxfield almshouse in exchange for land at Fyfield in 1877.[74]

Cirencester abbey (Glos.) appropriated Milton Lilbourne church, probably before 1195.[75] The *RECTORY* estate, consisting of great tithes and of land sometimes called *MILTON AB-BOT'S* manor, passed from the abbey to the Crown at the Dissolution.[76] In 1560 the land was granted to Richard Oakham and Richard Bittenson,[77] and in 1588 the tithes were granted to Edward Downing and Miles Dodding.[78] By 1591 William Jones (d. 1610) had acquired the whole estate, which descended in the direct line to John[79] (d. 1611), William[80] (d. 1632), and John.[81] In 1624 William Jones sold the tithes of Fyfield and Milcot, and by 1628 he had sold those of Clench.[82] In 1640 John Jones sold the rest of the estate to Thomas Mitchell (will proved 1678). Mitchell's estate, to which a holding almost certainly a former copyhold of Milton Lilbourne manor was added in 1648, passed in turn to his sons Thomas (d. by 1695) and John. In 1720 John sold it to Richard Stacey,[83] after whose death in 1740 it was held by his relict Anne.[84] It was acquired, almost certainly before 1761, by James Pulse (d. 1770),[85] who devised it to his son

Philip (d. 1824). From Philip the estate passed to his nephew S. E. Scroggs,[86] who *c.* 1842, when his tithes from Milton Lilbourne were commuted for a rent charge of £374, owned 242 a. there.[87] Scroggs (d. 1845) devised the estate in trust for his children.[88] By 1896 the rent charge had passed to his daughters Mary Scroggs (d. 1900), who held seven ninths of it, and Sibyl Dance (d. 1912). Mary devised her portion to Sibyl for life and afterwards to Milton Lilbourne vicarage as an endowment. Sibyl's portion descended to her daughter Mary Dance.[89] By the 1860s S. E. Scroggs's land had been bought by John Somerset, after whose death in 1892 it passed to Edward Somerset.[90] Between 1899 and 1905 *c.* 103 a. south of Milton Lilbourne village was bought by J. S. Haines and added to Lower farm, and *c.* 120 a. east of the village was bought by Mark Jeans[91] (d. 1924). As *KING HALL* farm, 156 a. in 1930, Jeans's land passed to his son G. M. Jeans. The later descent of the farm, which was offered for sale in 1930,[92] 1972, and *c.* 1989,[93] has not been traced. King Hall, a large Italianate house of brick, was built on the estate by John Somerset in the 1860s.[94]

The tithes of Clench were bought between 1611 and 1628 by Walter Bailey, who in 1628 sold them to his brother Thomas, rector of Manningford Bruce. In 1652 Thomas sold them to Richard Stephens, vicar of Stanton St. Bernard, who in 1657 settled them on the marriage of his son George (d. *s.p.* a widower and intestate *c.* 1672). The tithes were bought from George's administrators by his brother Nathaniel (d. 1678), a puritan divine, and they passed to Nathaniel's son Nathaniel. In 1679 Nathaniel Stephens sold the tithes to Christopher Willoughby, who in 1680 gave them to trustees for charitable purposes, including the provision of pensions for poor parishioners of Bishopstone in Ramsbury hundred.[95] The tithes were held by the trustees *c.* 1842, when they were commuted for a rent charge of £110.[96]

The tithes of Fyfield and Milcot were bought in 1624 by Henry Cusse.[97] They descended with Fyfield manor, and *c.* 1842 were commuted for a rent charge of £260.[98]

65   W.R.O. 9/21/1.
66   Ibid. 332/161, lease, Ashe to Whitehart, 1651; 549/35; 2037/138H.
67   Ibid. 192/50, ff. 2–3; Longleat Mun., Seymour papers, xii, f. 163.
68   P.R.O., CP 40/1360, Carte rott. 17–20.
69   Above, this section (Milton Lilbourne; Clench; Fyfield).
70   W.R.O., EA/119; ibid. tithe award.
71   Ibid. 2037/15, pp. 64, 70; 2037/16, p. 107; 2037/155.
72   Ibid. 942/15; B.L. Maps, 135, sale cat. of Broomsgrove estate, 1953; inf. from Mr. Derek Baxter, Broomsgrove Farm.
73   W.R.O., tithe award.
74   Ibid. 2037/15, pp. 64, 70.
75   *Cart. Cirencester*, i, ed. C. D. Ross, p. 154, ii, p. 433.
76   P.R.O., SC 6/Hen. VIII/1240, rot. 62; for the vicar's portion, below, church.
77   *Cal. Pat.* 1558–60, 463; P.R.O., E 318/46/2452, rot. 1.   78   P.R.O., C 66/1318, m. 6.
79   Ibid. C 142/680, no. 30; ibid. CP 25/2/241/33 Eliz. I Hil.
80   Ibid. C 142/325, no. 187.
81   *Wilts. Inq. p.m.* 1625–49 (Index Libr.), 120–4.
82   Below, this section.
83   W.R.O. 212B/5015; ibid. wills, archd. Wilts., Thomas

Mitchell, 1682.
84   P.R.O., PROB 11/702, f. 85v.
85   Phillipps, *Wilts. Inst.* ii. 79; *Musgrave's Obit.* v (Harl. Soc. xlviii), 94.
86   P.R.O., PROB 11/963, f. 222; W.R.O. 627/7; ibid. A 1/345/299.
87   W.R.O., tithe award.
88   *Misc. Geneal. et Her.* (5th ser.), iii. 76; P.R.O., PROB 11/2020, ff. 125–128v.
89   *Endowed Char. Wilts.* (S. Div.), 339; W.R.O. 672/1; Ch. Com. file 53775/1; ibid. file, NB 34/263B.
90   Princ. Regy. Fam. Div., will of John Somerset, 1892.
91   W.R.O. 672/1; ibid. tithe award; ibid. Inland Revenue, val. reg. 58; above, this section (Lower).
92   Ibid. G 10/500/64; *Wilts. Gaz.* 13 Mar. 1924; W.A.S. Libr., sale cat. xx, no. 17.
93   Wilts. Cuttings, xxvii. 102; W.A.S. Libr., sale cat. xlvii, no. 45.
94   Ferris, *Milton Lilbourne*, 2; Princ. Regy. Fam. Div., will of John Somerset, 1892.
95   *V.C.H. Wilts.* x. 117, 153–4; xii. 11; P.R.O., C 142/325, no. 187; W.R.O. 1364/25; ibid. wills, archd. Wilts., Geo. Stephens, 1672.
96   W.R.O., tithe award.
97   Ibid. 332/276, case respecting Fyfield tithes.
98   Ibid. tithe award; above, this section (Fyfield).

ECONOMIC HISTORY. MILTON LILBOURNE. By the 16th century Milton Lilbourne's open arable had been divided into six fields. East Sands field and West Sands field lay on greensand east, west, and a little south of the village; the present Burbage–Pewsey road may mark their north boundary. Between those fields and the scarp of Salisbury Plain, East Clay field and West Clay field lay on the Lower Chalk, and further south East Hill field and West Hill field lay on the downland. The fields were shared among the demesnes of Milton Lilbourne manor, Havering manor, and the Rectory estate, customary tenants of Milton Lilbourne manor and the Rectory estate, a small freehold, and the vicar's glebe. In addition to land in the open fields the demesne of Milton Lilbourne manor included, north of the sands fields and probably north of Deane Water, a mainly several pasture called Totteridge for cattle and, south of the hill fields, an extensive and apparently mainly several rough pasture for sheep;[99] both pastures were probably several from the 13th century[1] or earlier. Part of the downland pasture may have been assigned to the parish church when it was built and as Parsonage down was a several part of the Rectory estate.[2] The other holdings included rights to use an extensive common pasture for sheep, which evidently lay between Totteridge and the open fields, and a Cow down,[3] presumably the east–west scarp, called Great down and Little down in the 18th century, between the clay fields and the hill fields. Hockham bottom, 12 a., was also downland used in common,[4] and there were small areas of common meadow probably beside the stream south of the village.[5] In 1578 Havering farm included nominally 123 a. in the open fields, the seven copyholds of Milton Lilbourne manor nominally 287 a. At 80 to each yardland sheep stints were generous. By 1578 small areas of land, presumably near the village, had been inclosed, and a holding of 2 yardlands which in the earlier 17th century included 10 a. of inclosed meadows, nominally 64 a. in the open fields, and feeding in common for 6 horses, 12 cows, and 160 sheep was typical.[6]

The commonable land in the north half of Milton Lilbourne was inclosed in the 17th century or early 18th. By the earlier 17th century the common sheep pasture, probably c. 300 a., had been divided into two, and in 1686–7 both parts were inclosed, divided, and allotted;[7] by 1720 the two sands fields and part of the two clay fields had been inclosed. A farm which in 1680 included nominally 116 a. in the open fields, 13 a. of inclosed meadows, and 25 a. of inclosed

pasture, in 1720 included nominally 62 a. in the open fields and 112 a. in closes, of which 27 a. was former common pasture.[8]

By the earlier 18th century the demesne of Milton Lilbourne manor had been divided into three farms. About 1600 Totteridge was overgrown with briars: by 1613 it had been divided and some of the fields had been ploughed and sowed with corn.[9] In 1688 a right to feed eight beasts in Totteridge with the demesne cattle in summer, which had been given in 1236 or earlier, was bought by the lord of the manor,[10] and in the earlier 18th century the land, inclosed, several, and with farm buildings standing on it, was being leased as a separate farm.[11] Shortly before 1724 a farmstead was built on the demesne sheep pasture at the south end of Milton Lilbourne: as Milton Hill Farm it was held with that pasture, part of which was to be ploughed, and the demesne arable in the two hill fields.[12] Presumably to give Milton Hill farm pasture for cattle, in 1729–30 the lord of the manor acquired the right to feed 38 beasts on Cow down in exchange for nominally 11 a. in East Clay field and 1 a. in West Clay field.[13] Between Totteridge farm and Milton Hill farm the remaining demesne was leased as Home farm. In 1740 Totteridge farm, 157 a., included 143 a. of arable and 14 a. of water meadows, and Home farm, 65 a., included 25 a. in West Clay field.[14] Of the other farms, almost certainly all of which were based in the village, that comprising the land of the Rectory estate, with 17 a. of meadows, the 50 a. of Parsonage down, nominally 162 a. in the open fields, feeding for 400 sheep, and a new farmstead built c. 1750, is likely to have been the largest.[15]

In the later 18th century Milton Lilbourne had c. 440 a. of open fields. East Hill field and West Hill field were each of c. 150 a., East Clay and West Clay each of c. 65 a., and near the village there was c. 10 a. tilled every year. With Great down, c. 30 a., Little down, c. 5 a., and Hockham bottom, all pastures presumably for cattle, the fields were inclosed by Act in 1781, when lands were also exchanged. Milton Hill farm, c. 500 a., was confined to the extreme south. Between it and Totteridge farm in the extreme north each of five farms was allotted a north–south strip of former open field and down south of the village, and each had closes north, east, and west of the village; Havering farm consisted mainly of land inclosed earlier.[16]

In 1826 William Cobbett thought it noteworthy that a large field on Milton Hill farm was planted with swedes.[17] By c. 1842 some of the farms had been merged. Milton Hill farm was

99 P.R.O., CP 40/1360, Carte rott. 17–20; CP 43/19, Carte rott. 17–18; W.R.O. 212B/5015; 212B/5065; ibid. D 1/24/150/1; cf. *Cart. Cirencester*, ii, pp. 453–4; Geol. Surv. Map 1", drift, sheet 282 (1985 edn.); W.R.O. 2037/139H.
1 P.R.O., CP 25/1/250/9, no. 34; CP 25/1/252/22, no. 29.   2 W.R.O. 212B/5015; cf. 2037/139H.
3 P.R.O., CP 40/1360, Carte rott. 17–20.
4 W.R.O., EA/20.
5 Ibid. 212B/5065; Longleat Mun., Seymour papers, xii, ff. 310v.–311.
6 *Wilts. Inq. p.m.* 1625–49 (Index Libr.), 64–5; P.R.O., CP 40/1360, Carte rott. 17–20; CP 43/19, Carte rott. 17–18.
7 W.R.O. 130/49B/38; 212B/4975.

8 Ibid. 2037/109, lease, Pococke to Tarrant, 1720; 2037/169, deed, Keylway to Som., 1680.
9 P.R.O., C 2/Jas. I/G 4/59.
10 Ibid. CP 25/1/250/9, no. 34; W.R.O. 212B/4985.
11 W.R.O. 212B/4973.
12 Ibid.; ibid. 130/49B/27; cf. ibid. EA/20.
13 Ibid. 9/21/26A; 2037/169, deed, Clarke to Popham, 1729.
14 Ibid. 212B/4973.
15 Ibid. 130/49B/31; P.R.O., PROB 11/963, f. 222; cf. W.R.O., EA/20.
16 W.R.O., EA/20; ibid. tithe award.
17 W. Cobbett, *Rural Rides*, ed. E. W. Martin, 297.

then 533 a., including 196 a. of downland pasture and 19 a. in Everleigh, and Totteridge farm 174 a.; between them, and all based in Milton Lilbourne street, there were farms of 313 a., 246 a., 242 a., 123 a., and 107 a. The 313-a. farm was worked from buildings on the west side of the street at the north end later called Lawn Farm, at which a new farmhouse was built in 1867. The 246-a. farm was worked from Upper Farm and Lower Farm, and the 242-a. farm from the mid 18th-century farmstead later called King Hall Farm.[18]

In the later 19th century and earlier 20th most of the land between the village and Milton Hill farm became part of Lower (otherwise Sunnylands) farm, on which a new farmhouse and a field barn were built.[19] Much land was converted from arable to pasture between c. 1842 and c. 1932, and from the later 19th century the other farms were apparently used for dairying.[20] In 1910 Milton Hill farm measured 505 a., Totteridge farm 201 a., Lower farm 312 a., Lawn farm 240 a., and King Hall farm 134 a. or more.[21] By 1923 Milton Hill farm had been enlarged with Fyfield down, 100 a.;[22] a dairy was built on it c. 1945,[23] and a dairy herd was kept until c. 1992. In 1996 the farm, c. 625 a., was entirely arable.[24] From c. 1905 to 1954 Lower farm was worked with Manor farm, Easton, from 1922 included 225 a. of Fyfield, and from 1954 included 130 a. in Easton.[25] Lawn farm was a dairy farm of c. 192 a. in 1930,[26] had been increased to 320 a. by 1958, and was added to Lower farm in 1964. In 1989–90 extensive new farm buildings west of the village were erected for the composite farm, which, as Lawn farm and including the land in Fyfield and Easton, was an arable and dairy holding of 1,100 a. in 1996.[27] Totteridge farm, 237 a. in 1996, was an arable and dairy farm until 1989, when the cows were replaced by horses.[28] In 1996 horses were also kept on King Hall farm, c. 150 a.[29]

Milton Lilbourne's only woodland in 1773, in the extreme south and part of that associated with Everleigh Manor in Everleigh, may have been planted in the mid 18th century.[30] As Milton wood it covered 24 a. in 1996.

A water mill stood on Milton Lilbourne manor in the later 16th century.[31] It was presumably that, or on the site of that, called New mill in 1599,[32] the later 17th century,[33] and later.

New mill stands at the confluence of Deane Water and a stream flowing from Wootton Rivers village, gave a name to the nearby settlement in Clench,[34] housed two grist mills in the later 17th century and earlier 18th, and incorporated a malthouse in the 19th century.[35] It was rebuilt in brick in the 19th century, and from c. 1890 was driven partly by steam; it ceased to work in 1932.[36]

In the earlier 20th century F. C. Stagg, a locally prominent harness maker, had premises in Milton Lilbourne village.[37]

CLENCH. In the 16th century Clench, with meadow land beside the stream along its south boundary, a common lowland pasture, open fields on the greensand, and to the north rough pasture on the chalk and clay-with-flints of the scarp and the flat summit of the downs,[38] conformed to a normal pattern. In the later 13th century there were four or five farmsteads.[39] In the earlier 14th Battle abbey's demesne was in hand. On it 58 a. was sown in 1336–7, 79 a. in 1344–5, and 75 a. in 1346–7, and there was a flock of c. 115 sheep in the 1340s.[40] The demesne had been leased by 1400 and probably by 1386.[41] There were apparently four farmsteads in the earlier 15th century, when two holdings were added to the demesne because no tenant could be found for them.[42]

In the earlier 16th century the open fields were called North and South,[43] but references of 1575 to Man field and West field suggest that they were subdivided. Parts of them had been inclosed by the late 16th century.[44] The main period of inclosure seems to have been between 1596, when a holding of 91 a. included 66 a. in North and South fields, and 1612, when most of Clench's land, including the downland in the north-east corner, lay in closes.[45] The land not inclosed by 1612 was the scarp, Bowcliff, and c. 125 a. of flat downland north-west of it, Clench common.[46] From 1570 or earlier some land was worked from Wootton Rivers parish as part of East Wick farm,[47] and in 1622 a holding was sublet to the owner of Rainscombe in North Newnton.[48] Holdings based in Clench seem to have been of less than 100 a., although in 1672 a farmer had arable crops growing on 83 a., including 11 a. of peas and vetches, and 8 cows and 335 sheep. In the 18th century a holding of

[18] W.R.O., tithe award; ibid. 160A, mortgage, Astley to Lethbridge, 1842; 2037/15, p. 2.

[19] Ibid. 374/130/77; ibid. Inland Revenue, val. reg. 58 and map 42; above, manors (Lower).

[20] [1st] Land Util. Surv. Map, sheet 112; W.R.O., tithe award; ibid. 2037/16, p. 32.

[21] W.R.O., Inland Revenue, val. reg. 58.

[22] Ibid. G 10/500/63.   [23] Ibid. G 10/760/396.

[24] Inf. from Mrs. P. Brown, Manor Ho. Farm, Bishop's Cannings.

[25] Kelly's Dir. Wilts. (1903); W.R.O., G 10/500/62; above, manors (Lower); Easton, manors; inf. from Mr. G. E. R. Osborne, Lawn Farm.

[26] W.A.S. Libr., sale cat. xx, no. 19.

[27] Inf. from Mr. Osborne.

[28] Inf. from Mrs. F. Price, Totteridge Farm.

[29] Local inf.

[30] Andrews and Dury, Map (W.R.S. viii), pls. 9, 12; cf. V.C.H. Wilts. xi. 137–8; above, manors (Milton Hill).

[31] P.R.O., CP 25/2/241/28 & 29 Eliz. I Mich.

[32] B.L. Add. MS. 37270, f. 241.

[33] W.R.O. 212B/4973.

[34] O.S. Map 6", Wilts. XXXVI (1888 edn.); above, intro. (Clench).

[35] Harrod's Dir. Wilts. (1865); P.R.O., CP 25/2/889/11 Wm. III Mich.; W.R.O. 212B/4973; 2863/1.

[36] Kelly's Dir. Wilts. (1889 and later edns.); inf. from Mrs. Price.   [37] W.R.O. 1553/66.

[38] Ibid. 122/1, survey, 1612; 2037/141; Longleat Mun., Seymour papers, xii, ff. 162–3.

[39] P.R.O., E 315/57, rot. 43.

[40] Ibid. SC 6/1045/14; SC 6/1062/22–3.

[41] Ibid. SC 2/208/18–19.

[42] Ibid. E 315/56, f. 94.

[43] Longleat Mun., Seymour papers, xii, ff. 162–3.

[44] W.R.O. 192/50.

[45] Ibid. 122/1, survey, 1612; B.L. Add. MS. 37270, f. 311 and v.

[46] W.R.O. 9/21/19; 2037/119, pp. 44–6, 98–9.

[47] Below, Wootton Rivers, econ. hist. (E. Wick).

[48] V.C.H. Wilts. x. 130; W.R.O. 122/1, ct. bk., ct. 15 Apr. 20 Jas. I.

91 a., then lacking a farmstead, was worked as part of Fyfield farm.[49]

Parts of Bowcliff or Clench common had been divided and allotted for furze cutting by the late 18th century, but all their land remained common pasture on which 640 or more sheep could be fed. Common rights were eliminated and holdings consolidated in 1805, when lands were exchanged between the two owners.[50] About 1842 there were c. 365 a. of arable and c. 230 a. of grassland in Clench. To the south there were two farms of c. 50 a., one based where Brewers Cottages stands and one at buildings south-west of that; the second was held with Fyfield farm. Clench farm measured 184 a. including 20 a. in Milcot, and 306 a., including Clench common and most of Bowcliff, was part of East Wick farm.[51]

By 1879 both the 50-a. farms had been added to Broomsgrove farm, based in Milcot;[52] their land remained part of it in 1996 when it was used for arable and dairy farming.[53] Clench farm, 160 a., was a dairy farm in the earlier 20th century.[54] In 1929 c. 342 a. of Clench's land lay in East Wick farm, in 1996 c. 330 a. In 1996 Clench farm was worked in conjunction with East Wick farm, all the land of which was used for arable and dairy farming.[55] Clench common was probably ploughed for the first time in the Second World War.[56]

In the early 19th century there was c. 47 a. of woodland in Clench in c. 10 copses, the largest of which were one of 13 a. on Clench common and Rook grove, 6 a. Several of the smaller coppices were grubbed up between c. 1842 and 1886,[57] but the larger ones remained among c. 40 a. of woodland standing in 1996.

A mill may have stood in Clench in the 16th century,[58] and a windmill standing NNE. of Totteridge Farm in 1773[59] may also have been on Clench's land.

A wharf in Clench was built on the Kennet & Avon canal in 1810,[60] and a building was standing at the wharf in 1814.[61] There was probably little trade at the wharf; the building was demolished between 1842 and 1886.[62]

FYFIELD. In the 18th century the boundary between Fyfield's open land and its inclosed land ran east–west a little south of the stream flowing across Fyfield from the south end of Milton Lilbourne village. To the south there was c. 200 a. of arable in three open fields, East, Middle, and West, each field lying north–south on the greensand in the north and on Lower Chalk in the south; there was also c. 10 a. of open arable on the summit of Weed Hill and 25 a. in Titcombe bottom. The scarp face, the steep slopes of Weed Hill, and to the south Fyfield down, a total of 181 a., were common pastures, presumably for sheep.[63] Beside the stream East mead may earlier have been a common meadow.[64] By analogy with Easton and Milton Lilbourne it is likely that in the Middle Ages open fields also lay on the greensand east and west of Fyfield village and were roughly bounded to the north by the present Burbage–Pewsey road,[65] and east and west fields which were sown yearly in the 17th century may have lain there. Much of the land north of the Burbage–Pewsey road was a common pasture partly or wholly for cattle.[66]

In the 16th century few holdings were based in Fyfield. Most of Fyfield manor seems to have been demesne; the only holding of the manor known not to have been was of 1½ yardland.[67] A freehold of 3 yardlands may have been based there,[68] but the land of Fyfield in two copyholds of Milton Lilbourne manor, of 1½ and ½ yardland, may have been worked from Milton Lilbourne.[69] The demesne of Fyfield manor, Fyfield farm, was leased in 1567 with a stock of cattle said to be worth £200.[70] In 1638 it included nominally 122 a. in the open fields and feeding in common for 520 sheep and 62 cattle.[71] The pasture north of the village was inclosed in the mid 17th century,[72] and the land east and west of the village had been inclosed by 1711.[73]

In the late 17th century there were evidently only two owners of land in Fyfield,[74] and from 1703 nearly all the land was held by the lord of Fyfield manor as owner or lessee[75] and worked as Fyfield farm. About 1750, when it included land at Clench and Milcot, Fyfield farm measured 867 a., included 614 a. of arable, and was several de facto;[76] in 1810 it measured c. 880 a.[77]

The lands of Fyfield and Milcot were inclosed de jure, and lands were exchanged, by Act in 1823. Nearly all the land north of the Burbage–Pewsey road was assigned to Froxfield

[49] W.R.O., wills, archd. Wilts., Geo. Stephens, 1672; ibid. 332/276, poor rate, 1773; 2037/108, lease, Som. to Keylway, 1689; 2037/111, lease, Batson to Cannings, 1755; 2037/129.

[50] Ibid. 9/21/19; 2037/119, pp. 44–6, 98–9; 2037/140; ibid. tithe award.

[51] Ibid. tithe award; Wootton Rivers tithe award.

[52] Ibid. 2037/15, pp. 32, 85; for Broomsgrove farm, below, this section (Milcot).

[53] Inf. from Mr. Derek Baxter, Broomsgrove Farm.

[54] W.A.S. Libr., sale cat. xx, no. 18.

[55] W.R.O. 9/1/521; inf. from the agent for the Crown Estate Com., 42 High Street, Marlborough; Mr. R. C. Butler, E. Wick Farm, Wootton Rivers.

[56] A. J. and F. H. Hosier, *Hosier's Farming System*, 81.

[57] O.S. Map 6", Wilts. XXXVI (1888 edn.); W.R.O. 2037/141; ibid. tithe award.

[58] P.R.O., SC 2/208/27; Longleat Mun., Seymour papers, xii, f. 162; W.R.O. 192/50, f. 4.

[59] *Andrews and Dury, Map* (W.R.S. viii), pl. 12.

[60] W.R.O. 2037/13.

[61] Ibid. 2037/141.

[62] Ibid. tithe award; O.S. Map 6", Wilts. XXXVI (1888 edn.).

[63] Geol. Surv. Map 1", drift, sheet 282 (1985 edn.); W.R.O. 135/11; 2037/138H; ibid. EA/119.

[64] P.R.O., C 2/Eliz. I/W 26/35.

[65] Above, Easton, econ. hist.; this section (Milton Lilbourne).

[66] W.R.O. 332/159; 549/35; cf. 135/31.

[67] P.R.O., C 3/122/8.

[68] Ibid. C 142/254, no. 81.

[69] Ibid. C 2/Eliz. I/B 8/37; ibid. CP 40/1360, Carte rott. 17–20.   [70] Ibid. C 2/Eliz. I/F 8/62.

[71] W.R.O. 549/35.

[72] Ibid.; ibid. 332/159; 332/167; 2037/169, deed, Keylway to Som., 1680; cf. 135/31.

[73] Ibid. 332/286, survey, 1711; cf. 135/31.

[74] Above, manors (Fyfield).

[75] W.R.O. 332/166, deed, Devischer to Hungerford, 1725; 332/276, poor rate, 1773; 2037/12; 2037/26.

[76] Ibid. 332/286, measurement of Fyfield farm; 2037/12; cf. 135/31.

[77] Ibid. 332/181, lease, Penruddocke to Stagg, 1810.

almshouse, all that to the south as Fyfield farm to the lord of Fyfield manor.[78] The inclosure was agreed on in 1807,[79] and in anticipation of the award the land to the north had been separated from Fyfield farm by 1820.[80] North of the Burbage–Pewsey road 59 a. was held with Fyfield farm c. 1842,[81] and later, probably from c. 1845, most of the land north of the road was part of Broomsgrove farm.[82] On Fyfield farm, 599 a. in 1821, 56 a. of Fyfield down was ploughed in the 1820s. On the south part of the farm the arable inclosed in 1823 continued to be worked in large fields; on the north part 132 a. of arable lay in fields averaging 11 a., and 63 a. of meadows and pasture lay in fields averaging 4½ a.[83] About 1842, when it had two groups of farm buildings at Fyfield, a field barn, and land in Clench, Fyfield farm's 702 a. included c. 424 a. of arable, 151 a. of meadows and lowland pasture, and 125 a. of down.[84]

By the late 19th century Fyfield farm had been divided, and a small farm, Roadside, was being worked from Little Salisbury in 1896.[85] From 1922 the scarp face, Weed Hill, Titcombe bottom, and the arable in large fields south of the village have been part of Lower farm, Milton Lilbourne,[86] and from 1923 or earlier Fyfield down, 100 a., has been part of Milton Hill farm.[87] In the 1920s a dairy farm of c. 160 a. was worked from buildings in Fyfield village,[88] and in the 1940s and 1950s Lord Hudson, Minister of Agriculture and Fisheries from 1940 to 1945 and the owner of Fyfield Manor, kept pedigree Friesian, Jersey, and Ayrshire cattle at Fyfield and on Lawn farm, Milton Lilbourne.[89] In 1996 Fyfield down and the old East, Middle, and West fields were large arable fields; to the north c. 70 a. in Broomsgrove farm and 43 a. in Lawn farm was used for arable and dairy farming[90] and most of the other land was arable.

There was no more than a few acres of woodland in Fyfield in 1842[91] and 1996.

A windmill stood on the north-west side of the New Mill to Fyfield road in the early 19th century.[92] It had been demolished by 1842.[93]

In the 1920s and 1930s a slaughterer of horses was based at Roadside Farm,[94] where a new slaughterhouse was built c. 1931.[95] The slaughterhouse was closed in 1969.[96]

MILCOT. To the north Milcot had open fields and, on the south side of Martinsell Hill, a common downland pasture for sheep; to the south there were meadows beside the stream, and, as there was at Clench, probably a common lowland pasture for cattle.[97] The lowland pasture may have been inclosed in the later 16th century.[98] Much of the land was probably worked from Fyfield and Milton Lilbourne in the 16th century, when two holdings each of ½ yardland may have been the only ones based at Milcot.[99]

In the late 17th century Milcot's land was held by the same two owners as Fyfield's was,[1] and apparently from then nearly all of it was part of Fyfield farm.[2] Milcot's open-field land was probably what was referred to as the north field of Fyfield,[3] and apparently none but the tenant of Fyfield farm worked land in it or had a right to feed animals on the down. In 1820 Milcot's land was severed from Fyfield farm[4] and, as were lands in Fyfield, the arable, 65 a., and down, 20 a., were inclosed in 1823, when lands were also exchanged.[5] Of Milcot's 232 a. of agricultural land c. 1842, 209 a., on which there was no farmstead, was worked as one holding with West Wick farm based in Pewsey and the manor farm of Oare in Wilcot.[6]

In 1845 Broomsgrove Farm was built and nearly all the land of Milcot was leased with it.[7] By 1879 land in Clench and Fyfield had been added to Broomsgrove farm, then of 424 a. and including 300 a. of arable.[8] The farm had been little changed in area by the 1920s,[9] but between 1903 and 1919 it was converted for dairying and 185 a. was laid to grass.[10] In the early 1930s it still included more grassland than arable;[11] in the early 1950s a dairy herd was kept but the farm had more arable than grassland.[12] In 1996 Broomsgrove was an arable and dairy farm of 450 a., on which a herd of 120 cows was kept.[13]

Watercress beds were constructed at Milkhouse Water between 1899 and 1920, when they covered 2 a.[14] How long watercress was grown in them commercially is not clear. About 1974 the beds were converted to a trout hatchery, and in 1996 trout fry were reared there at the Avon Springs Hatchery.[15]

[78] W.R.O., EA/119.
[79] Ibid. 2037/13.
[80] Ibid. 332/181, lease, Penruddocke to Akerman, 1821; 2037/14. [81] Ibid. tithe award.
[82] Below, this section (Milcot).
[83] W.R.O. 332/181, leases, Penruddocke to Akerman, 1821; Penruddocke to Burfitt, 1829; ibid. EA/119.
[84] Ibid. tithe award.
[85] Ibid. 672/1; ibid. Inland Revenue, val. reg. 58; ibid. G 10/510/8.
[86] Ibid. G 10/500/62; inf. from Mr. Osborne.
[87] W.R.O., G 10/500/63; inf. from Mrs. Brown.
[88] W.A.S. Libr., sale cat. xvi, no. 4; xx, no. 33; W.R.O., G 10/500/64.
[89] D.N.B.; Wilts. Cuttings, xxi. 88; above, manors (Fyfield); inf. from Mr. Osborne.
[90] Inf. from Mr. Baxter; Mr. Osborne.
[91] W.R.O., tithe award.
[92] Ibid. 135/31; 549/38; C. Greenwood, Map of Wilts. (1820); O.S. Map 1", sheet 14 (1817 edn.).
[93] W.R.O., tithe award.
[94] Kelly's Dir. Wilts. (1923 and later edns.).
[95] W.R.O., G 10/760/110.
[96] Inf. from Mrs. Price.
[97] W.R.O. 2037/138H; ibid. EA/119; Longleat Mun.,

Seymour papers, xii, f. 163.
[98] W.R.O. 192/50.
[99] Ibid. 332/157; P.R.O., CP 40/1360, Carte rott. 17–20; ibid. REQ 2/206/64; Longleat Mun., Seymour papers, xii, f. 163.
[1] Above, manors (Fyfield; Milcot).
[2] W.R.O. 332/157; 332/181, deed, Popham to Penruddocke, 1721; 2037/26; above, this section (Fyfield).
[3] B.L. Add. MS. 37270, f. 311; W.R.O. 2037/169, deed, Keylway to Som., 1680.
[4] W.R.O. 2037/12; 2037/138H; above, this section (Fyfield).
[5] W.R.O., EA/119.
[6] Ibid. tithe award; Pewsey tithe award; Wilcot tithe award.
[7] Ibid. 2037/14; 2037/28.
[8] Ibid. 2037/15, pp. 32, 85.
[9] Ibid. 2037/155; ibid. G 10/500/64.
[10] Ibid. 2037/16, p. 18; 2037/125.
[11] [1st] Land Util. Surv. Map, sheet 112.
[12] B.L. Maps, 135, sale cat. of Broomsgrove estate, 1953.
[13] Inf. from Mr. Baxter.
[14] O.S. Maps 6", Wilts. XXXVI. SW. (1900, 1925 edns.); W.R.O., G 10/500/62.
[15] Inf. from Mrs. Price.

Milcot wood, mentioned in the 14th century,[16] may have been Broomsgrove wood, which was standing in 1567.[17] Broomsgrove wood was accounted 34 a. in 1638,[18] 41 a. c. 1842,[19] 51 a. in 1876,[20] 55 a. in the earlier 20th century, and c. 30 a. in the later 20th century.[21]

A mill stood at Milcot in 1289.[22]

LOCAL GOVERNMENT. In the Middle Ages Clench was in Battle abbey's liberty of Bromham,[23] the abbey's tenants attended courts held at Bromham, and the tithingman of Clench presented at the view of frankpledge held there twice a year. The tithingman was to be chosen from the abbey's tenants, but attendance at the view was required from all men living at Clench.[24] In the late 13th century and in the 14th assaults and the harbouring of strangers were punished, the raising of the hue was reported, and the assize of ale was enforced, but then and later presentments were few. Pleas were sometimes heard, and in the 15th century orders were occasionally made to repair roads, bridges, hedges, and ditches. A miller was amerced in the 16th century. Often in the 15th and 16th centuries the tithingman failed to attend the view, and in 1552 he explained his absence by implying that it would have cost him more to attend than to pay the fine for default. In the later 16th century and earlier 17th the use of the open fields and of Clench common was regulated at the view, orders were made to repair boundaries, and normal manorial business was done, but the amount of regulation and other business was very small.[25] From the 16th century or earlier land at Clench was held by copy of Huish manor,[26] the court of which dealt with matters concerning it.[27]

There are records of four meetings of a court of Fyfield manor 1683 × 1697. The poor condition of bridges and the pound, and the building of cottages on the waste, were among matters presented.[28]

In 1775–6 Milton Lilbourne parish spent £148 to relieve the poor, in the early 1780s an average of £143. In 1802–3, when at 2s. 8d. the poor rate was average for the hundred, £413 was spent to relieve 25 adults and 81 children regularly and 10 adults occasionally.[29] Spending reached a peak of £838 in 1812–13, when 69 adults were relieved regularly; it was less than half

that in 1814–15 but 50 adults were still being relieved.[30] Between 1815 and 1835 spending fluctuated between £818 and £393 and averaged £594. The parish joined Pewsey poor-law union in 1835[31] and was part of Kennet district from 1974.[32]

CHURCH. Milton Lilbourne church was appropriated by Cirencester abbey, and a vicarage had been ordained by 1195.[33] In 1929 the vicarage was united to Easton vicarage, and in 1991 the united benefice was united to Pewsey rectory and Wootton Rivers rectory.[34]

In 1278 Walter de Lillebonne quitclaimed the patronage of the church to Cirencester abbey,[35] and the advowson of the vicarage passed with the Rectory estate. Until the Dissolution all known presentations of vicars were by the abbey, and in 1546 Thomas Trussley presented by the abbey's grant.[36] In 1588 the advowson was granted by the Crown with the tithes of the Rectory estate, and it passed with the rectorial tithes of Milton Lilbourne[37] until 1846. In 1846 S. E. Scroggs's trustees presented J. H. Gale and sold the advowson to his father T. H. Gale, vicar until 1846.[38] The advowson passed to J. H. Gale (d. 1893).[39] After his death the patronage was exercised by his relict Augusta (d. 1913) and after hers by his daughters: in 1924 four of the surviving daughters and Oxford University in place of a fifth who had become a Roman Catholic presented jointly.[40] In 1931 the advowson was transferred to Wadham College, Oxford,[41] which shared the patronage of the united benefice formed in 1929 and became a member of the board of patronage for the united benefice formed in 1991.[42]

The vicarage was endowed, presumably at its ordination, with a house and ½ yardland, all tithes and 1 qr. each of wheat, barley, and oats from the Rectory estate, small tithes from the whole parish, and mortuaries, oblations, and other obventions. About 1300 tithes of milk and cheese from the whole parish and tithes of hay from Clench, Fyfield, and Milcot were added to the endowment,[43] and later the vicar was also given 46s. 8d. a year from the Rectory estate.[44] The vicarage was worth £7 13s. 6d. in 1535,[45] £40 in 1704,[46] and £70 in 1812.[47] In 1816 it was augmented by lot with £600 given by parliament[48] but, with a net income of £111, it was

16   V.C.H. Wilts. iv. 419.
17   P.R.O., REQ 2/206/64.
18   W.R.O. 549/35.
19   Ibid. tithe award.
20   Ibid. 2037/15, p. 64.
21   O.S. Maps 1/2,500, Wilts. XXXVI. 9 (1924 edn.); 1/50,000, SU 06/16 (1987 edn.).
22   P.R.O., JUST 1/1006, rot. 51.
23   Ibid. rot. 51d.; cf. Rot. Hund. (Rec. Com.), ii (1), 260; Collectanea (W.R.S. xii), 129–41.
24   P.R.O., E 315/56, f. 94.
25   Ibid. SC 2/208/15–19; SC 2/208/21–7; B.L. Add. MS. 37270; W.R.O. 84/35; 122/1, ct. bk.
26   W.R.O. 192/50, survey bk., f. 4; above, manors (Clench).
27   W.R.O. 2037/129–30.
28   Ibid. 332/254.
29   Poor Law Abstract, 1804, 566–7.
30   Ibid. 1818, 498–9.
31   Poor Rate Returns, 1816–21, 188; 1822–4, 228; 1825–9, 219; 1830–4, 212; Poor Law Com. 2nd Rep. App. D, 560.

32   O.S. Map 1/100,000, admin. areas, Wilts. (1974 edn.).
33   Cart. Cirencester, i, p. 154; above, manors (Rectory).
34   Ch. Com. file, NB 34/263B; ibid. file 85777.
35   Cart. Cirencester, iii, p. 1057.
36   Phillipps, Wilts. Inst. (index in W.A.M. xxviii. 226).
37   Ibid.; P.R.O., C 66/1318, m. 6; above, manors (Rectory).
38   W.R.O., D 1/2/34, ff. 182v.–183; Wadham Coll., Oxf., Mun. 101/1; for the Gales, below, this section.
39   W.R.O., D 1/56/7; ibid. 942/15.
40   Ibid. D 1/2/44, p. 389; D 1/2/45, p. 508; D 1/2/46, pp. 456–7; D 1/18/182.
41   Ch. Com. file 53775/1.
42   Ibid. NB 34/263B.
43   Cart. Cirencester, ii, pp. 453–4.
44   Valor Eccl. (Rec. Com.), ii. 469; P.R.O., SC 6/Hen. VIII/1240, rot. 62; W.R.O., D 1/24/150/1.
45   Valor Eccl. (Rec. Com.), ii. 151.
46   W.R.O., D 1/24/150/3.
47   W.A.M. xli. 134.
48   C. Hodgson, Queen Anne's Bounty (1845), p. cccxxxvi.

still poor *c.* 1830.[49] In 1866 the Revd. S. M. Scroggs gave £833 stock to augment it: the vicar was to receive the income and, from when it was possible to use the capital to buy it, to be given rent charge for which rectorial tithes of the parish had been commuted. In 1900–1 the vicar received £26 from Scroggs's charity. From 1912, by gift of the owner, the vicar also received seven ninths of the rent charge in respect of the rectorial tithes of Milton Lilbourne, and no rent charge was bought by Scroggs's trustees.[50] In the later 16th century and earlier 17th the vicar claimed, in addition to those assigned *c.* 1300 and earlier, tithes of hay from Milton Lilbourne and of 100 sheep.[51] No such additional claim was made in 1704[52] or later. In the later 18th century the owner of the Rectory estate paid £20 a year to the vicar in place of the tithes, corn rent, and pension from his estate.[53] About 1842 the vicar's tithes were commuted for a rent charge of £140.[54] In 1608 the glebe included a house, 1 a. of meadow, and nominally 15¼ a. of arable;[55] in 1704 feeding for 120 sheep and 6 beasts was held with the land.[56] There was 18 a. of glebe *c.* 1842.[57] The vicar sold *c.* 6 a. *c.* 1914, and 4 a. in 1917; the final 6 a. of glebe was sold in 1994.[58] The vicarage house was apparently rebuilt in the earlier 18th century.[59] In 1783 it was a thatched house with three bedchambers,[60] and in 1833 was unfit for the vicar.[61] It had been demolished by *c.* 1842.[62] A new house was built on its site *c.* 1855[63] and was sold in 1987.[64]

In 1553 quarterly sermons were not preached,[65] and by 1556 goods taken from the church in Edward VI's reign had not been returned.[66] From 1564 to 1986 it seems that few vicars were not resident or were assisted by a curate.[67] George Pinch was vicar from 1595 to 1645.[68] In the late 17th century and in the 18th each of several vicars was curate of Easton,[69] and John Swain, vicar 1777–1800, was also curate of Collingbourne Kingston. At Milton Lilbourne in 1783 Swain, who lived in Wootton Rivers, conducted a service on Good Friday, Christmas day, and every Sunday; there were *c.* 17 communicants, and communion was celebrated four times.[70] T. H. Gale was vicar from 1812 to 1846 and his son J. H. Gale from 1846 to 1893.[71] As Parson Gale the son became well known as a huntsman and a magistrate.[72] In 1864 he held two services each Sunday and a service on Ash Wednesday, Good Friday, and Christmas day, and he celebrated communion six times a year; there were 20–40 communicants at the great festivals.[73] From 1971 to 1986 the united benefice was held in plurality with Wootton Rivers rectory.[74] An iron cello played in the church *c.* 1800 and made at Milton Lilbourne was in Devizes museum in 1996.[75]

In 1906 Laetitia Penruddocke gave the interest from £100 for maintenance of the churchyard. The income, £3 11s. in 1907–8, £5.46 in 1975, was used as she intended. In 1996 the trustees of the charity resolved to spend the capital as if it was income.[76]

The church of *ST. PETER*, so called in 1763,[77] is built of flint and ashlar and consists of a chancel, a nave with north aisle and south porch, and a west tower. The proportions of the chancel and nave, and the thickness of their walls, suggest that they were built in the 12th century, the date of imposts on the chancel arch. The aisle was presumably first built in the later 13th century, the date of the arcade. In the 14th century the chancel was altered and in the south wall of the nave a doorway and a window were replaced. The tower is probably late 15th-century and the porch, to the west of which there is a 15th-century window in the south wall of the nave, may be contemporary with it; the aisle was rebuilt soon after the tower was built. Surviving windows which lit galleries, and surviving fragments of carved wood, suggest that the church was refurnished in the 17th century, and until 1874 it had south and west galleries, box pews, of which those in the aisle and those near the chancel arch were high, and a pulpit adjoining the east pier of the arcade.[78] The chancel was restored in 1859 to designs by G. E. Street.[79] In 1875 the nave, aisle, and porch were restored to designs by J. L. Pearson; much of the walling was rebuilt, the old windows being re-used or copied, and the box pews and galleries were removed.[80] In 1925 the arcade, which was leaning, was rebuilt with the old stone.[81]

An 8-oz. chalice was kept by the parish in 1553, when 2 oz. of plate was taken for the king. In 1891 and 1996 the parish had a silver paten cover apparently of the later 16th century, a

---

49 *Rep. Com. Eccl. Revenues*, 842–3.
50 *Endowed Char. Wilts.* (S. Div.), 337–8; W.R.O., L 2, Froxfield; above, manors (Rectory).
51 W.R.O., D 1/24/150/1.
52 Ibid. D 1/24/150/3.
53 Ibid. D 1/24/150/4.
54 Ibid. tithe award.
55 Ibid. D 1/24/150/1.
56 Ibid. D 1/24/150/3.
57 Ibid. tithe award.
58 Ibid. G 10/510/8; ibid. Inland Revenue, val. reg. 58; Wilts. Cuttings, xiv. 104; Ch. Com. file 53775/1; inf. from the Property Secretary, Salisbury Dioc. Bd. of Finance, Church Ho., Crane Street, Salisbury.
59 A. Tomlin, *Milton Lilbourne Church*, 32.
60 W.R.O., D 1/24/150/4.
61 *Rep. Com. Eccl. Revenues*, 842–3.
62 W.R.O., tithe award.   63 Ch. Com. file 53775/1.
64 Inf. from Ch. Com.
65 W.R.O., D 1/43/1, f. 142.
66 Ibid. D 1/43/2, f. 15.

67 e.g. ibid. 616/1–5; 942/1–5; 942/11–15; ibid. D 1/24/150/1; ibid. bishop's transcripts, bdles. 1–5.
68 Phillipps, *Wilts. Inst.* i. 234; ii. 22.
69 Above, Easton, church.
70 *Vis. Queries, 1783* (W.R.S. xxvii), pp. 159–60; W.R.O. 616/2.
71 *Alum. Oxon. 1715–1886*, ii. 504; W.R.O. 616/2; 942/15.
72 A. G. Bradley, *Round About Wilts.* 223; J. H. Chandler, *Vale of Pewsey*, 130; *W.A.M.* xxix. 340.
73 W.R.O., D 1/56/7.
74 *Crockford* (1971–2, 1987–8).
75 *W.A.M.* xxxix. 312; inf. from the Curator, the Museum, 41 Long Street, Devizes.
76 W.R.O., L 2, Milton Lilbourne; Char. Com. file.
77 J. Ecton, *Thesaurus* (1763), 406.
78 W.R.O., D 1/61/25/9.
79 Ibid. D 1/61/11/13.
80 Ibid. D 1/61/25/9; Pevsner, *Wilts.* (2nd edn.), 351; cf. J. Buckler, watercolour in W.A.S. Libr., vol. iv. 3.
81 W.R.O., D 1/61/65/6.

silver chalice hallmarked for 1655, and a silver-plated paten of 1875.[82]

There were three bells in the church in 1553[83] and in 1783, when one was cracked.[84] A new ring of six was hung; the bells were cast by Robert Wells at Aldbourne in 1789 and remained in the church in 1996. One of the bells was recast by Llewellins & James at Bristol in 1906.[85]

The registers begin in 1686 and are complete.[86]

NONCONFORMITY. In 1584 one of several parishioners who did not attend communion was the vicar's wife.[87] There was no nonconformist in the parish in 1676 or 1783.[88] A meeting house was certified in 1821 by Methodists, a newly built chapel in 1825 by Independent Methodists, and a chapel in 1843 by Primitive Methodists.[89] Only one chapel was open in 1864,[90] presumably that at Littleworth used by Wesleyan Methodists and said to have been built c. 1854.[91] In 1932 a new Methodist chapel was built a little north of the north end of Milton Lilbourne street,[92] and that at Littleworth was closed.[93] The new chapel was closed in 1967.[94]

EDUCATION. In 1818 there was no day school in the parish;[95] in 1833, when the population was c. 660, one for nine infant boys was the only school.[96] A school was provided with new premises, possibly c. 1854, but it was still attended only by very young children: the 30–40 children who were pupils in 1858 and 1864 left at an early age to go to work. Several evening schools were held in winter in 1864.[97] The day school had 52 pupils in 1871.[98] In 1876 the parish was compelled to form a school board, which replaced the old school with a new school and schoolhouse opened in 1878. The board was dissolved in 1903.[99] The school had 64 pupils in 1906–7, 75 in 1909–10; with fluctuations attendance had declined to 49 by 1937–8,[1] and to 29 by 1981. The school was closed in 1985.[2]

A residential school for deaf and dumb Jewish children was moved from London in 1940 and was held in Havering House from then until 1945.[3]

CHARITIES FOR THE POOR. Although land in all parts of the parish was given by Sarah, duchess of Somerset, to Froxfield almshouse,[4] which was opened c. 1695, in 1716 parishioners of Milton Lilbourne were declared inadmissible to the almshouse as manor widows.[5] No other eleemosynary charity is known.

PEWSEY

PEWSEY parish stretches from the Marlborough Downs to Salisbury Plain across the valley to which it gives a name.[6] It measured 1,935 ha. (4,782 a.) until 1987, when small areas were transferred to Manningford, Milton Lilbourne, and Savernake, and from Milton Lilbourne and Wilcot, and it was reduced to 1,909 ha.[7] In addition to Pewsey village the parish included villages and hamlets called Kepnal, East Sharcott, West Sharcott, Southcott, and West Wick.

About 940 an estate called Pewsey had a boundary apparently approximate to what became the parish boundary,[8] and later the villages and hamlets all stood on the land of Pewsey manor.[9] Pewsey village presumably originated where the church, probably the rectory house, and the large demesne farmstead of the manor stood close together on rising ground.[10] By contrast Kepnal, East Sharcott, and Southcott are all street villages, and they were almost certainly colonized from Pewsey, Southcott probably before Kepnal and East Sharcott.[11] To the east Milton Lilbourne and Easton apparently took their names from their relationship to Pewsey village,[12] but there is no other evidence that they were subsidiary settlements of it.

At the north end of the parish the eastern boundary of the estate called Pewsey ran c. 940 along the western ditch of an Iron-Age hill fort on Martinsell Hill,[13] thus excluding the hill fort

82 Nightingale, *Wilts. Plate*, 170; inf. from Mr. P. M. O. Springfield, Westering Ho.
83 *W.A.M.* xii. 364.   84 W.R.O., D 1/24/150/4.
85 Walters, *Wilts. Bells*, 140, 314; inf. from Mr. Springfield.
86 W.R.O. 616/1–5; there are transcripts for several periods earlier in the 17th cent. in W.R.O.
87 Ibid. D 1/43/5, ff. 17v.–18.
88 *Compton Census*, ed. Whiteman, 126; *Vis. Queries, 1783* (W.R.S. xxvii), p. 159.
89 *Meeting Ho. Certs.* (W.R.S. xl), pp. 93, 110, 157.
90 W.R.O., D 1/56/7.
91 *Kelly's Dir. Wilts.* (1895); O.S. Map 6", Wilts. XXXVI (1888 edn.).
92 *Kelly's Dir. Wilts.* (1939); W.R.O. 2193/17.
93 Inf. from Mrs. F. Price, Totteridge Farm.
94 W.R.O. 1464/46.
95 *Educ. of Poor Digest*, 1033.
96 *Educ. Enq. Abstract*, 1043; *V.C.H. Wilts.* iv. 354.
97 *Acct. of Wilts. Schs.* 34; W.R.O., D 1/56/7; ibid. F 8/600/195/1/2/1; ibid. 2037/14.
98 *Returns relating to Elem. Educ.* 426.
99 *Lond. Gaz.* 24 Mar. 1876, p. 2079; W.R.O., Milton Lilbourne sch. bd. rec.; ibid. F 8/600/195/1/27/1.
1 *Bd. of Educ., List 21, 1908–38* (H.M.S.O.).
2 Wilts. co. council, *Sched. of Educ. Establishments* (1982), p. 13; W.R.O., F 8/600/195/1/3/2.
3 W.R.O., G 10/132/20.
4 Above, manors (Lawn; Clench; Fyfield; Milcot).
5 W.R.O. 2037/12; for the almshouse and admittance to it, above, Froxfield, charities.
6 This article was written in 1997. Maps used include O.S. Maps 1", sheet 14 (1817 edn.); 1/25,000, SU 05/15, SU 06/16 (1987 edns.); 6", Wilts. XXXV–XXXVI, XLI–XLII (1888–9 and later edns.).
7 Statutory Instruments, 1987, no. 619, Kennet (Parishes) Order; *Census*, 1991.
8 *Arch. Jnl.* lxxvi. 247–51.
9 e.g. Alnwick Castle Mun. X.II.11, box 8, survey of Pewsey, 1755.
10 For the rectory ho., below, this section (Pewsey).
11 Ibid. agric. [preamble]; for W. Sharcott and W. Wick, below, this section.
12 Above, Easton, intro.; Milton Lilbourne, intro. (Milton Lilbourne).
13 *Arch. Jnl.* lxxvi. 248.

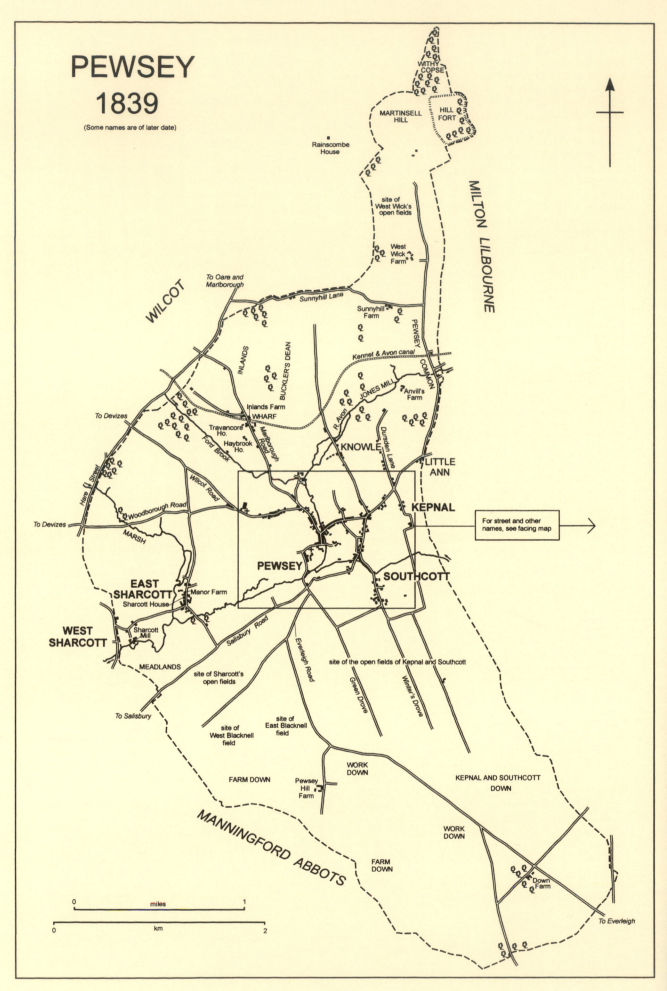

PEWSEY
1839
(Some names are of later date)

WITHY
COPSE

MARTINSELL
HILL

HILL
FORT

MILTON LILBOURNE

Rainscombe
House

site of
West Wick's
open fields

West
Wick
Farm

WILCOT

To Oare and
Marlborough

Sunnyhill Lane

Sunnyhill
Farm

PEWSEY COMMON

Kennet & Avon canal

INLANDS

BUCKLER'S DEAN

Jones Mill

Anvill's
Farm

To Devizes

Inlands Farm
WHARF

Travancore
Ho.

Haybrook
Ho.

R. Avon

Marlborough Road

Ford Brook

Dursden Lane

KNOWLE

LITTLE
ANN

Hare Street

Wilcot Road

Woodborough Road

To Devizes

MARSH

KEPNAL

For street and other
names, see facing map

EAST
SHARCOTT

Manor Farm

Sharcott House

PEWSEY

SOUTHCOTT

WEST
SHARCOTT

Sharcott
Mill

MEADLANDS

Salisbury Road

site of Sharcott's
open fields

Everleigh Road

site of the open fields of Kepnal and Southcott

Green Drove

Winter's Drove

KEPNAL AND SOUTHCOTT
DOWN

To Salisbury

site of
West Blacknell
field

site of
East Blacknell
field

WORK
DOWN

FARM DOWN

Pewsey
Hill
Farm

WORK
DOWN

MANNINGFORD ABBOTS

FARM
DOWN

Down
Farm

To Everleigh

0   miles   1

0   km   2

from the estate; later the parish embraced it, the parish's eastern boundary following the hill fort's eastern ditch.[14] West of the hill fort the parish boundary follows a prehistoric ditch, and south of the ditch it was set in 1280 to follow the contours at the foot of a west facing scarp.[15] South of Martinsell Hill, on the east the north part of the parish boundary follows the bottom of a north–south dry valley for 1.5 km.; also straight, the south part of the boundary ignored relief. On the west the boundary west of Pewsey village follows a road which may have been

west sides, and a triangle of gently sloping land north of it; the summit and much of the triangle are overlain by clay-with-flints. The more extensive southern downland, part of the northern edge of Salisbury Plain, consists of the north-facing scarp and of ridges and dry valleys south of it. The highest point is at 221 m. The centre of the parish is drained from north-east to south-west by the Avon, one of two principal head streams of the Christchurch Avon, and from the north-west by Ford brook, which joins the Avon north of Pewsey village; a tributary

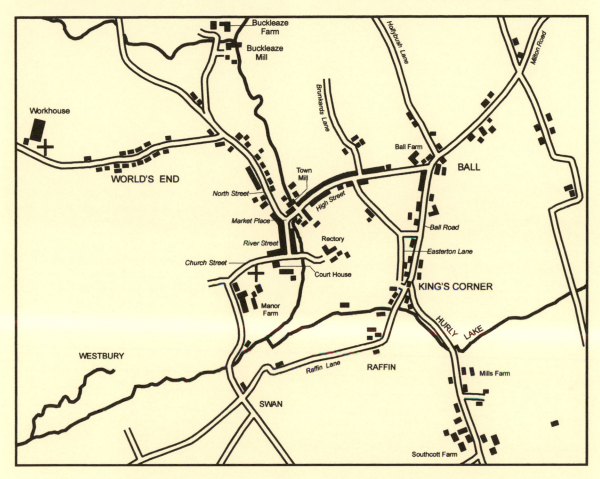

PEWSEY VILLAGE AND NEARBY SETTLEMENTS

ancient;[16] on the southern downland for *c*. 1 km. it follows the contours and what is probably a lynchet, and in several places it crosses the contours at right angles. On the south, two barrows stood on Pewsey's boundary with Everleigh *c*. 940;[17] the boundary was uncertain in 1290 and, possibly as a result of a decision of a commission then appointed to settle it,[18] later ran north of the barrows.

Chalk outcrops at both ends of the parish, Upper Greensand extensively in the centre. The northern downland, part of the Marlborough Downs, consists of the flat summit of Martinsell Hill, which reaches 289 m., its steep south and

which flows westwards through marshy ground called Hurly lake south-east of Pewsey village joins the Avon south of the village, and a tributary which flows south-eastwards through marshy ground west of Pewsey village joins the Avon south of East Sharcott village. The Avon leaves the parish at 102 m. Alluvium has been deposited by the Avon, Ford brook, and the stream flowing near East Sharcott village, and there are deposits of gravel on the south bank of the Avon west of Pewsey village, at Hurly lake, and in several places between the streams; brickearth has been deposited between Pewsey and Kepnal.[19]

14 Cf. below, this section [Savernake forest].
15 *Feet of F.* 1272–1327 (W.R.S. i), p. 12.
16 *Arch. Jnl.* lxxvi. 250; below, this section [roads: Hare Street].
17 *Arch. Jnl.* lxxvi. 249.
18 *Cal. Pat.* 1281–92, 400.
19 Geol. Surv. Maps 1/50,000, drift, sheet 266 (1974 edn.); 1", drift, sheet 282 (1985 edn.).

Open fields lay on the mainly flat land, where greensand and marly Lower Chalk outcrop, between the principal villages of the parish and the scarp of Salisbury Plain; a much smaller area of open fields lay mainly on the Lower Chalk south of Martinsell Hill. In the Middle Ages the greensand between the two areas of open fields was mostly pasture; between the 17th century and the 19th most of it was converted to arable. At both ends of the parish most of the downland was rough pasture for sheep; much of it was ploughed in the late 18th century or early 19th.[20]

Woodland at Pewsey was said to cover an area only 3 furlongs by ½ furlong in 1086,[21] and the parish has never been well wooded. In the triangle at the north end Withy copse was standing in 1300[22] and was accounted 11 a. c. 1700.[23] In 1767 Inlands grove north of Pewsey village was woodland accounted 20 a. and there was 10 a. of wood near the western parish boundary at Hare Street,[24] and by 1773 a copse had been planted beside Sunnyhill Lane north of Pewsey village.[25] In 1838 there was 70 a. of woodland in the parish. Withy copse then measured 28 a., there was 14 a. of woodland on the hill fort on Martinsell Hill, most of it planted in the period 1800–5, and most of the other woodland stood as copses of 5–12 a. in the north half of the parish.[26] By 1886 a few of those copses had been removed and additional trees planted on the west-facing scarp west of Martinsell Hill.[27] The distribution and amount of woodland changed little between 1886 and the late 20th century, when apparently less than 100 a. of the parish was wooded.[28]

The parish had 267 poll-tax payers in 1377,[29] apparently c. 648 inhabitants in 1676.[30] The population, 1,179 in 1801, increased rapidly in the earlier 19th century. It stood at 1,588 in 1831, 1,825 in 1841, when 69 people lived in the union workhouse built in the parish in 1836, and 1,921 in 1851, when 122 people lived in the workhouse. It was 2,027 in 1861, when labourers building a railway were temporarily resident in the parish. From 1,930 in 1871 it declined steadily to reach 1,574 in 1931. The conversion of the workhouse to a colony of mental defectives in the 1930s and the building of many new houses in the parish caused increases in the population, which stood at 2,351 in 1951, 2,579 in 1981, and, after the boundary changes of 1987, 2,831 in 1991.[31]

No road across Pewsey parish was turnpiked[32] and none had more than local importance until the 20th century. Pewsey village stands on a road

which, east of it, links villages below the northern scarp of Salisbury Plain; it may first have linked the villages from centre to centre, but in the later 18th century and later bypassed each one at its north end and, as Milton Road, approached Pewsey from the north-east.[33] As Salisbury Road it leaves Pewsey towards the south-west and joins the roads linking the villages in the Avon valley between Upavon and Salisbury. From the north Pewsey was reached from Marlborough by a road across Martinsell Hill which approached the village via Milton Road, and to the south was linked to Salisbury by a road leading from the village across the downs to join the main downland Marlborough–Salisbury road at Everleigh. The road across Martinsell Hill went out of use in the 19th century; alternative routes from Marlborough avoiding that hill ran to the east via Clench in Milton Lilbourne parish and to the west via Oare in Wilcot parish. The Marlborough–Oare road was part of a Marlborough–Salisbury road which led via Upavon and the Avon valley and bypassed Pewsey; Hare Street, which marks the parish boundary on the west, was part of its course.[34] South of Upavon the road was turnpiked in 1840,[35] and from c. 1900, when the main Marlborough–Salisbury road across the downs was closed to allow for military training,[36] it became more important. Presumably because its link with Pewsey village, serving Pewsey wharf and Pewsey station, was, as Marlborough Road, already well used, that link and Salisbury Road leading south-west from the village were improved as parts of what became a main Marlborough–Salisbury road through the village. Hare Street remains in use as a minor road, as does Everleigh Road leading south from Pewsey village to Everleigh. Westwards from Pewsey village roads leaving the parish as Wilcot Road and Woodborough Road lead to Devizes across, respectively, the north and south parts of the Vale of Pewsey.

The Kennet & Avon canal was built across the parish c. 1806–7 and a wharf was built north-west of the village; the whole canal was open from 1810. A windmill built on the south bank in Pewsey parish to supply water to the canal was removed between 1820 and 1839.[37] The canal was restored across the parish in the early 1970s.[38]

The Berks. & Hants Extension Railway was opened across the parish in 1862; Pewsey station was built immediately north-west of the village. The line led from Reading to Devizes and from

20 Below, agric.   21 V.C.H. Wilts. ii, p. 127.
22 B.L. Stowe MS. 925, f. 188.
23 Alnwick Castle Mun. X.II.11, box 6, survey of Pewsey, c. 1700.
24 Ibid. X.II.11, box 10, bdle. of draft deeds, Northumberland to Amor, 1767; W.R.O. 490/1060.
25 Andrews and Dury, Map (W.R.S. viii), pl. 12.
26 W.R.O., tithe award; ibid. 408/1, deed, Pyke and Ailesbury, 1807.
27 O.S. Maps 6", Wilts. XXXV–XXXVI (1888–9 edns.).
28 Cf. ibid. 1/25,000, SU 05/15, SU 06/16 (1987 edns.).
29 V.C.H. Wilts. iv. 309.
30 Compton Census, ed. Whiteman, 127.
31 V.C.H. Wilts. iv. 320–1, 323, 355; Census, 1981; 1991; for the workhouse, colony, and ho. bldg., below, this section

(Pewsey).
32 Cf. V.C.H. Wilts. iv. 257.
33 Andrews and Dury, Map (W.R.S. viii), pl. 12; apart from Hare Street, the names of roads given in this para. are 20th-cent.
34 Andrews and Dury, Map (W.R.S. viii), pls. 8–9, 11–12; C. Greenwood, Map of Wilts. (1820); O.S. Map 1", sheet 14 (1817 edn.); cf. ibid. 6", Wilts. XXXV–XXXVI (1888–9 edns.).
35 V.C.H. Wilts. iv. 257, 264.
36 Ibid. xv. 63, 65.
37 K. R. Clew, Kennet & Avon Canal (1985), 68–9, 73; Greenwood, Map of Wilts.; W.R.O., tithe award; above, plate 37.
38 R. W. Squires, Canals Revived, 112.

1900 to Westbury; from 1906 it has been part of a main line between London and Exeter.[39]

Artefacts from the Palaeolithic period and later have been found in various parts of the parish. In the north part, on the Marlborough Downs, the Iron-Age hill fort on Martinsell Hill covers 32 a. and has a prehistoric ditch leading west from its north-west corner; south-west of the hill fort another east–west ditch lies on the face of the scarp. On the downs in the south part of the parish there are barrows including a group of eight south-east of Down Farm, a pair of circular enclosures each of 3 a. and an enclosure of 2 a. all of the Iron-Age or Romano-British period, and, respectively on and astride the southernmost part of the parish boundary, a prehistoric enclosure of 4 a. and a prehistoric field system;[40] immediately north of the face of the scarp a cemetery of the mid 6th century A.D. was excavated over the period 1969–75.[41]

In 1237 the north half of the parish was defined as part of Savernake forest, the southern boundary of which apparently followed the line of what were later called Milton Road, High Street, North Street, and Wilcot Road.[42] It was disafforested in 1330.[43] The hill fort on the summit of Martinsell Hill, which was granted by the king to William Harding in 1302,[44] was defined as a detached part of the forest in 1330;[45] it was later part of Pewsey parish and probably of Pewsey manor.[46]

A gibbet stood on the downs in the south part of the parish in the later 18th century and earlier 19th.[47] On the north-facing scarp the figure of a white horse was cut in 1937; it was claimed that an earlier figure had been obliterated.[48] North of the scarp and to the west a part of the open fields was called the Hip end or the Heap end, and another part there was called Denny Sutton;[49] in the 19th century those names were agglutinated and as Denny Sutton Hipend transposed to a summit of the downs south of the scarp wrongly called Heap end on a map of 1773 and later maps.[50] North-east of Pewsey village 12 ha. beside the Avon has been managed as a nature reserve since 1980.[51]

PEWSEY. The church, a house which was probably the rectory house, and the demesne farmstead of Pewsey manor were built near each other on rising ground within a bend of the Avon.[52] The bridge called Parsonage bridge in 1615 presumably crossed the Avon east of

them.[53] In the early 18th century a new rectory house was built on lower land east of the river,[54] probably on a previously unoccupied site, and a red-brick three-arched bridge, built in the early 19th century across the Avon to link the new house to what was later called Church Street, presumably replaced Parsonage bridge. East of the church what was probably the old rectory house was called Court House in 1997.[55] It has as its core a late 16th-century, two-bayed, two-storeyed house with an east chimney stack; a blocked mullioned parlour window survives *in situ*. Soon after the house was built a new bay, adjoining the hall and incorporating decorative timber framing, was added on the east, and soon afterwards a lower timber-framed bay was added east of that. In the early 18th century a new block containing a staircase was built on the south side of the house at its west end, and a façade was built across the old and new parts of the west front; an oriel window was made in the façade in the earlier 19th century. In the later 19th century a verandah was added on the west front and a large south-east service block was built. On the north side of Church Street and opposite Court House a small house of red brick and thatch was said to have been built in 1734.[56] Also at the east end of Church Street a cottage incorporating timber framing was apparently built in the 18th century and several houses were built in the 19th and early 20th. South of the church most of the farmstead was rebuilt in the 1840s, the farm buildings mainly in 1845, the farmhouse, Manor Farm, in 1848–9.[57] Manor Farm was rebuilt as a plain three-storeyed house; the tall panelled chimney stack at each corner suggests that a roughly square house of the late 17th century or early 18th was incorporated in it. It was converted into flats between 1980 and 1982.[58] About then a farm building west of the house was rebuilt as three cottages, and on the site of farm buildings south of the house Manor Court, three two-storeyed buildings containing 20 cottages and 5 flats, was built *c.* 1980.[59]

In the Middle Ages customary tenants of Pewsey manor held many small farmsteads at Pewsey, presumably in the streets later called High, River, and North Streets.[60] In 1773 there were buildings on both sides of all three streets,[61] and near the north end of North Street on the east side an 18th-century house of red brick and thatch, refaced in the 19th century and standing

[39] *V.C.H. Wilts.* iv. 286–7, 289.
[40] Ibid. i (1), 95–6, 187, 210, 258, 268, 276; *W.A.M.* lxvi. 61–71.
[41] *W.A.M.* lxv. 206; lxx/lxxi. 142, 144–5.
[42] Ibid. xlix. 394; *V.C.H. Wilts.* iv. 418, 448; for the street names, below, this section (Pewsey); for Whipps hill, mentioned as a boundary mark, cf. W.R.O. 9/1/134, f. 222.
[43] *V.C.H. Wilts.* iv. 399–400, 450–1.
[44] *Cal. Pat.* 1301–7, 59.
[45] *W.A.M.* xlix. 423.
[46] Cf. W.R.O., tithe award; below, manors (Pewsey).
[47] Greenwood, *Map of Wilts.*; *Pewsey through the Ages,* i (copy in Wilts. local studies libr., Trowbridge), 8.
[48] M. Marples, *White Horses and other Hill Figures,* 105–7.
[49] e.g. Alnwick Castle Mun. X.II.11, box 8, survey of Pewsey, 1692; X.II.11, box 12, mins. of Pewsey cts., ct. 14 Aug. 1728; W.R.O. 9/1/82; 1634/34.

[50] *Andrews and Dury, Map* (W.R.S. viii), pl. 12; Greenwood, *Map of Wilts.*; O.S. Maps 1", sheet 14 (1817 edn.); 6", Wilts. XLI (1889 edn.).
[51] Wilts. Trust for Nature Conservation, *Jones Mill* (copy in Wilts. local studies libr.).
[52] Cf. W.R.O., tithe award.
[53] Ibid. 9/1/136, rot. 11d.
[54] Below, church.   [55] Above, plate 15.
[56] Local inf.
[57] Lond. Metro. Archives, H1/ST/E18, f. 115; H1/ST/E56/6/20; H1/ST/E56/8/1; H1/ST/E56/10/2; H1/ST/E56/10/36; H1/ST/E56/10/47.
[58] W.A.S. Libr., sale cat. xxxii, no. 31; xxxiv, no. 47.
[59] Wilts. Cuttings, xxix. 118–19.
[60] P.R.O., SC 6/Hen. VIII/3341, rott. 48d.–49d.; cf. B.L. Harl. MS. 1761, ff. 132–137v.; for those in other places in the par., below, this section.
[61] *Andrews and Dury, Map* (W.R.S. viii), pl. 12.

in 1997, is known to have been the farmhouse on a customary holding of 10 a.[62] From the late 18th century farms in the parish became larger[63] and the buildings of small farmsteads presumably went out of use, and in the 19th century, stimulated by the building of the canal, the opening of a market, and the building of the union workhouse and the railway, Pewsey assumed characteristics of a small town.[64] In 1839 apparently the only farmstead standing in the three streets was the small one near the north end of North Street,[65] and for most of the 19th and 20th centuries many of the houses were partly used as offices or for trade or retail;[66] in 1996 a large supermarket was built south of High Street, and in 1997 there were c. 45 commercial premises in the streets.

High Street[67] grew eastwards from a mill standing in the 13th century and driven by the Avon; industrial premises were built immediately north of the mill in the 19th century.[68] High Street was so called in 1797.[69] A red-brick three-arched bridge over the Avon at the west end was built in that year;[70] it presumably replaced the bridge called Town bridge in 1719[71] and was widened to the south in 1959.[72] On the north side of the street at the east end an 18th-century house of red brick and thatch has been much enlarged. In the main part of High Street an 18th-century house was apparently the only building older than 1800 to survive in 1997. Several new houses, of red brick and two storeys, were built in the early 19th century. On the north side of the street one 19th-century building is of three storeys, and there is a house in domestic Gothic style built c. 1870 of red brick with decoration in blue brick. Several terraces of cottages were built in the 19th century, on the south side a large detached red-brick house, in 1997 a bank, was built in the late 19th century, and on the north side a small bank was built in the earlier 20th century.

In River Street the oldest buildings to survive in 1997 were two red-brick houses on the east side each apparently of the early 19th century. A school was built on the east side in 1840.[73] On the west side two three-storeyed houses were built in the mid 19th century, one as an inn. On the east side a malthouse associated with the inn was converted to a village hall in 1898–9,[74] demolished in 1993,[75] and replaced by a block of flats.

In North Street,[76] in addition to the farm-house near the north end, a red-brick and thatched cottage, two other cottages, and part of the Royal Oak are all 18th-century. The Royal Oak was extended westwards in the earlier 19th century and northwards in 1886.[77] On the east side of the street most of the buildings standing in 1997 were early or mid 19th-century: they included a stone house, a terrace of four stone cottages, and a stone-fronted terrace of five cottages. Also on the east side two fire stations[78] and a bus shelter were built in the 20th century. On the west side most of the buildings standing in 1997 were of the later 19th century or early 20th: they included a nonconformist chapel,[79] the Greyhound inn, and a terrace of four houses incorporating shops.

In the 19th century the wide triangular junction of High Street, River Street, and North Street[80] became the site of a market and was given the name Market Place.[81] On the south-east side a pair of timber-framed and thatched cottages is apparently late 17th- or early 18th-century. On the west side stands Phoenix Row, a nine-bayed three-storeyed building of brick and thatch erected in 1823, the year before the market was granted,[82] and incorporating shops; four of the bays have been reduced to two storeys. North of Phoenix Row stands a thatched house of two storeys and attics, and north of that a terrace of four three-storeyed houses built in the mid 19th century each with a shop on the ground floor and a canted bay window on the first. On the north-east side of Market Place stand a red-brick house of the earlier 19th century and a building of 1959 incorporating a police station and a pair of police houses.[83] A statue commemorating King Alfred (d. 899), whose estates included Pewsey, was erected in the middle of Market Place in 1913.[84]

Church Street, High Street, Market Place, River Street, and the south part of North Street are part of a conservation area designated in 1985.[85]

By 1839 there had been settlement in several offshoots of Pewsey village. In the 17th century there was probably settlement on the waste at a place called the Bowling alley or the Bowling green[86] beside what was later called Wilcot Road. In 1713, when it apparently consisted of six or more cottages, settlement there was called the World's End; later it was sometimes called West End. In 1773 the World's End consisted of buildings on both sides of c. 200 m. of Wilcot Road,[87] in 1839 of c. 20 cottages and houses.[88]

62 W.R.O., tithe award; for such holdings, called worklands, below, agric. [preamble].
63 Below, agric.
64 Above, this section [canal; railway]; for the workhouse, below, this section; below, mkt.; trade and ind.
65 W.R.O., tithe award.
66 e.g. Kelly's Dir. Wilts. (1848 and later edns.).
67 Above, plate 43.
68 O.S. Map 6", Wilts. XLI (1889 edn.); W.R.O., tithe award; below, mills; trade and ind.
69 W.R.O. 493/49.
70 Gent. Mag. lxvii (2), 792; date on bldg.
71 Lond. Metro. Archives, H1/ST/E88/1, ct. 21 Apr. 1719.
72 W.R.O., F 4/150/35/2.
73 Below, educ.
74 W.A.S. Libr., sale cat. vii, no. 74; Wilts. Cuttings, vii. 15.
75 Pewsey Village Trail (copy in Wilts. local studies libr.), 4.

76 Above, plate 42.
77 Date on bldg.
78 Cf. below, this section.
79 Ibid. nonconf.
80 Above, plate 41.
81 Kelly's Dir. Wilts. (1875 and later edns.); below, mkt.
82 Date on bldg.; below, mkt.
83 For the police station, below, this section (public services).
84 Wilts. Gaz. 26 June 1913; below, manor (Pewsey).
85 Inf. from Dept. of Planning and Highways, Co. Hall, Trowbridge.
86 Alnwick Castle Mun. X.II.11, box 6, Pewsey ct. bk. 1692–1703, ct. 24 Mar. 1696; X.II.11, box 8, survey of Pewsey, 1692.
87 Andrews and Dury, Map (W.R.S. viii), pl. 12; O.S. Maps 6", Wilts. XLI (1889 edn.); 1/2,500, Wilts. XLI. 4 (1900 and later edns.); Lond. Metro. Archives, H1/ST/E88/1, ct. 16 Apr. 1713.
88 W.R.O., tithe award.

An inn was opened there *c.* 1870,[89] and, in an acute angle between the road and the railway, industrial premises were opened in the early 1920s.[90] Of the cottages standing in 1800 apparently only two, both thatched and one possibly 17th-century, survived in 1997. Of *c.* 40 houses and cottages standing in 1997 most were on the south side of the road and about half were 19th-century; on the north side they included a later 19th-century house of red brick, with dressings of buff brick, in mixed 17th-century styles. Four pairs of houses were built between Pewsey station and the north side of Wilcot Road in 1936,[91] and a large school was built on the south side of the road in 1958.[92]

West of the World's End a small group of cottages built on the waste at the junction of Wilcot Road and Woodborough Road between 1820 and 1839 was called Piccadilly in 1886.[93] A small group of cottages stood there in 1997. The union workhouse was built nearby;[94] on the north side of Wilcot Road at Piccadilly a house was built in 1924[95] for an employee at the workhouse, and 17 houses were built between 1941 and *c.* 1960 for staff at the colony which succeeded it.[96]

On the east side of former open arable called Easterton field allotted to the rector as glebe in 1777 buildings were erected along Easterton Lane in the 18th century. Several cottages of that date survive, including one timber-framed and thatched and one much altered and extended; *c.* 10 cottages and houses were built later. At the south end of Easterton Lane, King's Corner was so called in 1797, when cottages probably stood on the waste there.[97] In the mid and later 19th century a terrace of 10 small cottages called Wilderness Row, a school, and a mission room were built at King's Corner.[98] Easterton Lane and King's Corner are part of the conservation area designated in 1985.[99]

At Raffin, south of King's Corner, two attached timber-framed and thatched cottages of the 17th century, and a house of brick and thatch possibly of the early 19th, survived in 1997; two other cottages standing there in 1839 were replaced in the 20th century. In Raffin Lane west of Raffin six pairs of cottages were built between 1839 and 1874,[1] *c.* 10 houses and bungalows in the 20th century.

South of Manor Farm at the junction of Everleigh Road and Salisbury Road an alehouse open in the mid 18th century gave the name

Swan to a pocket of settlement.[2] The only building at Swan in 1839 stood on the waste, was long and narrow, and may have been the inn. In 1997 the south part of it survived as a three-storeyed house; the north part was replaced by a house built in the mid 19th century. A farmstead was built at Swan between 1839 and 1886,[3] and in the earlier 20th century a large farm was worked from it.[4] The farmhouse is square and of ashlar stone; in the late 20th century it was converted to flats, new houses were built to adjoin it, and two farm buildings were converted for light industrial use. In Green Drove south-east of the farmhouse three pairs of estate cottages were also built between 1839 and 1886.[5] Near Swan other houses were built in Green Drove, Everleigh Road, and Salisbury Road in the 20th century.

A little north of Pewsey village there may have been cottages on the waste at Knowle in 1713.[6] Hollybush Lane, a sunken road so called in 1797,[7] led to them from the south. In 1839 at Knowle there were about nine cottages or pairs of cottages,[8] of which three or four, thatched, apparently 18th-century, and extended, were standing in 1997. A few cottages were built at Knowle after 1839 and a few houses in the 20th century.

In the 20th century three large houses were built on the north side of Church Street, a timber-framed and thatched house *c.* 1925 and, *c.* 1928 and in 1974, successive rectory houses.[9] In the angle between North Street and Wilcot Road 36 council houses were built in the Crescent in 1926–7, 6 more in the Crescent over the period 1933–5, 20 in Haines Lane (later Haines Terrace) in 1938, and *c.* 105 between 1945 and 1954.[10] At the west end of the council estate *c.* 92 council houses and bungalows were built in Broadfields in the 1960s, and at the east end 4 bungalows and a block of 24 flats were built in the late 1960s, 24 bungalows in Aston Close in the early 1970s, and 69 houses in Goddard Road *c.* 1990. A private estate of *c.* 35 bungalows was built in Astley Close off Hollybush Lane in the late 1960s, one of 70 houses and bungalows was built in Swan Meadow off Raffin Lane in the late 1960s and early 1970s,[11] and several smaller estates were built in the village in the later 20th century. In the late 1980s and early 1990s *c.* 200 houses were built west of Hollybush Lane.[12]

Pewsey union workhouse was built in 1836[13] on the north side of Wilcot Road west of the

[89] *Kelly's Dir. Wilts.* (1867; 1875).
[90] O.S. Maps 1/2,500, Wilts. XLI. 4 (1900, 1924 edns.); W.R.O., G 10/760/66.
[91] O.S. Maps 1/2,500, Wilts. XLI. 4 (1924, 1936 edns.); W.R.O., G 10/760/232.
[92] Below, educ.
[93] Greenwood, *Map of Wilts.*; O.S. Map 6", Wilts. XLI (1889 edn.); W.R.O., tithe award.
[94] Below, this section.   [95] Date on bldg.
[96] W.R.O., G 10/505/1; G 10/760/463; ibid. J 6/130/13; for the colony, below, this section.
[97] W.R.O. 493/49.
[98] W.A.S. Libr., sale cat. viii, no. 5; below, church; educ.
[99] Inf. from Dept. of Planning and Highways, Co. Hall, Trowbridge.
[1] W.A.S. Libr., sale cat. viii, no. 5; W.R.O., tithe award.
[2] Alnwick Castle Mun. X.II.11, box 8, survey of Pewsey, 1755; W.R.O. 493/49.

[3] O.S. Map 6", Wilts. XLI (1889 edn.); W.R.O., tithe award.
[4] Below, agric. (Down Pewsey).
[5] O.S. Map 6", Wilts. XLI (1889 edn.); W.R.O., tithe award.
[6] Lond. Metro. Archives, H1/ST/E88/1, ct. 16 Apr. 1713.   [7] W.R.O. 493/49.
[8] Ibid. tithe award.
[9] O.S. Map 6", Wilts. XLI. NE. (1926 edn.); for the rectory hos., below, church.
[10] W.R.O., G 10/505/1; G 10/600/1; G 10/603/2.
[11] Ibid. A 1/355/390; A 1/355/415; A 1/355/440; A 1/355/465/2; A 1/355/540/4; A 1/355/550/4; for Broadfields, above, plate 38.
[12] W.R.O. 1634/41, agreement, Pewsey par. council and Ruralbrook, 1985.
[13] Date on bldg.: the date tablet is not contemporary with the bldg.

World's End. Of the buildings erected then, of stone and in a classical style, the principal block, the chapel, and an octagonal gatehouse and boardroom survived in 1997. By an agreement of 1915 between Wiltshire county council and the guardians of the union, mentally defective patients in the council's care were kept in the workhouse, and in 1932 the council appropriated the building for use as an industrial colony of the mentally defective.[14] New buildings were erected in the 1930s, and in 1938 *c.* 500 patients were housed.[15] In 1946, the year in which Haybrook House was added to its buildings, the colony was transferred from the county council to the National Council for Mental Health,[16] and as Pewsey mental hospital it was afterwards managed by various health authorities. In 1951 it had 400 patients, *c.* 100 staff, and grounds of 87 a.;[17] in 1960 it had 440 beds.[18] Haybrook House ceased to be part of the hospital in 1983.[19] In 1995 the hospital was closed,[20] and in 1997 large parts of it were being demolished.

Pewsey rural district council, created under an Act of 1872,[21] met in the boardroom at the workhouse until 1939, and from *c.* 1927 had offices in a house in Church Street.[22] In 1946 the council bought the old rectory house east of the Avon and accommodated itself there until local government was reorganized in 1974. In 1976 Kennet district council sold the building to Wiltshire county council,[23] which used it as offices until 1993 and sold it to the Barnabas Fund in 1997.[24]

Inns. There was an inn at Pewsey in 1538–9[25] and there were alehouses in the later 16th century and earlier 17th.[26] In 1646 the rector and other inhabitants petitioned at quarter sessions for the suppression of all alehouses in the parish; it was said that an inn, which had long been open there, was sufficient to cater for travellers.[27] In 1655 the innkeeper was hanged for his part in Penruddocke's rising.[28]

In the later 17th century and early 18th the Bear was an inn,[29] almost certainly in High Street; it had been closed by 1755.[30] The Phoenix has been open as an inn from *c.* 1700 or earlier;[31] from the mid 19th century or earlier and in 1997 it stood on the west side of River Street. The New inn, so called in 1767, was reopened as the Royal Oak in the 1820s, when it and the Phoenix were apparently the only inns in the parish.[32] The Royal Oak, in North Street, remained open in 1997.

The King's Arms, in High Street, was opened between 1848 and 1855, the New inn in North Street between 1855 and 1859, and the Plumber's Arms in High Street between 1867 and 1875;[33] as, respectively, the Moonrakers, the Greyhound, and Alfred's they remained open in 1997.[34] The Greyhound was rebuilt in the early 20th century.

At the World's End the Crown was opened between 1867 and 1875[35] and remained open in 1997. The Swan alehouse, at the place later called Swan, was open in 1755,[36] not in 1777[37] or later.

Public services. In the earlier 19th century there was a lockup in the triangle later called Market Place.[38] It was demolished probably in the early 1920s.[39] There was a police station at Pewsey from 1848[40] or earlier, presumably the earlier 19th-century house on the north-east side of Market Place which was the police station in 1886.[41] In the mid 19th century the county police stationed an inspector and two or three policemen there.[42] A pair of police houses incorporating a new police station was built in the garden of the old police station in 1959.[43] Petty sessions were held monthly at the Phoenix from the 1840s to the 1860s, at the police station in 1867 and to the 1950s, and from the 1950s to 1993 in the old rectory house.[44]

A fire engine was kept at Pewsey from 1800 or earlier.[45] In 1902 a new horse-drawn steam-powered fire engine was bought, and a building was erected in North Street to house it. In 1933 that fire engine was replaced by a lorry and a new trailer pump.[46] A new fire station for the Wiltshire fire brigade was built in North Street and opened in 1963.[47]

A gasworks had been built beside Marlborough Road north-west of the village by 1865; it was presumably built soon after the opening across the parish of the railway in 1862.[48] The streets of Pewsey were lit by gas until the First World War. In 1920 the Pewsey Electric Light

14 W.R.O., J 6/130/13.
15 *V.C.H. Wilts.* v. 332.
16 W.R.O., G 10/132/18; for Haybrook Ho., below, this section (other settlement).
17 W.R.O., G 10/132/26; ibid. J 6/130/13.
18 Ibid. J 6/130/15.
19 W.A.S. Libr., sale cat. xxxv, no. 56.
20 *Rep. E. Wilts. Health Care N.H.S. Trust* (1995–6): in W.R.O.
21 *V.C.H. Wilts.* iv. 335.
22 W.R.O., G 10/132/21.
23 Ibid. 1634/37.
24 Inf. from Dept. of Social Services, Co. Hall, Trowbridge; the Barnabas Fund, St. Andrew's Centre, St. Andrew's Road, Lond. E 13.
25 P.R.O., SC 6/Hen. VIII/3341, rot. 48d.
26 *Sess. Mins.* (W.R.S. iv), 18, 77; *Early-Stuart Tradesmen* (W.R.S. xv), p. 27; *W. Circuit Assize Orders*, ed. J. S. Cockburn, p. 15.
27 Hist. MSS. Com. 55, *Var. Colln.* i, p. 112.
28 *V.C.H. Wilts.* v. 149 n.
29 Lond. Metro. Archives, H1/ST/E88/1, ct. 22 May 1712; H1/ST/E88/3, cts. 31 July 1732, 19 July 1733.
30 Alnwick Castle Mun. X.II.11, box 8, survey of

Pewsey, 1755.
31 Ibid. X.II.11, box 6, survey of Pewsey, *c.* 1700.
32 W.R.O. 212B/5223; 1302/1; ibid. A 1/326/3.
33 *Kelly's Dir. Wilts.* (1848 and later edns.).
34 *Pewsey through the Ages*, iii (copy in Wilts. local studies libr.), 35; W.R.O. 1884/16.
35 *Kelly's Dir. Wilts.* (1867, 1875).
36 Alnwick Castle Mun. X.II.11, box 8, survey of Pewsey, 1755; above, this section.
37 W.R.O. 1634/34.
38 Ibid. tithe award.
39 Lond. Metro. Archives, H1/ST/E55/4; cf. O.S. Maps 1/2,500, XLI. 4 (1900, 1924 edns.).
40 *Kelly's Dir. Wilts.* (1848).
41 O.S. Map 6", Wilts. XLI (1889 edn.).
42 *Kelly's Dir. Wilts.* (1859); *Harrod's Dir. Wilts.* (1865).
43 W.R.O., F 1/100/2.
44 Ibid. F 1/101/3; *Kelly's Dir. Wilts.* (1848 and later edns.); Wilts. Cuttings, xxi. 229.
45 W.R.O. 493/49.
46 P. Thorpe, *Moonraker Firemen*, 127–8.
47 W.R.O., F 1/250/8.
48 *Harrod's Dir. Wilts.* (1865); cf. above, this section [railway].

Company converted Town mill to generate electricity, and from 1921 the streets were lit by electricity.[49] A waterworks was constructed in Wilcot Road west of the workhouse between 1899 and 1910,[50] and a sewage works was built beside the Avon south-west of the village in 1938.[51]

There has been a post office in Pewsey from the earlier 19th century.[52] Behind the post office, then on the west side of North Street, a telephone exchange was built in 1941.[53]

Pewsey burial board was formed in 1862 and, on the south side of Wilcot Road opposite the workhouse, a cemetery and a mortuary chapel were consecrated in 1863. The chapel was designed by C. J. Phipps.[54]

A branch of the county library was opened in a converted shop in High Street in 1959. In 1979 it was closed and replaced by a mobile building parked west of North Street; that building remained the public library in 1997.[55]

In the mid 20th century land south of the west end of High Street was used for a bus depot,[56] later for car parking. Land west of North Street was leased in 1946 to Pewsey rural district council for car parking;[57] later much more land west of North Street was used for car parking.

Recreation. The Bouverie hall, a converted malthouse on the east side of River Street, was opened as a village hall in 1899.[58] It was closed in 1989 when a Bouverie hall newly built on land west of North Street was opened. The new hall incorporates offices of the parish council.[59] A Foresters hall was built in High Street in 1886,[60] a British Legion club was opened in High Street in 1944,[61] and a scouts hall was opened in the Crescent in 1953.[62]

Cricket was played at Pewsey in the late 18th century.[63] In the late 19th century and earlier 20th land owned by the rector and lying between his garden and Easterton Lane was in use as a cricket ground;[64] the land was bought by Pewsey parish council in 1947 and since 1951 has been in use as a playing field.[65] In the 1920s and 1930s there was a golf course west of Manor Farm.[66] North-west of its buildings Pewsey hospital had a sports field in the later 20th century, when there was also a football pitch beside Wilcot Road. On land adjoining Pewsey Vale school a swimming pool was built in 1970[67] and a sports hall was built in 1976,[68] both partly for public use.

The Rex cinema was built at the west end, and on the south side, of High Street in 1938.[69] It was closed *c.* 1960, converted for industrial use,[70] and demolished in 1989.[71] A privately owned heritage centre was opened in a former foundry at the west end, and on the north side, of High Street in 1992.[72]

A feast or carnival has been held at Pewsey yearly in September from the 1890s.[73]

KEPNAL. The land of Kepnal probably lay as a strip along the eastern boundary of the parish,[74] and Kepnal was a street village almost certainly colonized from Pewsey. The village was called Tenhides, presumably from when it was founded,[75] although its land was apparently no more extensive than that of its eastern neighbour Fyfield (Fivehides) in Milton Lilbourne.[76] Kephill or Kepenhill had become the usual name of the village by the 13th century.[77]

From the 16th century to the 18th there were apparently 6–10 farmsteads in Kepnal. In the later 18th century and earlier 19th the number of farms in the parish was reduced,[78] and in 1839 no more than one small farm was worked from Kepnal; the farmstead stood at the south end of the street[79] and was demolished in the 20th century. New farm buildings were erected east of the street in the earlier and mid 20th century;[80] they were apparently little used in 1997.

Only one former farmhouse, built of red brick and thatch in the early 19th century and extended in similar materials in the 20th, stood in Kepnal street in 1997, near the north end on the east side. On the west side stood a small cottage, timber-framed, thatched, and apparently 17th-century, and a cottage of brick and thatch apparently built in the late 17th century and extended in the 18th. In the 20th century 10 houses and bungalows were built along the street.

The line of Kepnal street continues northwards as Dursden Lane, so called in 1755,[81] a sunken lane beside which, possibly on the waste, eight cottages, pairs of cottages, or houses had been built by 1839.[82] Three of those buildings

49 *Pewsey through the Ages*, iii. 11; W.A.S. Libr., sale cat. xiii, no. 9; Lond. Metro. Archives, H1/ST/E55/4; W.R.O. 1634/2; for Town mill, below, mills.
50 W.R.O., Inland Revenue, val. reg. 57; cf. O.S. Map 1/2,500, Wilts. XLI. 4 (1900 edn.).
51 *Pewsey through the Ages*, i. 12.
52 *Kelly's Dir. Wilts.* (1848 and later edns.).
53 O.S. Map 1/2,500, Wilts. XLI. 4 (1936 edn.); W.R.O., G 10/505/1.
54 W.R.O., D 1/60/8/19.
55 Inf. from Local Studies Librarian, Co. Hall, Trowbridge.
56 Local inf.   57 W.R.O., G 10/154/6.
58 Wilts. Cuttings, vii. 15.
59 W.R.O. 1634/41; 1634/50.
60 *Kelly's Dir. Wilts.* (1895); O.S. Map 1/2,500, Wilts. XLI. 4 (1900 edn.).
61 W.R.O., G 10/505/1.
62 *Pewsey through the Ages*, i. 15.
63 *V.C.H. Wilts.* iv. 378.
64 O.S. Maps 1/2,500, Wilts. XLI. 4 (1900, 1924 edns.); cf. W.R.O., tithe award.
65 *Pewsey through the Ages*, i. 15.

66 O.S. Map 1/2,500, Wilts. XLI. 4 (1936 edn.); W.R.O., G 10/500/72; G 10/518/6.
67 W.R.O., F 8/186/27; for the sch., below, educ.
68 W.R.O., F 8/186/25.
69 Ibid. G 10/505/1.
70 Ibid. 1634/4; *Pewsey through the Ages*, i. 14.
71 *Pewsey Village Trail*, 5.
72 Wilts. Cuttings, xxxii. 154; for the foundry, below, trade and ind.
73 *Kelly's Dir. Wilts.* (1895 and later edns.); *Pewsey Carnival* (souvenir programme in Wilts. local studies libr.).
74 Cf. below, agric. (Kepnal and Southcott).
75 B.L. Harl. MS. 1761, ff. 124, 126.
76 Cf. above, Milton Lilbourne, intro. (map; Fyfield).
77 *P.N. Wilts.* (E.P.N.S.), 351.
78 Below, agric.; for the farmsteads, ibid. agric. (Kepnal and Southcott).
79 W.R.O., tithe award.
80 O.S. Maps 6", Wilts. XLI. NE. (1926 edn.); XLII. NW. (1901, 1926 edns.).
81 Alnwick Castle Mun. X.II.11, box 8, survey of Pewsey, 1755.
82 W.R.O., tithe award.

survive, a thatched cottage of the early 18th century and two houses, each of red brick and thatch, apparently of the early 19th. A red-brick and thatched house was built in the earlier 20th century,[83] two other houses later in the century.

West of Kepnal street and beside Milton Road a brick and thatched house, built in 1762[84] and later called Kepnal Farm, was part of a farmstead in 1839 and 1997. In the early 19th century a house of red brick and slate was built beside the road south-west of it. Beside the road north-east of it a small farmstead was standing in 1839.[85] In 1997 its site was occupied by a large house, sometimes called Manor House,[86] of which the north-east part was apparently built c. 1840, the south-west part c. 1870. In the later 20th century several bungalows were built between Manor House and Ball.[87]

EAST SHARCOTT. Sharcott, like Kepnal and Southcott a north–south street village almost certainly colonized from Pewsey, had the epithet added to its name apparently in the 18th century.[88] In the 16th century the village probably consisted mainly of five farmsteads held of Pewsey manor by copy,[89] and in 1997 five farmhouses stood in the street, all on the west side. At the north end the Old Dairy House is a red-brick and thatched farmhouse of the late 18th century or early 19th. South of that Manor Farm is a house of red brick and slate built in the early 19th century; it has a three-bayed entrance front incorporating a Roman Doric porch and was extended in the mid 19th century. Further south Sharcott House is a red-brick house built in the 18th century, much enlarged c. 1900 when it was given a bracketed cornice and an entrance porch, and further enlarged c. 1904.[90] At the south end of the street stands a large timber-framed house all apparently built in the late 16th century or early 17th; it consists of a north–south range of one storey and attic, to which a bay was added on the south and a tall chamber block with decorative timber framing was added as a cross wing on the north. North of it a house consisting only of a north–south range and incorporating decorative timber framing[91] is of similar date. In 1839 only three of those houses were incorporated in farmsteads. The farm buildings at Sharcott House were removed between 1839 and 1886, and in 1997 the only farm buildings in the street stood behind Manor Farm. Of three houses or cottages and several farm buildings standing on the east side of the street in 1839[92] only a cottage of red brick and thatch built in the 18th century on the waste at the north end survived in 1997.

Beside the lane of which East Sharcott street forms part buildings were erected north and south of the village in the 19th and 20th centuries. To the north a terrace of four cottages, of brick and thatch, called Sharcott Barracks, and one house in 1997, was built on the waste in 1845. Between that and the village a cattle yard was built in the mid 20th century and extensive buildings for potato packing were erected in the late 20th century. To the south a small red-brick house was built in the 18th century. In the mid 19th century it was enlarged, farm buildings were erected near it, and the farmstead was given the name New Farm.[93]

WEST SHARCOTT. In 1225 Adam Sturmy was licensed to build a chapel at his house at Sharcott and to employ a chaplain to serve it. The house may have stood at West Sharcott where Adam's son Henry almost certainly owned a mill in the earlier 13th century.[94] West Sharcott hamlet was so called in 1538–9.[95] In 1839 it consisted of the mill and mill house, two small farmsteads, two other houses, and a cottage.[96] The mill house, of red brick and thatch, appears to have been rebuilt. The mill was converted for residence in the 20th century. On the parish boundary north-west of the mill a timber-framed and thatched house, built in the 17th century and extended eastwards in the 18th, survived in 1997; farm buildings beside it in the 19th century were added to in the late 20th.[97] Beside the lane leading from East Sharcott the cottage, built on the waste in the 17th or 18th century and timber-framed and thatched, also survived in 1997. The two other houses and a farmstead near the mill were demolished.

SOUTHCOTT. Of the three north–south street villages almost certainly colonized from Pewsey, Southcott was the largest and probably the first to be established.[98] It apparently consisted of the line of settlement, in the later 20th century called Southcott only at the south end, running north to join Milton Road and the east end of High Street.[99] Settlement at the junction had been given the name Ball by 1795,[1] and in the 20th century the northern part of what was apparently Southcott street was called Ball Road. Between what in 1997 was called Southcott and what in 1997 was called Ball Road there is unlikely to have been much building on the marshy ground called Hurly Lake.[2] In the 16th century probably c. 15 farmsteads stood in Southcott street;[3] among c. 25 houses in the street in the earlier 19th century two farmsteads stood at Ball and two at the south end,[4] and in 1997 there was no

83 Cf. O.S. Maps 1/2,500, Wilts. XXXV. 16 (1887 and later edns.).
84 Date on bldg. 85 W.R.O., tithe award.
86 O.S. Maps 6", Wilts. XLI (1889 edn.); XLI. NE. (1901 edn.).
87 For Ball, below, this section (Southcott).
88 *Andrews and Dury, Map* (W.R.S. viii), pl. 11.
89 Below, agric. (Sharcott).
90 W.R.O., G 10/760/15.
91 Dept. of Environment, list of bldgs. of hist. interest (1987); for the 2 hos., above, plate 13.
92 O.S. Map 6", Wilts. XLI (1889 edn.); W.R.O., tithe award.
93 O.S. Maps 6", Wilts. XLI (1889 and later edns.);

W.R.O., tithe award; for Sharcott Barracks, Lond. Metro. Archives, H1/ST/E66/47/3/1; for potato packing, below, agric. (Sharcott).
94 B.L. Harl. MS. 1761, ff. 130v., 132.
95 P.R.O., SC 6/Hen. VIII/3341, rot. 49.
96 W.R.O., tithe award; for the mill, below, mills.
97 O.S. Maps 6", Wilts. XLI (1889 and later edns.); W.R.O., tithe award.
98 Below, agric. [preamble].
99 Cf. *Andrews and Dury, Map* (W.R.S. viii), pl. 12.
1 *Coroners' Bills, 1752–96* (W.R.S. xxxvi), p. 132.
2 For Hurly Lake, above, this section.
3 Below, agric. (Kepnal and Southcott).
4 W.R.O., tithe award.

farmstead among *c.* 40 houses at Ball and in Ball Road or among the seven houses at what was then called Southcott. Probably *c.* 1768, the year in which Pewsey manor was divided,[5] a stone was placed at Ball to mark where the tithings of Down Pewsey, Kepnal, and Southcott met; by 1798 it had been unlawfully removed, and in 1805 it was replaced by triangular posts.[6]

The houses standing at Ball include Ball House, built of red brick and slate as a farmhouse in the early 19th century, and two 18th-century houses of red brick and thatch. Also at Ball, Ball Cottage is a timber-framed and thatched building on an L plan; it consists of a late-medieval front range, in which a cruck is visible, and a 17th-century rear wing.[7] Adjoining Ball Cottage, a red-brick and thatched house of the 18th century was refaced in the 19th century. At the north end of Ball Road on the west side stand four red-brick houses all apparently of the 18th century; also on the west side of the road there are two timber-framed cottages apparently of the 18th century. At the south end of Ball Road, where it meets Easterton Lane at King's Corner, several cottages had been built on the waste by 1839.[8] There was a cooperage on the east side of the road: a brick and thatched house, from the 1870s used to retail beer and called the Cooper's Arms, may have been built for the cooper *c.* 1800[9] and was open as the Cooper's Arms in 1997. In the 20th century *c.* 14 houses and bungalows were built in Ball Road, which was part of the conservation area designated in 1985.[10]

In 1997 at what was then called Southcott there were six houses on the east side of the street and one on the west. That on the west, Southcott Manor, is an early 19th-century farmhouse with a Doric porch; north of it a timber-framed, weatherboarded, and thatched barn of *c.* 1700 survives.[11] On the east side of the street, from north to south, Mills Farm is a thatched farmhouse apparently of the 18th century, there is a timber-framed and red-brick house of the 17th and 18th centuries, a red-brick and thatched house of the 18th century, a 20th-century house, and a large red-brick house of the earlier 19th century; at the south end Southcott House, which has an octagonal flint and brick gatehouse and is approached by a bridge over Winter's Drove, was built in the mid 19th century.

In the lane west of the south end of Southcott village farm buildings were erected in the 19th century and as Green Drove Farm greatly extended in the 20th, a trio of cottages was built between 1899 and 1923,[12] and a house was built in the later 20th century.

WEST WICK. In the 13th century, when it was so called and its men were mentioned, West Wick was the westernmost of three small settlements called Wick and probably consisted of several farmsteads.[13] Such a settlement may have stood on or near the dry-valley site occupied from the 18th century or earlier by West Wick Farm.[14] In the 16th century West Wick Farm was almost certainly the only farmstead.[15] West Wick House was the only house at West Wick in 1839, when farm buildings stood immediately north and east of it.[16]

West Wick House was built in the early 18th century, one room deep, of five bays, and of two storeys and a half; its staircase, which rises through all the storeys, remains *in situ.* On the south a parallel range, also of five bays and one room deep but of only two storeys, was added in the mid 18th century, probably soon after 1767, the year in which Henry Pyke bought the freehold of West Wick farm;[17] the south façade incorporates a straight parapet, a central pediment, and an open-pedimented Roman Doric doorcase. On the north an L-shaped east service wing was added about the same time as, or shortly after, the south range was built. Between 1937 and 1942 the south range was altered for B. G. Catterns. A marble fireplace was inserted in the drawing room, which was the west room on the ground floor, and rooms were made in the roof space. The range was altered again between 1946 and *c.* 1960 for Patrick Devlin (Lord Devlin from 1961) to designs by D. G. Collie. The drawing room and the entrance passage were thrown together, Corinthian columns being inserted at the east end of the room and two windows at the west end, and the adjoining east room was panelled. A north bow was added to the west room on the ground floor of the earlier range, and the east side of the house, where a semicircular portico was added on the east of the east room of the earlier range, was converted to the entrance front.[18] Among other farm buildings in 1997 a barn of brick and thatch apparently built in the late 18th century stood east of the house, and a building of limestone ashlar, in classical style and apparently early 19th-century, stood south of the barn.

South-east of West Wick House two pairs of cottages were built between 1886 and 1899,[19] and north-east of it a house was built *c.* 1938.[20]

OTHER SETTLEMENT. On the lowland between West Wick and the main villages in the parish several isolated farmsteads were built. A little north of Pewsey village Buckleaze mill was

5   Below, manor (Pewsey).
6   W.R.O. 679/3, cts. 1 Nov. 1798; 18 Nov. 1805; for the tithings, below, local govt.
7   Above, plate 14.
8   W.R.O., tithe award.
9   Ibid. 1075/1/85, sale cat. 1874; *Kelly's Dir. Wilts.* (1875 and later edns.); below, trade and ind.
10   Inf. from Dept. of Planning and Highways, Co. Hall, Trowbridge.
11   Dept. of Environment, list of bldgs. of hist. interest (1987).
12   O.S. Maps 6", Wilts. XLI (1889 and later edns.); W.R.O., tithe award.

13   P.R.O., E 32/199/10; B.L. Harl. MS. 1761, ff. 125v., 132v. sqq.; for Wick later Clench, above, Milton Lilbourne; for E. Wick, below, Wootton Rivers.
14   For the date, below, this section.
15   Below, agric. (W. Wick).
16   W.R.O., tithe award.
17   For Pyke and later owners of the ho., below, manors (Pewsey).
18   Inf. from, and plans in possession of, Madeleine, Lady Devlin, W. Wick Ho.
19   O.S. Maps 6", Wilts. XXXVI (1888 edn.); XXXVI. SW. (1900 edn.).
20   W.R.O., G 10/760/274.

standing in the Middle Ages, probably on its present site,[21] where a red-brick mill house of the late 18th century or early 19th survived in 1997. A farmstead, Buckleaze Farm, stood near the site from 1698, when a new farmhouse was built, or earlier.[22] The farmhouse is a square house, of brick, of two storeys, and with tall panelled chimney stacks; in 1997 it contained its original dog-leg staircase and refitted panelling of the earlier 17th century. Sunnyhill Farm, incorporating a red-brick farmhouse which survived in 1997, and Anvill's Farm, the farmhouse of which was greatly enlarged in the mid 19th century, were built between 1773 and 1817.[23] A pair of cottages north of Sunnyhill Farm was built in the late 19th century, and new farm buildings west of Sunnyhill Farm were erected in the 20th. East of Anvill's Farm a small house was built in the early 19th century and, respectively south-east and south of Anvill's Farm, Fairfield Farm, consisting of a pair of cottages and farm buildings, and Fairfield House were built between 1839 and 1886. North-west of Pewsey village Avebrick's Farm, including a thatched farmhouse, and Sharcott Penning Farm were also built between 1839 and 1886.[24] Additional buildings were erected at Sharcott Penning Farm in the 20th century.

On the downland in the south part of the parish two farmsteads have been built. Pewsey Hill Farm may stand on the site of a barn built in 1671.[25] In 1839 the farmstead incorporated an 11-bayed barn built in 1818 and a house;[26] by 1886 the house had been replaced by a pair of cottages,[27] and in the late 20th century the cottages were demolished and a new house was built.[28] In 1997 the barn, the house, and 20th-century farm buildings stood there. Down Farm was built in 1827[29] and incorporated a house[30] which, near mainly 20th-century farm buildings, survived in 1997. On the downland north of West Wick a keeper's cottage and a barn were standing in the earlier 19th century,[31] and in 1893 a small farmstead on their site incorporated a pair of cottages.[32] A farm building was all that remained on the site in 1997.

Settlement began along Marlborough Road north-west of Pewsey village in the early 19th century, probably from c. 1806–7 when the wharf on the Kennet & Avon canal was built beside the road.[33] A warehouse and wharfinger's house, red-brick, slated, and built c. 1806–7,[34] survived in 1997. Haybrook House had been built on rising ground near the canal by 1817;[35] it was rebuilt as a large stone house in 1902.[36] Haybrook House was used as an annexe of Pewsey hospital from 1946 to 1983[37] and by a school in 1997.[38] Its north lodge survives from the mid 19th century, its south lodge from c. 1902. Immediately north of Haybrook House a large house was built between 1817 and 1839; in the late 19th century it was replaced by Travancore House, a large stone house which was also used by the school in 1997. A few cottages had been built immediately north of the canal by 1839;[39] between 1859 and 1867 one of them was opened as the French Horn public house,[40] which was still open in 1997. North of the wharf, at a place called Prospect in 1886,[41] what was possibly a trio of cottages was standing in 1839,[42] a terrace of five small cottages was built in 1848,[43] and a few small farm buildings were erected later. In the 20th century the building standing in 1839 was demolished[44] and c. 20 houses and bungalows were built beside Marlborough Road north of the canal.

At the parish boundary north-east of Pewsey village a group of cottages on the waste beside Milton Road was called Little Ann in 1773.[45] Three cottages or rows of cottages stood there in 1839,[46] three pairs of cottages in 1899.[47] A pair of cottages in Milton Lilbourne parish was also part of the group.[48] Of the cottages in Pewsey parish, one pair was demolished in the earlier 20th century[49] and others, apparently 18th-century, were converted to a single house in the early 1960s.[50]

West of Pewsey village along Woodborough Road a pair of cottages was built in the early 20th century,[51] three bungalows in the mid 20th century, and a house later.

MANOR AND OTHER ESTATES. By his will made 879 × 888 King Alfred gave Pewsey to his son Edward,[52] who succeeded him as king in 899. The crown, and probably Pewsey, passed in turn to Edward's sons Athelstan (d. 939) and Edmund, who in 940 granted Pewsey to St. Peter's abbey, Winchester.[53] The abbey, otherwise called the New minster and from 1109 called Hyde abbey, held PEWSEY manor,

21 Below, mills.
22 Eroded date stone on bldg. recorded in 1992: rep. 7723, Wilts. Bldgs. Rec., Co. Hall, Trowbridge.
23 Andrews and Dury, Map (W.R.S. viii), pl. 12; O.S. Map 1", sheet 14 (1817 edn.).
24 O.S. Maps 6", Wilts. XXXV–XXXVI (1888–9 edns.); XXXV. SE. (1901 edn.); W.R.O., tithe award.
25 Below, agric. (Down Pewsey).
26 W.R.O., tithe award; date on bldg.
27 O.S. Map 6", Wilts. XLI (1889 edn.).
28 Inf. from Mr. P. H. Bowerman, Pewsey Hill Farm Ho.
29 Below, agric. (Kepnal and Southcott).
30 W.R.O., tithe award.
31 Ibid.; O.S. Map 1", sheet 14 (1817 edn.).
32 W.R.O. 628/48/1.
33 Above, this section [canal].
34 Ibid. plate 37.
35 O.S. Map 1", sheet 14 (1817 edn.).
36 Dept. of Environment, list of bldgs. of hist. interest

(1987).
37 Above, this section (Pewsey).
38 Below, educ.
39 O.S. Map 1", sheet 14 (1817 edn.); W.R.O., tithe award.
40 Kelly's Dir. Wilts. (1859, 1867).
41 O.S. Map 6", Wilts. XXXV (1889 edn.).
42 W.R.O., tithe award.
43 Date on bldg.
44 e.g. O.S. Map 6", Wilts. XXXV. SE. (1926 edn.).
45 Andrews and Dury, Map (W.R.S. viii), pl. 12.
46 W.R.O., tithe award.
47 O.S. Map 1/2,500, Wilts. XXXVI. 13 (1900 edn.).
48 Above, Milton Lilbourne, intro. (Fyfield).
49 O.S. Maps 1/2,500, Wilts. XXXVI. 13 (1900, 1924 edns.).
50 Pewsey through the Ages, iii. 2.
51 O.S. Maps 6", Wilts. XLI. NE. (1901, 1926 edns.).
52 Eng. Hist. Doc. i, ed. D. Whitelock (1979), pp. 534–7.
53 Finberg, Early Wessex Chart. p. 85.

which included nearly all of Pewsey parish and of Manningford Abbots parish, until the abbey was dissolved in 1538.[54] A claim by Ernulf of Hesdin, that the 2 hides which in 1086 he held in Pewsey was a separate fee, was apparently unsuccessful.[55] In two exchanges in 1545 the Crown gave the manor to, and received it from, Sir Thomas Wriothesley, Lord Wriothesley,[56] and in an exchange in 1547 granted it to Edward Seymour, duke of Somerset.[57] On Somerset's execution and attainder in 1552 the manor passed to the Crown, and in 1553 it was assigned to his son Sir Edward[58] (cr. earl of Hertford 1559, d. 1621), a minor. From 1553 to 1675 it descended with Tottenham Lodge in Great Bedwyn successively to William, duke of Somerset (d. 1660), William, duke of Somerset (d. 1671), and John, duke of Somerset (d. 1675).[59] In 1672 the duke settled Pewsey manor on himself for life, on the survivor of him and his wife Sarah (d. 1692), and on the heirs and assigns of the survivor.[60] By her will Sarah, from 1682 the wife of Henry Hare, Lord Coleraine, gave the manor to Charles Seymour, duke of Somerset (d. 1748).[61] It passed to Charles's son Algernon, duke of Somerset (cr. earl of Northumberland 1749, d. 1750), and to Algernon's daughter Elizabeth, the wife of Sir Hugh Smithson, Bt. In 1750 Sir Hugh succeeded Algernon as earl of Northumberland and took the surname Percy, and in 1766 he was created duke of Northumberland.[62] In 1766 Elizabeth and Hugh, for a fixed price and interest on it from that year, agreed to convey the fee simple of the manor, nearly all of which was then held by tenants for life, to Joseph Champion, and, by direction of Champion and for payments to defray the price and the interest, sold most of the manor in portions in 1767–8.[63] For what was left of the price and interest they conveyed what was left of the manor to Champion in 1769.[64]

In 1770 Joseph Champion sold his estate, which consisted of the lordship of the manor excluding Kepnal and Southcott, the reversion in fee of the demesne, mainly in Down Pewsey tithing and Manningford Abbots, and the reversion in fee of a few copyholds, mainly in Down Pewsey, to St. Thomas's hospital, London.[65]

The hospital owned 1,031 a. in Pewsey parish in 1839.[66] In 1919 it sold Inlands farm, 95 a., to Alfred Howse;[67] the later descent of the farm has not been traced. In 1927 the hospital sold Manor farm, 1,241 a. including c. 336 a. in Manningford Abbots, to the tenant J. M. Strong[68] (d. 1932),[69] who also owned 384 a. in Sharcott tithing.[70] In 1932 Strong gave Manor farm to his grandson J. V. Strong, who sold most of it to J. N. Bowerman and his wife Queenie in 1957. In 1997 the Bowermans' son Mr. P. H. Bowerman owned Manor farm, then 858 a. The part of the farm retained by J. V. Strong in 1957 passed as part of Green Drove farm to his son Mr. J. M. Strong, the owner in 1997.[71]

The reversion in fee of a copyhold mainly in Down Pewsey tithing, in 1755 comprising 144 a. and feeding rights, was bought in 1767 by John Winter[72] (d. 1797). Winter devised the land in trust for sale,[73] and in 1799 it belonged to Richard Chandler (d. 1823), who settled his estate on his wife Ann (d. 1833) for life with reversion to her son R. H. Alexander[74] (d. 1843).[75] About 1832 Alexander bought other land in Down Pewsey and land in Southcott tithing;[76] in 1839 he owned 430 a. in the parish.[77] All his land in Down Pewsey tithing passed to his son R. C. Alexander, who took the additional surname Prior.[78] Prior (d. 1902) devised the estate, 316 a., to his nephew F. H. Goldney.[79] In 1910 Goldney sold 196 a. to Walter Rawlins,[80] who added it to his farm based at Swan and partly in Kepnal and Southcott.[81] Rawlins (d. 1912) devised his farm in trust for sale.[82] From 1915 or earlier the farm, 378 a. in 1920 and 435 a. in 1950, belonged to S. H. Rawlins (d. 1950),[83] whose executors sold it c. 1956 to J. V. Strong (d. 1993). As Green Drove farm and greatly increased in area it passed from Strong to his son Mr. J. M. Strong, who owned Green Drove farm, 1,275 a., in 1997.[84] Also in 1910 Goldney sold Avebrick's farm, 99 a., to J. H. Smith Barry,[85] who in 1920 sold it to Wiltshire county council.[86] In the 1930s the council appropriated c. 75 a. of Avebrick's farm from its estate of smallholdings to Pewsey hospital; that land was transferred to the Minister of Health by Act of 1946 and 38 a. of it was sold in portions in 1970.[87]

54 V.C.H. Hants, ii. 117, 120; P.R.O., SC 6/Hen. VIII/3341, rott. 48d.–50d.; for Manningford Abbots, V.C.H. Wilts. x. 106–12.
55 V.C.H. Wilts. ii, pp. 127, 139.
56 L. & P. Hen. VIII, xx (1), pp. 524–5; xx (2), p. 220.
57 Cal. Pat. 1547–8, 121–3; for the Seymours, Complete Peerage, vi. 504–7; xii (1), 59–79.
58 P.R.O., E 328/117.
59 Above, Great Bedwyn, manors (Tottenham).
60 W.R.O. 1300/290.
61 Ibid. 1300/299.
62 Ibid. 1392, box 9, abstr. of title of duke and duchess of Northumb.; Complete Peerage, ix. 742–4.
63 Alnwick Castle Mun. X.II.11, box 10, bdle. of draft deeds; box 11, Champion's covenants for purchase of Pewsey; box 13, bdle. of draft deeds.
64 Lond. Metro. Archives, H1/ST/E66/47/1/8–9.
65 Ibid. H1/ST/E66/47/1/11–12; H1/ST/E112/1; W.R.O. 490/1060; for the lordship in respect of Kepnal and Southcott, below, this section; for the tithings, ibid. local govt.   66 W.R.O., tithe award.
67 Lond. Metro. Archives, H1/ST/E55/4.
68 Ibid. H1/ST/E66/47/6/1.
69 Princ. Regy. Fam. Div., will of J. M. Strong, 1932.
70 Below, this section.

71 Inf. from Mr. P. H. Bowerman, Pewsey Hill Farm Ho.; Mr. J. M. Strong, Green Drove Ho.; for Green Drove farm, below, this section.
72 Alnwick Castle Mun. X.II.11, box 8, survey of Pewsey, 1755; box 10, bdle. of draft deeds.
73 W.R.O., wills, archd. Wilts., John Winter, 1798.
74 Ibid. A 1/345/324A; ibid. 473/216, will of Ric. Chandler; 493/27.
75 P.R.O., PROB 11/1989, ff. 136–138v.
76 W.R.O., A 1/345/324B; ibid. 211/15/10–11.
77 Ibid. tithe award.
78 V.C.H. Som. v. 75; P.R.O., PROB 11/1989, ff. 136–138v.
79 Princ. Regy. Fam. Div., will of R. C. A. Prior, 1903; W.R.O., G 10/500/69.
80 W.R.O. 473/293.
81 Below, this section.
82 Princ. Regy. Fam. Div., will of Wal. Rawlins, 1912.
83 Kelly's Dir. Wilts. (1915); W.R.O. 1634/3; ibid. G 10/500/71.
84 Inf. from Mr. Strong; for land added to Green Drove farm, above and below, this section.
85 W.R.O. 473/293.   86 Ibid. F 9/120/56/7.
87 Ibid. J 6/130/13; inf. from Environmental Services Dept., Co. Hall, Trowbridge.

A copyhold mainly in Sharcott tithing, as-sessed at 4¼ yardlands in 1705[88] and 216 a. in 1733,[89] was held from 1663 or earlier by mem-bers of the Wroughton family,[90] and in 1767 the freehold of it was bought by George Wroughton[91] (d. 1779): the Wroughtons were lords of Wilcot manor in Wilcot, the land of which adjoined Sharcott. George Wroughton's relict Susannah Wroughton held the estate in Sharcott until her death in 1816, when it passed to his daughter Charlotte (d. 1839), the wife of Sir George Montagu (d. 1829).[92] About 1834 most of a holding of 213 a. in Sharcott was bought by Charlotte or her son and heir George Wroughton, who in 1839 owned 425 a. there including his mother's land.[93] George (d. 1871) was succeeded by his brother J. W. Montagu (d. 1882), who was succeeded by his grandson J. W. Montagu, a minor until 1898:[94] in 1899 in Shar-cott 318 a. belonged to the representatives of George Wroughton (d. 1871), 158 a. to the executors of J. W. Montagu (d. 1882), and 45 a. to J. W. Montagu.[95] Of the 476 a., 464 a. was offered for sale in 1900. Of that, Manor farm, 183 a., was bought by J. M. Strong[96] (d. 1932), the owner of Manor farm, Pewsey, from 1927,[97] who bought other land in Sharcott and in 1928 owned 384 a. there south of Woodborough Road.[98] That land passed as Manor farm, Shar-cott, like Manor farm, Pewsey, to Strong's grandson J. V. Strong, who sold the part of it north of the Avon, c. 210 a., as Manor farm to J. Ricketts in the 1950s.[99] In 1966 Ricketts sold the farm to S. G. Gates, whose son Mr. O. Gates owned the land east of East Sharcott village, 82 a., in 1997. In 1981–2 Mr. Gates sold the land west of the village: in 1981 he sold 60 a. south of the railway to Walter T. Ware Ltd. and in 1982 he sold c. 75 a. north of the railway to Malmesbury Potatoes Ltd., the respective own-ers in 1997.[1] About 175 a. south of the Avon descended as part of Green Drove farm to J. V. Strong's son Mr. J. M. Strong, the owner in 1997.[2] Of the 464 a. offered for sale in 1900 J. H. Smith Barry bought 160 a. in 1901, and in 1920 sold it to Wiltshire county council as Penning farm.[3] The county council owned the land in 1997.[4]

A holding of 213 a. in Sharcott tithing was accumulated after 1767 by George Gibbs[5] (d. 1813), rector of Woodborough. The estate de-scended to his son Sir George Gibbs, who c. 1834 sold most of it to George Wroughton or Wroughton's mother.[6]

The reversion in fee of another copyhold in Sharcott tithing, 162 a. in 1755, was bought in 1767 by Thomas Glass, whose family had held the land by copy from the later 17th century or earlier.[7] In 1806, after the death of a Thomas Glass in that year, the estate, 180 a., was offered for sale;[8] it was possibly bought by Thomas Smith, but by 1807 had been acquired by Wil-liam Gibbs.[9] Between 1860 and 1865 the estate was broken up on Gibbs's death.[10]

In 1767 the reversion in fee of several copy-holds with land mainly in Kepnal and Southcott tithings was bought by Sir John Astley, Bt., who in 1768 bought the lordship of Pewsey manor for those tithings and the reversion in fee of other copyholds there.[11] At his death in 1771 Astley's estate in Pewsey parish passed as part of his Everleigh estate to his cousin F. D. Astley (d. 1818),[12] who bought other holdings with land in Kepnal and Southcott.[13] F. D. Astley was suc-ceeded by his son Sir John Astley, Bt. (d. 1842), who owned 1,209 a. in Pewsey parish in 1839, and the estate passed with the baronetcy in the direct line to Sir Francis Astley (d. 1873), Sir John Astley (d. 1894), and Sir Francis Astley-Corbett.[14] Between 1874 and 1876 Sir John sold Southcott farm, 342 a., Sunnyhill farm, 220 a., a 74-a. farm in Sharcott, and other land,[15] and in 1918 Sir Francis sold Down farm, 407 a. adjoining Everleigh.[16] Southcott farm and Sun-nyhill farm were bought c. 1875 by Richard Pocock,[17] who in 1878 offered Southcott farm for sale.[18] In 1899 Southcott farm belonged to the Wilts. & Dorset Bank.[19] By 1910 it had been acquired by G. L. Cooke[20] (d. 1933), whose executors sold it c. 1933 to R. G. Cooke,[21] and in the 1960s R. G. Cooke sold nearly all of it in portions to J. V. Strong. As part of Green Drove farm the land bought by Strong descended to his son Mr. J. M. Strong, the owner in 1997.[22] In 1898 Sunnyhill farm belonged to Ellen Thomas Stanford, the owner of the Pythouse

---

88 W.R.O. 493/49.   89 Ibid. 212B/5217.
90 Ibid. 9/1/84.
91 Alnwick Castle Mun. X.II.11, box 10, bdle. of draft deeds.
92 V.C.H. Wilts. x. 194; Burke, Commoners (1833–8), ii. 53; W.R.O. 212B/7129.
93 W.A.S. Libr., sale cat. ix, no. 48; W.R.O. 211/15/11–12; ibid. tithe award; for the 213 a., below, this section.
94 Lond. Metro. Archives, H1/ST/E66/47/3/14.
95 W.R.O., G 10/500/69.
96 Ibid. 130/78, sale cat. of Stowell Lodge estate, 1900.
97 Above, this section.
98 W.R.O., G 10/500/72.
99 Inf. from Mr. Strong.
1 Inf. from Mr. O. Gates, the Old Rectory, Manning-ford Abbots; Malmesbury Potatoes Ltd., E. Sharcott.
2 Inf. from Mr. Strong; for Green Drove farm, above, this section.
3 W.R.O. 130/78, sale cat. of Stowell Lodge estate, 1900; ibid. F 9/120/56/7; ibid. Inland Revenue, val. reg. 57.
4 Inf. from Environmental Services Dept., Co. Hall, Trowbridge.   5 W.R.O. 493/46; 1634/34.
6 Ibid. 1737/9; ibid. tithe award; R. Royal Coll. of Physicians (2nd edn.), iii. 13; W.A.S. Libr., sale cat. ix, no. 48; above, this section.

7 Alnwick Castle Mun. X.II.11, box 8, survey of Pewsey, 1755; box 10, bdle. of draft deeds.
8 W.A.S. Libr., sale cat. ix, no. 49; W.R.O. 493/26.
9 W.R.O., A 1/345/324B.
10 Ibid. 211/15/26–7.
11 Ibid. 1392, box 11, deeds, Northumb. to Astley, 1767–8; for the land of Kepnal and Southcott, below, agric. (Kepnal and Southcott).
12 V.C.H. Wilts. xi. 137.
13 e.g. W.R.O. 1392, box 10, bdles. of deeds; 2523/1.
14 Ibid. tithe award; for the Astleys, Burke, Peerage (1949), 92–3.
15 W.R.O. 1075/1/85, sale cat. 1874; 1392, box 20, bk. entitled Astley Trustees.
16 Ibid. Inland Revenue, val. reg. 57; W.A.S. Libr., sale cat. xviii, no. 14; cf. V.C.H. Wilts. xi. 137.
17 W.R.O., A 1/345/324B.
18 W.A.S. Libr., sale cat. vii, no. 76.
19 W.R.O., G 10/500/69.
20 Ibid. Inland Revenue, val. reg. 57.
21 Ibid. G 10/505/1; Kelly's Dir. Wilts. (1935); W.A.S. Libr., sale cat. xx, no. 33; Princ. Regy. Fam. Div., will of G. L. Cooke, 1933.
22 Inf. from Mr. Strong; for Green Drove farm, above, this section.

estate, who sold it in portions in 1919.[23] Down farm was apparently bought from Sir Francis Astley-Corbett by Alfred Cook (d. 1923), who owned it in 1920 and added it to 70 a. of glebe bought in 1912 and 140 a. formerly George Winter's bought by 1914.[24] After Cook's death the court of Chancery ordered the sale of the farm, 613 a., which was bought by John Edwards in 1924.[25] Down farm belonged to A. J. Edwards in 1935,[26] and was bought c. 1937 by A. J. Hosier.[27] In 1997 it belonged to Mr. A. M. Hosier.[28] In 1962–3 c. 70 a. of the 140 a. was bought by J. V. Strong and, as part of Green Drove farm, belonged to his son Mr. J. M. Strong in 1997.[29]

The reversion in fee of a copyhold in Kepnal and Southcott tithings, 110 a. in 1767,[30] was bought in 1768 by Edmund Somerset[31] (d. 1789),[32] whose family had held the land by copy from the early 18th century or earlier.[33] In 1789 the estate passed to William Somerset (d. c. 1827), who held it with other land in the parish,[34] a total of c. 200 a. in 1817.[35] About 1830 the land in Kepnal and Southcott was divided between R. H. Alexander and Robert Lyne, apparently by purchase from William Somerset's executors.[36] Alexander devised his part, 116 a., to his son George[37] (d. 1885), who devised it to his wife Elizabeth, later Mrs. Collins (fl. 1899).[38] The land passed to the Revd. J. F. Collins, who offered it for sale in 1901,[39] and in 1910 belonged to Walter Rawlins.[40] It afterwards descended as part of Rawlins's farm based at Swan.[41] The other part of William Somerset's estate, 90 a. in 1839,[42] had descended by 1899 to Miss M. M. Lyne.[43] It belonged to a Mrs. Buchanan in 1910[44] and has not been traced further.

In 1767 John Winter bought the reversion in fee of one copyhold, and William Winter bought that of another. Both estates had lands in Kepnal and Southcott tithings,[45] from inclosure in 1777 the main parts of each were adjacent,[46] and from the death of William in 1789 Thomas Winter (d. 1819) owned both. Thomas's composite estate passed in turn to his son John (d. 1825) and that

John's son George (d. 1873),[47] who in 1839 owned 224 a. in the parish.[48] George Winter devised the estate to trustees,[49] who in 1902 sold the largest part, 140 a.[50] The purchaser may have been John Spackman, who owned that land in 1910.[51] In 1914 Alfred Cook, later the owner of Down farm, owned the 140 a. Since 1962–3 c. 70 a. of the 140 a. has been part of Green Drove farm; the rest was still part of Down farm in 1997.[52]

The freehold of West Wick farm, which as a copyhold had descended in the Pyke family from the earlier 16th century or earlier,[53] was bought in 1767 by the tenant Henry Pyke. On Pyke's death in 1797 the farm passed to his son Henry. The younger Henry (d. 1827) devised it to his nephew T. H. Pyke, who emigrated in 1835. In 1837 T. H. Pyke's trustees sold the farm, 371 a. in 1839, to the Revd. M. H. Goodman (d. 1856), who devised it to his nephew Edward Goodman. In 1893 Goodman sold it to Ebenezer Lane.[54] Between 1899 and 1910 F. E. N. Rogers of Rainscombe House in Wilcot acquired 55 a. on Martinsell Hill, and E. G. and A. L. Maidment acquired the rest of West Wick farm, 310 a., in each case presumably by purchase from Lane.[55] The 55 a. was added to the Rainscombe estate.[56] The Maidments owned West Wick farm until 1916 or later,[57] Daniel Cooke from 1920 or earlier.[58] In 1937 Cooke sold the farm to B. G. Catterns, in 1942 Catterns sold it to a Mr. Robinson, and in 1943 Robinson sold it to Patrick Devlin (Lord Devlin from 1961, d. 1992). In 1997 it belonged to Lord Devlin's relict Madeleine, Lady Devlin.[59]

An estate in Pewsey held by Edric in 1086, when it was assessed at 1 hide,[60] may have been that held freely by Henry Sturmy in the earlier 13th century; a mill stood on Henry's estate, which apparently descended to him from his father Adam.[61] The estate, called Buckler's in 1558,[62] assessed at 2½ yardlands and 29 a. in 1571,[63] and later called *BUCKLEAZE* farm,[64] was held by John Benger in the early 15th century.[65] The John Benger who held it in 1446[66]

23 *V.C.H. Wilts.* xiii. 211; W.A.S. Libr., sale cat. iv, no. 47; xiv, no. 13; W.R.O., G 10/500/71.
24 *W.A.M.* xlii. 244; W.A.S. Libr., sale cat. xxviiiD, no. 48; W.R.O., G 10/500/71; for the glebe, below, church; for Winter's land, below, this section.
25 W.A.S. Libr., sale cat. xviii, no. 14.
26 W.R.O., G 10/505/1.
27 A. J. and F. H. Hosier, *Hosier's Farming System*, 43.
28 Inf. from Mr. N. H. Hosier, Waglands Farm, Collingbourne Kingston.
29 Inf. from Mr. Strong; for Green Drove farm, above, this section.
30 W.R.O. 490/1060.
31 Alnwick Castle Mun. X.II.11, box 11, bdle. of draft deeds.
32 W.R.O. 493/25.
33 Alnwick Castle Mun. X.II.11, box 6, rent r. of Pewsey, 1702–3; Lond. Metro. Archives, H1/ST/E112/1.
34 W.R.O., A 1/345/324A–B.
35 Ibid. 493/46.
36 Ibid. A 1/345/324B; ibid. wills, archd. Wilts., Wm. Somerset, 1828, no. 15.
37 P.R.O., PROB 11/1989, ff. 136–138v.
38 Princ. Regy. Fam. Div., will of Geo. Alexander, 1885; will of R. C. A. Prior, 1903; W.R.O., G 10/500/69.
39 W.R.O. 473/292.
40 Ibid. Inland Revenue, val. reg. 57.
41 Above, this section.
42 W.R.O., tithe award.

43 Ibid. G 10/500/69.
44 Ibid. Inland Revenue, val. reg. 57.
45 Alnwick Castle Mun. X.II.11, box 10, bdle. of draft deeds.
46 W.R.O. 1634/34.
47 Ibid. A 1/345/324A–B; ibid. wills, cons. Sar., Thomas Winter, 1820, no. 117; wills, archd. Wilts., John Winter, 1825, no. 18; ibid. 493/25; 493/27–8.
48 Ibid. tithe award.
49 Princ. Regy. Fam. Div., will of Geo. Winter, 1874.
50 W.A.S. Libr., sale cat. xviii, no. 14.
51 W.R.O., Inland Revenue, val. reg. 57.
52 Ibid. G 10/511/1; above, this section.
53 e.g. W.R.O. 9/1/134; 493/49.
54 Ibid. 408/1; for the area, ibid. tithe award; for the date 1797, T. Phillipps, *Mon. Inscr. N. Wilts.* 183.
55 W.R.O., G 10/500/69; ibid. Inland Revenue, val. reg. 57.
56 For the Rainscombe estate, *V.C.H. Wilts.* x. 130.
57 W.R.O., G 10/511/1.
58 Ibid. G 10/500/71.
59 Inf. from Lady Devlin, W. Wick Ho.
60 *V.C.H. Wilts.* ii, p. 162.
61 B.L. Harl. MS. 1761, f. 132; P.R.O., CP 40/927, rot. 152.
62 P.R.O., REQ 2/62/59.
63 Ibid. C 142/254, no. 81.
64 O.S. Map 6", Wilts. XXXV (1889 edn.).
65 P.R.O., CP 40/927, rot. 152.
66 Ibid. C 143/450, no. 18.

probably held it in 1427 and 1452.[67] It was also held by a John Benger in 1494,[68] and it descended in the direct line from George Benger (d. *c.* 1538) to John (d. *c.* 1560), William[69] (d. 1571), and John Benger (d. 1609).[70] In 1615 the estate was sold by William Benger to Sir William Button.[71] Thereafter it descended with Lyneham manor in the Button and Walker families to John Walker-Heneage,[72] who in 1797 sold it to F. D. Astley (d. 1818), the owner of much land in Kepnal and Southcott tithings. In 1826 Sir John Astley gave it to the heirs and devisees of Anthony Mills in an exchange,[73] and in 1839, when it measured 60 a., Buckleaze farm belonged to Samuel Robbins.[74] Its later descent has not been traced.

From 1440 £10 11*s.* 8*d.* a year from Pewsey rectory was paid to Hyde abbey as a contribution to the pension of £20 a year paid by the abbey to Salisbury cathedral.[75] From the Dissolution to the Interregnum it was paid to the Crown.[76]

AGRICULTURE. In 1086 the estate called Pewsey belonging to St. Peter's abbey, Winchester, had land for 24 ploughteams. There were 3 teams and 6 *servi* on the demesne, which was assessed at 6 hides and 1 yardland, and 46 *villani*, 24 coscets, and 1 bordar had 18 teams. Another estate at Pewsey had land for 1½ team, and another was assessed at 1 carucate. There were 15 a. of meadow and 1 square league of pasture.[77]

The main area of open fields in the parish lay south and east of Pewsey village, north of the scarp of Salisbury Plain; south of the scarp there was extensive downland at the south end of the parish; to the north, mainly north and west of Pewsey village, there was extensive lowland pasture. All that land was shared by the four main villages in the parish, Pewsey, Kepnal, East Sharcott, and Southcott. All West Wick's land was in the parish's northern projection. Each of those five settlements probably had its own set of open fields. The southern downland was pasture for sheep and was apparently divided between Pewsey and Southcott; Pewsey was almost certainly the first, and Southcott probably the second, settlement to have been founded and have had land assigned to it. In Down Pewsey tithing, which comprised the land of Pewsey village, much of the land was demesne; in the tithing the demesne included land in the open fields and, in severalty, most of the downland and part of the lowland pasture. The other downland in Down Pewsey tithing was shared by a class of tenants called workmen, whose labour service on the demesne was onerous, and

by the rector. Except the demesne part all the lowland pasture in the parish was used in common. A part to the east and a part to the west were apparently assigned as pasture for sheep to, respectively, Kepnal and East Sharcott villages, which were probably founded after Pewsey and Southcott and apparently had no upland pasture. The remaining lowland, called Hatfield, was a cattle pasture for the men of all four villages.[78]

Pewsey manor included land in all parts of the parish.[79] In the early 13th century the demesne was apparently much less extensive than the customary land, as it was in 1086; there were many customary tenants, apparently some in each of the five settlements, and no more than *c.* 5 yardlands of the manor was held freely. The customary tenants were classified as yardlanders, half-yardlanders, cotsetlanders or workmen, mill-landers, crofters, and cottars. There were six holdings of ½ hide, probably at East Sharcott, *c.* 38 yardlanders, 24 half-yardlanders, and 22 workmen. The services of all classes included the various forms of labour associated with sheep-and-corn husbandry and were probably sufficient to cultivate the demesne. If he paid no rent a workman was apparently liable to be summoned to work on the demesne at any time; most of the crofters paid rent instead of working. Each workman held a workland, nominally 10 a. in the open fields; in the workmen's separate fold, later called Work down, by custom 26 workmen could each keep 10 sheep for 5*d.* a year paid to the lord of the manor, and the rector could keep 100 sheep.[80]

In the earlier Middle Ages the open fields of each village were presumably worked from farmsteads in the respective village. By the 16th century, however, all West Wick's land had apparently been accumulated by one farm, and Kepnal's and Southcott's open fields and common pastures had apparently been merged with each other's; also by then some tenants had acquired more than one holding, and some land in most parts of the parish was worked from farmsteads probably in other parts.[81] About 1700 there were *c.* 101 copyholders and lessees holding land of the manor for life,[82] and by the 18th century many of them had land and pasture rights in more than one part of the parish. In 1717, for example, a holding which included 35 a. of arable had land in open fields in Down Pewsey tithing, in Kepnal and Southcott tithings, and in Sharcott tithing.[83] In the mid 18th century, when only about five exceeded 100 a., most holdings remained small; nearly all included rights to feed animals in common.[84]

67 *Cal. Pat.* 1446–52, 555.
68 P.R.O., CP 40/927, rot. 152.
69 Ibid. C 3/11/72; ibid. REQ 2/62/59; ibid. SC 6/Hen. VIII/3341, rot. 48v.; W.R.O. 9/1/95, p. 1; 192/11A–B; Winchester Coll. Mun. 14907.
70 P.R.O., C 142/254, no. 81; W.R.O. 493/1.
71 Som. R.O., DD/WHb 238.
72 *V.C.H. Wilts.* ix. 94.
73 W.R.O. 1392, box 11, deed, Walker Heneage to Astley, 1797; ibid. EA/130; above, this section.
74 W.R.O., tithe award.
75 Ibid. D 1/2/10, ff. (2nd foliation) 46v.–48; cf. *Cal. Pat.* 1281–92, 230; cf. below, church.

76 *Cal. Pat.* 1547–8, 123; P.R.O., E 308/4/35, rot. 86; ibid. SC 6/Hen. VIII/3341, rot. 50.
77 *V.C.H. Wilts.* ii, pp. 119, 127, 162.
78 Below, this section; for the tithings, ibid. local govt.
79 e.g. Alnwick Castle Mun. X.II.11, box 8, survey of Pewsey, 1755.   80 B.L. Harl. MS. 1761, ff. 132–137v.
81 P.R.O., SC 6/Hen. VIII/3341, rott. 48d.–50; W.R.O. 9/1/95, pp. 2–19; cf. ibid. 9/1/141, rot. 4d.
82 Alnwick Castle Mun. X.II.11, box 6, survey of Pewsey, *c.* 1700.
83 Lond. Metro. Archives, H1/ST/E67/20/15.
84 Ibid. H1/ST/E112/1; Alnwick Castle Mun. X.II.11, box 8, survey of Pewsey, 1755.

Most of the land in the north part of the parish had been inclosed by the 17th century.[85] In the south part there remained in the 18th century 1,989 parcels of arable in open fields which measured 1,226 a., including 75 a. of roads and droves,[86] and c. 700 a. of commonable downland. In the late 18th century and early 19th farms were enlarged and consolidated, and by the earlier 19th century all the land in the parish had been inclosed and some of the downland ploughed. About 1838 there were 3,182 a. of arable, 250 a. of meadow and lowland pasture, and 838 a. of downland pasture.[87] From the mid 19th century much arable was laid to grass for dairy farming, and in the 1930s c. 75 per cent of the parish was under grass.[88] In the later 20th century most of the south part of the parish lay as arable in large fields; in the north part the farming was mixed.

DOWN PEWSEY. The open fields in Down Pewsey tithing were those of Pewsey village and measured 346 a. in the later 18th century. They lay mainly south of the village, and the two largest, East Blacknell and West Blacknell, lay in the west part of the parish between the open fields in Sharcott tithing and the scarp of the downs. Broomcroft, a 26-a. open field north of High Street, may also have been in Down Pewsey tithing. In the 18th century the 59 a. of the demesne of Pewsey manor in East Blacknell field and the 41 a. in West Blacknell field each lay as a single parcel, but all the other parcels were very small. South and south-east of those fields the tithing included the several demesne down, Farm down, c. 580 a., and Work down, c. 259 a., which was commonable.[89] The work-lands and other customary holdings possibly included part of what may have been a common meadow called Raffin immediately south of the village, and included rights to feed cattle on that part of Hatfield common west of Buckler's dean.[90]

The demesne of Pewsey manor was stocked c. 1210 with c. 60 cattle, 707 sheep and lambs, and 27 pigs.[91] It included several land called Inlands north of the village and called Westbury west of the village, and in the 16th century and later included land in Manningford Abbots. In 1552 it was said to have c. 126 a. of meadow and lowland pasture in severalty in Pewsey, 22 a. of meadow in Manningford Abbots, 600 a. of open-field arable, and feeding in common for 1,200

sheep and 20 cattle.[92] It also included Farm down:[93] a reference to the farmer's field in 1552 and the building of a barn on the down in 1671 suggest that part of the down was arable in the 16th and 17th centuries.[94] In the mid 16th century the lord of the manor licensed the farmer to use part of Westbury as a rabbit warren.[95]

The land called Raffin had been inclosed and divided into closes of 1 a. or less by the mid 16th century.[96] The part of Hatfield common which lay in Down Pewsey tithing was inclosed between the 1570s and 1609; it was apparently allotted at the rate of 1 a. for the feeding of two beasts, and most holdings were each allotted 3–10 a.[97] In 1777 the open fields and Work down were inclosed with the other open fields in the parish by Act.[98]

Probably from the 17th century or earlier the demesne, later called Manor farm, was worked from buildings immediately south of the church. Most other holdings were presumably worked from farmsteads in High, River, and North Streets; from 1698 or earlier one farm was worked from buildings near Buckleaze mill.[99] In 1755 Manor farm was possibly one of the largest farms in the Vale of Pewsey: it included 105 a. in the open fields in Down Pewsey tithing and 83 a. in the open fields in Kepnal and Southcott tithings; north and west of Pewsey village it had 43 a. of meadow, of which 20 a. was watered, 74 a. of inclosed arable, and 58 a. of inclosed pasture; in the south part of Pewsey parish it had 120 a. of downland arable, c. 460 a. of downland pasture, and feeding for 300 sheep on Kepnal and Southcott down; in Manningford Abbots it had 18 a. of meadow, 172 a. of arable, and downland or the right to feed sheep on down-land.[1] In 1767 the tenant was said to keep 1,700 sheep.[2] In 1755 only one other holding based in Pewsey village, probably that worked from buildings immediately east of the church, is known to have exceeded 100 a.[3]

In 1777 the whole of East Blacknell field and West Blacknell field was allotted for Manor farm,[4] from which Inlands farm, c. 90 a., was taken in 1818 or earlier.[5] The barn standing on Farm down in 1773 was possibly, or on the site of, that built in 1671;[6] a house and additional farm buildings, including a barn dated 1818 and all later called Pewsey Hill Farm, had been built on or near the site by the earlier 19th century.[7] In 1817 the farm worked from the buildings immediately east of the church had 346 a.[8] In

85   Below, this section.
86   Lond. Metro. Archives, H1/ST/E112/1.
87   Ibid.; W.R.O. 1634/34; ibid. EA/130; ibid. tithe award.
88   [1st] Land Util. Surv. Map, sheet 112.
89   Lond. Metro. Archives, H1/ST/E112/1; W.R.O. 1634/34; ibid. tithe award.
90   W.R.O. 9/1/95, pp. 5 sqq.; 9/1/134, ff. 175, 222; ibid. D 1/24/166/1.
91   *Interdict Doc.* (Pipe R. Soc. N.S. xxxiv), 28.
92   B.L. Harl. MS. 1761, f. 133v.; W.R.O. 9/1/95, p. 11; for the location of Inlands and Westbury, cf. ibid. tithe award.
93   Alnwick Castle Mun. X.II.11, box 8, survey of Pewsey, 1755; W.R.O. 490/1060.
94   W.R.O. 9/1/95, p. 12; 9/1/116.
95   P.R.O., C 3/112/11.
96   W.R.O. 9/1/95, pp. 5–15.
97   Ibid. 9/1/134; 9/1/141, ct. 4 Mar. 1619; ibid. D

1/24/166/1; Lond. Metro. Archives, H1/ST/E67/22/1; H1/ST/E88/3, ct. 5 Aug. 1737; Alnwick Castle Mun. X.II.11, box 6, copies taken 1706; X.II.11, box 8, survey of Pewsey, 1692.
98   W.R.O. 1634/34.
99   Above, intro. (Pewsey; other settlement).
1   Alnwick Castle Mun. X.II.11, box 8, survey of Pewsey, 1755.
2   W.R.O. 490/1060.
3   Alnwick Castle Mun. X.II.11, box 8, survey of Pewsey, 1755; cf. W.R.O. 1634/34; ibid. tithe award.
4   W.R.O. 1634/34.
5   Ibid. 493/46; Lond. Metro. Archives, H1/ST/E67/38/6.
6   *Andrews and Dury, Map* (W.R.S. viii), pl. 9; above, this section.
7   C. Greenwood, *Map of Wilts.* (1820); date on bldg.; cf. W.R.O., tithe award.
8   W.R.O. 493/46.

1838 that farm had 313 a., Manor farm had 1,277 a. including 935 a. in Pewsey parish, and the tenants of those farms each held an additional farm, of 54 a. and 78 a. respectively; Inlands farm then measured 124 a., Buckleaze farm 56 a.[9] The buildings of Manor farm immediately south of the church were largely rebuilt in the 1840s.[10]

Between 1838 and 1899 c. 113 a. of the 313-a. farm was taken to form Avebrick's farm for which buildings were erected north-west of Pewsey village; the buildings from which the remaining 200 a. was worked became new ones erected at Swan for the 54-a. farm and new ones erected south of Swan beside Everleigh Road, and the use of the farm buildings immediately east of the church may have declined. In 1899 Manor farm was c. 1,250 a. The farm based at Swan, 605 a., then lay almost entirely south of Pewsey village and included land formerly in the open fields of Kepnal and Southcott; north-west of the village Inlands farm was 155 a., Avebrick's farm 160 a., and Buckleaze farm 56 a.[11]

In 1920–1 Inlands, 97 a., Avebrick's, 93 a., and Buckleaze, 64 a., were dairy farms;[12] soon afterwards Avebrick's, with Sharcott Penning farm, was divided into smaller farms, and in the 1930s most of its land was used for Pewsey colony.[13] In 1927 Manor was an arable, dairy, and sheep farm of 1,241 a. including 106 a. of watered meadow and lowland pasture, 482 a. of arable, 232 a. of improved grassland on the downs, and 412 a. of rough downland pasture.[14] In 1928 the farm based at Swan, which included dairy farm buildings later called Green Drove Farm erected on land formerly in the open fields of Kepnal and Southcott, had 433 a.[15] In 1957 Manor farm was reduced to c. 860 a. About 1959 new buildings for it were erected beside Salisbury Road, those immediately south of the church were afterwards given up, and in 1997 Manor farm was an arable, sheep, and cattle farm of 858 a. worked from the buildings beside Salisbury Road and from Pewsey Hill Farm.[16] From 1957 the south-east part of Manor farm, the farm based at Swan, and other land have been worked together from Green Drove Farm. In 1997 Green Drove farm was a mainly arable farm of c. 1,275 a. on which some cattle were kept for beef.[17] The lowland north-west of Pewsey village formerly in Inlands farm and Buckleaze farm was then arable and pasture.

KEPNAL AND SOUTHCOTT. In the 16th century holdings based in Kepnal village and in Southcott village shared with each other common pastures and one set of open fields:[18] it is possible that the villages shared the lands from when they were founded, but more likely that each had a set of open fields and common pasture which were merged with each other's in the later Middle Ages. South of the villages c. 575 a. lay in open fields.[19] In the 16th century and early 17th that land was said to lie in an east field and a west field,[20] but in the 18th century there was a middle field and by then there may have been a further subdivision of the fields.[21] In addition Kepnal croft was an open field of 12 a. north-east of Kepnal village, and Garston was one of c. 48 a. south of Kepnal village.[22] The holdings included rights to feed sheep on a lowland common of 146 a., called Pewsey common in the 18th century, which lay along the parish boundary between Kepnal and West Wick and in the earlier Middle Ages may have been exclusive to holdings based in Kepnal; in the 1570s it was disputed whether the demesne of Pewsey manor included the right to feed 250 or 300 sheep on the common.[23] On the downland south-east of the open fields Kepnal and Southcott down, 456 a. which in the earlier Middle Ages may have been exclusive to holdings based in Southcott, could be fed on by 2,190 sheep.[24] East of Buckler's dean in the north part of the parish the holdings included rights to feed cattle in common on 200–300 a. of Hatfield common. By 1661 the 200–300 a. had apparently been inclosed, divided, and allotted,[25] and, like that part of Hatfield common in Down Pewsey tithing, it was possibly inclosed c. 1600.[26]

In the mid 16th century Pewsey manor had 6 holdings based in Kepnal with 171 a. in the open fields and feeding in common for c. 380 sheep and c. 66 cattle, and it had 13 holdings based in Southcott with c. 450 a. in the open fields and feeding in common for c. 950 sheep and c. 166 cattle: some of the open-field land and of the feeding rights were in Down Pewsey tithing, holdings based in that tithing had land and feeding rights in Kepnal and Southcott tithings,[27] and there were a few small freeholds, probably amounting to less than 5 yardlands, based in Kepnal and Southcott.[28] The holdings worked from the two villages apparently remained small, and their lands scattered, until the 18th century. In 1755 none seems to have had as much as 100 a. of closes and open-field arable.[29]

9 W.R.O., tithe award.
10 Lond. Metro. Archives, H1/ST/E18, f. 115; H1/ST/E56/6/20; H1/ST/E56/8/1.
11 O.S. Maps 6", Wilts. XXXV, XLI (1889 edns.); W.A.S. Libr., sale cat. xxviiiD, no. 48; W.R.O., tithe award; ibid. G 10/500/69.
12 W.A.S. Libr., sale cat. xvii, nos. 14, 29, 75.
13 W.R.O., G 10/500/72; above, manors (Pewsey); for the colony, above, intro. (Pewsey); for Sharcott Penning farm, below, this section (Sharcott).
14 Lond. Metro. Archives, H1/ST/E66/47/6/1.
15 W.A.S. Libr., sale cat. xviii, no. 14; W.R.O., G 10/500/72; cf. ibid. 1634/34.
16 Inf. from Mr. P. H. Bowerman, Pewsey Hill Farm Ho.
17 Inf. from Mr. J. M. Strong, Green Drove Ho.; for the other land of Green Drove farm, below, this section.
18 W.R.O. 9/1/134, f. 64; 192/11B, pp. 3–4, 10, 12–15.
19 Ibid. 1634/34.

20 Ibid. 9/1/82; 9/1/95, pp. 12–13; 9/1/141, rot. 4d.
21 Ibid. 212B/5218; Lond. Metro. Archives, H1/ST/E67/20/15; H1/ST/E88/3, ct. 6 Sept. 1742.
22 W.R.O. 1634/34.
23 Ibid. 9/1/134, f. 175; 9/1/141, rot. 4d.; 192/11B; 1634/34; Andrews and Dury, Map (W.R.S. viii), pl. 12.
24 Lond. Metro. Archives, H1/ST/E112/1; W.R.O. 1634/34.
25 Alnwick Castle Mun. X.II.11, box 8, survey of Pewsey, 1692; W.R.O. 9/1/134, ff. 66, 222.
26 Above, this section (Down Pewsey).
27 P.R.O., SC 6/Hen. VIII/3341, rott. 48d.–49d.; W.R.O. 9/1/95, pp. 2–19.
28 P.R.O., C 1/1392, nos. 7–9; C 3/128/23; C 142/662, no. 132; ibid. SC 6/Hen. VIII/3341, rot. 48d.; cf. W.R.O. 192/11B; 493/49.
29 Alnwick Castle Mun. X.II.11, box 8, survey of Pewsey, 1755; W.R.O. 1392, box 9, partic. of Ranger's.

The open fields and Pewsey common, with other land in the parish, were inclosed in 1777 by Act. The open fields, including Kepnal croft and Garston field, were laid out in *c.* 33 closes; Pewsey common was divided into 35. To replace its land in the open fields, feeding on the common, and feeding on Kepnal and Southcott down, land elsewhere in the parish was allotted for Manor farm. To replace the farm's feeding for 300 sheep on the down, some feeding rights in common were transferred from Work down, which was inclosed, to Kepnal and Southcott down, which remained commonable.[30] In the later 18th century and early 19th the land and feeding rights in Kepnal and Southcott tithings were concentrated in fewer and larger farms. On the lowland two new farmsteads, Sunnyhill Farm and Anvill's Farm, were built;[31] much of the lowland common became part of Sunnyhill farm, 183 a. *c.* 1810, when it included 145 a. of arable.[32] In 1817 Kepnal farm included 108 a., feeding for 250 sheep, and a farmstead in Kepnal's street, and Southcott farm included 195 a., feeding for 400 sheep, and a farmstead at the south end of Southcott's street; from 1824 the two farms were held together as Southcott farm. A farm which in 1817 had 131 a. and feeding for 210 sheep was almost certainly that later called Ball farm and worked from buildings at Ball.[33]

Kepnal and Southcott down was inclosed by Act in 1826.[34] A new farmstead, Down Farm, was built on it in 1827, and thenceforth *c.* 160 a. of Kepnal and Southcott down and 143 a. formerly part of Farm down and of Work down was worked as Down farm. A flock of 200 or more sheep was to be kept on the farm, which in 1828 included 175 a. of newly broken downland.[35] Other parts of Kepnal and Southcott down were also converted to arable between 1826 and 1838.[36] In 1838 Down farm had 306 a., Southcott farm had 463 a. including 105 a. of downland of which 20 a. was ploughed, and Ball farm had *c.* 400 a. including 118 a. of downland of which 23 a. was ploughed. Sunnyhill farm had 263 a. including *c.* 220 a. of arable, and Anvill's farm was 58 a. A 78-a. farm with buildings beside Milton Road, and a 54-a. farm with buildings in Southcott's street, belonged to the tenants of the two large farms with buildings near Pewsey church.[37]

Sunnyhill farm was mainly arable until 1874 or later;[38] it had been converted for dairy farming by 1898, when its 278 a. included 186 a. of meadows, 55 a. of permanent pasture, and only 30 a. of arable.[39] In 1899 Anvill's, 45 a., was probably another dairy farm.[40] Southcott farm remained 463 a. until the 1850s or later.[41] By 1878, when it had an additional farmstead called Mills Farm in Southcott's street, it had been reduced to 281 a., mainly by the loss of its downland.[42] In 1899 Southcott farm was held with Down farm and other land, a total of 627 a.; Mills farm was 121 a., and 101 a. of downland was worked from outside the parish. Ball farm had been divided by 1899; 140 a. of it south of Southcott village was then part of the farm worked from Swan and later part of Down farm; from 1962–3 *c.* 70 a. of the 140 a. was part of Down farm, *c.* 70 a. part of Green Drove farm.[43]

In 1919–20 Sunnyhill farm was reduced to 88 a. Part of its land was transferred to Fairfield farm, 162 a. in 1920,[44] for which buildings south-east of Sunnyhill Farm were erected between 1839 and 1886.[45] In 1997 the lowland north and north-west of Kepnal and Southcott villages, *c.* 350 a. formerly in Sunnyhill, Anvill's, and Fairfield farms, was mainly pasture. Sunnyhill farm, *c.* 140 a. then worked from 20th-century buildings west of the farmstead built *c.* 1800, was an arable and pig farm; a new Inlands farm, *c.* 80 a., was a cattle farm with buildings erected *c.* 1977 north of Pewsey village.[46] Down farm, including land formerly in Southcott farm and 613 a. in 1924,[47] was a mixed farm *c.* 1937. It was used for arable and dairy farming in the mid 20th century;[48] in 1997 it was a mixed farm of 501 a., of which 150 a. was grassland.[49] In 1933 Mills farm and the rest of Southcott farm, as Southcott Manor farm, measured 310 a., lay along the parish boundary south of Kepnal village, and was still worked from buildings in Southcott's street.[50] In the 1960s nearly all of it was added in portions to Green Drove farm and the farm buildings in Southcott's street were given up.[51]

SHARCOTT. The land in Sharcott tithing was bounded to the south by the open fields called East Blacknell and West Blacknell in Down Pewsey tithing.[52] In the 16th century it was shared mainly by five copyholds of Pewsey manor and by a small freehold. The copyhold farmsteads probably stood in East Sharcott's street; the freehold was held with Sharcott mill and was probably worked from a farmstead at West Sharcott.[53]

30 W.R.O. 1392, box 9, Southcott and Kepnal sheep leazes, 1792; 1634/34.
31 *Andrews and Dury, Map* (W.R.S. viii), pl. 12; O.S. Map 1", sheet 14 (1817 edn.).
32 W.R.O. 1392, box 9, plan of Sunnyhill farm.
33 Ibid. 493/46; 1392, box 9, val., 1824; 1392, box 9, terms of letting, 1824; ibid. tithe award.
34 W.R.O., EA/130.
35 Ibid. 628/41/3, outline for letting, 1827; 1392, box 9, val. of Kepnal Down farm, 1828; 1392, box 9, bdle. of vouchers, 1829; 1634/34; ibid. tithe award.
36 Ibid. EA/130; ibid. tithe award.
37 Ibid. tithe award; above, this section (Down Pewsey).
38 W.R.O. 1075/1/85, sale cat., 1874.
39 W.A.S. Libr., sale cat. iv, no. 47.
40 W.R.O., G 10/500/69.
41 Ibid. 1392, box 9, lease, Astley to Cook, 1847.
42 W.A.S. Libr., sale cat. vii, no. 76.

43 Ibid. sale cat. xviii, no. 14; W.R.O., G 10/500/69; inf. from Mr. Strong; for the farm worked from Swan and Green Drove farm, above, this section (Down Pewsey).
44 W.A.S. Libr., sale cat. xiv, no. 13; W.R.O., G 10/500/71.
45 O.S. Map 6", Wilts. XXXVI (1888 edn.); W.R.O., tithe award.
46 Inf. from Mr. S. Canning, Oak Leaze, Prospect, Pewsey.   47 W.A.S. Libr., sale cat. xviii, no. 14.
48 Hosier, *Hosier's Farming System*, 43, 67.
49 Inf. from Mr. N. H. Hosier, Waglands Farm, Collingbourne Kingston.
50 W.A.S. Libr., sale cat. xx, no. 33.
51 Inf. from Mr. Strong; for Green Drove farm, above, this section (Down Pewsey).
52 W.R.O. 1634/34.
53 Ibid. 9/1/95, pp. 2–3; P.R.O., C 142/254, no. 81; ibid. SC 6/Hen. VIII/3341, rot. 48d.

There was 180 a. of arable in Sharcott's open fields, which lay south of Salisbury Road and as the east part of Sharcott's land between the Avon and that road.[54] Meadlands, *c.* 35 a., the western part of the land between the Avon and Salisbury Road, was probably a common meadow; there was a common marsh, probably *c.* 25 a. north-west of East Sharcott village beside the head stream which is crossed by Woodborough Road, and there was an extensive common heath apparently east and west of East Sharcott's street and bounded to the east by the demesne pasture called Westbury. The holdings based in Sharcott tithing had no downland pasture, and the heath was probably for sheep. In addition, north and north-west of the marsh, the holdings apparently included pasture for cattle on the west part of Hatfield common.[55]

In 1552 the five copyholds had 44 a. of pasture in 50 small closes, presumably either side of the street; by then a particular part of Meadlands, 3–7 a., had been assigned to each copyhold and probably to the freehold, but the whole may still have been fed on in common after haymaking; there were rights to feed *c.* 1,000 sheep and 100 cattle on the open fields and common pastures.[56]

By the 1660s Meadlands, the marsh, the heath, and Sharcott's part of Hatfield had all been inclosed,[57] and from the 1660s or earlier the average size of the farms based in Sharcott tithing was probably *c.* 150 a. In 1733 one farm had 217 a., including 34 a. of open-field arable and 134 a. of arable in closes; the tenant was required to keep 300 sheep on the farm.[58] In 1755 there were farms of 163 a. and 161 a.[59] The open fields, which in the 18th century were worked as four fields and contained 170 strips,[60] were inclosed with the other open fields in the parish by Act in 1777.[61]

In 1817 there were farms of 221 a., 208 a., and 170 a., all apparently based in East Sharcott's street. That of 221 a. had been increased to 248 a. by 1838, when it was worked from two farmsteads, one incorporating the house later called Manor Farm and the other nearby on the east side of the street; that of 170 a. had been increased to 182 a. by 1838, when it was worked from the farmstead incorporating the house later called Sharcott House. Those two farms, 430 a., were held by one farmer in 1838, when a farm of 152 a. was worked from buildings at the south end of the street. A farm of 78 a. in 1817, 61 a. in 1838, was worked from a farmstead beside Sharcott mill.[62] In 1899 Manor farm, formerly of 221 a., was of 285 a. and was apparently the only farm worked from buildings in East Sharcott's street; a farm of 226 a. was worked from Sharcott Penning Farm, built between 1839 and 1886, and a farm of 84 a. was worked from West Sharcott.[63]

In 1900 Manor farm was reduced to 183 a. mainly south of East Sharcott village.[64] It had grown to 265 a. by 1928.[65] North of the village Sharcott Penning farm, 198 a. in 1910,[66] was divided into four smallholdings in 1920 or soon after,[67] and in 1928 there were about seven farms in Sharcott of less than 60 a.:[68] in the 1930s nearly all their land was pasture[69] and they were presumably dairy farms. In the 1950s Manor farm, then *c.* 384 a., was divided. About 175 a. south of the Avon was thereafter worked as part of Green Drove farm and in 1997 was mainly arable.[70] As Manor farm *c.* 210 a. between the Avon and Woodborough Road was a separate farm until 1966, from when it was worked with land in Manningford. In 1981–2 Manor farm's land in Sharcott was reduced to 82 a. east of the village; in 1997 that land, Manor Farm, and *c.* 150 a. in Manningford were used for rearing livestock.[71] The land of Sharcott Penning farm lay in three smallholdings in the 1950s and 1970s,[72] as a single mainly dairy farm of 160 a. in 1997.[73]

From *c.* 1910 Walter T. Ware Ltd., nurserymen, held Sharcott mill and *c.* 60 a. near it,[74] and from 1981 held *c.* 120 a. at Sharcott. All that land was used for market gardening in 1997.[75]

In 1982 Malmesbury Potatoes Ltd. bought *c.* 75 a. at Sharcott and in 1983 and later erected extensive buildings at East Sharcott called Ayrshire Farm. In 1997 the company grew potatoes on its land and on other land in the Vale of Pewsey leased to it, and used Ayrshire Farm for potato packing.[76]

WEST WICK. In the Middle Ages West Wick had open fields on the chalk and greensand south of the scarp of the Marlborough Downs. Fields which were called East, Middle, and West and were accounted 106 a. lay on the site in the 16th century.[77] Pewsey manor's men of West Wick, who presumably held farmsteads in a small settlement and land in the open fields,[78] had pasture on the downs. Some or all of it was apparently used in common with the men of Rainscombe, then in North Newnton parish,

[54] W.R.O. 1634/34.
[55] Ibid. 9/1/84; 9/1/95, pp. 2–3; 9/1/134, f. 222; cf. ibid. 1634/34; ibid. tithe award; for Hatfield, above, this section [preamble]; for Westbury, ibid. this section (Down Pewsey).
[56] W.R.O. 9/1/95, pp. 2–3; 192/11B, ct. 6 Sept. 1 & 2 Phil. and Mary.
[57] Ibid. 9/1/84; Alnwick Castle Mun. X.II.11, box 8, survey of Pewsey, 1692.
[58] W.R.O. 212B/5217.
[59] Alnwick Castle Mun. X.II.11, box 8, survey of Pewsey, 1755.
[60] Lond. Metro. Archives, H1/ST/E112/1; W.R.O. 212B/5217.   [61] W.R.O. 1634/34.
[62] Ibid. 493/46; 1392, box 9, plan of Goodman's estate, 1827; ibid. tithe award.
[63] Ibid. 130/78, sale cat. of Stowell Lodge estate, 1900; ibid. G 10/500/69; ibid. tithe award; O.S. Maps 6", Wilts. XXXV (1889 edn.); XLI. NE. (1901 edn.).

[64] W.R.O. 130/78, sale cat. of Stowell Lodge estate, 1900.
[65] Ibid. G 10/500/72.
[66] Ibid. Inland Revenue, val. reg. 57.
[67] Ibid. F 9/120/56/7.
[68] Ibid. G 10/500/72.
[69] [1st] Land Util. Surv. Map, sheet 112.
[70] Inf. from Mr. Strong; for Green Drove farm, above, this section (Down Pewsey).
[71] Inf. from Mr. O. Gates, the Old Rectory, Manningford Abbots.
[72] W.R.O., F 9/106/1; ibid. G 9/106/5.
[73] Inf. from Environmental Services Dept., Co. Hall, Trowbridge.
[74] *Kelly's Dir. Wilts.* (1907, 1911).
[75] Inf. from Mr. Gates; local inf.
[76] Inf. from Malmesbury Potatoes Ltd., E. Sharcott.
[77] W.R.O. 9/1/95, p. 4; 9/1/134, ff. 19, 21.
[78] Cf. B.L. Harl. MS. 1761, ff. 132v. sqq.

until 1280, when the men of West Wick gave up claims to feed cattle on land assarted before 1236 in the coomb in which Rainscombe House now stands, and the men of Rainscombe conceded to the men of West Wick all rights to feed cattle on the high ground east of the coomb.[79] The men of West Wick used the upland pasture, which included Martinsell Hill, in common,[80] but there is no evidence that they had rights to feed animals on Hatfield common.

In the 16th century all West Wick's land lay in severalty in West Wick farm, which was assessed at 7 yardlands. In 1538 the farm included 99 a. of arable in three fields, apparently the former open fields, 2¼ a. of meadows, 14 a. of lowland pasture probably near the farmstead, 60 a. of inclosed, and probably improved, pasture on Martinsell Hill, and 42 a. of rough downland pasture.[81] West Wick Farm has stood on its present site from the earlier 18th century or earlier.[82] In 1755 the farm measured 302 a., of which half lay on the downs.[83] In 1838 its 371 a. included 209 a. of arable, 20 a. of lowland pasture, 20 a. of improved pasture on the downs, and 66 a. of rough downland; the arable included 70 a. on the downs.[84] In 1893 its 365 a. included 213 a. of arable of which 76 a. lay on the downs.[85] Between 1899 and 1910 the steep slopes of the coomb in which Rainscombe House stands were taken from the farm, 310 a. in 1910,[86] and a dairy was built at West Wick Farm c. 1938.[87] By the mid 20th century West Wick farm had been increased to c. 460 a. by the addition of land west of the farmstead and in Wilcot parish. In 1997, when its land was used for arable and sheep farming, it was worked in conjunction with a larger farm from outside the parish.[88]

MILLS. There were seven mills at Pewsey in 1086.[89] In the earlier 13th century there were four: one was the Town mill, one probably stood on the site of Buckleaze mill, one almost certainly stood at West Sharcott, and one probably stood on the site of Jones mill.[90]

The Town mill stood on the north side of High Street at its west end and was driven by the Avon.[91] In the 16th century it was part of a customary holding of Pewsey manor.[92] In 1769–70 the reversion in fee of the mill passed like that of Manor farm, and St. Thomas's hospital,

London, owned the mill from 1770 to 1920.[93] The thatching of both the mill, which had three pairs of stones, and the mill house needed repair in 1758.[94] In 1849 the mill was said to have a well established business despite being old and small.[95] In 1920 it was converted to generate electricity[96] and it was later demolished.

Buckleaze mill was a water mill which stood at the confluence of Ford brook and the Avon 500 m. NNW. of the Town mill.[97] A mill on its site was probably one of the two mills of which Henry Sturmy was the freeholder in the earlier 13th century.[98] From the 15th century Buckleaze mill descended in the Benger family as part of the estate later called Buckleaze farm, and it descended with the farm until 1920 or later. In 1880 it was a flour and grist mill with three pairs of stones.[99] It may have gone out of use between 1915 and 1920,[1] and between 1920 and 1928 it was converted to generate electricity.[2]

Sharcott mill at West Sharcott was driven by the Avon. It was almost certainly one of the two mills of which Henry Sturmy was the freeholder in the earlier 13th century,[3] and it descended with Buckleaze mill in the Benger family from the 15th century to 1602, when John Benger sold it to Henry Goodman.[4] Sharcott mill descended in the Goodman family until 1687.[5] Later owners have not been traced. The mill was used for grinding corn in 1899;[6] between 1907 and 1911 it was acquired by nurserymen, and grinding had presumably ceased by then.[7]

Jones mill was standing in the 14th century, when it was held with land at East Wick in turn by William Harding (d. c. 1330) and his daughter Anstice (d. 1353), wife of William de Lillebonne and after of Sir Robert Bilkemore.[8] Its site was presumably where, above Buckleaze mill, land beside the Avon was called Jones mill from the 16th century or earlier.[9]

MARKET. The right to hold a Tuesday market at Pewsey was granted in 1824 to the lord of the Pewsey and Sharcott part of Pewsey manor.[10] From 1848 or earlier to the 1880s a weekly corn market was held on Tuesdays at the Phoenix inn,[11] and in the 1920s a monthly livestock market was held.[12] In the late 1970s a general market was revived;[13] in 1997 it was held on the car park west of North Street.

79 Ibid. ff. 125v., 127v.–128.
80 W.R.O. 9/1/95, p. 4.   81 Ibid. 9/1/134, f. 21.
82 Above, intro. (W. Wick).
83 Alnwick Castle Mun. X.II.11, box 8, survey of Pewsey, 1755.
84 W.R.O., tithe award.
85 Ibid. 628/48/1.
86 Ibid. G 10/500/69; ibid. Inland Revenue, val. reg. 57.
87 Ibid. G 10/760/323.
88 Inf. from Madeleine, Lady Devlin, W. Wick Ho.
89 V.C.H. Wilts. ii, p. 127.
90 B.L. Harl. MS. 1761, ff. 132, 136v.
91 O.S. Map 6", Wilts. XLI (1889 edn.).
92 W.R.O. 9/1/95, p. 9.
93 Lond. Metro. Archives, H1/ST/E66/47/4; above, manor (Pewsey).
94 Alnwick Castle Mun. X.II.11, box 8, survey of Pewsey, 1755; Lond. Metro. Archives, H1/ST/E88/4, ct. 12 Dec. 1758.
95 Lond. Metro. Archives, H1/ST/E56/11/32.
96 Ibid. H1/ST/E55/4; W.A.S. Libr., sale cat. xiii, no.

9.
97 O.S. Maps 6", Wilts. XXXV, XLI (1889 edns.).
98 B.L. Harl. MS. 1761, f. 132.
99 P.R.O., C 142/254, no. 81; ibid. CP 40/927, rot. 152; W.R.O., tithe award; ibid. 374/130/92; ibid. G 10/500/69; G 10/500/71; above manor (Buckleaze).
1 Kelly's Dir. Wilts. (1915, 1920).
2 W.R.O., G 10/500/71–2.
3 B.L. Harl. MS. 1761, f. 132.
4 P.R.O., CP 25/2/242/44 Eliz. I East.; CP 40/927, rot. 152; W.R.O. 9/7/714.
5 P.R.O., CP 25/2/803/3 Jas. II Mich.
6 O.S. Map 1/2,500, Wilts. XLI. 3 (1900 edn.).
7 Kelly's Dir. Wilts. (1907, 1911).
8 Wilts. Inq. p.m. 1327–77 (Index Libr.), 48, 256.
9 W.R.O. 9/1/95, pp. 3–4; ibid. Inland Revenue, val. reg. 57 and map 35.
10 Lond. Metro. Archives, H1/ST/E66/47/2/1.
11 Kelly's Dir. Wilts. (1848 and later edns.).
12 Wilts. Gaz. 5 May 1921.
13 Ibid. 25 Aug. 1977; Wilts. Cuttings, xxviii. 338.

TRADE AND INDUSTRY. Before the canal and the railway were opened across the parish in the 19th century there were few trades in Pewsey unconnected with agriculture. A pelterer, a maker of baskets and hives, and a fuller were mentioned in the 14th century,[14] glovers in the 16th and 17th.[15]

Bricks were made in the parish from the early 18th century or earlier[16] to the early 20th century. A kiln which in 1839 stood east of Hollybush Lane a little north of Ball had been demolished by 1886, when there was a brick field and a kiln between Kepnal village and Ball.[17] Brick making apparently ceased between 1895 and 1899.[18] A cooper had premises in the parish in the mid 18th century.[19] A cooperage said in 1806 to be newly built[20] was probably that in Ball Road used by members of the King family from 1838 or earlier to c. 1920:[21] the Cooper's Arms there was probably the cooper's new house.[22] Another cooper had premises in High Street in the mid 19th century.[23] Members of the Hunt family were watch and clock makers in Pewsey village from 1848 or earlier to c. 1903. About 1870 George Whatley & Son, agricultural engineers and iron and brass founders, opened the Avonside foundry near the Town mill.[24] The firm was managed by A. J. Hosier from 1904 to 1910; in 1922 it bought the assetts of Scout Motors Ltd. of Salisbury, makers of motor cars and buses. In the 20th century Whatley & Co. Ltd. specialized in various forms of mechanical engineering, including well boring from 1904 and car body repairing in the 1990s. It had c. 50 employees in 1952,[25] 16 in 1996.[26] A firm of agricultural, later motor, engineers had premises at Swan from c. 1910 to the 1980s.[27]

Innkeeping from the 16th century[28] and malting in the 18th and 19th centuries were apparently successful trades at Pewsey; there were three malthouses in 1767.[29] In the 19th century and until the mid 20th Pewsey was a local centre for retail and for trades connected to building, food and drink, and footwear and clothing. There was a bank in the village from the 1860s; c. 75 retailers and tradesmen and two banks had premises there in 1899. Coal was distributed from Pewsey wharf and Pewsey station, and from the early 1920s there was an oil depot on a site in Wilcot Road adjoining the railway station;[30] the site of the oil depot was a scrap metal yard in 1997. The number of shops in the village declined in the later 20th century despite the increase in its population.[31]

From c. 1961 to the 1980s glue packing was carried out by Copydex Ltd. in the former cinema in High Street.[32] Fordbrook industrial estate was built east of Marlborough Road in the early 1980s,[33] and Salisbury Road business park was opened c. 1991.[34] In 1997 several firms involved in computer technology were in business on the industrial estate, and a company which repaired telephone systems had premises in the business park.

LOCAL GOVERNMENT. There were four tithings in Pewsey parish, Down Pewsey, Kepnal, Sharcott, and Southcott. Pewsey village was in Down Pewsey tithing, West Wick in Kepnal tithing.[35] The tithings were probably in being in the 13th century[36] and remained fiscal units in the 19th.[37]

The lord of Pewsey manor exercised no leet jurisdiction in respect of it.[38] From the 16th century to the earlier 18th the manor court usually met twice a year. It recorded the death or default of tenants, dealt with the surrender of and admittance to copyholds and with other copyhold business, defined and enforced the customs which regulated the use of the open fields and common pastures, received presentments relating to agrarian misdemeanours, and made orders to remedy minor public nuisances. The condition and location of boundaries were frequently matters of concern, and pleas of debt or trespass were occasionally heard. In the 16th century and earlier 17th the court received presentments separately from each of the four tithingmen of Pewsey parish and from the tithingman of Manningford Abbots. In the early 17th century the court appointed tellers of sheep and of cattle for Kepnal and Southcott, in the 18th a hayward for Down Pewsey and Sharcott and for Kepnal and Southcott. From 1769 separate courts for Down Pewsey and Sharcott tithings and for Kepnal and Southcott tithings were held by the respective lords. Each met once a year as a court called a capital court baron and at other times, when required by copyhold busi-

14 V.C.H. Wilts. iv. 123; W.A.M. xxxiii. 394.
15 Sess. Mins. (W.R.S. iv), 77, 145; W.A.M. xxxviii. 574.
16 W.R.O. 493/49; Lond. Metro. Archives, H1/ST/E67/20/18; Alnwick Castle Mun. X.II.11, box 8, survey of Pewsey, 1755.
17 O.S. Map 6", Wilts. XLI (1889 edn.); W.R.O., tithe award; cf. ibid. G 10/500/69.
18 Kelly's Dir. Wilts. (1895, 1899).
19 Alnwick Castle Mun. X.II.11, box 8, survey of Pewsey, 1755.
20 W.R.O. 212B/5223, deed, Smith to Deadman, 1806.
21 Ibid. tithe award; Kelly's Dir. Wilts. (1848 and later edns.).
22 Above, intro. (Southcott).
23 Harrod's Dir. Wilts. (1865).
24 Kelly's Dir. Wilts. (1848 and later edns.); O.S. Map 6", Wilts. XLI (1889 edn.).
25 Hosier, Hosier's Farming System, 4–5; Kelly's Dir. Wilts. (1939); V.C.H. Wilts. iv. 196, 201; Pewsey Village Trail (copy in Wilts. local studies libr., Trowbridge), 5.
26 Wilts. co. council, Dir. of Employers (1996), p. 71.
27 Kelly's Dir. Wilts. (1907 and later edns.); Wilts. co. council, Dir. of Firms (1984).
28 Above, intro. (Pewsey: inns).
29 W.R.O. 490/1060; ibid. tithe award; Lond. Metro. Archives, H1/ST/E88/1; Alnwick Castle Mun. X.II.11, box 8, survey of Pewsey, 1755.
30 Kelly's Dir. Wilts. (1848 and later edns.); O.S. Maps 1/2,500, Wilts. XLI. 4 (1900, 1924 edns.); W.R.O., G 10/760/66.
31 Cf. above, intro. [population]; ibid. (Pewsey).
32 Pewsey through the Ages, i (copy in Wilts. local studies libr.), 14; W.R.O. 1634/4; 1634/50.
33 Wilts. co. council, Dir. of Firms (1984); O.S. Map 1/10,000, SU 16 SE. (1983 edn.).
34 Inf. from Messrs. Dreweatt Neate, 4–5 Mkt. Place, Devizes.
35 W.R.O. 9/1/95, pp. 2–19.
36 Crown Pleas, 1249 (W.R.S. xvi), p. 220; P.R.O., JUST 1/1006, rot. 51.
37 W.R.O., A 1/345/324A–B.
38 Ibid. 9/1/95, p. 19.

ness, as a special court. The court for Down Pewsey and Sharcott was held until 1819, that for Kepnal and Southcott until 1817 or later.[39]

Pewsey parish had four overseers in the earlier 17th century, afterwards two. In 1622 the overseers spent £10 10s. on the poor, in the 1650s £20–£30 a year. Spending was higher in the later 17th century, when at £97 it was highest in 1698–9. In several years in the period 1703–23 it was between £110 and £120. The parish provided a workhouse in 1773, presumably by converting the two houses which it bought in that year.[40] It spent £345 on relieving the poor in 1775–6, an average of £467 in the three years ending at Easter 1785. In 1802–3 the poor rate was low. The parish then spent £797 on outdoor relief of 113 adults and 217 children regularly and 85 people occasionally, and it spent £245 on indoor relief of 40; by their labour those in the workhouse contributed £52 to their maintenance.[41] In the three years to Easter 1815 the cost of poor relief averaged £1,735, at £2,284 being very high in 1812–13, and on average 122 adults were relieved regularly and 66 occasionally. Indoor relief is not referred to after 1813–14[42] and the workhouse may have been closed. Between then and 1835–6 the yearly cost was at £1,765 highest in 1817–18 and at £890 lowest in 1827–8. In 1835 the parish joined Pewsey poor-law union,[43] and in 1974 it became part of Kennet district.[44]

CHURCH. Pewsey church was standing in 1086, when it was held by Rainbold the priest: that it was then referred to as standing on the king's estate may suggest that it was built before 940.[45] In the 13th century and until the earlier 15th the church was served by both a rector and a vicar.[46] In 1440 the vicarage was consolidated with the rectory,[47] which in 1991 was united with the united benefice of Easton and Milton Lilbourne and the rectory of Wootton Rivers as Pewsey benefice.[48]

The advowson of the rectory belonged to Hyde abbey, the lord of Pewsey manor, until the Dissolution.[49] The king presented in 1408 while the abbey was vacant.[50] The advowson passed with the manor from 1538 to the attainder of Edward, duke of Somerset, in 1552. The king granted it in 1552 to William Herbert, earl of Pembroke,[51] and it descended with the Pembroke title to 1678.[52] For reasons that are not clear the Crown presented in 1558.[53] In 1678 Philip, earl of Pembroke and of Montgomery, sold the advowson to William Stanley, from whom it descended in the direct line to George, William, George (d. 1733), and Hans Stanley.[54] In 1706 John Thorpe presented under a grant of a turn by the elder George Stanley, and in 1736 Philippa Stanley, the relict and executor of Hoby Stanley, rector 1729–36, presented under a grant of a turn to her husband by the younger George Stanley.[55] In 1744 Hans Stanley sold the advowson to Mary Amyand. In 1763 Mary's daughter-in-law, Frances Amyand, and her five surviving children as her residuary legatees granted a turn to Chauncy Townsend, who presented in 1764, and, also in 1763, the legatees sold the advowson to Henry Fox[56] (from 1763 Lord Holland, d. 1774). Henry was succeeded by his son Stephen, Lord Holland (d. 1774), and he by his son Henry, Lord Holland, a minor.[57] For money paid in 1775 by William Bouverie, earl of Radnor (d. 1776), to that Lord Holland's trustees the advowson was conveyed to William's son Jacob Pleydell-Bouverie, earl of Radnor, in 1777.[58] It descended with the Radnor title,[59] and from 1991 Jacob Pleydell-Bouverie, earl of Radnor, was a member of the board of patronage for Pewsey benefice.[60] The advowson of the vicarage belonged to the rector. The king presented in 1401 while the rectory was vacant.[61]

In 1291 the church was valued at £25: at £20 the rectory was highly valued, the vicarage was worth £4 6s. 8d., and a pension of 13s. 4d. was paid to the sacrist of Hyde abbey.[62] From 1440 pensions of £10 11s. 8d. and 8s. were paid by the rector to Hyde abbey and Salisbury cathedral respectively,[63] and in 1535 the rectory was worth £27 net.[64] About 1830 the rectory, valued at £1,038, was the second most valuable parish living in Wiltshire.[65] The value of the vicarage in 1291 suggests that tithes had been assigned to it; if so, they were restored to the rector, presumably in 1440. The rector was later entitled to all tithes from the whole parish. Tithes from 107 a. of the demesne of Pewsey manor were

39 Ibid. 9/1/83; 9/1/134–7; 9/1/139–41; 9/1/143; 192/11A–C; 679/3; Alnwick Castle Mun. X.II.11, box 6, ct. bk. 1692–1703; X.II.11, box 12, ct. papers; X.II.11, box 13, ct. papers; X.II.11, box 27, notes of presentments; Lond. Metro. Archives, H1/ST/E88/1–4; Winchester Coll. Mun. 14905; 14907; 19646; for Manningford Abbots, cf. above, manor (Pewsey).
40 W.R.O. 493/49.
41 Poor Law Abstract, 1804, 566–7.
42 Ibid. 1818, 498–9.
43 Poor Rate Returns, 1816–21, 188; 1822–4, 228; 1825–9, 219; 1830–4, 212; Poor Law Com. 2nd Rep. App. D, 560.
44 O.S. Map 1/100,000, admin. areas, Wilts. (1974 edn.).
45 V.C.H. Wilts. ii, pp. 2–3, 119; cf. above, manor (Pewsey).
46 Tax. Eccl. (Rec. Com.), 189; Phillipps, Wilts. Inst. (index in W.A.M. xxviii. 227); B.L. Harl. MS. 1761, f. 130v.
47 W.R.O., D 1/2/10, ff. (2nd foliation) 46v.–48.
48 Ch. Com. file, NB 34/263B.
49 Cal. Pat. 1281–92, 230; Phillipps, Wilts. Inst. (index in W.A.M. xxviii. 227); above, manor (Pewsey).
50 B.L. Harl. MS. 1761, f. 122v.
51 Cal. Pat. 1550–3, 358; P.R.O., E 305/9/43; E 305/15/42A.
52 For the earls of Pembroke, Complete Peerage, x. 405–22.
53 Cal. Pat. 1557–8, 356.
54 Burke, Land. Gent. (1937), 2120; W.R.O. 490/479, abstr. of title of Hans Stanley.
55 W.R.O. 490/479, list of incumbents; 490/479, deed, Stanley to Thorpe, 1704; 490/479, add. abstr. of title of Hans Stanley.
56 Ibid. 490/479, abstr. of title of Hen. Fox; Phillipps, Wilts. Inst. ii. 81.
57 Complete Peerage, vi. 541–4.
58 W.R.O. 490/479, deeds, Holland to Collins, 1776; Collins to Radnor, 1777; 490/479, memo. 1777.
59 Complete Peerage, x. 717–21; Who's Who, 1997, 1601.
60 Ch. Com. file, NB 34/263B.
61 Phillipps, Wilts. Inst. i. 22, 24, 43–5, 63, 87–8, 119; Cal. Pat. 1461–7, 298.
62 Tax. Eccl. (Rec. Com.), 189.
63 W.R.O., D 1/2/10, ff. (2nd foliation) 46v.–48; P.R.O., E 315/100, ff. 331v.–332; for the larger pension, above, manor.
64 Valor Eccl. (Rec. Com.), ii. 151.
65 Rep. Com. Eccl. Revenues, 844–5.

exchanged for a 19-a. field, apparently between 1671 and 1704. The remaining tithes were valued at £1,230 in 1838 and commuted in 1839.[66] In 1086 the church was held with 1 carucate,[67] in the earlier 13th century with 1 yardland.[68] In 1341 it had arable and common pasture assessed at 2 yardlands, several meadow worth 40s., several pasture worth 20s., and two dovecots.[69] That land almost certainly included the house, garden, and agricultural land assigned by Hyde abbey to the vicarage: the abbey took that endowment back in 1440.[70] In the 17th century the glebe consisted of the rectory house, c. 18 a. in closes, c. 36 a. in open fields, and feeding in common for 100 sheep and c. 12 beasts.[71] In the mid 18th century a former copyhold was held by the rector or his patron on a lease for life: in 1768 the freehold was bought by the patron,[72] and between 1777 and 1817 the land was added to the glebe.[73] After the inclosure of the open fields and common downland, and the additions of 1671 × 1704 and 1777 × 1817, the glebe measured 125 a. in 1838.[74] The rector sold 107 a. in 1912,[75] the rectory house and 11 a. in 1928,[76] and 4 a. in 1957.[77] In 1408 the rectory house incorporated a hall with rooms at the upper and lower ends.[78] The rectory house standing in 1704, then said to be old and to have a fishpond in its garden,[79] was probably the house, later called Court House, immediately east of the church.[80] The rectory house sold in 1928 was built east of the Avon in the early 18th century, probably for John Thorpe, rector 1706–29.[81] It is a double-pile two-storeyed house of red brick with a hipped roof. Its west, entrance, front is of nine bays, of which the central five are recessed, and incorporates stone dressings; the three north bays of the central part are those of the entrance hall. An east bow of full height and a south-east service wing were built in the earlier 20th century, probably soon after 1928, and later in the 20th century the inside of the house was much altered for use as offices.[82] Features of the house to survive from the early 18th century include sashed windows at the north end of the east front, a broad staircase adjoining the entrance hall, the service staircase, and the fittings of the first-floor room at the south-east corner.

A new rectory house was built c. 1928[83] and another in 1974.[84] That built c. 1928 was sold in 1975.[85]

The rector from 1294 or earlier to c. 1305 was a pluralist in the 1290s and infirm in 1303.[86] His successor Henry of Ludgershall, rector from 1306 to 1327 or later, was a clerk of Edward II as prince of Wales in 1307 and also a pluralist.[87] Robert of Whitburgh, rector from 1349 to c. 1389, was the almoner of Queen Philippa and another pluralist; the vicar was appointed his guardian and assistant in 1388.[88] Licence to study at a university was given to the rector in the 1390s[89] and to the vicar in 1432.[90] The vicar who resigned when the vicarage was consolidated with the rectory in 1440 was instituted as rector in that year.[91] Goods taken from the church in Edward VI's reign had not been returned by 1556.[92]

From the 16th century the rector was often assisted by a curate.[93] Thomas Leche, rector 1612–46, was archdeacon of Wiltshire from 1614.[94] His successor Humphrey Chambers maintained a horse and a man under arms against Charles I, petitioned at quarter sessions for the suppression of alehouses in Pewsey, wrote *An Apology for the Ministers of Wiltshire*, was a leader of the Voluntary Association of Puritan Ministers in Wiltshire, and had been deprived by 1662.[95] Richard Watson, rector 1662–85 and a chaplain of James, duke of York, had several quarrels with his parishioners.[96] In 1671 it was not customary at Pewsey to stand at the creed or gospel or bow at the name Jesus.[97] The rector 1685–1702 was dean of Salisbury from 1691;[98] his curate at Pewsey from c. 1693 to 1702 was the subdean, the diarist Thomas Naish.[99] There were 48 communicants at Christmas in 1709, 44 at Easter in 1710.[1] Joseph Townsend, rector 1764–1816, was a geologist, a student of medicine, and an advocate of parliamentary reform. In 1783 he held two services each Sunday and communion at the great festivals. He was resident then,[2] but later, probably from 1799 or earlier, he was non-resident, and in 1812 there was only one service each Sunday and no more than 20 communicants.[3] Frederick Pleydell-Bouverie, rector 1816–57, and Bertrand

[66] W.R.O., D 1/24/166/2–3; ibid. tithe award.
[67] *V.C.H. Wilts.* ii, p. 119.
[68] B.L. Harl. MS. 1761, f. 133v.
[69] *Inq. Non.* (Rec. Com.), 173.
[70] W.R.O., D 1/2/10, ff. (2nd foliation) 46v.–48.
[71] Ibid. D 1/24/166/1–2.
[72] Ibid. 11/388–91.
[73] Ibid. 493/46; 1634/34.   [74] Ibid. tithe award.
[75] W.A.S. Libr., sale cat. xxviiiD, no. 48.
[76] W.R.O. 1634/38.
[77] Inf. from Ch. Com.
[78] *Reg. Hallum* (Cant. & York Soc.), p. 136.
[79] W.R.O., D 1/24/166/3.
[80] Court Ho. is described above, intro. (Pewsey).
[81] Phillipps, *Wilts. Inst.* ii. 48, 62.
[82] Above, intro. (Pewsey).
[83] W.R.O. 493/47.
[84] Ibid. 493/66.
[85] Inf. from Ch. Com.
[86] *Cal. Pat.* 1292–1301, 118; *Reg. Ghent* (Cant. & York Soc.), i. 120, 219.
[87] *Reg. Ghent* (Cant. & York Soc.), ii. 665; *Cal. Papal Reg.* ii. 26, 50; *Reg. Martival* (Cant. & York Soc.), i. 372.
[88] Phillipps, *Wilts. Inst.* i. 47, 74; *Cal. Papal Pets.* i. 416; *Reg. Waltham* (Cant. & York Soc.), p. 41.

[89] *Cal. Papal Reg.* iv. 527.
[90] Ibid. viii. 446.
[91] Phillipps, *Wilts. Inst.* i. 131; W.R.O., D 1/2/10, ff. (2nd foliation) 46v.–48.
[92] W.R.O., D 1/43/2, f. 13v.
[93] e.g. ibid. D 1/43/1, f. 142; D 1/51/4, f. 21; *Subscription Bk. 1620–40* (W.R.S. xxxii), pp. 23, 54; Hist. MSS. Com. 55, *Var. Colln.* i, p. 146; *Rep. Com. Eccl. Revenues*, 844–5.
[94] Le Neve, *Fasti, 1541–1857, Salisbury*, 18; Phillipps, *Wilts. Inst.* ii. 7.
[95] *L.J.* viii. 130; Hist. MSS. Com. 55, *Var. Colln.* i, p. 112; Phillipps, *Wilts. Inst.* ii. 25; *W.N. & Q.* viii. 14; *V.C.H. Wilts.* iii. 101.
[96] Phillipps, *Wilts. Inst.* ii. 25, 40; *D.N.B.*; Hist. MSS. Com. 55, *Var. Colln.* i, pp. 146, 150, 152; *V.C.H. Wilts.* iii. 46.
[97] *V.C.H. Wilts.* iii. 45.
[98] Le Neve, *Fasti, 1541–1857, Salisbury*, 7; Phillipps, *Wilts. Inst.* ii. 40, 46.
[99] W.R.O., D 1/48/3; D 1/51/1; cf. *Naish's Diary* (W.R.S. xx), 39.
[1] W.R.O. 493/49.
[2] *D.N.B.*; Phillipps, *Wilts. Inst.* ii. 81; *Vis. Queries, 1783* (W.R.S. xxvii), pp. 8, 174–5.
[3] *W.A.M.* xli. 135; lxxvi. 144.

Pleydell-Bouverie, rector 1880–1909, were each a canon of Salisbury. A second service each Sunday was restarted soon after 1816.[4] In 1850–1 the average attendance at each of the two services was said to be 408.[5] In 1864, when the rector was resident and had an assistant curate, there were three services each Sunday in winter, two in summer; at other services, held daily in Lent and Advent, on Thursday evenings, and at other times, the congregation was very small; there were c. 80 communicants, and communion was held at five festivals and on the first Sunday of each month. The rector protested that too many of the seats in the church had been appropriated, that the poor were almost excluded from the church because the only free seats were in the galleries where, because there was too little light, they, especially the women, would not sit, and that at evening service on Sundays the east end of the church was empty and the west end overcrowded.[6] A mission room built at King's Corner in 1878[7] had been closed by 1910.[8]

The church of *ST. JOHN THE BAPTIST*, so called in 1763,[9] is built of rubble and ashlar and consists of a chancel with north vestry and organ chamber and south chapel, an aisled and clerestoried nave with north porch, and a west tower.[10] The nave has unusually thick north and south walls, and the arcades have square piers: from that it appears that the nave is 12th-century and that the aisles were added later, possibly in the 13th century. The chancel was rebuilt in the later 13th century[11] and the tower was built in the early 16th. A west gallery had been constructed by 1710, c. 1738 a gallery was built in the north aisle,[12] and an early 19th-century statement that 105 seats had lately been added to the church[13] may refer to the building of a gallery in the south aisle. The porch was repaired or rebuilt in 1804–5 and the nave was ceiled in 1835.[14] The church was restored, to designs by Thomas Cundy, in 1853, when the floor was lowered, the north and west galleries were rearranged, and, at the west end of the north aisle, the vestry was altered.[15] In 1861, to designs by G. E. Street, the chancel was largely rebuilt and the south chapel was added.[16] In 1889–90, to designs by C. E. Ponting, the church was further restored: the north aisle was demolished and replaced by one which was wider and extended further east to form a new vestry and organ chamber, the gallery in the north aisle, a gallery in the south aisle, and the ceiling of the nave were removed, and the nave

was reroofed. The west gallery was removed, presumably before 1889.[17] The clock which had been installed in the church by 1670 was restored in 1982.[18] Several fittings inside the church incorporate carving in wood by Bertrand Pleydell-Bouverie.[19]

In 1553 a 5-oz. chalice was kept by the parish and 1½ oz. of plate was taken for the king. In 1891 and 1997 the parish had a silver-gilt chalice with paten cover hallmarked for 1679 and dated 1685. Plate given c. 1739 and c. 1750, two patens, two flagons, and two almsdishes, was recast in 1876 as a chalice, two patens, two flagons, and an almsdish. The recast vessels were retained in 1997. Other items of plate were given in the 1980s, and in 1995 the plate held until then for use in the chapel of Pewsey union workhouse (later Pewsey mental hospital) was given.[20]

In 1553 the church had three bells, by the 18th century a ring of six. A bell cast at Salisbury in the Middle Ages survives in the ring with a bell cast by a Purdue in 1620, three bells cast by Abraham Rudhall of Gloucester, two in 1709 and one in 1735, and a bell cast in 1792 by Robert Wells of Aldbourne. In 1961 the medieval bell and the bells of 1709 were recast, and the other bells were restored, by John Taylor & Company of Loughborough (Leics.). A sanctus bell cast at Devizes by James Burrough in 1754 hangs on the outside face of the east wall of the tower.[21]

The registers survive from 1568 and, apart from baptisms 1760–74, are complete.[22]

ROMAN CATHOLICISM. A chapel of ease, served from Devizes, was open at Pewsey in the 1930s.[23] A new church, small, **A**-framed, and dedicated to the Holy Family, was built in Broadfields in 1964.[24]

PROTESTANT NONCONFORMITY. In 1676 there was no dissenter at Pewsey.[25] A meeting house was certified in 1716[26] and John Wesley addressed a congregation in Pewsey church in 1764,[27] but in 1783 there was again no dissenter in the parish.[28]

Independents certified a meeting house in each of the years 1785, 1792, and 1794. One of the meeting houses, in Easterton Lane, was bought in 1817 by two members of the Congregational association from commissioners in bankruptcy.[29]

Baptists held services in a cottage in the early 19th century. A chapel used by Strict Baptists

4 Le Neve, *Fasti, 1541–1857, Salisbury*, 63, 105; B. P. Bouverie, *Par. of Pewsey*, 10, 17; *Crockford* (1915).
5 P.R.O., HO 129/261/2/1/1.
6 W.R.O., D 1/56/7.
7 *Pewsey through the Ages*, iii (copy in Wilts. local studies libr.), 22.   8 W.R.O., Inland Revenue, val. reg. 57.
9 J. Ecton, *Thesaurus* (1763), 406.
10 Above, plate 3.
11 Cf. J. Buckler, watercolour in W.A.S. Libr., vol. iv. 12.   12 W.R.O. 493/49.
13 Lewis, *Topog. Dict. Eng.* (1831), iii. 530.
14 *W.A.M.* xlii. 281; W.R.O. 493/49.
15 W.R.O., D 1/61/8/9.
16 Ibid. D 1/61/13/4.   17 Ibid. D 1/61/34/7.
18 Ibid. 493/49; *Pewsey through the Ages*, iii. 36; Wilts. Cuttings, xxix. 275, 307.

19 Bouverie, *Pewsey*, 19; *W.A.M.* liv. 35; W.R.O. 493/59.
20 Nightingale, *Wilts. Plate*, 171–2; Bouverie, *Pewsey*, 23; *W.A.M.* xii. 364; inf. from Mrs. S. M. Pope, 23 Astley Close.
21 Walters, *Wilts. Bells*, 156; W.R.O. 493/51, faculty, 1961; inf. from Mrs. Pope.
22 W.R.O. 493/1; 493/3; 493/5; 493/7–8; 493/15–16; 493/25–6; bishop's transcripts for 1760–74 are in W.R.O.
23 *V.C.H. Wilts.* iii. 97.
24 *Clifton Dioc. Dir.* (1997); above, plate 38.
25 *Compton Census*, ed. Whiteman, 127.
26 *Meeting Ho. Certs.* (W.R.S. xl), p. 18.
27 J. Wesley, *Jnl.* ed. E. Rhys, iii. 201.
28 *Vis. Queries, 1783* (W.R.S. xxvii), p. 174.
29 *Meeting Ho. Certs.* (W.R.S. xl), pp. 34, 40, 42; A. Antrobus, *Wilts. and E. Som. Congregational Union*, 23; cf. W.R.O., tithe award.

in 1835 stood in High Street near Brunkards Lane and was probably built in 1832. The first pastor was Thomas Godwin, a shoemaker, a friend of William Tiptaft and J. C. Philpott, and later pastor of Godmanchester (Hunts., later Cambs.).[30] In 1850–1 the average congregation at Sunday morning service was estimated at 200, at Sunday evening service at 100.[31] The chapel was replaced by one near the Town mill probably in the later 19th century.[32] The congregation had declined by the early 20th century and the chapel was sold in 1920.[33] The Independent chapel in Easterton Lane, or a replacement on its site, was later the Zion chapel and from 1886 or earlier was used by General Baptists.[34] It was closed in the 1950s.[35]

A metal chapel for Methodists was built off High Street in 1834.[36] On Census Sunday in 1851 morning service was attended by 55, afternoon service by 196, and evening service by 234.[37] Before 1873 the chapel was probably demolished and the Methodists shared the chapel in Easterton Lane. A new Methodist chapel was built in North Street in 1873, a schoolroom was added to it in 1928, and the inside of the chapel was restored in 1962.[38] Services were still held in the chapel in 1997. A chapel for Primitive Methodists had been opened at King's Corner by 1886.[39] By 1895 it had been replaced by one in Brunkards Lane;[40] that was closed apparently between 1915 and 1920.[41]

EDUCATION. A school was held in the parish church in the mid 17th century. It was apparently difficult to find a master for it, and it was closed c. 1673.[42] A room formerly used for malting was a schoolroom in the earlier 19th century.[43] Three day schools in the parish in 1818 had 95 pupils.[44] A National school was opened in 1824 and had 60 pupils in 1833, when the other three schools had 104; an additional 20 children attended an infants' school in 1833.[45] A new National school in River Street was built in 1840.[46] It had two teachers and 108 pupils in 1846–7, when the only other day school had 42 pupils.[47] In 1856 the National school was open on two evenings a week for boys and on two other evenings a week for girls.[48] In 1858 it had

80–90 pupils, an infants' school had 40, and five other day schools had 60.[49] A new National school was built at King's Corner in 1862–3,[50] was apparently opened in 1864,[51] and was enlarged in 1872;[52] in 1864 children were said to leave the school aged c. 10. The school in River Street was used for infants from when the school at King's Corner was opened.[53] It was apparently rebuilt in 1867[54] and was enlarged in 1871.[55] From c. 1888 until they were transferred to Wiltshire county council by Act of 1902 the schools were managed by a school board.[56] In 1899 a classroom was added to the school at King's Corner.[57] Various other small schools were held in the village in the later 19th century.[58]

In 1902 the primary school at King's Corner had 3 classrooms and 5 teachers, the infants' school had 2 classrooms and 2 teachers. Between 1902 and 1938 the average attendance at the two schools declined from 173 to 122 and from 93 to 63 respectively.[59] Cookery was taught at the primary school in the 1930s.[60] In 1953–4 older pupils from other parishes were transferred to the primary school, which in 1956 had 264 pupils aged from 8 to 15. In 1958 Pewsey Vale secondary modern school was opened in Wilcot Road and the primary school was renamed Pewsey junior school. In 1975 the secondary modern school was closed and a comprehensive school, Pewsey Vale school, was opened in its buildings.[61] In 1971 Pewsey infants' school was transferred from River Street to mobile buildings on a site adjoining that of Pewsey Vale school,[62] in 1985 the school at King's Corner was closed, and in 1986 a new Pewsey primary school for pupils aged from 5 to 11 was opened on the site adjoining that of Pewsey Vale school.[63] In 1996 the primary school had 199 pupils on the roll, the comprehensive school 407.[64]

A school held at the union workhouse had 30–40 pupils in 1858 and accommodation for 30 in 1871.[65] At Pewsey hospital a training centre for young people was transferred to the local education authority in 1971 when, as Pewsey Hospital (Special) school, it had 70 pupils, half living at the hospital and half elsewhere in Wiltshire. It was renamed Wyvern school in 1971 and closed in 1983.[66]

From 1911 or earlier to 1935 or later a private

30 Meeting Ho. Certs. (W.R.S. xl), p. 130; R. W. Oliver, Strict Bapt. Chapels Eng. (Strict Bapt. Hist. Soc.), v. 21–2; V.C.H. Wilts. iii. 139; W.R.O., tithe award.
31 P.R.O., HO 129/261/2/1/3.
32 Pewsey through the Ages, iii. 22; O.S. Map 1/2,500, Wilts. XLI. 4 (1900 edn.).
33 Oliver, Strict. Bapt. Chapels, 22.
34 O.S. Map 6", Wilts. XLI (1889 edn.); cf. W.R.O., tithe award.
35 Pewsey through the Ages, iii. 22.
36 Meeting Ho. Certs. (W.R.S. xl), p. 137; W.R.O. 2193/22.   37 P.R.O., HO 129/261/2/1/4.
38 W.R.O. 2193/22.
39 O.S. Map 6", Wilts. XLI (1889 edn.).
40 Kelly's Dir. Wilts. (1895); W.R.O., Inland Revenue, val. reg. 57 and map 41.
41 Kelly's Dir. Wilts. (1915, 1920).
42 W.R.O., D 1/54/4/1; ibid. 493/49.
43 Ibid. 493/46.   44 Educ. of Poor Digest, 1034.
45 Educ. Enq. Abstract, 1045.
46 P.R.O., ED 7/131, no. 220; W.R.O., F 8/600/220/2/2/1, deed, 1840.
47 Nat. Soc. Inquiry, Wilts. (1846–7), 8–9.
48 P.R.O., ED 7/131, no. 220.
49 Acct. of Wilts. Schs. 37.
50 W.R.O., D 1/56/7; ibid. F 8/600/220/2/3/1.
51 Ibid. F 8/600/220/2/6/1.
52 Bouverie, Pewsey, 44.   53 W.R.O., D 1/56/7.
54 Date on rainwater head.
55 Bouverie, Pewsey, 44.
56 P.R.O., ED 2/466, no. 10953; W.R.O., F 8/600/220/2/1, leases, 1888, 1908.
57 W.R.O., F 8/500/220/2/2.
58 Kelly's Dir. Wilts. (1855 and later edns.).
59 Bd. of Educ., List 21, 1938 (H.M.S.O.), 424; W.R.O., F 8/220/1.   60 W.R.O., G 10/505/1; G 10/518/6.
61 Ibid. F 8/500/220/2/4; F 8/700/17/1/2/1–2.
62 Wilts. Cuttings, xxix. 149; inf. from Mr. I. M. Slocombe, 11 Belcombe Place, Bradford on Avon.
63 W.R.O., F 8/600/220/1/24/1.
64 Wilts. co. council, Sched. of Educ. Establishments (1996), pp. 7, 21.
65 Acct. of Wilts. Schs. 37; P.R.O., ED 2/466, no. 10953.
66 W.R.O., F 8/500/220/3/1.

school was held in River Street; in 1939 it was held in North Street.[67] St. Francis's school, which was begun as a nursery school in 1941, was held in High Street from 1954 to 1984, in Haybrook House from 1984; Travancore House became one of the school's buildings in 1991 and was used by the older children.[68] In 1997 the school was for children aged from 2½ to 13 and was attended by c. 200.[69]

CHARITIES FOR THE POOR.

Instead of the £1 devised by Richard Foach (d. 1616) as a stock for the poor,[70] his executors apparently gave £3. A further 40s. was given in 1624 under the will of Avis Ring, and £3 in 1630 under the will of Richard Paple. Money lent at interest by the churchwardens in the early 18th century was presumably that of those three charities.[71] In 1786 Foach's and Paple's charities were said to have been lost, Ring's to have an income of £1 12s.;[72] Ring's had been lost by 1833.[73] Sir Thomas Fowle (d. 1692) gave £50 for apprenticing, and between 1699 and 1726 the charity paid for 13 children to be apprenticed. By 1786 Fowle's charity had been lost.[74] By will proved 1748 Philippa Stanley gave £100 to the second poor,[75] and in 1786 the income of the charity was £4.[76] That charity had also been lost by 1833.[77]

By will proved 1865 John Edmonds gave £150 to the poor for coal or meat. In 1901 the charity's income was £4, and 73 beneficiaries each received 2 lb. of meat. By will proved 1882 Richard Chandler gave £200 to the poor for coal. In 1901 the charity's income was £5 9s., and 44 beneficiaries each received 2 cwt. of coal. The two charities were managed together, and meat and coal were given until 1950. Thereafter the combined income, £8 12s., was given away as cash; in 1951 there were 30 recipients.[78] By will proved 1913 John Spackman gave £200 to the poor for provisions and coal. In 1921 the charity's income was £8, and 50 received gifts. By a Scheme of 1979 Edmonds's, Chandler's, and Spackman's charities were administered together as Pewsey Relief in Need charity. In 1994 the charity's income was £73, its expenditure £40.[79]

In 1891 Henry Trafford-Rawson and his wife gave £1,500 stock to pay for a nurse for the sick poor in Pewsey parish. Additional stock was bought with unreturned subscriptions for a cottage hospital which was not built; in 1901 the income of the charity was £65, and a nurse was employed.[80] From the 1920s only part of the nurse's salary was paid for by the charity,[81] and in the late 20th century the charity gave general help to the old or infirm. In 1995 its income was £162, and two gifts of £100 were made.[82]

Widows at Pewsey were presumably eligible for admittance to Froxfield almshouse, which was built and endowed under the will of Sarah, duchess of Somerset (d. 1692).[83]

SAVERNAKE

SAVERNAKE parish[84] lies immediately south of Marlborough. Its land is roughly conterminous with the main part of Savernake forest as defined in 1300[85] and was extra-parochial. In the later 18th century the west part, which was parkland and agricultural land from the 16th century, lay in two tithings, each of which relieved its own poor. To the north Savernake Park North was a tithing of Selkley hundred, and to the south Brimslade and South Savernake was a tithing of Kinwardstone hundred: under the Relief of the Poor in Extra-parochial Places Act of 1857 each was deemed a civil parish, respectively with the names North Savernake, and South Savernake with Brimslade and Cadley.[86] The east part of the forest as defined in 1300 remained uninclosed and mostly woodland,[87] and by the late 19th century some of it, and land which was probably some of it, had become parts of parishes adjoining it. On the south-east, land used in common by the men of Great Bedwyn and of Stock in Great Bedwyn and apparently part of the forest became part of Great Bedwyn parish, as did Tottenham park which was presumably part of the forest in the 16th century.[88] In the 18th century the boundary between the forest and Burbage parish, which seems to have run east–west immediately north of Durley village, was called into question: by 1886 c. 1,000 a. north-east of that line had been transferred from the forest to the parish.[89] In the 19th century land of the forest on the north-east may have been added to Little Bedwyn, and on the north was apparently added to Mildenhall.[90] The rest

[67] Kelly's Dir. Wilts. (1911 and later edns.).
[68] St. Francis's Sch. (prospectus in Wilts. local studies libr.).
[69] Guide to Independent Schs., S. and W., 1996–7 (Independent Schs. Inf. Service), p. 25.
[70] W.R.O., wills, cons. Sar., Ric. Foache, 1616; ibid. 509/1.   [71] Ibid. 493/49.
[72] Char. Don. H.C. 511 (1816), xvi (2), 1352–3, where the endowment of Ring's is wrongly given as £40.
[73] Endowed Char. Wilts. (S. Div.), 360.
[74] Char. Don. 1352–3; V.C.H. Wilts. x. 149; W.R.O. 493/49.   [75] P.R.O., PROB 11/765, f. 199.
[76] Char. Don. 1352–3.
[77] Endowed Char. Wilts. (S. Div.), 360.
[78] Ibid. 361–2; W.R.O., L 2, Pewsey, Edmonds's and Chandler's.
[79] Char. Com. files; W.R.O., L 2, Pewsey, Spackman's.
[80] Endowed Char. Wilts. (S. Div.), 362; Wilts. Cuttings, i. 113.   [81] W.R.O., L 2, Pewsey, Trafford-Rawson.
[82] Char. Com. file.
[83] Endowed Char. Wilts. (S. Div.), 980; for inf. about the almshouse, above, Froxfield, charities.
[84] This article was written in 1995. Maps used include O.S. Maps 1", sheet 14 (1817 edn.); 1/25,000, SU 06/16 (1987 edn.); SU 26/36 (1983 edn.); 6", Wilts. XXVIII–XXIX, XXXV–XXXVI (1888–9 and later edns.).
[85] V.C.H. Wilts. iv. 450–1.
[86] Ibid. 357, where the word Park is intruded in the name of each parish; Census, 1861; 20 Vic. c. 19; O.S. Maps 6", Wilts. XXIX, XXXVI (1888–9 edns.); W.R.O., A 1/345/353–4; below, econ. hist.; local govt.
[87] W.R.O. 1300/1840A; Savernake estate map, c. 1820 (copy in W.R.O.).
[88] Above, Great Bedwyn, intro.; manors (Tottenham; Bedwyn common); econ. hist. (Great Bedwyn; Stock; Tottenham park).   [89] Above, Burbage, intro.
[90] Ibid. Little Bedwyn, intro.; W.R.O., Mildenhall tithe award.

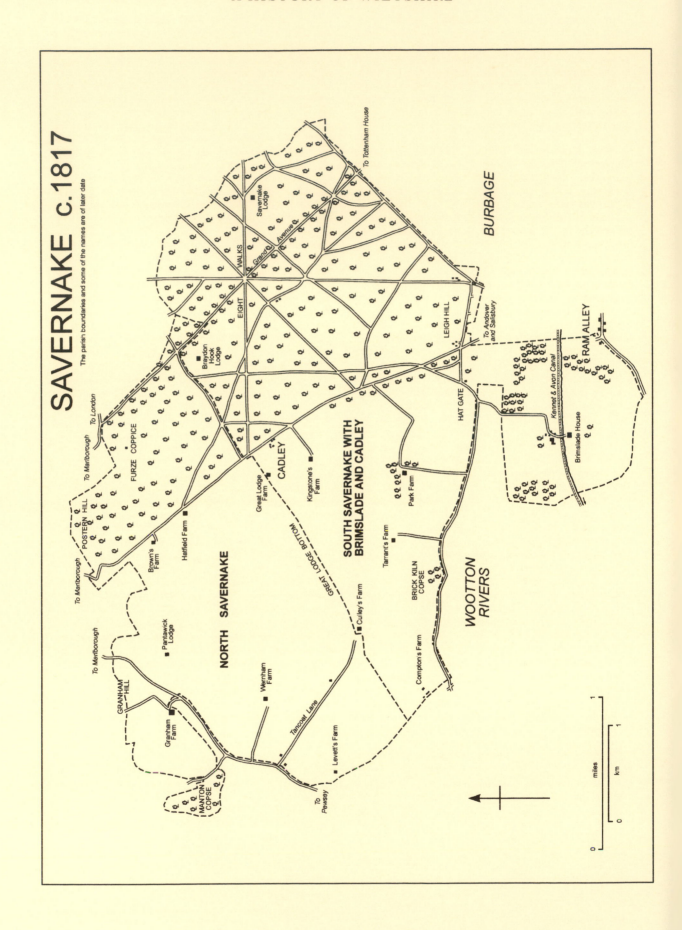

SAVERNAKE c.1817

The parish boundaries and some of the names are of later date

of the forest was divided between North Savernake, 2,315 a., and South Savernake with Brimslade and Cadley, 3,531 a. North Savernake parish was increased in 1901, when 78 a. of Preshute parish was transferred to it, and reduced in 1925, when 32 a. of that land was transferred to Marlborough.[91] In 1934 North Savernake parish and South Savernake with Brimslade and Cadley parish were merged as Savernake parish, 2,384 ha. (5,892 a.).[92] In 1987 land was transferred to Savernake parish from Fyfield, Milton Lilbourne, Pewsey, Preshute, Wilcot, and Wootton Rivers parishes, and from Savernake to Burbage, Preshute, and Wootton Rivers: as a result Savernake was reduced to 2,318 ha.[93]

Few of the features which defined the boundary of the forest in 1300 are unequivocally points on the parish boundary; on the north-west a road which marked the forest boundary[94] was presumably on the course of that which marks the parish boundary. A park pale was erected on, or adopted as, part of the parish boundary on the south, and on the north and south-east forest drives were adopted as parts of the boundary with respectively Mildenhall and Burbage fixed in the 19th century.[95]

Except for its southern projection the parish lies on the Marlborough Downs and in the valley of the river Kennet. Chalk outcrops over the main part of the parish, except where Reading Beds and Bagshot Beds outcrop in small areas near the south-east boundary. The outcrops are extensively overlain by clay-with-flints, and gravel has been deposited in several valleys. All the valleys are now dry. The highest point in the main part of the parish is at 220 m. on the boundary in the south-west, and the lowest points are at c. 145 m. on the boundary in the north and east. The southern scarp of the Marlborough Downs crosses the neck joining the projection to the main part of the parish. The projection lies in the valley of the Christchurch Avon and is crossed from east to west by a head stream now intermittent. The chalk of the scarp face, of which the highest point is at c. 190 m., outcrops in the north part of the projection, Upper Greensand in the lower part to the south; the stream leaves the parish at 135 m.[96] The clay-with-flints can support dense woodland, which had been cleared from the west half of the parish by the 18th century.[97]

The population of Savernake Park North tithing was 67 in 1801. It rose from 79 to 127 between 1811 and 1821 and remained roughly constant until 1861, when it was 108. North Savernake parish had 89 inhabitants in 1871, 85 in 1901. The transfer to it of part of Preshute parish, including a hospital, caused the population to increase; it was 146 in 1911, 145 in 1921,

and, after an increase in the number of patients at the hospital, 230 in 1931. The population of Brimslade and South Savernake tithing was 133 in 1801; if, as is likely, the Cadley which had 36 inhabitants in 1811 and 45 in 1821 was the Cadley in the tithing, the population was 136 and 155 in those years respectively. From 186 in 1831 it had risen to 230 by 1861. From 256 in 1871 the population of South Savernake with Brimslade and Cadley parish declined steadily to 147 in 1921. The population of Savernake parish declined from 355 to 197 between 1951 and 1981; in 1991, after the boundary changes of 1987, it was 194.[98]

The courses of two Roman roads, from Mildenhall to Old Salisbury, and between Cirencester and Winchester via Mildenhall, cross the parish.[99] In the Middle Ages a Marlborough–Salisbury road via Easton was probably on or near the course of the first, and an important Marlborough–Winchester road via Ludgershall and Andover (Hants) is likely to have been on a course south-west of and roughly parallel to the other. A Salisbury road via Easton would have been blocked by the imparking of the west part of Savernake forest in the 16th century, and in the later 17th century the Salisbury road, which north of Marlborough led from Chipping Campden (Glos.), shared the course of the Andover road between the parkland, then agricultural land, in the west part of the parish and the woodland in the east part.[1] The road was turnpiked in 1762 and disturnpiked in 1876;[2] it was still a main road in 1996. The north-west end of the parish is crossed by the Marlborough–Pewsey road, which, where it marks part of the parish boundary, is presumably on the course it followed in 1300.[3] Several public roads cross the woodland in the east part of the parish; apart from the Marlborough–Pewsey road, the west part, having been imparked, is crossed by none.

The Kennet & Avon canal was built c. 1807 beside the stream across the south projection of the parish. It was opened fully in 1810 and restored across the parish in the 1970s.[4] It has two locks in the parish.

The Berks. & Hants Extension Railway, built parallel to and immediately south of the canal, was opened across the parish in 1862. Since 1906 it has been part of a main London–Exeter line. Converging on it at Burbage a line from Marlborough was constructed as a loop through the west part of the parish and opened in 1864; a second Marlborough–Burbage line, the southern extension of a line from Swindon, was opened across the parish east of the first in 1898. The second line had a tunnel at the north end of Savernake parish. The line built in 1864 was closed in 1933; that built in 1898 was closed in 1964.[5]

91 V.C.H. Wilts. xii. 161, 199.   92 Ibid. iv. 357.
93 Census, 1991; Statutory Instruments, 1987, no. 619, Kennet (Parishes) Order.
94 V.C.H. Wilts. iv. 450–1.
95 For the Mildenhall boundary, cf. O.S. Map 6", Wilts. XXIX (1889 edn.); W.R.O., Mildenhall tithe award.
96 Geol. Surv. Maps 1/50,000, drift, sheet 266 (1974 edn.); 1", drift, sheet 267 (1971 edn.).   97 Below, econ. hist.
98 V.C.H. Wilts. iv. 326, 342, 357; Census, 1961; 1971; 1981; 1991; above, this section.
99 I. D. Margary, Rom. Roads in Brit. (1973), pp. 98–9.

1 J. Ogilby, Brit. (1675), pl. 85; above, Burbage, intro. [roads]; Easton, intro. [roads]; below, econ. hist.
2 V.C.H. Wilts. iv. 257, 262, 270; L.J. xxx. 205.
3 V.C.H. Wilts. iv. 450–1.
4 K. R. Clew, Kennet & Avon Canal (1985), 69, 73; R. W. Squires, Canals Revived, 112.
5 V.C.H. Wilts. iv. 281, 286–7, 289–90, 292–3; Clinker's Reg. Closed Passenger Sta. 1830–1977 (1978 edn.), 120, 172; K. Robertson and D. Abbott, Marlborough Branch: Railways of Savernake and Marlborough, 78–9; for more about the lines, above, Burbage, intro. [railways].

Prehistoric remains have been discovered in all parts of the parish. An artefact possibly of the Mesolithic period is the oldest; later artefacts include a gold torc of the later Bronze Age.[6] Barrows in the parish include a group of eight in the southern projection,[7] there are four ditches[8] and a later Iron-Age enclosure of 3½ a. in the north, and a small part of a similar enclosure was identified in the south-west.[9] A field system of 40 a., also of the later Iron Age, lies on Postern Hill on the boundary with Marlborough.[10] The parish lies near an area notable for Roman settlement, and there may have been a settlement of the Roman period at Pantawick in the north-west. A hoard of 4th-century coins was found on Granham Hill north-west of Pantawick,[11] and pottery was produced commercially from the late 1st century at kilns north of Leigh Hill in the south-east.[12] The east end of the East Wansdyke, a linear earthwork constructed probably between the 5th and 9th centuries, lies in the west part of the parish.[13]

Courts held to punish offences committed in Savernake forest were held at places which were afterwards in Savernake parish. A three-weekly court was held at Morley, possibly Leigh Hill, in the 13th century or earlier, and in the 16th century courts were held at Great Lodge and Bagden Lodge. Forest courts, known to have been held in the 17th century but not later, were attended by men from the villages with land bordering the woodland and mainly dealt with the unlawful killing of game, cutting of trees, and feeding of animals.[14]

Savernake parish contains no village. In the centre of it at Cadley, a hamlet so called in 1773,[15] a church, a vicarage house, and a school were built beside the Marlborough road in the mid 19th century.[16] A timber-framed and thatched cottage of the 17th century, a few estate houses of the 19th century built of red brick with patterning of blue and buff brick,[17] and a few later 20th-century houses also stood at Cadley in 1995.

In the west part of the parish, which apart from the land north-west of the Marlborough–Pewsey road was the land imparked in the 16th century, settlement was in isolated farmsteads built in the 17th century, when the land was converted to agriculture, or later.[18] None of the four lodges which stood in the park in the 16th century[19] survived in 1995.

Two farmsteads were built beside the Marlborough road. Brown's, so called in 1718,[20] incorporated a thatched and timber-framed house, presumably 17th-century, which was demolished in 1961–2 and replaced by a new house.[21] Hatfield, later High Trees, Farm, built

of sarsen in the 17th century, had a main north-west and south-east range with a cross wing at the north-west end. In the earlier 19th century a red-brick block was built on the south-west side of the main range, and in the later 19th century a red-brick tower and a service range were built on the north-west side of the cross wing.

Two farmsteads were built in the dry valley called Great Lodge bottom. Great Lodge Farm may stand on or near the site of the great lodge which stood in the park in the 16th century.[22] It was built in the later 17th century with a main north-west and south-east range, having one room on either side of a central chimney stack, and with a single-storeyed range on the south-east and brick gables. The lower courses of the north-east front were of sarsen and the higher ones of brick. The south-west wall may have been timber-framed; it was rebuilt in brick in the 18th century when the single-storeyed range was raised to two storeys and extended south-westwards to give the house an L plan. An 18th-century timber-framed barn and a granary on staddle stones stand north-east of the house. Culley's Farm was on an L plan when it was built c. 1700. Its south-east wall is partly of sarsen; otherwise its walls are of red brick. In 1995 the house contained an early 18th-century staircase and a room fitted with panelling partly of c. 1700 and partly of the early 17th century.

Three farmsteads were built south-east of Great Lodge bottom. Kingstone's incorporates a timber-framed house built in the later 17th century as a short north-west and south-east range. The house was extended north-eastwards in brick later in the 17th century and south-eastwards in sarsen in the early 18th century, thus acquiring an L plan. Park Farm possibly stands on the site of Witheridge Lodge, which was mentioned c. 1620.[23] A wall built of sarsen rubble in the 17th century is incorporated in the farmhouse, otherwise built of brick c. 1800, on an L plan, and still standing in 1995. Tarrant's Farm, standing in 1718,[24] was demolished in the later 20th century.[25]

North-west of Great Lodge bottom Wernham Farm was standing in 1718.[26] Part of an 18th-century garden wall survives south of the present farmhouse, which was built in the early 19th century. On the western edge of the former park Levett's Farm incorporates a farmhouse built in the earlier 18th century as a north-west and south-east range with walls of sarsen rubble and brick with ashlar dressings, and with a single room on each side of a central chimney stack. A lean-to was built on the north-east side of the house in the 18th century, and a two-storeyed

6   *V.C.H. Wilts*. i (1), 104; i (2), 392.
7   Ibid. i (1), 189.
8   Ibid. 258.
9   Ibid. 269.
10 Ibid. 277.
11 Ibid. 105.
12 Ibid. i (2), 450–1; *W.A.M*. lvii. 11, 235–6; lviii. 143.
13 *V.C.H. Wilts*. i (2), 477.
14 Ibid. iv. 422; W.R.O. 9/1/133; 192/25; 192/47; 1300/86–7; for the lodges, below, this section.
15 *Andrews and Dury, Map* (W.R.S. viii), pl. 12.
16 Below, church; educ.

17 Above, plate 30.
18 Cf. below, econ. hist.
19 W.R.O. 192/53.
20 Ibid. 1300/372, f. 27.
21 Date on bldg.; inf. from Mr. S. A. Hurd, Brown's Farm.
22 *W.A.M*. li. 308; W.R.O. 9/22/51; 192/53; 1300/87.
23 W.R.O. 9/22/17.
24 Ibid. 1300/372, ff. 25–6.
25 Inf. from the agent for the Crown Estate Com., 42 High Street, Marlborough.
26 W.R.O. 1300/372, f. 24.

block on the south-west side *c.* 1938.[27] South-east of Levett's Farm the west lodge of the former park was part of Compton's Farm, which was standing in the 17th century and early 18th.[28] In 1995 a red-brick cottage of the later 19th century stood on the site, from which the farm buildings were removed in the 20th century.[29] Near the northern edge of the former park Pantawick Lodge, standing in 1618, was demolished between 1840 and 1885.[30]

Levett's Farm and Compton's Farm stood on downland near several farmsteads and cottages in other parishes, each far from its parish church, and in the mid 19th century a room used as a school and a chapel of ease was built near Compton's Farm.[31] Near Levett's Farm, Overton Heath airfield was open from 1941 to 1948. Flying instructors were trained there and hangars and other buildings were erected. One of the hangars survived in 1995.[32]

North-west of the Marlborough–Pewsey road lies downland which was probably disafforested in 1330[33] and was not imparked in the 16th century. Granham Farm was standing there in 1718.[34] The farmhouse was rebuilt in 1788[35] of red and blue brick, is of two storeys and attics, and to the south-east has a main front of five bays.

In the east part of the parish, the land which remains mostly woodland, the sites of three lodges are known. A lodge on the site of Braydon Hook Lodge was standing *c.* 1600.[36] Braydon Hook Lodge, so called in the earlier 18th century,[37] was replaced in the later 19th century by a pair of cottages. Bagden Lodge, also standing *c.* 1600,[38] was replaced by a house built in 1717–18. The new house,[39] of two storeys and attics, consisted of a main north-west and south-east range with an east service wing, on a **L** plan, with its west corner attached to the east corner of the main range. The principal front, of seven bays with a pediment above the three central bays, was to the south-west. Some of the rooms were wainscotted.[40] In the later 18th century and early 19th a rectangular block was built on the north-east side of the main range, and a second rectangular block was built so that its west corner met the east corner of the first, and its south corner met the north corner of the service wing.[41] The house, which stood in a clearing called Savernake Lawn, was thereafter called Savernake Lodge.[42] In the later 19th century a single-storeyed extension incorporating a billiards room was built on the south-east side of the main range, but by 1886 the house, except

that extension, had been demolished. In the earlier 18th century a north-east and south-west range, partly single-storeyed and partly two-storeyed and incorporating stables and coach houses, was built south-east of the house, and by 1886 that had been linked to the surviving part of the house to form a new house on an **L** plan which was standing in 1995. A small park had been laid out south-west of the house by 1806.[43] The third lodge stood in Furze coppice in the earlier 18th century.[44] In the earlier 19th it was replaced by a pair of cottages of brick and slate; later in the 19th century the building was enlarged and converted to a house, around which specimen trees were planted in a large garden. The house was extended *c.* 1980. A cottage stood beside a forest gate at the south end of the woodland in 1773.[45] A 20th-century house stood on its site in 1995.

Between the 1720s and the 1740s the park of Tottenham House in Great Bedwyn was redesigned, and two straight rides were made from the house through the woodland in the east part of what became Savernake parish, Column ride, which was made across the south part to the Andover road, and the Grand Avenue, which roughly follows the course of the Roman road on a more direct route to Marlborough. Where the Grand Avenue joined the London road stone gate piers were erected in the early 19th century. Between 1764 and 1786 the woodland was brought into the overall design of the landscape around Tottenham House, and drives, paths, and clearings were made in it. Many of the features designed then, including the rond-point called Eight Walks, survived in 1995.[46]

BRIMSLADE. The southern projection of the parish was part of Savernake forest in the Middle Ages,[47] later parkland,[48] and from the 17th century agricultural land.[49]

Brimslade House was built in the park in the earlier 17th century and was standing in 1995. It was on an **L** plan and timber-framed and had principal south and west fronts each with two gables. The east range, which was the longer and had a central porch, was extended eastwards in the mid 17th century. In the early 18th century a new staircase was built in the centre of the west range, and the two principal rooms in the east range were refitted. Panelling from those rooms may have been that of the earlier 17th century reset on the first floor and incorporating an overmantel bearing the painted arms of Seymour impaling Stanhope.[50] The timber-framed walls

27 Ibid. G 8/760/320.
28 Ibid. 9/22/76; 9/22/112.
29 Cf. O.S. Map 6", Wilts. XXXVI. NW. (1925 edn.).
30 Ibid. 6", Wilts. XXIX (1889 edn.); W.R.O. 1300/372, f. 27; ibid. tithe award; Alnwick Castle Mun. X.II.11, box 26, deed, Hertford to Seymour, 1618.
31 O.S. Maps 6", Wilts. XXXV–XXXVI (1888–9 edns.); below, church.
32 C. Ashworth, *Action Stations*, ix. 235–7; inf. from the agent for the Crown Estate Com.
33 *V.C.H. Wilts.* iv. 399–400, 450–1.
34 W.R.O. 1300/372, f. 19.
35 Date on bldg.
36 *W.A.M.* li. 308.
37 Ibid. lii. 175.   38 Ibid. li. 308.
39 Above, plate 24.

40 W.R.O. 9/22/92.
41 J. Buckler, watercolour in W.A.S. Libr., vol. x. 16; archit. model in Savernake Lodge in 1996.
42 *W.A.M.* liii. 21.
43 O.S. Map 6", Wilts. XXXVI (1888 edn.); XXXVI. SE. (1900 edn.); Buckler, watercolour in W.A.S. Libr., vol. x. 16.
44 *W.A.M.* lii. 175.
45 *Andrews and Dury, Map* (W.R.S. viii), pl. 12.
46 W.R.O. 1300/360; above, Great Bedwyn, manors (Tottenham).
47 *V.C.H. Wilts.* iv. 450–1.
48 *Wilts. Inq. p.m.* 1625–49 (Index Libr.), 20–31.
49 Below, econ. hist.
50 *Complete Peerage*, xii (1), 64; B. Burke, *Gen. Armoury* (1884), 914, 961.

of the house have been partly covered by hung tiles and partly rebuilt in brick. From 1699 to 1787 the house was occupied successively by Michael Ernle, his son Edward (d. 1734), Sir Michael Ernle, Bt. (d. 1771), and Sir Edward Ernle, Bt. (d. 1787).[51]

By 1773 the head stream of the Avon, on the south bank of which Brimslade House stands, had been dammed to make ornamental canals, and a small park had been made around the house.[52] The canals were destroyed when the Kennet & Avon canal was built along the course of the stream c. 1807.[53] A formal garden survived on the north side of the canal in 1811,[54] but in the 19th century the house was a farmhouse and the park was not preserved.[55]

Brimslade House was linked to the north side of the Kennet & Avon canal by a bridge of stone and brick, and large farm buildings of red brick were erected on the north side in the early 19th century. In 1995 a 17th-century cottage, thatched and originally timber-framed, and a pair of mid 19th-century cottages, stood near the farm buildings; a lock keeper's cottage stood east of them.

East of Brimslade House a cottage in the parish is part of Ram Alley hamlet mainly in Burbage.[56] It is timber-framed and thatched and was built on the waste probably in the 17th century.

ESTATES. *SAVERNAKE* forest, the main part of which was roughly conterminous with what became Savernake parish, belonged to the Crown almost throughout the Middle Ages and was usually held with Marlborough castle and its site.[57] From 1415 or earlier to 1447 it was held in fee by Henry IV's son Humphrey, duke of Gloucester.[58] Under a grant of 1547 it reverted on the death of Catherine Parr in 1548 to Edward Seymour, duke of Somerset, the hereditary warden of the forest.[59] Somerset was deprived of the forest in 1549; it was restored to him in 1550 and forfeited on his execution and attainder in 1552. In 1553 it was assigned by Act to his son Sir Edward Seymour (cr. earl of Hertford 1559, d. 1621).[60] Of what became Savernake parish both the east part, which remained woodland, and the west part, which was parkland and agricultural land from the 16th century,[61] descended from 1553 in the Seymour, Bruce, Brudenell, and Brudenell-Bruce families with Tottenham

Lodge and Tottenham House in Great Bedwyn.[62] In 1939 George Brudenell-Bruce, marquess of Ailesbury (d. 1961), leased the woodland, c. 2,300 a., to the Forestry Commission for 999 years,[63] and in 1950 sold c. 3,200 a., nearly all the farmland, to the Crown, the owner in 1995.[64] The reversion of the woodland descended with Tottenham House and in 1995 belonged to David Brudenell-Bruce, earl of Cardigan.[65]

In 1618 Edward, earl of Hertford, sold 100 a. in the north-west part of the parish, part of what was later called *BROWN'S* farm, to his grandson Sir Francis Seymour (cr. Baron Seymour 1641, d. 1664).[66] The land presumably descended to Seymour's son Charles, Lord Seymour (d. 1665), and in turn to Charles's sons Francis, duke of Somerset (d. 1678), and Charles, duke of Somerset (d. 1748), who owned Brown's farm, 195 a., in 1718. From that Charles the farm descended to his son Algernon, duke of Somerset (d. 1750), and to his grandson Charles Manners, duke of Rutland, who in 1779 sold it to Thomas Bruce, earl of Ailesbury, the owner of the other land in the parish.[67]

The tithes of Savernake forest were taken by Salisbury cathedral from the 12th century, apparently by grant of the Crown as owner of the land.[68] In the earlier 17th century attempts to deprive the cathedral of tithes from land converted to agriculture were unsuccessful,[69] and in the early 19th century the dean and canons were taking all the tithes from what became Savernake parish. The tithes were valued at £690 in 1840 and commuted.[70]

ECONOMIC HISTORY. As the main part of Savernake forest, what became Savernake parish was probably mostly woodland in 1300[71] and until the later 16th century.[72] New plantations were made in the forest in the mid 16th century.[73]

In the later 16th century the west part of what became Savernake parish, excluding the land north-west of the Marlborough–Pewsey road, was impaled as Savernake great park. Much of the park was cleared of woodland, and red and fallow deer were kept in it.[74] In the 17th century the park was converted to agriculture. In the north part 100 a., later part of Brown's farm, was possibly used for agriculture from 1618,[75] and in 1633 c. 1,000 a. was pasture for sheep.[76]

[51] G.E.C. *Baronetage*, iii. 157; *Andrews and Dury, Map* (W.R.S. viii), pl. 12; W.R.O. 9/22/66; 9/22/78; 9/22/157.
[52] *Andrews and Dury, Map* (W.R.S. viii), pl. 12.
[53] Above, this section. [54] W.R.O. 9/22/232H.
[55] O.S. Map 6", Wilts. XXXVI (1888 edn.).
[56] For Ram Alley, above, Burbage, intro. (Ram Alley).
[57] e.g. *Pipe R.* 1194 (P.R.S. N.S. x), 10; *Cal. Pat.* 1266–72, 736–7; 1317–21, 115–16; 1334–8, 356; *V.C.H. Wilts.* iv. 450–1; for Marlborough castle, ibid. xii. 165–9.
[58] *Cal. Pat.* 1401–5, 320–1; 1413–16, 338; Rymer, *Foedera* (1737–45 edn.), v. 171.
[59] *Cal. Pat.* 1547–8, 124–33; *D.N.B.* (s.v. Catherine Parr); for the hereditary wardens, *V.C.H. Wilts.* iv. 420–1.
[60] *Cal. Pat.* 1549–51, 430–2; *Complete Peerage*, vi. 505–6; xii (1), 63–4; P.R.O., E 328/117.
[61] Below, econ. hist.
[62] Above, Great Bedwyn, manors (Tottenham).
[63] Burke, *Peerage* (1963), 35; W.R.O. 9/33/5.
[64] Inf. from the agent for the Crown Estate Com., 42

High Street, Marlborough.
[65] Above, Great Bedwyn, manors (Tottenham); inf. from the earl of Cardigan, Savernake Lodge.
[66] *Complete Peerage*, xi. 640–1; Alnwick Castle Mun. X.II.11, box 26, deed, Hertford to Seymour, 1618.
[67] *Complete Peerage*, xii (1), 76–81; *V.C.H. Wilts.* xii. 169, where more details of the descent 1750–79 are given; W.R.O. 1300/372, f. 27; Somerset Estate Act, 19 Geo. III, c. 46 (Priv. Act).
[68] *Close R.* 1231–4, 21. [69] *W.A.M.* xli. 127.
[70] W.R.O., tithe award.
[71] *V.C.H. Wilts.* iv. 419, 451.
[72] Below, this section.
[73] *W.A.M.* lii. 174.
[74] P.R.O., STAC 8/255/1; STAC 8/271/4; W.R.O. 192/53.
[75] Alnwick Castle Mun. X.II.11, box 26, deed, Hertford to Seymour, 1618.
[76] W.R.O. 9/22/22.

The farm later called Great Lodge, 127 a., was leased in 1633;[77] that later called Park, 385 a., and that later called Hatfield, 240 a., were leased in 1634.[78] Three farms, those later called Wernham, 210 a., Levett's, 200 a., and Culley's, 150 a., were made from the west part of the park in 1649.[79] The farm later called Kingstone's, 214 a. including a former colt park of c. 100 a., was probably leased in the later 17th century, the date of its farmhouse.[80] To the south Tarrant's farm, 140 a., was made from part of a sheep pasture before 1686,[81] and Compton's farm, 205 a., was made from the former West walk of the forest before 1689.[82]

In 1718 Savernake great park was accounted 2,562 a., of which the 10 main farms had 2,426 a. The largest farm was Park, 385 a., the smallest Culley's, 145 a.; Wernham's and Tarrant's had been enlarged to 376 a. and 261 a. respectively. All the farms were almost entirely arable and they had a total of only 33 a. of meadow and pasture. The largest field was of 54 a., and the average size of the fields was c. 20 a.[83]

North-west of Savernake great park and of the Marlborough–Pewsey road Granham farm, 180 a., was entirely arable in 1718. By 1770 it had been increased to 239 a. by the addition of 44 a. south-east of the road and of 15 a. of steep downland in Preshute parish used as pasture for sheep. By 1840, when it had c. 412 a. including 74 a. in Preshute, it had been extended further south-east by the addition of 107 a. in the north-west part of the park.[84]

South-east of Savernake great park in the southern projection of the parish land may have been converted from parkland to agriculture in the earlier 17th century, when Brimslade House was built on it.[85] Brimslade park was accounted 590 a. in 1642, when it included 77 a. of meadows, 31 a. of pasture, 236 a. of arable, and 241 a. of woodland.[86] Much of the woodland had been cleared by 1773, when there was a park of c. 30 a. around Brimslade House.[87] In 1811 Brimslade farm, 493 a., included c. 385 a. of arable, was worked from buildings recently erected on the north side of the Kennet & Avon canal, and was probably worked with 29 a. in Burbage. Its pasture, c. 87 a., lay west and south of the farmstead.[88]

In 1840 of c. 3,400 a. in the west part of what became Savernake parish c. 2,440 a. was arable, 292 a. was meadow or pasture, and 345 a. was rough pasture for sheep. There were 12 farms,

all mainly arable, but Brown's, Hatfield, and Great Lodge, a total of c. 670 a., were worked together, as were Kingstone's and Tarrant's, a total of c. 455 a., Levett's and Compton's, a total of c. 388 a., and Wernham's and Culley's, a total of c. 493 a.[89] In 1867 Levett's farm and Compton's farm were worked from Wootton Rivers as part of East Wick farm, and Brown's was a separate farm of 250 a., Park one of 372 a., and Granham one of 403 a. There were composite farms of 482 a. and 501 a.; Brimslade farm, 475 a., and Kingstone's and Tarrant's, then called Great Park farm, 482 a., were apparently worked together.[90] Between 1840 and 1886 New Buildings, a barn and other buildings, was erected on the composite Great Lodge and Hatfield farm.[91]

In 1867 sheep-and-corn husbandry was widely practised in the west part of what became Savernake parish, but from c. 1880 arable was laid to pasture and dairy farming increased. Pasture was at its most extensive c. 1930,[92] but c. 1933 there was slightly more arable than pasture.[93] Arable predominated c. 1995, when there were seven farms based in the parish. Brimslade, 568 a., Wernham, 378 a., and Levett's, 241 a., were entirely arable farms; Kingstone's, 703 a., was an arable and sheep farm, Brown's, 531 a., an arable and dairy farm, Culley's, 375 a., an arable, dairy, and beef farm, and Park, 384 a., a dairy farm. On Levett's farm free-range hens were kept.[94]

In 1718 only 9 a. of woodland was standing in Savernake great park. Manton copse covered 25 a. then,[95] 35 a. in 1840.[96] By 1885 it had been reduced to 14 a.,[97] roughly its size in the late 20th century.[98] In the south projection of the parish woodland stood north-east and north-west of Brimslade House in 1773.[99] In 1811, after several copses had been planted in geometrical shapes, and Ram Alley copse, 27 a., had been planted, there was 87 a.[1] A triangular copse of 2 a. was removed between 1811 and 1840, and a circular copse of 3 a. and a copse of 7 a. were removed between 1840 and 1886.[2] The others were standing in the late 20th century, by when a few small copses had been planted in the former great park.[3]

The ancient woodland in the east part of Savernake parish, although privately owned from the 16th century,[4] was not impaled. In the 18th century the men of villages on its periphery had the right to feed in it in summer as many cattle as they could keep on their holdings in

77   Ibid. 9/22/51.
78   Ibid. 9/22/24–5; 1300/372, ff. 25–6.
79   Ibid. 9/22/28–30.
80   Ibid. 9/22/33; P.R.O., C 5/153/22; above, intro.
81   W.R.O. 9/22/53; 1300/372, ff. 25–6.
82   Ibid. 9/22/76; 1300/372, f. 27.
83   Ibid. 1300/372, ff. 24–7.
84   Ibid. ff. 19, 24, 27; ibid. tithe award; Preshute tithe award.   85   Above, intro. (Brimslade).
86   W.R.O. 9/1/132, p. 99.
87   *Andrews and Dury, Map* (W.R.S. viii), pl. 12.
88   W.R.O. 9/22/232H; above, intro. (Brimslade).
89   W.R.O., tithe award.
90   Ibid. 9/1/110, ff. 96–111.
91   Ibid. tithe award; O.S. Map 6", Wilts. XXXVI (1888 edn.).
92   P.R.O., MAF 68/151, sheets 23, 26; MAF 68/493, sheets 13–14; MAF 68/1063, sheet 2; MAF 68/3319, sheets

11–12; MAF 68/3814, nos. 163, 170.
93   [1st] Land Util. Surv. Map, sheet 112.
94   Inf. from the agent for the Crown Estate Com.; Mr. H. M. Renwick, Kingstone's Farm; Mr. S. A. Hurd, Brown's Farm; Mrs. S. J. V. Faux, Culley's Farm; Mrs. G. J. Vigar-Smith, Wernham Farm; Mr. M. H. H. Pitt, Levett's Farm.
95   W.R.O. 1300/372, ff. 19, 24–7.
96   Ibid. tithe award.
97   O.S. Map 6", Wilts. XXXVI (1888 edn.).
98   Ibid. 1/25,000, SU 06/16 (1987 edn.).
99   *Andrews and Dury, Map* (W.R.S. viii), pl. 12.
1   W.R.O. 9/22/232H.
2   Ibid.; ibid. tithe award; O.S. Map 6", Wilts. XXXVI (1888 edn.).
3   O.S. Maps 1/25,000, SU 06/16 (1987 edn.); SU 26/36 (1983 edn.).
4   Above, estates (Savernake).

winter, and to each village the pasture of a separate part of the forest had been designated for its sheep to feed on. No farm in Savernake great park included any such pasture right.[5] The rights were probably largely extinguished in the later 18th century or early 19th when most of the holdings in those villages belonged to the owner of the forest.[6] In the 19th century some of the clearings which had been incorporated in the design of the landscape around Tottenham House in the 18th century were apparently used for agriculture.[7] In 1995 there was c. 200 a. of arable and pasture near Eight Walks.[8]

In the later 18th century coppices were amalgamated and areas of open heath were planted with oak and Spanish chestnut. In the later 19th century trees were damaged by herds of deer formerly confined to the park of Tottenham House. There was some replanting for commercial purposes between 1894 and 1911.[9] From 1939 the woodland was managed by the Forestry Commission.[10] Two nurseries were set up east of Cadley in the 1940s and abandoned in the 1960s.[11] In 1980–1 oak and beech trees were felled in the Grand Avenue, which was partly replanted in 1983, and in 1984 c. 1,000 beech, oak, and cherry trees were planted in the woodland.[12] Among many deciduous trees destroyed by storms in 1990 there were 700 beeches and 50 oaks. In 1995, when there was c. 2,300 a. of woodland in Savernake parish, coniferous trees were grown for timber on 20 per cent of Savernake forest, including the parts in other parishes. A site for camping was provided on Postern Hill in the 1960s; it remained in use in 1995, when the woodland was used for various leisure pursuits and contained a herd of fallow and roe deer.[13]

The clay deposits in the parish have been used for making bricks, and the sites of six brick kilns are known. A kiln east of Leigh Hill was in use in 1732[14] and closed between 1910 and 1922;[15] Wernham kiln, in Tancoat Lane south-west of Wernham Farm, was in use in 1840[16] and closed between 1886 and 1922.[17] A kiln west of Granham Farm was possibly in use in 1840; others north of Brown's Farm, where one was apparently in use c. 1820, and at Brick Kiln copse had apparently gone out of use by then.[18] A new kiln north of Brown's Farm was opened between 1885 and 1899 and closed between 1899 and 1922.[19]

At Cadley in 1995 the former school housed Dobie Wyatt Ltd., a company which made tarpaulins and employed 12 people there,[20] and the former vicarage house was a hotel. Horses were trained at Levett's Farm in the 1920s and 1930s.[21]

LOCAL GOVERNMENT. Savernake Park North tithing was relieving its own poor in 1783.[22] In 1802–3, when its population was c. 67, it spent £119 on relieving 9 adults and 25 children regularly and 2 adults occasionally.[23] From 1812–13 to 1814–15 an average of £90 a year was spent and on average 8 adults were relieved regularly and 4 occasionally.[24] In the following two decades expenditure, at £54, was lowest in 1816 and, at £132, highest in 1830.[25]

Brimslade and South Savernake tithing was relieving its own poor in 1775–6, when it spent £79. In 1802–3, when the population was c. 133, 12 adults and 48 children were relieved regularly and 15 adults occasionally at a total cost of £111.[26] Expenditure reached a peak of £197 in 1830.[27]

Neither tithing joined a poor-law union and, subject to the Relief of the Poor in Extra-parochial Places Act of 1857, as a civil parish each apparently remained responsible for relieving its own poor.[28] Savernake parish became part of Kennet district in 1974.[29]

CHURCH. In 1657, almost certainly after farmsteads had been built in Savernake great park and Brimslade park, it was proposed to build a church with the parks and the unimpaled forest as its parish. The proposal was not implemented until the 19th century. A church built at Cadley in 1851 or 1852 collapsed, was rebuilt, and was consecrated in 1854.[30] A district consisting of the later Savernake civil parish, except for the land north-west of the Marlborough–Pewsey road, and of the 78 a. of Preshute parish transferred to North Savernake civil parish in 1901, was assigned to the church as the ecclesiastical parish of Savernake, and a perpetual curate, from 1868 called a vicar, was licensed.[31] The ecclesiastical parish was renamed Savernake Christchurch in 1973, when the vicarage was united with Burbage vicarage. In 1975 the church was declared redundant and the parish was divided between Burbage, Marlborough, Preshute, and Wootton Rivers ecclesiastical parishes.[32]

5 W.R.O. 1300/1840A.
6 For the ownership, V.C.H. Wilts. xii. 131, 171; above, Little Bedwyn, manors (Puthall); Burbage, manors (Burbage; Durley); above, estates (Savernake); cf. W.A.M. liii. 30–1.
7 O.S. Map 6", Wilts. XXXVI (1888 edn.); Savernake estate map, c. 1820 (copy in W.R.O.).
8 Inf. from the earl of Cardigan, Savernake Lodge.
9 W.A.M. liii. 4–5, 29–30, 56–7.
10 Above, estates (Savernake).
11 Inf. from the Head Forester, Forest Enterprise, Postern Hill.
12 Wilts. Cuttings, xxix. 87, 109, 157, 335.
13 Inf. from the Head Forester.
14 W.R.O. 9/22/119.
15 Ibid. Inland Revenue, val. reg. 55; O.S. Map 6", Wilts. XXXVI. NW. (1925 edn.). 16 W.R.O., tithe award.
17 O.S. Maps 6", Wilts. XXXVI (1888 edn.); XXXVI. NW. (1925 edn.).
18 W.R.O., tithe award; Savernake estate map, c. 1820

(copy in W.R.O.).
19 O.S. Maps 6", Wilts. XXIX (1889 and later edns.).
20 Wilts. co. council, Dir. of Employers (1995), p. 27.
21 Kelly's Dir. Wilts. (1927 and later edns.).
22 Vis. Queries, 1783 (W.R.S. xxvii), p. 246.
23 Poor Law Abstract, 1804, 568–9; V.C.H. Wilts. iv. 357.
24 Poor Law Abstract, 1818, 500–1.
25 Poor Rate Returns, 1816–21, 189; 1822–4, 229; 1825–9, 220; 1830–4, 213.
26 Poor Law Abstract, 1804, 566–7; V.C.H. Wilts. iv. 357.
27 Poor Rate Returns, 1816–21, 188; 1822–4, 228; 1825–9, 218; 1830–4, 212.
28 V.C.H. Wilts. v. 254; 20 Vic. c. 19.
29 O.S. Map 1/100,000, admin. areas, Wilts. (1974 edn.).
30 W.A.M. l. 195; Pevsner, Wilts. (2nd edn.), 154; above, intro.; econ. hist.
31 Incumbents Act, 31 & 32 Vic. c. 117; W.R.O., D 1/36/4/4.
32 Ch. Com. file, NB 34/371B/2; inf. from Ch. Com.; for Burbage vicarage after 1973, above, Burbage, church.

In 1854 the patronage of the living was vested in Charles Brudenell-Bruce, marquess of Ailesbury.[33] It descended with Tottenham House to George, marquess of Ailesbury, who sold it to the dean and chapter of Salisbury in 1924. In 1915 the bishop of Salisbury had nominated by lapse. From 1973 the dean and chapter shared the patronage of the united benefice.[34]

In 1854 the incumbency was endowed with a house and £2,500 stock by Lord Ailesbury, and augmented with £100 of tithe rent charge by the Ecclesiastical Commissioners.[35] The house was sold in 1947.[36]

In the west part of the parish a room built near Compton's Farm c. 1855 for use as a chapel and a school was licensed in 1856 for divine service. Each Sunday in 1864 the curate held a morning service at Cadley church attended by c. 110 and an evening service there attended by c. 100. Weekday services in Lent and Advent and services on saints' days were attended by c. 75. Communion was celebrated monthly with c. 16 communicants and on Easter Sunday and Whit Sunday with c. 25. An afternoon service on Sundays held in the room near Compton's Farm was attended by c. 50, and in a similar room opened between 1861 and 1864 in or near Savernake Lodge in the east part of the parish a service was held on Friday evenings in winter.[37] There is no evidence of services after 1864 in the room in or near Savernake Lodge; the room near Compton's Farm has been closed apparently from the earlier 1960s.[38] The vicarage was held in plurality successively with Marlborough benefice from 1940 to 1947,[39] the vicarage of St. Katharine's, Savernake Forest, from 1947 to 1949,[40] Wootton Rivers rectory from 1965 to 1970, and Burbage vicarage from 1970.[41]

The church at Cadley, called *CHRIST-CHURCH*, was built of sarsen rubble, with dressings and banding of limestone, to designs by T. H. Wyatt.[42] It is in a 14th-century style and consists of a chancel[43] with south vestry, a nave, and a south-west tower which incorporates a south porch. A chalice and paten, both of silver, and a glass flagon with silver mounts were given in 1855,[44] and there was one bell.[45]

NONCONFORMITY. In the 1660s William Hughes, the ejected vicar of St. Mary's, Marlborough, preached to conventicles in Savernake forest.[46] There is no other evidence of nonconformity in what became Savernake parish.

EDUCATION. Cadley school was built in 1850 and had 40–50 pupils in 1858.[47] In the 1860s the curate held a poorly attended evening school in the building.[48] The day school had 51 pupils in 1906,[49] 66 in 1908–9. In 1939, when there were 13 on the roll, it was closed.[50]

In the room built c. 1855 near Compton's Farm 20–30 pupils were taught in 1858. No later evidence of the use of the building as a school has been found. A school said to stand at Birch copse in the park of Tottenham House probably stood near Savernake Lodge. It had been closed by 1858. The room opened between 1861 and 1864 in or near Savernake Lodge was for use partly as a school; no evidence of a school held there after 1864 has been found.[51]

CHARITY FOR THE POOR. None known.

TIDCOMBE

TIDCOMBE parish,[52] c. 15 km. both south-east of Marlborough and north-west of Andover (Hants), comprised Tidcombe, 895 a., and Fosbury, 1,444 a., which were detached from each other; 27 a. of the land of Oxenwood, otherwise in Shalbourne parish, had been added to Tidcombe parish by 1786.[53] Tidcombe parish church stood at Tidcombe and in the 19th century a church was built at Fosbury.[54] In 1894 Wiltshire county council gave the parish the name Tidcombe and Fosbury, and Hippenscombe, 911 a.,

a civil parish, formerly extra-parochial, and linking Tidcombe's and Fosbury's land, was then added to it.[55] In 1934 the land lying between Tidcombe's and Fosbury's, part of Shalbourne parish and until 1895 in Berkshire, was transferred to Tidcombe and Fosbury parish,[56] increasing it to 1,529 ha. (3,778 a.).[57]

The population of Tidcombe parish in 1801 was 220. Between then and 1881, when it was 238, it was at its lowest, at 204, in 1811 and its highest, at 274, in 1861. It had fallen to 199 by

33 W.R.O., D 1/60/5/32.
34 Ibid. D 1/2/47, p. 131; D 382/17; Ch. Com. file, NB 34/371B/2; above, Great Bedwyn, manors (Tottenham).
35 Ch. Com. file 6006/1; W.R.O., D 1/60/5/32.
36 Inf. from Ch. Com.
37 *Acct. of Wilts. Schs.* 41; W.R.O., D 1/4/2/21; D 1/56/7.
38 O.S. Map 1/25,000, SU 16 (1961 edn.); inf. from Mr. R. Gay, the Pearroc, Clench Common, Marlborough.
39 Ch. Com. file, NB 34/60B; ibid. file 25517/2.
40 *Sar. Dioc. Dir.* (1949, 1950); cf. above, Great Bedwyn, churches (St. Katharine's).
41 Ch. Com. file, NB 34/371B/1.
42 Pevsner, *Wilts.* (2nd edn.), 154.
43 Above, plate 9.
44 Nightingale, *Wilts. Plate*, 163.
45 Walters, *Wilts. Bells*, 194.
46 *V.C.H. Wilts.* iii. 105.

47 *Acct. of Wilts. Schs.* 41.
48 W.R.O., F 8/500/234/1/1.
49 *Return of Non-Provided Schs.* 27.
50 *Bd. of Educ., List 21, 1910* (H.M.S.O.), 510; *1938*, 425; W.R.O., F 8/500/234/1/3.
51 *Acct. of Wilts. Schs.* 41; W.R.O., D 1/56/7; cf. above, church.
52 This article was written in 1998. Maps used include O.S. Maps 6", Wilts. XLIII (1882 and later edns.); 1/25,000, SU 25/35 (1994 edn.).
53 W.R.O. 1933/11; ibid. tithe award.
54 Below, church; ibid. Fosbury, church.
55 O.S. Map 6", Wilts. XLIII (1882 edn.); W.R.O., F 2/200/3, order no. 31776; for Hippenscombe, below, Hippenscombe, intro.
56 *V.C.H. Wilts.* iv. 357, 359; O.S. Map 6", Wilts. XLIII (1882 edn.).
57 *Census*, 1961.

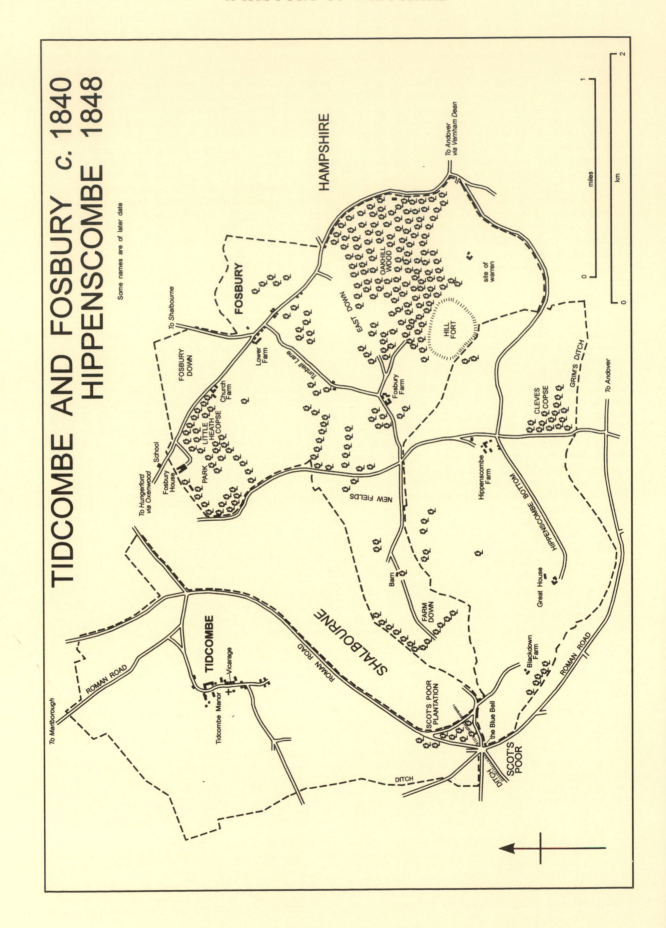

TIDCOMBE AND FOSBURY *c.* 1840
HIPPENSCOMBE 1848

Some names are of later date

1891 and, despite the addition of Hippenscombe to the parish, to 190 by 1901. A rise to 251 between 1901 and 1911 and a fall to 197 between 1911 and 1921 cannot be explained. Despite the addition of part of Shalbourne in 1934 the population of Tidcombe and Fosbury parish continued to fall. There were 158 inhabitants in 1951,[58] 97 in 1971. In 1991 the population was 105.[59]

The main part of this article deals principally with Tidcombe. Most aspects of Fosbury and Hippenscombe are dealt with separately in sub-articles under the name of each place.

The boundary of Tidcombe follows a Roman road for most of its length on the east and for a short distance on the north. Another road marks the boundary on the north-east, and the 27 a. of Oxenwood's land lies east of that road.[60] On the west the south part of Tidcombe's boundary follows a prehistoric ditch for c. 1 km.[61] On the south the point on the boundary where the Roman road crosses a prehistoric ditch was called Street gate in the 10th century.[62] All Tidcombe's land lies on chalk, a north facing scarp crosses the middle of it, and there is no stream on it. North and south of the scarp much of the land is flat. That to the north reaches its lowest point, at 150 m., on the north part of the boundary. That to the south is downland which falls gently from c. 260 m. immediately south of the scarp to c. 195 m. on the south part of the boundary; in two places the chalk is overlain by clay-with-flints.[63] Sheep-and-corn husbandry was for long practised on the land.[64]

No main road crosses Tidcombe's land. The Roman road followed by its boundary and crossing it north-east of Tidcombe village linked Cirencester and Winchester; the section on the east was part of a south-west deviation of the road from its otherwise straight course made to avoid broken relief.[65] Where it crossed and bounded Tidcombe all but a short part of the straight course was tarmacadamed and, leading north-west towards Marlborough and south-east towards Andover, was in use as a public road in 1998. A long barrow, a bowl barrow, and several prehistoric ditches lie on the downland south of Tidcombe village.[66] Tidcombe lay within Savernake forest until 1330.[67]

Most of the buildings of Tidcombe village have long stood in a north–south street immediately below the face of the scarp, with the church in the middle on the west side.[68] In the Middle Ages there were probably c. 16 small farmsteads in the street,[69] and in 1377, when it had 50 poll-tax payers,[70] Tidcombe village may have been more populous than at any time later. It had 76 inhabitants in 1841.[71] In the mid 18th century a manor house was built north of the church,[72] and in the earlier 19th century a vicarage house was standing on the east side of the street and east of the church. About 1840 there were two farmyards at the north end of the street, one on each side, and a house and a farmyard stood immediately north of the vicarage house. There were then nine cottages in the street, including a terrace of five at the south end.[73] In the mid 19th century the vicarage house was rebuilt and, south of the church and on the west side of the street, a school was built;[74] the school was converted to a house c. 1947.[75] Of the buildings standing c. 1840 only the church, the manor house, a small house apparently of 17th-century origin, and a possibly 19th-century cottage survived in 1998. At the north end of the street 20th-century buildings stood in the two farmyards; buildings on the site of the third farmyard were used for keeping horses. Only two new houses were built in the street in the 20th century.

About 1840 two cottages stood beside the lane by which the north end of Tidcombe street is approached. One of them, of brick, flint, and thatch and possibly of the late 18th century, survived in 1998. North-east of it two pairs of estate cottages were built between c. 1840 and 1879 and rebuilt in the mid 20th century. Beside a track leading to the street from the south four cottages were standing c. 1840; three were demolished between 1899 and 1922, the fourth in the mid 20th century.[76]

Tidcombe village was designated a conservation area in 1975.[77]

MANOR AND OTHER ESTATE. Tidcombe was probably part of the estate called Bedwyn which passed with the crown almost certainly from the 8th century. The estate was held by Abingdon abbey (Berks., later Oxon.) from 968 to 975 or later, and from 978 apparently again passed with the crown.[78] By 1066 Tidcombe had been granted away: it was held then by Wenesius, in 1086 by his relict.[79]

In the late 12th century *TIDCOMBE* manor was held by Henry Hussey.[80] Formerly it may have been held by members of the Beauchamp family, and in 1249 William de Beauchamp of Elmley Castle (Worcs.) confirmed it to Hussey's successor.[81] The overlordship of the manor was held by William's son William, earl of Warwick (d. 1298),[82] and descended with the earldom.[83]

58 V.C.H. Wilts. iv. 359.   59 Census, 1971; 1991.
60 W.R.O., tithe award.
61 For the ditch, inf. from Arch. section, Co. Hall, Trowbridge.   62 Arch. Jnl. lxxvii. 76.
63 Geol. Surv. Map 1/50,000, drift, sheet 283 (1975 edn.).
64 Below, econ. hist.
65 I. D. Margary, Rom. Roads in Brit. (1973), pp. 98–9.
66 V.C.H. Wilts. i (1), 144, 192, 254, 259; inf. from Arch. section, Co. Hall, Trowbridge.
67 V.C.H. Wilts. iv. 399–400, 448, 450–1.
68 Cf. Andrews and Dury, Map (W.R.S. viii), pl. 12.
69 Cf. W.R.O. 192/52, ff. 11v.–13v.
70 V.C.H. Wilts. iv. 309.
71 P.R.O., HO 107/1180.
72 For a description of the ho., below, manor.

73 W.R.O., tithe award.   74 Below, church; educ.
75 W.R.O., G 8/760/468.
76 Ibid. tithe award; O.S. Maps 6", Wilts. XLIII (1882 and later edns.); 1/25,000 SU 25 (1958 edn.).
77 Inf. from Dept. of Planning and Highways, Co. Hall, Trowbridge.
78 W.A.M. xli. 284, and map at p. 281; above, Great Bedwyn, manors [preamble], where, in n. 28, there is comment on a chart. of 968.   79 V.C.H. Wilts. ii, p. 164.
80 Cal. Chart. R. i. 394.
81 P.R.O., CP 25/1/251/16, no. 84.
82 Rot. Hund. (Rec. Com.), ii (1), 260; Complete Peerage, xii (2), 368.
83 e.g. Cal. Inq. p.m. v, p. 401; xviii, p. 171; P.R.O., C 139/40, no. 44.

Tidcombe manor passed from Henry Hussey to his son Geoffrey, to whom the king confirmed it in 1198. It presumably descended like Figheldean manor to Geoffrey's son Geoffrey (d. c. 1218), whose estate passed to another Henry Hussey (d. 1260 x 1263).[84] Tidcombe manor passed from that Henry Hussey to his son Sir Hubert (d. by 1275),[85] whose heirs were his infant daughters Margaret (d. c. 1320), who married Henry Sturmy (d. c. 1305), Maud (d. c. 1285 unmarried), and Isabel, who married John Thorney.[86] From c. 1285 to the later 14th century moieties of the manor apparently descended separately. In the 1320s what was probably one of the moieties was apparently disputed between Margaret Sturmy's sons Henry Sturmy and John Sturmy, as a moiety of Figheldean manor was,[87] and in 1331 John held an estate in Tidcombe, presumably the moiety.[88] John's estate may have passed to Henry (d. c. 1338) and probably passed to that Henry's son Henry (d. 1381).[89] By 1289 Isabel Thorney's moiety had apparently been acquired by (Sir) John of Kingston,[90] who in 1322 forfeited his lands for contrariance.[91] By 1329 it had apparently been recovered by Sir John (d. 1332 × 1339), who settled it on himself and his wife Constance for life with reversion to his son Thomas: in 1329 Sir John's right to the estate was acknowledged by John and Isabel Thorney, and in 1339 it was disputed by Henry Sturmy and by Isabel's grandson John Thorney and her daughter-in-law Maud Thorney.[92] The estate passed to Thomas Kingston's son John, who in 1375 conveyed a moiety of Tidcombe manor to Henry Sturmy and the younger John Thorney.[93] In 1382 the whole manor belonged to Henry's nephew and heir (Sir) William Sturmy.[94]

From Sir William Sturmy's death in 1427 Tidcombe manor was held for life by his relict Joan (d. 1429). Sir William's heirs were his grandson (Sir) John Seymour and his daughter Agnes, the wife of John Holcombe.[95] Tidcombe manor may have been assigned to Agnes and in 1447, as part of the settlement of a dispute over the partition of Sir William's lands, it was assigned to her son William Ringbourne[96] (d. 1450). It was held for life by William's relict Elizabeth and passed in turn to his son Robert[97] (d. 1485), Robert's brother William (d. 1512), and that William's grandson Thomas Brown,[98] who held it until 1532 or later.[99] By 1540 the manor had been acquired, probably by purchase, by Edward Seymour, earl of Hertford (cr. duke of Somerset 1547).[1]

On Somerset's execution and attainder in 1552 Tidcombe manor passed by Act to his son Sir Edward Seymour (cr. earl of Hertford 1559, d. 1621), a minor.[2] From 1553 to 1675 it descended with Tottenham Lodge in Great Bedwyn successively to William, duke of Somerset (d. 1660), William, duke of Somerset (d. 1671), and John, duke of Somerset (d. 1675).[3] Under a settlement of 1672 the manor passed in 1675 to Somerset's relict Sarah (d. 1692), and from then until c. 1767 it descended in the Seymour family with Pewsey manor.[4] About 1767 Hugh Percy, duke of Northumberland, and his wife Elizabeth, by direction of Joseph Champion, sold it to Edward Tanner.[5]

The manor descended from Edward Tanner (d. 1779) to his son John (d. 1797)[6] and passed to John's daughter Martha (d. 1855), from 1798 the wife of the Revd. W. R. H. Churchill (d. 1847). It passed to Martha's son the Revd. William Churchill, who in 1871–2 sold it to Thomas Hayward[7] (d. 1921). The manor descended in the direct line to Thomas Hayward (d. 1947), who sold the manor house and c. 25 a., T. P. Hayward (d. 1985), and Mr. J. W. Hayward, who owned Tidcombe farm, c. 940 a., in 1998.[8]

Tidcombe Manor was built in the mid 18th century, possibly for John Tanner soon after c. 1767.[9] It is a two-storeyed house of red brick with, on the south, a main front of five bays, of which the central bay is pedimented and incorporates an open-pedimented doorcase.[10] On the ground floor the house originally had four rooms, two on each side of a central staircase hall. In the 1930s a rear service wing was enlarged, the interior of the house was much altered, a garden with rustic walls of flint was made to the west, and a swimming pool house was built in a Moorish style. In the 1960s stables were converted to cottages, in the 1970s a bay was added to the service wing and a coach house was converted to a library,[11] and in 1990 the south forecourt was altered to designs by Sir Geoffrey Jellicoe.[12]

A licence of 1331 for Easton priory to appropriate Tidcombe church[13] was void. A licence for the priory to appropriate it as soon as it was vacant was granted in 1392,[14] and between 1401 and 1403 the priory appropriated the church.[15] The *RECTORY* estate belonged to Easton priory

84 *Cal. Chart. R.* 1226–57, 394; *V.C.H. Wilts.* xv. 109.
85 *Rot. Hund.* (Rec. Com.), ii (1), 260; W.R.O. 1300/111.
86 *Wilts. Inq. p.m.* 1242–1326 (Index Libr.), 160, 312–14; P.R.O., JUST 1/1006, rot. 26.
87 *Reg. Martival* (Cant. & York Soc.), iii, p. 125; *V.C.H. Wilts.* xv. 109.
88 *Wilts. Inq. p.m.* 1327–77 (Index Libr.), 78–9.
89 Cf. *V.C.H. Wilts.* xv. 109; below, church.
90 P.R.O., JUST 1/1006, rot. 26.
91 Ibid. SC 6/1148/19A.
92 *Feet of F.* 1327–77 (W.R.S. xxix), pp. 20, 58–9.
93 W.R.O. 1300/111.
94 Ibid. 1300/32; *Cal. Inq. p.m.* xv, p. 202.
95 P.R.O., C 139/28, no. 22; C 139/40, no. 44.
96 W.R.O. 1300/141; cf. *V.C.H. Wilts.* xv. 109.
97 P.R.O., C 139/138, no. 18.
98 Ibid. C 142/27, no. 68; *V.C.H. Wilts.* xv. 109.
99 W.R.O. 192/52, f. 13d.
1 *Complete Peerage*, vi. 504; P.R.O., E 328/117.

2 *Complete Peerage*, vi. 505–6; P.R.O., E 328/117.
3 Above, Great Bedwyn, manors (Tottenham).
4 W.R.O. 1300/290; 1300/299A; above, Pewsey, manor (Pewsey).
5 Alnwick Castle Mun. X.II.11, box 10, bdle. of draft deeds; cf. above, Pewsey, manor (Pewsey).
6 P.R.O., KB 122/471, no. 573; W.R.O. 1836/6; 1933/1.
7 Burke, *Land. Gent.* (1937), 412; W.R.O., A 1/345/392.
8 P. Bushell, *Tidcombe Manor* (copy in Wilts. local studies libr., Trowbridge), 11; W.R.O. 1933/26; inf. from Mrs. J. M. Hayward, Downside.
9 Cf. above, this section; Edw. Tanner lived at Wexcombe in Great Bedwyn: W.R.O. 347/5.
10 Above, plate 21.
11 Inf. from George Jellicoe, Earl Jellicoe, Tidcombe Manor.
12 Drawings in possession of Lord Jellicoe.
13 *Cal. Pat.* 1330–4, 122.   14 W.R.O. 9/15/48.
15 *Cal. Papal Reg.* v. 354; Phillipps, *Wilts. Inst.* i. 89.

until the Dissolution,[16] and in 1536 it was granted to Sir Edward Seymour, Viscount Beauchamp (cr. earl of Hertford 1537, duke of Somerset 1547).[17] In 1547 Somerset gave it to the Crown in an exchange and the Crown granted it to St. George's chapel, Windsor.[18] It was confiscated by parliament in 1643, assigned to the almshouses of Windsor castle in 1654, and recovered by the chapel at the Restoration.[19] In 1838 the estate consisted of 48 a. and all the tithes from the whole of Tidcombe and Fosbury; the tithes were valued at £481 in 1839 and commuted.[20] In 1867 the estate passed to the Ecclesiastical Commissioners,[21] who sold the land in 1920.[22]

ECONOMIC HISTORY. In 1086 Tidcombe had land for 3 ploughteams: 1 team and 1 *servus* were on the demesne, and 2 *villani* and 6 bordars had 2 teams. There were 4 a. of woodland and 10 square furlongs of pasture.[23]

Until the later 18th century Tidcombe's only inclosed land, c. 25 a., lay in the home closes of farmsteads in the village and in a few closes of meadow and pasture near the village. North of the scarp which crosses Tidcombe immediately south of the village there were three open fields, North, East, and West, a total of 431 a. The scarp face and the downland south of it, 392 a., were common pasture.[24]

In the 16th century all the land of Tidcombe manor was apparently held customarily. There were then 14 holdings, with an average of nominally 38 a. in the open fields; the largest had nominally 67 a., the smallest nominally 13 a. Each holding included land in each of the fields, common pasture for sheep and cattle, and a tenement presumably in the village.[25] The only other holdings of Tidcombe's land were a freehold, about the size of the largest copyhold of the manor and apparently of 2 yardlands, and the land of the rectory estate, about the average size of a copyhold and of 1 yardland.[26] Sheep stints, at 60 to 1 yardland, were generous.[27] In the late 17th century there was a cow down, on which sheep were kept in winter. From 1692 or earlier no more than three beasts to 1 yardland was permitted on the common pasture, and from 1702 or earlier no more than 40 sheep or 80 lambs on the cow down.[28]

By 1774 all but one of the copyholds of Tidcombe manor had been agglomerated as one farm; the last was added in 1791–2.[29] The open fields and common pastures were inclosed in 1775 by Act. In respect of the farm later called Manor farm the lord of Tidcombe manor was allotted 295 a. of the open fields and 296 a. of the downland. Other allotments lay east of his: 47 a. was allotted to the owner of the Rectory estate, 90 a. to the freeholder, and 95 a. to the copyholder. The Act required that after inclosure no less than 230 a., shared proportionately among the owners, should be ploughed.[30] By c. 1840 little of the land north of the scarp face had been laid to grass and 137 a. of the downland had been ploughed.[31]

About 1840 Tidcombe had c. 590 a. of arable, c. 42 a. of meadows and lowland pasture, and c. 236 a. of downland pasture. Manor farm, then and later worked from two farmyards at the north end of the street, had 718 a., and a farm worked from the farmstead east of the church had 145 a.[32] Both were apparently arable and sheep farms.[33] The smaller was added to Manor farm in the later 19th century or early 20th. In 1910 Manor farm had 850 a.[34] In 1998 it was a farm of c. 940 a. on which corn was grown and sheep and beef cattle were kept.[35]

Tidcombe had little woodland. Scots Poor plantation, 18 a. at the southern boundary, was standing c. 1840 and in 1998. No other wood as extensive as 10 a. seems to have been planted.[36]

LOCAL GOVERNMENT. Although the lord of Tidcombe manor in the late 12th century held the manor quit of suit to shire and hundred courts,[37] no separate view of frankpledge or court leet is known to have been held in respect of it. Records of the court baron survive for 1615–16, 1620, 1692–1702, and 1711–89. In the early 17th century the homage presented the death of tenants, and orders were made for hedges and boundaries to be repaired. In the late 17th century and early 18th it seems that the court usually met once a year, occasionally more often. Then and later in the 18th century it witnessed surrenders of and admittances to copyholds, endorsed regulations, most of them stereotyped, for common husbandry, and occasionally penalized the contravening of custom or of a regulation. The court met less often after the early 18th century: not at all between 1716 and 1719, only thrice in the 1740s, infrequently after 1760, and last in 1789.[38]

To relieve the poor of Tidcombe and Fosbury the parish appointed two overseers, each of whom relieved poverty throughout the parish. In 1775–6 the parish spent £142 on poor relief.

[16] *Valor Eccl.* (Rec. Com.), ii. 149.
[17] *L. & P. Hen. VIII*, x, pp. 526–7; *Complete Peerage*, vi. 504.
[18] P.R.O., E 305/15/F 42–3.
[19] *V.C.H. Berks.* iii. 26; *Acts & Ords. of Interr.* ed. Firth & Rait, ii. 1021.
[20] W.R.O., tithe award.
[21] *Lond. Gaz.* 28 June 1867, pp. 3630–4.
[22] Ch. Com. file 28633.
[23] *V.C.H. Wilts.* ii, p. 164.
[24] P.R.O., KB 122/471, no. 573; W.R.O. 192/52, ff. 11v.–13v.
[25] W.R.O. 192/52, ff. 11v.–13v.
[26] *W.A.M.* xli. 36; P.R.O., KB 122/471, no. 573.
[27] Alnwick Castle Mun. X.II.11, box 22B, survey of Tidcombe, 1705.
[28] Ibid. X.II.11, box 22A, ct. bk. of Tidcombe, 1692–1702.
[29] P.R.O., KB 122/471, no. 573; W.R.O. 347/5; ibid. A 1/345/392.
[30] P.R.O., KB 122/471, no. 573.
[31] W.R.O., tithe award.
[32] Ibid.
[33] P.R.O., IR 18/11171.
[34] W.R.O. 756/77; ibid. Inland Revenue, val. reg. 60.
[35] Inf. from Mrs. Hayward.
[36] O.S. Maps 6", Wilts. XLIII (1882 and later edns.); W.R.O., tithe award.
[37] *Cal. Chart. R.* 1226–57, 394.
[38] Alnwick Castle Mun. X.II.11, box 22A, ct. bk. of Tidcombe, 1692–1702; W.R.O. 9/1/135, rot. 12; 9/1/137, rot. 8; 9/1/143, rot. 1; 1005/1.

In the late 1780s much more was spent on monthly doles than on making occasional payments for shoes, clothing, medical help, and funerals and in meeting other needs. The parish had a workhouse, in which there were usually three paupers in 1780; it stood at Fosbury and was probably closed in 1783. From Easter 1782 to Easter 1785 poor relief cost an average of £106 a year. In 1802–3 £160 was spent on relieving 15 adults and 14 children regularly and 10 people occasionally; by their labour the poor contributed £27 to their maintenance, and at 3s. the poor rate was about the average for the hundred.[39] In 1814–15 £344 was spent on relieving 5 adults regularly and 41 occasionally.[40] The cost of poor relief reached a peak of £441 in 1817–18; it had fallen to £146 by 1822–3, and between then and 1833–4 exceeded £300 only twice.[41] By 1848 Tidcombe parish had joined Hungerford (Berks.) poor-law union, which was formed in 1835.[42] Tidcombe and Fosbury parish became part of Kennet district in 1974.[43]

CHURCH. Tidcombe church was standing in the mid 13th century.[44] It was served by a rector until, between 1401 and 1403, it was appropriated by Easton priory. In the licence to appropriate, which was given in 1392, the bishop required the priory to appoint a resident stipendiary chaplain who was to be presented to him to receive cure of souls,[45] but by 1403 a vicarage had been ordained.[46] Vicars were presented until 1575.[47] From when the vicarage was vacated by the vicar instituted in 1575 the church was apparently served by stipendiary curates.[48] From 1789 it was served by a perpetual curate licensed by the bishop[49] and from 1868 called a vicar.[50] Tidcombe ecclesiastical parish was reduced in 1856, when Fosbury, where a church was consecrated in that year, was made a separate ecclesiastical district,[51] and increased in 1879, when Hippenscombe was added to it.[52] In 1926 the vicarages of Tidcombe and Fosbury were united,[53] and in 1962 the united benefice was united to East Grafton vicarage.[54] In 1979 that united benefice was united to others to form Wexcombe benefice, and the ecclesiastical parishes of Tidcombe and Fosbury were united.[55]

The advowson of Tidcombe rectory belonged to Henry Hussey (d. 1260 × 1263), the lord of Tidcombe manor, and descended with the manor to his son Sir Hubert (d. by 1275). From

c. 1275 to 1335 it was disputed.[56] In 1275 and 1276, when as overlord he was keeper of Sir Hubert's daughters and heirs, the king presented,[57] and Sir Hubert's daughters Margaret, the wife of Henry Sturmy, and Isabel, the wife of John Thorney, later claimed to share the advowson with each other and attempted to present alternately; Margaret's claim passed to her son Henry Sturmy. Against that claim it was said in 1324 that the advowson had passed by successive conveyances from Sir Hubert Hussey to his brother John, to Richard de la Mote, and to William Mauduit; it was said to have descended to William's son Thomas Mauduit and to have been conveyed in 1324 by him to the rector Vincent Tarent,[58] on whose resignation in 1324 his claim was disputed by the younger Henry Sturmy. Tarent claimed that the candidates presented by the king had not been instituted, ignored a successful claim by Margaret Sturmy and Isabel Thorney against William Mauduit's relict Joan Mauduit in 1305,[59] and claimed that candidates presented successively by John Hussey and Richard de la Mote had been instituted; he himself had been presented in 1318 by Thomas Mauduit. Sturmy claimed that a candidate presented by his parents before c. 1305 had been instituted and, although the bishop recorded that it had been disputed by John Thorney,[60] claimed that the presentation of 1318 had been by grant of Isabel Thorney's turn. Jurors found for Tarent, who presented his own successor in 1324 and presented unchallenged in 1325.[61] At the following vacancy, in 1335, Henry Sturmy and John Sturmy, who were apparently disputing what was probably a moiety of Tidcombe manor with each other, each presented a rival to the candidate as rector presented by Tarent: Tarent's candidate was instituted, and between 1336 and 1349 Tarent presented five rectors without challenge. In 1361 William of Wykeham and John Froile, probably feoffees, presented,[62] and by 1374 the advowson had been acquired, possibly by purchase, by the younger Henry Sturmy's son Henry (d. 1381), who probably held a moiety of Tidcombe manor.[63] The advowson passed with Tidcombe manor to Sir William Sturmy, under a licence of 1390 Sir William gave it to Easton priory in an exchange,[64] and the priory was patron in 1392 when it was licensed to appropriate the church.[65] From 1403 to the Dissolution the priory presented vicars.[66] The patronage passed with the

39 *Poor Law Abstract, 1804*, 566–7; W.R.O. 1933/11.
40 *Poor Law Abstract, 1818*, 498–9.
41 *Poor Rate Returns, 1816–21*, 188; *1822–4*, 228; *1825–9*, 219; *1830–4*, 212.
42 *Kelly's Dir. Wilts.* (1848); *Poor Law Com. 1st Rep.* App. D, 242.
43 O.S. Map 1/100,000, admin. areas, Wilts. (1974 edn.).
44 P.R.O., CP 40/253, rot. 49.
45 Phillipps, *Wilts. Inst.* i. 14, 16, 21–2, 30–1, 38, 42–3, 46, 53; W.R.O. 9/15/48; above, manor (Rectory).
46 W.R.O., D 1/2/6, f. 91.
47 Phillipps, *Wilts. Inst.* i. 89–90, 116, 118, 132, 167, 181, 187, 202, 228.
48 *MSS. St. Geo.'s Chap., Windsor*, ed. J. N. Dalton, pp. 430–1; e.g. *W.A.M.* xli. 36; W.R.O., D 1/48/1–4.
49 W.R.O., D 1/2/28, f. 40v.; D 1/2/31, f. 53.
50 *Clergy List* (1870); Incumbents Act, 31 & 32 Vic. c. 117.
51 W.R.O. 1933/25; below, Fosbury, church.
52 W.R.O., D 1/36/4/8, no. 10.
53 Ibid. D 1/36/4/11, no. 57.
54 Ch. Com. file, NB 34/371B/2.
55 W.R.O. 1933/32; inf. from Ch. Com.
56 P.R.O., CP 40/253, rot. 49, where the dispute to 1324 is rehearsed; for the descent of the manor and for Sir Hubert Hussey's successors, above, manor (Tidcombe).
57 *Cal. Pat.* 1272–81, 83, 135.
58 *Feet of F.* 1272–1327 (W.R.S. i), p. 111.
59 P.R.O., CP 40/154, rot. 6.
60 For the presentation of 1318, *Reg. Martival* (Cant. & York Soc.), i. 128–9.
61 Ibid. 304–6, 340–1.
62 Phillipps, *Wilts. Inst.* i. 30–1, 38, 42–3, 46, 53.
63 W.R.O., D 1/2/3/1, f. 216; above, manor (Tidcombe).
64 *Cal. Pat.* 1388–92, 179.
65 W.R.O. 9/15/48.
66 Phillipps, *Wilts. Inst.* i. 89–90, 116, 118, 132, 167, 181, 187, 202.

Rectory estate to Edward Seymour, duke of Somerset, and to St. George's chapel, Windsor,[67] and in 1575 William Ernle, the chapel's lessee, presented a vicar. Thereafter stipendiary curates were appointed by successive lessees or their nominees,[68] apparently until the late 18th century. In 1789 and later the perpetual curates and the vicars were nominated by St. George's chapel.[69] In 1926 the patronage of Fosbury church was given to the chapel in an exchange, and the chapel was the sole patron of the united benefice of Tidcombe with Fosbury.[70] From 1962 the chapel shared the patronage of the united benefice and from 1979 had a seat on the board of patronage for Wexcombe benefice.[71]

In 1291, when it was worth £5 6s. 8d., the rectory was of below average value for the diocese.[72] Apparently the rector held 1 yardland and was entitled to all the tithes from Tidcombe and Fosbury.[73] The vicar was entitled to no tithe and, apart from a house, had no glebe. In 1535 the vicarage was worth £6 13s. 4d.[74] From 1612 the lessee of the Rectory estate was required to pay £13 6s. 8d. for services in the church, £14 6s. 8d. from 1627, £38 from 1669,[75] £45 10s. in the earlier 19th century. The living was augmented in 1723 by £400, of which Queen Anne's Bounty gave £200, and in 1830 by £400 given by Queen Anne's Bounty.[76] The incumbent's average income from 1829 to 1831 was £77.[77] The living included a thatched house in 1812.[78] In 1833 the house was said to be unfit for residence[79] and in 1843 was dilapidated.[80] A new house was built c. 1865.[81] It was sold c. 1926.[82]

In the late 1320s an obligation to pay for the daily service of the church by two chaplains and a holy water clerk was placed upon the rector; the patron, Vincent Tarent, endowed the rectory with 100 wethers, 4 oxen, 2 horses, and 10 pigs to meet, or to help meet, the cost. The obligation was removed in 1374.[83] In 1553 quarterly sermons were not preached and the church had no communion table.[84] From 1612 or earlier a condition of the lease of the Rectory estate was that eight sermons a year were to be preached.[85] In 1783 services were held by a curate who lived at Chute and served the cure there. At Tidcombe one service was held each Sunday, alternately morning and afternoon, and communion was celebrated four times a year; there were 8–12 communicants.[86] In the earlier 19th century large new private pews were built and the incumbent complained that as a result some poor parishioners attended nonconformist meetings because there was too little room for them to worship in the church. Alterations to provide more free seats were made c. 1845.[87] From 1810 or soon after, services attended by inhabitants of Fosbury were held in a schoolroom standing in Shalbourne parish beside the Oxenwood road near Fosbury House. Sunday service was held there in the morning in 1851 with a congregation, presumably including inhabitants of Oxenwood, said to average 200.[88] In 1851 there was still only one service held each Sunday in Tidcombe church; the congregation numbered only 50 on Census Sunday.[89] In 1864 two services were held each Sunday and additional services on Good Friday and Christmas day; communion was celebrated every two months and at Easter, Whitsun, and Christmas with 6–8 communicants. Between 1862 and 1864, after Fosbury church was built, the average congregation at Sunday services was said to have risen from c. 16 to c. 35.[90] In the late 19th century and early 20th the vicar held services in a chapel of ease at Wexcombe in Grafton parish.[91] The vicarages of Tidcombe and Fosbury were held in plurality from 1916 to 1925;[92] that of Tidcombe with Fosbury was held in plurality with the rectory of Ham with Buttermere from 1952, with East Grafton from 1955.[93]

The church of *ST. MICHAEL*, so called in 1763,[94] is built of rendered flint rubble and consists of a chancel and an aisled and clerestoried nave with north porch and, within its westernmost bay, a tower. Apart from the porch and tower it was built in the 14th century; on the north wall of the chancel an arch, now blocked, may have led to a chapel. In the 15th century the chancel was reroofed and the clerestory was built. The tower was built, and the west bay of each aisle was altered, c. 1600. The porch, of brick, was built in 1675. West buttresses were built of brick in 1707.[95] Proposals to build a gallery were made in 1724 and 1750;[96] there is no evidence that one was built.[97] The church was lightly restored in 1882 to designs by Ewan Christian.[98]

Plate weighing 2½ oz. was confiscated from the church in 1553 and a chalice of 9 oz. was retained. A silver chalice of the earlier 18th century, a silver paten hallmarked for 1727 and probably given to the church in 1736, and a silver-plated flagon given in the later 19th century were held for the church in 1891 and 1998.[99]

67 *L. & P. Hen. VIII*, x, pp. 526–7; P.R.O., E 305/15/F 42–3; above, manor (Rectory).
68 Phillipps, *Wilts. Inst.* i. 228; *MSS. St. Geo.'s Chap.* pp. 430–1.
69 *Clergy List* (1856 and later edns.); W.R.O., D 1/2/28, f. 40v.; D 1/2/31, f. 53.
70 W.R.O., D 1/36/4/11, no. 57.
71 Ch. Com. file, NB 34/371B/1; inf. from Ch. Com.
72 *Tax. Eccl.* (Rec. Com.), 189.
73 *W.A.M.* xli. 36; W.R.O., tithe award.
74 *Valor Eccl.* (Rec. Com.), ii. 151.
75 *MSS. St. Geo.'s Chap.* pp. 430–1.
76 C. Hodgson, *Queen Anne's Bounty* (1845), pp. cxxxvi, cccxxxvi; W.R.O. 1933/36.
77 *Rep. Com. Eccl. Revenues*, 850–1.
78 *W.A.M.* xli. 135.
79 *Rep. Com. Eccl. Revenues*, 850–1.
80 W.R.O. 1933/36.
81 *MSS. St. Geo.'s Chap.* p. 36.
82 W.R.O., D 1/36/4/11, no. 57.
83 Ibid. D 1/2/3/1, ff. 215v.–216v.
84 Ibid. D 1/43/1, f. 142v.
85 *MSS. St. Geo.'s Chap.* p. 430.
86 *Vis. Queries, 1783* (W.R.S. xxvii), pp. 214–15.
87 W.R.O. 1933/36.
88 Ibid. Shalbourne tithe award; P.R.O., HO 129/121/1/8/13; cf. below, Fosbury, educ.
89 P.R.O., HO 129/121/2/2/1.
90 W.R.O., D 1/56/7.
91 *Kelly's Dir. Wilts.* (1899 and later edns.).
92 *Crockford* (1930); W.R.O., D 1/36/4/11, no. 57; Ch. Com. file 100594.
93 Ch. Com. file 102353; W.R.O. 1933/30.
94 J. Ecton, *Thesaurus* (1763), 406.   95 Dates on bldg.
96 W.R.O., D 1/61/1/31; ibid. 1933/10.
97 Cf. ibid. 1933/36.   98 Ibid. 1933/39.
99 Nightingale, *Wilts. Plate*, 172; inf. from Mrs. J. M. Hayward, Downside.

Three bells hung in the church in 1553. The treble was replaced by a bell cast by John Wallis in 1608, the middle bell by one cast by Wallis in 1622, and the tenor by one cast by John Danton in 1636. In 1907 the treble cast in 1608 was replaced by a bell cast by Llewellins & James at Bristol,[1] and the bells were rehung.[2] The bells of 1907, 1622, and 1636 hung in the church in 1998.[3]

The registers begin in 1639. They are lacking for 1702–30, and registrations of burials are also lacking for 1676–9.[4]

NONCONFORMITY. Inhabitants of Tidcombe village may have been among parishioners who refused communion in the 1580s and 1686[5] and among the five nonconformists, including four papists, who lived in the parish in 1676.[6] In 1816 a meeting house in Tidcombe was certified, probably by Independents, and Independents certified a meeting house there in 1828.[7] In 1864 there were eight Primitive Methodists and four Baptists in Tidcombe, some or all of whom met in a cottage in the village.[8] No nonconformist chapel is known to have been built.

EDUCATION. A National school in Tidcombe village was opened between 1846 and 1855.[9] It was held in a cottage until 1858, when it was attended by c. 20 children, probably including some living in Wexcombe. A new school was built in 1858.[10] It was apparently closed c. 1879.[11]

CHARITIES FOR THE POOR. Ann Crook (d. 1825) gave by will nearly all the income from £100 for blankets and fuel for four poor inhabitants of Tidcombe village, and by will proved 1849 Edward Tanner gave a similar amount for fuel for four similar people. In 1904, when each charity had an income of £2 10s., the trustees of the two charities gave coal to 14 people.[12] In the 1950s coal was given away every few years.[13] In 1998 the charities were being wound up.[14]

FOSBURY

FOSBURY'S boundary on the east, two thirds of which is with Hampshire, follows the bottom of deep dry valleys. Parts of the boundary on the north and west also follow dry valleys, and a prehistoric earthwork marks part of the boundary on the south. All Fosbury's land lies on chalk, and there is now no stream. Gravel has been deposited in a north-west and south-east valley across the north part of the land and in the valleys, of which that is one, followed by the boundary on the north and east.[15] The land is broken downland with high points at 262 m. and 258 m. in the south and a low point at 135 m. at its easternmost corner. It was apparently long used for sheep-and-corn husbandry.[16]

A minor road leading north-westwards via Oxenwood towards Hungerford (Berks.) and south-eastwards via Vernham Dean towards Andover (both Hants) follows the valley across the north part of Fosbury's land and the main one along the boundary on the east; where it passes through Fosbury hamlet it is joined by a minor road leading from Shalbourne along the valley followed by the boundary on the north. Those two roads and Tunball Lane, leading south-west from Fosbury hamlet, were on their present courses in the later 18th century and are the only roads across Fosbury to have been tarmacadamed.[17]

An Iron-Age hill fort adjoins Fosbury's southern boundary; east of it a field system of c. 190 a. may be associated with it. Another field system lies in the south-west corner of Fosbury's land.[18] Fosbury lay within Savernake forest until 1330.[19]

Fosbury had 37 poll-tax payers in 1377,[20] a population of 150 in 1841.[21] In the Middle Ages most of the farmsteads on its land probably stood in a small village in the valley followed by the road from Oxenwood to Vernham Dean, and a hamlet on that site was called Fosbury in 1773[22] and later. In the earlier 19th century only one farmstead stood there, and there were pockets of settlement elsewhere.[23] Most of the buildings standing in 1998 were erected in the early or mid 19th century.

The farmstead in Fosbury hamlet was called Lower Farm in 1879[24] and later. In 1998 it incorporated a farmhouse with a main south-east front of brick and other walls of flint and brick; the house was probably built in the early 19th century, and a back range was added in the mid 19th century. A barn and part of a high boundary wall, each of flint and brick and apparently early 19th-century, survived in 1998, when the farmstead also included large 20th-century farm buildings. Between Lower Farm and Tunball Lane a cottage and a pair of cottages were built

1 Walters, *Wilts. Bells*, 215.
2 W.R.O., D 1/61/43/23.
3 Inf. from Mrs. Hayward.
4 W.R.O. 1933/1–2; 1933/4; 1933/28; bishop's transcripts for several years in the 1620s and 1630s and for some of the missing years are in W.R.O.
5 Ibid. D 1/43/5, f. 19; D 1/43/6, f. 38; D 1/54/11/2/20.
6 *Compton Census*, ed. Whiteman, 127.
7 *Meeting Ho. Certs.* (W.R.S. xl), pp. 78, 118.
8 W.R.O., D 1/56/7.
9 Nat. Soc. *Inquiry, 1846–7*, Wilts. 10–11; *Kelly's Dir. Wilts.* (1855).
10 *Acct. of Wilts. Schs.* 44.
11 *Kelly's Dir. Wilts.* (1875, 1880); O.S. Map 6", Wilts.

XLIII (1882 edn.).
12 *Endowed Char. Wilts.* (N. Div.), 943–5.
13 W.R.O., L 2, Tidcombe.
14 Inf. from Mrs. Hayward.
15 Geol. Surv. Map 1/50,000, drift, sheet 283 (1975 edn.).
16 Below, econ. hist.
17 *Andrews and Dury, Map* (W.R.S. viii), pls. 9, 12.
18 *V.C.H. Wilts.* i (1), 270, 278; inf. from Arch. section, Co. Hall, Trowbridge.
19 *V.C.H. Wilts.* iv. 399–400, 448, 450–1.
20 Ibid. 309.   21 P.R.O., HO 107/1180.
22 *Andrews and Dury, Map* (W.R.S. viii), pl. 12.
23 W.R.O., tithe award.
24 O.S. Map 6", Wilts. XLIII (1882 edn.).

beside the Oxenwood road apparently between 1773 and 1817.[25] Both were replaced in the 19th century, the cottage by a pair of cottages, and the pair in the mid 19th century by an asymetrical terrace of four cottages with Gothic doorways. Beside the road and a little south-east of Tunball Lane a house and a terrace of four cottages had been built by c. 1840,[26] and a pair of cottages was built in the mid 19th century. Much of the walling of the cottages in Fosbury hamlet is brick and flint.

About 500 m. south-east of Lower Farm a small group of buildings may have been called the Tang in 1773.[27] Two cottages stood on the site c. 1840,[28] apparently those, with walls of brick and flint, which stood there in 1998. About 500 m. north-west of Lower Farm a new farmstead, which by 1879 had been given the name Church Farm,[29] was built between 1820 and c. 1840.[30] The farmhouse was largely rebuilt in the 1990s. A timber-framed, thatched, and weatherboarded barn and a timber-framed and weatherboarded granary on staddle stones stood near it in 1998.

In the 17th and 18th centuries a manor house called Little Heath apparently stood off the south-west side of the Oxenwood road at the north end of Fosbury's land. A small group of buildings standing there in 1773 was replaced by Fosbury House, apparently shortly before 1820.[31] A school was built nearby in Shalbourne parish,[32] and east of the house and off the north-east side of the road Fosbury church and a vicarage house were built c. 1856.[33] Two lodges for Fosbury House were built beside the road: the south-eastern is of brick and flint, stands where a drive from the house and the drive from the church join the road, and was probably built c. 1856; the north-western stands in Shalbourne parish.

On the downland south-west of Fosbury hamlet Fosbury Farm had been built by 1773 and possibly by the early 18th century.[34] A large farmhouse and large farm buildings stood there in the 19th century.[35] The farmhouse was largely or entirely rebuilt in domestic revival style in the later 19th century or early 20th. By 1998 some of the farm buildings had been demolished. Buildings standing north of Fosbury Farm in 1773 were probably cottages;[36] two pairs of cottages stood on their site c. 1840.[37] In the later

20th century one pair was demolished and the other was rebuilt as a house.[38] East of the hill fort a farmyard was built between 1773 and 1817,[39] and a pair of cottages was built near the farmyard between c. 1840 and 1879.[40] In 1998 only the cottages, then occupied as a house, survived. On downland west of Fosbury Farm a pond had been made by 1773 and a barn was built near it between then and 1817.[41] A barn stood on the site in 1998.

MANOR. There were two estates called Fosbury in 1066, one of 10 hides held by Vitel and one of 2 hides held by Alwin. In 1086 both were held by Robert son of Gerald and of him by Rainer. By 1122 the smaller had been granted to the abbey of Shaftesbury (Dors.) by Jocelin Rivers, a forbear of whom held land of Robert son of Gerald in 1086;[42] the abbey may not have kept it long.[43] In 1275 the priory of Noyon-sur-Andelle (now Charleval, Eure) was overlord of *FOSBURY* manor.[44] The priory's property was confiscated during the wars with France and in 1414 was granted to the priory of Sheen (Surr.) when it was founded.[45] Sheen priory was overlord of Fosbury manor in 1428[46] and at the Dissolution.[47]

The lordship in demesne of Fosbury manor was held in 1275 by Peter Fosbury,[48] in 1412 and 1428 by William Sparsholt,[49] and at her death in 1475 by Margaret Ernle, whose heir was her son William Ernle.[50] The manor passed to Edmund Ernle (d. 1485), whose heir was his son John (born c. 1481),[51] and it descended to Mary, the daughter and heir of, presumably that, John Ernle. Mary Ernle (fl. 1562–3) married Walter Skilling, and Fosbury manor passed in turn to her sons William Skilling (d. 1608) and Swithun Skilling (d. shortly after 1608). It descended to Swithun's son Edward (d. 1651),[52] who by 1647 had forfeited it for recusancy.[53] In 1654 the manor was apparently settled on Henry Skilling[54] (d. 1670) and it descended in the direct line to Henry (d. 1686) and Henry,[55] who in 1748 was foreclosed by the mortgagee Thomas Trevor, Baron Trevor, from all of it except the woodland, 167 a., and 3 a. adjoining woodland.[56] The 170 a. passed to Henry Skilling's heir, his sister Elizabeth, the wife of Sir Jemmett Raymond, and to Elizabeth's heir, her daughter

[25] Ibid. 1", sheet 12 (1817 edn.); *Andrews and Dury, Map* (W.R.S. viii), pl. 12; W.R.O., tithe award.
[26] W.R.O., tithe award.
[27] *Andrews and Dury, Map* (W.R.S. viii), pl. 12.
[28] W.R.O., tithe award.
[29] O.S. Map 6", Wilts. XLIII (1882 edn.).
[30] C. Greenwood, *Map of Wilts.* (1820); W.R.O., tithe award.
[31] *Andrews and Dury, Map* (W.R.S. viii), pl. 12; Greenwood, *Map of Wilts.*; O.S. Map 1", sheet 12 (1817 edn.); below, manor.
[32] W.R.O., Shalbourne tithe award; below, educ.
[33] Below, church.
[34] *Andrews and Dury, Map* (W.R.S. viii), pl. 9; below, econ. hist.
[35] O.S. Map 1/2,500, Wilts. XLIII. 10 (1880 edn.); W.R.O., tithe award.
[36] *Andrews and Dury, Map* (W.R.S. viii), pl. 9.
[37] W.R.O., tithe award.
[38] Cf. O.S. Map 1/25,000, SU 35 (1958 edn.).
[39] *Andrews and Dury, Map* (W.R.S. viii), pl. 9; O.S. Map

1", sheet 12 (1817 edn.).
[40] O.S. Map 6", Wilts. XLIII (1882 edn.); W.R.O., tithe award.
[41] *Andrews and Dury, Map* (W.R.S. viii), pl. 9; O.S. Map 1", sheet 12 (1817 edn.).
[42] *V.C.H. Wilts.* ii, pp. 153, 159; *Reg. Regum Anglo-Norm.* ii, App., no. clv.
[43] Cf. Dugdale, *Mon.* ii. 474–88; J. Hutchins, *Hist. Dors.* iii. 84–8.   [44] *Rot. Hund.* (Rec. Com.), ii (1), 260.
[45] O. Manning and W. Bray, *Hist. Surr.* i. 417–18.
[46] *Feud. Aids*, v. 264.
[47] P.R.O., SC 6/Hen. VIII/3464, rot. 41.
[48] *Rot. Hund.* (Rec. Com.), ii (1), 260.
[49] *Feud. Aids*, v. 264; vi. 534.
[50] P.R.O., E 149/235, no. 11.
[51] *Cal. Inq. p.m. Hen. VII*, i, p. 88.
[52] *V.C.H. Wilts.* x. 195; P.R.O., C 2/Jas. I/S 35/15.
[53] *W.A.M.* xxvi. 387.
[54] P.R.O., CP 25/2/609/1654 Trin.
[55] Ibid. C 5/336/22; W.R.O. 1933/28.
[56] P.R.O., C 78/1863, no. 1.

Elizabeth Raymond, the wife of the Revd. John Craven. The Cravens sold it to John Poore in 1773.[57] The main part of Fosbury manor passed from Lord Trevor (d. 1753) to his daughter Elizabeth (d. 1761), the wife of Charles Spencer, duke of Marlborough (d. 1758), and to Elizabeth's son George, duke of Marlborough,[58] who sold it to John Poore in 1776.[59]

John Poore (d. 1787) devised the whole of Fosbury manor to his son John.[60] In 1804 John conveyed the manor to trustees, who in 1805 sold it to trustees of Joseph Gulston (d. 1786). The beneficiary of Gulston's trust was his great-grandson Joseph Gulston, a minor,[61] who in 1810 sold Fosbury manor to Silvanus Bevan.[62] From Bevan's death in 1830 the manor passed, from father to son, to David Bevan (d. 1846), R. C. L. Bevan (d. 1890), and F. A. Bevan,[63] who owned it in 1899. Between 1899 and 1903 the manor was bought by A. H. Huth (d. 1910),[64] whose relict Octavia Huth held it until her death in 1929. It passed in 1929 to A. H. Huth's brother Edward, who in 1934 sold it to Sir Eastman Bell, Bt.[65] In 1956 Sir Eastman sold it to C. W. Garnett, and between 1982 and 1987 Garnett conveyed it in portions to his stepson Mr. William Govett. In 1998 Mr. Govett owned c. 1,000 a. of Fosbury's land. In 1993 he sold Fosbury House and c. 330 a. of Fosbury's land to the Hon. Erskine Guinness, who in 1998 owned that estate with other land outside the parish.[66]

Members of the Skilling family lived at Fosbury, apparently in a manor house called Little Heath which stood at the north end of Fosbury's land.[67] Fosbury House,[68] of two storeys and with plain classical elevations faced in limestone ashlar, was built there in the early 19th century, apparently for Silvanus Bevan shortly before 1820.[69] It was rectangular with north-west and south-east fronts of four bays and longer fronts, of nine bays or more, incorporating the main entrance on the north-east and facing the garden to the south-west; on the garden front there was a three-bayed bow of full height. Two parallel ranges of brick, presumably stables and service rooms, extended north-west from the north-west front to form an open court. Between c. 1840 and 1879 the north-west part of the house, except those ranges, was demolished; on the garden front five bays, including the bow, survived. The south-east part of the house was linked to the north-west ranges, which were partly rebuilt, by three new brick ranges built on a **U** plan and creating an enclosed courtyard.

In the early 20th century the main elevations of the three ranges were in early Georgian style. The south-west range was of one tall storey and housed the books collected by Henry Huth and his son A. H. Huth, who lived in the house from c. 1900 to 1910. It was widened, presumably in that period, and between 1899 and 1922 a billiards room was built at its north-west end. The north-east range was of two storeys and about eight bays. The south-east part of the house was altered in the earlier 20th century, probably in the mid 1930s: a large entrance hall was made and a new staircase in early 18th-century style was constructed in it, and three wide bays were made at the centre of the north-east façade and a semicircular Ionic portico was built at their centre. In 1958 the three ranges built between c. 1840 and 1879 were demolished, leaving the surviving part of the original house and the two north-west service ranges detached from each other; the billiards room, attached to one of the service ranges, survived. In or soon after 1958 two short north-west wings were built, a partition was built to separate the entrance hall and the staircase, and the upper flights of the staircase were turned. A new kitchen was built at the south corner of the house in the 1990s.[70]

South-west of, and apparently contemporary with, Fosbury House a walled garden incorporating a hot house and a melon yard was built. A glasshouse had been added to the hot house by 1879. Only the garden walls survived in 1998. Three plantations of trees stood south, east, and south-west of the house c. 1840; between them and the house lay a park of 32 a. Between c. 1840 and 1879 two lodges were built beside the Oxenwood to Vernham Dean road, one east and one north-west of the house; long drives were made through woodland and parkland between them and the house, and the short drive between the road and the north-east front of the house was obliterated.[71]

All tithes from the whole of Fosbury were part of the Rectory estate of Tidcombe.[72]

ECONOMIC HISTORY. In 1086 Fosbury had land for 7 ploughteams. There was demesne land on which there were 2 teams and 2 *servi*, and 7 *villani* and 5 bordars had 2½ teams. There were 18 square furlongs of pasture, and woodland accounted ½ league by 3 furlongs and 4 square furlongs. Neither of the two estates which shared the land was fully cultivated.[73]

Fosbury had open fields and common pas-

57 *V.C.H. Berks.* iii. 488; W.R.O. 562/18, deed, Craven to Poore, 1773.
58 *Complete Peerage*, viii. 499–500; xii (2), 32; W.R.O. 562/19, deed, Marlborough to Bedford, 1756.
59 W.R.O. 562/22, Marlborough to Poore, 1776.
60 Ibid. 562/19, deed, Poore to Poore, 1795; 562/23, deed, Child to Poore, 1805.
61 Ibid. 562/23, deed, Poore to Gulston, 1805; 562/23, abstr. of title to Fosbury manor, 1805.
62 Ibid. 562/23, deed, Gulston to Bevan, 1810.
63 Ibid. A 1/345/392; Burke, *Land. Gent.* (1898), i. 108–10; Princ. Regy. Fam. Div., will of R. C. L. Bevan, 1890.
64 *Kelly's Dir. Wilts.* (1899, 1903); *W.A.M.* xxxvii. 165–6.
65 Burke, *Land. Gent.* (1937), 1199; W.A.S. Libr., sale

cat. lii, no. 35; W.R.O., G 8/516/1.
66 Inf. from Mr. J. Wallis, Messrs. Humberts, 19 High Street, Pewsey.
67 e.g. Williams, *Cath. Recusancy* (Cath. Rec. Soc.), p. 232; W.R.O. 562/18, deed, Skilling to Smith, 1710; cf. O.S. Map 1", sheet 12 (1817 edn.).
68 Above, plate 25.
69 Cf. Greenwood, *Map of Wilts.*; O.S. Map 1", sheet 12 (1817 edn.).
70 O.S. Maps 1/2,500, Wilts. XLIII. 6 (1880 and later edns.); W.R.O., tithe award; inf. from, and photo. in possession of, the Hon. Erskine Guinness, Fosbury Ho.; for the Huths, *D.N.B.*
71 O.S. Map 1/2,500, Wilts. XLIII. 6 (1880 edn.); W.R.O., tithe award.   72 W.R.O., tithe award.
73 *V.C.H. Wilts.* ii, p. 153.

tures, and Fosbury manor included demesne land and customary tenants.[74] On downland to the south-east the demesne included Oakhill wood and a warren, a total of *c*. 350 a.,[75] and on the downland which constituted Fosbury's south-west tongue it included Farm down, *c*. 236 a.; it also included a warren on Silver down in Shalbourne parish adjoining Farm down. The main area of common pasture seems to have been the rising ground north-east of the Oxenwood to Vernham Dean road, *c*. 165 a., the north-west part of which was called Fosbury down in the 19th century. Little heath, perhaps *c*. 50 a., the northernmost land south-west of the road, and East down, *c*. 35 a. north-west of Oakhill wood, may also have been common pastures.[76] Presumably the open fields lay mainly between the Oxenwood to Vernham Dean road and the downs to the south-east and south-west and amounted to *c*. 500 a.

In the early 17th century Fosbury farm included Oakhill wood, 201 a. *c*. 1840, Oakhill warren, *c*. 150 a. south of it, and presumably the agricultural land of the demesne;[77] where the farmstead stood in the early 17th century is uncertain. In the early 18th century the copyholders of Fosbury manor may have been few. Between 1708 and 1710 the open fields and common pastures were divided and allotted by private agreement; in 1709 one copyholder was refusing to inclose land allotted to her. In 1710 there were apparently three main farms: Fosbury farm included the demesne land and may then have been worked from a farmstead on the downs on the site of that standing in 1773, a farm consisted of newly inclosed and other land formerly held by several copyholders, and Henley Woods farm may have included land north-east of the Vernham Dean road abutting that of Henley in Buttermere parish. Farmland may also have been worked from buildings near what was apparently the manor house called Little Heath. It is unlikely that much land was held with any of the 13 other tenements on Fosbury manor in 1710.[78]

By 1716 the east end of Farm down had been converted to two new arable fields, of 35 a. and 36 a., and by *c*. 1840 five other arable fields, 155 a., lay on the downland west of them; a barn was built in the middle of the downland. Also by *c*. 1840 the warren south of Oakhill wood had been converted to five arable fields, each of 30–32 a., and a farmyard had been built among the fields; the hill fort and the land between it and the new fields remained rough pasture.[79]

The farmstead later called Church Farm was built between 1820 and *c*. 1840 presumably to replace farm buildings on Little heath demolished when Fosbury House was built, apparently shortly before 1820, and *c*. 1840 there were three farms in Fosbury. Fosbury farm had 675 a., including *c*. 500 a. of arable; the farm later called Lower had 301 a., including 236 a. of arable; the farm later called Church had 153 a., including the park of Fosbury House and only 72 a. of arable. Each farm included small areas of woodland.[80] Fosbury's agricultural land was apparently worked in those three farms until the late 20th century. In 1910, without the woodland, Fosbury farm had 647 a., Lower farm 304 a., and Church farm 103 a.; the park was not then part of a farm.[81] In the late 20th century the three farms were merged, Farm down was separated from them, and Church Farm went out of agricultural use. In 1998 the composite farm had in Fosbury, excluding woodland, *c*. 700 a.; it was an arable and sheep farm with its principal buildings at Lower Farm. In 1998 Farm down was mainly arable and was worked from outside the parish.[82]

Oakhill wood was standing in the early 13th century,[83] Little Heath copse in the early 18th.[84] About 1840 they measured 201 a. and 19 a. respectively and there were plantations of 8 a. and 7 a. near Fosbury House, 8 a. of woodland in two belts on Farm down, several other coppices of 1–5 a., and other woodland in rows. Several plantations were made between *c*. 1840 and 1879 including one of 16 a. adjoining Oakhill wood.[85] In 1910 there was 288 a. of woodland in Fosbury,[86] all of which was standing in 1998. In the 20th century some copses were enlarged and, between 1923 and 1956, a copse of *c*. 15 a. was planted on Farm down.[87]

A saw mill was built in Fosbury hamlet between 1909 and 1922.[88] Its buildings were not used for milling in 1998.

CHURCH. Fosbury church was consecrated, an ecclesiastical district was assigned to it, and a perpetual curate was licensed to serve it, in 1856. The district consisted of Fosbury and of Oxenwood.[89] From 1868 the perpetual curate was called a vicar.[90] In 1926 the vicarage was united to Tidcombe vicarage,[91] in 1962 the united benefice was united to East Grafton vicarage, and in 1979 that united benefice was united to others to form Wexcombe benefice, the ecclesiastical parishes of Tidcombe and Fosbury were

74 P.R.O., C 5/268/10.
75 Ibid. STAC 8/111/18; STAC 8/211/29; W.R.O., tithe award.
76 *Andrews and Dury, Map* (W.R.S. viii), pl. 12; W.R.O. 562/18, assignment of mortgage, 1738; ibid. tithe award; cf. O.S. Map 6", Wilts. XLIII (1882 edn.).
77 P.R.O., STAC 8/111/18; STAC 8/211/29; W.R.O., tithe award.
78 *Andrews and Dury, Map* (W.R.S. viii), pl. 9; P.R.O., C 5/268/10; C 5/336/22; C 5/595/43; W.R.O. 562/18, deed, Skilling to Smith, 1710.
79 W.R.O. 562/18, assignment of mortgage, 1738; ibid. tithe award; above, intro.
80 Greenwood, *Map of Wilts.*; W.R.O., tithe award; above, manor.
81 *Kelly's Dir. Wilts.* (1939); W.R.O., Inland Revenue, val. reg. 60.
82 Inf. from Mr. J. Wallis, Messrs. Humberts, 19 High Street, Pewsey.
83 *V.C.H. Wilts.* iv. 419.
84 W.R.O. 562/18, deed, Skilling to Smith, 1710.
85 Ibid. tithe award; O.S. Map 6", Wilts. XLIII (1882 edn.).
86 W.R.O., Inland Revenue, val. reg. 60.
87 O.S. Maps 6", Wilts. XLIII. SW. (1926 edn.); 1/25,000, SU 35 (1958 edn.); SU 25/35 (1994 edn.).
88 Ibid. 1/2,500, Wilts. XLIII. 7 (1910, 1924 edns.).
89 W.R.O. 1933/25; ibid. D 1/2/36, p. 421.
90 Incumbents Act, 31 & 32 Vic. c. 117.
91 W.R.O., D 1/36/4/11, no. 57.

united,[92] and Fosbury church was declared redundant.[93]

In 1856 the curate was nominated by R. C. L. Bevan, the lord of Fosbury manor, who was apparently patron until his death in 1890. Between 1889 and 1894 the patronage was transferred to the Church Patronage society,[94] and in 1926 the society gave it to St. George's chapel, Windsor, in an exchange.[95] From 1926 the chapel was sole patron of the united benefice of Tidcombe with Fosbury.[96]

A house for the perpetual curate had been built beside the church by 1856. It was designed by S. S. Teulon,[97] is of flint with dressings of stone and decoration in brick, and is in Tudor Gothic style. It was sold in 1956.[98]

In 1864 a service was held in Fosbury church twice each Sunday and once both on Christmas day and Good Friday; average attendance was below 100. About 1864 communion was celebrated at Christmas and Easter, sometimes on Whit and Trinity Sundays, and monthly; the average number of communicants was c. 25.[99] From 1916 to 1925 the vicarage was held in plurality with Tidcombe vicarage,[1] and the united benefice of Tidcombe with Fosbury was held in plurality with other benefices from 1952.[2]

CHRISTCHURCH at Fosbury was built 1854–6 to designs by S. S. Teulon.[3] It is of flint with dressings of Bath stone, is in Decorated style, and consists of an undivided chancel and nave of six bays with north vestry and south-west tower. The tower is prominent and of three stages, and there is a porch in its base. A slender octagonal stair tower with a crocketed spire is attached to the tower and the nave in their east angle. There is a hammer-beamed roof over the chancel, a trussed roof over the nave, and the floor of the chancel is higher than that of the nave.

A chalice, a paten, and an almsdish, all hallmarked for 1856, were given to the church, presumably in that year, and a pair of chalices and a silver-mounted glass flagon, all hallmarked for 1889, were given in 1890.[4] The church has one bell.[5]

NONCONFORMITY. Francis Browning of Fosbury was a popish recusant in 1577.[6] Members of the Skilling family, probably living at Fosbury, refused communion at Tidcombe church in the 1580s[7] and may also have been recusants. Edward Skilling, the lord of Fosbury manor, was a recusant in 1646,[8] and the four papists who lived in the parish in 1676 probably included Skillings.[9]

In the early 19th century Silvanus Bevan, the lord of Fosbury manor, supported Independent meeting houses, and in 1816 a house at Fosbury was certified, probably by Independents. Services were held by J. B. Walcot, who was later the pastor of a Strict Baptist chapel at Ludgershall.[10] In 1864 there were two Baptists, a Congregationalist, and two families of Primitive Methodists in Fosbury ecclesiastical district.[11] No chapel is known to have been built at Fosbury.

EDUCATION. In or soon after 1810 a school was built in Shalbourne parish by Silvanus Bevan, the lord of Fosbury manor, apparently for children living at Fosbury and Oxenwood: it stands beside the Oxenwood road near Fosbury House.[12] In 1858 it had 45–60 pupils, including infants.[13] It was closed in 1904 and was replaced by a school in Oxenwood village open from 1905 to 1967.[14]

HIPPENSCOMBE

UNTIL c. 1240 Hippenscombe, consisting of a deep east–west coomb and a northern tributary coomb, lay in Savernake forest. From c. 1240 the north part lay in Savernake forest and the south part in Chute forest, and from 1330 the whole was a detached part of Chute forest.[15] Hippenscombe was extra-parochial, its inhabitants relieved their own poor, and, possibly under the Relief of the Poor in Extra-parochial Places Act of 1857, it was deemed a civil parish. It remained a civil parish until 1894,[16]

when it was added to Tidcombe and Fosbury parish.[17]

Hippenscombe's boundary on the north and south ran along the top of the steep sides of the coombs. On the south it followed a ditch; on the north, part of it was marked by the Iron-Age hill fort in Fosbury. On the east the boundary crosses the contours to exclude the lower end of the coomb. All Hippenscombe's land lies on chalk, and each coomb is now dry; the river which cut the main coomb, the floor of which is

92 Above, Tidcombe, church.   93 W.R.O. 1933/32.
94 Ibid. D 1/2/36, p. 421; D 1/2/41, pp. 421–2; *Clergy List* (1889 and later edns.); above, manor.
95 W.R.O., D 1/36/4/11, no. 57.
96 Above, Tidcombe, church.
97 Pevsner, *Wilts.* (2nd edn.), 250.
98 Ch. Com. file 102353.   99 W.R.O., D 1/56/7.
1 Ibid. D 1/36/4/11, no. 57; *Crockford* (1930); Ch. Com. file 100594.   2 Above, Tidcombe, church.
3 Pevsner, *Wilts.* (2nd edn.), 250.
4 Nightingale, *Wilts. Plate*, 168.
5 Walters, *Wilts. Bells*, 249.
6 *Misc.* xii (Cath. Rec. Soc. xxii), 107.
7 W.R.O., D 1/43/5, f. 19; D 1/43/6, f. 38.
8 *W.A.M.* xxvi. 367; above, manor.
9 *Compton Census*, ed. Whiteman, 127; cf. Williams,

Cath. Recusancy (Cath. Rec. Soc.), 232.
10 *Meeting Ho. Certs.* (W.R.S. xl), p. 79; R. W. Oliver, *Strict Bapt. Chapels Eng.* (Strict Bapt. Hist. Soc.), v. 24; J. B. Walcot, *Memorials of Fosbury Ho.* (priv. print. 1847: photocopy in Wilts. local studies libr., Trowbridge), 1–4; above, manor.   11 W.R.O., D 1/56/7.
12 Ibid. Shalbourne tithe award; P.R.O., HO 129/121/1/8/13; above, manor.
13 *Acct. of Wilts. Schs.* 24.
14 W.R.O., F 8/500/124/1/2–3.
15 Ibid. 9/17/1; *V.C.H. Wilts.* iv. 418, 448, 450–3; *W.A.M.* xlix. 407; the hist. of Chute forest and Savernake forest is written in *V.C.H. Wilts.* iv. 417–27.
16 *Poor Law Abstract, 1804*, 566–7; *V.C.H. Wilts.* iv. 350; *Census*, 1861; 20 Vic. c. 19.
17 Above, Tidcombe, intro.

now called Hippenscombe bottom, deposited a small amount of gravel.[18] Near the boundary on the north the land reaches 260 m., on the south boundary 245 m.; on the eastern boundary Hippenscombe bottom lies at *c.* 150 m. Grim's ditch, which marks the boundary on the south, is probably prehistoric, and prehistoric field systems have been identified on the high ground on either side of Hippenscombe bottom.[19]

The population of Hippenscombe numbered 47 in 1801. For reasons that are obscure it had fallen to 21 by 1811 and risen to 40 by 1821 and to 58 by 1831. At 59 it reached its peak in 1841. From 1871 to 1891 it fell from 57 to 35.[20]

Four sites of settlement are known, three of them in Hippenscombe bottom. A lodge was standing in the earlier 16th century.[21] A building which in 1707 was called the lodge or dwelling house of Hippenscombe farm probably stood on its site.[22] The most likely site of both is that of a farmstead called Hippenscombe at which a notable house was standing in 1773.[23] In 1955 that house was said to be ruinous,[24] and it was later demolished. In 1848 there were extensive farm buildings around it and a pair of cottages stood north of it. The cottages were apparently derelict in 1923 and were demolished later; a farm building of flint and apparently early 19th-century was converted to cottages probably soon after 1923[25] and was a house in 1998. Two bungalows and a house were built in the 20th century, and in 1998 most of the farm buildings were 20th-century.

Another possible site of the 16th-century lodge and the early 18th-century house is that of buildings which stood south-west of Hippenscombe farmstead in 1773.[26] A new farmstead was built there, probably *c.* 1830, and in 1834 and until 1899 or later a terrace of six cottages there was called the Great House.[27] The farmyard apparently went out of use between 1879 and 1899 and was later demolished; Great House was apparently ruinous in 1923[28] and was later demolished.

Blagden Farm, later called Blackdown Farm, was built in Hippenscombe bottom west of Great House between 1773 and 1817.[29] In 1849 it consisted of a house and a barn,[30] in 1929 of a thatched house with walls of flint and brick and several small farm buildings.[31] The farm-stead was in ruins in 1957[32] and was afterwards demolished.

On the downland west of Hippenscombe bottom where several parishes met and several tracks joined the Roman road, a place called Scott Poor in 1773,[33] later Scot's Poor, a thatched cottage with walls of flint and brick was built in the 18th century and survived in 1998. In 1822 it was an alehouse called the Bell, from 1827 the Blue Bell.[34] It was closed in 1914.[35]

ESTATES. As part of Savernake forest and later of Chute forest the land of Hippenscombe parish belonged to the Crown in the Middle Ages.[36]

In 1544 *HIPPENSCOMBE*, apparently *c.* 90 per cent of the parish, was granted to an agent of Edward Seymour, earl of Hertford[37] (cr. duke of Somerset 1547), on whose execution and attainder in 1552[38] it passed to the Crown. In 1553 it was assigned by Act to Somerset's son Sir Edward[39] (cr. earl of Hertford 1559, d. 1621),[40] and from then to 1827 the estate descended in the Seymour, Bruce, Brudenell, and Brudenell-Bruce families with Tottenham Lodge and Tottenham House in Great Bedwyn.[41] In 1827 Charles Brudenell-Bruce, marquess of Ailesbury, sold it to William Fulbrook[42] (d. by 1834),[43] who owned it until 1831 or later.[44] It was offered for sale by mortgagees[45] and bought, probably from them in 1834, by James Wheble (d. 1840). Wheble devised it to his son E. J. Wheble[46] (d. by 1863),[47] who in 1848 owned it as an estate of 825 a.[48] In 1879 E. J. Wheble's executors sold the estate to Edward Bates[49] (from 1896 Sir Edward Bates, Bt., d. 1899),[50] whose representatives held it in 1903. By 1907 the estate had been acquired by F. W. Lillywhite, who held it until 1911 or later.[51] In 1922 it was offered for sale by mortgagees[52] and may have been bought by A. W. Crawford.[53] From the late 1920s to the mid 1930s it belonged to members of the Stephens family,[54] from *c.* 1936 to 1949 to A. J. Hosier.[55] In 1955 it was bought by John Cherrington, who in 1962 sold it to his son Daniel Cherrington.[56] In 1998, as Hippenscombe farm, it belonged to Mr. Anders Bergengren.[57]

18 Geol. Surv. Map 1/50,000, drift, sheet 283 (1975 edn.).
19 *V.C.H. Wilts.* i (1), 278; inf. from Arch. section, Co. Hall, Trowbridge.
20 *V.C.H. Wilts.* iv. 350.
21 *L. & P. Hen. VIII*, iv (1), p. 58.
22 P.R.O., C 5/331/21.
23 *Andrews and Dury, Map* (W.R.S. viii), pl. 9.
24 J. Cherrington, *On the Smell of an Oily Rag*, 176.
25 O.S. Map 1/2,500, Wilts. XLIII. 10 (1880 edn.; endorsed copy of 1924 edn. in W.R.O.); W.R.O., tithe award.
26 *Andrews and Dury, Map* (W.R.S. viii), pl. 9, where one is called Blackdown barn; cf. below, this section.
27 O.S. Map 1/2,500, Wilts. XLIII. 14 (1900 edn.); W.R.O. 374/128/74; ibid. Ch. Com., chapter, 153/24.
28 O.S. Maps 6", Wilts. XLIII (1882 edn.); 1/2,500, Wilts. XLIII. 14 (1900, 1924 edns.).
29 *Andrews and Dury, Map* (W.R.S. viii), pl. 9; O.S. Map 1", sheet 14 (1817 edn.).
30 W.R.O., Blagden tithe award.
31 Ibid. 9/1/521.
32 O.S. Map 1/25,000, SU 25 (1958 edn.).
33 *Andrews and Dury, Map* (W.R.S. viii), pl. 9.
34 W.R.O., A 1/326/3.
35 *W.A.M.* xli. 285.
36 *V.C.H. Wilts.* iv. 418, 450–3.
37 *Cat. Anct. D.* iii, B 4134; W.R.O. 9/17/1; cf. ibid. tithe award; Blagden tithe award.
38 *Complete Peerage*, xii (1), 59–63.
39 P.R.O., E 328/117.
40 *Complete Peerage*, vi. 505–6.
41 Above, Great Bedwyn, manors (Tottenham).
42 W.R.O. 9/17/4.
43 Ibid. Ch. Com., chapter, 153/19.
44 Ibid. A 1/345/219.   45 Ibid. 374/128/74.
46 Ibid. Ch. Com., chapter, 153/19; ibid. Ch. Com., chapter, 153/21.   47 Burke, *Land. Gent.* (1863), 1647.
48 W.R.O., tithe award.
49 Ibid. A 1/345/219; ibid. 2132/195.
50 Burke, *Peerage* (1915), 202.
51 *Kelly's Dir. Wilts.* (1903 and later edns.).
52 W.R.O. 2132/195.
53 *Kelly's Dir. Wilts.* (1923).
54 Ibid. (1927 and later edns.); W.R.O., G 8/516/1.
55 A. J. and F. H. Hosier, *Hosier's Farming System*, 43, 242.
56 Cherrington, *Smell of an Oily Rag*, 176–7.
57 Inf. from Mr. P. van Vlissingen, Conholt Ho.

Part of Chute forest called *BLAGDEN*, *c.* 10 per cent of Hippenscombe parish, was granted by the Crown in 1632 to Sir William Russell, Bt., who in 1633 conveyed it to the lessee Sir Edward Wardour. Also in 1633 Wardour sold it to William Seymour, earl of Hertford.[58] From 1633 to *c.* 1929 Blagden descended in the Seymour, Bruce, Brudenell, and Brudenell-Bruce families with Tottenham Lodge and Tottenham House, until 1827 also with Hippenscombe.[59] In 1849 it consisted of Blagden (later Blackdown) farm and the Blue Bell at Scot's Poor, a total of 89 a.[60] In 1929 it was offered for sale by George Brudenell-Bruce, marquess of Ailesbury.[61] Blackdown farm, *c.* 80 a., was sold by Lady (Eleanor) Yarrow to Friend Sykes *c.* 1936, has since been part of the Chantry estate based in Chute parish, and in 1998 belonged to Mr. Michael Sykes.[62]

The tithes of Savernake forest were taken by Salisbury cathedral from the 12th century, as those of Chute forest probably were,[63] and the cathedral owned the tithes of the Hippenscombe estate.[64] In 1848 those tithes were valued at £132 and commuted.[65]

For reasons which are obscure the tithes of Blagden were not part of the cathedral's estate. In 1848 they belonged to Charles, marquess of Ailesbury, were valued at £12, and were commuted.[66]

ECONOMIC HISTORY. Land at Hippenscombe had been inclosed by the Crown by 1343 and was thereafter managed as a park in which deer were kept and grass was mown for hay.[67] The park was presumably what later descended as the Hippenscombe estate.[68] The estate was said to contain 314 a. of woodland in 1544, 450 a. of woodland and 250 a. of pasture in 1586,[69] and a warren in the 1630s. Until 1633 it was kept in hand[70] and presumably used for sport and as a source of rabbits and timber.

In 1633 the Hippenscombe estate was leased as a farm, and the tenant undertook to destroy the rabbits. In the 1640s, however, the rabbits multiplied, and those killed in 1657 were worth *c.* £130. The woodland was much damaged by the rabbits, many trees were felled, and some coppices were grubbed up for arable; in the late 17th century there was said to be little woodland standing on the farm. In 1693 the farmer was licensed to clear rabbits from and to plough 250 a., and authority was given for a 16-a. coppice to be grubbed up; sheep-and-corn husbandry

was practised, and in 1695 a flock of 160 ewes was kept. In 1702 the farmer was licensed to clear rabbits from and to plough a further 220 a., and he covenanted to plough no more than 400 a. a year. In 1709 it was estimated that Hippenscombe farm comprised 600 a. of arable, 15 a. of meadows, 40 a. of pastures, 15 a. of wood, and 160 a., presumably steep downland, considered more suitable for feeding sheep than preserving rabbits.[71]

In 1834 Hippenscombe farm, 825 a., included two farmsteads, 530 a. of arable, 34 a. of meadows, 21 a. of woodland, and, on the high ground on the north and south, 226 a. of downland pasture.[72] It remained a sheep-and-corn farm in 1867, when it had *c.* 600 a. of arable and temporary grassland, *c.* 200 a. of permanent pasture, a flock of *c.* 1,000 sheep, and a herd of pigs.[73] By 1886 much of the arable had been laid to grass and a herd of *c.* 100 cattle was kept in addition to sheep and pigs.[74] In the early 20th century the farm was used to rear game birds.[75] In the 1930s it contained no arable,[76] from *c.* 1936 to 1949 was used to rear cattle, and in 1955 was largely unproductive.[77] In 1998 Hippenscombe farm was an arable, cattle, and poultry farm.

In 1632 Blagden was described as waste land.[78] In the late 18th century or early 19th a farmstead was built on it,[79] and in 1849 the land was an 85-a. farm, later called Blackdown farm, which included 77 a. of arable and 7 a. of woodland.[80] In 1929 Blackdown farm was apparently a dairy farm and included the farmstead, 2 a. of woodland, 21 a. of arable, and 51 a. of pasture in Tidcombe and Fosbury parish, and 5 a. of rough pasture in Chute parish.[81] From *c.* 1936 and in 1998, when it was used to produce seeds and for sheep rearing, that land was part of a large farm based in Chute parish.[82]

Of the woodland which in 1834 stood on Hippenscombe farm 17 a. stood as Cleves copse.[83] Most of the 7 a. of woodland on Blackdown farm was cleared in the mid 19th century.[84] In the 20th century part of Cleves copse was cleared and trees were allowed to grow in several other places, especially on the high ground on the south;[85] in 1998 there was *c.* 35 a. of woodland.

LOCAL GOVERNMENT. Hippenscombe spent £13 on the relief of its poor in 1775–6, an average of £5 in the three years ending at Easter 1785. In 1802–3 eight adults and nine children

58 W.R.O. 9/17/32, deed, Wardour to Hertford, 1633.
59 Above, Great Bedwyn, manors (Tottenham).
60 W.R.O., Blagden tithe award.
61 Ibid. 9/1/521.
62 Inf. from Mr. M. Sykes, Chute Farms Ltd.; for the estate, above, Chute, manors (Chantry).
63 *Close R.* 1231–4, 21; above, Chute Forest, estates [tithes].   64 W.R.O., Ch. Com., chapter, 153/1–24.
65 Ibid. tithe award.
66 Ibid. Blagden tithe award.
67 *Cal. Fine R.* 1337–47, 328; *Cal. Pat.* 1377–81, 619.
68 Above, estates (Hippenscombe).
69 W.R.O. 9/17/1–2.
70 Ibid. 9/17/34, notes by Simkins.
71 Ibid.; 9/17/34, case concerning Hippenscombe; 9/17/35, papers about Hippenscombe, 1639; P.R.O., E 134/1658 Mich./24; E 134/9 Wm. III East./3.
72 W.R.O., Ch. Com., chapter, 153/24.
73 P.R.O., MAF 68/151, sheet 14.
74 Ibid. MAF 68/1063, sheet 3.
75 *Kelly's Dir. Wilts.* (1907, 1911).
76 [1st] Land Util. Surv. Map, sheet 112.
77 Cherrington, *Smell of an Oily Rag*, 176.
78 W.R.O. 9/17/32, deed, Wardour to Hertford, 1633.
79 Above, intro.   80 W.R.O., Blagden tithe award.
81 Ibid. 9/1/521.
82 Inf. from Mr. Sykes; for the farm, above, Chute, econ. hist. (Chute).
83 W.R.O., Ch. Com., chapter, 153/24.
84 Ibid. Blagden tithe award; O.S. Map 6", Wilts. XLIII (1882 edn.).
85 Cf. O.S. Map 6", Wilts. XLIII. SW. (1900 edn.).

were relieved regularly, three people occasionally; £54 was spent and the poor rate, at 6d., was very low.[86] Expenditure had risen to £73 by 1812–13 and fallen to £26 by 1814–15.[87] In the early 1830s no poor rate was levied.[88] By 1864 Hippenscombe had joined Hungerford poor-law union.[89] As part of Tidcombe and Fosbury parish it became part of Kennet district in 1974.[90]

WOOTTON RIVERS

WOOTTON RIVERS village lies 6 km. south of Marlborough.[91] Besides the village, the parish contains East Wick Farm, which possibly stands on the site of what was a small village in the Middle Ages.[92] The suffix in the parish's name is the surname of lords of the principal manor and was in use in the 14th century.[93] In 1300 the land between the eastern arms at the north and south ends of the parish, which either was or might soon have become part of the parish, was probably woodland and was defined as a southern tail of Savernake forest. It remained part of the forest in 1330, when the land east and west of it was disafforested,[94] and as Brimslade it remained extra-parochial until the 19th century.[95] Wootton Rivers parish measured 1,200 a. (486 ha.). In 1987 Brimslade was transferred to it from Savernake parish, and a small area was transferred from it to Savernake. Wootton Rivers parish thereafter measured 705 ha.[96]

The parish boundary follows a dry valley and a ridge on the south-east, but no prominent natural feature marks it elsewhere. On the north and in several other places it is marked by roads and paths. Sharp bends in the boundary with Milton Lilbourne may be partly the result of a compromise between the rector of Wootton Rivers and the appropriator of Milton Lilbourne church who disputed tithes c. 1215 and c. 1327.[97] The line of the boundary with Easton along a road was confirmed in 1908.[98]

Upper Greensand outcrops over the whole parish except its north end, where chalk outcrops and the southern scarp of the Marlborough Downs crosses the parish from east to west. A small area in the extreme north is overlain by clay-with-flints.[99] An intermittent head stream of the Christchurch Avon flows from north-east to south-west across the south half of the parish. To the north the land reaches 205 m. on the down at the western boundary, to the south, where it is undulating, it reaches 170 m. at the eastern boundary. The stream leaves the parish at 130 m. Open fields lay in the centre and north parts of the parish, common pasture in the south

and on the downland in the north. The parish contained very little woodland.[1]

There were 51 poll-tax payers at Wootton Rivers in 1377; they presumably included the inhabitants of East Wick.[2] The population of the parish was 313 in 1801 and 367 in 1811. It was over 400 between 1821 and 1871, reaching a peak of 470 in 1841; it was between 300 and 400 in the period 1881–1911, between 300 and 200 thereafter. The parish had 247 inhabitants in 1981 and, after the boundary changes of 1987, 271 in 1991.[3]

The Roman road from Mildenhall to Old Salisbury, and in the Middle Ages a main Marlborough–Salisbury road, may have run north–south across the parish. The direct course of a Marlborough–Salisbury road through Wootton Rivers would have been blocked in the 16th century when north of the parish the west part of Savernake forest was inclosed as Savernake great park, and later the main Marlborough–Salisbury road ran further east.[4] Wootton Rivers village is linked to the present main road from Marlborough to Salisbury and Andover (Hants) by a lane leading north-eastwards and by others leading to Burbage. It is linked to another main Marlborough–Salisbury road, which runs through Pewsey, by three lanes, one via East Wick, one via Milton Lilbourne, and one via Clench in Milton Lilbourne; the lane via East Wick had been diverted south of the farmstead by 1732. The road along the northern boundary, in use in the early 18th century, has never been tarmacadamed and was a track called Mud Lane in 1997.[5]

The Kennet & Avon canal was built across the parish c. 1807 and was opened fully in 1810.[6] A wharf, a lock, and a lock keeper's house were built immediately south of the village, and there is another lock in the east part of the parish. The canal was restored in the 1970s and the locks were reopened in 1973.[7]

The Berks. & Hants Extension Railway, built parallel to and immediately south of the canal, was opened across the parish in 1862. Since 1906

---

86   *Poor Law Abstract, 1804,* 566–7.
87   Ibid. *1818,* 498–9.   88   W.R.O. 374/128/74.
89   *P.O. Dir. Berks.* (1864).
90   O.S. Map 1/100,000, admin. areas, Wilts. (1974 edn.).
91   This article was written in 1997. Maps used include O.S. Maps 6", Wilts. XXXVI (1888 and later edns.); 1/25,000, SU 06/16 (1987 edn.); SU 26/36 (1983 edn.); 1", sheet 14 (1817 edn.).
92   Below, this section (E. Wick).
93   *P.N. Wilts.* (E.P.N.S.), 357; below, manors (Wootton Rivers).
94   *V.C.H. Wilts.* iv. 399–400, 450–1.
95   Above, Savernake, intro.
96   *Census,* 1991; Statutory Instruments, 1987, no. 619, Kennet (Parishes) Order.
97   *Letters of Innocent III,* ed. C. R. and M. G. Cheney,

pp. 165–6; *Cart. Cirencester,* ii, ed. C. D. Ross, p. 433; *Reg. Martival* (Cant. & York Soc.), iv, p. 123.
98   W.R.O., F 8/200/3/1, no. 36.
99   Geol. Surv. Maps 1/50,000, drift, sheet 266 (1974 edn.); 1", drift, sheet 282 (1985 edn.).
1   St. John's Coll., Camb., Mun., D110.311; below, econ. hist.
2   *V.C.H. Wilts.* iv. 309.
3   Ibid. 361; *Census,* 1961; 1971; 1981; 1991.
4   I. D. Margary, *Rom. Roads in Brit.* (1973), 99; W.R.O. 1300/47B; cf. above, Easton, intro.; Savernake, intro.; econ. hist.
5   For the early 18th cent., St. John's Coll. Mun., MPS714, sheet 7510.
6   K. A. Clew, *Kennet & Avon Canal* (1985), 69, 73.
7   R. W. Squires, *Canals Revived,* 112.

it has been part of a main London–Exeter line. A passenger halt was opened at the south end of the village in 1928[8] and closed in 1964.[9] Two railways from Marlborough, one opened in 1864 and the other, part of a Swindon–Andover line, in 1898, crossed the north-east tip of the parish. They were closed in 1933 and 1964 respectively.[10]

A barrow at the north-east end is the only evidence of prehistoric activity in the parish.[11] The parish was in Savernake forest until 1330, when the whole of what was the parish until 1987 was disafforested.[12]

The church, the rectory house, and the demesne farmstead of Wootton Rivers manor stand as a group at the south end of the village.[13] The church stands on rising ground and, when it was built in the 14th century, replaced a church which may have stood on a lower site.[14] The demesne farmhouse, called Manor Farmhouse in 1997, is two-storeyed and mostly thatched.[15] At its west end it incorporates part of a medieval house built of large blocks of limestone; that part may have been the chamber wing of a house which c. 1600 was probably large. There survive in it a timber ceiling with heavily moulded beams and chamfered joists on the ground floor, a heavily moulded beam on the first floor, and three four-centred headed doorways. One of those doorways is in the west wall and is double-chamfered; a large, blocked, chamfered, three-centred arch abuts it and may be older. The surviving walls of the medieval house were patched with flint and rubble in the 17th century and with brick in the 18th; a mullioned window was inserted in the north wall in the 17th century. The part of the house which stood east of the medieval walls was replaced by a timber-framed range of three bays and a half built in the 17th century, possibly in 1680.[16] In the 18th century the lower part of the south wall of that range was rebuilt in brick and rubble, two bays built of brick were added on the east, and the house was reroofed. In the west wall, probably in the 18th century, large segmental-headed openings were made and a brick arch was built within the medieval one. In the 19th century an outbuilding was attached to the house at the east end of the north front. In the late 20th dormer windows were constructed, the outbuilding was converted to part of the house, and there were many minor alterations.

The copyhold farmsteads of Wootton Rivers manor were built north of the demesne farmstead beside a curving north–south street.[17] The street runs along a valley a little west of the floor, and at its north end was served by a pond in which the water of a stream flowing, perhaps intermittently, southwards down the valley was trapped.

Between Manor Farm and the pond, which was apparently filled between 1732 and 1842, there were probably 25–30 houses beside the street in 1732[18] and most, including several built in the late 16th or early 17th century, were standing in 1997. There was some rebuilding in the 18th century, and in the 19th a school and a nonconformist chapel were built,[19] but the main period of building after the 17th century was the 20th.

Most of the village was designated a conservation area in 1975.[20] In 1997 c. 25 houses built before 1800, nearly all of them thatched, stood in the street. On the east side near the south end Church Farmhouse, built c. 1600, is of three bays with stone chimney stacks between the bays. The heavy, square-panelled, timber frame of its back wall survives; its front wall was rebuilt in brick in the 18th century. After a fire in 1978 the house was raised from 1½ storey to 2 storeys and its roof was changed from thatch to tiles.[21] Further north on the east side Somerset Farm is a three-bayed timber-framed house of the 17th century, and the Royal Oak is an extended and altered house of 17th-century origin. The Royal Oak was open as a public house from 1848[22] or earlier and in 1997. On the west side of the street Noyes Farmhouse is another three-bayed, timber-framed, 17th-century house; in the 18th century its east and main front was clad in brick, in the early 19th century it was extended south by two bays, and in the mid 20th century its interior was altered and a single-storeyed west extension was built. Further north on the west side of the street St. John's Cottage, timber-framed and of the late 16th century or early 17th, unusually for Wootton Rivers was built on an L plan.

By 1732 cottages, including a timber-framed one and a brick one dated 1717, both of which survive, had been built on the waste at the north end of the street near the pond.[23] In the main part of the street a village hall and c. 15 houses were built in the 20th century. Off the street to the west four council houses and two council bungalows were built in South Bank in the early 1950s,[24] at the south end of the street four estate cottages were built in 1961, and at the north end of the street north of the site of the pond several houses and four bungalows for old people were built in the 20th century. In the later 20th century that north part of the street was called Forest Road.

When the railway was built in 1862 a lane to Milton Lilbourne was diverted to run beside and south of it for c. 150 m.;[25] that part of the lane was later called Station Road. Off Station Road 10 council houses were built between 1924 and 1945.[26]

East of Wootton Rivers village a farmstead called Heathy Close was standing in 1732: a mid 20th-century house stood on the site in

8   V.C.H. Wilts. iv. 286–7, 289, 291.
9   Wootton Rivers Village Appraisal (Wootton Rivers par. council, 1985), 3.
10   Above, Burbage, intro. [railways], where more inf. about the lines is given.
11   V.C.H. Wilts. i (1), 204.
12   Ibid. iv. 399–400, 418–19, 448, 450–1.
13   For the rectory ho., below, church.
14   Below, church.   15   Above, plate 12.
16   Dept. of Environment, list of bldgs. of hist. interest (1987).
17   Cf. St. John's Coll. Mun., MPS714, sheet 7510; ibid.

D110.311.
18   Ibid. MPS714, sheet 7510; W.R.O., tithe award.
19   Below, nonconf.; educ.
20   Inf. from Dept. of Planning and Highways, Co. Hall, Trowbridge.
21   Inf. from Mr. M. D. Rowell, Church Farmhouse.
22   Kelly's Dir. Wilts. (1848).
23   St. John's Coll. Mun., MPS714, sheet 7510.
24   W.R.O., G 10/505/1.
25   Cf. O.S. Map 6", Wilts. XXXVI (1888 edn.); W.R.O., tithe award.
26   W.R.O., G 10/505/1; G 10/603/2.

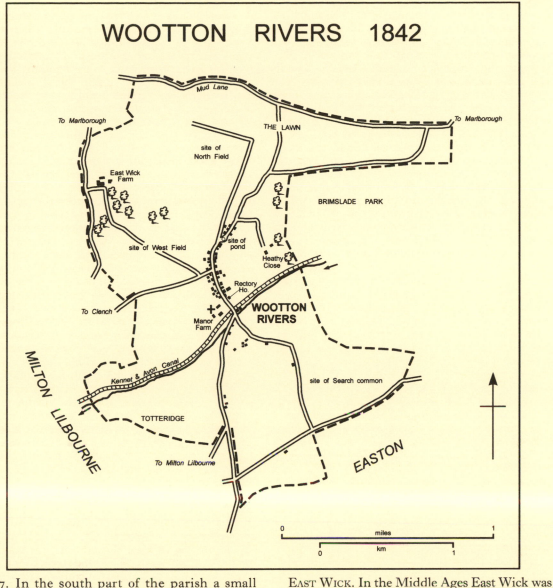

WOOTTON RIVERS 1842

1997. In the south part of the parish a small group of cottages and houses stood *c.* 350 m. south-east of the church in 1732. Of five houses standing there in 1997 one, of red brick and thatch, survived from 1732, and another, Flit-wick House, was built of red brick with decorations of grey brick between 1842 and 1886. On other sites south-east of the village buildings standing in 1732 and 1842 had been demolished or replaced by 1997. South of the village a hamlet beside the Milton Lilbourne lane had taken the name Cuckoo's Knob by 1886. A thatched house standing there in 1732[27] and possibly of 17th-century origin sur-vived in 1997, as did a brick house, built in 1738[28] and extended later, and two pairs of 19th-century cottages. A pair of council houses was built at Cuckoo's Knob in the 1930s and four bungalows for old people later. West of the village a new farmstead, Lady Margaret Farm, was built *c.* 1972.[29]

EAST WICK. In the Middle Ages East Wick was the name of a manor on which there were customary tenants[30] and, like its neighbours Wick (later Clench) in Milton Lilbourne parish and West Wick in Pewsey parish,[31] may have been a small village. East Wick Farm may stand on the site of a demesne farmstead which was probably standing in the 14th century;[32] it was the only farmstead at East Wick in the 18th century and almost certainly in the 16th.[33] The present farm-house, tall, three-bayed, and of red brick and flint, was built in the late 18th century or early 19th; it was extended in the later 19th century. In 1997 it stood among extensive farm buildings of the 19th and 20th centuries. South of it a pair of cottages of 1977 and a house of 1984 replaced buildings of the mid or later 19th century.[34]

MANORS AND OTHER ESTATE. Between 801 and 805 Byrhtelm gave Wootton, almost

27 Ibid. tithe award; O.S. Map 6", Wilts. XXXVI (1888 edn.); St. John's Coll. Mun., MPS714, sheet 7510.
28 Date on bldg.
29 Inf. from Mr. R. C. Butler, E. Wick Farm.
30 *Wilts. Inq. p.m.* 1327–77 (Index Libr.), 47–8, 274–5.
31 Above, Milton Lilbourne, intro. (Clench); Pewsey, intro.

(W. Wick).
32 *Wilts. Inq. p.m.* 1327–77 (Index Libr.), 47.
33 St. John's Coll. Mun., MPS714, sheet 7510; Longleat Mun., Seymour papers, xii, f. 311 and v.
34 O.S. Map 6", Wilts. XXXVI (1888 edn.); W.R.O., tithe award; dates on bldgs.

certainly including what was later the land of Wootton Rivers, to Ealhmund, bishop of Winchester, and his see in an exchange.[35] There is no evidence that it belonged to the see later. A large estate called Wootton was held by Queen Edith in 1066 and by the king in 1086. The estate, which was assessed at 30 hides and on which two churches stood,[36] almost certainly included more land than what was later Wootton Rivers parish. The additional land most likely to have been included in the estate is that of Easton, which may then have had a church and, because in the mid 12th century it was the marshal's, may have been the king's in 1086. The estate may also have included the land of Wick in Milton Lilbourne parish which, because it was later an endowment of Battle abbey (Suss.), may also have been the king's in 1086. Neither Easton nor Wick was mentioned in Domesday Book. Of other nearby places not mentioned in Domesday Book, Froxfield was held with Wootton in the early 9th century, and Milton Lilbourne is likely to have been part of an estate other than Wootton in 1086.[37]

WOOTTON RIVERS manor was held by Walter Giffard, earl of Buckingham (d. 1164), half of whose estates had been acquired by William Marshal, earl of Pembroke (d. 1219), by 1190.[38] The manor had been subinfeudated by 1202, when Marshal was overlord.[39] Thereafter the overlordship descended with the lordship of Wexcombe manor in Great Bedwyn.[40]

By 1202 the lordship in demesne of Wootton Rivers manor had been held by Walter de Leites, surrendered by him to William Marshal, and granted by Marshal to Walter de Rivers (fl. 1212) for 1 knight's fee.[41] In 1222 Rivers's relict Margaret and William de Rivers had interests in the manor,[42] which in 1242–3 was held by another Walter de Rivers.[43] The manor passed to Walter's son Richard (d. by 1304), to Richard's son John[44] (d. c. 1314), and in turn to John's sons Thomas,[45] a minor,[46] and John, who, while a minor, held it in 1325.[47] In 1330 Rose, the relict of, presumably the younger, John Rivers, held a third of it as dower. Sir Robert Bilkemore and his wife Anstice held the manor, including the reversion of Rose's portion, from 1330 or earlier.[48] In 1346 they were disputing the title to all or part of it with Simon Simeon, perhaps Rose's husband, and Thomas Rivers,

perhaps her son,[49] and in 1351 Sir Robert and Anstice conveyed the manor to Thomas[50] (d. 1375). From the death of Thomas, who had a son John, the manor was held for life by his relict Isabel;[51] it was held by Isabel in 1377,[52] by Hugh Craan, perhaps her husband, in 1384 and 1403.[53] By 1412 the manor had passed, presumably by inheritance, to Thomas Rivers.[54] In 1428 it was held by Roger Rivers,[55] and in 1441 was sold by Henry Rivers to Sir John Seymour.[56]

From the death of Sir John Seymour in 1464 Wootton Rivers manor was held by his relict Isabel, on whose death in 1485 it passed to his grandson John Seymour.[57] From John's death in 1491[58] it was held by his relict Elizabeth (fl. 1536).[59] It reverted to John's grandson Sir Edward Seymour (cr. Viscount Beauchamp 1536, earl of Hertford 1537, duke of Somerset 1547), on whose execution and attainder in 1552 it passed by Act to his son Sir Edward (cr. earl of Hertford 1559, d. 1621), a minor. From 1553 to 1675 it descended with Tottenham Lodge in Great Bedwyn successively to William, duke of Somerset (d. 1660), William, duke of Somerset (d. 1671), and John, duke of Somerset (d. 1675),[60] and it passed like Pewsey manor to Sarah, duchess of Somerset (d. 1692).[61] By her will Sarah gave Wootton Rivers manor to St. John's College, Cambridge.[62] The college owned c. 850 a. in the parish in 1840,[63] 675 a. in 1997.[64] In 1964 it sold Church farm and Somerset farm, a total of c. 150 a., to Charles Antrobus, whose relict Mrs. Pamela Antrobus owned them in 1997.[65]

At his death c. 1330 William Harding held 2 yardlands at East Wick in chief and land, not held in chief, consisting of what was later called *EAST WICK* manor and of land which, near East Wick, lay in Milton Lilbourne and Pewsey parishes. The whole estate descended to his daughter Anstice[66] (d. 1353), wife of Sir Robert Bilkemore (d. 1361). Probably on Bilkemore's death it passed to Anstice's grandson (Sir) John Lillebonne,[67] who by 1368 had given it to Thomas Hungerford in an exchange.[68] In 1369 Hungerford conveyed the estate to trustees,[69] and in 1371 Henry Sturmy conveyed that part of it which was not held in chief to Easton priory.[70] By an exchange licensed in 1390 the priory apparently gave the land near East Wick and in other parishes to Sir William Sturmy.[71]

35 Finberg, *Early Wessex Chart.* p. 72.
36 *V.C.H. Wilts.* ii, p. 118.
37 Above, Easton, manors; Froxfield, manors; Milton Lilbourne, manors.
38 *Red Bk. Exch.* (Rolls Ser.), i. 69; *Complete Peerage*, ii. 387; x. 358–63. 39 *Pipe R.* 1202 (P.R.S. N.S. xv), 130.
40 *Bk. of Fees*, ii. 745; *Wilts. Inq. p.m. 1242–1326* (Index Libr.), 397; *Cal. Inq. p.m. Hen. VII*, i, pp. 327–9; above, Great Bedwyn, manors (Wexcombe).
41 *Pipe R.* 1202 (P.R.S. N.S. xv), 130; *Cur. Reg. R.* vi. 251.
42 *Ex. e Rot. Fin.* (Rec. Com.), i. 88.
43 *Bk. of Fees*, ii. 711.
44 P.R.O., CP 40/152, rot. 93d.
45 *Wilts. Inq. p.m. 1242–1326* (Index Libr.), 397.
46 P.R.O., SC 6/1145/12.
47 Ibid. SC 6/1148/24.
48 *Feet of F. 1327–77* (W.R.S. xxix), pp. 56–7.
49 *Cal. Close*, 1346–9, 76.
50 *Feet of F. 1327–77* (W.R.S. xxix), p. 98.
51 *Wilts. Inq. p.m. 1327–77* (Index Libr.), 384–5.

52 Phillipps, *Wilts. Inst.* i. 61.
53 Ibid. 68; *Cal. Inq. p.m.* xviii, pp. 280–1.
54 *Feud. Aids*, vi. 533.   55 Ibid. v. 263.
56 *Feet of F. 1377–1509* (W.R.S. xli), p. 116.
57 P.R.O., C 140/14, no. 32; C 141/571, no. 26.
58 *Cal. Inq. p.m. Hen. VII*, i, pp. 327–8.
59 Phillipps, *Wilts. Inst.* i. 205; *Valor Eccl.* (Rec. Com.), ii. 149.
60 *Complete Peerage*, vi. 504–6; xii (1), 59–64; P.R.O., E 328/117; above, Great Bedwyn, manors (Tottenham).
61 W.R.O. 1300/290; above, Pewsey, manor (Pewsey).
62 W.R.O. 1300/299.   63 Ibid. tithe award.
64 Inf. from the senior bursar, St. John's Coll., Camb.
65 Inf. from Mrs. P. Antrobus, Wootton Ho.
66 *Wilts. Inq. p.m. 1327–77* (Index Libr.), 46–8; for the 2 yardlands, below, this section.
67 *Wilts. Inq. p.m. 1327–77* (Index Libr.), 231–3, 256, 274–6; P.R.O., KB 27/399, Rex rot. 8 and d.
68 *Cal. Pat. 1367–70*, 106.
69 W.R.O. 9/21/2–3.   70 *Cal. Pat. 1370–4*, 145.
71 Ibid. 1388–92, 179.

East Wick manor was held by the priory until the Dissolution[72] and was apparently granted with Easton Druce manor in Easton to Sir Edward Seymour, Viscount Beauchamp, in 1536.[73] From 1553 East Wick manor passed with Tottenham Lodge and Tottenham House in Great Bedwyn in the Seymour, Bruce, Brudenell, and Brudenell-Bruce families and, from 1552 or earlier to 1675, with Wootton Rivers manor.[74] George Brudenell-Bruce, marquess of Ailesbury, sold it to the Crown in 1950. In Wootton Rivers parish in 1997 the Crown owned c. 200 a., of which c. 150 a. was part of East Wick farm.[75]

In 1268 Gillian Bowcliffe held 1 yardland at East Wick which was later held with the keeping of part of Savernake forest. William Bowcliffe held it in 1275,[76] and in 1315 he or another William Bowcliffe conveyed it to William Harding,[77] who held other land at East Wick with the office of a forester of Savernake forest.[78] At his death c. 1330 Harding held 2 yardlands for service as keeper of the west bailiwick of the forest.[79] The land descended with East Wick manor until 1371 when, as land held in chief, it was retained by Henry Sturmy.[80] It descended with Burbage Sturmy manor from Henry (d. 1381) to Sir William Sturmy (d. 1427) and Sir John Seymour (d. 1464).[81] From 1441 it also descended with Wootton Rivers manor and was presumably merged with that or East Wick manor.[82]

ECONOMIC HISTORY. In 1086 the estate called Wootton, which almost certainly included land not later part of Wootton Rivers parish, had land for 30 ploughteams. On 13 hides 1 yardland of demesne there were 2 teams and 12 *servi*; 40 *villani* and 17 coscets had 14 teams. There were 6 a. of meadow and 18 square furlongs of pasture.[83]

There is no evidence that the demesne of Wootton Rivers manor included land in open fields. In 1314 it consisted of 118 a. of arable, 6 a. of meadow, a several pasture of 20 a., and a pasture called Totteridge which lay south-west of Wootton Rivers village adjoining pasture called Totteridge in Milton Lilbourne parish.[84] In the later 16th century the demesne consisted of c. 110 a. and lay, as it probably did in 1314, in closes south-west of the village and near the demesne farmstead. Totteridge close was then accounted 20 a. The demesne also included the right to feed cattle and 300 sheep on the common pastures of Wootton Rivers.[85]

In 1314 the customary tenants of Wootton Rivers manor were seven yardlanders, three ½-yardlanders, and five cottars; none of them owed labour service.[86] In the later 16th century the manor included 10 yardlands in 10 copyholds; there was c. 22 a. to each yardland, most of which lay in the open fields. The largest holding was of 45 a., the smallest of 11 a.; each had a farmstead presumably in the village street. There were also six copyholders each with a cottage and between 2 a. and 12 a. Around the village there was then 10–20 a. of home closes and, mainly east of the village where land lay inclosed as Heathy closes, the copyholders had c. 35 a. in small closes of meadow and pasture and the glebe included 14 a. in closes.[87]

The open fields of Wootton Rivers, shared by the copyholders and the rector, lay mainly north-west of the stream which flows across the south part of the parish from north-east to south-west; the scarp of the downs, which lies east–west across the north part, diminishes in steepness from west to east and was ploughed. In the Middle Ages there were probably two main fields, one north of the village and one west. By the later 16th century, when there were fields called North-east and North-west, the north field had apparently been subdivided. Southbrook was an open field of c. 6 a. lying south-east of the village and of the stream. In the 16th century the downland, called the Lawn, north of the scarp, and much of the land south-east of the stream was common pasture for sheep and cattle, and there was a small common meadow called West moor. The copyholders had feeding in common for 727 sheep, the rector for 60, the lessee of the demesne for 300, and the lessee of East Wick farm for 120; as many cattle could be fed in common as could be kept on each holding in winter.[88]

In 1607 West field, the common pasture, then called Search, south-east of the village, and a common pasture called Inlands were inclosed by agreement. Common rights over West field, probably c. 75 a., were eliminated, but the land continued to be worked in small parcels and in 1842 most of the fields west of the village were of less than 5 a. Search, 275 a., and Inlands, 10 a., were allotted at the rate of 13 a. for the right to feed 60 sheep, and in 1842 there remained c. 10 fields of c. 13 a. south-east of the village.[89] The Lawn, 160 a., had been inclosed, divided, and allotted by 1682.[90]

Southbrook field and 130 a. north of the village remained open arable, and in the later 17th century the 130 a. lay as Great North field and Little North

72 Cf. *Wilts. Inq. p.m.* 1327–77 (Index Libr.), 275; *Valor Eccl.* (Rec. Com.), ii. 149.
73 Longleat Mun., Seymour papers, xii, f. 311 and v.; above, Easton, manors (Easton Druce).
74 Above, Great Bedwyn, manors (Tottenham); this section (Wootton Rivers); cf. *Wilts. Inq. p.m.* 1625–49 (Index Libr.), 20–31; P.R.O., E 328/117; W.R.O., A 1/345/455; ibid. tithe award; ibid. Inland Revenue, val. reg. 55.
75 Inf. from the agent for the Crown Estate Com., 42 High Street, Marlborough.
76 *Rot. Hund.* (Rec. Com.), ii (1), 259; P.R.O., JUST 1/998, rot. 34d.
77 *Feet of F.* 1272–1327 (W.R.S. i), p. 92.
78 *Abbrev. Rot. Orig.* (Rec. Com.), i. 230.
79 *Wilts. Inq. p.m.* 1327–77 (Index Libr.), 46–7.

80 Above, this section (E. Wick).
81 *Cal. Inq. p.m.* xv, p. 202; P.R.O., C 139/28, no. 22; C 140/14, no. 32.   82 Above, this section.
83 *V.C.H. Wilts.* ii, p. 118; for the estate, cf. above, manors.
84 *Wilts. Inq. p.m.* 1242–1326 (Index Libr.), 397; above, Milton Lilbourne, econ. hist. (Milton Lilbourne).
85 W.R.O. 9/21/44; cf. ibid. tithe award.
86 *Wilts. Inq. p.m.* 1242–1326 (Index Libr.), 397.
87 W.R.O. 9/21/44; cf. ibid. tithe award.
88 Ibid. 9/21/44; cf. ibid. tithe award; for E. Wick farm, below, this section (E. Wick).
89 W.R.O. 9/21/44; ibid. tithe award.
90 Ibid. D 1/24/231/2; St. John's Coll., Camb., Mun., MPS714, sheet 7510; cf. Phillipps, *Wilts. Inst.* ii. 31, 38.

field.[91] Southbrook field and the 130 a. were inclosed by Act of 1836: the land lay inclosed in 1838 although an award was not made until 1842.[92]

In the early 18th century the demesne of Wootton Rivers manor was held on leases in portions. In 1732 it was a single farm, later called Manor farm, of 237 a. In 1795 the farm had 274 a. Most other farms in the parish apparently remained small; apart from East Wick farm none is known to have exceeded 100 a. in the 18th century.[93] In 1842 Manor farm had 265 a., copyholds totalling 291 a. may have been worked as a single farm, c. 240 a. of Wootton Rivers's land was held by the tenant of East Wick farm, and there may have been three farms each of c. 50 a. worked from farmsteads in the street. All but c. 100 a. was arable.[94]

Manor farm remained largely arable in the mid 19th century, and in 1860 the principal crops grown on it were wheat and legumes.[95] Later in the 1860s c. 20 cattle and 500–600 sheep were kept on it and wheat and a feed crop of turnips were grown.[96] In the later 19th century and the early 20th dairying was increasingly important in the parish and milk was sent to London by rail.[97] In 1910 Manor farm had 328 a. and there were apparently five other farms, of which the largest was 167 a., based in Wootton Rivers village. East of the village 55 a. was then worked from Savernake parish as part of Brimslade farm,[98] as it was in 1997.[99] From 1912 to 1942 the farm of 167 a. was held on lease by Wiltshire county council and sublet as smallholdings.[1] After 1945 some dairy herds were replaced by cattle reared for beef.[2] From 1972 most of Wootton Rivers's land has been worked with land outside the parish as part of East Wick farm and devoted to arable and dairy farming.[3]

The estate called Wootton in 1086 had on it 36 square furlongs of woodland.[4] A few small copses were standing on Wootton Rivers's land in the earlier 18th century, the earlier 19th, and in 1997; one of 4 a. east of the village was grubbed up between 1842 and 1886.[5]

A mill said in 1194 to stand at Wootton[6] probably stood at Wootton Bassett.[7]

In the 19th century coal was unloaded at Wootton Rivers wharf on the Kennet & Avon canal, and a passenger boat plied between Wootton Rivers and Devizes until 1851.[8] Thomas Holmes, an iron founder and machine maker,

was working at Wootton Rivers in 1848, and between 1855 and 1859 a firm of iron founders, engineers, and agricultural implement makers, Oatley & Morris, later Oatley & Whatley, began trading there. The firm apparently left the parish between 1865 and 1867, presumably for Pewsey.[9] From 1975 to 1985 SSI Ltd. made scientific instruments at Wootton Rivers;[10] in 1997 the company was in business in Pewsey.

EAST WICK. In the Middle Ages East Wick may have been a small village with its own small open fields. In 1330 the manor had as demesne 93 a. of arable and the hay from 4 a. of meadow and had on it 2 yardlanders and 12 cottars as customary tenants.[11] East Wick farm, 113 a., probably included all East Wick's land in the earlier 16th century, when it had 4½ a. of meadows, 77 a. of pastures, and 31 a. of arable, all in severalty. Its arable lay in fields of which the names, North and South,[12] suggest that they were formerly open, and the farmer was presumably entitled, as he was later, to feed cattle and sheep in the common pastures of Wootton Rivers. The farmstead from which the farm was worked almost certainly stood on or near the site on which the present East Wick Farm had been built by the 18th century.[13]

From 1570 or earlier East Wick farm had land in Clench in Milton Lilbourne parish in addition to that in Wootton Rivers.[14] About 1600 it had 210 a. and included 106 a. of arable, 22 a. of meadow, and 76 a. of pasture; the farmer then had feeding for 120 sheep in Wootton Rivers and for 240 in Clench.[15] To replace feeding for cattle and sheep on Search common in Wootton Rivers 25 a. was allotted in 1607.[16] In Wootton Rivers parish in 1732 East Wick farm had 143 a. lying as a strip along the parish boundary north and south of the farmstead.[17] In 1842 the farm, 449 a., consisted of that land and 306 a. adjoining it in Clench; the tenant also held c. 240 a. elsewhere in Wootton Rivers.[18] In 1910 the farm had c. 470 a., including the 143 a. but not the other land in Wootton Rivers.[19] In 1972 most of the land of Wootton Rivers was added to East Wick farm, thereafter an arable and dairy farm of c. 1,500 a. A new dairy, Lady Margaret Farm, was built c. 1972, and in 1997 a dairy herd of over 300 cows was kept.[20]

A copse of 7 a. stood immediately south of East Wick Farm in 1732.[21] It was grubbed up between 1842 and 1886.[22]

91 W.R.O., D 1/24/231/2; St. John's Coll. Mun., MPS714, sheet 7510.
92 W.R.O., EA/163; P.R.O., IR 18/11209.
93 St. John's Coll. Mun., D110.311; ibid. SB7.4A, p. 376.
94 W.R.O., tithe award.
95 St. John's Coll. Mun., D110.258A; D110.289.
96 Ibid. D110.264.
97 Ibid. SB1.20, pp. 89–90; SB1.22, p. 241.
98 Kelly's Dir. Wilts. (1911); W.R.O., Inland Revenue, val. reg. 55.
99 Inf. from the agent for the Crown Estate Com.
1 St. John's Coll. Mun., SB1.73, p. 209; SB13.30.
2 Ibid. SB1.78, p. 219.
3 Inf. from Mr. R. C. Butler, E. Wick Farm; for E. Wick farm, below, this section.
4 V.C.H. Wilts. ii, p. 118.
5 O.S. Map 6", Wilts. XXXVI (1888 edn.); St. John's Coll. Mun., MPS714, sheet 7510; W.R.O., tithe award.
6 Rot. Cur. Reg. (Rec. Com.), i. 89.

7 Cf. V.C.H. Wilts. ix. 197–8.
8 Ibid. iv. 274.
9 Kelly's Dir. Wilts. (1848 and later edns.); Harrod's Dir. Wilts. (1865); cf. above, Pewsey, trade and ind.
10 Inf. from Mr. W. Davison, 2 Cuckoo's Knob.
11 Wilts. Inq. p.m. 1327–77 (Index Libr.), 47–8.
12 Longleat Mun., Seymour papers, xii, f. 311 and v.
13 St. John's Coll. Mun., MPS714, sheet 7510; above, intro. (E. Wick).
14 W.R.O. 9/21/42.
15 Ibid. 9/15/326.
16 Ibid. 9/21/44; above, this section.
17 St. John's Coll. Mun., MPS714, sheet 7510.
18 W.R.O., tithe award; Milton Lilbourne tithe award.
19 Ibid. Inland Revenue, val. reg. 55, 58.
20 Inf. from Mr. Butler.
21 St. John's Coll. Mun., MPS714, sheet 7510.
22 O.S. Map 6", Wilts. XXXVI (1888 edn.); W.R.O., tithe award.

LOCAL GOVERNMENT. Records of the court of Wootton Rivers manor survive for 1455–6, 1561–4, and 1575, for several years in the 17th century, for 1702, and for 1710–1900. From the 17th century the court was called a court baron. It was not usually held more than once a year and its main business was always to record the death of tenants and surrender of and admittance to copyholds. In 1455–6 it ordered the repair of tenements and the making of hedges, in 1575 the inheritance customs of the manor were presented, and from the 17th century rules were made for feeding animals in common.[23] A court was apparently held for East Wick manor in the 14th century.[24]

The parish spent £49 on poor relief in 1775–6, an average of £81 in the three years beginning 1782–3, and £107 in 1802–3 when regular relief was given to 14 adults and 6 children, occasional relief to 21 people.[25] The number receiving regular relief had risen to 32 by 1813, when £371 was spent.[26] In the 1820s and early 1830s spending fluctuated between £131 and £348: it was usually between £200 and £250.[27] Wootton Rivers became part of Pewsey poor-law union in 1835,[28] and of Kennet district in 1974.[29]

CHURCH. A church belonging to the abbey of Mont St. Michel (Manche) stood at Wootton Rivers in 1086; it was one of two churches on the estate called Wootton, the second of which may have stood at Easton.[30] In the early 13th century Wootton Rivers church was served by a rector, and the abbey was entitled to a pension from its revenues.[31] In 1991 the rectory was united to Pewsey rectory and the united benefice of Easton and Milton Lilbourne to form a new Pewsey benefice.[32]

In 1212 the abbey of Mont St. Michel and Walter de Rivers, lord of Wootton Rivers manor, agreed that each should present alternate rectors.[33] There is no evidence that the abbey ever presented, and the advowson descended with the lordship of the manor. In the name of the lord of the manor, who was then a minor, three separate claimants each presented a candidate for the rectory in 1321; a fourth candidate was collated by the ordinary.[34] Simon Simeon, who presented in 1349 and 1350, possibly had an interest in part of the manor.[35] In 1425 Sir William Sturmy presented, possibly by grant of a turn, in 1555 the Crown presented because the

lord of the manor was its ward, and in 1629 Roger Sherfield presented by grant of a turn.[36] Sarah, duchess of Somerset (d. 1692), devised alternate rights of presentation to St. John's College, Cambridge, and Brasenose College, Oxford:[37] the first presentation after 1692 was by St. John's College in 1728.[38] From 1991 the colleges have been members of the board of patronage for Pewsey benefice.[39]

In the Middle Ages the rectory was poor: it was valued at £5 in 1291,[40] was exempt from taxation because of its poverty in the late 15th century,[41] and was valued at £8 in 1535.[42] At £379 its value was close to the diocesan average c. 1830.[43] The rector was entitled to all tithes from the parish.[44] They were valued at £405 in 1838 and commuted in 1843.[45] The glebe was accounted 40 a. in 1341,[46] later as 1 yardland. In the later 16th century it consisted of 15 a. in closes, the first cut of ½ a. of meadow, a nominal 10 a. in the open fields, and feeding for cattle and 60 sheep. The rector was allotted 13 a. of Search common when it was inclosed in 1607[47] and 8 a. of the Lawn when it was inclosed. In the late 17th century he held 41 a. in closes and the nominal 10 a.[48] He was allotted 6 a. at the inclosure of c. 1836[49] and held 49 a. of glebe in 1842.[50] The rector sold 44 a. in 1917.[51] The rectory house was replaced by one built in the early 18th century and said in 1732 to be new.[52] The new house, double-pile and red-brick, had a main west front of five bays, the central three of which project; in 1997 early 18th-century fireplaces and panelling remained in the principal rooms of the west part of the house. In the earlier 19th century a tall façade, of red and blue chequered brick with a pedimental gable flanked by chimney stacks, was built on the south, which was converted to an entrance front; in the same period a similar façade and a service room were built on the north, and a large drawing room raised over a basement was added on the east. In the 1960s a south doorcase in neoclassical style was added and steps were built from the drawing room to the garden.[53] The house was sold in 1960.[54] A new one built north of it was sold in 1971.[55]

In 1550, when the rector lived outside the parish, communion could not easily be administered in the chancel because its roof was in such bad repair.[56] Peter Waterman, rector from 1630, was accused in 1646 of preaching and of using the threat of exclusion from communion in support of the royalist cause. He was also said

23 W.R.O. 9/1/137; 9/1/166; 9/21/43–4; 192/22; St. John's Coll. Mun., D94.80; D97.331; D97.333–5; D109.274; D109.281.
24 Wilts. Inq. p.m. 1327–77 (Index Libr.), 275.
25 Poor Law Abstract, 1804, 566–7.
26 Ibid. 1818, 498–9.
27 Poor Rate Returns, 1816–21, 188; 1822–4, 228; 1825–9, 219; 1830–4, 212.
28 Poor Law Com. 2nd Rep. App. D, 560.
29 O.S. Map 1/100,000, admin. areas, Wilts. (1974 edn.).
30 V.C.H. Wilts. ii, p. 118; for the estate, above, manors.
31 Cur. Reg. R. vi. 251.
32 Ch. Com. file, P34/409/1.
33 Cur. Reg. R. vi. 251; above, manors (Wootton Rivers).
34 Reg. Martival (Cant. & York Soc.), i. 233, 235–6, 242–3; above, manors (Wootton Rivers).
35 Phillipps, Wilts. Inst. i. 47, 49; above, manors (Wootton Rivers).
36 Phillipps, Wilts. Inst. i. 116, 218; ii. 15; above, manors

(Wootton Rivers).
37 W.R.O. 1300/299.
38 Phillipps, Wilts. Inst. ii. 62.
39 Ch. Com. file, NB 34/263B.
40 Tax. Eccl. (Rec. Com.), 189.
41 Reg. Langton (Cant. & York Soc.), p. 59.
42 Valor Eccl. (Rec. Com.), ii. 149.
43 Rep. Com. Eccl. Revenues, 854–5.
44 Inq. Non. (Rec. Com.), 173; W.R.O., D 1/24/231/2.
45 W.R.O., tithe award.
46 Inq. Non. (Rec. Com.), 173.
47 W.R.O. 9/21/44.   48 Ibid. D 1/24/231/2.
49 Ibid. EA/163.   50 Ibid. tithe award.
51 Ch. Com. file, NB 34/409.
52 W.R.O., D 1/24/231/1–3; St. John's Coll., Camb., Mun., D110.311.   53 Inf. from Mrs. P. Antrobus, Wootton Ho.
54 Ch. Com. file, P 34/409/1.
55 Inf. from Mr. W. Davison, 2 Cuckoo's Knob.
56 W.R.O., D 1/43/1, f. 34v.

to have done manual labour unfitting for a minister. He had been sequestrated by 1653, restored by 1660.[57] Under the will of Sarah, duchess of Somerset, from 1728 to 1905 each rector held a scholarship endowed by the duchess at either St. John's College or Brasenose College.[58] In 1783 a morning and an afternoon service were held each Sunday and services were held on fast days and on days following great festivals. Some poor parishioners rarely went to church, saying that they had no suitable clothes, and few attended the weekday services. Communion was celebrated at Christmas, Easter, and Whitsun and on the Sunday after Michaelmas. The number of communicants, c. 40 at Easter, was said to be rising because religious tracts had recently been distributed in the parish. Inhabitants of Brimslade and South Savernake tithing, which was extra-parochial and in which no church was built until c. 1854, attended Wootton Rivers church.[59] By 1812 the number of communicants in Wootton Rivers had fallen to 12.[60] On Census Sunday in 1851 a morning service was attended by 147 people, an afternoon one by 92.[61] In 1864, in addition to Sunday services, there were services at the great festivals. Communion was celebrated at Christmas and Easter, on Whit and Trinity Sundays, and on the first Sunday of each month; of 20 communicants, between 7 and 10 usually received.[62] From 1965 to 1970 the rectory was held in plurality with Savernake (Christchurch) vicarage and from 1971 to 1986 with the united benefice of Easton and Milton Lilbourne.[63]

The church of *ST. ANDREW*, so called in 1763,[64] is built of flint with sarsens and has an undivided chancel and nave with south porch and west bell turret. Most of the building is 14th-century. The roof, incorporating turned posts, which rest on collars, and cusped braces is apparently 17th-century. A wooden screen separating the chancel and the nave had been removed by 1812.[65] In the early 19th century the church had a plain weatherboarded bell turret with a pyramidal cap and a vane.[66] About 1861 it was restored conservatively to designs by G. E. Street:[67] the roof covering was renewed and the bell turret was replaced by a taller one with decorative bracing and a tiled broached spire.

In 1553 plate weighing 2½ oz. was confiscated and a chalice of 11 oz. was left in the parish. A chalice and paten cover made later in the 16th century belonged to the parish in 1891 and 1997.[68]

Three bells hung in the church in 1553. A ring of five bells cast in 1793 by Robert Wells of Aldbourne hung in the turret in the 1920s and in 1997.[69]

Registers of baptisms, marriages, and burials survive from 1728.[70]

NONCONFORMITY. A meeting house for Methodists was licensed in 1821.[71] A Methodist chapel was built in 1881[72] and closed in 1967.[73]

EDUCATION. In 1783 a few children were taught at a school probably in the parish.[74] Four schools were open in 1818,[75] two, with a total of 39 pupils, in 1833.[76] A Church of England school was opened in 1845;[77] in 1846–7 there were 74 pupils at that and one other school in the parish.[78] In 1848 the church school was endowed with £150 raised by Ann Briant; in 1858, when it had 90–100 pupils and was probably the only school in the parish, its income from the endowment was £4 10s., in 1901 £4 2s.[79] A new school was built in 1864.[80] From the 1860s to 1907 there were usually c. 80 pupils.[81] Average attendance was 41 in 1918–19, higher in the 1920s, and 43 in 1937–8.[82] The school was closed in 1979.[83]

CHARITIES FOR THE POOR. Boys born on the land of Wootton Rivers manor were entitled to benefit from the Broad Town charity for apprenticing endowed by Sarah, duchess of Somerset (d. 1692),[84] and widows living on it qualified as manor widows for admittance to Froxfield almshouse, which was also endowed by the duchess.[85]

Probably in 1901 a Mrs. Merriman endowed a coal charity for the poor of Wootton Rivers. It and an associated charity, the Carey trust, had ceased to exist by 1994.[86]

57 *Walker Revised*, ed. Matthews, 381; *Calamy Revised*, ed. Matthews, 489; Phillipps, *Wilts. Inst.* ii. 15.
58 *Crockford* (1898, 1909); A. Tomlin, *St. Andrew's Church, Wootton Rivers* (priv. print. 1989), 17.
59 *Vis. Queries, 1783* (W.R.S. xxvii), pp. 245–6; above, Savernake, intro.; church.
60 *W.A.M.* xli. 135.
61 P.R.O., HO 129/261/2/3/6.
62 W.R.O., D 1/56/7.
63 *Crockford* (1965–6 and later edns.).
64 J. Ecton, *Thesaurus* (1763), 406.
65 *W.A.M.* xli. 135.
66 J. Buckler, watercolour in W.A.S. Libr., vol. iv. 12.
67 W.R.O., D 1/61/13/5.
68 Nightingale, *Wilts. Plate*, 173; inf. from Mr. Davison.
69 Walters, *Wilts. Bells*, 242; inf. from Mr. Davison.
70 W.R.O. 1085/1–7; 1085/9; 1085/20; bishop's transcripts for some earlier years are in W.R.O.
71 *Meeting Ho. Certs.* (W.R.S. xl), p. 94.
72 Date on bldg.
73 Wilts. Cuttings, xxiii. 27.
74 *Vis. Queries, 1783* (W.R.S. xxvii), p. 246.
75 *Educ of Poor Digest*, 1042.
76 *Educ. Enq. Abstract*, 1053.
77 P.R.O., ED 7/131, no. 330.
78 Nat. Soc. *Inquiry, 1846–7*, Wilts. 12–13.
79 *Endowed Char. Wilts.* (S. Div.), 923; *Acct. of Wilts. Schs.* 51.
80 W.R.O., F 8/600/300/1/1/1; ibid. 782/117.
81 *Rep. Com. Children and Women in Agric.* [4202-I], p. 258, H.C. (1868–9), xiii; *Return of Public Elem. Schs. 1875–6* [C. 1882], pp. 286–7, H.C. (1877), lxvii; *Bd. of Educ., List 21, 1908* (H.M.S.O.), 508.
82 *Bd. of Educ., List 21, 1910–38* (H.M.S.O.).
83 W.R.O., list of primary schs. closed since 1946.
84 *Endowed Char. Wilts.* (S. Div.), 972; for a hist. of the char., *V.C.H. Wilts.* ix. 42–3.
85 *Endowed Char. Wilts.* (S. Div.), 980; cf. above, manors; Froxfield, charities.
86 Char. Com. file.

INDEX

INDEX

LIST OF CONTRIBUTORS TO THE WILTSHIRE V.C.H. APPEAL FUND

(as at 30 June 1999)

The countess of Iveagh, Wilbury Park
Mr. Paul van Vlissingen, Conholt House
The Weinberg Foundation
Mr. D. K. Newbigging, Fyfield Manor
Lord Congleton, Ebbesborne Wake
Mr. B. R. Taylor, Marten
The Walter Guinness Charitable Trust
The Revd. J. Gosling, Wilton
Mr. C. J. Bunyan, Pewsey
The earl of Cardigan, Savernake
Mr. O. Lodge, Hindon
Mr. P. Maundrell, Bradford on Avon
Miss S. Reynolds, London
Mr. M. J. Duckenfield, Pewsey
Sir Anthony Lees, Bt., Fiddington, Somerset
Mr. B. G. Baycliffe, Brockworth, Gloucestershire
Sir Donald and Lady Hawley, Little Cheverell
Mr. J. R. Arkell, Kingsdown, Swindon
Miss J. M. Backhouse, Richmond, Surrey
Mr. E. J. G. Balley, Welwyn Garden City, Hertfordshire
Mr. M. E. and Mrs. M. F. Balston, Patney
Mr. D. H. Bartlett
The marquess of Bath, Longleat House
Bedwyn History Society, Great Bedwyn
Mr. A. M. Berrett
Mr. D. Box, Reading, Berkshire
Bradford on Avon Preservation Trust Ltd.
Bradford on Avon town council
Mr. F. S. Brazier, Devizes
Mr. R. I. Bullough, West Hatch
Mr. J. B. Bush, Heywood
Mr. R. M. Charles, Great Bedwyn
Mrs. R. A. Currie, Aldbourne

Mr. J. F. Dennis, Crowood House
Mr. R. J. Field, Warminster
Mr. D. H. and Mrs. D. Fitzwilliam-Lay, Great Bedwyn
Mr. R. D. Harding, Fordingbridge, Hampshire
Mr. R. Hatchwell, Malmesbury
Miss A. M. Hutchison, Mere
Earl Jellicoe, Tidcombe Manor
Dr. I. Keil, Loughborough, Leicestershire
Mrs. V. C. S. Landell Mills, Bradford on Avon
Mr. M. J. Lansdown, Trowbridge
Mr. J. McNeile, Fisherton de la Mere
Mr. R. F. Moody, East Harptree, Somerset
The Hon. A. J. Morrison, Fonthill Bishop
Mr. J. G. Peel, Fairford, Gloucestershire
The earl of Pembroke and of Montgomery, Wilton House
Purton Historical Society
Mrs. J. L. Repton, Bradford on Avon
Mr. W. J. Riley, Bradford on Avon
The bishop of Salisbury
Salisbury Civic Society
Mr. and Mrs. J. M. Scott, Great Bedwyn
The earl of Shelburne, Bowood House
The Ven. B. J. Smith, Chippenham
The Swindon Society
Prof. L. Symon, Shalbourne
Mr. P. Q. and Mrs. B. N. Treloar, Calne
A. M. J. Walker
Mr. G. J. Ward, Chilton Foliat
Mr. P. Ward, Great Bedwyn
Warminster History Society
Mrs. A. R. Wilson, Bremhill
Wiltshire Family History Society
Wiltshire Local History Forum